Reading Hemingway's *For Whom the Bell Tolls*

READING HEMINGWAY SERIES
MARK CIRINO, EDITOR
ROBERT W. LEWIS, FOUNDING EDITOR

Reading Hemingway's *The Sun Also Rises*
    H. R. Stoneback

Reading Hemingway's *Men Without Women*
    Joseph M. Flora

Reading Hemingway's *Across the River and into the Trees*
    Mark Cirino

Reading Hemingway's *To Have and Have Not*
    Kirk Curnutt

Reading Hemingway's *The Old Man and the Sea*
    Bickford Sylvester, Larry Grimes, and Peter L. Hays

Reading Hemingway's *A Farewell to Arms*
    Robert W. Lewis and Michael Kim Roos

Reading Hemingway's *Winner Take Nothing*
    Edited by Mark Cirino and Susan Vandagriff

Reading Hemingway's *The Garden of Eden*
    Carl P. Eby

Reading Hemingway's *For Whom the Bell Tolls*
    Alex Vernon

Reading Hemingway's
For Whom the Bell Tolls

GLOSSARY AND COMMENTARY

Alex Vernon

The Kent State University Press

KENT, OHIO

© 2024 by The Kent State University Press, Kent, Ohio 44242
All rights reserved
ISBN 978-1-60635-472-8
Published in the United States of America

No part of this book may be used or reproduced, in any manner whatsoever, without written permission from the Publisher, except in the case of short quotations in critical reviews or articles.

Cataloging information for this title is available at the Library of Congress.

28 27 26 25 24   5 4 3 2 1

For CHRISTIN

Who ere thou beest that read'st this sullen Writ,
Which just so much courts thee, as thou dost it,
Let me arrest thy thoughts; wonder with mee,
Why plowing, building, ruling and the rest,
Or most of those arts, whence our lives are blest,
By cursed Cains race invented be,
And blest Seth vext us with Astronomie,
Ther's nothing simply good, nor ill alone,
Of every quality comparison,
   The onely measure is, and judge, opinion.

       —John Donne, "Metempsycosis"

CONTENTS

Acknowledgments   ix
Introduction   xi
Abbreviations Used in This Book   xxxvii
Series Note   xxxix
Maps   xli
Front Matter   3
The first calendar day [28 May 1937]
    Chapter 1   11
    Chapter 2   35
    Chapter 3   51
    Chapter 4   60
    Chapter 5   66
    Chapter 6   70
    Chapter 7   77
The second calendar day [29 May 1937]
    Chapter 8   83
    Chapter 9   90
    Chapter 10   96
    Chapter 11   113
    Chapter 12   130
    Chapter 13   133
    Chapter 14   153
    Chapter 15   165
    Chapter 16   169
    Chapter 17   174
    Chapter 18   175
    Chapter 19   204
    Chapter 20   209
The third calendar day [30 May 1937]
    Chapter 21   217
    Chapter 22   219

Chapter 23 222
Chapter 24 225
Chapter 25 229
Chapter 26 230
Chapter 27 234
Chapter 28 240
Chapter 29 244
Chapter 30 245
Chapter 31 255
Chapter 32 265

The fourth and final calendar day [31 May 1937]

Chapter 33 271
Chapter 34 272
Chapter 35 273
Chapter 36 275
Chapter 37 277
Chapter 38 286
Chapter 39 289
Chapter 40 291
Chapter 41 294
Chapter 42 298
Chapter 43 303

Appendix A: Composition 321
Appendix B: In Memoriam Frank G. Tinker Jr. 336
Appendix C: "For Whom the Gong Sounds" by Cornelia Otis Skinner 338
Works Cited 342
Index 353

ACKNOWLEDGMENTS

My task and purpose with this book have been, as much as possible over eighty years later, to make *For Whom the Bell Tolls* come alive again, as it lived for its writer and its first readers, as it might for a new generation. It has been a joy. I owe its successes to a battalion's worth of colleagues, friends, and family. Foremost, my gratitude goes to Mark Cirino and Kent State University Press for entrusting me with this contribution to their vital Reading Hemingway series. Mark's support throughout the process and his editing acumen have been exemplary.

I first taught *For Whom the Bell Tolls* in the fall of 2002 at Hendrix College, my professional home. At the time, my understanding of the novel amounted to a couple or three inklings. To the Hendrix students who have studied the book with me—truly with me, alongside me, in our conversations, in your essays—and to those I anticipate studying it with, I owe so very much. You brought the novel alive for me; you energized and still energize me; you made connections and braved ideas that I missed.

Many of the book's insights and the lion's share of whatever brilliance readers discover in it I credit to my Hemingway brain trust, those fellow scholars and dear friends whom I've bombarded with questions and puzzles over the years. In alphabetical order: Mark Cirino, Kirk Curnutt, Suzanne del Gizzo, Carl Eby, Stacey Guill, Hilary Justice, Verna Kale, Miriam Mandel, Mark Ott, Sandra Spanier, André Stufkens, Robert Trogdon, Linda Wagner-Martin, and Frederick White. Others who have supported me along this scholarly journey: Milt Cohen, Marc Dudley, Ruth Hawkins, Jennifer Haytock, Pat Hoy, David Krause, Adam Long, Tim O'Brien, Steve Paul, H. R. Stoneback, and Steven Trout. We all owe a debt to Allen Josephs, whose afición and good work helped sustain the study of the novel for decades. My great appreciation to Michael Katakis and Stacey Chandler for making materials at the JFK available. And to my friends expert in Spain and the Spanish Civil War: Almudena Cros, Sebastiaan Faber, Alberto Lena, Garbiñe Vidal-Torreira, and Alan Warren. My Hendrix College colleague, friend, and neighbor Bobby Williamson fielded many theological and Biblical questions over the years, for which I'm very grateful. Thank you, Jenny Emery Davidson and Martha Williams of the Community Library in Ketchum, for the opportunity to present a version of the introduction to an amazing audience. Some individual contributions are acknowledged in the annotations—thank you! I am grateful to the Ernest Hemingway Foundation for permission to include brief excerpts from nine unpublished letters (©2024), soon to appear in volumes 7 and 8 of *The Letters of Ernest Hemingway* by Cambridge University Press.

Hendrix College has supported my work as a teacher and scholar since my arrival in 2001. I cannot imagine a better professional home. My colleagues' talents and dedication to our students inspire me. Y'all're world class. Thanks to the College, to the Julia Mobley Odyssey Professorship, and to the M. E. and Ima Graves Peace Distinguished Professorship, for their support. John Shutt's and Britt Murphy's help getting my hands on books and articles was invaluable.

Kent State University Press has been a stalwart and patient supporter of this project from the get-go. This book would not be the book that it is without the work and intelligence of Susan Wadsworth-Booth, Mary Young, Christine Brooks, Julia Wiesenberg, Darryl Crosby, Kat Saunders, Clara Totten, and the outside readers and editorial board members.

I've dedicated this book to my wife, Christin, partner of partners, whose love and support make everything possible. Ten years and counting! Anna Cay and Quinn, your geniuses are my world. And finally: Townsend Ludington. Bright-smiling, kindhearted, towering Towny led me from West Point to graduate school at the University of North Carolina–Chapel Hill, and as a result, in countless ways, to the rest of my life. Peace is yours now, always and forever.

INTRODUCTION
Once Upon a Time in Spain
Hemingway's Revolutionary Romance

> The function of criticism should be to show *how it is what it is,* even *that it is what it is,* rather than to show *what it means.*
> —Susan Sontag, "Against Interpretation"

In a 2008 interview, the novelist Robert Stone captured the appeal for many readers of Ernest Hemingway's *For Whom the Bell Tolls* from 1940: "Robert Jordan is really a great and admirable character. . . . Above all, stoicism, grace under pressure, the 20th century heroism. In fact, Hemingway kind of created the whole idea of the anti-fascist hero. I mean you can't really have *Casablanca* and Humphrey Bogart and all those characters without the Hemingway character. They all kind of derive from Robert Jordan" ("Robert Jordan").[1]

Growing up, John McCain, a US Naval Academy graduate, veteran of the war in Vietnam where he was a prisoner of war in the infamous Hanoi Hilton for six years, longtime US senator from Arizona and presidential candidate, wanted to be Robert Jordan ("Avatar"). The romance and idealism of the novel "had a lot to do with" Matt Gallagher's joining the army and serving in Iraq before becoming a writer (Gallagher).

Stone, McCain, Gallagher, and so many others across the generations (men especially) have met Robert Jordan and gobbled him up, hook, line, and sinker. Some readers have found in this hero's journey a mythic, even sacred dimension. Twelve years into the twenty-first century, the US Library of Congress recognized Hemingway's accomplishment by ranking the novel one of the eighty-eight "Books that Shaped America."

For over eighty years, many readers have loved the book. The *New York Times Book Review* considered it "the best book Hemingway has written, the fullest, the deepest, the truest. It will . . . be one of the major novels in American literature" (Adams 1). Most contemporary reviews shared this assessment.

For over eighty years, many readers have not cared much for it at all.

Right out of the gate, the novel met with acrimony from the North American volunteers who fought in Spain with the International Brigades. They trounced it as a political betrayal and as an unrealistic adventure tale that resembled their soldiering experiences not in the least. As Hemingway's war friend and volunteer Milton Wolff phrased the latter charge (more kindly than his peers), "These guys had no Abercrombie & Fitch sleeping bags. They slept on the ground using their ponchos for both cover and blanket. There were no Marias to share their bedding" (qtd. in Nelson 3). The Catalonian writer Joan Sales mocked *For Whom the Bell Tolls* in his own novel of the Spanish Civil War, as his characters imagine how novelists will distort the war they are living, the war Sales himself experienced:

> "But the worst side to the wars is the fact that they are turned into novels; at the end of this war—and I assure you it's a war as shitty as any—novels will be written that are especially stupid, as sentimental and risqué as they come; they'll have wonderfully courageous heroes and wonderfully buxom little angels.... Foreigners will turn this huge mess into stirring stories of bullfighters and gypsies.... A bullfighter has never been sighted in the army, let alone a gypsy, but foreigners have a good nose for business." (312)

The very title of Sales's novel, *Uncertain Glory* (its original version published in 1956), rebuffs the apparent certainty of Hemingway's novel's romantic vision. Sales's practical assessment that for the non-Spanish audience "anything else is a waste of time and time is money" also speaks perspicaciously to a biographical truth: headed toward divorce from his second wife, Pauline Pfeiffer, and separation from her family's wealth and generosity, Hemingway needed money.

A review from November 1940, C. V. Roberts's "Hemingway Lets Down Followers," accused the novel's bombastic style of having "nullified" the subject's promise and import (33). Susan Sontag slammed the book in her famous 1964 essay "Notes on 'Camp.'" It and works like it "are bad to the point of being laughable, but not bad to the point of being enjoyable," because "they are too dogged and pretentious" (*Against* 284). The most renowned novelist of the US war in Vietnam, Tim O'Brien, has charged Hemingway with pushing "a pretty dubious moral code," with "the novel's concluding scene ... weirdly Victorian in its celebration of self-sacrificial military values (honor, duty, discipline)" along the lines of Tennyson's "The Charge of the Light Brigade" rather than Owen's ironically titled "Dulce et Decorum Est" (246–47). The novel's ultimate plot point distracts O'Brien to no end:

> I'm thinking not about the pending extinction of Robert Jordan but rather about the improbable contrivance of the novel's final paragraphs. How unlikely, I think, that Lieutenant Paco Berrendo—the one and only enemy soldier we've come to know over hundreds of pages—suddenly dashes into the story to become the one and only human being whom Jordan will slay as his final earthly act. How tidy. How symmetrical. How heart-tuggingly convenient....

The scene is not just contrived. It's heavy-handed. It's a Gary Cooper movie. (247)

As O'Brien well knows, Cooper played Jordan in the 1943 film adaptation.

Along with these potential frustrations, the twenty-first century audience must contend with the impediment of its unfamiliarity with the Spanish Civil War, and the book's daunting length. So which is it: grand, even mythic, or preposterous? The above estimations have made their determinations based upon the same evidence—namely, *For Whom the Bell Tolls*'s apparent gravitas, its portrayal of martial self-sacrificing heroism, its happenstances, and its instant and urgent love story. In other words, upon matters of story.

Yet could the novel be grand, and realist, and preposterous, all at once? Once upon a time, in Spain?

Differently regarded, the word *preposterous* can serve colloquially to distinguish a text by genre, specifically as a Romance. The history of book-length fictional prose is complicated, and its alternative explanations are not always readily compatible. Dating roughly to the 1970s, the rise of new modes of literary criticism—feminism, New Historicism, postcolonial studies, and race and ethnic studies (pioneered in the United States by African American studies)—has proven a welcome paradigm shift in understanding literary history (e.g., see 404:31). Genres aren't stable, uncontestable forms. According to the tradition that Hemingway knew, writers since the seventeenth century have contrasted the novel from the Romance in long-form fiction, the former dedicated to Realism and the latter to "works with extravagant characters, remote and exotic places, highly exciting and heroic events, passionate love, or mysterious or supernatural experiences," or in a more nuanced way to "works relatively free of the more restrictive aspects of realistic verisimilitude" (Holman and Harmon 413). Emily Brontë's *Wuthering Heights*, for example.

In his preface to *The Great Crusade*, a quasi-autobiographical 1940 novel of the Spanish Civil War by Hemingway's friend Gustav Regler, Hemingway calls *Wuthering Heights* a "great tour de force" because of its inventiveness and poetry—qualities he implies Regler's book, in its obligation to actual events, lacks (Regler xi). Hemingway dashed off this preface in April 1940 while deep into the writing of his own Spanish Civil War novel. Elements of Brönte's novel color Hemingway's. Her moors and wilds become his Guadarrama Mountains. Heathcliff, the Romani outsider yet foundling English insider, becomes Jordan, the *Inglés* outsider yet Spanish insider among a circumstantial family that includes Romani. And Catherine Earnshaw, the near-sister with whom Heathcliff frolics in the wild and who declares "I *am* Heathcliff" (102), becomes Maria, the young woman who looks like she could be Jordan's sister, with whom he frolics in the wild, and who similarly declares, "I am thee" (262:26; see Spilka, chapter 5).

Northrop Frye's *Anatomy of Criticism* could provide a template. In Frye's vision of the Romance, whose lineage stretches back to medieval literature, the hero's inevitable "epiphany," whereby the "undisplaced apocalyptic world and the cyclical world of nature come into alignment," frequently happens on a mountaintop (203). There are also "analogous forms" the epiphany might take. "For instance, it may be presented in erotic terms as a place of sexual fulfillment, where there is no apocalyptic vision but simply a sense of arriving at the summit of experience in nature" (205). Jordan's final feeling of complete integration in the mountains, in a scene resonant with his and Maria's lovemaking, resembles just such an experience. The final phase of Romance "is a reflective, idyllic view of experience from above, in which the movement of the natural cycle has usually a prominent place"; its mood is a contemplative withdrawal from or sequel to action"; and it is "an erotic world"—a sensuous world—that "presents experience as comprehended and not a mystery" (202).

Owen Wister's 1902 *The Virginian*, which Hemingway biographer Michael Reynolds sees as a strong influence on *For Whom the Bell Tolls* ("Ringing"), is a cowboy Romance. Edgar Rice Burroughs—who lived in Oak Park, Illinois, during Hemingway's adolescence there—subtitled his 1912 *Tarzan of the Apes* "A Romance of the Jungle." Hemingway's fiction shares with Burroughs's extravagant characters, remote and exotic places, highly exciting and heroic events, passionate love, Victorian ideals, and absurd coincidences. Clambering around the bridge trestlework to rig explosives, Jordan likens himself to "a bloody Tarzan in a rolled steel forest" (436:33–34). Each hero represents a Great Hope *Inglés* (despite their American origins) who, in a different way, saves the love interest from rape; both question the difference between killing animals and people, between animals and people. The novels feature at least one animal's perspective (64:14+). Books such as *The Virginian* and *Tarzan of the Apes* are deeply nostalgic, a trait Frye relates to the "perennially childlike quality of Romance" (186).

For O'Brien, everything about Jordan's situation "combine[s] to produce the impression of war as romance, both literal and figurative. It is an example of what Wilfred Owen called 'The old Lie'" (336). But couldn't this be, at least partially, Hemingway's point? The author of *A Farewell to Arms* knew the old lie; that novel's most quoted passage spells it out (see 165:31+). Hemingway recognized the unrealistic literariness of the romance with Maria—in the draft, Jordan dismisses the very possibility: "They have that sort of life only in stories" (*HLE* 491). Parody and irony were constants of Hemingway's style. The high adventure and romance of this novel are genuine while also self-conscious, anxious, and a shade sardonic. Jordan's Romance of the sierras manifests the difficulty in reconciling the high idealism and adventuresomeness of the International Brigades with the cruel realities of their doomed war.

Within a month of *For Whom the Bell Tolls*'s 21 October 1940 publication, Hemingway received an incisive personal assessment from Nobel laureate Sinclair Lewis:

> Jesus, that's a great book, "Bell Tolls." I guess it's even greater than "Sun Also Rises" or "Farewell to Arms"—I say it almost regretfully, such favorites of mine have they been. But you damned near killed me, waiting for Would he blow up

Ernest Hemingway with Sinclair Lewis in Key West, 1940. (Photo by Toby Bruce. Toby and Betty Brue Collection of Ernest Hemingway, #10077, Special Collections Library, Pennsylvania State University, University Park, PA)

the bridge and get away with it, holding myself from skipping a word but wanting to know. Funny thing is that if I were a critic, I could prove—completely—either that it is as "realistic" as Zola, or as "romantic" as Kipling.[2]

Lewis's letter implies that a richer understanding involves not an either/or, but a both. And then some—Realism and Romance are not the only narrative traditions and influences in play.

My understanding of Hemingway's novel as a novel accords with the argument made by Thomas O. Beebee's *The Ideology of Genre:*

> [We] should be less interested in generic classification than in discovering, first of all, the kinds of systems and intertextual relationships (rather than individual genres) that have given them the classifications they take for granted, and second, the tensions within texts between contradictory generic features. Above all, critics should note that such tensions are of the utmost importance for authors and readers. . . . Genre is seen here as a balancing between alternate possibilities, rather than as the construction of a logical system. (256)

The more a text originates from and stays true to a particular genre, the more it limits its characters to their genre-function. Human complexity is achieved through generic interplay. Colliding genres transcend the generic.

Not what it means, but how it is what it is; not story, but genre. *For Whom the Bell Tolls* mashes up genres, influences, and traditions so as not to be overly beholden to any one of them. Yet if any genre subsumes the others in *For Whom the Bell Tolls,* it's the American subspecies of Romance identified by C. Hugh Holman and William Harmon: a fictional work whose story is just larger-than-life enough, whose effect is only slightly more tall tale than verisimilitude, and by virtue of that nature becomes a meditation—in this case a dramatized meditation, on, among other things, its own genre identity and functions. According to Holman and Harmon, "[i]n America in particular, the romance has proved to be a serious, flexible, and successful medium for the exploration of philosophical ideas and attitudes, ranging through such differing works as Hawthorne's *The Scarlet Letter,* Melville's *Moby-Dick,* Fitzgerald's *The Great Gatsby,* Faulkner's *Absalom, Absalom!,* and Warren's *World Enough and Time*" (413). They could have easily included Hemingway's *For Whom the Bell Tolls,* which is as much a meditation on a host of ideas as it is an adventure story, a love story, and a war story.

The modern Romance has proven to be an expansive genre, hardly limited to the cowboy masculinity of Wister or the troubling colonialism of Burroughs and Kipling. *Moby-Dick* makes for an instructive comparison, as it grounds its larger-than-life tale in the mystifying technical details of whaling, just as *For Whom the Bell Tolls* grounds its tale in the mystifying political details of the Spanish Civil War. Both books involve a crew led by a single man on a doomed mission; both involve an Orientalizing element. More to the point, in both books—as Beebee has written about Melville's—"genres collide" (25). In Nina Baym's language, "*Moby-Dick* manages to be interpretable even while submitting itself to no single genre" (qtd. in Beebe 27). Readers who insist on *For Whom the Bell Tolls*'s Realism should remember that the novel emerged in literary history as an alternative or challenge to the Romance. For Frye, realistic fiction amounts to "parody-romance" dominated by "[c]haracters confused by romantic assumptions about reality," from Don Quixote and Emma Bovary to Henry Fleming and Jay Gatsby (*Secular* 38–39, 161). Robert Jordan, too.

As he lies dying, relishing the earth and sun for the last time, Jordan reaches the conclusion that "[t]here's no *one* thing that's true. It's all true" (467:20). Jordan's line can be helpfully reformulated: *There's no one genre that's true. They're all true.* Inversely, they are each false. The novel's Romance is as false as its Realism. Who can deny the ugly Realism of Pilar's tale of a small town's neighbors murdering other neighbors by driving them off a cliff? To admire Robert Jordan's selfless heroism, to uphold the high Romance, is to blunt the novel's unpleasant Realism. It's to hoodwink oneself. Jordan's willingness to kill Pablo for mission expediency has precedent in his past approval of the execution of citizen-militia deserters (235:34+); his own murder of defenseless prisoners (304:17–18); and his offer to his Soviet handler to disappear a fellow American volunteer working for the Republic (239:26+). He knows that even the perception of dereliction of his duty to try to blow the bridge could result in his own execution (151:30). The ending, his ending, is not a straightforward selfless sacrifice. In going ahead with the mission, Jordan at least stands a fighting chance, even knowing some of the Spaniards he leads will die, probably futilely. Or selfless *and* selfish—not either/or, but both. The novel needs its Romance and idealism because people need them in their lives.

Symptomatic of its yoking together of genres, the novel registers its language as both Realist and as something else. Take its use of second-person pronouns. In Early Modern English, the pronouns *thou/thee/thy* were the singular, informal pronouns, and *you/your* the plural, polite, and formal pronouns that eventually supplanted the others. *Thou, thee,* and *thy* accurately document the Republic's employment of the informal pronoun for everyone and its rejection of the formal pronoun for anyone—typically used for strangers, elders, and people in positions of authority. As George Orwell writes in his memoir of the war, *Homage to Catalonia,* "Waiters and shopwalkers looked you in the face and treated you as an equal. Servile and even ceremonial forms of speech had temporarily disappeared. Nobody said 'Señor' or 'Don' or even 'Usted'; everyone called everyone else 'Comrade' and 'Thou'" (5). Thus when addressing someone in Spanish, Hemingway's characters use *thou* as a translation of *tú* (singular familiar subjective) rather than saying *usted* (singular formal subjective). The French equivalent would be to use *tu* instead of *vous* (as singular formal). The novel's *thou/thee/they* sounds more elevated to modern ears, reminiscent of Shakespearean and Biblical language, such that this realistic, plebeian detail counterintuitively effects the heightened quality of an Epic, Tragedy, or Romance.

For Whom the Bell Tolls's style departs from readers' expectations. The familiar Hemingway spare prose and minimalist dramatic mode have turned into longwinded cogitation. Because Ernest Hemingway loved making books. He loved making different kinds of books. *In Our Time, Green Hills of Africa, Death in the Afternoon, A Moveable Feast,* and *The Garden of Eden* display his lifelong experimentation with prose form and genre. When works of art become canonical, it becomes difficult to experience their original strangeness. For all its deceptively conventional qualities, *For Whom the Bell Tolls* is rich in revolutionary strangeness.

The Spanish Civil War was and continues to be a polestar for the creative arts. Spain sat out the First World War, falling behind the rest of Europe's transition from monarchy. The war had its immediate roots in the elections of 1931, which resulted in the end of the monarchy and the declaration of the Second Spanish Republic. The new national leadership committed itself to progressive reforms, naming itself after the short-lived Spanish Republic of 1873–1874, itself the result of the glorious revolution—la Gloriosa—of 1868. But the reforms proved too many, too deep, and too fast for much of the country. It couldn't catch up to the decades of democratic developments of other Western European countries overnight. The political power struggle between liberal and conservative Spain over the next several years included outbreaks of violence. The various moderate, liberal, and far-left factions eventually coalesced into the Popular Front to secure a tenuous hold on the country with the February 1936 elections—until the conservative military rebelled on 17–18 July 1936. The planned coup failed, and the consequent civil war lasted until April 1939 with a victory by the conservative forces, the Nationalist rebels or insurgents, under the command of General Francisco Franco, over the Republican government's loyalists. Franco's dictatorship ruled Spain until his death in 1975.

Outside Spain, non-interventionists argued that increased involvement would precipitate the next world war; interventionists argued that non-intervention would precipitate the next world war. It was the great conflict purportedly between anti-communists (many of whom were fascists) and anti-fascists (many of whom were communists), a battlefield where the era's major political ideologies converged to clash: fascism, communism (Stalinists and Trotskyites), socialism, democratic republicanism, anarchism, syndicalism, theocracy, monarchism, and Catalonian and Basque separatism. And more. It was "a war more cruel and complicated than historians would ever sort out" (Reynolds, *1930s* 262). The 40,000 or so International Brigade volunteers fighting for the Republic came from fifty-two countries across the globe: Europe, North America, Central America, South America, the British Commonwealth nations, the Middle East, and Asia. About 2,800 came from the United States. While Germany and Italy provided military support for Franco's Nationalists, breaking the Non-Intervention Pact that the United States, Great Britain, and France observed, individual Germans and Italians joined the International Brigades. Germans and Italians sometimes fought their own compatriots.

Hemingway traveled to Spain four times during the war: in the spring of 1937, the fall and winter of 1937, the spring of 1938, and briefly in November 1938. He believed in the Republic's legitimately elected government and its anti-fascist cause. He was not a communist, but he threw his lot in with them. The war, he wrote on 5 February 1937 on his way to it, is "none of my business and I'm not making it mine but my sympathies are always for exploited working people against absentee landlords even if I drink around with the landlords and shoot pigeons with them. I would as soon shoot them as the pigeons" (to Harry Sylvester; *SL* 456). His journalism for the North American Newspaper Alliance (NANA) wire service made little pretense of reportorial neutrality; the documentary film he helped Joris Ivens make, *The Spanish Earth*, was used to raise funds for Republican ambulances. He held off writing fiction until late in the war, with a play and several short stories that wrestled with its complexity and, importantly, his compromised role in it, in ways his journalism could not. *The Fifth Column* has always struggled for critical respect. Hemingway attributed the play's troubles in part to the fact that he wrote it in wartime Madrid, resorting to snatches of dialogue and occasional stage direction because he couldn't craft descriptive prose while under regular bombardment.[3] The four stories—"The Denunciation," "The Butterfly and the Tank," "The Night Before

Battle," and "Under the Ridge"—are among the most underesteemed of Hemingway's astonishing body of short fiction.

The Spanish Civil War was a controversial, pivotal, and fascinating moment in twentieth-century global history; writers like to repeat the claim that it has inspired more books than the Second World War. Plenty of Hemingway scholarship has already plunged headfirst into the rabbit hole of trying to read his and Robert Jordan's politics each in terms of the other's. Reynolds partially blamed the flagging interest in *For Whom the Bell Tolls* fifty years after its publication to the undue scholarly attention given to political and biographical interpretations rather than to the literary dimensions and pleasures of the text ("Ringing"). One of its foremost experts, Allen Josephs, has speculated that its historical rootedness has worked against its prevalence in classrooms and scholarship (*Undiscovered* 21).

Yet the tension between this particular war's particulars and the implied commonalities in the human condition—the former impeding and the latter contributing to the text's relatability, to use classroom parlance—is part of the book's artistry. When trying to step inside a character's life, the details matter. One can't relate without knowing the terms of the circumstances. All wars are not the same, and humans find themselves in all sorts of conflicted positions. *For Whom the Bell Tolls* may very well transcend its historical context, but for the novel to communicate that accomplishment, it must provide the historical context it then transcends.

Hemingway began writing material for a novel as early as October 1938 in Paris that might have led to *For Whom the Bell Tolls*. The first draft page, and most of his letters, date that first page to 1 March 1939. Hemingway completed the draft in July 1940 (see appendix A). Between first page and last, the Second World War erupted. Although it received some negative and lukewarm reviews, as Robert Trogdon summarizes in his history of the book's composition, publication, and reception, "The novel was widely regarded as one of the best novels of 1940" (*Lousy Racket* 223; for another summary of the reviews, see Mazzeno 37–39).

The book suffered two disappointments. First, it did not win the Pulitzer Prize. By one account, the prize committee had selected the novel, but Columbia University President Nicholas Murray Butler shamed the committee members into giving no award that year rather than honoring a lesser novel or endorsing Hemingway's novel, which Butler found offensive. For the nonprofanity? For the nongraphic sex? Many scholars suspect Murray objected to the leftist politics of the Republic's supporters. He may have been behind a statement in the *New York Times* distancing the prize and the university from the politics of the prior year's winner, John Steinbeck's *The Grapes of Wrath* (Stuckey 118). In another account, the committee selected a different novel, which upset the advisory board, and Murray managed the disagreement by convincing the committee to forgo the award (see Stuckey 122–23; Hohenberg 144–45; and Mazzeno 39).

Second, Hemingway's American wartime comrades, the veterans of the Abraham Lincoln Brigade, rejected it. They wanted Robert Jordan to represent them as they saw themselves, to be an everyman of a brigader, not a puffed-up hero or a warts-and-all soul; they wanted unambiguous praise for the Republic and condemnation of all Nationalists. Jordan's atypical role in an invented and fantastical military scenario should have prevented accusations of inaccuracy.

If Murray objected on ideological grounds, then the two disappointments came from opposing political extremes—suggesting, perhaps, that Hemingway took the high road of the middle way and got it right. Franco's fascist Spain banned publication of the novel until 1968 (LaPrade 67), for the obvious reason of its author's and characters' anti-fascism, its "Red" ideology. Yet the Soviet Union also banned the novel, for "depict[ing] the superiority of the bourgeois-democratic ideology . . . over communist ideology" (White, "Most Outstanding" 16). Like its detractors, the novel's fans have ranged across the political spectrum, from John McCain, the moderately conservative US senator; and Barack Obama, the moderately liberal forty-fourth US president; to Fidel Castro, the communist Cuban dictator. The contradictory responses testify to the novel's complexity and richness.

Although their rancor festered for many years to come, in 1947 the Lincolns invited Hemingway to speak at a New York City banquet marking the tenth anniversary of the Battle of Jarama, the first combat action for the US volunteers. Hemingway could not break away for the dinner, but he recorded a reading of "On the American Dead in Spain," his 1939 eulogy for those killed at Jarama two winters earlier: "For our dead are a part of the earth of Spain now and the earth of Spain can never die. Each winter it will seem to die and each spring it will come alive again. Our dead will live with it forever" (3). At least in this rhetoric, Robert Jordan's death lives up to the spirit of what the Lincolns wanted for *For Whom the Bell Tolls*. Fully aware of his impending death and preparing to open fire one last time against the approaching fascist soldiers, Robert Jordan settles into the earth: "He was completely integrated now and he took a good long look at everything. Then he looked up at the sky. There were big white clouds in it. He touched the palm of his hand against the pine needles where he lay and he touched the bark of the pine trunk that he lay behind" (471:12+).

Robert Jordan would rather be Spanish than American (15:30). *For Whom the Bell Tolls* mimics that aspiration. Language is one means, as Hemingway frequently attempts to approximate Spanish syntax and diction with his English. In dialogue especially, the text, for example, avoids contractions and uses the prepositional possessive, but the narration also sometimes employs a Spanish rhythm over the common English one—the "floor of the forest" instead of the forest floor (1:1+). If twenty-first-century readers find the prose stilted, forced, or even corny, the negative reviews suggest it was no more palatable to some of its original readers.

Beyond language, the book perhaps aspires to Spanishness in an expansive sense of the word *genre*. In *The Soul of Spain* (1908), Havelock Ellis identified the Spanish character as expressed in literature and art as the Spanish Gothic, which he linked to the "romantic spirit." It was "a mixture . . . of the mysterious and grandiose with the grotesquely bizarre, of the soaringly ideal with the crudely real" (20); a "combination of mysteriously grandiose splendor with detailed realism," of "massiveness and extravagance" with "realistic naturalness" (21). First published in 1908, Ellis's book went through many printings. Hemingway owned a 1937 edition, and he was well-versed in Ellis's psychological theories about sexuality. Hemingway's prewar friend John Dos Passos promoted a similar characterization of the relationship between the Spanish character and its art and literature in his own creative treatise on Spanishness, the 1922 *Rosinante to the Road Again*:

> Spanish art is constantly on the edge of caricature. Given the ebullient fertility of the Spanish mind and its intense individualism, a constant slipping over into the grotesque is inevitable. . . . Their image of reality is sharp and clear, but distorted. Burlesque and satire are never far away in their most serious moments. Not even the calmest and best ordered of Spanish minds can resist a tendency to excess of all sorts, to over-elaboration, to grotesquerie, to deadening mannerism. All that is greatest in their art, indeed, lies on the borderland of the extravagant, where sublime things skim the thin ice of absurdity. (27)

Hemingway's novel aspires less to Spanishness than to a widely held foreigner's idea of it.

Furthermore, for Ellis, "Interwoven with the manifestations of the romantic spirit of Spain, indeed a part of its texture, there is a perpetual insistence on suffering and death" such that, as "it has been said, the Spaniard has a natural passion for suicide, has always been a note of the romantic mood" (24). One does not have to subscribe to a fulfilled desire-for-death thesis to acknowledge Jordan's preoccupation with suicide and the text's romanticizing of his end. The English poet W. H. Auden spent a brief time in Spain in the spring of 1937 and afterward wrote and published a poem titled simply "Spain." In it, Auden assumes the voice of the Second Spanish Republic as it appeals to those with its fate in their hands:

"I am whatever you do. I am your vow to be
Good, your humorous story.
I am your business voice. I am your marriage.

"What's your proposal? To build the just city? I will.
I agree. Or is it the suicide pact, the romantic

Death? Very well, I accept, for
I am your choice, your decision. Yes, I am Spain." (Auden 24)

The spirit of Auden's poem moves in Jordan's heart. His romantic death mirrors the Republic's.

Michele Haapamaki's essay "Writers in Arms and the Just War: The Spanish Civil War, Literary Activism, and Leftist Masculinity" provides another tradition to consider. Haapamaki examines British leftist writers of the 1930s, including their relationship to the Great War as well as to British identity and nationalism. The terms of Jordan's heroism narrative match what Haapamaki finds in British leftist writing about the war, namely "the embrace of a certain leftist form of militia soldiering, as well as the persistence of traditional motifs of sacrifice and quasi-religious symbolism" (34). In Britain, the challenge was in reconciling the left's post–Great War pacifism and the war-against-war movement with the increasing realization that the democratic nations had to go to war to stop fascism: "The path from these resoundingly pacifist editorials in the early *Left Review,* to the glorification of the intellectual warrior, necessitated a re-orientation of war along leftist lines to counter the anti-heroic legacy of the Great War. The most striking feature of the hagiography surrounding the Spanish Civil War was the glorification of the individual soldier" (39). The path from Frederic Henry to Robert Jordan, from the antiheroic Great War novel *A Farewell to Arms* to the glorifying Spanish Civil War novel *For Whom the Bell Tolls,* follows just such a reorientation.

Haapamaki describes British writers' idealized volunteer militiamen as having a "strong military masculinity, but one constructed outside of the confines of the nation-state" (24). The absence of real uniforms and of professional structures "became a means for the left to accept a warrior role in Spain without simultaneously accepting the baggage of an outdated military ideal" of "hierarchy and authoritarianism" (39). Lawrence of Arabia "served as an example of heroic masculine fantasy that would prove an important element in the Spanish narrative" of the leftwing British intellectual "as a model of a writer hero who retained a sense of independence and nonconformity" (44). Readers have long considered T. E. Lawrence and his Great War memoir of guerilla warfare *The Seven Pillars of Wisdom* as models for Robert Jordan and *For Whom the Bell Tolls.* Unlike nearly all other International Brigaders, Jordan doesn't function within a military unit, he wears no uniform, apparently has no rank, and refuses a proper soldier's haircut. He started fighting alongside the Loyalist militias months before the first International Brigades showed up (235:32). What exactly is his relationship to military command structures? His service is as irregular, autonomous, and individualized as it could possibly be. In the spirit of British narratives of the Spanish Civil War and Lawrence of Arabia, Jordan's tale partakes of "masculine adventure and fantasy," is "bound with the notion of the foreign," and partially relies upon "an image of Latin military ineptitude," to evoke a traditional colonial mythos (45–46).

This trajectory of leftist British war writing of the 1930s dovetails with a longer trajectory of US war literature. For Jonathan Vincent, the story of American war literature from the late nineteenth century to well into the Cold War moves from a foundational notion of laissez-faire liberal citizenship—for which the "call for sacrifice sounded by war administrators" was "an anomaly" (15)—to a normalization of the disciplinary and regulatory prerogative of the nation-state. As Vincent argues in *The Health of the State: Modern U.S. War Narrative and the American Political Imagination, 1890–1964,* this era's war writings helped construct a sanctification of the individual's willful yielding of autonomy and identity, of flesh and blood. Henry Fleming, the protagonist of Stephen Crane's novel of the American Civil War, *The Red Badge of Courage,* struggles to reconcile his visions of warfare as an expression of individuality with his cog-like role in the US Army's blue machine, a role he inevitably accepts. For Vincent, this novel is "the urtext, perhaps, of twentieth-century US war writing, . . . an allegory of political selfhood in a process of transformation: its central aesthetic concern is to frame the translation of individual sovereignty into corporate combination as the advent of a kind of sacramental nationality" (25). Self-abnegation through military service, ultimately through the possibility of secular martyrdom, becomes the means to realizing full selfhood. (One can then regard Fleming's running away from the battle as actually his running away from utter subjugation to the state.)

It makes sense, then, that Jordan's thoughts frequently return to the American Civil War, the war mined for its raw material by American writers revisiting it thirty years later in order to sort through their generation's conflict between individualistic laissez-faire citizenship and selfhood through incorporation. By sacrificing himself, not for the country that bore him but the country he adopts (in death), Jordan at once preserves autonomy, resisting the claim of happenstance soil, and reenacts that earlier literature's plotline toward actualization through submission. The vestigial pull of the laissez-faire lingers in his service as a lone-wolf guerilla, in the presence of Romani and anarchists, and in Jordan's foil, Pablo, whose leadership over his quasi–militia band favors preservation and independence. The novel's timeframe, the spring of 1937, coincides with the Republic's incorporation of its many autonomous militias into the single organization and command structure of the People's Army. In Spain since before the war, Jordan fought as a part of those militias before the arrival of the International Brigades, much less the creation of the People's Army. Perhaps, in the end, he couldn't survive such incorporation into the state. "Who wants to be in an army?" asks the Romani Raphael: "Do we make the revolution to be in an army? I am willing to fight but not to be in an army" (26:25+).

The book's evocation of an American frontier nostalgia—of nineteenth-century heroes created by writers such as James Fenimore Cooper and Owen Wister—permits Jordan to wear the guise of "cultural icons" such as "Paul Revere or Davy Crocket, Daniel Boone or Lewis and Clark, George Washington or Andrew Jackson," who for Vincent helped nineteenth-century Americans "bridge the identification gap between their isolated, individual identities and the non-cognizable abstractions of 'society,' 'the state,' and 'the republic'" (29). Vincent's hypothesis also relegates Jordan's obsession with the idea of suicide into a moot distraction. He has already given himself over, given himself up, as his revered grandfather had during the American Civil War, enjoying zero identity outside his military function.

Whether Jordan gives himself over to the Republic or to a vision of himself, however, remains brilliantly ambiguous. Since boyhood, he has idolized the nineteenth-century frontiersman and cavalryman George Armstrong Custer, a career officer who belonged to the state's apparatus but also bucked against it at every turn. His last misadventure proved fatal. Custer famously died at the Battle of the Little Bighorn, on 25 June 1876, in the Montana Territory near Jordan's hometown. The book with the most direct influence on *For Whom the Bell Tolls* may well have been Frederic F. Van de Water's *Glory-Hunter: A Life of General Custer*. It appeared in 1934: "Few books have had so immediate and dramatic an impact as Van de Water's biography did on historical interpretation and the popular mind" (Hutton 11). Hemingway owned the book and included its climatic episode, Custer's last stand, in his 1942 *Men at War* anthology. Van de Water figures the west as Custer's lover (158, 237); he describes the beauty and romance of the Black Hills (259); he discusses the unexpected, unseasonal snowfalls on several expeditions, including on the first of June during Custer's final mission (307); and he emphasizes Custer's uncharacteristic nervousness and the foreboding throughout his unit as the last stand approached (317–19). According to his subordinates, the general was anxious and gloomy that day: "I believe Custer is going to be killed," said one lieutenant: "I have never heard him talk that way before" (327). As Van de Water summarizes, "It may have been the nervousness of their leader; it may have been the prescience of impending disaster. Whatever its source, many of the officers were in the jumpy state of mind that is receptive to ill omen" (329). In Hemingway's draft, Jordan worries his nervousness will spread to others (*HLE* 492).

Several times Van de Water writes about Custer's life story in terms of a literary Tragedy. The most extensive of these passages portrays him like a Robert Jordan prototype:

[Custer] was not the fury-hounded hapless man of Greek drama, unless it be that the Eumenides nest in a man's own heart. The tragedy in which he went down had grandeur. The part he played therein was less exalted. He was not the austerely innocent, the God-destroyed. Fate whirled him along, with many others, white and red. He was less the doom-overwhelmed hero than the puppet, whose movements were directed, whose death was devised, by the guiding strings of conduct a willful life had spun.

Men whispered, for long after his naked body had been found on the brown slope above the Little Bighorn, that Custer had killed himself. Indian bullets had stopped his hungry heart, yet in a broader sense the fable had its truth. (250)

Nothing in *The Virginian* or *The Seven Pillars of Wisdom* approaches *Glory-Hunter* in matching the mood, structure, and pace of *For Whom the Bell Tolls*. Moreover, from Van de Water Hemingway would have seen Custer as more the swashbuckler than a soldier, a man whose cruelty toward the enemy during the Civil War was exceeded by his racist cruelty toward Native Americans. His boss in both wars was Phil Sheridan, the general to whom we popularly attribute the phrase, *the only good Indian is a dead Indian*. Hemingway wants his readers to question Jordan's attraction to Custer and his last stand; by extension, it seems reasonable that he expects his readers to question their attraction to Jordan and his last stand. The two bullets shot into Custer's body had encouraged the rumors that he killed himself—one to his chest or torso, but the second to his temple. In this scenario, he would have faced the same decision as Robert Jordan, already dying, in pain, the enemy but steps away. It was also whispered that Custer's brother Tom fired the fatal shot, to spare Custer any indignities or torture. The ambiguity of whether self or brother shot Custer suggests the ambiguity of whether Jordan or his look-alike comrade, Kashkin, killed the latter, who was already wounded, to spare him capture and torture.

The late spring and early summer of 1937 is an apt chronological setting for a more palpable reason. Hemingway in retrospect very likely believed that period to have been the war's tipping point, or at least knew his novel could dramatize it as such. The Republic had recently won its most resounding battlefield victory to date, the Battle of Guadalajara (or Brihuega). The failed Segovia Offensive, the battle of Jordan's mission, frustrated that momentum. Full of various omens, *For Whom the Bell Tolls* finally hints at an inevitability to Jordan's death, to the failed Segovia Offensive, and by extension to the Republican war effort. A self-derived futility and doom suited to the literary trappings of the Tragic.

Tragedy has certainly been a reliable touchstone genre for scholars of *For Whom the Bell Tolls*. In his early study *Hemingway: The Writer as Artist*, Carlos Baker categorizes the novel as "a tragic epic," the word *tragic* seeming to mean nothing more than the inevitable "doom" of the story (250). Baker admires the way Pilar creatively resurrects the premonition of superstition in the service of Naturalism (253). In a letter to his publisher, Hemingway discusses how Pilar's disquisition on the scent of death reunites the supernatural with the natural, through the question about forebodings which I know is not phony from haveing [sic] seen people walking around with it sitting on their shoulders (this is not being romantic) There is the balanceing [sic] of Jordan's good sense and sound skepticism against this gypsy crap which isn't at all crap. And to make the gypsy thing valid and not just seeming phony as all that stuff always does I needed some complete naturalistic thing which gives some of the horror that is in Madrid. (To Charles Scribner, ca. 15 August 1940, *SL* 508; see 251:16)

The supernatural is not above nature, is not *supra*natural—it is of nature's essence. For Baker, the supernatural omen is the stuff of "the old epics and the great dramatic tragedies" (253). Baker does not define the Epic with much precision; his description of its elements fits Frye's breakdown of the Romance and could apply to all sorts of texts. Gerry Brenner provides a different list of the novel's Epic aspects, concluding that these concealed genre mechanics invite judgment by the standards of "the great epic," and in this the "novel fares poorly" (125–33).

Baker's "tragic epic" neglects one traditional distinction between the Epic and the Tragic, whether one suffers the will of the gods or the foibles of self-determination. "The will," to quote the modernist Spanish critic José Ortega y Gasset, "is the tragic theme" and it has become the novel's turf (152). Just as Madame Bovary and Helen of Troy do not exist in the same cosmology, Ortega writes, "The novel and the epic are precisely poles apart" (126–27, 119). Yuval Noah Harari summarizes Friedrich von Blanckenburg's argument, in *Versuch über den Roman* (1774), on the novel's superiority to the Epic as being "because the latter described only external events while the former focuses on the protagonist's inner development (*Bildung*)" (146). For Harari, epic heroes come fully formed, and while they face decisions, their characters do not change. Heroes of novels, on the other hand, accrete experiences toward the evolution of thought and the formation of self. A reader can recognize Hemingway's failed effort to combine the Epic with the modern novel, as Brenner does, or can insist on the two forms' fundamental incompatibility, as Ortega and Harari do. A third option places the two forms in a productive rivalry to view the incompatibility of the novel's Epic strains within its modern situation as exactly the point. *The Red Badge of Courage*'s Henry Fleming pines for Homeric heroism but settles for his role as another cog in the Union army and lamely compensates for that resignation by dubbing himself, for the umpteenth time, a *man*.

As Terry Eagleton wryly begins his study *Sweet Violence: The Idea of the Tragic*, "The truth is that no definition of tragedy more elaborate than 'very sad' has ever worked" (3). But not even that vague definition works, because sadness isn't always there. Were sadness a baseline criterion, it would prove challenging to consider the novel's tragic dimension as denoting "an unambiguous, spiritual triumph," with Jordan's death "exalted and transcendent," as Wirt Williams does in *The Tragic Art of Ernest Hemingway* (137). For Frye, "The tragic hero is normally a person capable of being an agent and not merely a victim of violence, but tragedy is mainly a form in which an actual or potential agent of violence becomes a victim of it" (*Secular* 66). For Ortega, on the other hand, "it is essential for the hero to want his tragic destiny.... All the sorrow springs from the hero's refusal to give up an ideal part, an imaginary role he has chosen" (154).

Ortega avoids distinguishing between character or volition as the source of that desire and choice, of the tragic flaw or tragic virtue. More than once, *For Whom the Bell Tolls* calls attention to these differences and distinctions. Pilar's palm reading suggests that Jordan's fate is inescapably embodied. But is it figuratively as well as literally in his hands, and so a matter of volition? Or of character? Or is it written there, written on him, an externally imposed destiny, either a predetermination or simply the randomness of an indifferent universe? What is one to make of the bullfighter Finito's hubris-driven aphorism that "the bull never gored the man; rather the man gored himself on the horn of the bull," which his lover Pilar dismisses as poppycock (55:3–4)?

An understanding of the Tragic as the consequence of an individual's failure to relinquish a self-appointed role would seem to fit *For Whom the Bell Tolls*. But so would a seemingly opposite understanding: Susan Sontag's, of the Tragic as a "heroic or ennobling vision of nihilism," of character confronting "the implacability of the world" (*Against* 136). Sontag's approach accords with one widespread conception of Hemingway and his art. As Verna Kale writes, for Hemingway, "everyone loses" against "the unfeeling natural world" (1). Jordan muses that the sudden late snowfall obeys the "pattern of tragedy into which the whole operation had seemed grooved" (393:11–12). This is the sense in which Hemingway considers the bullfight a tragedy for the bull toward whose death the whole system is grooved. The novel's language and imagery here and elsewhere convey the metaphysic of Naturalism, a late-nineteenth-century post-Darwin literary movement that has continued in various guises ever since—from *The Call of the Wild* to *The Jungle*, *Native Son*, and beyond. If in the Tragic text, character becomes the determining factor, in the Naturalist text, external environment (natural or social) and internal biological fundamentals (one's animal nature) become the determining factors. Random, indifferent, and consequential weather events—like an unexpected snowstorm—exemplify this tradition. Per Ortega, "The will—that paradoxical object which begins in reality and ends in the ideal, since one only wants what is not—is the tragic theme; and an epoch for which the will does not exist, a deterministic and Darwinian epoch, for example, cannot be interested in tragedy" (152).

Yet *For Whom the Bell Tolls* refuses stark opposition between Tragedy and Naturalism. It honors life's complexity, which exceeds generic explanation. It is a meditation. The novel's narration, a third-person omniscient dominated but not defined by Jordan's interior monologue, structurally enacts the Naturalist-Tragic collision. The two modes persist all the way to Jordan's dying, poetic assertion of the true and the beautiful inhabiting all things. In post-nineteenth-century literature, Ortega laments, the "environment is the only protagonist" and art "submits" to the rule of "verisimilitude." But, he asks, "does not Tragedy have its own internal independent verisimilitude?" Is there no room for "the beautiful" and the "true" outside the cold laws of "what is probable" and of "physics"? (165). Hemingway and Ortega believe in the dignity of individual human experience and subjectivity.

By the "'realism' of Zola," Sinclair Lewis meant Naturalism, the species of Realism practiced and originated by Émile Zola. Zola's social conscience led him to a nearly documentary style involving thick descriptions of his characters' unremitting environment. A foundational American war story, Stephen Crane's *The Red Badge of Courage* is also a committed work of literary Naturalism. Crane was the original American novelist, war correspondent, and celebrity author. Hemingway appreciated how Crane's novel dramatizes a character's quaint belief in character as determinant rather than the overwhelming forces of (animal) nature, the environment (of war), and chance. In a 1926 letter, Hemingway called *The Red Badge of Courage* a "tour de force" (to Maxwell Perkins, 19 Nov.; *SL* 230, *Letters 3* 158). A year before the start of the Spanish Civil War, his nonfiction book *Green Hills of Africa* grouped Crane with Henry James and Mark Twain as the nation's three "good writers" (17)—one could argue that this trio served as the literary muses for *For Whom the Bell Tolls*: Crane for his Naturalism, graphic stories of war and violence, and common-man politics; James for his lengthy treatments of human interiority; and Twain for his humor. Hemingway included *The Red Badge of Courage* in its entirety in the 1942 *Men at War* book he helped assemble. It's the only novel included in its entirety, and it appears in the same section with an excerpt from *For Whom the Bell Tolls*, from El Sordo's last stand (chapter 27), titled in the anthology "The Fight on the Hilltop." In his introduction to the anthology, Hemingway writes that *The Red Badge of Courage* was "that boy's dream of war that was to be truer to how war is than any war the boy who wrote it would ever live to see. It is one of the finest books of our literature" (xvii).

Most timely, Hemingway repeats the "tour de force" label in his preface to Regler's *The Great Crusade*, pairing *The Red Badge of Courage* with *Wuthering Heights* in their inventive and poetic powers (xi). Readers often discuss Crane's novel as an intertext for *A Farewell to Arms*, given the similarity of the protagonists' names—Henry Fleming and Frederic Henry—and the central issues of fleeing from war and being wounded. Yet *The Red Badge of Courage* has its legacy realized in *For Whom the Bell Tolls*. The "youth" of the former becomes the "young man" of the latter; the Battle of Chancellorsville becomes the Segovia Offensive. The actions of both occupy a condensed period of a few days in May—in both cases, to use Robert Jordan's tally, over four calendar dates, but in real time, "not quite three days and three nights" (466:30–31). Fleming's and Jordan's sides lose their respective historic battles to the rebelling army, and in neither battle does either side gain any ground. There is a tragic irrelevance to both protagonists' personal victories. If Henry Fleming struggles to reconcile his nostalgic fantasy for Greek mano-a-mano warfare with the dehumanizing regimentation of his war, Robert Jordan struggles to reconcile his nostalgic fantasy of pre-twentieth-century war adventure narratives with the messy reality of his war—which, although occurring eighty years after the American Civil War, is defined by its own clash of the modernist and the premodernist.

The narratives of *The Red Badge of Courage* and of *For Whom the Bell Tolls* consist largely of a representation of the protagonist's frustratingly mercurial thoughts, which often as not debate the nature of his manhood, particularly regarding cowardice and the decision of whether to enter the fight. Both narratives employ a third-person limited frame that sometimes shifts into first-person and free indirect discourse and sometimes introduces an omniscient narrator. Fleming and Jordan are quite unreliable in their self-narrations. Given that the reader meets the middle-aged Jordan in the final days of his life, it is easy to overlook that his war story, like Fleming's, pretends to be a bildungsroman, a story of education and maturation. "Christ," Jordan tells himself as the novel wraps up, "I was learning fast there at the end" (467:14–15).

Crane's protagonist survives his war, but a year after *Red Badge*, in the short story "The Veteran," a much older Henry Fleming gives up his life to save horses from a burning barn. As with Jordan's motive, Fleming's isn't clear-cut selflessness. Does he do it to prove to himself, finally, what kind of man he is? To silence his interminable self-questioning? "Why, it's suicide for a man to go in there!" an onlooker exclaims just before Fleming rushes into the barn: "When the roof fell in, a great funnel of smoke swarmed toward the sky, as if the old man's mighty spirit, released from its body—a little body—had swelled like the genie of a fable. The smoke was tinted rose-hue from the flames, and perhaps the unutterable midnights of the universe will have no power to daunt the color of his soul" (174). Fleming's final moment anticipates Jordan's romanticized integration with the Spanish earth and sky. But neither hero's death carries a straightforward message. What Donald Pizer has written about Fleming's applies to Jordan's: its "purposeful ambivalence" combines "sympathetic identity and irony" to chart "the complex impact of experience" and portray "the unresolvable complexities of inner life" (in Crane 137–38).

As a Naturalist work, Crane's novel emphasizes humanity's animalism when first Henry Fleming's flight instinct and then his fight instinct kick in—when the latter happens, the text at different times describes him as fierce as a "dog" (71), a "barbarian, a beast" (72), a "savage" (92), and a "mad horse" (93). Hemingway's novel often relates human behavior to mere animal activity and also poses the question of war's naturalness, in, for example, conversations about the difference between hunting animals and hunting people as well as the use of natural imagery for such instruments of war as combat aircraft. Nor do the natural imagery and the mechanical imagery for the war planes—"sharks" as well as "mechanized doom" (87:3+)—necessarily contradict, as both are standard techniques of literary Naturalism for communicating the indifferent mechanisms of the world. *The Red Badge of Courage* describes soldiers, military units, and war itself in both bestial and mechanistic language, sometimes at the same time (e.g., 89–90). When Jordan spies a squirrel among the pines as it flees the battle, and reflects upon it, the potential allusion to Fleming's meditation upon a scampering-away squirrel is hard to ignore.

In addition to the opposition between Tragedy and Naturalism, the two novels incorporate religious language and imagery to place another pair of incompatible metaphysical frameworks, the godless Naturalist world and the Christian universe, on the same textual battleground. As one example: After Fleming's squirrel meditation—by which he comically justifies his natural and superior wisdom in running away from the battle, but only by declining to read the next page of nature's book, when a small mammal "pounces" into the swampy pond to emerge with its prey—after this meditation, he enters a natural chapel-like space, bathed in "a religious half light" and inhabited by a corpse with a disfigured face crawling with ants (36). Then there is Hemingway's scene with the Carlist Lieutenant Paco Berrendo riding away from the killing of El Sordo and his men, his troops carrying their heads: "He went on with the prayer, the horses' hooves soft on the fallen pine needles, the light coming through the tree trunks in patches as it comes through the columns of a cathedral" (326:25+). The two scenes involve a piney chapel, the gruesome results of war, and a sincere question about the place of God.

One might agree with Cleanth Brooks's early argument against a Christian interpretation: "For Jordan is not a supernaturalist. He is a naturalist in all the senses, including his tremendous sensitivity to the realm of nature. He dies as he has lived, loving the feel, smell, and quality of the earth. . . . These are the certainties of the Hemingway world—the intense vibrations of the senses," not the certainties of the divine spheres (18). Yet what about Paco Berrendo's death? The novel instructs us exactly how to imagine it: Robert Jordan will pull the trigger when Berrendo reaches "the sunlit place where the first trees of the pine forest joined the green slope of the meadow" (471:33–34). The text draws this second cathedral-like natural space as liminal, as a threshold between the sloping meadow and the forest above, between earth and heaven, and blessed by the sun. Is Anselmo, in his genuine yearning for spiritual answers, merely, in Brooks's language, "a dying animal in a purely mechanistic universe"? (20). Hemingway's novel gives far more credence to the Christian view than Crane's. The genius of *For Whom the Bell Tolls* stems from its ability to vitalize and validate seemingly incompatible narratives—discourses, worldviews, genres—and thereby realize the complex world its characters inhabit, continuing *A Farewell to Arms*'s investigation into this world as God-filled or godless.

Like *For Whom the Bell Tolls*, *The Red Badge of Courage* saw instant popular and commercial success. And like Hemingway's novel, Crane's met with some telling confusion among critics due to its generic and stylistic unfamiliarity. One contemporary reviewer praised it exactly for its unfamiliarity: "It is a book outside of all classification. So unlike anything else is it that the temptation rises to deny that it is a book at all" (Frederic). Dorothy Parker said much the same thing about *For Whom the Bell Tolls:* "I think that what you do about this book of Ernest Hemingway's is to point at it and say, 'Here is a book.' As you would stand below Everest and say, 'Here is a mountain'" (qtd. in Trogdon, *Lousy Racket* 220).

The action of the novel occurs exclusively in the Sierra de Guadarrama, the mountain range just north of and commanding the view from Madrid. The Guadarrama stand between the capital and La Granja and Segovia, the objectives of the Republican offensive that Jordan's mission supports. As suggested in the earlier comparison of the landscapes of *Wuthering Heights* and *For Whom the Bell Tolls*, the mountains are key to Hemingway's novel's status as Romance.

Allen Josephs first recognized that while the front lines in the area were "somewhat ill-defined" in late May 1937—as all front lines are, especially in mountainous terrain—"at no time was the bridge *behind* Nationalist (enemy) lines," and the novel's military geography is "Hemingway's invention," a "fictional necessity" (*Undiscovered* 53). This invention enables Hemingway to write toward the more general fact of the Guadarrama Mountains as the natural and contested division between the Nationalist and the Republican forces. *Liminality* is the term for such between and betwixt spaces, where one straddles two spaces yet occupies neither, those spaces

In the Guadarrama Mountains, looking south toward the Republican lines from a Nationalist fighting position. (Photo by author. May 2019)

signifying states of being. The term comes from anthropologists Arnold van Gennep and Victor Turner in studies of ritualized rites of passage, such as from childhood to adulthood. If these liminal or threshold ceremonial spaces exist of and between and beyond actual places, of and between and beyond states of being, the ritual events also exist outside ordinary time. By creating a liminal space of (and within) the Sierra de Guadarrama, a site whose imagined details Josephs reports do not correspond with a precise location (*Undiscovered* 52–57), Hemingway encourages a reading of the novel as a transformational journey for Robert Jordan.

One of Jordan's favorite writers on Spain, George Borrow, retells a Spaniard's description of the Guadarrama Mountains in his nineteenth-century travel book, *The Bible in Spain*:

> *Caballero*, there is not another such range in Spain; they have their secrets, too—their mysteries. Strange tales are told of those hills, and of what they contain in their deep recesses, for they are a broad chain, and you may wander days and days amongst them without coming to any *termino* [ending]. Many have lost themselves in those hills, and have never again been heard of. Strange things are told of them: it is said that in certain places there are deep pools and lakes, in which dwell monsters, huge serpents as long as a pine-tree, and horses of the flood, which sometimes come out and commit mighty damage. One thing is certain, that yonder, far away to the west, in the heart of those hills, there is a wonderful valley, so narrow that only at mid-day is the face of the sun to be descried from it. That valley lay undiscovered and unknown for thousands of years; no person dreamed of its existence. . . . *Caballero*, I am proud of yonder hills; and were I independent, and without wife or children, I would . . . travel amongst them till I knew all their mysteries, and seen all the wondrous things which they contain. (151–52)

The Spanish barber's characterization of the valley as "undiscovered and unknown" conveniently resembles Hemingway's working title for his novel, "The Undiscovered Country," Shakespeare's metaphor for death from *Hamlet* (see frontmatter: title and epigraph). The romantic rumors of people being lost forever to the mountains, and the barber's fantasy of traveling the mountains without wife or child as if to both find himself and lose himself in their mysteries, could perhaps be read into Robert Jordan's motives.

The barber accurately references the mountain range as the division between Old Castile and New Castile. One must extend the division along the entire Central System mountain chain and extend it further back in time, to the border between the Moorish state to its south and the old Spanish kingdoms to its north. The Moor's domain in Spain varied over several centuries. At its height, it covered most of the peninsula before being reduced to Grenada in the far south and its final demise after the Reconquista of 1492. But for much of its duration, the Central System served as the frontier.

The historic division becomes far more interesting and provocative in setting the novel at the very juncture of white Christian Europe and dark and so-called savage Africa. "Spain is a mountain country," Hemingway writes in *Death in the Afternoon,* "and a good part of it is African" (101). Hemingway writes the modernist aphorism that "Africa begins at the Pyrenees" (the mountains between France and Spain) into *The Garden of Eden:*

> "They always say that Africa begins at the Pyrenees," Catherine said. "I remember how impressed I was when I first heard it."
> "That's one of those easy sayings," David said. "It's more complicated than that."
> "But how can I tell about where Africa begins if I've never been there? People are always telling you tricky things.
> "Sure. You can tell."
> "The Basque country certainly wasn't like Africa or anything I ever heard about Africa."
> "Neither is Asturias nor Galicia but once you're in from the coast it gets to be Africa fast enough." (52)

Although wary of oversimplifying the Moorish legacy in Spain, this passage confirms that Spain's African-ness, at least for Hemingway, begins a little deeper and more centrally than the French border. The aphorism could be rewritten as "Africa begins at the Guadarrama."

It is impossible to overstate the pervasiveness and depth of racialized attitudes toward Spaniards. Richard Ford's *A Hand-book for Travellers in Spain and Readers at Home*—another book Jordan knows (248:22)—describes Spain as a "singular country, which hovers between Europe and Africa, between civilization and barbarism" (77), between "the hat and the turban" (ix). Spain's role as the "connecting link between Europe and the African continent," writes Havelock Ellis, "is the cause of the almost savage primitiveness and violence which we find in all the burnt-brown soil of Spain, wherever it is most characteristic, and of the independence, equally savage in its aboriginal primitiveness, which we may detect in the Spanish temper" (29). W. H. Auden's poem "Spain" calls the country "that arid square, that fragment nipped off from hot / Africa, soldered so crudely to inventive Europe" (25). Spain's women have a "bearing and carriage," Ellis believes, that can sometimes mimic that "of the Hottentot Venus" or "the Ogowe woman of tropical Africa" (71–72). Because of the North African Moors' Islamic heritage, Victor Hugo asserted that "Spain is half African, and Africa is half Asiatic" (52; trans. by author).

For Hemingway and his modernist peers, the Western Orientalizing of Spain, as María DeGuzmán has demonstrated, condescendingly idealized Spaniards as "representatives of a primal, authentic relationship to the land, if not actual embodiments of both its creative and destructive forces" (*Spain's Long Shadow* 188). Spain symbolized "a place with ties to the land, ties that, it was felt, had been lost in the United States through industrialization, mechanization, increasing urbanization, physical and psychological dislocation, and discontinuity." In Spain, one could find "what was missing from life in the United States—ritual, passion, a sense of the sacred" (190). Ultimately, this modernist fantasy of the Spanish landscape belongs to a racialized, romanticized, and colonial or imperialist discourse.

Sinclair Lewis celebrated Hemingway's new novel for being as "'realistic' as Zola, or as 'romantic' as Kipling." Hemingway grew up on the novels and stories of Rudyard Kipling, and throughout his life cited Kipling as a significant writer and major influence. "*Enlistment* may be the appropriate word for Kipling's youthful readers," writes Mark Spilka. "In his imperial largesse he liked to imagine for them heroic children performing quasi-military deeds" (95). Per Spilka, Kipling "had impressed Hemingway more profoundly than he ever quite acknowledged" (97). If Hemingway's experiences in World War I did not lend themselves to Kiplingesque patriotism, he found a far more conducive setting in the idealized, romanticized Spanish Civil War. Spilka's otherwise excellent study of Kipling's impact on Hemingway insufficiently attends to *For Whom the Bell Tolls*, but the novel resonates throughout. A "staunch imperialist," Kipling nevertheless in his fiction preferred subalterns, "loyal natives," and "raffish but heroic types" (Spilka 100). He loved "'inside' outsiders" like "mischievous sons of colonial officers and administrators" who grew up to "become the minor officers and officials who kept the Empire going" (Spilka 101). Even Mowgli, the famous feral native child of the *Jungle Book* and its sequel, grows up to work for the Department of Woods and Forests in an imperial land management posting (Spilka 95). This hanging of native sympathies onto a colonial framework fits Ernest Hemingway—and the "inside" outsider Robert Jordan—to a tee. Kipling's fictions are inevitably tales of conceptual miscegenation between the paternalistic British empire and its colonized subjects.

Kipling's early novel, *The Light That Failed* (1891), charts the life of a painter who signs on as a newspaper-syndicate illustrator covering the British army fighting in the Sudan and Egypt. At the end of the novel, with failing eyesight and a broken heart, Dick Heldar arranges to return to the military campaign in search of a "redeeming death at the front" (Spilka 109). Kipling, Spilka conjectures, sparked or fed Hemingway's admiration for "the death-urges of those who try to die valiantly in battle" and "a self-destructive and perhaps even a romantic edge to his own active courage" (117). Kipling also contributed to the young Hemingway's "emerging attitudes toward women as they served or threatened [male] independence" (92). Soldiers in Kipling "never indulge in romantic leanings" because "marriage and the military life do not mix well" (99). Jordan initially adheres to this injunction. Until meeting Maria. As he carries out the mission, he does his damnedest to separate the girl from the combat.

The Maria plot conforms to the "deathly consequences" when a Kipling man, especially a military Kipling man, becomes romantically entangled (116). Jordan consistently predicates the intensity and nature of his love for her on the certainty of his death. No death, no love; no love, no redeeming death at the front.

Hemingway's affection for Kiplingesque Romanticism and his inclination to ruthless Naturalism would seem hard to reconcile. Yet one of the foremost American literary Naturalists, Frank Norris, aligned Naturalism with Romanticism rather than with Realism. For Norris, Realism belonged to the "teacup tragedies" of "ordinary and bourgeois" lives, "not adventurous or not rich or not unconventional" (168). In Naturalism as in Romance, characters "must be twisted from the ordinary, wrenched out from the quiet, uneventful round of every-day life, and flung into the throes of a vast and terrible drama that works itself out in unleased passions, in blood, in death" (168). In Romance, invention exceeds punctilious verisimilitude to "be truer than Life itself" (170), a principle Hemingway would also hold.

Naturalism's male characters struggle against a fickle universe whose agent is often a woman, as in Norris's *McTeague*. In many Naturalist novels, Susan Donaldson writes,

> we discover depictions of a diminished, shrunken masculinity that is eventually destroyed by competing narratives of womanhood and a newly assertive female sexuality, and by an increasingly complicated and heterogeneous public sphere of multiple voices and stories. In the brave new world of turn-of-the-century America, both novels assert, even the very space allocated to manhood seems in danger of disappearing altogether. (141)

Hemingway's novel structurally admits an "increasingly complicated and heterogeneous" (and not always compatible) gathering of "voices and stories"; it also misdirects his audience's attention to Pilar as the emasculating woman.[4] Maria is hardly the blatant Spanish femme fatale of *The Devil Is a Woman*, the extravagant, almost campy 1935 cinematic caricature of Spanishness starring Hemingway's new friend Marlene Dietrich and loosely based on a John Dos Passos screenplay. Nevertheless, *For Whom the Bell Tolls* obeys a pattern of so much Naturalist and Modernist fiction that ends with the man's demise through romance. Jordan experiences conflicting nostalgias, for everlasting romantic love and for a frontier autonomy that harkens back to Rip Van Winkle, and by his interlinking of Maria and Spain he accomplishes both. The space allocated to undomesticated manhood has shrunk to a spot in the Guadarrama Mountains into which he can rapturously integrate himself.

Consider *For Whom the Bell Tolls*, then, to be a success story of an American's fantasy of becoming Spain. It's a failed fantasy, but he doesn't know it. Hemingway's go-to intellectual, Havelock Ellis, in *The Soul of Spain*, called Spain "the home of romance," its literature and arts the product of the "special character of the Spanish temperament," their admixture of the ideal and the crude, the over-the-top and the down-to-earth, "the natural outcome of the experiences and feelings of the men who created it" (19–20). By this standard, the novel's unartful excesses constitute its artfulness as it formally and ironically achieves Robert Jordan's failed aspiration. What, then, of Jordan's final epiphany?

> That is in Madrid. Just over the hills there, and down across the plain. Down out of the gray rocks and the pines, the heather and the gorse, across the yellow high plateau you see it rising white and beautiful. That part is just as true as Pilar's old women drinking the blood down at the slaughterhouse. There's no *one* thing that's true. It's all true. The way the planes are beautiful whether they are ours or theirs. The hell they are, he thought. (467:15+)

The romantic vision of Madrid rising white and beautiful is just as true as the realism of its death stench. Not either/or, but both, just as the planes are both beautiful and not—aesthetically commanding romantic visions as well as instruments of the absolute ugliness of death and destruction.

It is October 1940. The Second Spanish Republic is dead. France has fallen as fascist Germany has conquered western continental Europe. Can a war novel contain the Romance and the Real, the genres' conflicting expectations? Can it hold beauty and ugliness? Can it deliver pleasure and appall? Can art appease?

Absolutely, Hemingway says. The hell it can, himself says.

NOTES

1. Like Jordan, Bogart's character in *Casablanca* served in the Spanish Civil War's International Brigades, the volunteers who traveled to Spain to fight for the Republic against the insurrection.

2. Sinclair Lewis to Ernest Hemingway, TLS 17 Nov. 1940, NY, 1p. Museum Ernest Hemingway Collection, Incoming Correspondence, Box 4, "Lewis, Sinclair."

3. To Maurice Speiser, 11 July 1938 (USC).

4. In *Facing the Abyss,* his study of 1940s postwar fiction, Hutchinson credits Pilar as an early incarnation of the decade's "powerful, emasculating, sexually uninhibited female figure" (299). Hutchinson fails to note the novel's anticipatory flirtation with gender fluidity and same-sex desire, despite the fact that he devotes an entire chapter to "Queer Horizons." See also Allan Bérubé, *Coming Out Under Fire: The History of Gay Men and Women in World War II* (1990).

ABBREVIATIONS USED IN THIS BOOK

ARIT	*Across the River and into the Trees*
CSS	*Complete Short Stories of Ernest Hemingway,* Finca Vigía Edition
DIA	*Death in the Afternoon*
FTA	*A Farewell to Arms*
GHOA	*Green Hills of Africa*
GOE	*The Garden of Eden*
HLE	*For Whom the Bell Tolls,* Hemingway Library Edition
HRC	Harry Ransom Humanities Research Center, University of Texas, Austin
Incoming	Ernest Hemingway Incoming Correspondence, John F. Kennedy Presidential Library (JFK)
JFK	Ernest Hemingway Personal Papers, JFK
Letters 1	*The Letters of Ernest Hemingway Volume 1, 1907–1922*
Letters 3	*The Letters of Ernest Hemingway Volume 3, 1926–1929*
Letters 5	*The Letters of Ernest Hemingway Volume 5, 1932–1934*
MW	*Men at War*
Outgoing	Ernest Hemingway Outgoing Correspondence, JFK
PUL	Department of Rare Books and Special Collections, Princeton University Library
Residencia	Centro de Documentación, La Residencia de Estudiantes, Madrid
SAR	*The Sun Also Rises*
SL	*Ernest Hemingway: Selected Letters, 1917–1961*
SS-HLE	*The Short Stories of Ernest Hemingway,* Hemingway Library Edition
UIL	University of Illinois Rare Book and Manuscript Library
USC	Irvin Department of Rare Books and Special Collections, Ernest F. Hollings Special Collections Library, University of South Carolina

REFERENCES TO PREPUBLICATION VERSIONS OF THE NOVEL

Draft: JFK 083
Armstrong typescript: JFK 084
Galley Proofs: JFK 086

SERIES NOTE

All page references in this volume are keyed to the First Scribner trade paperback edition of *For Whom the Bell Tolls* (2003), which begins on page 1 and ends on page 471. This has been the standard pagination since the book's 1940 publication.

Annotations and comments follow a page:line format. A reference to the third line of page 17, for instance, would be 17:3. A reference to the first three lines of page 40 would be 40:1–3. A reference to a long passage beginning on line 20 of page 320 would be 320:20+. Keyed words from a long passage appear in boldface.

When citing, the volume adapts the standard abbreviations for Hemingway texts used by the *Hemingway Review,* in concert with the Hemingway Letters Project, available online at https://www.hemingwaysociety.org/abbreviations-works-ernest-hemingway.

MAPS

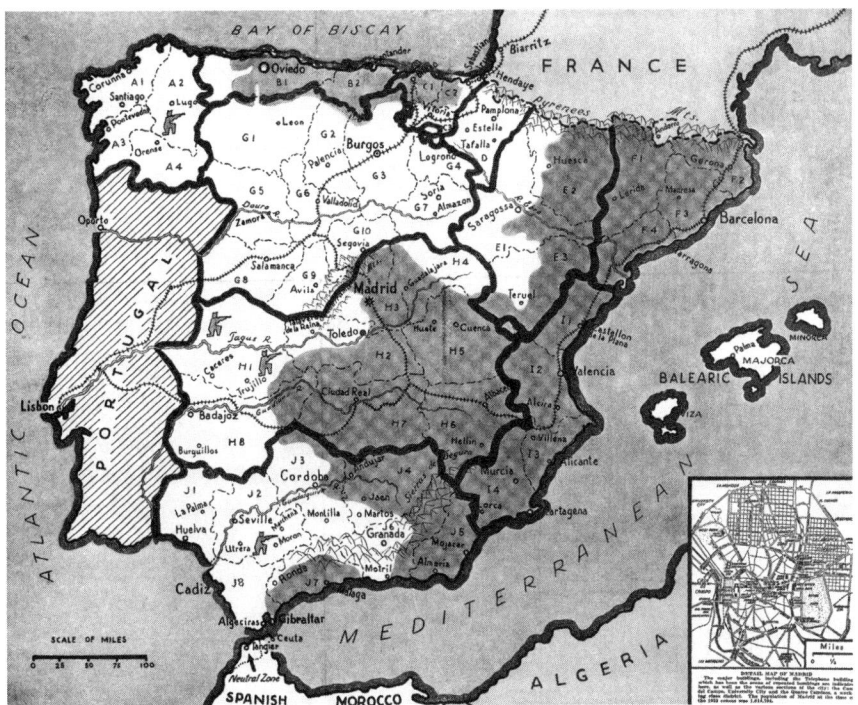

1937 Special Map of Spain by *Soviet Russia Today*. Republican Territory is shaded. (WikiMedia Commons / Public Domain [cropped])

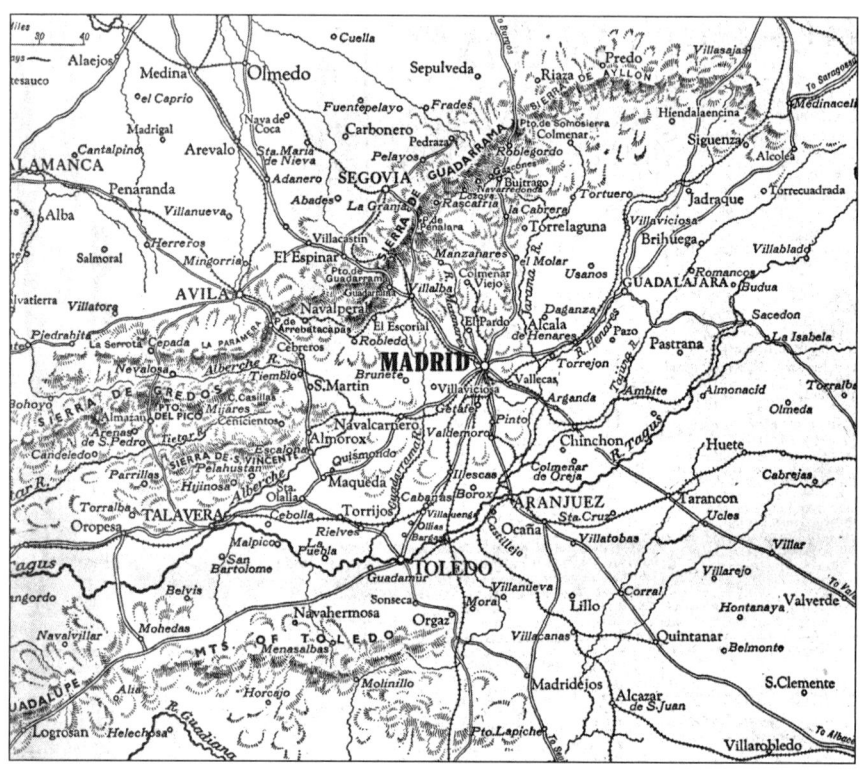

"Heart of Spain," *The Observer* on 4 October 1936 (cropped). (Courtesy of Modern Records Centre, University of Warwick Library, Coventry, UK)

Reading *For Whom the Bell Tolls*

FRONT MATTER

Dedication to Martha Gellhorn: A formidable young writer whom Hemingway met in December 1936. Gellhorn's writing career already included significant journalism, the novel *What Mad Pursuit* (1934), and the story collection *The Trouble I've Seen* (1936). The two writers pursued a romantic affair in wartime Spain beginning in the spring of 1937, where she wrote for *Collier's Magazine*. The memoir of a Spaniard with the government's Foreign Press Bureau, Constancia de la Mora, gives this description of Gellhorn:

> The soldiers love to see her coming [to the front], her slacks setting off her slim figure, her fair hair, so unusual in Spain, blowing in the wind. She was one of those women, rare in any country, who managed to do a man's job well and at the same time look like a debutante. I never failed to marvel at Martha's clothes, always simple, to be sure, but always fresh and immaculate and charming—in the middle of a war. (296–97; on de la Mora, see 317:36)

In the summer of 1937, Gellhorn arranged for a screening of *The Spanish Earth* for herself and Hemingway at the White House with the Roosevelts. Hemingway divorced his second wife, Pauline Pfeiffer, to marry Gellhorn. The marriage took place on 21 November 1940, exactly one month after *For Whom the Bell Tolls*'s publication. They divorced in 1945.

Many readers ascribe the intensity of Jordan and Maria's romance, and the sensuality of the novel's description of it, to Hemingway and Gellhorn's wartime love. In unpublished and quasi-autobiographical fragments set in Madrid during the war, the first-person male narrator calls his companion "Rabbit," Jordan's pet name for Maria (JFK Items 522a & 824). Gellhorn seems also to have influenced the Pilar character. Early in their relationship, before either got to Spain and probably before they consummated their relationship, Gellhorn communicated to Hemingway that she could have been, should have been, or wanted to be a man, a desire reflected (if muted) in one of the "Rabbit" fragments ("We used to quarrel before attacks"; JFK Item 824). Pilar tells Jordan very much the same thing (97:31+). Like Pilar and

Jordan, Gellhorn and Hemingway met their match in the other's strength of personality; both pairs shared the art of storytelling.

(The relationship between Pilar and her husband, Pablo, predicts Gellhorn and Hemingway's a few years after the novel. Gellhorn left to report on the Second World War, in the process shaming Hemingway for his lack of interest in the war and his decision to stay home, drink, and play. Pilar takes over the guerilla band's leadership due to Pablo's similar shirking. Pablo and Hemingway both professionally betray their partners—Pablo by stealing the dynamite, Hemingway by stealing Gellhorn's *Collier's* war correspondent credential—and both eventually if begrudgingly come around and join the effort.)

Title and epigraph: Hemingway considered "thirty some titles" for the novel (to Maxwell Perkins, 21 Apr. 1940; *SL* 504). The runner-up was "The Undiscovered Country" in reference to a metaphor for death in the famous "to be or not to be" soliloquy from Shakespeare's play *Hamlet*. Hamlet has a popular reputation for indecisiveness and excessive rumination. Robert Jordan worries about worrying too much, in a forty-three-chapter book told mostly through his ruminations. Hemingway once used the word "soliloquy" to describe some of the book's content (to Charles Scribner, ca. 15 Aug. 1940; *SL* 509). Hamlet's soliloquy agonizes not on death per se but on suicide as a release from self-torment, "a consummation / Devoutly to be wished" (III.i.71–72). The idea of suicide stalks Jordan until the very end as an inheritance from his father, who shot himself with his father's American Civil War pistol. In their own ways, the protagonists of the play and novel wrestle with the legacy of the father's demise. Hamlet's language of desire, devotion, and consummation implicates Jordan's precipitous fondness for Maria, a romance he recognizes as dangerous. The temptation of suicide also strikes Horatio in the play's final scene, but Hamlet charges him to live to tell the tale. Horatio's description of his mission to bear witness might as well be Hemingway's purpose for writing this novel of the Spanish Civil War, of "carnal, bloody, and unnatural acts, / Of accidental judgments, casual slaughters, / Of deaths put on by cunning and forced cause" (V.ii.423–25).

Hemingway could have known of *Hamlet*'s possible source in Thomas Kyd's *The Spanish Tragedy*, perhaps from T. S. Eliot's 1921 essay "Hamlet and His Problems." *Hamlet* and *For Whom the Bell Tolls* end in a climactic battle of certain risk, orchestrated by protagonists preoccupied with suicide, resulting in their deaths. Hemingway mulled over suicide a great deal during the late thirties, and in two letters imagined figuring out how to have other people shoot him so he wouldn't need to, so he could have it both ways—could leave life and avoid burdening his sons with his shame the way his father's suicide had burdened him (to Archibald MacLeish, 26 Sept. 1936, *SL* 453; to Hadley Mowrer, 31 Jan. 1938, *SL* 463). Jordan unconsciously accomplishes what Hemingway consciously entertained (undoubtedly more than twice).

The "to be or not to be" soliloquy concludes in a way that complicates Jordan's dismissal of his father's suicide as an act of cowardice. Hamlet worries that his "conscience" makes him a "coward" in not taking his own life, that "the native hue of resolution / Is sicklied o'er with the pale cast of thought, / . . . And lose the name of action" (III.i.91–96). Suicide demands bravery; cowards are those who choose niggling indecision over discovering the country beyond.

Allen Josephs uses the phrase *undiscovered country* in the subtitle to his important 1994 study of Hemingway's novel, finding it the less "poetic" if "more accurate description of what Hemingway was really about," although for reasons other than suicide:

> But in the novel [the phrase] encompasses much more than death. The "undiscovered country" suggests, particularly in Hemingway's view, the nature of Spain itself; more specifically, within the novel it hints at the unknown but fateful and omen-ridden nature of the episode of blowing the bridge; for Robert Jordan and Maria it also describes the ecstasy of love and, finally, for Robert Jordan, the ultimate uncertainty of death. I chose to use the phrase in the title of the book because, above all, the "undiscovered country" is the realm of the artist's imagination where all the other elements are given a life of their own. (*Undiscovered* xix)·

Hemingway's published title argues against Josephs's romanticized vision of the *Hamlet* allusion by drawing on another literary meditation on death.

Hemingway provided the title and the book's epigraph in a letter of 21 April 1940 to his editor Max Perkins (*SL* 504). They come from "Meditation XVII" of John Donne's *Devotions upon Emergent Occasions,* published in 1624, in a passage Hemingway spotted while flipping anxiously through *The Oxford Book of English Prose.* Given the anecdote of Hemingway's landing upon the meditation in an anthology, one should perhaps proceed no further than a cursory reading of the passage, perhaps intended to be received by readers in 1940 as a call to action, to global citizenship, to war against the fascist threat. The Second World War had begun, although the United States had not yet entered. The war against European fascism had begun in Spain with the Republic's war against General Franco, who was Hitler and Mussolini's ally and Spain's dictator as of April 1939. Donne's use of the second-person singular-familiar pronoun *thee* might have caught Hemingway's ear. It befits the novel's language; it prepares the reader.

Lawrence Broer argues for a pessimistic interpretation of the novel's ending and an ironic title. For Broer, "the failure of the establishment of a human community" among the characters leaves the survivors islanded "within themselves, destined to die alone in corrosive solitude." Jordan "resumes the old familiar pose of the rebellious individualist," the "protective and egocentric stance of the matador" by which he can imagine "some sense of form and dignity to his life" (94–95). Or perhaps the irony slices geopolitically at the failure of the Western democracies to see themselves in the beleaguered Spanish Republic and come to its aid.

But "Meditation XVII" has nothing to do with international politics. The *Devotions* often uses body-politic analogies . . . as analogies. The passage references the death knell, the literal tolling of a real bell announcing someone's passing. Donne wrote *Devotions* during an illness he believed fatal. By declaring a collective loss for any departed soul, Donne pleads that his own inevitable death will diminish humanity. That his life will have mattered. The stakes are highly personal; they have nothing to do with idealized community or politics. (When Hemingway picked the passage, did he remember the church tower bells Republican Spain used as an alert for approaching enemy aircraft, or the Sanctus Bell rung before an execution?)

A number of scholars place Catholicism at the center of their studies of Hemingway. Because it is a theological reflection written by an Anglican priest, *Devotions* tempts as evidence for reading the novel as intentionally bearing a Christian message (e.g., Nickel 162–70). Yet Jordan never speaks of himself as possessing a Christian faith. The opposite, in fact. Nowhere does Jordan hear God in tolling bells or pray for deliverance unto God. An argument that he is Christian despite himself does not square. While the Bible provides some theological justification for God bestowing the grace of heavenly entrance on those unwitting of their own Christianity (Matthew 25:31–40), the Catholic Church more decidedly requires a conscious commitment and declaration (especially the Spanish Church, the church of the Inquisition). As does John Donne. Donne would understand Jordan's willing death as sinful.

At their heart, the *Devotions*'s twenty-three meditations express Donne's acceptance of the death he believes will soon befall him. Moreover, they express relief that he won't need to kill himself, even as they mull over the will's complicity. "Meditation XII" most directly concerns how "we are . . . active . . . to our own destruction," how we perchance "kill ourselves with our own vapors" (72), the reference here to his immediate illness and to God's regard of mortal life as but a vapor (James 4:14). "But I do nothing upon myself," Donne ascertains, "and yet am my own executioner" (*Devotions* 72–73). A decade earlier, Donne wrote two treatises on the question of self-homicide's inherent sinfulness, *Biathanatos* and *Pseudo-Martyr*. The *Devotions* continues that line of inquiry by considering how one kills oneself by dint of being oneself: "They tell me it is my melancholy; did I infuse, did I drink in melancholy into myself? It is my thoughtfulness; was I not made to think? It is my study; doth not my calling call for that? I have done nothing willfully, perversely toward it, yet must suffer in it, die by it" (72).

Donne's *Biathanatos* and *Pseudo-Martyr* regard sacrificing one's life for others and placing oneself in harm's way as forms of suicide. These two works do not differentiate among the willingness to be killed, the allowing of oneself to be killed, the wish to die, and self-homicide; and they see a willing or willed death as not necessarily sinful, as proven by Christ's example. At the novel's and his own life's end, however, Jordan concludes that "[t]he world is a fine place and worth the fighting for and I hate very much to leave it" (467:8–9). This lovely sentiment flies in the face of Donne's theology, according to which people should hold "a just contempt of this life" and a natural "desire of supreme happiness in the next life by the loss of this" one (*Biathanatos* 5443–5445). These are the fundamental conditions for a self-homicide to avoid being a sin. Nowhere does Jordan maintain a contempt for earthly life (certainly not while making love to Maria on the pine needles), a devoutness to God, or an anticipation of His embrace in the afterlife. However noble they might be, in no way do Jordan's actions, whether in his heart or by any divine reckoning, serve the glory of God. They are profane acts, not sacred ones. Per Donne, Jordan's death doesn't qualify as martyrdom, it counts as sin. Hemingway's choice of title and epigraph doesn't mean Hemingway fully agreed with Donne's theology; readers should take considered care, however, when applying that choice to their interpretations.

None of which should be taken to say that *For Whom the Bell Tolls* absents Christian sympathies altogether. Hemingway's novel recognizes the virtues of Paco Berrendo's Catholic devotion and in other ways calls its readers to meditate on Christianity's presence in it. Just not in its title or epigraph, nor through its main character.

One might discover Donne's spirit in Jordan in two other ways. *Devotions* is nothing if not an anxious and personal contemplation with unresolved dilemmas more akin to a Montaigne essay or a Jordan self-debate than to a treatise. As Andrew Motion writes about the conflicted voice in these meditations, "The self that longs to be transfigured is also the self that feels insulted by extinction, and clings to a dramatic identity in spite of itself." At its best, this "mind delighting . . . prevents his faith from becoming complacent or merely passive." One of the voice's most troubled issues involves the self's relations to others—the very matter of the no-man-is-an-island passage, which Motion understands as Donne's solution to the problem that his writing, that a proper devotion to God which eschews worldly affairs, and that his present illness, all keep him apart from others, from a life of public service and engagement (xvii).[1] The passage adopted by Hemingway professes the opposite of a call to action in the world. It is instead a consolation for solitude. Biographically, Hemingway has retreated from the world, taking up residence in a secluded home outside Havana, Cuba, to write this book.

The more visible trace of Donne in Jordan is in the former's romantic love poetry, which couples sexuality's sacred and profane elements. Robert Jordan's valedictory assurance to Maria that his death doesn't matter because he lives on in her matches the language of Donne's most famous poem, "Valediction: Forbidding Mourning." The poem might also be the source of Hemingway's describing the lovers as having moved the earth when making love:

Moving of th' earth brings harms and fears,
   Men reckon what it did, and meant;

> But trepidation of the spheres,
> > Though greater far, is innocent. (9–12)
>
> [. . . .]
>
> Our two souls therefore, which are one,
> > Though I must go, endure not yet
> A breach, but an expansion,
> > Like gold to airy thinness beat. (21–24)

NOTE

1. Donne's poem "Satire 3" rejects such profane misadventures as Englishmen supporting the Dutch war against Spain and the Spanish auto-da-fé, the torture and execution of nonbelievers in a tag-team ritual conducted jointly by state and church. In this poem, earthly conflicts presumptuously and falsely claim righteousness while distracting individuals from the proper devotion of their whole selves to God, the first and only cause. To engage in worldly wars is to be a "desperate coward" who avoids God—"th'appointed field"—to "seem bold" only (lines 29–32). Donne wrote "Satire 3" during the period he turned away from his Catholic upbringing to become Anglican, and while still very much engaged in the world, joining two naval expeditions (one against the Spanish at Cádiz) and serving in the government.

THE FIRST CALENDAR DAY
[28 MAY 1937]

CHAPTER ONE

1:1+ **on the brown, pine-needled floor of the forest:** The novel begins in medias res. The image of Jordan prone on the needle-covered ground establishes a pattern the novel repeats during soldiering and sex scenes. The book culminates with a final return to this originating image (and its language) as Jordan lies dying "against the pine needle floor of the forest" (471:35–36). For this reason, critics have called the novel circular. With its ending built into its beginning, Jordan's story attains an inevitability.

The Segovia Offensive, the historic Republican offensive for which the fictional bridge mission plays a role, launched on 31 May, and as the entire novel occurs over four calendar days (with three mornings to come), it opens on the 28th—although see the inconsistency in the day of the week at 89:13. At the end of the novel, Jordan muses that almost three days' worth of clock time has passed (466:30). *For Whom the Bell Tolls* is Hemingway's most chronologically compressed novel to date, yet at nearly five hundred pages his most narratively protracted (*The Old Man and the Sea* and *Across the River and into the Trees* will have very similar time frames). Its relative unity of time and place makes it a more formally dramatic novel suggestive of Aristotelian tragedy. The three days resembles Hemingway's characterization of the bullfight as a tragedy staged in three acts; it covers the same length of time as the Battle of Chancellorsville, the battle of Crane's *The Red Badge of Courage;* and it corresponds to the Easter (Paschal) Triduum, the Three Days from the evening of Maundy Thursday to the Sunday evening of Christ's Resurrection. The Triduum's three days' worth of time over four calendar dates matches Jordan's final days (if the days of the week are off by one. See the Easter parody, 185:28–30).

The possessive construction of the first sentence obeys Spanish syntax ("floor of the forest," or *suelo del bosque*, rather than "forest floor") and provides a more rhythmic opening. Hemingway fills the novel with similar Spanish possessive constructions, such as "the *mujer* of Pablo" (*la mujer de Pablo*) instead of "Pablo's *mujer*" ("wife" or "woman"). For further discussion of the novel's rendering of Spanish in English, see 2:36–37.

1:13 **photostated military map:** Essentially a photocopied map. The clunky language disturbs the otherwise pastoral language and scene as its crude interruption introduces the novel's war story. Photostat machines were large cameras that captured negative images directly on photographic paper. Jordan is either looking at such a map, with terrain contour lines, roads, text, and other symbols in white on a black background, or at a map that underwent the process twice—a photostated negative image of the original photostated negative image. Either way, he has placed upon the real ground a mechanical reproduction of a representation of it.

Thomas Strychacz reads the novel through the lens of "what Martin Jay has called the 'Empire of the Gaze': the fascination with the ability of the gaze to survey, organize, discipline, and master the entire terrain of modernity" (105). For Strychacz, this gaze partakes of despotic, fascist, and decidedly male domination. He doesn't mention the map as a symbol of this terrain-mastering gaze, but he very well could have. To beat the fascists, for Strychacz, Jordan must function fascistically (108–9), a dilemma Jordan acknowledges after describing his tactical mindset as "clear and hard and sharp as when a camera lens is brought into focus" (161:26; 162:3–5). An older interpretative scheme, pitting the technologically modern Nationalists against the earthy Republicans (see next entry), becomes amended here in opposing modern foreigners on both sides against the Spaniards. As a contemporary Spaniard living in Pittsburgh wrote Hemingway after the novel's publication, "as compared with the immensely powerful and devilish organizations of Moscow and Berlin everything in Spain was innocent and powerless," and Spaniards "were like babes in the woods" (José Alemany to Hemingway, 2 Nov. 1940, Incoming). The novel ends with the American hero, armed with a German submachine gun recently carried by a Russian comrade, receiving a fatal wound from a Russian tank in the hands of the fascists. Such an approach, however, encourages stereotypes of a less-than-modern Spain, stereotypes often coated with a romanticized or exoticized (racist) varnish.

1:19 the bridge: The Puente de la Cantina, on present-day CL-601, about two-thirds the distance from Navacerrada to Valsaín and crossing over Arroyo del Puerto del Paular, is the only bridge in the vicinity sufficiently like the novel's. The immediate terrain is similar enough. The actual arched bridge crosses a brook, not a "deep gorge" with water coursing white-tipped over boulders (35:8). At the point of crossing, the bridge runs north–south, the brook west-to-east, where it joins the Eresma. The actual bridge and the fictional one are both single span, although the actual one is stone, the fictional one steel, a change Hemingway made perhaps to align it with the militarily better-equipped Nationalists by decoupling it from the earthiness of his Republican characters and their peasant cause.[1] The Arganda Bridge, the low steel bridge over the Jarama River southeast of Madrid and the military objective in the film *The Spanish Earth*, on which Hemingway collaborated, has three through-truss spans (see 334:31+). At the time of the Segovia Offensive, the Puente de la Cantina was several kilometers from the front in Republican territory—not behind the Nationalist lines. Hemingway once indicated this bridge as the basis for the novel's (Josephs, *Undiscovered* 50–60; Tremlett 311).

1:27 who was studying the country: At the moment, Jordan is analyzing the military aspects of the terrain. But as a professor of Spanish and a Hispanophile, he has traveled to Spain to study the country. The stilted English approximates Spanish syntax and for the first time calls attention to the language disjuncture as well as the narrative disjuncture between third-person limited perspective and the omniscient narrator. These disjunctures occur as Jordan, who longs to be Spanish, studies the Spanish earth.

2:23 many men now here in the hills: A number of Spaniards retreated into the mountainous areas of Spain to escape the war and, to a lesser extent, to wage guerilla warfare on behalf of the Republic. Although guerilla warfare in Spain had a long history of success, the mountainous terrain an ideal environment for it, "guerrilla warfare never became a vital military problem for the Nationalists" (Seidman 81). For one thing, guerrillas were hardly the friends of the locals. "Republican *guerrillos* might have plundered even more than regular troops" (79), antagonizing the very people on whose support they depended. In the area of the novel's setting, one Republican military commissar reported that "'any desire of peasants to work for our cause'" was squandered (in Seidman 97). Additionally, "Nationalist terror and torture made civilians reluctant to cooperate with partisans. To get supplies, the latter had to raid farmhouses and small towns and regularly exposed themselves to enemy forces" (81). Pablo and his comrades are not native to the Guadarrama Mountains. This motley amateur crew attests to another problem— the lack of military skills, discipline, and resources among those who took to the hills. Republican leadership minimally supported irregular warfare, especially by civilians. In the spring of 1937, the Guadarrama was settling into being a relatively quiet front for the rest of the war. When Jordan introduces himself to the band, Pablo has become an early adopter of the self-preservation mentality that gradually afflicted Republican supporters. After the war, mountains became the home of the anti-Franco militant resistance known as the *maquis*.

The fact that, per Seidman, the "presence of Spanish *guerrilleros* in the mountains and cities of Spain from 1936 to 1960 was unprecedented in modern Western Europe" (80) lent Hemingway's novel another appeal to the exotic, the different, the strange, the novel.

2:36–37 How are you called?: Whereas an English speaker would ask, "What's your name?", a Spanish speaker would ask, *¿Cómo se llama?*, or "How are you called?" (the formal construction used for strangers and elders, like Anselmo). On the novel's replicating the rhythm of Spanish syntax, see 1:1.

Throughout the novel, Hemingway's translation of Spanish dialogue aims to preserve the foreignness of the culture to English readers and even to Jordan, a professor of Spanish. A smooth translation into a familiar English idiom would fail to remind readers that they are experiencing spoken Spanish, that in a sense they are privy to Jordan's on-the-fly interpretation. It would fail to immerse them in the scene. When the novel's Spaniards think to themselves, they do so in smooth English. In other words, the novel's sometimes clunky, sometimes too-literal translations have a mimetic effect. What some readers find distracting and distancing is a kind of realism. The effect on English ears is untranslatable in Spanish-language versions of the novel. In an early article from 1943, Edward Fenimore illustrated this point with (among other examples) Hemingway's direct rather than idiomatic translations of *raro* into "rare" and *mucho* into "much." The former strikes contemporary English ears as practically Elizabethan—a bit like *thee/thou/thy* (see introduction)—while the latter "will hold something of the primitive" in pidgin phrases such as "much horse" and "much woman" (74–75).

As a fluent nonnative Spanish speaker, Jordan wouldn't always bother translating what he hears. He would likely receive and process *raro* as "rare" without translating it to himself into "odd," "strange," "unique," or "singular." Again like the novel's *thee/thou/thy*, for Jordan the direct translation is realism that for the reader resonates with the romanticized. The outstanding ambiguity involves how much, and in which instances, one attributes what Fenimore calls the novel's "phonetico-semantic" translations (75) to their effect on readers, to their associations for Jordan, or to both. Jordan or the narrator often translate idiomatically, with mixed results.

The biographer James M. Hutchisson, while not finding Hemingway's technique entirely successful, nevertheless lauds Hemingway for its experimental aims: "the writing calls attention to itself," creating a style "nothing like his early prose, in which he sought to make the language transparent and let the ideas present themselves" (168–69). Noël Valis sees the novel as "an experiment in cross-cultural translation" (258). For Valis, "Hemingway's use of language (both English and Spanish) highlights a complex interplay between insider-outsider cultures, some, but not all, of which the novelist was acutely aware" (261). Sometimes, for example, his rendering of Spanish dialogue is "awkward and contrived" such that, "[o]n the one hand, he does what a number of translation theorists now encourage: he foreignizes his novel, rather than naturalizing or domesticating the foreign. . . . On the other hand, he often falls into the trap of exoticizing the foreign" (264). Thus, the novel's language challenge becomes a metaphor for the predicament of Jordan, in its "modes of simultaneous insider-outsiderness" (265). Another way to think about how Hemingway's translations foreignize the novel is to credit him for attempting to respect the original language regardless of its palatability to the English ear.

Ilan Stavans finds the book's 1940 conjunction of Spanish and English a creative forerunner to the playful Spanglish of the late-twentieth- and early-twenty-first-century United States (Cirino, "One"). After all, every speech act, even entirely in one's native tongue, is an imperfect improvisation. Who ever speaks perfectly all the time?

Some readers, critics, and scholars have objected to certain instances of the novel's use of Spanish. For Michael Reynolds writing in 1991, scholarly attention paid to the novel's Spanish joins attention paid to the war's politics as detrimental to the novel's chances of continuing to be widely read. After all, "this novel was no more written for a Spanish-speaking audience than *A Farewell to Arms* was written for an Italian one" ("Ringing"). Some of the published novel's Spanish-language words and phrases were revision suggestions from Hemingway's wartime Spanish friend Gustavo Durán (see 335:24); Hemingway's Spanish was also influenced by the Basque population in Cuba, where he wrote much of the novel (see 293:2–3).

That Jordan's forgetting Anselmo's name is a **"bad sign"** is the novel's first of many ill omens. The language of calling recalls the famous first line of *Moby-Dick,* "Call me Ishmael," another American romance of doom.

3:2 **Barco de Avila:** A small town a little over one hundred miles west of Madrid, southwest of the novel's setting, nestled at the foot of the Sierra de Gredos on their northern side. The Gredos belong to the Central Mountain chain that includes the Guadarrama and splits Spain in half. They are a probable destination for Pablo and Pilar's band after the bridge mission.

3:3+ **The young man . . . with sun-streaked fair hair:** The original draft begins in first person. With this "young man," Hemingway began typing in the third-person. Did he make the change because of an early realization that Jordan will die? Because he decided against tethering the novel's perspective to a single character? In March 1939, when the new novel took him away from his plans to write a few stories, Hemingway wrote that he "would like to be able to write understandingly about both deserters and heroes, cowards and brave men, traitors and men who are not capable of being traitors" (to Ivan Kashkin, 23 Mar. 1939, *SL* 480). That would have been difficult in the first-person. The use of *sun* three times in the sentence could allude to the Greek god Apollo; it could also reinforce how much Jordan struggles with being his father's son.

Ever since Cecil Eby's 1966 article "The Real Robert Jordan," which names Robert Merriman as the model for Jordan, readers have repeated Eby's hypothesis as fact. As summarized elsewhere: "Jordan and Merriman shared a first name, were both professors from the American west (of Spanish in Montana and economics in California, respectively) fighting in Spain, and they both disappeared in battle, presumed dead," behind enemy lines, "while some of their cohort got away" (Vernon, *Second War* 167). Friends called both "Bob." The description of Merriman in a 1937 report by an American military observer fits the bill: "He is a fine manly type, over six feet in height, physically sound with the endurance of an ox, pleasing personality, filled with initiative, overflowing with energy, he moves about everywhere in the command honored and respected by all, he is unquestionably the dominant figure of the brigade and the 'Star' American in the 'Volunteer' group" (qtd. in Cortada 185). Hemingway and Merriman crossed paths a few times in Spain. Merriman, however, was not just a regular soldier but an officer—the Lincoln Battalion's adjunct, then its commander, then a training officer, and finally the XV International Brigade's chief of staff. Merriman had studied in Moscow. His subordinates considered him a sycophant; some called him "Captain Murderman" (Vernon, *Second War* 167). He didn't tumble into bed with a Spanish woman, because his wife accompanied him to Spain, working in Albacete, the headquarters of the International Brigades. (As an epithet, Murderman isn't entirely inapt for Jordan; see 239:26+ and 304:17–18.)

For Whom the Bell Tolls is an intensive character study about a man whose preoccupations dovetail with Hemingway's such that looking for Jordan in a historical person is futile and, in terms of improving one's understanding of the novel, ultimately moot. Other names have been floated. Martha Gellhorn and another correspondent, Sefton Delmer, liked the *New York Times* reporter and Hemingway's dear friend Herbert Matthews—the two were nearly as inseparable as Hemingway and Gellhorn. Hemingway knew Hans Kahle, the German commander of the XI Brigade, far better than he did Robert Merriman. Like Merriman and Matthews, Kahle cut a tall, loping figure. According to Hemingway and Kahle's mutual friend Gustav Regler, Hemingway "loved [Kahle] for reasons which went so deep that he proposed to write a whole book about him" (*Owl* 297; see 233:34+). Two volunteer guerillas have caught scholars' attention: the Soviet Hadji Mamsurov, who had a leadership role in behind-the-lines operations, and the Polish Antoni "Antek" Chrost, who actually operated behind the lines. The evidence for these two is provocative but tentative. Beyond their background in irregular warfare, they had little to contribute to Hemingway's complex vision of Robert Jordan.

What about James Lardner, the son of the writer Ring Lardner (a Hemingway favorite), an idealistic young man who joined the war against Hemingway's advice, only to disappear in the Pàndols Mountains on or about 21 September 1938, the very day the Republic announced the cessation of the International Brigades and a month before Hemingway finished drafting two chapters of an abandoned novel (see appendix A)?[2] Lardner may have been the last international killed in Spain; the futility of the sacrifice for a lost cause resonates with Jordan's death. Less, then, a model for Jordan's character than the emotion behind the novel's tenor—although the draft bears some evidence that Hemingway thought about writing Jordan as youthful and inexperienced (91:20+).

Another possibility whose personality might have rubbed off on Jordan was the soldier-adventurer Charles Sweeny, about whom see the entry below (8:4).

A 1941 *Life* magazine article about the upcoming film version of *For Whom the Bell Tolls* included photos of Spaniards representing the Spanish characters, and a photo of

Gary Cooper as the hoped-for actor to play Jordan ("Hemingway: *Life*" 53). Hemingway "originally sold it to Paramount" so "Cooper could play" Jordan (to Prudencio de Pereda, 14 Aug. 1941, *SL* 526). Cooper had played Frederic Henry in the 1932 film adaptation of *A Farewell to Arms,* and in personal history resembled Jordan more than anyone Hemingway knew in Spain. He grew up in Helena, Montana, spending his summers at the family ranch learning to ride, shoot, hunt, and fish. To cowboy, as it were. His Hollywood career started with gigs as a stunt rider before he became one of the most accomplished Western film actors. Cooper's breakout role was the title character in *The Virginian* (1929), a film adaptation of Owen Wister's 1902 novel. In *Morocco* (1930), Cooper starred as an American serving in the French Legion during the 1920s Rif wars which saw the French and the Spanish fighting to maintain their colonies (see 229:31+). This Josef von Sternberg film included a controversial scene in which Marlene Dietrich, dressed as a man for a cabaret number, kisses another woman; during the war, Hemingway apparently enjoyed dreams about the bisexual Dietrich (137:16+). Hemingway had written the main character of his Spanish Civil War play *The Fifth Column* "with Cooper in mind."[3] He first met Cooper, however, as the novel headed to the printers in the fall of 1940, in Sun Valley, Idaho.[4] The fantasy that is Jordan, the Romance that is this novel, derive from films like the kind Cooper made. The names Robert Jordan and Gary Cooper sound alike—they poetically scan the same and share "r" sounds—a similarity that perhaps contributed to the text always calling its hero by both his names.

3:5 **peasant's trousers and rope-soled shoes:** For his work behind enemy lines, Jordan dresses as a local. His choice of dress also speaks to his desire to go native. As he soon says, he'd rather have been born a Spaniard (15:30). Today the shoes are commonly known as espadrilles, the traditional footwear of Spanish lower classes and of the Spanish infantry from the fourteenth century. For his American audience, Hemingway describes the shoes rather than names them; he names them without description when he introduces Pablo a few pages later, possibly to disguise an association between Jordan and Pablo. *Espadrilles* is the Catalan word (originally from French); for Pablo's footwear, Hemingway employs the Castilian Spanish *alpargatas*. In the later passage, Jordan also thinks about the impracticality of such shoes when riding horses (12:27), yet another potential foreshadowing, as he will be riding a horse when he is fatally injured.

3:27 **How do they call thee?:** In Spanish, *¿Cómo te llamas?* For the novel's historically accurate use of the Early Modern English familiar second-person singular pronoun forms *thee, thou,* and *thy* during the Spanish Civil War, see the introduction. While it would seem Anselmo's use of it here, the first time in the novel, emphasizes his Spanish foreignness, the "you" of Jordan's earlier "How are you called?" to Anselmo is a consistent and correct translation of the Spanish reflexive pronoun for someone older than the speaker: ¿Cómo se llama? (see 2:36–37). Jordan on first meeting Anselmo would not risk saying ¿Cómo te llamas?

3:28 Roberto: Hemingway possibly takes Jordan's first name from Robert Merriman (see 3:3+), but equally possibly from the Spanish artist Roberto Domingo Fallola, a leading painter of bullfights. Hemingway owned a few of his works; used one, *Saltando la Barrera* ("Jumping the Barrier"), for the dust jacket of his earlier Spain-inspired book, *Death in the Afternoon* (1932); and hung them on the walls at his new Cuban home, the Finca Vigía, where he wrote much of *For Whom the Bell Tolls*. In a letter to his editor Max Perkins, Hemingway wrote of Domingo: "He is one of the best birds I have ever known and a damned good friend—also only painter of bull ring who is really good" (to Maxwell Perkins, 15 Aug. [1932], *Letters 5* 200).[5]

4:6 The young man, whose name was Robert Jordan: The protagonist of *The Red Badge of Courage* is called a "youth" and goes unnamed until a few pages into the story. Given that a river is fundamental to the plot and the protagonist's military mission, it's reasonable to see his name as alluding to the Jordan River. Jordan will acknowledge as much (438:7+). The Bible describes the river's fertile plain as "well-watered everywhere . . . as the garden of the Lord" (Genesis 13:10); the Israelites crossed it to settle in the Promised Land, ending the long exodus from Egypt (Joshua 3:15–17); and John the Baptist baptized Jesus in the Jordan River (Matthew 3:13; Mark 1:9; Luke 3:21, 4:1). These transformational moments of physical and spiritual arrival and blessing have made *crossing the River Jordan* into a metaphor for the arrival into and blessing of Heaven—that is to say, for death. Additionally, in crossing the river the Israelites gained political freedom, the essential Republican cause.

The ungainliness of this naming calls attention to itself, reflecting the novel's tension between the third-person limited perspective and an omniscient narrator, a nondiegetic voice pronouncing from beyond the action. The phrase announces the novel's commitment to telling its story from multiple perspectives. The tension potentially bespeaks what Jordan later calls his "schizophrenic" thinking (394:4). That the narration always calls him "Robert Jordan," first and last name, might evidence a need to insist upon a stable identity, to shore up a vulnerable self.

Offering his full name in the past tense, for a man who goes by Bob (337:7, 31), and interrupting the familiarity already established with the limited perspective, suggests an act of eulogy. Hemingway's eulogy "On the American Dead in Spain" appeared in *New Masses*'s 14 February 1939 issue, days before the writing of *For Whom the Bell Toll* got seriously under way. The Spanish communist leader Dolores Ibárruri (La Pasionaria) used similar eulogizing language in her 28 October 1938 farewell address to the International Brigades (see 471:12). Hemingway was in Paris when the farewell parade took place in Barcelona. That very day, he wrote to his editor that he had finished two chapters of a novel—perhaps the germinating seeds of *For Whom the Bell Tolls*—felt "a little bit gloomy," and planned to work on the novel that day: "Writing is a hard business Max but nothing makes you feel better" (to Maxwell Perkins, 28 Oct. 1938, *SL* 474; see appendix A).

4:21 **walk him to death:** In the novel's final chapter, the two men die having walked to the place where it happens.

4:30–31 **La Granja:** A small town on the northern edge of the Guadarrama Mountains in the direction (from Madrid) of Segovia. The military operation under way is sometimes known as the Segovia Offensive, sometimes the La Granja Offensive.

4:31 **Golz:** The model for General Golz was the Polish-born Karol Wacław Świerczewski, who joined the Bolshevik Revolution, fought with the Red Army during the Russian Civil War, and eventually became a high-ranking Soviet officer. In Spain, he operated as "General Walter." Walter commanded the XIV International Brigade before becoming commander of the 35th International Division for the Segovia Offensive. He blamed his soldiers for the division's poor performance and carried out reprisal executions against his own (see 151:30). Golz briefly had operational command of the division taken away (Beevor 276), but regained it in time for the next major operation and held on until August 1938.

4:33 **the Escorial:** The town of San Lorenzo de El Escorial sits at the southern base of the Guadarrama Mountains, not far from Madrid. It contains the Royal Site of San Lorenzo de El Escorial (Monasterio y Sitio de El Escorial en Madrid), commonly called El Escorial, a grand structure designed as a monastery, a royal palace, and the final resting place for Spain's future monarchs. When completed in 1584, it was one of the largest buildings in the world, "surely the greatest mass of granite existing upon earth," one of the "eighth wonders of the world," wrote Théophile Gautier in an 1845 travelogue Hemingway knew. Gautier devotes an entire chapter of *A Romantic in Spain* to this "architectural leviathan," this "colossus" (100–101).

Prior to the war, the Spanish right used El Escorial as a meeting place to organize their resistance as well as to stage rallies. It and the town became important objectives for both sides in the first months of the war, for operational and symbolic reasons. When the Nationalist offensive toward Madrid through the Guadarrama failed, the town and palace became the Republican's base for military support activity in the area for the rest of the war. Jordan and Golz meet a stone's throw away.

Gautier also calls El Escorial a "monkish necropolis" (107), just as Havelock Ellis in *The Soul of Spain* (1908) calls it "The Royal Spanish Temple to Death," because Philip II designed it to house not just his and his father's remains, but those of all descendent monarchs for the next five hundred years. The living "Spanish monarch may here descend the dark marble staircase to the little vault below the high

El Escorial circa 1880s. (Author's collection)

altar, to view in its own small niche the sarcophagus which was prepared for him centuries before he was born" (24). Philip II built this "Palace of Death . . . so that he might lie on his dying bed with its outlook on the high altar, fingering the same crucifix as his father," Charles I, the Holy Roman Emperor, "also held when he lay dying" (25). The novel's originating moment, Jordan's acceptance of the bridge mission, occurs in the shadow of this enormous anticipatory edifice to death, a house of death wrapped up in patrimonial inheritance. Although Jordan forswears women for the mission beside this monastery, he later admits to having sex in El Escorial and indirectly associates Maria with it (see 166:16+).

Francisco Franco built his cathedral tomb, Valle de los Caídos (Valley of the Fallen), into a mountainside a few kilometers from, and higher than, El Escorial. The proximity linked him to the monarchy and to Philip II, under whom Spain's empire and the Church's influence reached its most expansive, while the elevation enshrined Franco's presumptive superiority.

Before the war, the Escorial held in its large art collection one of Hemingway's favorites, Hieronymus Bosch's *The Garden of Earthly Delights* (1490–1500). Conventionally read, Bosch's triptych tells a linear story of the Garden of Eden, an earthly life of sensual pleasures experienced outdoors, and the resultant afterlife of nightmarish damnation. Jordan is heading into the mountains to experience the middle panel with Maria and then face mortal consequences. Carl Eby understands the painting not as chronologically linear and causal but as communicating the "simultaneity" of innocence, pleasure or sin, and damnation (Eby, *Reading* 123–24). For Jordan, the novel's three-day triptych presents confusions of innocence and sin, when, for example, cold-blooded killing comes from the innocence of naïve idealism before his "corruption" (e.g., 239:15+).

In September 1936, Hemingway wrote John Dos Passos that he hoped Spain managed to safekeep its great paintings, but to "hell with the Architecture—Anything looks better after being shelled. That's just what the {Escorial} needs—" (to John Dos Passos, 22 Sept. 1936, Outgoing).

5:19+ **never my attacks:** Golz expresses his reality as a subordinate commander who must follow the instructions of his superiors and compete with other units for scant resources like artillery support. But he's also expressing a more complicated and dangerous political reality: "That is the least of it. There are other things." The International Brigades answered to two chains of command, that of the Spanish Republic and that of the Communist International (Comintern), in the latter case often by direction of a political commissar with military rank but frequently no military experience or training (see 387:31).

6:16+ **If you do not want to:** It isn't entirely clear whether Golz's request and Jordan's agreement are genuine such that Jordan could reasonably decline without consequence, or pro forma in the context of their military orders. For Golz's operation, the hour is late. The personal risk for Jordan comes from both sides, from enemy hands in battle and friendly hands by disciplinary execution, sometimes carried out in the heat of postbattle rage without due process or much warrant—as was the case after this particular battle (see 151:30; 335:11). This might be the implied risk in Golz's insistence on Jordan's willingness in light of "all of the possible difficulties."

6:32 **Vicente Rojo:** A major at the beginning of the war, Vicente Rojo Lluch was quickly promoted to lieutenant colonel and placed in charge of planning the defense of Madrid. His success there launched his wartime career. By spring, he had become a full colonel and the Chief of the General Staff of the Republican Army, in which capacity he planned the Segovia Offensive. Observers then and historians today consider Rojo one of the war's most talented military leaders. In the 1920s, as a captain, Rojo taught cadets and designed curricula at the military academy in Toledo (the Alcázar). Calling him an "unsuccessful" professor reflects Golz's low opinion of the Spanish officer corps and the army's tactics, which Rojo helped develop.

6:36 **Segovia:** The objective of the Segovia (La Granja) Offensive, the historic battle which Jordan's guerilla operation supports. The coronation of Queen Isabella took place in Segovia in 1474; she and her husband, Ferdinand of Aragon, led the Reconquista, the reconquest of the last Moorish territories, and were the first royal couple to rule over an entirely unified Spain. For the novel anyway, Segovia thus serves as a symbol of a reunified Spain for the present civil war. With its dramatic Roman aqueduct, its eleventh-century Moorish citadel (*alcázar*), and its sixteenth-century Gothic cathedral, the small city visually compacts Spanish history.

7:7–8 **the one thing:** Presumably when Jordan must blow the bridge, and perhaps the personal consequences if he were to fail to detonate at the right time (see 6:16+). It is not unusual, however, for a Hemingway character to have some "one thing" in mind that is not shared with the readers, as in for example "Soldier's Home" and *A Farewell to Arms*. Hemingway's protagonist writer in *The Garden of Eden* enacts just such a withholding: "Finally, he knew what his father thought and knowing it, he did not put it in the story. He only wrote what his father did" (146–47).

7:18 **a better name:** Many International Brigaders (especially officers) used a nom de guerre (see 4:31).

7:21–22 ***partizan* work . . . guerilla work:** These terms are not exact synonyms. In English military parlance, the term *partisan* emphasizes the person, and *guerilla* the tactics. *Partisans* are typically nonprofessional—civilian—inhabitants of an occupied area who disrupt the military occupation by whatever means possible. They generally conduct small operations due to resource constraints and the need to survive, and they remain anonymous in order to continue the work for the duration. Sometimes their methods are those only civilian inhabitants could carry out. Historically, they have worked independently, with varying degrees of communication with other partisans and with the military command. Resistance fighters are the classic example. Guerilla warfare also consists of disruption and harassment work conducted behind enemy lines by independent or quasi-independent armed groups. Its operations tend to be more military in nature—ambushes, demolitions, and so forth. Additionally, it can be more integrated within the conventional military command structure. Like T. E. Lawrence (of Arabia) in the Great War, Robert Jordan operates under the orders and authority of the army. Their missions directly support and are supported by the regular military effort (Lawrence was a British officer). On guerilla warfare in the Spanish Civil War, see 2:23.

According to Yuval Noah Harari's history of war narratives, guerilla warfare was "either invisible or disreputable" until the late eighteenth and early nineteenth centuries, when "above all in Spain" it achieved "central stage in war culture" (187). The term itself comes from Spanish, essentially translating as "little war," in describing the resistance to Napoleon during the Peninsular War. For Harari, the "changing cultural attitude" and "drastic shift in the image of guerilla warfare" (187) occurred "within a much larger shift in Western civilization . . . tagged 'the culture of sensibility'" (135), which privileged and in fact democratized individual experience: "And if an illiterate soldier directly experienced something that a learned theologian only read about, then the soldier was a better authority on it than the theologian" (137). The eighteenth century was also the first great age of the novel, a prose genre suited for dramatizing the interior life's struggle between reason and sensation.

Even before Hemingway arrived in wartime Spain, he was thinking about guerilla warfare. In October 1936, he wrote in a letter about getting to Spain "to see what and who's left. There may still be plenty guerilla war going on. Imagine there will be. They can't disarm that amount of people even if Madrid is taken by now. I want to see the truth of what's happened."[6] His correspondence that fall never explicitly says that he wants to see the war to look for writing material, but the motive is apparent nevertheless—he told an aspiring writer considering going to fight that he'll certainly find great stuff to write about in Spain (to Prudencio de Pereda, 9 Dec. 1936, Outgoing), and called war "the best thing for our lousy trade there ever was" to fellow novelist John Dos Passos. The comment to Dos Passos assumes that Madrid had fallen and the war was already over; it expresses regret for not having witnessed it (22 Sept. 1936, Outgoing).

7:38+ **no time for girls:** Jordan rejects wartime romance and sex because they would distract from his mission—he has "enough to think about without girls" (8:6). By 1937, one of the Republic's justifications for removing Spanish women from the front lines drew on old-fashioned notions of a body's limited vital "biological energy," both male and female, which needed to be conserved for the war effort; more directly, sexual restraint would prevent casualties due to venereal diseases (Nash 114–15). One Republican poster equates a casualty due to a sexually transmitted illness to desertion, its image featuring a snake wrapped around a naked woman, its head placed phallically and aiming for a soldier.[7] In another, the forearm of the naked woman becomes skeletal, becomes death, where it wraps around the soldier.[8]

In terms of genre, Jordan perhaps sought a chanson de geste, a song of heroic deeds uncomplicated by love, such as the famous eleventh-century *Chanson de Roland,* in which Roland dies a military martyr's death against the Moors at Roncesvalles in Navarre, Spain. Not the messy chivalric Romance business of Sir Thomas Malory's fifteenth-century *Le Morte d'Arthur.*

8:4 **my hair cut as it needs it:** By resisting a shorn military look like Golz's, Jordan asserts an identity and autonomy outside military service. The longer hair also strengthens his connection with that unruly and unduly romanticized US cavalry officer, George Armstrong Custer, whose death at the Battle of the Little Bighorn in Montana quite near Jordan's childhood home has acquired a popular reputation as tragically heroic (see introduction).

Throughout Hemingway's texts, a male character's having his hair cut can signify emasculation. In the Spanish context, the cutting of a bullfighter's coleta—the short, braided pigtail useful for supporting the headgear—denigrates his professional identity and undermines his masculinity. The character Joaquín failed as a bullfighter and lost his coleta but now grows it back, having overcome wartime fears and perhaps become a man (133:31+). Carl Eby links this novel with other Hemingway works through a shared castration complex. *For Whom the Bell Tolls* references lost testicles, scalping, and decapitation; Eby sees Jordan's flirtation with becoming one with Maria as symptomatic of "the intensity of castration anxiety in fetishists" that "is *partly* the result of a profound, but threatening, desire to identify with the phallic woman in her 'castrated' aspect" (*Fetishism*, 69). Both Maria's rape by fascist soldiers and their slicing off her braids beforehand amount to symbolic castration (*Fetishism*, 55–85). Jordan eventually suggests she have her hair cut just like his, shoulder-length, an idea that sexually excites him (345:34–35; 346:7+). If for Hemingway's men short hair on a woman approaches the androgynous or gender-fluid, then they potentially render their masculinity more fluid with identical haircuts.

Hemingway would have known from Van de Water's *Glory-Hunter* that many of the soldiers' bodies at the Little Bighorn were left naked, some mutilated (355). *Glory-Hunter*'s language disguises the fact that Custer was also stripped bare. In fact almost all the bodies were unclothed and most were mutilated, limbs hacked off, heads scalped. Had it not been for Custer's recent haircut, he probably would have been scalped as well. He did receive the slash on the right thigh by which the Sioux claimed their kills. The displaced castration symbols of scalping, amputations, and thigh-cutting aside, Custer may have had an arrow jammed into his penis.[9]

Hemingway knew a dashing, opportunistic soldier-adventurer who flaunted long hair in the face of military authority, his friend since the early 1920s, Charley Sweeny. Sweeny found wars to fight wherever he could, beginning with the French Foreign Legion in the First World War in 1914, in several Latin American conflicts, in the Polish-Soviet War, and in 1925 the Rif Wars in Morocco (229:31+). On his way to the war, Hemingway visited Sweeny in Paris in March 1937 (Reynolds, *1930s* 261), and saw him at least once in Spain, where Sweeny advised the French. Like Jordan, Sweeny cherished independence in war and hated uniforms and regulations, and in Spain others took note of his nonmilitary long hair. In a 1940 letter, Hemingway described Sweeny as having "one of the most brilliant military brains I have ever known" but also "really absolutely goddamned insufferable sometimes" (to Maxwell Perkins, ca. 4 or 11 Feb. 1940, *SL* 500)—the Sweeny who lectured Republican officers and advisors how to fight resembles Jordan giving unwelcome military instructions to El Sordo and Pablo (see 147:34). Sweeny and Jordan also share a remorseless willingness to shoot people on one's own side.

Years later, Hemingway will write Sweeny into *The Garden of Eden* as Colonel Boyle. The manuscript for that unfinished novel describes Boyle as "a 'romantic' who loves France," for whom "'France is his only illusion'" (Eby, *Reading* 151). Is Spain the romantic Jordan's only beloved illusion? Boyle is the character who intuits when Catherine Bourne visits the Prado Museum "as though [she] were the young chief of a warrior tribe" (*GOE* 62).

8:13–16 ***Général Sovietique.* I never think:** The intolerant Comintern (Soviet) power structure did not allow it. During Joseph Stalin's Great Purge of 1936–1938, making contrary opinions known, much less acting on them, could get one disappeared—mysteriously vanished to a life of imprisonment and hard labor if not outright killed. Regular Soviet military officers such as this general rarely enjoyed real command authority (5:19+).

8:24–25 **Guadarrama:** Jordan and Anselmo have traveled a little over seven miles northeast of El Escorial to pass the town of Guadarrama, then another approximately seven miles to the town of **Navacerrada** at the entrance to the primary pass and route through the Guadarrama Mountains to La Granja and on to Segovia. The bridge is up this road. The Spanish **Alpine Club** (Club Alpino Español) built cabins in Navacerrada, the closest place to Madrid for winter sports.

8:30 **outside the Escorial:** In imagining the troops preparing to move "[t]omorrow night" to begin the doomed offensive, Jordan can't help but envision them alongside this architectural herald of death (4:33). The published version mutes the unabashedly ominous tone in the draft, which gathered the soldiers beside "the looming, angled stone of the Escorial" (*HLE* 492).

9:16–17 **carbine:** A rifle with a short barrel, either a shorter version of a standard rifle or a weapon designed to be short. Carbines were developed as military cavalry rifles but proved useful for infantry soldiers due to their mobility and their handiness in tight spaces such as trenches and building interiors. Probably a bolt-action carbine.

9:20 ***Salud:*** Literally "health," a shortening of "good health." Among Republicans during the war, it was accompanied by the raising of the clenched right fist in salute. Republicans also addressed one another as ***Camarada,*** or comrade, as an egalitarian gesture that refuses aristocratic, hierarchical, or other distinctions of authority, adopted from the communists. *Camarada* does not inflect for gender (*el camarada* and *la camarada*), befitting the Republic's efforts across to extend its egalitarianism to gender.

10:12–13 **S. I. M. . . . General Staff:** The Servicio de Información Militar (**SIM**) is an anachronism, as it did not exist until August 1937, over two months after the events of the novel. Until this point in time, many Republican affiliated organizations ran their own intelligence and espionage operations. Ideally, SIM was to be a centralized and thus more efficient means of combating Nationalist espionage and providing order, security, and constraint. Unfortunately, the SIM suffered from Russian and communist influence, and its ends justified its means a little too readily: bribery, blackmail, coercion, torture, imprisonment, and political executions were commonplace. Agents frequently lacked professional background or training and could manipulate military commanders. Jordan's presenting papers with the SIM seal amounts to a nasty threat. The **General Staff** commanded all Republican military forces. That Pablo has seen the General Staff seal but not the SIM seal suggests that Hemingway recognized the anachronism.

10:28+ **I have heard much good of you:** Hemingway decided to trust his reader to hear the empty rhetoric here and in the next few lines, as in the draft Jordan admits to himself that he is spewing bunk and has heard about Pablo's untrustworthiness and brutality (MS10–008).

10:36 **from Buitrago to the Escorial:** Buitrago del Lozoya, located farther northeast in the Guadarramas (the small town of Buitrago outside Soria, much farther to the northeast, was in Nationalist territory). On the Escorial, see 4:33.

11:3 **Avila:** A town in southern Castile, about fifty kilometers west of the Guadarrama Mountains. Pilar later tells Jordan that Pablo lied and he is not from Ávila (98:38). Ávila was the home of Saint Teresa of Ávila, or Saint Teresa of Jesus, a sixteenth-century mystic nun and one of the most important Catholic theologians in history, known for embracing the pain of Christ. Gian Lorenzo Bernini's *The Ecstasy of Saint Teresa* sculpts her vision of an angel repeatedly plunging a golden spear into her body, causing enormous pain but also a "surpassing . . . sweetness" from the love of God (*Life of St. Teresa* 274). In 1817, she joined Saint James to become a co–patron saint of Spain.

11:16 **Quevedo . . . old Castilian:** The poet and writer Francisco Gómez de Quevedo y Villegas, born sixteen years after Shakespeare, was one of the great writers of the Spanish Renaissance. Compared to that of his contemporaries, Quevedo's style was concise and straightforward. As Jordan's translation of Anselmo's dialogue shows, reading Quevedo for Spanish speakers was like reading Shakespeare for English speakers. Quevedo was also a realist and satirist, the author of the exemplar picaresque novel, *Historia de la vida del Buscón, llamado Don Pablos, ejemplo de vagamundos y espejo de tacaños,* or The History of the Life of the Sharper Called Don Pablo, the Pattern of Vagabonds and Mirror of Rogues, known in Spanish as simply *El Buscón*—The Sharper, or The Swindler—and translated into English as *Pablo de Segovia, The Spanish Sharper.* The picaresque is an anti-Romantic genre of Spanish origin. It typically follows the mock adventures of a lower-class knockabout living by his wits, making fun of both the lower-class antihero and the dated literary chivalric tradition to which he often aspires. On the one hand, Hemingway alludes to Quevedo's Don Pablo of Segovia as he introduces the reader to his novel's Pablo, a peasant presented in the scene as knocking about and surviving by his wits just on the other side of Segovia (11:25). Up until the galleys, Hemingway has Agustín call Pablo *picaro,* using the noun as an adjective to mean clever and wily like a picaro, the picaresque's protagonist (95:1). *El Buscón*'s humor comes at the expense of its Pablo's impossible and laughable fantasy of becoming a *caballero,* a gentleman, but the word literally translates as *horseman;* at the end of the first chapter, Jordan silently ridicules Pablo's affection for horses in class-based terms (16:36+), where Jordan's disdain might be the text's real target of critique. On the other hand, the picaro descended from the literary posturing of the chivalric knight-errant. As in the case of Cervantes's *Don Quixote,* he was a man of a bygone spirit—of a bygone literature. He's as much Jordan nostalgic for the nineteenth century as he is Pablo. According to H. E. Watts, the picaresque "was a return to nature"—the triumph of the real over the romantic"—a veritable revolution, which doubtless led the way to a healthier taste and a higher art" (xv). *For Whom the Bell Tolls* isn't a picaresque novel, but the picaresque resides in it, as does the genre's ambition. Hemingway owned a 1927 Spanish edition of *Vida del Buscón.*

In labeling Quevedo's and Anselmo's language "**old Castilian**," Jordan isn't making the equivalent mistake of labeling Shakespeare's Modern English as either Old or even Middle English. He speaks more colloquially than academically, and while that would be odd for a professor of Spanish, he achieves a common understanding of the more formal Castilian of older generations. For Gayle Rogers, "the Spanish in the novel, which draws on Quevedo and vernacular speech, is not the stable, uncorrupted, autochthonous tongue that even Hemingway himself dreamed at times." Rather, the text "implies . . . the existence of an original Spanish text that appears realistic yet is linguistically impossible. To unpack this novel's linguistic world is to realize that Hemingway points to a Spanish ur-text that is . . . corrupted and contorted" (215). The novel's ur-Spanish reflects Jordan, the ur-Spaniard, his ur-Spain, his romanticized dream.

Diego Velázquez painted a portrait of Quevedo, housed at the Instituto Valencia of Don Juan in Madrid. The painter and writer admired one another's frank depictions. In a moment, horses painted by Velázquez cross Jordan's mind (13:18–19), perhaps primed by subconscious association with Quevedo.

11:25 beyond Segovia: Segovia's city center is about thirteen kilometers from the cave Pablo's guerillas inhabit. Pablo's tactical intelligence is sound. He does not operate in his own area, but conducts missions on the other side of Segovia, deeper into Nationalist territory.

11:29 **the principle of the fox:** The American Civil War's most famous tactician, the Confederate army's General Robert E. Lee, was sometimes called the Grey Fox in recognition of his cunning and mobility in the face of much larger enemy forces.

12:8 **I will take it:** Pablo's future-tense declaration foreshadows his later stealing of Jordan's dynamite, the backpack's content. Jordan registers the "sadness" in Pablo's demeanor, recognizing it as the "sadness they get before they quit or before they betray" (12:30).

12:19–20 **picket pins had been driven into the earth:** stakes for tethering horses to a spot of ground. Jordan knows horses and knows how to read the ground. He grew up and lives in Montana, where horses were indispensable.

12:27 *alpargatas:* see 3:5.

12:28 **outfit:** A double-entendre referencing Pablo's wardrobe and his guerilla band, the former meaning indicative of the latter's motley, ill-equipped state (a state analogous to the state of the Republic, especially militarily).

13:8–9 **Pablo stood now proud . . . watching them lovingly:** Pablo once transported goods by horse-drawn carts (182:17–18), in another job handled horses for a dealer who sold them to bullrings and the military (182:25), and also "led picador horses in the ring" (190:5). His pride is that of someone who labored for others, for owners that didn't know their horses as well as he did, and who dreamed of ownership but never thought it possible before the Republic.

13:19 **Velásquez:** Art scholars consider the Spaniard Diego Rodríguez de Silva y Velázquez one of the most important European painters in history. Famous for his naturalist portraits, Velázquez created many works depicting mounted royalty. In the draft typescript, Hemingway handwrote himself an instruction to add a description of the painting Jordan has in mind, but he never did (MS10–008). It was probably *White Horse* (1634–1635), in which the horse appears alone with only a simple flat saddle and harness, allowing the painting to concentrate on the powerful body. During the same period, Velázquez painted *Prince Baltasar Carlos on Horseback* (1634–1635), which shows a late spring snow on the Guadarrama peaks in the background. Ironically, considering the politics of the Spanish Civil War, Velázquez until his death served the court of King Philip IV and is strongly associated with royal life. Equestrian portraits epitomized dynastic rule.

Hemingway might have had *The Dead Soldier* in mind when writing the novel, an anonymous seventeenth-century painting initially attributed to Velázquez, an attribution upheld by Ellis in *The Soul of Spain* (160–61). The painting is of a soldier lying alone, dead, sword in hand, on barren terrain among other emblems of death—skull, bones, and a wisping, just-extinguished lamp hanging inexplicably from a single bare tree branch:

Left: Diego Velázquez, *White Horse* (1634–1635). (WikiMedia Commons / Public Domain)

Below: Anonymous, *The Dead Soldier* (17th Century). (WikiMedia Commons / Public Domain)

14:8 **a pair of *guardia civil*:** The Civil Guard has been a national police force in Spain since the mid-nineteenth century. They traditionally operate in pairs and are easily recognizable by their distinctive tricorn headgear. During the war, about half of the Civil Guard sided with the Republicans, half with the Nationalists. Jordan's reference to them as "big game" is the novel's concrete introduction to its meditation on the relationship between hunting and warfare.

14:11–12 **between Segovia and Santa Maria del Real:** The town Santa María la Real de Nieva is indeed "beyond Segovia" (11:25), about thirty kilometers northwest, in the same province.

14:17 **blew up the train at Arevalo:** Due west of Santa María la Real de Nieva, Arevalo is south of Valladolid, north of Ávila, so still "beyond Segovia" and on the train route from Valladolid to the south. This operation resulted in the freeing of Maria, who was being moved from the prison at Valladolid to somewhere south (23:22–25). The timing fits history. As Franco's military continued to succeed in the north, it transported prisoners to more stable Nationalist areas, including sites in Extremadura and Andalusia in the south. It had also begun transforming its ad hoc prisoner-of-war system into a proper organization. That spring and summer saw the establishment of more permanent facilities designed with the ideological goal of purging prisoners of impurities through "a process of political reeducation, 're-Catholicization,' humiliation, torture, and finally reutilization as forced laborers" (Perez 6). Nationalist Spain regarded its Spanish enemies as racially compromised, as infected.

14:26 **Kashkin:** Hemingway named Jordan's predecessor to Pablo's band after Ivan Kashkin, Hemingway's Soviet translator and the person responsible for establishing his reputation in the Soviet Union in a manner palatable to the authorities. The real Kashkin "was the leading Soviet translator of the era and the main theorist of a school of creative translation that aimed to capture an author's literary style while making a work relevant for a Soviet readership" (White, "Ideological Profit" 48). Hemingway and Kashkin never met, but their correspondence shows a mutual admiration and friendly familiarity. While working on *For Whom the Bell Tolls*, Hemingway wrote to Kashkin that he considered him the person "who wrote the best and most useful, to me, critique on my stuff I ever read and probably knows more about it than I do" (23 Mar. 1939, *SL* 480).

15:6–7 **Sierra de Gredos:** See 3:2.

15:10 **hunt for us with planes:** An allusion to the Spanish and French names for certain military aircraft. See 38:19.

15:11 **Moors:** The historical term describes North Africans who came to rule over parts of Europe during the Middle Ages, most especially in Spain. The Moors conquered and held sovereignty over most of the Iberian Peninsula from 711 to the Reconquista (reconquest) by northern Christian Spain in 1492. Ironically, the Nationalists used Moors in their Catholic crusade against the Republican government. At the beginning of the civil war, Spain's Army of Africa was transported from Morocco to Spain by ship and by the first major military airlift in history, using Italian and German aircraft and crews. Legionnaires, consisting of both Spanish and non-Spanish volunteers, and *regulares,* consisting of indigenous Moorish troops, formed the ranks of the Army of Africa. Its initial success in quickly securing southern Spain gave the rebellion a foothold and momentum such that historian Paul Preston credits the airlift with "turn[ing] a *coup d'état* going wrong into a bloody and prolonged civil war" (*Spanish Civil War* 119). Moors were in northern and central Spain (the Guadarrama) by the fall of 1936. As the war progressed, propaganda on both sides took full advantage of the age-old popular belief in African savagery—the Nationalists to subjugate through terror, the Republicans to inspire resistance (see 117:15+).

15:36 **another capitalist more:** This accusation complicates the question of political faith as it relates to personal circumstances. Pablo's acquisition of horses and a tribe has altered his attitude into a more conservative perseveration of the status quo. See 16:34.

16:22–23 **Anselmo must have known what he was doing:** Anselmo has chosen Pablo's guerilla band for the mission instead of one of the others in the area. In the draft, Hemingway changed "what he [Pablo] is about" to "what he [Anselmo] was doing" (MS10-008), both versions meaning *Anselmo must have known all about Pablo.* The draft clarifies that Jordan did not know to which guerrilla band Anselmo was bringing him. Hemingway considered having Jordan ask Anselmo "Who are these people?" as the two climbed away from the bridge to meet Pablo (MS10-008). The draft has Jordan ask Pablo for his name listing five possibilities, including El Sordo and Pablo (MS10-008; this question with the five names came between Pablo's "What is that to you?" and Anselmo's "He is Pablo" [10:25–26]).

16:34 **the way those horses make Pablo feel:** The thing that will make Jordan feel that way is Maria, whom he describes as moving like a "colt" (25:17; 137:10) and who has a similar effect on his political commitment as the horses do on Pablo's (15:36). Pablo also thinks of Maria as a colt (64:4). Like Pablo's horses, Maria gives Jordan something to coddle and possess, and a taste for life outside war. Immediately after sleeping with her the second time, he tells himself he has no politics "now" (163:23) and fantasizes about domestic life with her.

16:36+ **he can't join the Jockey Club. . . . Pauvre Pablo. Il a manqué son Jockey:** Dating to the 1830s, the Jockey Club of Paris, originally the Society for the Encouragement of the Improvement of Horse Breeding in France, quickly became one of the most elite social institutions for Parisian aristocratic men and the ruling class and remained so well into the twentieth century. This Right Bank institution for the ruling class should not be confused with the Cabaret Le Jockey, in Montparnasse on the Left Bank, a popular party spot for the creative set, where the singer, nude model, and professional lover Kiki captivated audiences (Hemingway wrote the introduction to her memoir). Hemingway knew the cabaret well, with its "large painted figures on the outside of the building [including] an Indian on an Appaloosa" and inside walls decorated "with cowboy scenes by Hilaire Hiler, an American painter" (as well as Kiki's piano accompanist) (Fitch 125). Jordan the Montanan elsewhere likens these Spaniards to Native Americans; readers have linked Jordan's outlook and the novel's spirit to the American West and the Western genre.

Hemingway translates the French phrase in an adjacent sentence. The verb *manquer* literally translates "to miss"—one could read the line as sarcastically saying that Pablo sentimentally misses *his* ("*son*") Jockey Club—as if he could ever belong to such a club. Jordan's dig testifies to his bourgeois cosmopolitanism, when Loyalist Spaniards refused to wear ties, hats, even eyeglasses, or use the formal second-person pronoun, because they signaled class difference. As with its English equivalent, the French *pauvre* indicates pity or poverty. Jordan's using French for his slight, which Pablo can't understand and which was the second language of the European and American elite, widens the gap between Pablo and the elite, between Pablo and Jordan. Jordan uses French to distance himself from Pablo again later (404:22–23).

The first time Jordan thinks in a foreign language, he does it in French, not Spanish. This passage is the first time Jordan reveals a familiarity with Paris unexplained by what little the novel gives of his biography. During the 1920s and 1930s, the French Line sometimes made a port call in Vigo, Spain, on its way from New York City to Le Havre, France; more often, however, US travelers to Spain would have shipped from New York City to either Le Havre or Southampton (England) and passed through Paris. If Jordan never actually lived in Paris, as Hemingway did, he most likely stopped in Paris for a lengthy stay in his travels to and from Spain. Alternatively, these passages could be moments when Hemingway drafted himself into the text, as he often did in his writing process, but neglected to remove later.

17:10+ **All the best ones:** Hemingway expressed a similar idea about the gay ones being the best and the shortest-lived in his Spanish Civil War short story "The Denunciation," published by *Esquire* magazine in November 1938. The story's narrator observes that the "really cheerful people are usually the bravest, and the bravest get killed quickest" (*CSS* 421). The second of *Esquire*'s three so-called Chicote stories about the war, "The Butterfly and the Tank" (Dec. 1938), recounts the mistaken killing of a man celebrating a wedding. A waiter at Chicote's concludes that he dies because his "gaiety comes in contact with the seriousness of the war" (*CSS* 435). Jordan's reflection gives him little room to survive the war. He isn't a gay one—he isn't cheerful or brave—and he has been fighting in the war since the beginning. If he were one of the best, he ought to be dead. But the alternative personality trait to which he seems predisposed, serious thinking, will also get him killed. In war, Hemingway will write in his introduction to the 1942 anthology *Men at War*, "worrying does no good," and "learning to suspend your imagination and live completely in the very second of the present minute with no before and no after is the greatest gift a soldier can acquire" (xxvii) (a mental state Jordan enters the second time the novel describes his lovemaking with Maria).

17:17–18 Not a thinker. Man, I'm hungry, he thought. I hope Pablo eats well: Jordan hopes for good eats right after Anselmo accuses Pablo of acting only to "eat well," not fight the war (16:2–3), right after Jordan wonders what could make him feel the way Pablo feels about his horses (16:34), and right after Jordan realizes he is "getting gloomy" like Pablo (17:5). The two men are more similar than either care to admit. The lines' movement away from thinking to hunger echoes *A Farewell to Arms*, from Frederic Henry's decision to quit his war: "I was not made to think. I was made to eat. My God, yes. Eat and drink and sleep with Catherine" (*FTA* 233). Enter Maria—

NOTES

1. On the novel as "dramatizing the conflict between the values associated with the natural world and the values associated with the tank and other machines," see Guttmann (170). Per Guttmann, "The Nationalists hold the bridge. It is their armor that must not cross" (173). Guttman's simple and dated scheme has merit but lacks the novel's nuance. As one small example, what would such a scheme make of Maria's fantasy of riding her love's happiness "in the sky like the little pursuit planes" (161:19)?
2. Hemingway wrote about Lardner twice: "James Lardner, Loyalist Volunteer," dateline 25 April 1938 (in Watson 84–85): and "The Writer as Writer," *Direction* 2 (May–June 1939), reprinted in Trogdon, *Literary Reference*, 214–15.
3. To Maurice Speiser, 26 Aug. [1938] (USC).
4. To Max Perkins [Sept. 1940] (PUL).
5. On Domingo, see Mandel, *Hemingway's DIA*, 127–28; also the website robertodomingo.com, where one can see *Saltando la Barrera* (http://robertodomingo.com/en/saltando-la-barrera/). The painting is alternatively known as *Toros*, or Bull, a truncation of *Corrida de Toros* or The Bullfight, because the word appears prominently on it, as it was the poster art for the 1923 Valencia bullfights. It has mistakenly been called *La Cogida*, or The Goring (*Letters 5* 83n7, 201n1).
6. To Arnold Gingrich, 3 Oct 1936 (Bentley Historical Library, University of Michigan).
7. "Una Baja por mal venéreo es una deserción," (1937), Universitat de Barcelona, Collecció Cartells del Pavelló de la República (https://mdc.csuc.cat/digital/collection/pavellorepu/id/550/).

8. Francisco Rivero Gil, "¡Atención¡ Las Enfermedades Venéreas Amenazan Tu Salud. ¡Prevente Contra Ellas¡", Museum of Modern Art (https://www.moma.org/collection/works/5335).

9. As the single report of this specific mutilation was never publicly disclosed, it is unlikely that Hemingway heard of it, although he might have understood that it was not an uncommon Sioux and Cheyenne practice. See Hardorff, *Casualties*, 21; *Casualties II*, 20.

CHAPTER TWO

18:7 **a bear's den:** See 40:15+.

18:9 **a large cave in the rim-rock formation:** The Guadarrama is a granite mountain chain without caves. While Hemingway later has Jordan observe the "limestone upper basins" and imagine the caves throughout (138:13), everywhere else he identifies it as granite and in a letter wrote that "there are many caves in the Guadarrama and Gredos where people have lived" (to José Alemany, 8 Nov. 1940, Outgoing). Hemingway was familiar with several caves elsewhere in central Spain, used for dwellings and military functions around Fuentidueña de Tajo and Teruel. The Monk's Cave (Cueva del Monje) is a large rock formation—a boulder pile, really—whose dramatic suggestion of a cave entrance lends it as a possible model. Its location relative to the actual bridge loosely fits the novel. It's a bit far, at 5.4 kilometers north-northeast of the bridge, with some uphill walking and with some high ground above (the high ground of the Nationalist positions in the introduction's photo), but it sits on a slope closer to the valley floor than to any rimrocked ridgetop.

18:20 **dark, good-looking lazy gypsy face:** The character Rafael. Pilar has Romani blood, and later tells a story involving three of the most famous Romani flamenco artists. The novel's unrealistic use of Romani contributes to its exotic appeal to its American audience and, more deeply, to a primitivist, Orientalist vision of Spain exacerbated by Spanish Romani's purported affinity with the Moors (see 40:31). Conversely, the ethnic color provided by the Romani offsets the racialized portrayal of the Spaniards, who would appear more conventionally European by comparison. David Murad argues that although Hemingway creates Rafael as "a caricature of a person of Romani descent" in being "carefree, easygoing, and even clown-like, as well as lazy, unreliable, and lacking seriousness"—and a folksy musician to boot—"*For Whom the Bell Tolls* also complicates and examines these traditions and associations" (87).

The racial stereotyping notwithstanding, Hemingway's inclusion of Romani characters on the Republican side reminds readers of the thoroughly racist nature of the Nationalist cause. Franco's propaganda machine intellectually contorted itself to claim that political opponents such as communists were racially—genetically—not Spanish. Romani in Spain and elsewhere suffered centuries of ethnic persecution. In Spain, the Inquisition targeted them. In the late nineteenth and early twentieth century, conservative Spaniards resented the global popularity of the flamenco musical arts for the association of true Spain with its Romani population. Some Spanish Romani did fight for the Republic; some fled the country. During the Second World War, Romani became victims of the Holocaust. For a political perspective on Romani in the novel, see 19:37.

18:23 **unprintable:** The first of many instances in which Hemingway substitutes a placeholder for an actual Spanish vulgarity. The creative variety of substitute words suggests the colorful richness of these expressions, a richness Hemingway thought untranslatable and unbelievable.[1] He thus made the substitutions in the name of realism. This creative constraint contributes to the originality of the novel's voice by making it unique and more memorable than the actual language would have been. In his revisions, Hemingway sometimes changed "obscenity" to distinct and forceful words like "besmirch," "vileness," and "defile," as well as to their Spanish versions, such as "mierda" for *shit* and "joder" for *to fuck*. Two years after the novel's publication, Hemingway offered another explanation:

> There are certain words which are a permanent, but usually unpublishable part of the language. They are how men have talked actually, when under stress for hundreds of years. But to substitute slang expressions for these words, slang being a language which becomes a dead language at least every three years, makes a defect in writing which causes it to die as fast as the slang expressions die. It is the "Twenty-three skidoo" and "Ish ka bibble" school of American writing. (*MW* xvii)

Using these substitutes also showed off Hemingway's sense of humor. Avoiding profanity became something of a game.

After being forced to remove vulgarities from *The Sun Also Rises* and still seeing it banned in Boston in 1927, Hemingway had his next confrontation over obscenities and sexual references in *A Farewell to Arms*. The second installment of its serialized version led the Boston police to confiscate *Scribner's Magazine* from sellers, and to further expurgations (Trogdon, *Lousy* 70–83). Just before *For Whom the Bell Tolls*, Hemingway's editor and publisher allowed him to include the word "fucking" once but only once, and for the first time, in *To Have and Have Not*, resulting in its ban from bookstores and libraries in Detroit. This was the era of the Motion Picture Production Code—the Hays Code—and the (Catholic) National Legion of Decency. Hemingway did not need additional reasons or excuses for bans or boycotts. After a decade of underperforming books, he desperately needed critical, popular, and *commercial* success:

The composition of *For Whom the Bell Tolls* coincides with the end of Hemingway's marriage to Pauline Pfeiffer, his second wife, and his developing relationship with Martha Gellhorn, the woman he would marry in November 1940. In order to gain freedom from Pauline, Hemingway had to produce a best-seller, a work which would replace the income he would lose after his divorce. (Trogdon, "Money and Marriage" 11)

To replace the financial support of Pauline's family money, particularly from Uncle Gus, Hemingway sought serialization and a Book of the Month Club contract. Obscenities would have been nonstarters. The serialization did not come through, but the Book of the Month Club deal did.

19:1 **He catches rabbits:** Rafael, the one who catches rabbits, "found [Maria] where she had run from the train to the rocks" (30:15–16). Rabbit will become Jordan's pet name for her. Two mornings from now, Rafael will kill two hares copulating in the snow all but simultaneously with Jordan and Maria's lovemaking in Jordan's sleeping bag in the snow (274:7+).

19:37 **They keep on being gypsies:** Politically speaking, on the one hand, the Romani lifestyle agreed with Hemingway in being peripatetic and ungoverned by anyone save themselves. Hemingway believed in minimal government interference in one's affairs, and he located his homes more or less beyond society's reach—in Key West, then Cuba, and eventually Ketchum. "A writer is like a Gypsy," Hemingway wrote his Russian translator, an "outlyer" [sic] who "owes no allegiance to any government" (to Ivan Kashkin, 19 Aug. 1935, *SL* 419). For Murad, "Jordan envies the unattached Gypsy lifestyle" but "realistically and rationally" opposes it, as the conflict between individual sentiment and social duty is at the heart of the novel (91).

To the degree that Hemingway has fashioned Pablo's band into an allegory of the Republic, the Romani's unlikely presence corresponds to the unlikely participation of anarchists in the government and the military. But a random anarchist in Pablo's crew wouldn't fit the story. Plus, Hemingway shared with his wartime communist and socialist colleagues an abiding spite for the anarchists on full display elsewhere in the novel. Treating Pablo's crew as a loose allegory allows Hemingway to have it both ways.

22:8+ **the strange thing about her:** The "strange thing" is her "cropped hair," an instant point of erotic fascination. Later Jordan uses the word "strange" to describe his insides whenever she catches his eye (168:1). This passage introduces Jordan's relating Maria to Spain, her "skin and eyes . . . golden tawny brown," her hair "the golden brown of a grain field." Jordan thinks the adjective "tawny" seven times in the novel, only ever for the landscape and for Maria. As with any quickening romantic love, theirs springs from a fair amount of fantasy. Jordan's attraction to Maria involves his vision of Spain and his envisioned role in saving Spain.

The strangeness that is Maria's shorn hair opens the text to other readings of the word "strange," for example as being of a piece with a strangeness underneath, an eroticized quality not unlike the "darkness underneath" her tanned skin that carries sexual and racial undertones (43:38). "Hemingway not only fetishized hair, he also fetishized racial otherness," observes Eby, "and, for him, the two fetishes were linked" (Eby, *Reading* 66). Well into the nineteenth century, the adjective **tawny** was nominalized to mean a person of color. In *Vanity Fair* (1848), William Thackeray used it for a woman of mixed Jewish and Jamaican heritage (247). It often signified people from northern Africa, as in the compound *tawny-moor* (related to *blackamoor*). The *Oxford English Dictionary* cites F. E Smedley's 1850 novel *Frank Fairlegh* for its reference to "Rajah somebody or other . . . on his elephant, attended by a train of tawnies" (def. B.3). *Tawny* is a favorite adjective of one of Jordan's preferred travel writers, Richard Ford, who usually employs it for all of Spain, but sometimes to distinguish Andalusia—the region closest to northern Africa and with the strongest Moorish influence (332). Jordan sees tawny Spain the way Ford did before him, with a romanticizing nineteenth-century Othering gaze. Hemingway did not originally type "tawny" in this passage—he inserted these instances later by hand (MS10-009).

Jordan's comparison of Maria's short hair to a "**beaver pelt**" initiates a pattern whereby he connects the sexualized Maria with the violence perpetrated toward the hunted (e.g., 378:6+). Because the forced shaving of her head preluded her multiple rapes, Jordan's erotic excitement is deeply troubling—even more so when one takes into account Hemingway's own pleasure in cutting women's hair (Eby, *Fetishism* 79–82). Whether Hemingway intended to evoke the cultural association of a beaver to a woman's genitalia is unknowable. The association emerged in the 1920s, although the use of pubic wigs, or merkins, has a much longer history; in the New World, some may have been fashioned from beaver pelts (Poliquin 109). Regardless, per Rachel Poliquin, the "beaver has always been an overdetermined metaphor for human sexuality" (117). Poliquin notes the mammal's biological intersexuality, pseudohermaphrodism, and androgyny (118). In the draft, Hemingway first typed "beaver's fur," then in a handwritten revision replaced it with "the fur on a marten" but instantly crossed over "marten" to restore *beaver* for the final language: "the fur on a beaver pelt" (*HLE* 492–93). The decision process might have involved the sexual suggestion. Adding "pelt" highlights the violence; a pelt requires a killed thing. When Jordan later compares touching Maria's head to caressing and stroking the fur of a small mammal just caught in a metal trap, it's a marten (378:6+).

The Garden of Eden's Marita verily reincarnates Maria. As Eby summarizes an unpublished manuscript scene, when "David meets Marita at the café in Cannes [he] is shocked by her hair 'cropped as close as a sheared beaver.' . . . He wants to know 'what kind of boy' she is supposed to be. . . . It's 'wonderful,' David tells her, but a 'shock.'

The hairstyle looks North African, like a 'waterfront Arab's,' and it 'mixe[s] up the genders'" (Eby, *Reading* 311). Maria and Marita present at once as conventional and androgynous, and to various degrees flirt with bisexuality. North Africa figures into the Maria erotic imaginary too, complicated by the fact that Moors repeatedly shaved and raped her (see 117:15). Imagine Maria's state of mind in knowing that the public site (and sight) of her traumatic violation is the very "strange thing" that excites her new beloved. *The Garden of Eden* also draws on the *Hamlet* allusion to death as an "undiscovered country," mixing together gender and sexual exploration, geographic adventure, and self-destruction (see front matter: title and epigraph).

22:24–25 They gave me this haircut in Valladolid: The shaving and rape of women were common terrorist practices by Nationalist forces. Maria was first shorn and raped in her unnamed home village (350:25), most likely near Valladolid in Old Castile. By referencing her subsequent periodic haircuts and implied rapes while imprisoned in Valladolid (see 23:21–22), she avoids revisiting her original traumatic assault as the book whets (disturbingly) its reader's curiosity. Falangist militiamen originally shaved and raped her, and Valladolid was the region's wartime Falangist hub (Payne 65). It makes sense that her Falangist tormentors transported her to the Valladolid prison. A very conservative party, the Falange sought a strict authoritarian nationalism, refused regional autonomy, regarded Catholicism as integral to Spanish identity, and hoped to recover the glory of imperialist Spain. Racism permeated its ideology, as did very traditional gender roles consigning women to a submissive and domestic status. Franco would come to co-opt the Falange as his dictatorship's single political party.

22:37 rabbit cooked with onions: According to Richard Ford, Spaniards traditionally preferred hare over rabbit, but in any event when the meat is stewed the "*sauce is everything; . . . it is a brown sauce—salsa morena*. Brown is in fact the epithet for *tawny* Spain, and for *las cosas de España* [all things Spanish]—cloaks, sierras, women, and ollas" (*Hand-book* 63). Jordan finds the sauce the tawny Maria serves him in the mountains "delicious" (23:2). Ford characterizes Spanish cooking and eating habits as "Oriental" (63). Hemingway had originally typed "It was beef," but *x*'d over those words and typed "It was rabbit" before continuing (MS10–009). That night, when Maria joins Jordan in his sleeping bag, he calls her "little rabbit," and Rabbit then becomes his pet name for her, making yet another association of her with Spain (see 69:23). DeGuzmán convincingly argues that the novel "attempts to transubstantiate the act of eating from colonialist consumption into the very act of communion with the country and its inhabitants" as the novel "actually conflates people with food," most especially Maria (*Shadow* 218–19).

Two friendly amendments to DeGuzmán's argument are in order. First, mirroring the colonialist-imperialist appetite for consuming native bodies was the colonialist-imperialist anxiety and titillation about consumption by the colonized—as popularly reinforced by countless print and screen narratives featuring African cannibals, an ur-narrative Hemingway's novel acknowledges when Jordan compares himself to Tarzan (436:33). Jordan's desire for incorporation in the Spanish earth suggests a willingness to be consumed by Maria-as-Spain. Second, the colonizing imagination's titillation by the idea of consuming and being consumed by the racial Other (visually evidenced in exaggerated depictions of mouths) has always borne a palpable subtext of male homoeroticism. Cannibalism's entanglement in the colonizing world's imagination with ideas of so-called primitive sexuality includes incest in addition to miscegenation and homoeroticism, another taboo of the self-proclaimed civilized world that plays out in Jordan's attraction to Maria—and between the lovers in Hemingway's later Spain-inflected novel, *The Garden of Eden* (see hooks, "Eating the Other"; Woodard, *Delectable Negro;* Tompkins, *Racial Indigestion;* and Vernon, *On Tarzan*).

23:12 **How art thou called?:** So, *¿Cómo te llamas?* Jordan has already asked Anselmo and Pablo for their names, the text both times using "you" and "your," the formal or plural second-person English pronoun that in Early Modern English was used for an elder or superior (2:36–37; 10:23–24). On those occasions, readers can assume he did not utter *¿Cómo te llamas?*, the familiar second-person-form pronoun used democratically throughout the Republic for all fellow citizens, but *¿Cómo se llama?* because he needed to show initial deference and perhaps suspected that the abandonment of the hierarchical, bourgeois, formal second-person pronouns had not reached the mountains. The exact same question posed now to Maria elicits the familiar form. The text linguistically inscribes Maria as the personification of democratic Spain for Jordan's desire for integration. At the same time, it expresses a tone of romantic interest (which Pablo recognizes). With the familiar form, Jordan positions himself as either her equal or her better.

23:17 **Three months:** Pablo's band and Kashkin attacked the train and liberated Maria in April (23:32). As this scene occurs on 28 May, she has been free of prison for eight weeks at most. She could not have been in the mountains for three months (although she had just started her third month). Hemingway perhaps intended to refer to the fact that her last head-shaving and rape occurred three months earlier—the length of time she says her hair has had to grow (23:22)—such that she did not suffer these abuses her last month in prison. The time problem is somewhat mitigated by the fact that Hemingway initially had the novel's actions taking place sometime in June, not May, changing it with the galley proofs (see 153:24).

23:20 **as a grain field in the wind on a hillside:** Hemingway added this line by hand to the original typescript, beginning with "that was as thick and short" (MS10-009). Jordan's attraction to her "rippling" hair still mostly connects to his vision of her as the Spanish landscape (see 22:8+; 345:29). He has not yet learned that the hair shearing preceded her rape. The moment mutes Jordan's erotic attraction to the visible site of the sexual violence done to Maria, an attraction that increasingly manifests (starting at 67:16+).

23:21–22 They shaved it regularly in the prison at Valladolid: Given that Maria's later detailed story of her initial violent head-shaving by several Falangists serves as a surrogate description for the gang-rape by these men that immediately followed (351:35+), and given her testimony of being gang-raped more than the one time (350:19+), serial gang-rapes should be read into her language of the periodic head-shavings by her imprisoners. Moors were among her rapists (117:15). Hemingway added this line by hand to the original typescript (MS10–009).

23:38 Three trains: Jordan's expertise at blowing trains behind enemy lines is one reason readers have seen Thomas Edward (T. E.) Lawrence—Lawrence of Arabia—as a model. Lawrence fought among Arabs using guerilla tactics during the First World War and told that story in his 1926 memoir, *Seven Pillars of Wisdom* (he published an abridged version, titled *Revolt in the Desert,* the next year).

24:2 Estremadura: A region southwest of central Spain, most of which was under Nationalist control during the time Jordan describes. Hemingway's colleague Jay Allen reported on the fall of the Extremaduran town of Badajoz early in the war, and the slaughter of government loyalists:

> They were young, mostly peasants in blue blouses, mechanics in jumpers, "The Reds." They are still being rounded up. At 4 o'clock in the morning they were turned out into the ring through the gate by which the initial parade of the bullfight enters. There machine guns awaited them.
> After the first night the blood was supposed to be palm deep on the far side of the ring. I don't doubt it. Eighteen hundred men—there were women, too—were mowed down there in some 12 hours. There is more blood than you would think in 1,800 bodies. (2)

On Jordan's time in Extremadura, see 162:30 and 148:12+. He shot Kashkin there (149:17).

24:17 leave the women alone: Jordan has now expressed two reasons for avoiding romance: because with his mission he has enough to think about already (8:5–6) and because it interferes with good relations with the Spaniards on whose cooperation he depends. He willfully courts trouble. His sudden lack of care whiffs of fatalism (and admits Maria's power over him).

25:9 **You are blushing:** Blushing is a defining feature of Maria—as it will be for Marita in *The Garden of Eden*. In both texts, the American man teases the woman about it. In the latter, David gives Marita the nickname Haya, "the one who blushes," a Swahili term (142; see Eby, *Reading* 180). While one can't readily apply a term from a much later work onto this one, Maria and Marita come from the same imaginative locus and are colored by Hemingway's African otherness complex, which the nickname Haya reinforces (e.g., 22:8+).

25:17 **as a colt moves:** The first of two times Jordan likens Maria to a colt (137:10). The line contributes to Jordan's association of Maria with animals and natural Spain. Jordan's colt simile answers his earlier wondering about "what could make me feel the way those horses make Pablo feel" (16:33–34). Pablo, who also lusts for Maria, corroborates Jordan's simile when he tells his bay stallion that it is "no colt of a girl with cropped head" (64:4). Maria thus poses a threat to Jordan's political commitment, per Anselmo's judgment of Pablo (15:35–36). Once he sleeps with Maria, Jordan declares he has quit politics (163:23) and imagines bourgeois domestic life with her. He dies from an injury sustained when his wounded mount falls on and crushes his leg.

A colt is a young male. Tom Burnam suggests replacing the word "colt" with "lad." For Burnam, a "boy-like" Maria fits a pattern whereby "Hemingway's 'good' women seem really to be Hemingway men only slightly changed"; Burnam cites Maria's slender figure, cropped hair, and long, trousered legs (22). A coltish Maria aligns with the ambiguously gendered Greta Garbo, about whom Jordan muses right after the second colt simile (137:16+); and with Comley and Scholes's reading of her as a younger version of a sexually ambiguous Pilar (46–49).

25:35 **seven and there are two women:** At this point in typing the draft, Hemingway had not yet finalized the men's names. On the backside of the prior typescript page, he jotted a list: two brothers, Primitivo and Segundo; Rafael; Fernando; "Augustin"; one [other]; and Pablo (MS10–009). A folder with Hemingway's word counts ranging from 16 July to 13 August [1939], which includes an insert to chapter 11, the beginning of chapter 14, and beyond, has two different lists. One folder flap lists Pablo, Rafael, Fernando, "Augustin," Primitivo, and Andres as the brothers, and a tentative "Manolo?"; another flap includes the final names and sibling set: Pablo; Raphael; "flat-faced" Primitivo; the old man [Anselmo]; the brothers Andres and Eladio; Fernando; and "Augustin" (MS12–005).[2] Durán corrected the spelling of Agustín's name in the galley proofs.

Primitivo's possibly having a younger brother named Segundo intrigues. The older brother of someone named Segundo, or Second, would properly be Primero, or First. If Hemingway intended Primitivo to be a firstborn even after finally pairing Andres and Eladio, the text's exclusion of Primitivo's younger brother, of any mention of him, quietly disquiets in this novel of a civil war. Is Segundo dead? Does he fight on the other side?

26:10+ **than the cholera . . . than the typhoid fever . . . than the bubonic plague:** The first chapter of *A Farewell to Arms* ends with the line "At the start of the winter came the permanent rain and with the rain came the cholera. But it was checked and in the end only seven thousand died of it in the army" (4). One way of defining the beginning of modern warfare is to date it to the war in which direct combat deaths for the first time in history exceeded death by disease and other "natural" (even if collateral) causes, such as malnutrition. That would be the Great War. As Spain did not participate in that war, its weaponry and tactics remained stuck largely in the pre–Great War era. Rafael's hyperbolic comparison perhaps suggests Spain's civil war as its transitional event, although it seems he means for Jordan to consider Pablo a force of nature beyond those other forces rather than an agent of modern industrial warfare.

26:19 **retire like a *matador de toros*:** Like a bullfighter. See Pilar's story of the start of the war, comparing the day's events under Pablo's leadership with a bullfight (chapter 10).

26:22 **make him go in the army:** Although Hemingway's journalism and propaganda film *The Spanish Earth* (filmed from February through early May 1937) boasted of waves of volunteers joining the Republican cause, both sides relied on conscription, often under duress. The side on which one fought could be a matter of happenstance geography rather than personal allegiance.

27:11 **a Lewis gun:** A thirty-caliber, gas-operated, and pan-fed light machine-gun with foldout legs. Designed in 1911 by an American and made in Belgium, manufacture moved to companies in Great Britain and the United States by 1914 because of Germany's threat to Belgium. These two countries obeyed the Non-Intervention Treaty and did not provide material support. The Soviet Union supplied the Republic with Lewis guns it had purchased earlier, but Pablo's crew captured this particular gun—it isn't clear how the Nationalists acquired it, unless the Spanish army bought some before the civil war or the Nationalists had previously captured it from Republican forces. The "three legs that fold" (27:3) refers to the bipod and its support arm, as when Jordan later "clamped the tripod against the barrel" (454:19).

27:33 **The *mujer* of Pablo reads in the hands:** Because of her "gypsy blood" (28:8) and her gender, as traditionally only Romani women practiced fortune-telling. From his travels and reading George Borrow, Jordan should know better than to ask Rafael to read his palm (27:29). Either Jordan has forgotten, or he knows less

"Marine Corps Rifle Range, Lewis Machine Gun Tests" (1917), Harris and Ewing, photographers. (Library of Congress Prints and Photographs Division. Public Domain. Cropped from original. Reproduction No.: LC-DIG-hec-07932. Call No.: LC-H261-7659)

than he thinks, or Hemingway is playing to his reader's unfamiliarity. Pablo has no such heritage, yet he and Pilar ply the typical Romani gendered trades according to Borrow: the man dealing in horses, the woman telling fortunes (Borrow, *Zincali* 7, 10–11). Moreover, the women only practiced it on non-Romani as a means of income. Pilar's reading Jordan's palm signifies his outsider status, where it becomes an interesting power dynamic, as she performs it for the white-dominant-culture male while the implied fortune—his imminent death—works almost as a curse.

Pilar the fortune-telling Romani is frank about her sexuality. Such paintings as Caravaggio's *The Fortune Teller* (ca. 1594) and Régnier's *Cardsharps and Fortune Teller* (ca. 1626) convey the Western imaginary of the woman fortune teller's sexuality as bewitchment, distraction, and swindling or sharping. The tradition of mothers passing their fortune-telling art to daughters, combined with Pilar's motherly role toward and the sexual instruction she imparts to Mari, might give a tinge of bewitchment to Jordan's instant love for Maria, a love which betrays his principle of romantic abstaining (7:38–8:6), arguably deflates his political commitment (163:23), and perhaps contributes to his death. Borrow asserts—contra popular myth—that gitanas were not themselves harlots, but "at all times willing to encourage licentiousness in others, from hope of gain" (108).

27:34 **such a barbarousness:** Hemingway has chosen an archaic English word, dating to the sixteenth century, in place of the more modern "barbarity," to convey the foreignness of the language to English readers by grounding that otherness as if from a time out of mind. The effect cannot be achieved in Spanish translations of the novel, which might use *barbarie*, *bárbaro*, or *barbaridad*. According to Ilan Stavans, *bárbaro* can connote a mentally ill or merely passionate person, and *barbaridad* connects to "how a man looks at a woman and feels there's this heat and passion inside that is overwhelming" (Cirino, "One"). That connection would fit the novel's characterization of Pilar's sexuality, a potentially emasculating sexuality, and it fits the reference to her reading Jordan's hand with its fatal prognostication. The translation by Lola de Aguado uses *salvaje*, "wild" or "savage" (40), to suggest a certain animality and physicality.

28:38+ **making him pick her up again and loading the gun for him:** This description of Pilar as the driving force behind saving Maria, using her mighty if profane rhetorical talent and supporting the men in their fighting, provides some corroboration for seeing Pilar as La Pasionaria (see 30:24+). She reloads Pablo's rifle but does not fire herself.

29:23+ **Then it came chu-chu-chu-chu-chu-chu:** The length and rhythm of Rafael's sentence, the movement of the earth that "seemed to rise," and the reference to the train as an animal resemble the earth-moving lovemaking scenes between Jordan and Maria. Hemingway took care to create the rhythm, length, and pace of this sentence, adding to the typescript by hand a couple of commas, two mostly iambic phrases—"of blackness and a roar" and "rising in the air"—two words to enhance the overall iambic meter: "in the cloud of dirt and ^*of* the wooden ties," and "as in a dream and then ^*it* fell onto its side." A third added phrase appropriately jars readers out of the metrical pattern's spell: "like a great wounded animal" (MS10–009).

Rafael uses the word *máquina* five times in the passage, thrice with a metaphor of "speaking" for firing, after the text has already had him say the English "machine gun" (26:38; 29:15). Fenimore has smartly concluded that Hemingway's choice of the Spanish term expresses the mysteriousness of the weapon to Rafael, "and the Spanish term provides the English reader something of the almost animate quality which the gun may be supposed to have had for the gypsy" (76). The effect cannot be replicated in Spanish translations of the novel.

30:5 **at the point of a pistol:** Leaders on both sides of war sometimes led by gunpoint.

30:20+ **said a deep voice . . . unsayable son of an unnameable unmarried gypsy obscenity:** This is Pilar, Pablo's partner, although the novel does not provide her name until chapter 4 (55:8). After Pablo's band has introduced Pilar's personality to Jordan and the reader several times, her entrance does not disappoint. In literature, Pilar resembles Chaucer's Wife of Bath and Falstaff, the stage-commanding ribald older mentor (of sorts) to Prince Hal in Shakespeare's plays of civil war, *1 Henry IV* and *2 Henry IV*. The novel's several allusions to Shakespeare suggest Hemingway might have had Falstaff in mind. Pilar's physical presence and other evidence have led scholars to postulate a few models and influences. See the next entry. She also seems to have been a Spanish type—Josephine Herbst, in her memoir of the

Spanish Civil War, recalls "women of sixty" who came "proudly home, erect, magnificently wrathful as they shook their fists at far distant towers of enemy smoke piercing the sky, or burst out into gorgeous obscenities oddly mixed with symbolic religiosity, which reduced my memory of fashionable ladies back home, with their little stereotyped lavender curls and their mincing high heels, to a parody of a potential they had forfeited" (161).

30:24+ **a woman of about fifty:** In two letters Hemingway identifies Pilar as Pastora Imperio (to Charles Scribner, ca. 15 Aug. 1940, *SL* 508; to José Alemany, 8 Nov. 1940, Outgoing).[3] Born Pastora Rojas Monje to a Romani family in Seville, Andalusia, Pastora Imperio was one of the most famous flamenco dancers in history. According to Josephs, she "was well known for her long repertory and particularly for her 'arm dance'—*baile de brazos*—and for her spontaneous, unchoreographed dances." Seeing Pilar as "the essence of Spain," Josephs concludes that her character "works so well and is so complex that she truly is Pastora" (*Undiscovered* 76–77). Pilar is also an Andalusian Romani.[4] Pilar and Pastora appear together in chapter 14, in a fascinating scene where Hemingway has fun with their shared personality.

Pastora Imperio for personality; for political development and leadership, Dolores Ibárruri, also known as La Pasionaria (*the passionflower*), a prominent Spanish communist politician, inspirational spokeswoman, and figurehead for the Republic. Agustín accurately judges Pilar to be "brave" and "loyal," to have "[m]uch decision and much heart," and says to her: "You for energy and resolution, . . . [b]ut Pablo for the moving" (94:17–19; 95:8–9). La Pasionaria visited soldiers on the front; she organized women's support efforts; she ran orphanages. She appears in *The Spanish Earth*, the propagandistic documentary on which Hemingway collaborated. His narration for the film introduces her as "the most famous woman in Spain today" who "speaks of the new Spain. It is a nation disciplined and brave. It is a new nation forged in the discipline of its soldiers and the enduring bravery of its women." As the film makes plainly visible, La Pasionaria shares Pilar's physicality and arresting passion. Pilar's language of saving "other projects" until after the Republic wins the war (53:35–36), by which she means revolutionary projects, matches the communist party's and Pasionaria's wartime message. Some of the guerillas assert allegiance to her, not the bridge (53:20+). One might see Pilar's other statement in that passage, "That which must pass will pass" (54:3–4), as an ironically fateful allusion to La Pasionaria's rallying cry, "¡No Pasaran!": *They shall not pass!* That Hemingway might have expressed distaste for La Pasionaria does not exclude her ipso facto as contributing to his creation of Pilar. Jordan, too, sometimes finds Pilar's motivational chatter tiresome (387:31).

For spiritual development, the least definite Spanish candidate is less a person than an icon, Nuestra Senora del Pilar, or Virgen del Pilar. For adherents to Catholic readings of Hemingway, the novel's comparison of Pilar to a granite monument makes her a "secular reincarnation" of the Virgin Mary as the Patroness of Spain, who appeared to Saint James in the year AD 40 on a stone pillar on the bank of the Ebro River in Zaragoza. As H. R. Stoneback argues, Pilar's "assumption of the leadership of the guerilla band corresponds with Pilar's role as the patroness of the Spanish Army" ("Priest," 103). Nuestra Senora del Pilar was and is the patron saint of the *guardia civil,* not the Spanish Army—that would be Saint James—plus historically, most of the Spanish army sided with the Nationalists anyway. Another challenge to this identification: the Virgen del Pilar enshrined in the Cathedral-Basilica of Our Lady of the Pillar in Zaragoza is a wooden statue atop a jasper column. Hardly a granite monument. One can't easily reconcile this identification with Pilar's denouncement of God and Church, nor how the novel's actual quasi-virginal Maria (*Mary*) fits into this symbolism. To make this point another way, it is not clear what meaningful purpose such an association serves. How exactly does it help us understand Robert Jordan or the novel?

From Spanish models to more personal influences:

The literary legend and an early mentor of Hemingway, Gertrude Stein, elicited similar monumental adjectives from her contemporaries. She reminded W. G. Rogers of a "sculpture," and he cites one writer on her "statuesque appeal" and a caricaturist who called her "striking as Stonehenge" (12). The novel reminds us that *stein* means "stone" in German (289:16), and Pablo also thinks of Pilar as a "rock" (64:3). Rogers's description of Stein reads like one of Pilar: "The mouth was wide, the complexion weathered, the dark brown eyes mellow and magnetic. Her voice carried easily, and her infectious laughter would sometimes rumble like thunder" (12). Hemingway's description of Stein in *A Moveable Feast,* written years later, matches the novel's of Pilar (see Comley and Scholes 46; Eby, *Fetishism* 46–50). Stein shares with Pastora, La Pasionaria, and Pilar a fullness of figure and personality, and this commonality is at the heart of Hemingway's invention. Hemingway's distaste for La Pasionaria fits with his feelings at this point in his life for Stein (and for his own mother—see below). Her politics preclude too much overlap with Pilar, for despite being Jewish and gay, Stein was in other ways conservative. Her dislike of communism and her taste for old Spain apparently tilted her sympathies toward the Nationalists (Knapp 71; Malcolm 31).

Pilar's exemplary storytelling reflects Stein's literary talents. Stein was why Hemingway first traveled to Spain, inspired by her talk of bullfights and a photo of herself and her partner, Alice Toklas, "at the bull ring at Valencia" (*DIA* 1). Pilar's backstory involves bullfights and bullfighters, and her stories and rhetoric draw on her life in that world. Stein's Jewish heritage links her to Pilar's Romani blood: white Spaniards treated Moors, Gypsies, and Jews as racial and religious enemies even as these groups came to be perceived by the rest of Europe and America as part of the Spanish essence (DeGuzmán, *Shadow* 74, 77, 79, 81). That Pilar expresses sexual desire toward Maria has been debated, but to the extent that one accepts Pilar's more fluid

Left: Pastora Imperio ca. 1940. (Fotografia Archivo ABC). *Center:* Dolores Ibárruri / La Pasionaria cropped from Reunion of the Cortes of the Republic held on 30 September 1938 in the historic Monastery of Sant Cugat del Vallées, Public Domain (La Biblioteca Digital Hispánica de la Biblioteca Nacional de España). *Right:* Portrait of Gertrude Stein, New York, 1934, by Carl Von Vechten. (Library of Congress / Public Domain. LOT 12735, no. 1051 [P&P]. LOC Control No. 2004663582)

gender and sexuality—at the very least her nonfeminine presentation—and recognizes Hemingway's psychosomatic response to such women—Hemingway once wrote that he "always wanted to fuck" Stein, "a good healthy feeling" that "made more sense than some of the talk" (to W. G. Rogers, 29 Jul. 1948, *SL* 650)—the presence in Pilar of the openly gay Stein is hard to deny.

La Pasionaria, Stein, and Pilar are all gruff nurturers with what Hemingway's generation would have regarded as mannish traits. La Pasionaria was known to dress in a male soldier's uniform when visiting the troops. Another non-Spanish influence on Pilar was Grace Hall Hemingway, Ernest's mother, who shared the robust figure, prideful strength of personality, and rhetorical ability. Pilar's emasculation of Pablo corresponds to Hemingway's perception of his mother's emasculation of his father. There's also Grace's apparent flirtation with same-sex romance. In her forties, Grace took in Ruth Arnold, a young teenager with a troubled home life, as domestic help. Eventually, after Hemingway's father's death, she became Grace's companion. Although unverified, the family suspected an amorous relationship between Grace and Ruth—the latter something of a daughter figure as well as a mother's helper in taking care of the children. An ambiguous same-sex intimacy between a rescued daughter and her maternal boss characterizes the relationship between Maria and Pilar.

Pilar was Hemingway's nickname for his current wife, Pauline, who had a tomboyish quality that attracted him (although as early as 1946, observers saw all four of Hemingway's wives' short haircuts in terms of Maria's [Stone 6–7]). *Pilar* was also his beloved made-to-order fishing boat, purchased back in 1934. His wartime lover and next wife, Martha Gellhorn, early in their budding romance, confessed to

Hemingway that she sometimes thought about being a man, a sentiment Pilar also feels (97:31). Pilar and Maria are common names for a Spanish mother and daughter. Hemingway's friend the painter Joan Miró and his wife, Pilar, had a daughter named Maria. Finally, the word "pilar" in English means "pertaining to hair," a fact which potentially reinforces the connection between Pilar and Maria as well as the gender ambiguity that is part of Jordan's attraction to Maria.

31:25 **a stagnation that is repugnant:** After the Nationalist advance on Madrid from the north through the Guadarrama failed in late summer of 1936, the lines stabilized and indeed sat mostly stagnant for the duration of the war (but for the major exception of the novel's action).

32:23+ **homes to care for such as her . . . she can work with children:** The Spanish Communist Party spokeswoman La Pasionaria, on whom Hemingway partially based Pilar (30:24+), organized wartime group homes and orphanages for the displaced (see Vernon, *Second War* 175–76).

33:9–10 **I am not of those who speak gloomily . . . Let me see thy hand:** Pilar has just reminded Jordan of the bad fortune brought by anxious, gloomy, speech, the very kind of talk to which Kashkin fell prey—this follows on the heels of her having seen the sickness for Maria rising in Jordan (32:17). Rightly concerned, Pilar immediately asks to read his palm.

33:17 **Nothing:** In Spanish, *nada*, a term Hemingway used for the nothingness of death, most famously in his story "A Clean, Well-Lighted Place," first published in *Scribner's Magazine* in March 1933. The story takes place in Spain, features a suicidal old man, and includes this late reflection by the older of two waiters:

> It was all a nothing and a man was a nothing too. It was only that and light was all it needed and a certain cleanness and order. Some lived in it and never felt it but he knew it all was *nada y pues nada y nada y pues nada*. Our *nada* who art in *nada*, *nada* be thy name thy kingdom *nada* thy will be *nada* in *nada* as it is in *nada*. Give us this *nada* our daily *nada* and *nada* us our *nada* as we *nada* our *nadas* and *nada* us not into *nada* but deliver us from *nada*; *pues nada*. Hail nothing full of nothing, nothing is with thee. (*CSS* 291)

Most readers conclude that Pilar sees Jordan's impending death. The palm-reading reveals that he holds his fate in his own hands, that it is embedded in his character.

NOTES

1. To Max Perkins from Cuba, late December 1939 or early January 1940 (PUL).
2. See appendix A. The first page of published chapter 14's draft word count is dated 28 July, although the daily word count beside the final name list corresponds to a total daily count dated 29 July on the folder. The folder contents are published chapter 31.
3. The Scribner letter indirectly associates her husband, Rafael el Gallo, with Pilar's Finito.
4. Interested readers should see DeGuzmán's discussion of the controversy around John Singer Sargent's 1882 painting *El Jaleo,* a flamenco scene visibly marked by gender and sexual ambiguity. For DeGuzmán, the painting "works to encode its historical, literary, and erotic tropes about Spain into the visual language of the real, thus transforming legend about hot, dark, queer, passionate, and fatal Spain into essence" (*Shadow* 128).

CHAPTER THREE

35:6 **a steel bridge:** See 1:24.

35:8–9 **deep gorge at the bottom of which, far below, a brook leaped:** Also described as "almost a canyon" (37:13). The terrain is difficult to visualize. Chapter 1 describes a stream that "flows gently" before it "drops suddenly" into a "steep gorge" (1:21–22). But *steep* references contour, not depth, and nowhere does the novel mention a waterfall or cataract. Moreover, much later Pablo crosses from one side to the other by descending the "gorge" on one side (452:37), "climbing down into the gorge like a goat" (453:1–2), and what could only be a few minutes later "coming over the edge of the gorge, pulling himself over on hands and knees" (454:9–10). The gorge could not possibly be too deep and steep; not as deep and steep anyway as most visual representations dramatize.

38:19 **pursuit planes:** Throughout the novel, Hemingway uses the English term for this aircraft rather than translating the Spanish term, even when Jordan speaks in Spanish. The Spanish term *caza* translates as *hunt* or *hunter* functioning adjectivally, or *hunter* functioning as a noun to replace the two-word term—so, *cazas* is used for "pursuit planes." The Spanish word contributes to the novel's interrogation of the line between hunting and warring, most pointedly in passages in which the characters talk about being hunted by the enemy and the enemy's planes (e.g., 15:10). The Spanish term derives from the French *chasse* for planes developed during WWI as the first anti-aircraft aircraft, which had fixed-position machine guns whose mechanism synced the bullets to fly between the spinning propeller blades and which "the pilot aimed simply by flying" (Hynes 21). In the earlier war—the first modern, industrialized war—and to some degree, every war since—only in aerial dogfights did combat cling to a romantic vision of duels and gladiatorial contests. No such romance exists in this novel, where military aviation serves up only terror. (The male protagonist of *The Sun Also Rises* and of *The Garden of Eden* were Great War pilots.)

Jordan's confession to the reader that he lets his inexpert comrades believe any aircraft to be friendly, even when he knows better (as he realizes a few lines later), suggests his tactical complicity in the morale-building disinformation campaign waged by the Republic.

38:22 **Moscas:** Jordan describes these aircraft as "the green, red wing-tipped, low wing Russian conversion of the Boeing P32" (38:30–31). The Polikarpov I-16 was an innovative Russian design that beat the P32 to production in the mid-1930s. Both were low-wing monoplanes; the Russian version featured retractable landing gear. *Mosca*, its Republican nickname, translates as "fly"; *rata*, the Nationalist nickname, as "rat". The Soviet Union sold the aircraft to the Republic.

38:33 **Fascist Patrol:** While the Republican side commonly referred to the Nationalists as fascists, the language also points to the very real possibility that these planes, probably of German make, are being flown by German pilots from the Condor Legion (see 87:3+; 89:22).

39:14 **I do not like to kill animals:** Hemingway's active hunting life was very much part of his public persona, and then as now readers have sought the writer inside his male protagonists. Hemingway considered having Jordan in this passage admit to having hunted, "[b]ut I like this more" (*HLE* 493). Beyond this line's contribution to the novel's exploration of the difference between killing people in war and hunting animals, it distinguishes Jordan from Hemingway, who in the fall of 1936 observed the new war from a hunting trip in the Wyoming-Montana borderlands, the area of Jordan's childhood. Hemingway filled his letters that fall with details of his kills.

Jordan certainly has hunting experience. He knows horses, animal traps, and firearms. The men on his list of close friends share names with some of Hemingway's hunting and fishing pals (381:8–9), although the novel does not associate their fictional counterparts with hunting. Later he will say that he has "liked to kill as all who are soldiers by choice have enjoyed it" (287:7–8). During the Spanish Civil War, Hemingway crossed the combatant status line at most by helping a Republican soldier unjam his rifle. A few years after the Second World War, Hemingway bragged about killing twenty-six German soldiers while serving as a correspondent.[1] That number increased over the years to 122—see Cirino and Elder for a discussion of these claims as exaggerations if not outright fabrications. Hemingway anticipated Jordan's attitude in his 1936 article "On the Blue Water": "Certainly there is no hunting like the hunting of man and those who have hunted armed men long enough and liked it, never really care for anything else thereafter" (31). The line is the sardonic opening of an article about deep-sea fishing written with the forbidding certainty of the Second World War's approach.[2]

39:28+ **an eagle stuffed by an embalmer of birds of Avila:** With spread wings, "yellow" eyes "real as the eyes of an eagle alive," this "very beautiful thing" that gave Anselmo "great pleasure to contemplate" resembles representations of crucified Christ, a possibility enhanced by Anselmo's thrice mentioning his lost house, suggestive of both the Catholic Church where he, a loyal Republican, no longer spiritually resides, and of Saint Peter's three denials of Christ prior to the crucifixion. Isabel I, Isabel la Católica, adopted an eagle with spread wings—the eagle of John the Evangelist—for her heraldic banner. A striking example hangs in her throne room at the Alcázar of Segovia, the city that is the offensive's objective. That Hemingway might have had Isabel's eagle device in mind—yellow halo becoming yellow eyes—is suggested by the draft, in which he located the embalmer in Segovia (MS10-010); he corrected Anselmo's hometown to Ávila in the galley proofs (although he might have simply confused the cities).

Isabel's escutcheon sometimes bore the phrase *sub umbra alarum tuarum protege nos* ("protect us under the shadow of your wings"). Isabel and her husband Ferdinand led the Reconquista, the final victory over Moorish Spain and the unification

Throne Room, Alcázar of Segovia. (Alcázar of Segovia)

CHAPTER THREE · 53

of (Catholic) Spain under the Spanish monarchy in 1492. The queen and king later added a yoke and arrows to symbolize their union—the banner phrase *Tanto Monta,* "they amount to the same," sounds like Maria and Jordan. Francisco Franco adopted and adapted their heraldic device for Nationalist Spain, the Falange (353:24) having already co-opted the yoke and arrows (merged into a single image).

39:34+ **on the door of the church:** Anselmo's recollection of "the paw of a bear that I killed in the spring" that was "nailed through the palm" (40:1–2) to the church door and, thusly nailed, looked "like the hand of a man," again recalls Christ's springtime crucifixion. Hemingway added "through the palm" to the draft, having added but then crossed out "with the pads of the paw out" (MS10–010). The language also recalls Martin Luther's legendary nailing of his *Ninety-Five Theses* to the door of All Saints' Church in Wittenberg on 31 October 1517. In its rejection of the Catholic Church as the final spiritual authority and arbiter, the *Theses* is the founding document of the Protestant Reformation. Anselmo's "pleasure" in seeing the paw appears to be the simple, profane pleasure of self-satisfaction, however, without intimations of the sacred.

40:15+ **So do the Indians in America:** Native Americans aren't Romani, Jordan states, yet in relating both to beliefs about bears in the prior line he has made an association that persists. He finds that Pilar has "high Indian cheekbones" (298:37) and her bed smells like an "Indian's bed" (360:27–28). DeGuzmán *Spain's Long Shadow* documents how in nineteenth-century American travel literature, "the Spaniard is likened to or becomes the Moor, the Gypsy, and/or the 'Indian' in terms of empiricizing and fetishizing detail[s] of physical appearance, behavior, gesture, dress, and other exotic and yet banal particularities of daily life" (79). Anselmo and Jordan add the topic of Moors to their conversations in short order (40:31). Jordan doesn't restrict his comparison to Romani, either, as he sees something "Indian" in El Sordo and Fernando as well (141:12; 198:37). Something banal, but also exotic and dangerous: "For many Anglo-Americans of the nineteenth century, the Moor, the Gypsy, and the Indian were represented as seductive or even hypnotizing and, therefore, potentially threatening" (80). The present passage also spiritually relates Romani and Native Americans—and by extension all Spaniards—to animals. To bears. Jordan has already likened the band's hideout to a "bear's den" (18:7). El Sordo's gang also lives in a cave.

Jordan's recourse to the word "Indian" is further complicated because the grandfather he emulates likely took part in the genocidal war against North America's indigenous peoples (336:12+). The draft and galley proofs specify that the grandfather went west as part of the 7th Cavalry, the regiment commanded by George Armstrong Custer. Custer reported to his old Civil War boss, Phil Sheridan, the person who earned the reputation for having said, "The only good Indians I ever saw were dead" (see 233:12+).

To Hemingway, "[r]eal gypsies are a very strange people and the ones in this book are not book-gypsies anymore than my indians were ever book-indians" (to Maxwell Perkins, 26 Aug. 1940, *SL* 513). They do seem to be literary clichés to Jordan, quite possibly an intentional distinction from Hemingway's perspective.

40:31 Like the Moors: Elsewhere, the Romani Rafael sings a song expressing a degree of kinship with the Moors, and a preference for that kinship over one with Catalonians (60:3+). George Borrow's nineteenth-century writings assert that the Zincali—the Spanish Romani, also called Gitano—and the Moors felt more kinship with one another than with the Catholic Spaniards. Borrow records a belief that the Zincali hailed from Egypt, and he writes about the oppression and discrimination both groups suffered under the Spaniards. Andalusia, the region with the deepest Moorish roots and the home of the last Moorish communities in Spain, "has ever been the province where the Gitano race has most abounded since its arrival," where "living even as wanderers among these people, the Gitanos naturally became acquainted with their tongue and with many of their customs," the Moors being "a people almost as wild as themselves" (83–84).

41:9–10 live in such a way . . . that it will be forgiven: "Anselmo, that 'rare' old Christian (287) who thinks a good deal about the expiation or atonement that will be necessary after the war, has certain traits in common with Saint Anselm, including age and dignity and the reputation of a wise and reformist (not radical) commitment to his cause. Most striking, perhaps, is the fact that Saint Anselm's most famous work, *Cur Deus Homo,* was the most important medieval contribution to the theology of atonement, and the expiation motif in the novel centers on Anselmo" (Stoneback, "Priest," 104).

41:12+ Since we do not have God here any more: Anselmo renounces the Christian (Catholic) God based on the horrible things he has seen, which "never would He have permitted." His pronouncement "Let *them* have God" is the novel's first reference to the role of the Church in Spanish life and the war. Historically, the Spanish Church and the Spanish monarchy, in league with the landed aristocracy, jointly ruled the country. In Madrid today, the Royal Palace and Almudena Cathedral face each other across a shared courtyard. The origin of the Second Spanish Republic involved casting the Church out of power as much as replacing the monarchy. Many of the new Republic's reforms dating from 1931 aggressively targeted the Church. As Thomas writes, "the inclusion of such sweeping anti-clerical clauses in the constitution of the Republic was ambitious" and probably just, "but foolish," a result of how "Spanish liberalism had come to look on the church as a scapegoat for all Spain's ills" (73). Due to the Church's centuries-old hold on daily life and identity, many Spaniards saw the Republic's anticlericalism as anti-Spanish. The spring of the Republic's birth saw "[s]ome hundred churches... damaged throughout Spain" by leftist mobs (Thomas 56). Convictions against the Church ranged from anticlericalism to antireligiosity, from antagonism toward the institution's sins to antipathy toward religion's deluding superstitions. Unsurprisingly, the defense of Spanish Catholicism became fundamental to the right and to the Nationalist cause.

When the civil war broke out, the so-called uncontrollables (*incontrolables*) in towns and villages across Spain murdered anyone they associated with the ruling classes, including priests, as Pilar recounts in detail in chapter 10. On 19 August 1936, Don Saturnino Garcia, the priest of Fuentidueña de Tajo, the village of *The Spanish Earth* film, was escorted just outside of town and shot on the side of the road heading to the river (Vernon, "*Spanish Earth*" 39–40). Anselmo, who arguably embodies the novel's moral center, refuses to kill bishops or proprietors for the mere fact of being clergy and businesspersons (41:32). He only agrees to kill when necessary for a military purpose, and even then "not with pleasure" (42:10).

Hemingway's relationship to Catholicism is too complex, important, and divisive for a short comment. For some scholars, Hemingway's Christian faith is integral to the man and a primary interpretative lens for the literature. Others conclude that he was a nominal Catholic who understood that we emerge from nada and return to nada. For a Hemingway character to miss the consolation of past religious belief does not validate the old belief; people can pine for something they realize does not exist. Understood this way, Anselmo, in missing a God whose certainty he does not accept—whose certainty the novel does not accept—resembles the main characters of *The Sun Also Rises* and *A Farewell to Arms*.

Hemingway became a practicing Catholic in 1927 upon his second marriage, to Pauline Pfeiffer, whose parents had an altar installed and sanctified in their Piggott, Arkansas, home because there were no Catholic churches around. Pauline was his wife during the war, yet the wife he divorced immediately after to marry his wartime lover Martha Gellhorn. He subscribed to the Republican profound objection to the oppressive role of the Church in Spain and its unholy alliance with fascism, in public for example by accompanying an article with a photograph of clergy gathered with Nationalist officers and making the Nazi salute ("Cardinal," 38–39). On the other hand, while in Barcelona, Hemingway's Catholicism obliged him to fast on Good Friday, 1938, the very day (15 April) the Nationalists reached the Mediterranean coast at Vinaròs below Barcelona to split the remaining Republican territory in half, signaling the irreversibility of the Nationalist victory (Sheean 79). In letters from December 1936, he identified as Catholic but asserted that he did not write as a Catholic,[3] presumably meaning that he was more interested in exploring the human condition than upholding any religious faith or institution.

41:24–25 But with or without God, I think it is a sin to kill: Anselmo raises the significant question about whether sin can exist absent the moral authority of an absolute divinity (typically realized via organized religion). The question is at the heart of the novel's interrogation of the difference between hunting and war, and the difference between animals and people. Anselmo has already offered a pagan perspective on the fraternity and sanctity of all life (40:13–14). When, a little later in the conversation, he tells Jordan that he will kill the bridge sentry "with a clear heart" (42:10), he is not wholly convincing. Whereas Jordan struggles in the novel with the matter of self-murder (absent theological considerations), Anselmo wrestles with spirituality.

41:33 **make them work each day:** Anselmo's plan fits the ideological rationale for forced labor camps common with communist countries. His idea that they work "all the rest of their lives" reveals his naïveté; many such imprisoned laborers died pitifully early. Franco sentenced former Republicans to postwar labor units with similar results (including for the construction of his own mausoleum at the Valley of the Fallen).

42:16 **ever been in a battle?:** Anselmo's negative response in the next line, even though he has already acknowledged killing many people (42:6) and goes on to talk about fighting in Segovia, indicates that the two men understand "battle" to mean organized military combat.

42:21 **Mausers:** In the late nineteenth and early twentieth centuries, Mausers were quite popular for military and private use. The *guardia civil* would have been using the Mauser Model 1893, also known as the Spanish Mauser (or one of its variants), with a cartridge that held five smokeless 7×57mm, designed for rapid reloading.

42:38 **Very few of these people read:** Illiteracy dominated pre-Republic Spain. The monarchy and the Church had no motive to educate the peasants, on whose labor and ignorance their wealth, power, and position depended. The new government committed itself to rectify this situation. This line appropriately appears in the chapter introducing the Republic's anticlericalism. Literacy campaigns became part of military life for Republican soldiers. In *The Spanish Earth*, scenes of soldiers reading newspapers and writing letters show these progressive efforts, although due to the film's minimal commentary, most viewers miss the import.

43:7 **a great tendency to run at Segovia:** Anselmo's initially joining his comrades in running from the fight (42:17–19), and his preoccupation with how he might fare the next time, echoes Henry Fleming's story in Crane's *The Red Badge of Courage*.

43:13–14 **felt a little theatrical but it sounded well in Spanish:** The novel is aware of its style's effect.

43:33 **Stop worrying, you windy bastard:** Hemingway displays his wry humor, as the worry-filled windiness has a few hundred pages to go. Jordan's interior monologue does not bode well, according to his own judgment of his predecessor Kashkin (21:20–22; 149:6–7; 171:14–16).

43:35 **So he thought about the girl:** Jordan's thoughts travel here as his antidote to thinking too much about his mission (43:33), ironically so, because he already observed that a romantic entanglement would compromise thinking about the mission and because Maria, in the end, may be indistinguishable from his ultimate motives and fate.

43:38 **a darkness underneath:** Physically referencing Maria's skin, the language suggests a subcutaneous darkness, a matter of character that is racialized, exoticized, eroticized. Only a few pages earlier, Anselmo and Jordan compared Romani, Moors, and indigenous Americans (and bears) (40:13–15). Perhaps the only other sex scene Hemingway ever wrote in prose similar to that of the two moments between Jordan and Maria was one involving a white man and an Ojibwe woman ("Fathers and Sons," *CSS* 375–76).

Jordan fantasizes about the summer sun lightening Maria's hair while darkening her skin. This visual contrast drives the erotic storyline in *The Garden of Eden,* a novel set largely in Spain, which Hemingway began writing within the decade. *The Garden* explicitly presents the Bournes' tanning as a fantasy of racial fluidity, of playing African, in a sexual relationship that also plays with gender fluidity, homoeroticism, incest, and sameness. Whatever latent fluidities or taboo vulnerabilities Jordan harbors swim in the darkness beneath this text's surface; Jordan dies before he and Maria have a chance to live as newlyweds in Madrid. In the draft, Hemingway ties the word *darkness* to queer sexuality in one of several lines excised or revised to downplay the same-sex attraction of Pilar for Maria: "There is a darkness in us that you know nothing of," Pilar tells Maria while running her fingers over the younger woman's cheek and down her throat, "But all have it and I say this to thee now" (*HLE* 499). Hemingway's generation regarded Spain as essentially African, and "not only African," as Havelock Ellis wrote in *The Soul of Spain,* "but primitive, and—in the best and not in any depreciative sense of the word—savage" (36). As if admired savagery could avoid the depreciative (see Vernon, *Second War* 190–95).

If Catherine Bourne's "insistence on being 'Kanaka' clearly connects her to the supposedly innocent, Edenic, sexually-liberated, tropical islands of Margaret Mead's Pacific, it also carries an implicit threat so long as we remember Captain Cook's reputed fate at the hands of cannibal Kanakas" (Eby, *Fetishism* 161). For Eby, the implicit threat is castration anxiety. Jordan perhaps experiences the death-by-incorporation threat differently—in the ominous image of two dead hares to be eaten, having been killed while copulating (323:21+), and in his merging into Maria, which is idealistically transformed, in death, into his integration with the Spanish earth (see 22:37).

The Spanish artist Luis Quintanilla, Hemingway's dear Republican friend, provides one small piece of contextual evidence for the Western association of racial otherness with sexual "perversion" (the novel's word). In his 1938 book *Franco's Black Spain,* the text accompanying drawing 9 reads, "Quite often, fascism seems to go hand in hand with sexual degeneracy. Black Spain has proved no exception to this rule" (L. Quintanilla). The drawing clearly shows Moors as the initiators with their male Spanish Nationalist same-sex partners. Other Quintanilla illustrations depict Moors as creatures of unrestrained appetite, whether looting, squabbling with each other over loot, murdering civilians, or raping Republican women.

44:7–8 **a difficulty in walking:** Jordan has an erection.

45:15 **You look like the other one:** Kashkin and Jordan are blonde-haired Caucasians. Because of the presence in Spain of Soviet advisors and military specialists, and of Russia's much-trumpeted material aid and support, Spaniards often believed any white foreigner working for the Republic a Russian. El Sordo is curious that Jordan isn't *Ruso* (141:28). Hemingway personally experienced this confusion (to John Dos Passos, 26 Mar. 1938, *SL* 464; to Ivan Kashkin, 23 Mar. 1939, *SL* 481). Kashkin and Jordan's similarities run deeper: their nervous windiness, their talk of death, their ambiguous fates—Kashkin by Jordan's hand, Jordan arguably by Jordan's hand.

45:31 **the principal obscenity:** The word "fuck" in various forms.

NOTES

1. To Archibald MacLeish, 27 Aug. 1948, Archibald MacLeish Papers, Manuscript Division, Library of Congress, Box 10, Folder "Hemingway."
2. The article ends with the monetary gains to be had by war, which was the main subject of Hemingway's article in the same magazine seven months earlier, "Notes on the Next War: A Serious Topical Letter" (*Esquire,* Sept. 1935). Almost presciently, the reference to war profits in "On the Blue Water," published three months before the outbreak of the Spanish Civil War, cites as evidence the Spanish-American War of 1898.
3. To Elizabeth Huling, 15 Dec. 1936 (Swann Galleries, Sale 2316 Lot 227; https://catalogue.swanngalleries.com/). See also: to Harry Sylvester, 15 Dec. 1936 (PUL).

CHAPTER FOUR

50:17+ **Jordan smiled at her:** The drama of this chapter comes from the contested leadership of the guerrilla band. That Jordan positions his pistol in preparation while smiling at Maria with Pablo watching furthers the novel's use of Maria to symbolize Republican Spain and Spain itself.

50:29 **anis:** Jordan clarifies the contents of his flask as "real absinthe" (see 51:17–19).

51:4+ **of all the old evenings:** The references are all to Paris, where Hemingway lived in the 1920s. The nostalgia seems to belong more to Hemingway than to Jordan. The typed draft stuck to generalities; Hemingway revised to insert the named places (MS10–011).

Parc Montsouris and **Butte Chaumont** are both parks. The **Ile de la Cité** is the island on the Seine where the city began, where the Notre Dame Cathedral stands. **Hotel Foyot**, once located on the Rue de Tournon near the Luxembourg Gardens, was demolished in November 1937 due to structural weaknesses (Roth, *Life* 518).[1] If by "old hotel" the text means *no longer there,* it would be an anachronism for Jordan, as the demolition occurred six months after the events of the novel. Established in 1848 by Emperor Louis-Philippe's chef (Foyot), the restaurant's royal lineage could be somewhat problematic for a good Republican like Jordan. As Stoneback notes, "It was a very expensive restaurant, frequented by senators and politicians from the nearby Palais de Luxembourg" (*Reading* 36).

Le Stade Buffalo was a stadium for cycling races, named after the American cowboy entertainer Buffalo Bill Cody, whose circus appeared at the original stadium site before it moved outside the city. Cody was a veteran of the American Civil War and the Indian Wars; his show sold nostalgia for a romanticized nineteenth-century America. Carl Eby sees Buffalo Bill as "an equally long-haired substitute [for George Armstrong Custer] whose identity was inextricably bound up with the Custer myth." As Eby describes the Custer-Cody interchangeability,

> [i]t was after a meeting with Cody that Custer adapted the "scout" image in dress and manner that characterizes his style between 1874 and his death. Cody re-

turned the compliment after the Last Stand by "modifying his own appearance and dramatizing his adventures" to emphasize "his Custer likeness and his close relation to the Custer story" (Slotkin 408). With Custer safely buried, Cody became Custer's sidekick on stage and in dozens of dime novels, and after 1886 Cody regularly "reenacted" Custer's Last Stand for cheering fans in his Wild West show. (Eby, *Fetishism* 217)

Eby follows Richard Slotkin in emphasizing Custer's androgynous qualities and his hybrid image of the white soldier-hero and the uncivilized indigenous American warrior (217–23).

51:17–19 **wormwood [is] supposed to rot your brain:** At the turn of the twentieth century, absinthe was widely purported to cause different mental conditions, from hallucinations and psychoses to criminality and deviancy. Rumors linked it to serious physical ailments such as epilepsy and tuberculosis, and to death (none of these dangers turned out to be true). After France banned production in 1914, the Pernod distillery moved operations to Spain. That Jordan drinks absinthe suggests a self-destructive tendency. Hemingway's description in "The Strange Country" might apply here: "But almost everything bad that had ever happened to him had happened when he was drinking absinthe; those bad things which were his own fault" (*CSS* 643; for more on absinthe, see Stoneback, *Sun* 32–33; Eby, *Reading GOE* 84–85 passim).

51:30 **the other three men:** The flat-faced one is Primitivo (57:30–31), which translates as it sounds, to *primitive*—yet another way the novel depicts Spaniards as racially lesser. Andrés bears a scar (57:35–36), presumably from his days at their village's bullfights (364–65); his older-looking brother, Eladio, isn't named until chapter 17 (218:10). On Hemingway's naming process, see 25:35. Hemingway added the detail about the scar by hand to the typescript once he sorted out his characters (MS10–011).

53:25+ **if it should be necessary, half hoping it would be:** Jordan's willingness and half-eagerness to murder Pablo is one way the novel engages the practice and problem of political killings of one's own comrades. Hemingway's apparent acceptance of this practice in the instance of José Robles in the spring of 1937 led to the permanent rupture of his long friendship with novelist John Dos Passos (see Muller 72–78). However Hemingway discussed Robles's fate early on—one should keep in mind the precarity of his position in doing his work and of his actual safety in wartime Spain—his later writings expressed a more troubled moral position over such murders. By the fall of 1937, writing the play *The Fifth Column,* he was wrestling with the problem; the play acknowledges that "regrettable mistakes" had been made (38). Publicly, however, in *Ken* magazine in June 1938, with the war still raging and himself still traveling to Spain, he justified Robles's execution when denouncing Dos Passos's outcry. But then his November 1938 story "The Denunciation" problematizes the role of an American correspondent in Republican Spain who betrays a former friend, condemning him to death. At the end of "Under the Ridge," a general instructs the story's American correspondent that he can't write about an execution of a fellow officer beyond the official line, not now, but then instructs him: "Write it afterwards. You can write it all afterwards. . . . Now, get out of here" (CSS 469). The story appeared after the war, in October 1939, while he was writing *For Whom the Bell Tolls*. The novel takes up the moral meditation over seemingly expedient, seemingly necessary political murders. Readers sharing Jordan's half-eagerness for gunning down Pablo should pause and reconsider.

Jordan's language on Kashkin talking openly about his worries, as "doing more harm than good" (21:25), strongly echoes Hemingway's and Joris Ivens's on Dos Passos talking openly about the Robles execution as wrongheaded, ill-advised, and dangerous. Kashkin's death and the Robles–Dos Passos episode both occurred in April 1937. Jordan's changing account of his role in Kashkin's death perhaps obliquely reflects Hemingway's frustrating attitude toward Dos Passos.

This entire sentence, with its long parenthetical moment that includes one *perhaps* and two *yets*, resembles the prose of the novelist William Faulkner, especially in *The Sound and the Fury* (1929) and *Absalom, Absalom!* (1936), the two novels detailing the agonizing interior life of Quentin Compson, a young man who takes his own life.

53:34+ **for the Republic:** Pilar's statement of having time after the war resembles the practical, nonrevolutionary position of Spain's Communist Party (PCE) and the rhetoric used by its spokeswoman, Dolores Ibárruri, aka La Pasionaria (Ibárruri 162; see 30:24+). Jordan's comparison of Pablo with War Minister Prieto (163:30–33) tightens the soft political allegory whereby the guerilla band's internal strife comments on the Republican government's.

54:3–4 **That which must pass, will pass:** Another association of Pilar with La Pasionaria. In November 1936, Ibárruri exhorted Madrid's Republican defenders with the phrase "¡No Pasarán!"—*they shall not pass*. The phrase instantly became a rallying slogan, appearing on banners, posters, and postcards (and wherever else, whenever inspiration struck), and repeated by faithful Republicans throughout the war. The postwar resistance to Franco's dictatorship kept it in circulation and various leftist causes throughout the world have adopted it ever since. As graffiti, it continues to pop up in Madrid and elsewhere. Pilar the prophesying Romani's inversion of the phrase bespeaks a fatalism and inevitability that reflects the historical outcome and participates in the novel's heavy foreshadowing. At chapter's end, she knowingly suppresses "a feeling of the thwarting of all hope and promise" (58:20), an apparent rebuttal to Jordan's imaging that "she doesn't see it, yet" (54:23). The phrase originated with the French army at the Battle of Verdun in 1916.

54:28–29 **for the good of the foreigners:** Even though theirs began as and fundamentally was a civil war, many Spaniards understood their country to have become the battleground for global powers. Spain had a long history of violent conquest by other nations, as a character in Hemingway's "Under the Ridge" reminds the narrator: "In Badajoz, we have been sacked and pillaged and our women violated by the English, the French and now the Moors. What the Moors have done now is no worse than what the English did under Wellington" (*CSS* 464).

55:3–4 **rather the man gored himself on the horn of the bull:** Finito's claim gets at the heart of the novel's genre-play, particularly with respect to where it falls on the Tragic-Naturalist spectrum. Finito's assertion of proud self-determination against the facts also engages the related Romanticism-Realism spectrum. On genre questions, see the introduction. Finito gored himself in the sense that he put himself in the ring; Jordan has similarly agreed to enter this war and join this battle. Before the novel's final fight, Pilar compares Jordan to a frightened matador (405:2). For John Donne, fatally placing oneself in harm's way can amount to self-murder (see front matter: title and epigraph).

55:7 ***Buenas, Compadre:*** Good, friend-companion-partner.

55:8 **Pilar:** The first mention of Pilar's name. It is significant that she names herself, and does so relationally, by telling a story and in that story revealing her name in dialogue from her former lover. Immediately after this act of relational self-appellation, she usurps command from Pablo. After this usurpation, the text never again refers to Pilar as the *mujer* (wife, or woman) of Pablo.

55:9 ***Chico:*** Boy, as a term of endearment.

55:24 **one year of war:** The war began in mid-July 1936. It is late May, so it has not yet been a full year.

55:32 ***la gente:*** The people. The mini-Republic that is the guerrilla crew operates more or less democratically. Students of American military history will recall the officer elections in the Revolutionary War and the Civil War for militias and volunteer units of nonprofessional citizen-soldiers. Popularity and persuasion did not always result in competent leadership.

57:30+ **who was named Primitivo . . . who was called Andrés:** Both these phrases Hemingway added by hand to the draft after finally determining their names (MS10–011; see 25:35 and 51:37). The reader encounters these names immediately after the band has switched allegiance to Pilar. The narrator announces these names nondiegetically, so it remains unclear whether Jordan knows them. Andrés's name has been spoken aloud once, in his absence and not to Jordan (30:37); Primitivo's is not spoken aloud until chapter 9 (92:34). The reader (and Jordan?) still has two names to learn, Fernando (80:34) and Eladio (218:10). Jordan's focus on his mission, and his preference for not staying long enough to care about his mission-mates, would explain a lack of effort to learn their names.

58:12–13 **suddenly remembering what she had seen:** This is the first time the novel enters the consciousness of a character other than Robert Jordan, the adverb *suddenly* signaling this abrupt textual shift as well as Pilar's abrupt memory. The second time occurs with Pablo's chat with the horses at the end of the next chapter (63:34+). Hemingway's editor objected to this departure from Jordan's perspective, to which the author responded: "I do not agree with you on the passage where something is written about Pilar at the end of galley 18. You thought it was o.k. when it was Pablo and the horses. I know it was necessary. It was simply that the first time it was done it would always be a shock to you. The second time o.k." (to Maxwell Perkins, 26 Aug. 1940, *SL* 513). Hemingway crafted the novel in such a way that the time spent inside the heads of other characters, or with them absent Jordan, gradually increases, from this short paragraph to the two paragraphs with Pablo and the horses (63:34+), to the long conversation between Fernando and Pilar that finishes chapter 9 (92:23+), and eventually to entire chapters. Structurally, the novel gyres from Jordan outward. The penultimate chapter includes a third-person omniscience that, in another letter, Hemingway calls God-like (see 423:28+). The ending of the novel holds in tension the central, still point of Robert Jordan's death and the centrifugal movement of the rest of the characters. And of history.

Hemingway had considered including an epilogue that began at the same time Jordan lay dying, but with General Golz riding back to El Escorial, where Jordan's mission had begun (*HLE* 520), and that would have provided some information on life after Jordan's death. Such a denouement would have created a different and less tangible approach to the full circle of seeing Jordan prone on pine needles that opens and closes the published novel. In the same letter about the sudden move to Pilar's remembrance, Hemingway appealed to Perkins for support in deciding against the epilogue, which would have "everything completely knit up and stowed away ship-shape. I can write it like Tolstoi and make the book seem larger, wiser and all the rest of it. But then I remember that was what I always skipped in Tolstoi." As described to Perkins, the drafted epilogue "only shows that good generals suffer after an unsuccessful attack (which isn't new); that they get over it (that's a little newer) Golz haveing killed so much that day is forgiveing of Marty because he has that kindliness you get sometimes. I can and do make Karkov see how it will all go" (to Maxwell Perkins, 26 Aug. 1940, *SL* 514).

Hemingway wisely decided to leave the reader with the vibrations of that still point. For Jordan, the world ends when he does. There is no after.

It is tempting to see in this structure an analog to the content of W. B. Yeats's famous poem "The Second Coming" (1921), with the ominously approaching "rough beast" of that poem as Adolf Hitler and the coming of the Second World War:

> Things fall apart; the centre cannot hold;
> Mere anarchy is loosed upon the world,
> The blood-dimmed tide is loosed, and everywhere
> The ceremony of innocence is drowned [. . .] (Yeats 211)

Carlos Baker conceives of the novel's "form" as "that of a series of concentric circles with the all-important bridge in the middle" (Baker, *Artist* 245). Looking out from the imagined locale of the bridge, the reader "will see his horizons lifting by degrees towards a circumference far beyond the Guadarrama mountains," and beyond "the trans-European aspect of the struggle," until finally he sees the "outermost ring," which "is nothing less than the great globe itself" (246). Baker's hopeful vision imposes a thematic "form" consistent with a heroic interpretation of the novel.

58:21+ **this feeling from when she was a girl:** Pilar knows but does not name "the things that caused it all through her life." Refusing thorough backstory explication (especially of the childhood drama variety), preserving a little personal mystery, helped Hemingway create more interesting, fully alive characters rather than flat ideas of characters. For Pilar, not expressing the thing performs a valuable psychological function by refusing it the energy of attention. Her "put[ting] it away from her" so that it could not "touch her" markedly contrasts with Jordan's wallowing in his paternal legacy of violent heroism and violent cowardice. The text subtly slides toward that wallowing on the next page, when Rafael sings the "gypsy" song about an inheritance from one's father that one can never be done with (59:24+).

NOTE

1. A German exile, Roth frequently lived in the hotel. In 1938, he published an essay about its final days, "Rest while Watching the Demolition" (*Report* 238–41).

CHAPTER FIVE

59:24+ ***I had an inheritance from my father:*** Hemingway heard this song from a Republican soldier during the Teruel Offensive of December 1937. The novel's version is slightly altered from what he reported: "I had an inheritance from my father. It was the moon and the sun and I can move all over the world and the spending of it is never done." The dispatch provides a pointed coda: "Where is your father now?" Hemingway asked the Republican soldier. "'Dead,' he said" (in Watson 62). Rafael's song resonates with Jordan, burdened with the legacy of his father's suicide until the moment after the last page of the novel.

60:3+ ***My nose is flat:*** In terms of the novel's racial dynamics, Rafael's second song expresses a perceived affinity between Romani and Moors (see 40:31).

Hemingway included this song in a 1939 letter to his mother-in-law as an expression of the disgust he and other Republican sympathizers felt for their allies in Catalonia, whom they believed wouldn't bother to fight (to Mary Pfeiffer, 6 Feb., *SL* 476–77). This conclusion oversimplifies a complicated situation that involved the competing factions within the Republic as well as the larger strategic situation. The Catalonian militias holding the Aragon front were an assortment of anarchists and (reputedly Trotskyite) revolutionary communists—the POUM (Partido Obrero de Unificación Marxista, or the Workers' Party of Marxist Unification) in whose militia George Orwell fought (see 120:6–8)—who "blamed the lack of aggressivity on inadequate support from the Republican government, especially the shortage of arms and the absence of an offensive plan" (Seidman 53). Orwell and his fellow *poumistas* firmly believed that "arms were deliberately withheld [by the government] lest too many of them should get into the hands of the Anarchists" (68). In November 1940, Hemingway received a letter from a Catalan living in the United States criticizing the novel for its aspersions against the Barcelona POUM and syndicalist militias:

> At the outbreak, in 24 hours of terrific fighting, the government of Catalonia and the workers of Catalonia had defeated the heavy Spanish garrisons throughout the region. Shortly after, those workers went of their own initiative hundreds of

miles from Barcelona to establish a front in the Aragon desert. Then they took boats and landed in the Balearic Islands. The Madrid government never gave them cannon nor airplanes for the Aragon front and a few months later ordered them to get the hell out of the islands and turn them over to the fascists, so that the Italians could carry out their daily bombings of Barcelona in comfort.

While the Catalans were taking these offensive actions, the Madrid government did nothing except post a few people on the Guadarrama overlooking Madrid. You know that nothing had been done to put obstacles, to establish a front, to stop the long Franco advance from Andalusia to Toledo. (from José Alemany, 2 Nov. 1940, Incoming)

On the other hand, the Aragon front was quiet for this period of the war, and the government legitimately declined to dedicate precious military resources to a stable front that did not appear threatened. And it is questionable whether the Catalan militias defending Aragon possessed the necessary motivation and martial talent to pull off a successful offensive operation.

60:35 **Qué va:** This utile idiomatic expression has a flexible meaning depending on context, all in the neighborhood of: Nonsense. That is nothing. What of it. So. So what. What are you going to do? Come on. No way. Before the novel's publication, Hemingway had his Spanish friend from the war Gustavo Durán review the galley proofs (see 335:24+). Among other changes, Durán suggested alternatives for *qué va,* which Hemingway had strewn throughout the novel because, as he wrote Durán, "It is the most common expression used here for disbelief, dis-sent, etc. and is in the mouths [sic] of Gallegos, Basques, Islenos here about every third word. I am sure you are right, positive, about it not being used to such an extent in Madrid."[1] The "here" means in Cuba (see 293:2–3). In the end, Hemingway replaced twenty-six instances of the expression, removed three, and kept fifty-two.

61:4–5 **the flight of the big bird:** An orgasm. The prostitute wants her male customer to get it over with, as Rafael says Pilar waited for Jordan to kill Pablo already. Hemingway used this expression at least three other times in his writing, all with positive connotations of pleasure, not as ugly business to finish: in "Fathers and Sons" (*CSS* 376), *Across the River and into the Trees* (144), and an unpublished piece, "Crime and Punishment" (JFK Items #340 and #341).

61:8+ **to assassinate . . . is repugnant to me:** Jordan distinguishes between killing Pablo when Pablo has been provoked into action and Jordan can claim self-defense or other immediate necessity, versus killing Pablo any time because of the overall risk he poses. Really? Jordan splits moral hairs. He has offered to dispose of a fellow

American correspondent who profited off the Republic (239:25+) and did not mind carrying out such shootings (that he has a reputation for not minding them suggests he has carried them out [245:21–23]).

The characters' conversations about killing Republican comrades partake of the novel's larger meditation on language. Fernando justifies the need to kill Pablo by making what Pilar calls "a bureaucracy with his mouth" (219:30). He uses the word "eliminate." Jordan finds himself talking like him, and then uses the word "liquidate" (220:6; 221:17). His Soviet handler, Karkov, differentiates between executing or destroying and assassinating (245:10–13). Elsewhere, Jordan contends with the ready-mades of political rhetoric that he wants to get outside of and critique yet regards nevertheless as "true" (164:7). He quips about roses being roses and being onions and about different words for rocks (289:12+) and will cogitate on the difference between different languages' words for the same signified idea, for what the English language calls *now, tonight, life, wife, death, war,* and *sweetheart* (166:32+). Different language for the same thing doesn't really matter, is the stuff of quips and puns, but also matters profoundly. No two people, the novel seems to say, ever truly speak the same language.

63:34 **Pablo was saying to the horse:** The novel has just acknowledged that Jordan cannot "see what Pablo is doing, nor hear what he was saying to the horse" and that another matter now occupies his thoughts, thoughts the reader does not learn (63:30+). The final two paragraphs of this chapter are the second instance in the novel, a more extended instance than the first, of the third-person narration presenting a perspective other than Jordan's. The second of these two paragraphs introduces two additional perspectives, that of the narrator opining that it "would have been very interesting" for Jordan to overhear Pablo, and that of Pablo's horse (64:13+). For the first instance of a different perspective and commentary on this novel's gradual widening of perspectives to encompass more characters and for longer durations, see 58:12–13.

64:3–4 **no woman like a rock that is burning:** Pablo means Pilar, the rock descriptive of her physical presence and perhaps her coldness toward him, the burning her passionate personality devoted at present to the Republic in accord with Pilar as an avatar of La Pasionaria. The rock language echoes Jordan's description of her as a "granite monument"—see 30.24+ on the monument description and the possible associations with Our Lady of the Pillar and Gertrude Stein (on "stein" as rock, see 289:16–17).

64:4–5 **no colt of a girl:** Pablo and Jordan are the only characters who think of Maria as a colt. The shared term, the shared perspective, links the two men (in what Eve Kosofsky Sedgwick would call a homosocial bond; see 404:31).

64:14+ **The horse understood nothing that he said:** See 63:3–4. Yet the horse does understand the tone, and the horse experiences and communicates impatience and annoyance that Pablo does not understand. This moment almost comically demonstrates the pointed differences in perspectives, in subjective truths, at the heart of the novel. Different truths were the heart of the civil war. Such a stark, instantaneous presentation of opposed perspectives occurs again when Jordan attributes arrogance to an enemy soldier who only feels sadness at the death of a friend and remorse at the necessity of his duty (325:38+). At novel's end, when the dying Robert Jordan comes to utter, "There's no *one* thing that's true. It's all true" (467: 20), he is right. But the realization hardly provides the reader with any political hope, only a Keatsian consolation in the recognition of beauty that the novel can't even fully embrace.

Hemingway added this passage by hand to the draft typescript (MS10–012).

NOTE

1. To Gustavo Durán, 13 Aug. 1940 (Residencia).

CHAPTER SIX

65:30 **Don't call me Don Roberto:** *Don* is a traditional honorific reserved for nobles, the upper class, men of duly respectable positions such as priests and teachers, and for a man above one's own station. Republican Spain refused language that confirmed social hierarchy.

65:32 **Señorita Maria:** *Señorita* can function as a noun or title of address for a young, unmarried woman, often as a term of respect for teachers and other such roles, the equivalent of *Miss*. The Republican faithful replaced all such titles with *camarada*, as Jordan does in the next line (66:1).

66:4 **very religious about thy politics:** Many international volunteers went to Spain out of a quasi-religious conviction and faith. As Peter N. Carroll discovered in studying personal accounts of American brigaders, "[t]he bravery of the Lincoln volunteers had ideological roots. To many young communists, joining the part involved genuine psychological conversion, similar to the experience of religious rebirth" (118). The novel captures their fervor in its descriptions of the Spanish communists' Fifth Regiment headquarters and Velázquez 63, which housed some of the International Brigades' leadership operations (see 234:38). Hemingway meant for Jordan to be a communist—see the next entry. He later transfers his devotional ardor to Maria.

66:14+ **I am an anti-fascist:** Up through the galley proofs, Jordan answers in the affirmative to Pilar's question about his communist status; when she asks how long, he says two years.[1] Hemingway changed Jordan's answer to "anti-fascist" to ease negotiations with the Book of the Month Club (Trogdon, *Lousy* 212). He had to change a later passage as well (163:17+). This language was much more acceptable to a 1940 America watching Nazi Germany's conquest of most of Europe. Seventy-two percent of American volunteers to Spain belonged to either the Communist Party or the Young Communist League (Brooks, "Analysis"). The term *anti-fascist* signaled communist for those in the know. For example, a 29 December 1937 list of candidates for special work at Albacete—the headquarters village for the International Brigades—describes one volunteer as a "[v]ery good anti-fascist '33. Politically reliable." This volunteer,

Paul Wendorf, joined the American Communist Party in 1933, as noted by other International Brigade documents.² Once the Second World War began, supporters of the Republic took to calling themselves "premature anti-fascists."

When the novel's copyright expires, editors of future editions will have to decide whether to restore the original language here and below (see 66:37) or preserve the published language. Both Hemingway's intent and his contemporary audience's mores have a valid historical claim.

66:19–21 **a Republican for twenty years . . . a Republican all his life:** There was never a Spanish Republican party, and before the proclamation of the Second Spanish Republic in April 1931—only six years before the events of the novel—*republican* was not a widespread term of political identity. The [First] Spanish Republic effectively lasted less than a year, from February 1873 to January 1874, after the dissolution of the Cortes (Spain's legislature or parliament). It nominally persisted until December 1874 when the monarchy returned to power. For Pilar and for Maria's father to identify retroactively as republican would mean they were anti-monarchist centrists or leftists.

66:23 **My father was also a Republican his entire life:** Since the beginning of the twentieth century, the Republican Party has been one of the two primary parties in American politics. Jordan doesn't bother to explain that his father's republicanism did not align with Spain's. From its abolitionist, profederalism roots, it had become the party of big business, industry, and wealth generation over egalitarianism. The influence of the communists on the Spanish Republic's affairs was anathema to most American Republicans. The leading American industrialist Henry Ford, for example, was infamously antisemitic and Nazi-sympathizing. On 30 July 1938, Ford received the Grand Cross of the German Eagle, the highest honor awarded by Nazi Germany to non-Germans. The first such medal, awarded the year before, went to Italian fascist dictator and Nationalist Spain's benefactor Benito Mussolini. Ford is an extreme example, and undoubtedly a complicated one—Nazism wasn't exactly pro-laissez-faire-capitalism or -individualism, after all—but the visual association of that medal ceremony of Ford the triumphant businessman with fascism is undeniable. Meanwhile, Texaco broke its oil contract with the Republican government (Hochschild 169), subsidized the Nationalist war machine by providing it cut-rate oil on credit and arranging shipment to get around the United States' export embargo (173–74, 249), and fed intelligence to the Nationalists about oil shipments to Republican Spain for targeting by bombers, naval surface vessels, and submarines (249). "Like many executives of his day," the giant company's chief executive, Torkild Reiber, "had no love for unions or for Franklin D. Roosevelt's New Deal" (Hochschild 169).

Little about the US political response to the Spanish Civil War was straightforward. The Catholic situation is a case in point. In the 1930s, most Catholic Americans voted Democratic and supported Roosevelt's New Deal. Many were first- and second-generation European immigrants, working-class folk seeking a foothold into middle-class life, focused with the rest of the country on domestic challenges. Yet the Republic's anticlericalism and its ties to international communism offended the Church and much laity. The cultural war trumped the economic, democratic one. Some of the loudest clamorers for nonintervention—because the United States would have intervened on the Republic's behalf—were the print editor Father Francis X. Talbot and the radio personality Father Charles Coughlin. While their ilk promoted nonintervention from a pro-Nationalist stance, the *Catholic Worker* argued for neutrality based on its long-standing advocacy of pacifism and its inability to choose the lesser of two evils (see Prudlo).

As J. David Valaik writes in his study of the American Catholic response to the war, "[t]he summer of 1936 marked the beginning of one of the most bitter debates in American history, for the outbreak of the Spanish Civil War tore huge rents in the fabric of American society" (73). Jordan's unstated communism aside, the text reveals a man who loves his sixty-five-dollar sleeping bag and colt of a pretty girl, a man as divided as America itself.

66:32 My grandfather was on the Republican national committee: Jordan's grandfather fought for the Union in the American Civil War. His Republican party was that of Abraham Lincoln, the party that fought slavery and promoted a strong federal government in support of equal citizenship, minority and labor rights, education, and social welfare. In other words, the grandfather's version of republicanism had more in common with the Spanish republicanism for whom the grandson—along with the American volunteers of the Abraham Lincoln Brigade—fights (the novel never clarifies Jordan's exact position within the International Brigades; he joined the war before their formation). Jordan thus speaks this line with pride, not with the knowing irony of identifying his father as Republican. Maria *should* be impressed.

Thus there's a political dimension to Jordan's conflicted patrilineal loyalty. Perhaps the death drive that threatens to replicate his father's suicide, that risks his becoming his father, harbors an inherent urge toward his father's brand of American Republicanism.

66:37 He shot himself: Before this line, the drafts up through the galleys (where Hemingway changed it by hand as well as with a typed insert) maintained Jordan's communism, playing up the political irony for American readers:

> "And in America have many republicans become communist?" the woman asked.
> "Not so many," Robert Jordan said. "A few."
> "And was not your father disappointed when you renounced the republic to become a communist?" Maria asked.
> "He was dead." (*HLE* 495)

Maria is still thinking about the Spanish Republic's internal conflict between its republicans and communists. Hemingway's father, Clarence, killed himself in 1928. The actual and fictional fathers both used the grandfather's Civil War pistol. Hemingway's mother gave this pistol to her oldest son, who eventually disposed of it exactly as Jordan disposed of his grandfather's (337:14+). The father's inheritance of Rafael's song (59:24+) is, for Jordan, the suicide. See the removal of other language identifying Jordan as a communist in chapter 13 (163:17+).

67:7 **we are the same:** The immediate cause for Maria's identification with Jordan is her misunderstanding of their fathers' similarities, a misunderstanding Jordan has encouraged. This is not the last time the lovers declare their sameness. Jordan typically follows Maria's lead. Here, Maria's declaration ignites her desire, as Jordan finds her eyes "suddenly hungry and young and wanting" (67:10–11). The fact that this desire follows on the heels of identification through the fathers' apparent likeness suggests a different dimension to their mutual attraction and contributes to Pilar's observation in the next line that they resemble siblings.

67:12 **brother and sister by the look:** Although the affair will hardly be chaste, the lovers conceive it as restoring Maria's innocence (71:25–26; 73:14; 73:30–31). The sibling comparison works with the setting and with Maria's connection to the landscape to tease the reader with one phase of the Romance genre as described by Northrop Frye:

> In literature this phase presents a pastoral and Arcadian world, generally a pleasant wooded landscape, full of glades, shaded valleys, murmuring brooks, the moon, and other images closely linked with the female or maternal aspects of sexual imagery. . . . The archetype of erotic innocence is less commonly marriage than the kind of "chaste" love that precedes marriage; the love of brother for sister, or of two boys for each other. (*Anatomy* 200)

Chaste yet erotic—Frye's casual mention of two boys resonates with the gender ambiguities of this novel and other Hemingway texts.

The lovers' superficial kinship affords readers a specious prophylactic against the miscegenation with which the novel elsewhere titillates. They safely become like Hemingway's white couples who announce their sameness, such as the very Anglo Frederic Henry and Catherine Barkley do in *A Farewell to Arms*. While it is easy to suppose the blonde couple as having north-of-the-Pyrenees European roots, the reverse is also possible: the promise for Jordan of Spanish consanguinity. Pilar's language of "by the look" references not only a physical similarity but also "the look" the couple just exchanged, the sexually charged gaze. Thus, even as Pilar's language mitigates the miscegenation taboo, it flirts with the incest taboo (67:7). Pilar's authority stems from her attitude toward the couple, namely Maria, which is both maternal and erotic. Walter Benn Michaels's *Our America* offers an insightful study of the overlapping phenomena of American literary modernism and the 1920s American nativist movement, which he defines as "commitment to race as a political category and to whiteness as the foundation of the new nation" (44). In this cultural moment, as expressed time and again in its literature, Michaels contends that "[w]hat's at stake in the desire to keep someone in the family is thus the sense that what is outside the family is thus outside the race" (7–8).

Michaels's analysis does not use *For Whom the Bell Tolls,* but it does include *The Sun Also Rises, The Garden of Eden, The Torrents of Spring,* and several Hemingway short stories. In this moment, "the purely American family must be the nonreproductive family" as the "homosexual family and the incestuous family thus emerge as parallel technologies in the effort to prevent half-breeds" (49). For Michaels, *The Garden of Eden* serves as an example of "when these technologies are invoked simultaneously" (49). Although written decades after the high modernist, high nativist 1920s, *Garden* for Michaels transforms the twenties' discourse of racial purity "almost completely" into "a discourse of perversity" (50). In this vein, *For Whom the Bell Tolls* transitions from "the nativist writings of the '20s where the stakes are more national than the personal, which is to say, when the ultimate question is always the 'half-breed'" (50) to the "almost entirely psychological register" of *Garden* (5)—all complicated by the Spanish Civil War adventure plot. However personal and psychological these "technologies" in *Garden,* the novel is largely set in Spain with characters who have clearly internalized the cultural discourse of Africa and the primitive. The published novel's newlyweds repeat the adage that Africa begins at the Pyrenees, and their honeymoon experience has in its background the husband's time as a boy in Africa, complete with suspicious hints of miscegenation, half-breeds, homosexuality, and cannibalism. *For Whom the Bell Toll*'s "quietly titillating transgressions—racial, gender, and familial—link it to *The Garden of Eden* and to the West's imaginings of primitive polysexuality" (Vernon, *Second War* 221–22). In the posthumous novel, as Michaels concludes, "the incestuous couple and the homosexual couple are made identical" (50), not just brother and sister, but brothers in their sameness.

One could perhaps see a more disguised and fledgling version of such gender sameness between Jordan and Maria. In her own language, "[a]fterwards we will be as one animal of the forest and be so close that neither one can tell that one of us is one and not the other. . . . I am thee and thou art me and all of one is the other" (262:22–27). The two opposite readings—the one regarding incest and homoeroticism as bulwark against miscegenation and racial corruption, the other regarding them as part and parcel of miscegenation and immersion in the native—are, finally, complementary interpretations drawing on the same Western fantasies and fears of the nonwhite. Jordan adopts two other technologies to avoid raising a mixed child. First, he sleeps with a woman who might not be able to have children because of months of sexual violence. Second, he dies—arranges to die?—three days after meeting her. Michaels would theorize Jordan's death another way. "[A]lthough marrying your twin may be as close as you can come to marrying yourself," he writes about Hemingway's "The Battler," "even a twin may be lost, even the incestuous marriage may jeopardize rather than preserve identity" (97).

Rabbits and ambiguous incest connect *For Whom the Bell Tolls* to "The Battler," whose chief couple are rumored to be siblings, about whom one character says, "they wasn't brother and sister no more than a rabbit" yet who also looked alike enough "to be twins" (*CSS* 103). Rabbit is of course Jordan's pet name for Maria. Many scholars read the sibling-lover trope that appears in Hemingway's oeuvre as rooted in Hemingway's mother's "elaborate pretense that little Ernest and his sister were twins of the same sex" (Lynn 40). Thus Hemingway's identity is at once constituted through and compromised by sameness and gender fluidity. *For Whom the Bell Tolls* summons that sister once, when Hemingway gives Jordan a memory of an event that she witnessed, of a lynching of an African American (see 116:30). The novel enacts the porousness between Ernest and his one-year-older sister, Marcelline, in other words, in a violently racist context in keeping with Jordan and Maria's rhetoric of porous sameness and their affair's racial and violent underpinnings. Actual or purported miscegenation, or the threat thereof, was often the motivation for a lynching.

67:16+ **he ran his hand ... on her neck:** Jordan's hand reenacts hers from an earlier "rippling," which he likened idyllically to "a grain field in the wind on a hillside" as she broached to him the serial violence she suffered (23:19–20). In Hemingway, short hair on a woman suggests a certain gender ambiguity on her part and thus a certain ambiguity of desire on his part. Such ambiguities shade Jordan's attraction to Maria. In this passage and elsewhere, Robert Jordan finds himself titillated, with swelling throat, by petting the site of her sexual victimization. Several readings suggest themselves: that the possibility of his love aiding in her recovery feeds his excitement; that an emotional or psychological violence lurks in Jordan's physical response to Maria; that (in this scene, anyway) such violence expresses a desire for separation from the thing that threatens to overtake the integrity of his individuality.

67:33+ ***Inglés:*** English. It was common for Spaniards to call all English-speakers "English." Even though Robert Jordan immediately corrects Pilar and she calls him "American," it is the only time. She reverts to *Inglés* for the rest of the novel. When El Sordo asks about Jordan's nationality, he comments that North Americans are the "[s]ame as *Inglés*" (141:34).

Pilar is the first to call him *Inglés*, but everyone else follows suit—although Maria drops it as their romance deepens (see 172:11+). The moniker constantly emphasizes foreignness and difference as well as international solidarity. Using the moniker allowed the partisans to avoid his actual name for political reasons (many international volunteers in Spain fought under a nom de guerre), or for emotional reasons, to blunt their personal attachment to someone who might die and who is asking them to possibly die.

68:30 **She stroked under his hand like a kitten:** When Maria isn't compared to a colt, she's a small mammal. When she gets into Jordan's sleeping bag at the beginning of the next chapter, he calls her "little rabbit" for the first time (69:23). Maria's nuzzling her head into his hand resembles her stroking it along Pilar's thighs in an excised phrase (see 154:30).

NOTES

1. MS10–012. The original language of Jordan's communism was changed by hand and also by typed insert to the galley proofs (MS17–006). *HLE* does not include this removed text.
2. *Documents of the Soviet Era* online: "Organizations and Institutions (Including Public Ones) / Section 9. Interbrigades of the Republican Army of Spain / Fund 545. International Brigades of the Republican Army of Spain / Inventory 6. Lists, personal files of fighters and commanders of international brigades / File 1011. Personal files of American volunteers (Wel–Wes). RGASPI F.545, DP 6 D.1011 (IMG0064). http://sovdoc.rusarchives.ru/sections/organizations//cards/234445.

CHAPTER SEVEN

69:23 **little rabbit:** Jordan's first use of his pet name for Maria. The two writers on Spain that Jordan knows, Borrow and Ford (248:22), both observed that Spain derives its name from the word rabbit. Borrow's *The Bible in Spain* includes an image of a Roman military monument featuring a rabbit, prompting an editor's note that "[r]abbits were so numerous in the south of the Peninsula in Carthaginian and Roman times, that they are even said to have given their name (Phoen. 'Pahan') to Hispania" (25). Ford's *Gatherings from Spain* makes the same assertion: "Spain abounds with them to such a degree, that ancient naturalists thought the animal indigenous, and went so far as to derive the name Spain from *Sephan*, the rabbit which the Phoenicians found here for the first time" (123). Phoenicians shipped rabbits from Spain throughout the Mediterranean at a time when the animal "remained a novelty, found only in Spain or on certain islands"; Roman coins depicted *Hispania* as a woman seated on the ground holding an olive branch and with a rabbit at her feet (Dickenson 31–32). For DeGuzmán, naming Maria after this totem animal of Spain solidifies the case that "the fusion" of Jordan's "body with the Spanish earth/soil is accomplished through his romance with Maria" ("Dirt," 20).

The criticism has had to work through the challenge that the Spanish word *coño* for "rabbit" is slang, equivalent to "cunt." Some scholars have lambasted Hemingway for this misogynist diminutive. Others have countered that the lewdness allows one to envision Maria as an emblem of sensual and fertile Spain, celebrating Jordan's physical and spiritual consummation with hill and dale (see Link 135). Josephs doesn't believe Hemingway knew the obscenity, and sees it simply as "a natural, innocent and pure word" (Josephs, *Undiscovered* 158). The fact that Jordan first uses the pet name when inviting Maria to join him in his sleeping bag—even insisting upon it—suggests that Hemingway may have intended the idiomatic obscenity. Lewdness and innocence aren't necessarily mutually exclusive. Carl Eby argues for the coexistence of innocence and sexual pleasure in Bosch's *The Garden of Earthly Delights* (see 4:33). Hemingway's rabbit language ties this coexistence to the animal world. As Pilar reminds Agustín, it is spring, after all (93:14). Lovers can say "cunt" affectionately (e.g., D. H. Lawrence's *Lady Chatterley's Lover*).

Eby offers a different explanation: "Jordan's tender feelings for Maria mask an element of hostility that is somehow bound up with 'the strange thing about her,' and thanks to a split in Hemingway's ego, one part of him knew exactly what it was doing . . . while another part of him was entirely innocent" (*Fetishism* 113). Eby interprets Hemingway as conflating "hare," "hair," and "cunt" in the formation of "a substitute female phallus" that "testifies to his fluid ego boundaries and satisfies his narcissistic desire to recapture the world of primary identification and blissful twinship" (114), the psyche's prelapsarian world.

The paper-doll caricature of Hemingway as "NEANDERTHAL MAN" in the March 1934 *Vanity Fair* magazine has him wearing a leopard-skin loincloth, one hand grasping a club, the other a dead rabbit (29).

69:25 **I am afraid:** Maria is afraid because of her recent history as the victim of repeated extreme sexual violence. She expresses this fear immediately after Jordan calls her "little rabbit" ("little cunt"?) for the first time, a pet name loaded with discourses of being hunted and consumed.

70:1 **Do not be afraid. That is the pistol:** Maria has mistaken the pistol for Jordan's erect penis. In the context of a violent strain in Jordan's psychology toward her, her fear has merit. Consider also that the novel associates Jordan's pistols with suicide: Jordan's father killed himself with an inherited pistol, and he and Maria make a suicide pact involving this very pistol (170:24–26). Separate from the danger Jordan's penis-as-pistol poses Maria, then, is the danger it poses for Jordan via the self-destructive nature of his romancing her (of which he is aware). The suicide pact occurs in the very chapter after their lovemaking has made the earth move. The literal confusion of weapon and sex organ bespeaks cultural messaging that conflates discourses of gender, sex, and war.

70:9 **Put thy hand on my head:** At chapter's end, Maria tells Jordan to sleep with her now to erase her recent history of sexual victimization (73:30–31). The instructions to touch her head and then make love summons the pattern of her rapes, always preceded by head shavings, and reinforces the displacement of the trauma site to her hair, where the loss is visible.

71:6 **By various:** Maria has survived several acts of sexual violence. See 23:21–22; 117:15; 350:19–22.

71:11 **something had happened to him:** Twice characters in this chapter, including Jordan, insist that nothing happens to one that one does not accept (71:25–26; 73:13–14). What is a reader to make of whatever has happened to Jordan in learning of the sexual violence done to Maria?

72:5–6 unthinking and untired and unworried . . . My little rabbit: Just before sleeping with Maria for the first time, Jordan associates the experience as approaching the condition of animals, an idea corroborated elsewhere (93:14–15; 262:22). The negative prefix sounds like Faulkner as well as the language Hemingway used in overseas cables, such as his war dispatches (to save word count costs).

72:20 lo sabes?: Do you know?

72:26 one o'clock. The dial showed bright: It is now 29 May 1937, the second calendar day. This is the first appearance of Jordan's watch, which plays a role in the military operation and in the romance (378:1–2). The text's introducing it during Jordan's and Maria's first embrace moments before sex tenders an incipient carpe diem theme. The male lover of *A Farewell to Arms* quotes the most famous carpe diem poem, Andrew Marvell's "To His Coy Mistress"—"But at my back I always hear / Time's wingèd chariot hurrying near" (*FTA* 154). Because Jordan's arms wrap around Maria, the watch is "behind [her] back" (72:22). Although Jordan wears a modern field watch, it resonates with the watch that Hemingway inherited from his father upon the latter's suicide along with the grandfather's pistol his father used to kill himself, like the grandfather's pistol Jordan's father used to kill himself (Dearborn 273).

In the following chapter, Rafael comments on the watch's fanciness (79:8+), a sly dig at its expense. Jordan's is the watch of a bourgeois, not a peasant or a gitano. Accoutered with a fancy watch and a luxe sleeping bag (179:18–20; 180:15), Jordan acquires Maria: "[T]hou art my woman now" (73:21–22). The text is too familiar with revolutionary ideologies, capitalist inclinations, and traditional patriarchal Spain for readers to dismiss the possessive language as unadulterated endearing, mutual romantic exclusivity and commitment. The novel never writes him as hers.

72:33 Not before the bridge: Frederic Henry, the protagonist of *A Farewell to Arms*, grows a beard after deserting the Italian army and fleeing with his war-found love. Henry's early stubble scratches Catherine's skin, too (*FTA* 114). In the context of the earlier novel about an American fighting in another country's military, this line might portend that Jordan will not survive the bridge mission to take Maria to Madrid (or anywhere else).

The two novels explicitly connect beards with masculine authority. Henry feels like a "fake doctor" with his beard (*FTA* 319); Jordan endures Pablo's taunting that he's a "false professor" of Spanish because of his lack of a beard, which Jordan rebuts by touching his fuzz (210:37–38). Eby reads beards in Hemingway's work as "ward[ing] off the cross-gender identification and reinforc[ing] the anatomical *difference* between the sexes"; Frederic Henry grows a beard "to ward off the more threatening aspects of merger with the split-off feminine part of himself" (*Fetishism* 215). In that novel, Catherine wants them to have the same hair length so they can be "all mixed up" (*FTA* 300); in this novel, Maria flirts with the idea of their having the same-length hair (345:37–38). Both women talk about being one with their man. That Jordan and Maria discuss his potential beard right before they make love the first time suggests a similar playful measure against the loss of self (mostly his masculine self) in merged identities.

73:4 **I am not sick:** According to Pilar, Maria does not have a sexually transmitted infection (see 7:38+).

73:13–15 **nothing is done to oneself that one does not accept . . . I wished to die:** In this instance, Pilar and Maria insist on Maria's right to define herself regardless of what happened to her. The line joins the novel's interrogation of the question of character, will, and fate. Pilar's logic here would appear to contradict her dismissal of Finito's claim that bulls don't gore matadors, but "the man gore[s] himself on the horn of the bull" (55:3–4). Pilar's logic applies to his death—he does accept it—but doesn't speak to his desire for it. Maria conditions her refusal to accept what happened, her refusal to let it define her, upon her being loved by another man. The last line, about her wish to have died, becomes complicated when she later tells Jordan that she "die[s] each time" they make love (having at that point only done so twice; 160:4).

73:21+ **I cannot have a woman doing what I do. But thou art my woman now:** Jordan reaffirms the incompatibility of his military role with romance and appears to accept the consequences. Maria's next line calls him out on the ambiguity of "**now**"—does he mean *for now*, as in for the moment, or *starting now* and lasting forever? Readers ought to follow her lead and trouble the word every time Jordan uses it, such as in their last great lovemaking scene (379:6+) and his death-bound feeling of complete integration "now" (471:12). Note the possessiveness in these lines; note who possesses whom (also 70:31; see 72:26).

73:33 **Yes. Yes. Yes:** Jordan and Maria have sex for the first time in the break between chapters. The act happens off the page because it is more functional than sensual or poetic. She wants it done "quickly"; she implores him "almost fiercely." To paraphrase Rafael, she hurries up the flight of the big bird. She also affirms her voice in the developing relationship, as the repetition of "yes" three times revises the triple repetition of "no" earlier in the chapter, when she insisted on living with Jordan as his woman, not in a home for the war-displaced as he had suggested (70:29–31). Some readers might also hear in the chapter's last words an echo of Molly Bloom's that end James Joyce's *Ulysses*.

THE SECOND CALENDAR DAY

[29 MAY 1937]

CHAPTER EIGHT

74:19 **corralling the horses:** Jordan's speculation on Pablo's predawn activity corresponds to his own early morning activity, as he has just been corralling—so to speak—his "colt" Maria. The text fully answers his early question about what would make him feel what Pablo feels toward the horses and foreshadows his priorities shifting away from the war cause. It might be too far-fetched to read a sly joke in having Pablo smoke a cigarette afterward (a well-known twentieth-century postcoitus cliché).

74:28 **Qué más da:** What difference does it make? What does it matter? Why not? Hemingway had originally typed *Qué va;* the revision occurred to the galley proofs. Hemingway often typed *Qué va* in the draft only to replace the phrase with a more precise or colorful one at the galley stage on the advice of, and almost certainly provided by, Gustavo Durán (see 335:24+).

74:30 **fascist patrol of three Fiats:** The Fiat CR.32 was a single-seat sesquiplane fighter (a biplane whose lower wings have no more than half the surface area of the upper wings) of Italian make. Italy's Legionary Air Force was created to support the Nationalists in Spain and operated the majority of the Fiats (about four hundred), although over a hundred Fiats were flown by the Nationalist Air Force. Spaniards might have flown some or all of the Fiats Jordan sees; during the Battle of Jarama (February 1937), Fiats from both the Nationalist Air Force and the Legionary Air Force worked together to clear the sky for the Condor Legion's bombers (Beevor 214).

74:31–32 **headed in the direction from which Anselmo and he had come:** In the direction of the bridge, which would be to the south. Although the novel's geography isn't necessarily precise, the actual bridge in the vicinity (1:19) is south of the Monk's Cave location (18:9).

75:5–6 **Heinkel one-elevens, twin-motor bombers:** The Heinkel He 111 was a German gull-wing fast medium bomber with a five-man crew. Its twin engines would have been their chief identifying feature for observers on the ground. Most Heinkels were operated by the Condor Legion, the unit of the German Air Force created specifically to support the Nationalists. As the war progressed, Germany gave some older Heinkels to the Nationalist Air Force, although this transfer occurred after the novel's time frame. In early 1937, US military observers of the war reported that Italy's Legionary Air Force and Germany's Condor Legion cooperated by having Italian fighters (Fiats) provide protection for the German bombers (Cortada 60).[1]

76:6 **in echelon of echelons like a wild-goose flight:** The planes are headed south as birds in winter. Perhaps the simile predicts the coming snowfall, in which case the fascist military and the weather become allies of sorts. Later the chapter compares the planes to "sharks" (76:30) and "lions" (79:34). Employing natural imagery to fascist military formations and equipment suggests a natural order that can be read ironically, sincerely, or both—in an honest appraisal of the complex questions about war, violence, industry, and human nature (see 87:3+; 467:20–22). Hemingway was an avid bird hunter, and his simile associates the planes as the unlikely prey of Jordan and his cohort. The association is corroborated below (76:36–37).

76:13 **chasers:** Pablo says *cazas,* the Spanish term for pursuit planes, after the French *chasse;* the singular for both translates directly as *hunter* (see 38:19).

76:27+ **with Castile all yellow and tawny . . . as the shadows of sharks:** Castile is the central region of Spain, where Madrid sits. The Heinkels now out of sight, Jordan imagines them as predatory sharks. Seeing Castile in his mind's eye as "yellow and tawny" echoes his descriptions of Maria as "golden tawny" (22:14; 43:36). The beginning of the next chapter confirms this language as Jordan's, not the narrator's (87:3+).

76:32 **no bump, bump, bumping. . . . His watch ticked on:** If the text adumbrates "tawny" Maria in the prior paragraph, it follows that Jordan's anticipation of the "bumping thud of bombs" textually anticipates his lovemaking with Maria. The repetition of "bump" prefigures the rhythmic repetition of language in the two sex scenes. The observing of his watch and imagined stopped time in those scenes, and Jordan's current observation that his watch ticks on—that time hasn't stopped, that the bombs have not been dropped—strengthens the connection. Jordan's making love to Maria as making love to the Spanish earth becomes tangled up with the fascists' bombing of the Spanish earth (the planes probably piloted by foreigners such as himself). See the description of Jordan checking his watch while feeling Maria's hair "as alive and silkily rolling as when a marten's fur rises under the caress of your hand when you spread the trap jaws open and lift the marten clear and, holding it, stroke the fur smooth" (378:7–10).

76:34–35 **to Colmenar, to Escorial, or . . . Manzanares el Real:** All three are on the other (southern) side of the Guadarrama, in Republican territory. Colmenar Viejo and Manzanares el Real sit in the flight path between Segovia and Madrid, although they do not come to Jordan's mind in the order the planes would fly over them, as Colmenar Viejo is closer to Madrid. Escorial is to the west.

76:36–37 **above the lake with the ducks in the reeds . . . with the dummy planes:** The reference to ducks in the reeds, combined with the wild geese simile above (76:6), extends the simile such that the dummy planes become like decoys that hunters use to attract waterfowl.

76:38+ **They can't know about the attack:** But the Nationalists do, as Jordan soon learns (81:23). The planes very well may have traveled beyond the three targets he supposes; see the next entry.

77:17 **ten minutes:** At 250 miles per hour (76:25), the planes have now traveled over forty miles from when Jordan started timing them. While they could still be going after Colmenar Viejo, Escorial, and the airfield at Manzanares el Real, as he continues to suspect (80:24–25), the forty miles could have taken them deeper into the Republic, in range of Madrid.

77:33–35 **make a mark for tanks thus . . . and when there are four, cross the four strokes for the fifth:** Hemingway initially drafted these pages by hand and drew on the manuscript an example of what Jordan draws for Anselmo (MS10-013), recreated here:

Author's rendition of Hemingway sketch that appears in the manuscript (MS10-013)

79:8+ **What a watch:** One few Spaniards could ever expect to own. See 72:26. It is indeed the "watch to end watches" for Jordan, who will never need another. A thematic complication is the watch's role in Jordan's carpe diem urge as well as in his military mission, which will result in a fair number of deaths. The two are related: he must die to have his transitory bliss (168:28+). Strychacz begins his discussion of the power and authority of the masculine gaze with Rafael's comment about the watch, which for Rafael "implies a new and unfamiliar scopic regime built on 'watching'" (104). As a Romani, Rafael has a different relationship with time as an organizing principle than the American's mechanical one.

79:34 **you ask me:** The paragraph begins "thou askest," so in Spanish Jordan has switched from second-person familiar to second-person formal. But really Hemingway changed to modern English, according to his margin note in the galley proofs, "to avoid archaic dialogue which would become a bore to the reader." The text is intentionally inconsistent for the reader's sake.

81:9 **It still goes badly in the north:** The strategic purpose of the Segovia Offensive was to relieve military pressure on the resource-rich Republican-held Basque and Asturias areas to the north.

81:22 **the broadcast of Quiepo de Llano:** In the 1920s, Gonzalo Queipo de Llano y Sierra publicly clashed with General Miguel Primo de Rivera, the monarch-sanctioned dictator; in 1930, Queipo de Llano was one of the leaders of a failed coup against the monarchy, after which he exiled himself to Portugal. In 1931, the new Second Spanish Republic brought him back and promoted him from brigadier to major general. He lauded the Republic in populist terms those early years. Although Queipo was widely regarded as an unpredictable wildcard capable of going rogue, the government expected his command to hold Seville against the 1936 uprising.

Instead of supporting the Republic when war broke out, Queipo joined the insurgency. The Republican government had thwarted his ambitions. Narcissism, defiance against whoever presumed authority over him (regardless of politics), and a penchant for excessive violence drove him. Seville fell to Nationalist control in the opening days of the war. Queipo declared martial law (*bando de Guerra*) on 18 July 1936, which served as the initial rationale for indiscriminate killings and the foundation of Queipo's purge. As the war progressed, Queipo remained in the south, ruling over an unofficial principality of central and western Andalusia as terrorist in chief. Thousands of civilians were killed under his reign.[2] "Sometimes [southern] villages were literally wiped off the map by repression" (Graham, *Short* 32).

Well into 1938, every night at 10:00 he made a nationwide radio broadcast exaggerating his leadership, spreading gross misinformation, and boasting of Nationalist atrocities with messages such as this one: "Our brave Legionaries and Regulares have shown the red cowards what it is to be a man. And, incidentally, the wives of the reds too. These Communist and Anarchist women, after all, have made themselves fair game by their doctrine of free love. And now they have at least made the acquaintance of real men, and not milksops of militiamen. Kicking their legs about and struggling won't save them."[3] These broadcasts worked to cow the government loyalists and to exhort rebel soldiers and thugs to cruelties against them.

Among the lies he broadcast was one from 18 August 1936, a month into that war: in the small Andalusian town of Ronda, perched on a tall, steep plateau, Republicans murdered upstanding traditional Spaniards by throwing them off a cliff (Preston, *Holocaust* 171). Queipo's propaganda seems to be the source for Pilar's version of events at Ronda in chapter 10. It is interesting to speculate whether Hemingway believed Queipo's fabrication, and if not, why he immortalized the fabrication in his novel. Did fictionalizing the fiction score some wry point? Or did Hemingway simply recognize the dramatic potential of Queipo's imagination?

81:23 **It seems that the Republic is preparing an offensive:** The Segovia Offensive failed "partly because the nationalists appeared to have got wind of what was being prepared" (Beevor 276).

82:1 **over the Alto del León:** Also known as the Guadarrama Pass, this is the primary large pass through the mountains between central and northern Spain, the main route from Madrid to Segovia and Valladolid. At the beginning of the war, the Nationalists failed to capture Madrid through this pass; Jordan fought during that battle (235:32+; 236:8+). At the galley proof stage, this language replaced "beyond the Guadarrama." Presumably, Gustavo Durán, who commanded a Republican brigade during the offensive and who reviewed the galleys, suggested the change.

82:13–14 **troops to be sent to clear out these mountains:** At least one cavalry company has been sent, the one that kills El Sordo's gang and ultimately comes for Jordan. Throughout the conversation, Fernando reminds his audience (and the novel's) of the rumor mill that churns out endless speculation in all wars. *The Red Badge of Courage* opens with yet another false rumor. Pilar accuses Fernando of stupidity, which might be true, but he's also a realist.

82:22 *Tonto:* Fool, or more harshly, idiot or imbecile.

84:13 **Fernandito:** The suffix *–ito* can serve as a diminutive, indicating a smaller version of the thing, or it can indicate endearment. "Little Fernando" is too literal a translation, but it does suggest the familiar and almost familial affection Maria expresses toward Fernando.

84:18 **The people had no manners:** In *Death in the Afternoon,* Hemingway describes the Valencians as "local, patriotic, bullfighter worshippers" (42), meaning patriotic toward Valencia, not Spain, and suggesting an insular local pride that non-Valencians (such as Fernando) might have found unwelcoming and without common courtesy. Hemingway harshly judges how Valencians "worship" Valencian bullfighters "rather than enjoy the bullfights" and are quick to "turn on" their homegrown idols who disappoint in the ring (45–46).

84:27 *Vamos!:* Literally, Let's go. Here, it means Oh, come on.

84:33+ **three fights at the Feria:** Spanish bullfights often occur in conjunction with a city's, town's, or village's annual festival—its *feria*—that traditionally celebrates the local patron saint or another event on the Catholic calendar. According to *Death in the Afternoon,* the first fight of the major feria at Valencia begins on 25 July, followed by "seven to nine fights on successive days until and through August 2" (480). This matches Pilar's story that follows, of being at the feria in the summer. The initial paragraphs of her story—being on the beach, eating paella—are very similar to Hemingway's description of being there in *Death in the Afternoon;* it is "hottest when the wind blows from Africa" (44).

85:7–9 **Pastries:** One pastry served on the Valencia beach, the Granero, was named after Manuel Granero, Valencia's "greatest bullfighter," killed by a bull in 1922 (*DIA* 45; see 251:21).

85:12–13 *paella* **with fresh sea food:** Paella de marisco is a traditional Valencian frypan dish consisting of seafood in saffron-flavored rice cooked in oil and seafood broth.

85:33 **firecrackers of the** *traca:* firecrackers of the fireworks.

86:24–25 **But no one can speak against Valencia either:** In addition to protecting her memory of Valencia, Pilar might also be defending the Republican government, which relocated to Valencia in November 1936 when Madrid's fall to the Nationalists appeared imminent.

NOTES

1. See also Juntunen, who further comments that the American attachés did not observe this arrangement after this period of the war: "[W]ith the introduction of the Messerschmitt Bf.109, in the summer of 1937, the Germans had a fighter capable of providing protection for

their bombers. And with the increased speed of their new bombers, they even questioned the need to provide fighter cover on bombing missions" (49).

2. On Queipo de Llano and Seville, see Preston, *Holocaust* 137–45; and Rúben Emanuel Leitão Prazeres Serém, *Conspiracy, Coup d'État and Civil War in Seville (1936–1939): History and Myth in Francoist Spain,* 2012, London School of Economics and Political Science, PhD dissertation.

3. Preston quotes this broadcast in *The Spanish Civil War* (206) and *The Spanish Holocaust* (149). On the evening hour and the end of the broadcasts, see Thomas (732, 734).

CHAPTER NINE

87:2 **fast, ugly arrow-heads:** The phrase might be aesthetically oxymoronic for readers who visualize arrowheads as lovely in their crafted, purposeful sleekness. The issue turns on whether one regards the adjective "ugly" from a purely visual perspective or from a perspective that highlights their purpose: killing, in this case of allies and friends. On the conflict between beautiful form and terrible purpose, see 467:20. The phrase "beating the sky" suggests a bird in flight, creating a mixed metaphor—see the next entry.

87:3+ **shaped like sharks. . . . move like mechanized doom:** Jordan does not favor the natural or the mechanical simile. He distinguishes *shape* from *movement*—the enemy aircraft are like sharks in their shape and mechanized doom in their movement. Both similes are true. Commentators who only cite "mechanized doom" to characterize the fascists neglect the context of the full passage. If in the second simile Jordan wants to communicate their terrifying ugliness, he falls prey to the fact that the rhythm of the line "They *move* like *mech*-a-nized *doom*" is rather poetic—two iambs followed by an anapest—as is the repeated *m*-sound that slyly revised the repeated sibilant pattern in "shaped like sharks." He falls into the catch-22 of any artistic effort to represent the ugliness of war, violence, brutality, atrocity. The claim that they "move like no other thing that has ever been" differentiates their movement from the natural world (without denying their natural shape) while also crediting them with one of the prime criteria of artistic merit and of most human endeavors: originality. Indeed his recognition of the originality and poetry of his language leads him, in his very next thought, to the notion that he should write again someday (87:9). Is his language accurate, or just evocative? The natural imagery and the mechanical imagery do not necessarily contradict, as both are standard techniques of literary Naturalism for communicating the indifferent universe (see introduction). The descriptive excess of arrowhead, bird, shark, and machine, suggests that the planes—or rather, the emotional response they stir—exceed the potency of a single simile or metaphor.

In the draft, Hemingway identified the pilots as Germans from the Condor Legion, then described the planes as moving like "no birds," which he crossed out and replaced with "mechanized doom" (MS10–015). The bird imagery perhaps followed from the legion name as well as the "beating the sky" language.

87:5 the Gulf Stream: As with Jordan's familiarity with France, the text never explains his experience of the Gulf Stream, which it references again when Jordan recalls approaching Cuba by boat at night (260:31). Hemingway had been deep-sea fishing in the Gulf Stream between Florida and Cuba since January 1931 (Ott 110). Jordan's travels indicate a privileged cosmopolitanism in sharp contrast to the lives of the guerilla cohort. The next chapter, Pilar's account of the atrocities committed under Pablo's leadership at the beginning of the war, Hemingway wrote while making frequent fishing outings aboard his boat *Pilar* in May and June, 1939. In the boat's log for 8 June 1939, he recorded his "[b]iggest week's work on novel yet" (Chamberlin 212).

87:9+ You ought to write: Jordan has written one mediocre book on Spain and fantasizes about writing another after the war (248:28). Jordan's writing fantasy implies the enabling lifestyle of bourgeois, middle-class life. His descriptive musing on the bombers prompts this moment's writing fantasy, but so does the fact that he has just heard Pilar's colorful story about life with Finito, the novel's first instance of Pilar's remarkable oral storytelling talent. After her long story about the start of the war, Jordan finds himself the lesser storyteller (134:33+), a feeling of inadequacy he returns to later (248:30). In his introduction to the *Men at War* anthology published two years after this novel, Hemingway writes about the incompatibility for most people between creative imagination and successful soldiering (xxvii). The imaginative soldier worries, and both pieces of writing regard worrying as detrimental to war fighting. One might understand Jordan as someone who vacillates between the demands of art and the demands of war. Sometimes he plunges into the "now" of bridge-blowing or lovemaking; sometimes he imagines his immediate future, sometimes his postwar future (as in this fantasy of writing). Maria complicates and embodies his problem, at once a focus of his commitment to the now but also a vision of what might or could happen, at the bridge, after the bridge. Jordan expressed a version of the character problem earlier, in his discussion of the "the gay ones." To be gay and worry-free ends in death; but to be the other sort, the sort who thinks these very thoughts, promises the same short future (17:10+).

87:11 *guapa*: Very attractive, the equivalent of using gorgeous or beautiful as a noun.

88:2–3 like a finger faintly touching: Of all the similes Jordan uses for the combat aircraft, this is the strangest in its intimation of erotic touch. He thinks it in response to Maria's statement about the planes' surreality—"It seems as though they were a dream that you wake from" (87:32)—and it precedes his eerily similar language about her: "Maybe you dreamed it. . . . Maybe you would be afraid to touch her to see if it was true" (137:12; 137:37–38). See also Jordan's late thoughts about life as but a dream (452:3+).

89:13 **Sunday:** Dating the days according to the historical start of the Segovia Offensive would make this Saturday (see 1:1+). Hemingway revised other passages that originally placed the novel's action in June in order to fit the historical time frame (see 153:24). He either overlooked changing "Sunday" to "Saturday," did not learn the precise dates, or decided against the change. Readers should consider the interpretative implications of his intending to have this day's activities take place on Sunday. For example, for the possible reading of the massacre in chapter 10 in terms of the auto-da-fé (104:26–27); for Jordan's and Maria's first extended lovemaking scene (chapter 13); and for Finito's tale as possibly alluding to Easter Sunday (185:28–30).

89:22+ **The sight of those machines does things to one:** The German Condor Legion, a month before this novel's action, bombed Guernica on 26 April 1937. Guernica was (and is) a small Basque town of zero military or industrial significance. Its bombing was a terror campaign waged against civilians, the first on European soil,[1] and the inspiration of Hemingway's friend Pablo Picasso's painting *Guernica*. Airpower in the First World War was limited to observation, dogfights, and some bombing of military positions; in the Second World War, it will progress to massive bombing campaigns—think of the Battle of Britain and the firebombings of Tokyo and Dresden. The Spanish Civil War was the transition. American military attachés in Spain paid special attention to aviation. It is difficult for twenty-first-century readers to imagine the shock of this new warfare and the effect of the previously unimaginable on the people who underwent it (see Guill, "'Los Avióñes!'").

The "does things to one" language is potentially complicated again by the idea that "nothing is done to oneself that one does not accept" (73:13–14).

90:1 ***Vamos a ver:*** Let's see.

90:19 **God and the *Virgen*:** "Why Virgen rather than an English 'Virgin' to match the English 'God?'" asks Fenimore. "Because here and again the Spanish word sets off the idea in the ear and imagination of the English reader" (76), the idea of the uniquely Spanish relationship to the Virgin Mary. See 380:21+ on the Spanishness of "La Gloria."

90:22 ***Tengo miedo de morir:*** Fenimore argues that the Spanish carries more emotion for English ears than the provided literal translation. English readers unfamiliar with Spanish will associate the conjugated *tengo,* from the infinitive *tener,* with its root etymological meaning of *to hold:* "For the English ear it is not simply that

Pablo 'has' fear of death: he holds it, desperately, in his two hands" (77). It makes sense, then, that the Spanish original follows the English translation, rather than the novel's usual other way around. The repetition adds to the emphasized emotion.

91:17 **But not to interfere with my work:** Jordan's wartime relinquishing of "the things of life" corresponds to Hemingway's experience, at least according to a letter to his mother-in-law: after "the first two weeks in Madrid had an impersonal feeling of haveing [sic] no wife, no children, no house, no boat, nothing. The only way to function" (to Mary Pfeiffer, 2 Aug. 1937, *SL* 461). He neglects to mention his wartime lover, Martha Gellhorn.

91:20+ **And women?:** The next several lines, from "I like them very much" to "Maybe a little," were added by hand, replacing a dialogue in which Jordan says that he had little knowledge about women before the war because of shyness but that his military duties rid him of insecurity and gave him confidence. This version of Jordan has mostly or has only ever had relations with women in Spain—and only since the beginning of the war (MS10-015). Spanish women, but possibly another international volunteer. Unlike with his traveling life, Jordan makes no passing reference to anyone he might have loved, or dated, crushed on, or even known before the war. This insecurity and lack of romantic experience might corroborate a more youthful protagonist—although his well-traveled self would be somewhat at odds with such a person, and after all Hemingway rewrote this passage. Perhaps he realized that he had been writing a version of himself, not yet twenty years old, on the way to the Great War.

Wartime romances between international men and Spanish women or female volunteers occurred with some frequency, sometimes resulting in marriage.

91:32–33 **he said it quite formally in Spanish:** In the Lola de Aguado translation, Jordan says, *La quiero mucho* (113). It isn't clear why Hemingway doesn't write Jordan's words in Spanish. A few pages earlier, he revised by hand Pablo's "I am afraid" to *Tengo miedo de morir* (90:22; MS10-015). "Quite formally" could suggest a foreigner's textbook version of a language, conveying the limit of Jordan's intimacy with the language, the country, the people. But Jordan seems to deliberately switch to the formal register to dignify his affection for Maria in reaction to his physical response to her (his "thickening" voice). The more formal register risks a deference to the proper that is characteristic of a conservative, bourgeois mentality.

92:6–7 **dark under the tawny skin:** On Maria's darkness beneath the tawny, see 43:38. Hemingway replaced "gold coloured" with "tawny" by hand (MS10–015). She is putting up dishes. Much of the flirtation occurs when she is doing domestic tasks, which was strictly women's work.

92:14 **Don Juan Tenorio:** The title character of José Zorrilla's 1844 play *Don Juan Tenorio: Drama religioso-fantástico en dos partes* (Don Juan Tenorio: Religious-Fantasy Drama in Two Parts), one of the most famous plays in Spain, performed every year on All Saints' Day. Don Juan has slept with more women and killed more men than anyone. In Part II, he has one day to live and determine his beloved's fate: heaven or hell? On his way to hell, his beloved's spirit miraculously saves him when he pleads for divine mercy.

92:28 **her *novio*:** Her fiancé or boyfriend.

93:13–14 **Nothing, . . . *Nada*. We are, after all, in the spring, animal:** Pilar's "nothing" and *nada* answer what Jordan and Maria are doing and adumbrate the "nowhere" language of their first depicted lovemaking (159:17+). On *nada* as spiritual nothingness, as the absolute absence of anything metaphysical (also from Pilar), see 33:17. This is the chapter's second attribution of human behavior to animal nature, the first being Pablo's crying (90:7). In counterpoint, the chapter offers two expressions of belief in God, by Pilar (88:22) and by Pablo (90:15+).

93:17 **Daughter of the great whore of whores. I befoul myself in the milk of the springtime:** Later Hemingway will have Jordan, El Sordo, and Andrés use the expression "son of the great whore" or "son of a whore" in Spanish without providing a translation (274:15; 320:26; 422:8).

The Spanish word for milk, *leche*, is also slang for semen. Agustín's use of the word as a generic expletive now takes on the literal slang meaning after Pilar's comment about what animals and people do in spring. Thus the following joke about the "difficult[y] of execution" involving semen and aircraft motors (93:21+).

93:25 ***Desde luego*:** Of course.

95:1 ***Pero es muy vivo*:** But he is very alive, as in still alive. Changed from *picaro* to *vivo* at the galley proofs (likely suggested by Durán). This change happened twice on this page (95:21; see also 95:11). Pablo is a shifty survivor in the *picaro* tradition (see 11:16).

95:8 **You for energy and resolution:** The text here affirms Pilar's function as the Dolores Ibárruri (La Pasionaria) of the guerilla group, the inspirational spokesperson.

95:11 **But *sin picardía*:** Without cunning. Changed in the galley proofs from "But *picaro*, no" (see 95:1). Pablo uses the term *picardia* himself later (332:38).

NOTE

1. Under the fascist dictator Benito Mussolini, Italian warplanes targeted civilians in Ethiopia during the Second Italo-Ethiopian War. Because the 1935–1937 war overlapped the one in Spain, some Italian soldiers fighting in Spain had believed they were headed to Ethiopia.

CHAPTER TEN

96:29 *guapa:* Jordan called Maria *guapa* first (87:11). In having Pilar (who was there) now do so, the text sets up the desire triangle that surfaces in chapter 12 (154:19+).

97:10 **Pero, venga:** But, come. Equivalent English expressions in this context: Come on, Oh, please, or Give me a break.

97:31 **I would have made a good man:** Not long after meeting Hemingway, and before they traveled (separately) to Spain where they became lovers, Martha Gellhorn expressed something similar to him, as he wrote in response: "And Marty if you want to be a man in this or the next world that is fine and I'll swear you are to you whenever it hits you because I am crazy enough myself to understand a good healthy streak of insanity in a pal."[1]

98:23 **If Roberto says:** Jordan and Maria have tumbled into a very gender-traditional relationship of a Spanish sort. The feminist, emancipatory voices on the left and the Republic's progressive propaganda aside, most Spaniards on both sides of the war, men and women, continued to live and propagate the patriarchal social order they inherited over generations. Hemingway and Ivens's pro-Republican film *The Spanish Earth* maintains rigid gender spheres. The Republic's granting women the right to vote backfired, as most women in 1934 voted for politicians who gave control of the government to the right. Maria's deference fits Jordan's longing to become Spanish and undergirds his attraction to her.

98:33 **the start of the movement:** July 1936, corroborated at 107:23. See commentary at 99:18–19.

98:39 **she named a town:** Hemingway uses the anonymous to fictionalize the typical and apply dramatic license while avoiding petty criticisms of inaccuracy. Writing as the Nationalists came to power and instituted their wartime terrorist reprisal practices into the state's justice system, Hemingway might have worried about how the fascist government could misuse his writing.

Years later Hemingway identified the town as Ronda in Andalusia (Hotchner 131). Conflicts with landowners had been quite severe in Andalusia prior to the war, resulting in some of the most brutal treatment of them by the rebels anywhere in Spain. According to Preston, murders were "carried out by anarchists from Málaga as well as by locals," but there is no evidence of "large numbers of prisoners" herded over the cliff to their death; instead, "[t]he many rightist victims were shot in the cemetery" (*Holocaust* 171); Thomas cites 512 "murdered in the first month of the war" in Ronda, also noting that in Ronda the perpetrators were "a gang from Málaga" and the victims might have been shot in the valley rather than thrown or forced over a cliff (263). Pilar's version has its roots in a radio broadcast of 18 August 1936 by the Nationalist General Queipo de Llano; it was one of the many atrocity stories Queipo fabricated to inspire and justify his own terror campaign (see 81:22). Ronda's location deep in southern Spain presents a moderate challenge for a novel set in central Spain. And whereas the novel compresses the time until the Nationalists' arrival to "three days" (129:19) after the massacre that took place at "the start of the movement" (98:3), the Nationalists did not conquer Ronda until 16 September, a month after Queipo's broadcast. The *New York Times* reported, during the two weeks between, the execution of over "800 prosperous persons" by government loyalists and the arrival of the rebels ("Reports"). Preston writes that an anarchist known as El Gitano (171), "the Gypsy," led the leftist terror. If Hemingway knew this, he deflects the Romani association from Pablo to Pilar and the anarchist association to a few drunks.

Since the executions take the form of local bullfight, Ronda makes sense because of its storied connection to bullfighting (see 103:25). Hemingway's description in *Death in the Afternoon* is strongly suggestive of the town as the novel's massacre site, regardless of whether Hemingway knew anything about what happened at Ronda at the beginning of the war, whether it was a total invention, or whether it was a creative adaptation of whatever he might have heard:

> It is built on a plateau in a circle of mountains and the plateau is cut by a gorge that divides the two towns and ends in a cliff that drops sheer to the river and the plain below.... [The bull ring] stands at the edge of the cliff and after the bullfight when the bulls have been skinned and dressed and their meat went out for sale on carts they drag the dead horses over the edge of the cliff and the buzzards that have circled over the town and high in the air over the rig all day, drop down to feed on the rocks below the town. (43)

The geographical language of *gorge* resembles that of the fictional mission's bridge, the discarding of horse corpses the fictional massacre's discarding of human corpses (126:30–31).

"Imposing Gorge of the Guadalevin and the New Bridge, Ronda, Spain," 1908, H. G. White Co. From stereoscopic card by J. J. Killelea & Company (New York and London). (Author's collection)

99:18–19 **the start of the movement in any small town:** Spanish Morocco fell to the Nationalists on 17 July 1936. The next day, the Spanish mainland war broke out. The text confirms the July date (107:23). As Pilar's tale dramatizes, local, isolated, and impromptu outbreaks of horrendous violence by party and union militias, anonymous gangs, and everyday Spaniards filled those early days. Calling it "the movement" is accurate, as even though the Nationalist rebellion began the war, those aligned with the progressive government or with more radical ideologies seized the rebellion as an opportunity to begin a revolution and take revenge on whomever could be said to represent the power structures: "In country districts, revolution itself often consisted primarily of the murder of the upper classes or the bourgeoisie" (Thomas 263). Neither the state nor in many places local authorities had much control. Personal grievances and the feeling of sport got mixed up with political motives. Those carrying out the violence that Thomas characterizes as "frivolous, sadistic cruelty" (260) are sometimes referred to as the *incontrolables* (uncontrollables). Thomas estimates 55,000 or more were killed in these circumstances (259). Historians contrast these populist Republican-allied atrocities with the Nationalist program, the former unofficial and mostly limited to the war's initial phase, the latter sanctioned, encouraged, and carried out by Nationalist authorities for the duration of the war (and beyond; although executions and disappearances by the Republican security regime throughout the war must be kept in mind; see Guill, "Red and White Terrors"; see 129:19).

99:21 **Then thou hast seen nothing:** See 106:21–23.

99:26 **tell it truly as it was:** Pilar's promise is potentially paradoxical. Hemingway always considered fiction a better medium for truth-telling than nonfiction. In the excised draft ending of his first book, for example, he wrote (as Nick Adams but truly as himself), "Writing about anything actual was bad. It always killed it. The only writing that was any good was what you made up, what you imagined. That made everything come true" (*NA* 237). Nick and Ernest don't mean total invention but an imaginative riffing on the real. Or, as Hemingway wrote his younger brother in August 1938, having just written two stories based on Chicote's Bar in wartime Madrid, "When you write a story try to invent truly ie make up as well as record and remember and invent something of interest and significance (Sounds easy huh?)."[2] Does Pilar's story take creative liberties to get after the truth beyond or within the happened? Is this why she is the better storyteller than Jordan (134:23+), because she is bolder in marrying invention with remembrance? Consider the conflict Hemingway articulated between imagination and soldiering in *Men at War* (see 87:9), as well as the complication that Pilar's potentially quasi-imagined truthful story has its roots in Queipo de Llano's propagandist lie (see 81:22).

99:36 **their two hands against the heather:** Hemingway added this short paragraph by hand to the draft typescript, presumably at the same time he added the three instances of the word "heather" to the descriptive passage setting the scene at the beginning of the chapter (96:8+; MS10–016).

The repetition of "heather" contributes a sensuousness appropriate to the lovers reclining together, holding hands, and listening to a story. Their settling into the heather unsettles in framing Pilar's tale of the massacre as a species of entertainment, as if Jordan and Maria were on a date, an unsettling echoed in the repetition of "heather" in their upcoming lovemaking (159:8+) and related to Jordan's fantasy of entertaining his (male) students by having Maria tell her story of sexual victimization (165:2+). The novel calls attention to the problem of war porn, of stimulation's usurping abhorrence in one's response to representations of such violence. How can the sought-after pleasure of art reconcile with the ugliest of subject matter? See 101:13. The exchange about whether Pilar's tale might "molest" Maria (99:27–28) reflects a "provocation" Susan Sontag has identified that motivates looking at graphic images of human pain, suffering, and disfigurement: "There is the satisfaction of being able to look at the image without flinching. There is the pleasure of flinching" (*Regarding* 41). In *Death in the Afternoon*, Hemingway argues that a writer couldn't relate violent death with clarity or truthfulness if he "had physically or mentally shut his eyes" when confronting it (2–3).

99:38 **civiles:** *Guardia civil;* see 14:8.

101:13 **ugly:** The word appears three times on this page, twenty-three times in the chapter. *Beauty, beautiful,* and *guapa* appear fifteen times, most notably in the statement about the "beauty" of the collective nature of the killings (105:35). As Jordan later reflects, Pilar's horrible tale is magnificently told (134:23+). The novel is very conscious of the problem of aesthetic representation of the repugnant (see 99:36; 129:19).

102:2 **too grave for a joke:** The men about to die are "too grave" for a joke about death, but the narrator isn't.

102:9–10 **I can hear the pistol still . . . and see the barrel jerk:** Pilar's tale is a model of ekphrasis as practiced by Classical rhetoricians—not a literary engagement with a work of visual art (e.g., Keats's "Ode on a Grecian Urn") but a style of oratory "that worked an immediate impact on the mind of the listener, sparking mental images of the subjects it 'placed before the eyes'" (Webb 193). Battles were a common exercise topic in Roman handbooks; historians, not poets, were the exemplar practitioners. Rhetorical definitions and instructions for ekphrasis uniquely focus "in terms of its effect" on the audience of turning listeners into virtual spectators (Webb 51–52). Whereas with other tale-tellers Jordan "only *heard* the statement," through evocative details and other techniques "Pilar had made him *see* it in that town" (134:23, 32; emphasis added). The comparison to a local bullfight (*capea*) employs one ekphrastic technique, the practice of relating to the familiar and recognizable to provoke an immediate response that mimics the story's immediacy in order to push onward without the need to stop and think (Webb 109–10, 122).

Pilar's inserted reminder of her remembering self is an ekphrastic technique that makes the subject more vivid by virtue of being consciously, subjectively processed. Ruth Webb describes the technique in *Ekphrasis: Imagination and Persuasion in Ancient Rhetorical Theory and Practice*, particularly for the communication of a memory:

For what *enargeia,* and thus *ekphrasis,* seeks to imitate is not so much an object, or scene, or person in itself, but the effect of seeing that thing. . . . It is the act of seeing that is imitated, not the object itself. . . . In communicating through words his own mental image of a murder or a sacked city, Quintilian is not primarily attempting to convey information about a specific reality, but rather to prompt his audience to re-enact internally the act of seeing such a sight, and therefore to achieve an approximation of what an actual witness might have felt. (127–28)

Through *enargeia,* ekphrasis solves the literal impossibility of painting with words, the paradox of literary descriptive realism, by representing "not reality itself, but the impact of the perception of reality" (Webb 128). The speaker, whether witness or fabricator, enables the listener to cocreate the visualization. One only need contrast Pilar's sentence with the less potent remainder of the paragraph. The sentence serves as a mise en abyme of how Pilar's tale functions in its entirety—for many readers, this is the novel's most memorable, most powerful chapter. Ironically, ekphrasis joins the full catalogue of classical rhetorical moves contributing to an elite education, which Pilar seemingly has come by naturally.

102:26 **as powdered as men are at a threshing:** Pilar introduces one of her two articulated similes for the massacre, agricultural reaping and threshing. The people use agricultural tools to kill the town's bourgeois element as they "thresh fascists" (107:28). The simile invites comparison to the Republican rhetoric of its own dead reflowering Spain (see 471:12). The other articulated simile is the bullfight (see 103:25). A third potential simile is the auto-da-fé (see 104:26–27).

102:36 **Vaya:** Well. Damn. What a day that commences. Here we go.

103:25 **a *capea*:** Hemingway defines *capeas* in *Death in the Afternoon* as "informal bullfights or bull baitings in village squares" for aspiring bullfighters and amateurs (*DIA* 393). They typically occur as part of annual festivals, and they vary according to local tradition. In chapter 34, Andrés reflects on his village's annual *capea* (364:34). Local *capeas* were often collective efforts where, when things got out of hand, people could "swarm" the bull "with knives, daggers, butcher knives and rocks. . . . All amateur or group killing is a very barbarous, messy, though exciting business and is a long way from the ritual of the formal bullfight" (*DIA* 24).

"Bullfight" is the inexact English term for the *corrida de toros,* the running of the bulls. Channeling the upper class through two lines of murderous, tipsy peasants resembles the "drunken, dancing, bull-running public of Pamplona," the *encierro* that ends for the bull in certain death in the bullring (*DIA* 42), which Hemingway captured for the ages in *The Sun Also Rises.*

Bullfighting provided wartime Spaniards a way of wrapping their heads around the violence. A man from a town near Madrid "was taken to a corral filled with fighting bulls, where he was gored to unconsciousness. Afterwards, one of his ears was cut off, in imitation of the amputation of the ear of a bull in honour of a matador, following a successful *faena* [conclusion]. Ears of priests were often passed around." However the murders occurred, "[o]ften, the moment of death would be greeted with applause, as if it were the moment of truth in a *corrida*" (Thomas 261). On the other side, the Nationalists used bullrings like the ones in Llerena and Badajoz to carry out mass executions (see 24:2). Hemingway's friend Luis Quintanilla, an artist and staunch Republican who participated in early fighting, was proud to be listed as one of "the first twelve to be shot in the Burgos bullring in the manner of a spectacular bullfight" (in P. Quintanilla 177).

Ronda is lauded as the birthplace of the modern bullfight whereby the main event takes place on foot rather than mounted, an apt setting for depicting the beginning of Spain's first modern war. One of the greatest bullfighting legacies is that of the Romero family, dating back more than two hundred years. Hemingway borrows the name of the family's most famous son, Pedro Romero (1754–1839), for the idealized matador of *The Sun Also Rises*, whose style he models on a contemporary *rondeño* matador Hemingway greatly admired, Cayetano Ordóñez. With Pedro Romero's Ronda as the hidden backdrop to the massacre, the new novel revisits the earlier novel, reframing the bullfighting bloodlust in in the context of the civil war:

> *For Whom the Bell Tolls* is blunter than *The Sun Also Rises* in terms of the war-*corrida* correlation . . . [as the latter] novel's bullfighting references emphasize the barbarity of that collective. . . .
>
> Pilar's story . . . discloses the ugly truth of the communal ecstasy and social responsibility undergirding all wars and sanctioned violence, in stark contrast to the idealized matador of the earlier novel. (Vernon, "Afterthoughts")

The character Pedro Romero's calling the bulls he fights his brothers, the dynamic predator-prey relationship between matador and bull that can reverse in an instant, the way the two can appear to blur into one another—one might consider the novel's sympathetic equivalence of people on both sides of the war (e.g., the bridge sentries, 36:11+; 192:35+). The predator-prey relationship reverses three days later, when the Nationalists take the town (129:16+). For Barbara Ehrenreich, in *Blood Rites: Origins and History of the Passions of War*, "Rituals of blood sacrifice both celebrate and terrifyingly reenact the human transition from prey to predator, and so . . . does war" (22). The essay "The Rites of War and *The Sun Also Rises*" draws on Ehrenreich:

> In short, communities organized themselves to protect against predation, first passively by avoiding the beasts, then confrontationally by standing their ground,

then offensively in hunting. Initially hunting included everyone through "such techniques as driving animals over cliffs" (83). Eventually it belonged to specialized groups, and finally, especially with the drastic decline in large game, these specialized groups for various reasons sustained themselves by basically inventing war. Animal sacrifice meanwhile became a sanctified vestigial reenactment of the prey-to-predator transition. In sum, blood sacrifice and war share this origin and thrive on its emotional legacy.

Astonishingly, though Ehrenreich mentions large horned ungulates several times as a chief predatory threat to humans, she never once invokes the bullfight. When *The Sun Also Rises* gives us the farmer Vicente Girones's death during the *encierro* and the crowds outside and inside the arena, I can think of no other ritual that approaches the bullfight in so perfectly reenacting the prey-to-predator (and predator-to-prey) transition. (Vernon, "'Rites'" 22)

For Whom the Bell Tolls's massacre scene as told by Pilar manifests the predator-prey equivalence, blurring, slippage, and reversal by having the crowd call its victims bulls (109:16–17) and referring to what its victims face as bulls (113:1; 115:3). The scene forcefully dramatizes and historicizes the novel's comparative inquiry into hunting and war.

104:24–25 **rope pulling contest, or . . . a bicycle road race:** Bullfighting too is a sport and, like sport-hunting, descended from actual, necessary hunting. The uncontrollables (*incontrolables*) who conducted the killings at the start of the war often came from somewhere else, their raucous wantonness sometimes playing out, for them, as a kind of sport. Outsiders form part of the murderous crowd in Pilar's tale (105:38). Local fiestas combine the sacred of the holy days with the profane of the sporting spirit, experienced congruously. At the end of *The Sun Also Rises,* after Jake Barnes fails to find peace of mind or social harmony at the Fiesta de San Fermín, he enjoys an unexpected introduction to the Tour du Pays Basque cycling race, the novel contrasting the two events. Even in that novel's idealized *corrida,* its centerpiece spectacle act of violence at once spills out into and is reflective of the interpersonal violence outside the ring.

104:26–27 **the passage of a holy image in a procession:** The religious imagery in this line might support reading the event as a parody of the auto-da-fé, the ritual execution of supposed apostates and heretics during the Spanish Inquisition, which involved imprisoning ahead of time, a morning breakfast feast for the citizens, (forced) confession inside, then the public procession of infamy through the streets led by priests bearing religious emblems, toward execution at the town plaza, often by burning. In Pilar's tale, Pablo rounds up the victims the night before (103:35) and has his morning coffee at the café (104:6); the crowd jokes about their victims' recounting of sins inside city hall (107:13+) before parading them across the plaza toward death. A drunk anarchist twice tries to set one of them on fire (122:37; 126:10+). Officiants avoided holy days for the auto-da-fé, and the text says that today was not a feria day (107:24–25), so probably not a holy day. The novel mentions the auto-da-fé in chapter 23, calling this "act of faith" a furtherance of pre-Christian Spanish bloodlust (286:34–38). During the Inquisition, Church and Crown collaborated to conduct the auto-da-fé. It makes sense that this scene's revolt against the old order would employ a version of its methods.

In *Virgin Spain*, a book Hemingway knew, Waldo Frank speculates that Spanish communities of old might have alternated public events on the *plaza mayor* between the bullfight and the auto-da-fé. He refers to both as sport: "In the one sport, the actors were nobles and the victims were bulls. In the other, officiated captains of the Church and the victims were Jews." He also surmises that the youth of the nobility turned to bullfighting after the Reconquest to replace the killing of Moors (229). The local *capea* and auto-da-fé were favored subjects of the nineteenth-century Spanish painter Eugenio Lucas Velázquez, his composition and style remarkably similar for both (the Prado did not acquire its collection of his work until after Hemingway's day).

105:4–5 as today is clear . . . as there are now: In *A Moveable Feast*, Hemingway describes "transplanting" as the technique whereby the writer transplants his or her immediate environment into the fiction scene presently being written (17). The repetition of the two days' similarities suggests Pilar might be using this fiction trick, especially since hers is an oral story. In an oral setting it would be another instance of ekphrasis by providing immediacy of visualization.

105:22–23 There are no women: A very pointed difference between this atrocity and the one in Maria's hometown—at least in Pilar's and Maria's tellings—is the treatment of women. This Republican mob leaves them alone, but the fascists murder Maria's mother and rape Maria and other young women. In a separate event, the fascists executed Joaquín's mother apparently for having voted Socialist (138:21–22). The novel debunks the Nationalists' traditionalist view of women, revealing it as the opposite of reverential. Pilar's declaration to men that "[w]e are not killing women," as much order as report, gives her a public authority that rightist Spain would never permit a woman.

105:37 They have taken Valladolid. They have Avila: Valladolid and Ávila fell to the Nationalists practically overnight when the rebellion began. The emphasized *they* echoes Hemingway's voice-over script for *The Spanish Earth*, where it vaguely references prewar anti-Republican conservatives as well as wartime opponents, such as when the film accuses the landowners of refusing to improve irrigation to better feed the people, by saying, "*They* held us back." The novel's language—"*This* town is ours" (106:1)—echoes the film twice. First: "This is the moment that all the rest of war prepares for, when six men go forward into death to walk across a stretch of land and by their presence on it prove—this earth is ours." Second: "The bridge is ours. The road is saved. The men who never fought before, who were not trained in arms, who only wanted work and food, fight on."

Chapter 10 exposes the emptiness of such simplistic, tribal, oppositional rhetoric that pretends no differences among individuals, no internal conflicts for either side. Pilar gives the enemy names, personalities, and various degrees of guilt or innocence, while presenting their killers as hastily forming a rather fractious, tenuous alliance. This chapter encapsulates the novel's deconstruction of an unsympathetic us/them attitude. It also participates in the novel's critique of ideological and bureaucratic rhetoric.

106:21–23 **in a small town where all know all:** "The memory of war, however, like all memory, is mostly local" (Sontag, *Regarding* 35). Stathis N. Kalyvas begins *The Logic of Violence in Civil War* wondering how neighboring Spanish towns, with very similar social and political profiles, experienced startlingly different first months of the war. One had thirty-eight men killed "at the hands of right-wing Falangists," the other, none (2). Kalyvas's book explores the enormous gap between macrohistorical narratives and microhistorical happenings: "the habitually cited causes of group division (e.g., ideological, social, or ethnic polarization) often fail to account for the actual dynamics of violence: the game of record is not the game on the ground" (5). On the ground, the interpersonal and the intimate dictate a community's fate: settling old scores, dealing with a rival suitor, putting a competitor forever out of business. Local "cleavages" can order allegiances and behaviors as much if not more than the other way around, appropriating the terms of the national conflict "to serve ends that often have only local significance" (371). The study of the "black box of intracommunity dynamics and individual behavior" belongs to "the province of anthropological and microhistorical studies, literature, and novels" (11). Hemingway's novel imaginatively witnesses the *pico*historical, the very instant the crowd turns especially cruel in response to two early victims facing violent death, the defiant Don Ricardo and the simpering Don Faustino (114:35–37; 116:11–12).

107:23–25 **It is July . . . not yet in the time of fairs and festivals:** Although bullfights occur throughout Spain from spring through the fall, and the second week of July is the time of Pamplona's Fiesta de San Fermín, whose bullfights Hemingway immortalized for his American audience in *The Sun Also Rises*, September is the "great feria month," according to Hemingway (*DIA* 482). Carrie B. Douglass calculates that between August 15 and September 8, "twice the number of towns celebrate fiestas than during other months" (31). This season corresponds to the beginning of the autumn harvest and the war; the many farming implements used during the execution scene become both a realistic detail in terms of available weaponry—which was the case for a lot of Republican spontaneous militias at the start of the war—and also a connection to the bullfighting fiestas. Ronda's major feria began on May 20 (*DIA* 39, 479).

107:34 **three-cornered patent leather hats:** The civil guard's tricorn is very distinctive.

108:20 **the Mayor:** Maria's father, executed at the beginning of the war by the fascists, was also the town mayor.

108:27 **Qué pasa:** Hemingway translates connotatively as "[w]hat is the matter?" A more direct translation would have a sarcastic bite: How's it going? What's up? What's happening? What's going on?

108:38 **Cabron:** Bastard. An English speaker might say son-of-a-bitch or asshole.

110:32 **The priest would not speak to Pablo:** For H. R. Stoneback, the failed dialogue between Pablo and the priest is the essence of Pilar's tale, and it is a Catholic essence. Concluding that Pablo has been "mocking" the priest, Stoneback writes that "there is nothing the priest can answer to Pablo, for the situation is unanswerable, just as the tragedy of Spain is unanswerable; and there is nothing even the best Republicans—such as Anselmo—can do in the end except pray and long for expiation, for atonement" ("Priest" 108). For Stoneback, the Donne epigraph signals the novel's "core Christian vision of the oneness of humankind and the relationship of the individual soul to fate"; Pilar's tale reveals "the subsumptive Christian truth of the epigraph: every death diminishes everyone, and the complicity, for all of Spain and for everyone involved, which spreads beyond mere knowing, demands . . . expiation and penance" ("'Priest'" 109).

Stoneback is right to challenge scholars and readers who, so enamored of the Republican cause, at best overlook and at worst dismiss Hemingway's profound affection for traditional (and Catholic) Spain. The novel does indeed anguish over what Stoneback calls "the irreconcilable tensions in the very fabric of Spanish life" that troubled Hemingway (100). Stoneback reconciles the novel to these tensions by arguing that by "design," it "shows most of the Spanish characters—and Jordan with them—moving toward a reclamation and deeper acknowledgement of the very mystery"—the Christian truth—"that the Republic . . . had attempted to eradicate" (103). Another interpretation of the novel's engagement with the tensions, the one to which this *Glossary and Commentary* is partial, maintains their anguishing irreconcilability. "There's no *one* thing that's true," Jordan reflects in his dying minutes. "It's all true" (467:20). That formulation is at once hearteningly capacious and frustratingly insolvent. It understands the novel moving not toward spiritual reclamation but fraught resignation. Jordan's romanticized death spares him, Hemingway, and the reader of continuing to beat their heads and hearts against the impossible task of reconciling tensions of and far beyond civil war–era Spain. In the actual spirit of Donne, the novel becomes rending meditation, not ready catechism.

111:10 **canalla:** Rabble, as in a common, vulgar, even ignorant mob.

111:17 **Arriba España!:** Up with Spain! Long live Spain! by which Don Ricardo means a traditional, aristocratic, and potentially monarchist vision of true, pure Spain. Changed from *Viva España* in the galley proofs, likely per Durán's suggestion.

112:3+ **Whose Lord?:** The next several lines exhibit the delicate fault lines of the Republic's political coalition. Beyond that, they illustrate how tribalist partisans of any political movement contend among themselves to demonstrate the superior correctness of their thinking.

112:29–30 **on horseback in the Andalucian style:** The main event in modern bullfighting, invented in Ronda, occurs dismounted, the matador in the position of the infantryman (see 103:25). Don Faustino's doing it the old-fashioned mounted way, the way of the nobility, is the height of pretension.

113:16–17 **but time was shortening and there was only one direction to go:** The entire chapter reviews various men moving toward certain death. One could easily imagine this exact line appearing in one of Jordan's interior monologues as he looks toward his three last days on earth. Pilar's story entrances him as a mise en abyme. This story-within-the-story, this one line within the story-within, crystallizes one of Hemingway's major preoccupations. For the novelist Tim O'Brien, most famous for transmuting into fiction his experiences of the American war in Vietnam, Hemingway isn't a war writer, but a death writer: "Figuratively, but also literally, I'm quite certain that when Ernest Hemingway sat down to write in the early mornings, and as he slipped into the ballet of imagined events and imagined human beings, he was often engaged in something close to a dress rehearsal for his own coming extinction. He was practicing" (344).

116:8 **El Debate:** See 398:6–8.

116:30 **a Negro was hanged:** Hemingway borrows his sister Marcelline's witnessing of a lynching (Baker, "Empirical" 105). The fact that Black American men were often lynched upon accusation of sex with or rape of white women subtextually prompts Maria's reference to unspeakable, personal knowledge of being raped by

Moors (117:15). The lynching memory connects the two civil wars through their racism. The Nationalist vision of a *pure* Spain and of *true* Spaniards was fundamentally racist. Nationalist rhetoric figured Spanish leftists as corrupted by non-Spanish influences. It figured leftists, through the vulgar association of communism with Jewishness, as a different or at least a tainted race. Hanging was used during the war.

Jordan repeatedly muses on the American Civil War, a war fought over slavery. The American volunteers dubbed themselves the Abraham Lincoln Brigade to proclaim emancipation as their cause. Some Black American members of the Lincoln Brigade joined as a way of fighting racist ideology and oppression. They could no longer defend Ethiopia against Italy, and they couldn't wage war against the institutionalized racism of the United States, so they went to Spain. Jordan's childhood witnessing of the lynching serves as a warning that racist violence doesn't end with the end of a war, regardless of the victor.

In the United States, the large audiences that formed to watch lynchings proved spectatorship to be complicity. For global supporters of the Spanish Republic, the Non-Intervention Pact obeyed by potential allies resulted in a spectatorship tantamount to complicity. As the window blinds and Robert Jordan's mother's pulling him away from the window show, remote spectators sometimes engaged in a partial and sometimes willful ignorance (116:37–38). For Cirino, "[t]he image neatly reverses a moment from Pilar's extended narrative in which she scrambles onto a chair to see through a window, to better view the violence" (*Thought* 110).

116:34 How barbarous!: Maria's colloquial ejaculation is empty, reflexive language that tires Jordan (134:15+), as Hemingway indicates through its parallelism with her prior utterance, "How nice!" (116:29).

117:15 Not as I can: See 116:30. When Maria later tells the story of her capture, she identifies her initial rapists as Falangists. It is textually near-certain as well as historically plausible to conclude that she suffered sexual violence by Moors while imprisoned in Valladolid. The first time readers learn "things were done" to her, she says her assailants were "various" (71:3–6).

Maria was raped multiple times throughout her months-long imprisonment (23:21–22; 350:19–22). The Army of Africa's Second Bandera of European legionnaires joined with General Mola's northern forces in Valladolid in mid-August 1936 (Álvarez 78–79), on the way to fight in such critical operations as Irún and Huesca (Álvarez 181–92), and newspapers reported the participation of Moors at Irún in the opening days of September, as in this sensationalist headline and article from the *Daily News* (Perth, Australia): "Half-Naked Moors Leave Trail of Carnage in Irun." The US ambassador to Spain and Hemingway's acquaintance, Claude Bowers, also notes that as the battle initially developed, Moorish troops had been seen in Burgos, and that Mola's censor "instructed the correspondents to refer to the

Moors as 'the army from Morocco,' *if they had to mention them at all.* But soon the presence of Moors would be proclaimed from Burgos, and the Moorish cavalry would act as the guard of honor when the Hitler Ambassador would present his credentials to General Franco" (278). In October, the Foreign Legion's Third Bandera, also dispatched to the north, fought in the Asturian campaign and its siege of Oviedo alongside at least one *tabor* of *regulares* (Álvarez, 193–212; see also Fraser 250–54). Republicans faced some "African troops" during the Segovia–La Granja offensive during which *For Whom the Bell Tolls* is set (Seidman 100). In 1937, the year of the novel's action, Moorish units passed through Valladolid on their way to the Aragon front (see González and del Río). The Nationalists also established a segregated medical facility for Moorish soldiers in Valladolid.

Whether Moorish troops were posted for any length of time to Valladolid during Maria's imprisonment doesn't matter. The town served as something of a hub. Their occasional presence in the area sufficiently serves Hemingway's purpose. His novel capitalizes upon the widespread wartime fears and rumors of rape by Moors, which became a propaganda tool used by both the Republicans and the Nationalists. The domestic racism of Hemingway's 1940 American audience might have conditioned its response to Maria's line (Richard Wright's *Native Son* came out the same year).

120:6–8 **Viva la Anarquia! . . . Viva la Libertad!:** Long live Anarchy! . . . Long live Liberty! By the turn of the twentieth century, anarchy had become a serious political movement in the Western world, including in the United States and especially in Spain. Its intellectual roots trace to the Frenchman Pierre-Joseph Proudhon and two Russians, Mikhail Bakunin and Pyotr Kropotkin. Kropotkin's vision of anarcho-communism adopted cooperative elements of communism but demanded the dissolution of the state and the end of traditional forms of government. His 1892 book *The Conquest of Bread* greatly influenced Spanish anarchism leading up to the civil war. Spanish anarchism evolved into organized syndicates over the first decades of the new century, and by the beginning of the war the two major ones with goals of revolutionary liberation were the Confederación Nacional del Trabajo (CNT; National Confederation of Workers) and the Federación Anarquista Ibérica (FAI; Anarchist Federation of Iberia). Although rival organizations, they united during the war under the banner CNT-FAI and used red and black as their colors, as seen in the handkerchiefs in the novel.

In his 1922 book about Spain, *Rosinante to the Road Again,* John Dos Passos wrote the following about Spanish anarchy:

> Spain is the classic home of the anarchist. A bleak upland country mostly, with a climate giving all varieties of temperature, from moist African heat to dry Siberian cold, where people have lived until very recently,—and do still,—in villages hidden away among the bare ribs of the mountains, or in the indented coast

plains, where every region is cut off from every other by high passes and defiles of the mountains, flaming hot in summer and freezing cold in winter, where the Iberian race has grown up centerless. The pueblo, the village community, is the only form of social cohesion that really has roots in the past. On these free towns empires have time and again been imposed by force. (44–45)

During the first years of the Second Spanish Republic, dissatisfied with the slow pace of change and realizing that middle-class professionals rather than revolutionaries ran the Republican government, the anarchists resumed their tactics of disruption through strikes and minor militancy. But after the right regained control of the government in 1934, the anarchists joined the new Popular Front in 1935 to help return the left to power. The victory of the left in that election resulted in the armed insurrection that turned into the civil war.

The anarchist alliance with the Republic remained strained, to say the least. While a few anarchists became members of the Spanish parliament (the Cortes), many objected to this partnership and most saw the alliance as a temporary necessity to defeat the Nationalists. Mainstream Republicans often perceived them to be in league with POUM (the Workers' Party of Marxist Unification), the more radical and revolutionary Trotskyite communist organization than the arguably conservative Stalinist Communist Party of Spain (PCE). POUM and anarchist militia held the Aragon front defending the Republic's northeastern territory, including the vitally important Catalonia, with the industry and port in Barcelona. The stalemate on that front led many Republicans—especially the PCE—to believe the POUM and anarchist militias to be incompetent, undisciplined, cowardly, self-interested, and even secret allies of the fascists (see 60:3+).

The strain reached a breaking point in early May 1937 in Barcelona, weeks before the action of the novel, with the May Days civil war within the Republic, as the anarchists and revolutionary communists sided against the mainstream communists that by this point had thoroughly integrated themselves into the Republican government and military. The classic account of this civil-war-within-the-civil-war is George Orwell's *Homage to Catalonia*. Orwell, an Englishman, fought in the POUM, not the International Brigades. The anarchists and POUM lost. Reprisals were swift and fierce. The POUM leader, Andrés Nin, was tortured and executed, his organization decimated.

These events would have been fresh on the characters' minds. The anarchists do not fare well in this novel. Hemingway shared the Republican government's distrust of the anarchists. Nevertheless, in his distaste for government and his desire to be left alone, he appreciated the aspirations of anarchy: "I think Anarchy is the noblest religion in the world but it does not work in a war once the war has become formalized" (to José Alemany, 8 Nov. 1940, Outgoing).

120:25 **red-and-black handkerchief:** The colors of the anarchists. See 120:6–8.

123:22 **a dealer in horses:** Pablo worked for a horse contractor in Zaragoza who supplied horses for bull rings (182:25); part of his job was leading "picador horses in the ring" (190:5). There's a prominent ring in Ronda. Don Pepe and Pablo may have had past business dealings.

129:19 **when the fascists took the town:** The historical record bears out Pilar's implication that Nationalists' crimes against humanity surpassed Republicans' (see 99:18–19). "In Baena for example, near Córdoba, the revolutionaries killed 92 people of the Right. The repression after the right-wing recovery of the town accounted for about 700" (Thomas 246). Towns that did not violently rise up against their conservative populations faced repercussions regardless. Nationalist retributions were especially awful in Andalusia. In one of his notorious radio broadcasts, Queipo de Llano commanded fascist troops and sympathizers to "start digging graves. I authorize you to kill like a dog anyone who dares oppose you and I say that if you act in this way, you will be free of all blame" (Preston, *Spanish Civil War* 206; see 81:22).

Pilar promises to tell this story to Jordan but never gets the chance. The novel asserts the story's ability to be told while textually not being able to tell it. Some stories do exceed representation; yet the very acknowledgment of that truth serves as its own form of representation. In "War and Words," Kate McLoughlin defines *adynaton* as a recognition of the impossibility of adequate language for the task that conveys its extreme reality. The "rhetorical trick of communication-by-implication is that absence conjures up presence: a reader informed that a battle is too shocking to be described is likely to envision horrors exceeding anything that straightforward description could invoke" (21–22). It achieves its effect by soliciting the reader's active involvement. Veterans of the International Brigades upset that Hemingway narrated the Republican atrocities but not the Nationalist ones missed the point that the novel judges the latter as far more atrocious, as literally unrepresentable. Pilar does say that it is only "fair" to report the worst of both sides (129:37), and the novel's treatment of Maria's relating her rape story—with its own act of *adynaton* in not recounting the sexual violation—should not be overlooked.

129:38 **But you shall never hear it:** Pilar says she will tell Jordan sometime when Maria is not around, but as she has read Jordan's death in her palm, the line more ominously indicates she'll never tell the story to him, never tell it at all in this novel. The "you" becomes the reader.

130:5 **that the afternoon should come:** Are either Pilar or Maria in this passage thinking about sex? After leaving El Sordo's cave, the first thing Jordan and Maria do when alone together is make love. Then they talk. Maria's impatience for the afternoon to "come flying," and Pilar's repetition of that language, recalls Rafael's expression for sexual climax—"the flight of the big bird"—in describing Pilar's impatience to have Jordan kill Pablo (61:4–5). Maria has come to think of lovemaking as a cleansing, something she might need after hearing Pilar's tale.

NOTES

1. To Martha Gellhorn [February 1937] (Thomas A. Goldwasser Rare Books Catalogue 23, p. 51).
2. To Leicester Hemingway, 3 Aug. 1938 (HRC). On the stories: To Max Perkins, 3 Aug. 1938 (PUL). The stories were "The Denunciation" and "The Butterfly and the Tank."

CHAPTER ELEVEN

131:7 **But with a Christian name:** A Christian name originally meant one's baptismal name (what one was christened as) but has come to mean one's given or first name. Pilar intends something else. *Roberto* is the Spanish, Italian, and Portuguese version of Robert; the name stems from Latin, the language of the Church. It would thus be a "Christian" name rather than an Anglo-Saxon name such as one would expect for an *Inglés*, a name such as Eric, Edward, Harry, or Richard (though Maria addresses Jordan as *Inglés* later in this chapter [138:7]). Less likely: Pilar is saying that Jordan does not use a nom de guerre, as non-Spaniards often did during the war, but his actual name. Finally, Pilar could be contrasting his name with Kashkin's. Because most of Russia's land falls in Asia, Europeans sometimes employed *Oriental* or *Asian* as a synonym for *Russian* (as Muriel Rukeyser does in her contemporaneous Spanish Civil War novel, *The Savage Coast*). In this case, Pilar's "Christian" would mean "not Russian" (*Ruso*)—Spaniards often assumed internationals working for the Republic were Russian (see 45:15).

132:15 **By any names they are as bad:** Another instance of the novel's inquiry into language, in this case by a straightforward allusion to Shakespeare's Juliet's famous rejection of her lover Romeo's family name because of their families' bitter rivalry: "What's in a name? that which we call a rose / By any other name would smell as sweet" (II.ii.890–91). Hardly an instant later, however, Joaquín asserts that sometimes what one calls a thing does in fact matter. Using "terms" that are "more military" improves clarity and order (132:21–22).

132:18 **chief:** In Spanish, *jefe*. Joaquín's or the novel's distaste for the word might be political: Less than eight months earlier, in October 1936 in nearby Burgos, Francisco Franco officially became General of the Nationalist military as well as the Nationalists' Jefe del Estado—Head of State (Franco later adopted the title El Caudillo, the Supreme Leader). See 132:15.

133:31+ **Why did you fail at it?:** Pilar has recognized in Joaquín the build and gait of a bullfighter as well as the beginnings of a new coleta, what she calls a **pigtail**, the braided tress of hair traditionally worn by bullfighters. Joaquín's coleta indicates his rural upbringing. By this point in the sport's history, professional and urban matadors used fake coletas to secure their hats. Only hopeful country youth wore what had long been the pride of all matadors (*DIA* 397). Two Hemingway stories feature the cutting of the coleta, "Chapter IX" from *In Our Time* and "The Undefeated" from *Men without Women* (on the coleta's relationship with masculinity and its cutting with emasculation, see 8:4).

134:33+ If that woman could only write. . . . God, how she could tell a story: Hemingway has, of course, just admired his own writing prowess. Pilar's speaking talent reinforces her connection to Ibárruri, La Pasionaria. The draft includes several lines that do not appear in the galleys, having been replaced by the single line, "Pilar had made him see it in that town" (134:32). Continuing from "you saw the bodies":

> . . . but no Goya had yet made the pictures.
>
> Pilar had made him see what the things were that we had done. No Goya could make that any better. He must make her tell him, before this business was over, about what happened when the fascists came. I have to have that too, he thought. He had the other now forever. (*HLE* 498)

And straight into, "If that woman could only write."

In his *Men at War* introduction, Hemingway praises this quality of Stendhal's writing: "Once you have read it you will have been at the battle of Waterloo and nothing can ever take that experience from you" (xx). Jordan in the novel's draft cites the same Stendhal novel, *The Charterhouse of Parma* (*HLE* 497). Here is *The Garden of Eden*'s David Bourne on his own writing: "It was not him, but as he wrote it was and when someone read it, finally, it would be whoever read it and what they found when they should reach the escarpment, if they reached it, and he would make them reach its base by noon of that day; then whoever read it would find what there was there and have it forever" (*GOE* 129). Both novels collapse and merge identities, from the characters in the fiction's told story, to the fictional storyteller, to the fictional audience, to Hemingway, to Hemingway's reader. Jordan, Hemingway, and Hemingway's reader became Pilar the storyteller and Pilar the character in her told story. The preceding paragraph's use of second-person, about what "you" did or did not see and hear, enacts this merging. As Webb writes about effective ekphrasis, "the poet's mental image, to which the reader has access through the text, is itself a representation of the character's mental image. This chain of images ultimately allows the reader or listener to share in the experience of the character and to admire the skill of the poet" (97).

Francisco Goya, *No se puede mirar / Can't look.* Plate 26 from *The Disasters of War* (1810; published 1863). (WikiMedia Commons / Public Domain)

The excised allusion to the Spanish painter and engraver Francisco José de Goya y Lucientes would have been the only one in the novel. Hemingway might have removed it to avoid the comparison, perhaps to sidestep the question of influence, as one can easily imagine his being directly inspired by Goya's work in writing Pilar's tale. Allen Josephs's study of Hemingway's novel *The Undiscovered Country* uses for its cover art Goya's 1814 painting *The 3rd of May 1808 in Madrid, or "The Executions."* Hemingway cites Goya's *Los desastros de la guerra* (Disasters of War) on the third page of *Death in the Afternoon*. The titles of the individual images from the *Disasters of War* lithograph series (1810–1820), along with the images themselves, pointedly suggest the mood of Pilar's tale-telling. One atrocity scene is called *Fuerte cosa es / This is too much*. Especially provocative is how Goya extends the scene to include the viewer in the imagined space, as with the rifles poking into the frame in *No se puede mirar / Can't look*.

Goya is also one of Spain's great painters and illustrators of the bullfight. Hemingway knew the Prado's extensive Goya collection. Preserving the Goya reference, with its implicit comparison between the visual and the narrative arts, the rivalry and conundrum at the heart of ekphrasis, would have distracted from the section's real comparison, the contrast between printed and oral storytelling, the latter grounded in embodied knowledge and the occasion of the telling (time, place, people, conditions), with no pretense to art, only faithful conveyance (see Broadwell-Gulde). Pilar made him see that horrible day "in that story she had told by the stream" (134:24–25)—he doesn't separate the story from the stream. Jordan's envy of Pilar's talent partakes of the romanticized vision of the Spaniards, of these Spaniards anyway, as more of the earth (less civilized) and therefore more genuine. Works such as Walter Ong's *Orality and Literacy* and David Abrams's *The Spell of the Sensuous* contend that the cultural turn from orality to literacy corresponds to and exacerbates the inward turn to isolated, self-conscious interiority. The novel presents Jordan's first long-winded interior monologue just when it raises awareness of the orality and literacy difference. The fact (not just the content) of his internal windiness troubles him. The passage's pronouns manifest the complexity of the turn. The *you* is at once Jordan talking to himself, inventing an audience within himself, the narrator talking to the reader, and the reader literally saying "you" to . . . Jordan? *You, he,* and *I* become uncertainly interchangeable—later he'll have a conversation between "himself" and "him" (304:21). In contrast, when Pilar silently recalls, the text sticks firmly, unjarringly to third-person (182–84). Of course he envies her integral self; she will never suffer the internal splitting he calls "schizophrenic" (394:4). (Andrés's monologue uses first- and second-person, but the text frames them with a third-person *he thought* [e.g., 367:36–37].) The novel's always calling Jordan "Robert Jordan," by first and last name, as it slips between the narrator's and Jordan's perspectives, contributes to the dizzying effect of his too-insistent (desperate?) self-articulation.

Jordan's monologues aren't diary entries, his pronouns aren't committed to the page, but they exhibit the problem of the diarist who, in speaking to the self, careens haphazardly among selves. As Ong writes, the diary form implies that its content's "verbalized solipsistic reveries . . . are a product of consciousness as shaped by print culture." For Ong, the perplexities a diarist faces about addresser and addressee can "lead to discontinuation of diaries" as the anxiety-ridden "diarist can no longer live with his or her fiction" (101). Fast-forward to the end of the novel?

134:36 **Quevedo:** See 11:16. Hemingway lets Quevedo stand for all literary representation. Originally, Hemingway had drafted a complicated passage beginning "Nothing you ever read was very like it really was," followed by qualifications. First, the excised passage moves from representing anything to representing battle, noting that only the rare writer and book wrote battle well and got it right. It cites Tolstoy and Stendhal. Then it differentiates between battle and revolution: "But never had he read how revolution really was; both sides of how it truly looked." Finally, the draft pairs Quevedo with Cervantes in comparing their "invention[s]" to Pilar's powerful story (*HLE* 497; MS11-001). Such twisting reflections would have pulled the reader away from the primary comparison between orality and literacy (see prior entry); they were half-baked ideas that belonged more to Hemingway than Jordan; and they risked breaking the reading spell by turning attention to Hemingway's well-known war writing and his own position, as the actual author and inventor of Pilar's tale, in these comparisons.

134:37–38 **I wish I could write well enough to write that story:** As with Pablo, Jordan now finds himself put in his place by Pilar's rhetorical forcefulness. Jordan resigns himself to being the lesser storyteller to Pilar, and his conversations with Kashkin show his awareness of his limited literary talents (248:15+). Besides his talent, part of the trouble is the difference between oral and written storytelling. Also, if "[u]ntranslatability becomes a sign of authenticity" (Rogers, *Incomparable* 138), Jordan's inability to translate Pilar's tale—from speech to print, from Spanish to English, from Spain to America—evidences his insurmountable foreignness. He can't write what he hasn't lived.

134:38 **What we did:** The first-person plural pronouns shift meanings throughout the next few paragraphs, sometimes meaning all those who fight for the Republic, Spanish or otherwise, and sometimes *partizans,* or guerrilla fighters (Spanish or otherwise) not native to the area where they operate. When Jordan laments about what "we did to them" (135:14), by "them" he means the local villagers, the peasants, the Spanish people. The language continues the passage's confusion about belonging, familiarity, and responsibility.

135:24–25 **only really loyal to his village:** This was true enough before the political divisions of the early 1930s; for John Dos Passos, village-centric Spain helped explain the appeal of anarchy to Spaniards (see 120:6–8). The civil war set neighbors against neighbors.

135:30+ **He never felt like a foreigner:** The passage resists resolving the question of Jordan's feelings of foreignness, with waffling language—"did not really" and "most of the time"—and the final turn that they betrayed one another too, so betrayal alone does not a foreigner make.

135:38+ **who censored his thinking?:** As a civil war based on ideological rifts, with trust a precious commodity, political parties vying for control, and fears of enemy agents operating among the loyal, demonstrating one's correct thinking could be a matter of life and death. A simple disagreement could lead to accusations of fascism. People disappeared. Hemingway's journalism underwent routine censorship—his sources were constrained in speech, and his dispatches had to be approved by government officials before being sent out (a fact one of his dispatches tells its readers; in Watson 34). For radiograms, an interpreter sat beside foreign correspondents to ensure they did not depart from the approved copy. When a teenager from Cleveland published a limited-edition book of Hemingway's narration for *The Spanish Earth* with an anarchist banner on the inside back cover—after the Barcelona May Days of 1937—Hemingway fired off an incensed telegram demanding its removal from future printings, as he feared for his life on his return to Republican Spain. In a letter to a Catalonian, Hemingway claimed that a Republican military commander, Cipriano Mera, wanted him shot (to José Alemany, 8 Nov. 1940, Outgoing).

Hemingway's wartime nonfiction was sometimes criticized for its Republican bias, amounting at times to propaganda. A communist dupe, the critics accused. Whether willing or unaware was beside the point. Accordingly, some scholars regard this passage as an autobiographical, supratextual retort that he hadn't been a dupe and was collecting plenty of truths to write about after the war, in this very novel, in admitting "[w]hat we did. Not what the others did to us" (134:38). The argument that passages such as this one function as revisionist autobiography, that he had been naïve his first months at the war in 1937, too much under the spell of people like the Russian Mikhail Koltsov (231:20+), have some merit. Yet if his wartime writing had violated the trust of Republican authorities, he wouldn't have been allowed to stay in Spain to continue bearing witness. One should also consider his correspondence the month before he traveled, which condemns both sides for their wrongheadedness—he knew Republican sympathizers were murdering priests—and reveals his distrust of Soviet leadership (to Harry Sylvester, 5 Feb. 1937, *SL* 456; to Paul and Mary Pfeiffer, 9 Feb. 1937, *SL* 458).[1] His journalism was also baldly first-person and did not differ from much US reportage of the Second World War (see Vernon, *Second War*, ch. 2).

136:21 a Belgian boy in the Eleventh Brigade: The XI International Brigade, which included the Franco-Belgian battalion, was commanded by **Hans Kahle** (see 233:34+).

137:16+ Garbo still, and Harlow: Greta Garbo and Jean Harlow, two cinema stars of the day. The Swedish-born Garbo, the better actor, imprinted more deeply in his imagination. She receives first mention, the word "still" suggesting a persistent affection, and he revisits a specific fantasy of Garbo, whom "he loved . . . much more than Harlow" (137:26). Later, Maria recognizes that the hair length he wishes for her would match Garbo's; Maria's intoning of the name "Garbo," in reference to herself as Jordan's lover, causes his throat to swell (346:5–8). The "Garbo still" might refer to Jean Harlow's death in 1937. This would have been a slight anachronism, since Harlow died on 7 June, a week after Jordan. Or it might refer (also mildly anachronistically) to the fact that Garbo's 1937 film *Conquest* was a critical and commercial flop. On 3 May 1938, Harold Brandt published "Wake Up! Hollywood Producers," an article in *Hollywood Reporter* grouping her with other women stars who now ranked as "poison" for the box office. In a draft version of one of Hemingway's Spanish Civil War short stories, "The Butterfly and the Tank," the narrator makes a joking allusion to Garbo, prompting his Spanish interlocutor to say, "A very beautiful woman . . . But past her best epoch" (*SS-HLE* 537). Jordan's love of an actor in an apparently irrecoverable slump reflects his love of the failing Republic.

The Swedish actor Ingrid Bergman played Maria in the 1943 film adaptation of the novel—so a Swedish actor plays the Spanish beloved whom her lover's fantasies conflate with a Swedish actor. David Archibald claims that by casting Bergman, the film "allows Maria to fulfill the role of exotic European other" (39). Jordan's preference for Garbo over the Kansas City-raised Harlow underscores his attraction to Maria as an exotic European other. The person Paramount first named to play Maria, the actor and ballerina Vera Zorina (Haver 13), born Eva Brigitta Hartwig, had a German father and a Norwegian mother. The film conveniently dodged the potentially racial complications a Spanish lover risked, tucking the miscegenation fantasy safely away.

The mention of **Jack Gilbert** (137:25), Garbo's periodic lover on- and off-screen, probably points to a specific Garbo film. Gilbert did not appear in *The Painted Veil*, the 1934 Garbo film in Madrid theaters in spring 1937.[2] He was her love interest, however, in *Queen Christina*. Released in 1933 in the United States, the film was widely publicized for reuniting her with Gilbert as the love interest. Garbo plays Queen Christina of Sweden and Gilbert plays Antonio, the Spanish envoy with whom she falls in love. They become lovers the night of their first meeting, snowbound in an inn for three days. The camera follows her as she moves about their room, touching and studying various objects. "In the future, in my memory," she tells Antonio. "I shall live a great deal in this room," as if she lived the whole of her life in and for those three days. Because this Protestant queen cannot marry a Catholic Spaniard (Europe at the time was embroiled in the Thirty Years' War between Protestant and Catholic countries), Christina abdicates the throne to marry Antonio. Before they can rendezvous, he is killed in a duel. The last scene takes place aboard ship as she travels with his body back to Spain, where he will be interred and she will live out her days—the film ends not unlike Hemingway's novel. Like Jordan, Christina must choose between self-sacrificing public duty and a domestic life sprung from love. But she makes the opposite choice; her deliberate memorization of the brief affair feels like the more measured response in comparison with Jordan's effort to fix his moment of love to eternity.

Jordan plausibly saw the film in Spain (if not in the United States). *Queen Christina* played in Republican-held Madrid at the Panorama Theater until the first days of August 1936,[3] right after the rebellion. Jordan was in Spain prior to the rebellion. As the revolutionary spirit took deeper hold, no film with the word "queen" in the title would have been welcome. The problem was compounded by the historic queen's wartime support for the Catholics and her conversion to Catholicism. The real Christina relinquished Sweden and moved to Rome, a spiritual commitment the film fictionalizes with the engagement to a Catholic Spaniard.

Two aspects of *Queen Christina* sharply reflect *For Whom the Bell Tolls*. First is the man's death. Antonio's fate is compounded by the film's being Gilbert's last

Greta Garbo and Jack Gilbert in *Queen Christina* (1933). (Author's collection)

with Garbo as well as the penultimate film of his life—Gilbert died in January 1936, another portent of Jordan's fate, in connection with his love fantasy. The allusion to Garbo in "The Butterfly and the Tank" draft involves three dead Republican soldiers in front of their disabled tank. The narrator jokes that a cartoon of the scene could carry the caption, "They tank they go home now," a riff on a line popularly attributed to Garbo (and her Swedish accent), *I tank* [or *tink*] *I'll go home now,* said to a producer or director before walking off a set (*SS-HLE* 537). Witnesses to the bombardment of Madrid reported that the Nationalists often timed their artillery to fall when the cinema let out and people clustered together in the open street. Plenty of Garbo pictures made wartime Madrid movie houses, where they drew sizeable audiences: *The Painted Veil* (1934), *Anna Karenina* (1935), *Camille* (1936), and three of her films from the early thirties revived in the last two years of the war, *Mata Hari* in 1938 and *Grand Hotel* and *As You Desire Me* in 1939. In this light, Jordan's "still" can be read as saying that he loves her despite the risk.

Second, *Queen Christina* foregrounds ambiguities of gender and sexuality after the fashion of a Shakespearean comedy, ambiguities central to certain readings of *For Whom the Bell Tolls*. When Christina takes the throne to be the new monarch as a child, the audience learns that her father raised her as a tomboy, and the assembly proclaims her their liege by shouting, "Long live the king!" She next appears as a young woman wearing a man's hunting kit, who in short order enthusiastically kisses a young countess on the lips before riding into the wooded mountains. Thusly cross-dressed she meets Antonio, they begin their flirtation, and they are asked—as two presumed noble*men*—to share a room in the small inn. Antonio's obvious attraction to her precedes her revelation to him that she's a woman; before they share a bed, a woman inn worker invites the masculine-clad queen into her bed, in a room

Sébastien Bourdon, *Christina of Sweden on Horseback* (1663–1664). (© Photographic Archive Museo Nacional del Prado)

down the hall. One morning of Christina and Antonio's stay together at the inn, one of his men enters the chamber to ask after his lord. From the curtained bed he occupies with Christina, Antonio replies that he plans to spend the day there. As his facial expression indicates, the man believes Antonio wants to stay in bed with another nobleman.

Beyond the frame, the film capitalized on the public curiosity about the sexuality of the Swedish queen and the Swedish actor. The young countess whom Garbo's Christina kisses is based on one of the androgynous (and possibly intersex) real queen's closest companions and potential romantic interests, Countess Ebba Sparre. Descriptions of Queen Christina by contemporaries likened her in dress, body shape, demeanor, interests, and deep voice to a man—something of a Gertrude Stein or Pilar figure. Hemingway was familiar with just such an image of her, Sébastien Bourdon's 1663–1664 hunting portrait *Christina of Sweden on Horseback*, housed at the Museo Nacional del Prado in Madrid.[4]

The bisexual Greta Garbo cultivated an androgynous image, often sporting men's fashions, whether in trousers, tie, vest, blazer, or trench coat. Contemporary publicity and commentary on the film noted the similarity between Garbo and Queen Christina. According to one review, Garbo "might easily be the reincarnation of Christina," whose eyes like Garbo's "might have belonged to either sex" (Dale 28–29); another observed that "Garbo is Queen Christina's counterpart to an astonishing degree," that the two have a very "close character resemblance" (Rankin 35). *Picture Play* attributed Garbo's superb performance to her "spiritual belief in the part," to her "acting com[ing] from within herself," her "characterization not a disguise that she slips on like a garment" (Lusk 40). Another American war correspondent in Spain, Virginia Cowles, writes in her memoir about Kaja von Rothman, "a Swedish girl who dressed in men's clothes and wore her hair in a Greta Garbo bob" who worked during the war as a nurse and then "as a semi-official interpreter for the foreign journalists" (32). In 1934, Irving Thalberg entertained the idea of a screen adaptation of *The Sun Also Rises* with Garbo playing the short-haired Lady Brett Ashley (Leff 195).

Jordan harbors a truer connection to Garbo rather than Harlow, to the gender-bending foreigner rather than the conventional blonde bombshell starlet from the American Midwest. That he dreams more often of Harlow speaks to the cultural construction of attraction—he turned to her because he was supposed to, despite his deeper desires. For Sontag, "the haunting androgynous vacancy behind the perfect beauty of Greta Garbo" personifies the aesthetic of camp, and "[a]llied to the Camp taste for the androgynous is something that seems quite different but isn't: a relish for the exaggeration of sexual characteristics and personality mannerisms" (279). Allied to Jordan's relish for Garbo is his taste for Harlow. Maria is at once androgynously vacant and the epitome of conventional femininity.

One of Garbo's rumored lovers was the actor Marlene Dietrich, who wore men's clothes even more brashly, whose screen persona openly flirted with queerness, and with whom Hemingway developed an enduring friendship. In spring 1938, Hemingway described his typical dreams (and possibly daydreams) as involving big-game hunting, up-close urban warfare in Madrid, and—in language nearly identical to Jordan's—"lovely experiences with Miss Dietrich, Miss Garbo, and others in dreams too, they always being awfully nice (in dreams)" (to Eugene Jolas [ca. late Mar 1938], *SL* 465).

One can only speculate why Hemingway chose Garbo over Dietrich for Jordan's sexual psyche. A native German whom Hemingway would affectionately call the Kraut and *Vanity Fair* labeled "the Teuton siren"[5] a month before he met her in 1934,

Dietrich might have vexed Jordan and an anti-Nazi readership. Because Hemingway had never met Garbo, Dietrich already represented less of a fantasy. And in her forthrightness, Dietrich could not have embodied the subtle possibility of gender transgression, the mystery and intimation, of Garbo and Maria. In the 1930 film *Morocco,* Dietrich played a cabaret singer who, while dressed in a tuxedo and top hat, kisses a woman audience member full on the lips, then tosses the flower from the woman's hair to the soldier who will soon enough become her love interest—played by Gary Cooper, who will soon enough play Robert Jordan.

Closer in release date and in setting to Hemingway's novel was the 1935 film *The Devil Is a Woman* featuring Dietrich as a Spanish femme fatale. Based on a draft screenplay by Hemingway's prewar friend John Dos Passos, the film mocked male romantic passion as ridiculous and self-destructive. Jordan could hardly associate by fantasy this Spanish woman with his beloved Maria; it would have seriously undermined Jordan's love and the entire romance even as it hinted at a truth about him: "If you really loved me," Dietrich's Spaniard taunts one of her male suitors, "you would have killed yourself."

137:19 **the attack at Pozoblanco:** See 238:35.

137:25 **Jack Gilbert:** The actor John Gilbert. See 137:16+. In the 1920s, Gilbert rivaled Rudolph Valentino as the great on-screen male lover. He starred with Greta Garbo in three other films: *Flesh and the Devil* (1926), *Love* (1927), and *A Woman of Affairs* (1928). He was also the first actor cast to play Frederic Henry in *A Farewell to Arms* (Leff 168), replaced by Gary Cooper.

137:34 *corrales* **and the** *cortijos:* Pens and farmhouses.

138:13–14 **limestone . . . full of caves:** See 18:9.

138:22–23 **the first time she had ever voted:** Joaquín's mother voted Socialist, presumably in the February 1936 election that restored the left to governmental power and resulted in the right's July military rebellion. She could vote only because the first government of the Second Spanish Republic granted women suffrage for the first time in history. That she voted Socialist perhaps reflects the fact that the civil strife pitting left versus right forced people to choose sides. In this war and countless other hostilities, conflict drove partisanship rather than the other way around. This entire paragraph underscores the complexity of the war's politics, of any civil war's: "almost every macrohistorical account of civil war points to the importance of preexisting popular allegiances for the war's outcome, yet almost every microhistorical account points to a host of endogenous mechanisms, whereby allegiances and identities tend to result from the war or are radically transformed by it" (Kalyvas 3).

Joaquín's brother-in-law, who was "without politics," joined a syndicate for a job, and was shot for it. In Spain, one's "side," the side one fought for, often had nothing to do with ideological identification. A few reasons: geographical or family circumstances, economic need, coercion, or response to a local cruelty.

140:26 **economically. It gives employment:** See 184:29+

141:12 **like an Indian's:** See 40:15+.

141:28+ ***Inglés? . . . Not Ruso?:*** English, not Russian? See 45:15. Jordan's accent and his hankering for Scotch whiskey (not vodka) leads El Sordo to this conclusion (142:35). El Sordo considers English and American the same because of their shared language (see 135:21+) and due to the United States' and the United Kingdom's shared nonintervention in the war, versus Russia's active role on behalf of the Republic.

142:10 **pinch bottle:** Usually used for whiskey, a pinch bottle has indentations on the sides for ease of gripping.

142:22-23 **the deaf man:** El Sordo translates as the Deaf One. His real name is Santiago (149:7).

143:21-22 **Villacastín . . . San Rafael:** Villacastín is halfway between Segovia and Ávila to its southwest—the road parallels the Guadarrama. Southeast of Villacastín sits San Rafael, a small village at the base of the Guadarrama Pass—the Alto del León (82:1), the major route through the mountains to Madrid.

144:16 **Don't trouble:** Because most if not all of these Spaniards are illiterate. The chapter continues the thread of orality and literacy it started with Jordan's reflections on Pilar's tale (134:23+) and revisits at its close with a reference to an adage that becomes at once about military orders and literary representation (152:28). Written military instructions also risk falling into enemy hands; the Nationalists could use them as evidence against the guerillas afterward.

145:3 **With pans:** Another Lewis gun. See 27:11 and 320:33.

146:8 ***Dentro de la gravedad:*** The text (Jordan?) translates this as "[w]ithin the limits of the danger." A more literal and perhaps better translation might be "given the gravity of the situation."

146:15 **Worse every day:** The draft included additional characterizations along these lines, of Rafael as "worth little" and Fernando as "stupid" but "honorable" and "stubborn," a "good thing in fight." Fernando does not suffer from the imaginative intelligence that makes most writers bad soldiers. Jordan tells El Sordo he only likes a fight "when it's over." El Sordo does like a fight (MS11-002).

147:19 Sierra de Paramera: The smaller chain constituting the northern edge of the Gredos Mountains touching Ávila.

147:34 There was no friendliness: In the draft, this line replaces "He seemed angry at Jordan taking a part in this discussion" (MS11-002). Jordan soon realizes his mistake in presuming to give advice (148:26+). He compounds the presumption with a language error, calling the mountains "the Gredos" (147:31–32) instead of simply "Gredos" as Spaniards do—this error immediately precedes and may have sparked El Sordo's "What?" (147:33). In his list of galley proof corrections sent to his editor, Hemingway insisted on the error, on the gap between Jordan's high opinion of his Spanish expertise and his actual level of familiarity (to Maxwell Perkins, 26 Aug. 1940, *SL* 516).

148:9–10 Barco de Avila: Not Ávila, Anselmo's home village, on the northern side of the Gredos Mountains (see 3:2). **Béjar** and **Plasencia** are southwest of Ávila, on the edge of the Gredos and the Central Range; the valley between them is the major western route between northern and southern Spain. Since the Nationalists did not control the Guadarrama Pass, this was their primary secure line of communications, supply, and troop transport. As he did with Pablo's horses, Jordan wants to prove himself to El Sordo as someone who knows Spain and who knows irregular warfare. It backfires (148:26+).

148:15 *guerrilleros*: Hemingway justified his use of this term, along with the term *partisan* used by all the Russians (and everyone who worked with them), because *guerrillero* sounded more "archaic" than *guerillas* and to Hemingway like the word *toreador* (bullfighter).[6]

148:25 You see what I mean?: Pilar appears to mean that Kashkin and Jordan are similar, continuing her earlier thoughts on this subject. Her reference to Kashkin's being dead, in addressing Jordan, feels ominous given her reading of his palm and her reading of the military situation.

149:6–7 in a very rare and windy way: Jordan earlier catches himself being full of worry and too "windy" (43:33). The echo in Pilar's characterization of Kashkin reinforces Jordan's resemblance to his predecessor. The resemblance to Kashkin spells trouble for Jordan's own fate, as reinforced by Jordan's hunch that Kashkin "had a hunch" (171:15–16). To Pablo, this resemblance must have felt somewhat like Jordan's metaphor of the ever-turning merry-go-round of situations challenging him to kill Pablo (225:1+; 226:24); both Jordan and Pablo want off of their differently dangerous merry-go-rounds.

149:7 **Santiago:** The Spanish name for Saint James, the country's patron Saint and a common Spanish given name. Hemingway will use this name for the protagonist of *The Old Man and the Sea,* another man who nobly fights a doomed fight. Interestingly, Pilar thinks to use this martyr's name in this conversation about Kashkin's fate, with its implications for Jordan's.

149:9–12 *Algo raro . . . pero bueno:* Something strange (rare), something else . . . but good.

149:17 **I shot him:** Earlier Jordan claimed Kashkin had killed himself, having been wounded and captured (21:1+). Now he admits to killing Kashkin, whom he resembles (45:15). At the end of the novel Jordan finds himself, like Kashkin, too injured to travel, and holding Kashkin's gun—in his differing reports on Kashkin, he has already blurred the line between committing a militarily necessary suicide and being killed. Jordan admits that he shot Kashkin to El Sordo and Pilar; Pilar later tells Pablo's band (249:23).

149:21–22 **He was always talking of such a necessity and it was his obsession:** Jordan's repetition of Pilar's characterization of Kashkin underscores the similarities between the two men. Jordan does not obsess about killing himself to avoid capture, as Kashkin did, but he does obsess about his father's suicide and the potential lurking within himself, he fixates on the idea of these few days with Maria being his final ones in this life, and he worries about the increasingly dangerous and seemingly inevitable bridge-blowing mission.

149:31 **Are you sure your nerves are all right?:** Perhaps Pilar, with her Romani intuition, senses the resemblance between Jordan's and Kashkin's windy worrying (149:6–7).

149:35–37 **go to the Gredos. . . . a flood of obscene invective:** Jordan teases Pilar. Having realized he insulted El Sordo and Pilar in advising them on where to go and what to do after the bridge, he owns up to the mistake and saves face by kiddingly doubling down, provoking Pilar's amusing torrent. This move earns him the respect of El Sordo (150:2–3), who stops with the pidgin Spanish he uses for foreigners he doesn't yet trust (151:2).

150:16–17 **do not shut the door on others who are not foreigners:** Pilar intuitively responds to Jordan's earlier internal reflection on his in-and-out operations, where after his departure his Spanish peasant abettors "stayed and took the punishment" (135:12–13). Hence the hostility in her voice and in her and El Sordo's initial reaction to Jordan's suggestions for their lives after the bridge. Pilar uses the word "Republic" in two different ways. By telling Jordan to get back to the Republic, she means Republican territory—the government, the politics, the hotels, the bourgeois vestiges—where she wants to go but never can. The Republic she and others have loved since his babyhood is also their idealized democratic vision for Spain.

151:30 **I would be shot for it:** This is one of the most important and neglected lines of the novel. However else readers evaluate Jordan for carrying out an ill-advised mission, he believes he faces execution if an officer or commissar were to perceive him as having shirked his duty or as giving them a reason to scapegoat him. After the historic Segovia Offensive, General Walter—the novel's Golz—ordered the immediate, on-the-battlefield slaughter of any of his soldiers who gave up ground (Beevor 277; Tremlett 314–15). Hemingway knew about Walter's humiliation and murderous order because everyone in touch with Republican military leadership did. If from no one else, he would have learned about it from his friend Gustavo Durán, one of Walter's subordinate officers during the offensive. Hemingway wrote about how "in that La Granja attack . . . Walter shot so many damned people," in an April 1940 letter to the poet and Lincoln Brigade veteran Edwin Rolfe.[7] A captain in the XIV Brigade shot five random men in the back of the head (Beevor 276).

The mission briefing Jordan receives from Golz takes place at El Escorial, that anticipatory edifice to death; the corporal in Golz's division who carried out executions for the International Brigades' top political commissar, André Marty, names El Escorial as the site for "I don't know how many" such killings (419:2). The novel plainly reviews such executions carried out by order of Marty (418:32+). Five months earlier, in late December 1937 on the Córdoba front, Marty blamed Major Gaston Delasalle for a failed operation and, without evidence, had him summarily executed for cowardice and spying. Jordan fought near Córdoba at Pozoblanco in early spring (137:19). The well-connected Jordan would have been aware of the French major's death. Delasalle fought under Walter (Golz), and Marty arrested him at Walter's headquarters (Thomas 477). Disciplinary killings and assassinations for military expediency were open knowledge. Jordan "had approved and understood" the executions of "cowards" at Guadarrama (235:34+); still considers killing Pablo; discusses the elimination of "treacherous dogs" with Karkov (245:10+); in excised material, offers to kill an American journalist (239:25+); and makes no objection to Pablo's plan to kill several guerrilla comrades during the bridge mission, to get their horses for his people's escape. One wonders if Jordan's tolerance for murder stems from his desire to become Spanish, a people to whom he attributes a "complete . . . lack of respect for life" (234:23), for whom killing is "their extra sacrament" (286:34).

For corroborating moments during which execution is on Jordan's mind, see 6:16+ and 335:11. Executions of one's own form the basis of Hemingway's play *The Fifth Column* and the story "Under the Ridge." His *Men at War* anthology cites the same execution of a French company commander mentioned in "Under the Ridge" (xix). Jordan's direct statement about being shot by comrades occurs shortly after he directly states that he shot his comrade Kashkin (149:17).

152:28 **Paper bleeds little:** The immediate context is the difference between military plans and the human lives that suffer to carry them out. The proverb becomes metacommentary by Hemingway on the failure of literary representation to inhabit human emotion and physical pain, a brilliant way to end a printed chapter that began with Jordan's aesthetic regret that he could never *write* a story that would make his readers *see* the war (134:23+). It's the insurmountable aesthetic truth that enables representations to become mere war porn.

Jordan can't write it, but Hemingway can, and did. Jordan's saying he can't write it is another instance of adynaton, a way of expressing a thing by acknowledging its inexpressibility. The film director and Second World War veteran Sam Fuller said this on the subject:

> See, there's no way you can portray war realistically, not in a movie nor in a book. You can only capture a very, very small aspect of it. If you really want to make readers understand battle, a few pages of your book would be booby-trapped. For moviegoers to get the idea of real combat, you'd have to shoot at them every so often from either side of the screen. The casualties in the theater would be bad for business. Such reaching for reality in the name of art is against the law. (123)

Pilar's tale marries her oral telling with Hemingway's written telling, integrating (perhaps speciously) the primitively genuine and the artificial, perhaps the Romance and the Real.

152:36 ***Ya irás, mujer:*** You go now. Go, woman.

NOTES

1. The recipients were Catholic; and Paul and Mary, his in-laws.
2. E.g., "Cartelera madrileña: cinematógrafos," *ABC Madrid* (1 Apr. 1937), 16.
3. "Cartelera madrileña: cinematógrafos," *ABC Madrid* (30 Jul. 1936), 36; and 2 Aug. 1936, 33.

4. The painting occupied a prominent position in the Goya rotunda from at least 1907 through 1915 (see Prado Museum, "View of the High Roundabout of Goya. 1907–1915," José Lacoste Y Borde, photographer; Juana Roig Villalonga, editor). It appears in the museum's 1920 catalog, the same year that the French painting room was established on the first floor, in the same entrance hall gallery (xlix) where Bourdon's painting is listed as being displayed in the 1933 catalog. It is safe to conclude that the museum consistently featured the painting during this period such that Hemingway would have encountered it on his visits.

5. *Vanity Fair* (Mar. 1934), 44. This is the same issue with the caricature paper-doll cutout Hemingway (29).

6. To Gustavo Durán [ca. 20–27 Aug. 1940] (Residencia).

7. To Edwin Rolfe [April 1940] (UIL).

CHAPTER TWELVE

153:24 **late May:** In the draft, Hemingway originally inserted "June" before "afternoon" in pencil, then at some later point replaced "June" with "late May" in red ink (MS11-002). The red ink change occurred sometime after he sent the draft to Jane Armstrong to prepare the full typescript ("June") but before the publisher created the galley proofs ("late May").

Throughout the draft, Hemingway set the novel in June. Unlike this instance, Hemingway made most of the changes by hand to the galley proofs. In chapter 13, "In June?" becomes "Now? Almost in June?" (177:1); in chapter 14, "Now in June" becomes "Now in this month" (181:11); and twice in chapter 15, "June" had to become "almost in June" (194:24) and "coming on June" (195:8)—all at the galley proof stage. In addition to this instance in chapter 12, two other changes happened between the Armstrong typescript and the galley proofs: The first line of chapter 24, which takes place the following calendar day, changed from "June" to "late May" (288:1); and in chapter 37, "June" again becomes "this month" (381:21). In the draft for the novel's last chapter, Hemingway changes "June" to "end of May" by hand (434:9) but does not change "lovely June day" to "lovely late May morning" later in the same paragraph (434:18)—a discrepancy that Armstrong faithfully typed (there are no surviving galley proofs for the last two published chapters).

The revisions suggest that Hemingway made the change fairly late in the composition process. The original June dating could reflect an honest misremembering or confusion about the dates of the Segovia Offensive. He knew it took place sometime in June, so he used June for the novel—and only on realizing the Segovia Offensive began on 31 May did he go back and correct his months. Conversations in the late spring and early summer of 1940 with Gustavo Durán, who participated in the military operation, might have led to the realization. Hemingway might have initially and knowingly used the wrong month to separate his fictional events and people from real events and real people, only to change his mind.

The late change from June to May helps with—but does not completely solve—the problem of Maria's being free for three months since early April (23:17+) when it is still May. Hemingway forgot to adjust that page. The most interesting ramification of the change upsets the conversation between the Nationalist sentries in chapter

15. In the draft, the dialogue begins and ends "in June"—published as "almost June" (194:23–24) and "coming on June" (195:8)—with everything in between referencing May in the draft as well as the published novel. The draft better captures the difference between the Roman calendar and the lunar calendar, where "May" refers to the period after the May full moon, which in 1937 happened on 25 May. The divergence between the solar and lunar calendar months envisioned in the draft—between urban Spaniards, who think in solar calendar terms, versus rural and coastal Spaniards, who think in lunar calendar terms—is less clear in the published novel.

154:21 **Maria moved close to her:** "and laid her head across the woman's big thighs" is crossed out in the draft (*HLE* 498).

154:30 **Do not talk like that:** In the draft, the sentence continues with this crossed-out clause: "and stroked her head across the big woman's thighs, then patted her where her hands lay" (*HLE* 499). The deleted movement echoes an earlier moment when Maria "stroked" her head under Jordan's hand "like a kitten" (68:30).

154:33 **Do not talk thus:** In the draft, the sentence replaces: "I love thee and thou hast no cause to be jealous" (corrected from *HLE* 499).

155:1 **But with me there is not. Truly there is not:** In the draft, these sentences replace the following: "and for me to find it now in me. But you understand" (*HLE* 499). Although throughout this scene Hemingway revised Pilar's dialogue to insist upon her heterosexuality, the draft's ambiguity about her sexuality lingers, in Pilar's caresses, her jealousy, and her "wish" to "take" Maria "the rabbit" from Jordan (156:11+).

Many scholars have read Pilar as bisexual. Comley and Scholes's *Hemingway's Genders* reads this line's replacement "as a suppression by the author, or, more richly, as a repression and excessive protest by Pilar herself" (48). They use as evidence their decided opinion that Hemingway principally based Pilar on Gertrude Stein (46) and an understanding of the excised term "darkness" (see 155:14) in a racially charged way indicative of a wide range of gender identities and sexual proclivities (48–49). It is also reasonable to conclude that by revising away the suggestiveness early in the process—before handing the manuscript to the typist—Hemingway rejected a fleeting characterization, a whim, to which he never seriously committed the text.

The other major work of scholarship to analyze Pilar's queer sexuality is Eby's *Hemingway's Fetishism*. Both works interpret Hemingway texts in the context of one another and of Hemingway's biography. Other criticism takes her queerness as a point of fact. Writers in Hemingway's time had a very limited vocabulary for (and understanding of) the varieties of gendered and sexual identities, desires, and experiences. Pilar herself could only understand and discuss her gender in strict binary terms. Comley and Scholes, writing in the 1990s, couldn't benefit from the positivity and inclusiveness that the word *queer* has come to enjoy. The richness of twenty-first-century approaches to this element of the human condition, the expansion and refinement of language for it, opens up possibilities for reconsidering Pilar.

155:6 **tracingly over the contours of her cheeks:** In the draft, the sentence continues, "and over her chin and then swept three fingers down the smooth curve of her throat" (*HLE* 499).

155:7 **I am no *tortillera*:** Derogatory slang for a lesbian, something like "faggot" for a gay man.

155:14 **You are for the *Inglés*:** Before this line, the draft includes this crossed-out sentence: "There is a darkness in us that you know nothing of. But all have it and I say this to thee now" (*HLE* 499). See 43:38.

155:36 **You swallowed it yourself:** An interesting choice of language when one considers the novel's ambiguity about Jordan's role in his own death. Readers of *The Garden of Eden,* particularly those disposed to the word associations made by Eby's *Hemingway's Fetishism,* might see David and Catherine Bourne in Jordan's wondering whether a "cat" got his tongue (155:30)—David is a writer in a contest with Catherine over his own writing voice. See Jordan's reference to a snake eating its own tail (386:32–33).

157:26 **Let her go!:** Jordan has resisted being left alone to have sex with Maria. He is impatient to return to camp and continue preparing for the bridge mission. His reluctance seems related to the fear of how she might complicate and endanger the mission as well as his sense of self. Maria, on the other hand, from the moment she "sat on the ground under the tree" (157:4–5), has every intention of resisting his resistance until he accedes. When they make love at the beginning of the next chapter, the little death of that act for him—a "dark passage" to "nowhere" for "always and forever" (159:17–19)—prefigures his actual death, which is immediately preceded by Maria's only other disobedience toward him (458:35).

CHAPTER THIRTEEN

158:1 **heather:** The scene's repetition of the word "heather" five times in this extended lovemaking scene connects it with the repeated heather of Jordan and Maria's audience for Pilar's tale (99:32+). After this chapter, the novel does not employ the word until Jordan receives his fatal wound and, lying on the forest floor, awaits death (467:17; 470:15).

158:2+ **the brushing of the heather ... tawny as wheat:** The sex scene begins here, Jordan's sensual interaction with the land and sun and air mixing with his holding Maria's hand. Her hair "tawny as wheat" and her "gold-brown" complexion reinforce the connection to the Spanish earth (22:14–16). The first sentences nestle "the weight of his pistol ... against his thigh" among the other pleasant, stimulating sensations (158:3–4) as the text declines to separate potential violence from the sexual. Jordan's pistol appeared the first time the couple made love as well (70:1). Note the reference to the "glassy surface" of a calm body of water (158:11); Jordan disposed of his father's suicide pistol in the "still" waters of a mountaintop lake (337:21–22).

159:5 **Everything as you:** Maria echoes Catherine Barkley from Hemingway's earlier wartime romance, *A Farewell to Arms,* and anticipates the behavior of Renata in *Across the River and into the Trees* and Catherine Bourne in *The Garden of Eden.* In all four cases, the women have suffered great traumas—Barkley the death of her fiancé in the Battle of the Somme, Renata the loss of her father and her home to war, Bourne the deaths of her parents in a car accident that was possibly a murder-suicide committed by her father, and Maria the murder of her parents as well as months of being regularly gang-raped. All four women seek to be relieved of the burden of their very selves. In Maria's case, this interpretation is corroborated by her statement that she "dies" each time she and Jordan make love, that she seeks a kind of death in sexual congress (160:4+). With all four couples, one of the lovers winds up dead or in some other way destroyed.

159:8+ **Then there was the smell of heather:** This is the second time the couple makes love and one of two the text describes. The absence of graphic language and imagery involves the social mores of the times. The rhythmic lyricism of the two passages suggests a yoking together of Romance and Realism, of the emotional flight and the physical act. The feeling that "the earth move[d]" is the most famous phrase from the novel. A possible source is Donne's poem "A Valediction: Forbidding Mourning" (see front matter: title and epigraph). Some readers find Hemingway's phrase laughable. This was the passage singled out by C. V. Roberts's November 1940 negative review as evidence of what he considered the novel's awful style (33). The actor and writer Cornelia Otis Skinner invokes it twice in her 1941 friendly parody of the novel, "For Whom the Gong Sounds" (appendix C). Nobel Prize–winning writer Mario Vargas Llosa cackles over the phrase in Ken Burns and Lynn Novick's 2021 *Hemingway* film.

Jordan's physical awareness of place, his smelling the heather and feeling the stalks and sun while gazing at Maria, gradually blurs into a nonliteral expressionist depiction of his interior experience that culminates with a pace and rhythm in sync with sexual orgasm: "now beyond all bearing up, up, up and into nowhere, suddenly, scaldingly, holdingly all nowhere gone and time absolutely still and they were both there." The repetition simultaneously evokes the repetitive bodily motion of sex and reinforces the passage's movement away from body to a space that forgets its place, the particularities of its place, where *where* no longer matters. For many readers, Jordan's forgetting of place amounts to a transcending of place that becomes a transcending of the earthly and an entering into the spiritual. Josephs relates the astute observation by one of his students that the word "nowhere" can be a compound of *no-where* and of *now-here* (*Undiscovered* 108). Not just place transcended, but also time stilled. For Josephs, the moved earth does not correspond to reached orgasm—or not simply to orgasm—what a "supreme pathetic fallacy" that would be (*Undiscovered* 104)—but to achieved spiritual ecstasy. Jordan does not feel the earth shudder, after all. He feels it "move out and away from under them" as if the lovers have momentarily left it behind, almost as if they've left their bodies behind (as Frederic Henry temporarily does when nearly mortally wounded [*FTA* 54]).

The language of this scene is the language of death, as in "a dark passage which led to nowhere." The French phrase *la petite mort* refers to the postorgasmic state of release, even to the orgasmic spasms. Afterward, Hemingway's lovers discuss their experience in terms of whether they had died (160:2+). George Bataille's *Erotism: Death and Sensuality* connects sex and death as the two means through which "discontinuous" birthed beings regain the "primal continuity linking us with everything that is" (15). The dissolution of the self in erotic union approximates the dissolution of the self in death. After they finish, Jordan articulates the death simile as aspirational: "I feel as though I wanted to die when I am loving thee" (160:2–3). *Dissolution* is one word for it; *integration* is another, the word that Robert Jordan will discover as he lies dying (471:12).

Throughout the novel, Jordan's association of Maria with Spain's terrain, flora, and fauna informs his romantic desire for her. A union with her manifests a union with Spain. The passage's sensuality merges Maria's body with the land and the sun. Union with Maria partakes of whatever drives Jordan to die for Spain and end his problems, including the problem of his father's suicide (466:7+).

Any analysis of this passage must address the fact that the marriage of mental state and sensations belongs to Jordan alone, to his interiority: "all his life he would remember" these sensations; "[f]or him it was" that "dark passage." This passage represents his perspective—what he sees, smells, feels, and thinks, consciously and unconsciously. Her perspective is more complex, on the one hand an experience of "the roughness of the bent stalks under her head" which was "pushed back," but also an experience of "possessing" and "having" as opposed to being possessed or had, with the sun's bright colors through her closed lids in what seems a more private transaction with herself.

If the repetitious language enters the prose stylings of Hemingway's former mentor Gertrude Stein (see Brogan 90), a potential model for Pilar, it thereby keeps Pilar around for the lovemaking. The triangle of desire developed in chapter 12 remains, at least in spirit. From that chapter, see also the potential relationship between Maria's resistance to Jordan's authority and death (157:26).

159:33 **Hello, my *Inglés*:** Maria's first words after the couple's lovemaking suggest that Robert Jordan's desire to integrate with Spain, to become Spanish, has not yet succeeded. Throughout this chapter, Maria insists on calling him her *Inglés* over his objections. The inaccuracy of the pet name on which she insists, which conflates English and American, perhaps corresponds to the Anglo-European perception of the African within the Spanish.

160:2–3 **I feel as though I wanted to die when I am loving thee:** The wish to die echoes Maria's wanting to die every time she was raped (73:14–15). Jordan's motives for union differ from Maria's. Their understanding of death through sexual consummation also differs. Their experiences have not been the same: she dies every time; he only nearly does. She felt sunlight on her eyes; he plunged into darkness (159:9+). To ignore the differences between their romantic needs and visions is to fall prey to one's own desire and (genre) expectation for romance, a desire and expectation that also results in overlooking Jordan's act of murder (see 304:17+).

Jordan has acknowledged the risk he's taking in loving Maria during the military operation, and later in this chapter decides to intensify his love because he suspects he will die in two days (168:28). It seems, then, that on some level he does feel as though he wanted to die when loving her. Since his language of wanting to die echoes hers, does he experience her love deep down as violating his psychic integrity, his autonomous masculine selfhood?

160:4 **each time:** Each? This is their second time together, and the only time the earth moves. She wanted to die each time Nationalist soldiers violently violated her (73:14–15), in which case her expression here amounts to a reclamation of her sexuality—a killing of the victimized self as well as repurposing of the repeated word. Nevertheless, her use of the same language for what she desired, with her rapists and with her lover, is troublingly suggestive.

160:6–7 **Yes. As I died:** Maria reasserts the difference (160:3+) even as she affirms that she felt the earth move. In both cases of figurative language, of dying and of the earth moving, Maria follows Jordan's lead as he proffers the language she then takes up. Maybe she's only saying what she knows he wants to hear, as she perhaps does later when she tells him the sex didn't hurt (379:36). With *dying*, however, the phrase "each time" makes her emotions and language feel more genuinely hers, more considered, and less influenced by her desire for unity of experience.

When Maria asks Jordan to put his arm around her, he declines because he has (possesses) her hand, which he says is "**enough**"—either he means enough for him, disregarding her expressed need, or he patronizingly tells her what is enough for her.

160:8–9 **a hawk was hunting and the big afternoon clouds were coming:** A classic example of Naturalist foreshadowing. More than just an ominous symbol, the approaching clouds indicate the upcoming snow that directly influences the course of events. The hawk adumbrates the fascist aircraft that will kill El Sordo and generally haunt and hunt the Republicans. Hawks prey on small ground mammals like rabbits, martens, and squirrels, all of which Jordan connects to Maria. The line contributes to the text's tendency to frame Robert and Maria's lovemaking with hunting imagery and give it a violent undercurrent. As the foreshadowing follows the lovemaking, it becomes a consequence of it. The compounded foreshadowing of hawk and storm clouds seems purposefully overdone.

160:25 **stroke thy hand across my head:** This is the second of three times Maria requests that Jordan touch her head, a site of her sexual trauma (70:9; 262:14).

161:18+ **in a plane:** Jordan's absent-minded response turns Maria's natural imagery of riding horses into riding aircraft. The novel has already memorably associated aircraft with the "mechanized doom" of the Nationalist warplanes (87:8). When Maria picks up the pursuit plane imagery for their love, flying "in loops and in dives," the novel confuses any simple association of technology with the evil of modern fascism. As for his absent-mindedness, Jordan soon comments that he is "fighting against exactly what [he is] doing and being forced into doing to have any chance of winning" (162:4–5)—that he fights fascism fascistically, by emotionally and mentally detaching himself from others, from those he must use.

161:26 clear and hard and sharp as when a camera lens is brought into focus: In *The Garden of Eden,* David Bourne discusses the "deadly clarity" that comes after sex, and the loneliness required to write after the arrival of that clarity (13–14). Jordan's focus does not last out the paragraph. On the technology simile, see 1:13.

162:2 Certainly it may happen: The draft continues the paragraph with these crossed-out sentences, both typed and with handwritten insertions:

> It was a damned shame to have gotten that woman in on it and it was a shame to have Sordo in too. Not to mention the girl, what? Not to mention the girl. But what the hell were they supposed to be in the war for? Not the girl, all the rest of them. Was it any worse on them than on anybody else? It would be. It was. Only that it had been easier on them so far and that they were picturesque. It was always hardest on the picturesque. That was another of the things that Golz knew. That was one reason why he permitted no deviation of any sort in uniform and why he wanted everyone to have their heads shaved. The nearer you all were alike, the uglier and the less differentiation the easier it was. Of course it had always been that way. (corrected from *HLE* 502–03)

The word "picturesque" accompanies a racialized gaze. The idea that being less differentiated mitigates the loss of death would slant Jordan and Maria's conversation about having their hair the same length and becoming one as Jordan journeys toward death.

162:30 That swine Gomez in Estremadura: Wilhelm Zaisser, an internationally prominent communist originally from Germany, served in Spain under the nom de guerre "Gomez." A Great War veteran in the German army who became a Bolshevik during the Russian revolution, Zaisser "was a classic example of the type of professional revolutionary who performed the Comintern's work throughout the world," with training and experience in intelligence, espionage, and internal security (Richardson 68–69). In Spain, he initially commanded the XIII International Brigade. Jordan killed his immobilized predecessor Kashkin in Extremadura in April (23:32–33; 24:2), a fact that would exacerbate his disgust for Gomez.

The novel gets the history wrong. Hemingway honestly confused the facts, or wanted to assert his understanding of events, or needed to reinforce Jordan's party-line understanding. The inaccuracy is one of the novel's several anachronisms, but the only anatopism (besides the location of the fictional bridge). Gomez's XIII operated on the Córdoba front dividing Andalusia, at coastal Motril (south of Granada) where the Nevada Mountains descend to the Mediterranean, from 12 February to 28 March 1937, and from 29 March to 26 June 1937 at Pozoblanco. Jordan rightly locates Pozoblanco on the Córdoba front (238:35; 239:10), not Extremadura to its west.¹ Pozoblanco was also a successful defensive operation, not the failed offensive implied by Jordan's criticism. Jordan's accusation refers to events in June 1937—after his death—when Gomez objected to orders to participate in the upcoming Brunete offensive, what Jordan regards as a cowardly refusal of orders that only seemed "impossible." Having been in constant operation for six months, Gomez's brigade was exhausted, undermanned, and underequipped. Gomez was relieved of command on 26 June 1937 and briefly imprisoned. After the Republic's disastrous failure at Brunete, the XIII mutinied under its new commander. Gomez, meanwhile, wound up as the training commander and then the base commander at Albacete, the International Brigades' primary headquarters.²

163:17+ under Communist discipline: For Jordan, this means accepting nonbattlefield, extrajudicial killing—comrades shooting comrades—and his willingness to be on either side of such actions. When Hemingway changed Jordan to an antifascist at the galley stage (66:14+), he also removed party affiliation here. The full passage had read:

> But why did he tell Pilar and Maria that he was a Communist? He was a Communist for the duration of the war. Here in Spain the Communists offered the best discipline and the soundest and saneness for the prosecution of the war. Then he was not really a Communist? No. But he had been for two years. He had a party card and he accepted their discipline for the duration of the war because, in the conduct of the war, they were the only party whose program and whose discipline he could respect. It was lucky then that he had joined the party at the university the year before he came because if he had not he would never have been trusted here.
> What were his politics then? He had none now, he told himself. But do not tell anyone else that, he thought. Don't ever admit that. But you were a Communist at one time, weren't you? Yes. And I still am now for the duration. (*HLE* 503–04)

This is the moment Jordan renounces communism as an ideology. He had been a communist for two years, and as he had joined the party a year before coming to Spain, his political convictions remained for his many months in Spain up until now. He had certainly felt the crusading fervor at the International Brigade headquarters as well as the Spanish communists' Fifth Regiment headquarters in Madrid (234:37+).

While Jordan's disillusion likely swelled over the past month, the immediate cause of articulating his renunciation for the first time is the just-finished sexual congress with Maria. Jordan's new apolitical sentiment reprises that of Frederic Henry in *A Farewell to Arms,* who deserts his voluntary war after falling in love with a woman who, like Maria, wants to become one with her man. Jordan confirms the lovemaking's influence when he blames sexual continence for "bigoted . . . surety and righteousness" (164:11). Tellingly, Jordan now wants to discuss Pablo's political development with that war dropout who once caused him to wonder "what could make me feel the way those horses make Pablo feel" (16:33–34).

163:30+ **The classical move from left to right . . . the politics of horse thieves:** Alejandro **Lerroux** García was a socialist, never a particularly radical one, who served in various Republican government minister roles and thrice as prime minister—including a term during the conservative government after the right-wing victory in the 1933 election. After being caught up in a messy overpayment of a contract for two ships (Bowers 168), he became a persona non grata as a result of a corruption scandal involving a fraudulent gambling business (rigged roulette wheels), and at the outbreak of the war, Lerroux hightailed it to the safety of Portugal. Indalecio **Prieto** Tuero was another moderate socialist who served in different ministerial roles for the Republic. As the war developed (beyond the novel's time frame), he increasingly objected to the communists' agenda and was called "an impertinent pessimist" by the Republican newspaper *La Vanguardia;* the communist leader La Pasionaria also publicly denounced Prieto (Thomas 788–89). Other government officials, including Prime Minister Juan Negrín López, shared this estimation of Prieto's 1938 leadership (Bowers 380).[3] Jordan objects to Lerroux's apparent capitalist greed and corruption. His objection to Lerroux's moderate politics and to Prieto's anti-communist stance reveals his (former) allegiance to communism. La Pasionaria's speeches against Prieto resemble Pilar's berating of Pablo that leads to his loss of command. Soon after these public criticisms, Prieto lost his job as war minister. His purported pessimism resembles Pablo's as this ad hoc militia's commander. Anselmo called out Pablo's "classical move from right to left," because of his possessive love of his horses, in chapter 1 (15:34–36). Pablo has stolen horses, and will again before the novel ends.

Although Pablo is a popular Spanish name, there is a remote possibility that Hemingway had in mind another socialist, Pablo Iglesias Posse, the founding father of Spanish socialism, whom Jordan later mentions (370:3). In the mid-1930s, Hemingway's friend Luis Quintanilla painted the murals for the Monument to Pablo Iglesias in the Parque del Oeste. The monument was dedicated on 3 May 1936 (with one incomplete panel), and within two months the civil war began. The monument was destroyed during the war. Like Prieto, Pablo Iglesias was far more honorable than the novel's Pablo. In naming his Pablo after the famous one, Hemingway would have achieved a subtle irony and further evidenced Jordan's prejudice against the socialists.

164:9+ **Bigotry:** See next entry. At the galley proof stage, Hemingway deleted a misogynist passage about another source of bigotry: "Being married to an unattractive wife and being faithful to her. Something with spectacles and a square bottomed haircut and good stiff underwear. Something that worked hard in the party and was a true intellectual helpmeet." Such a spouse was "twice as strong a force for bigotry" as not having sex (*HLE* 504).

164:18+ **the sin of Mayakovsky:** The Russian poet, playwright, and editor Vladimir Vladimirovich Mayakovsky believed strongly in Vladimir Lenin's Bolshevik Revolution, yet as time went by, he publicly criticized aspects of the Soviet state and Soviet communism. Mayakovsky had many love affairs, and he lived intimately and publicly with a married couple for several years, hence Jordan's reference to his "Bohemianism" and the connection drawn between his active sexual life and his political heresy. After Mayakovsky's death in 1930, his official reputation unexpectedly reversed, from black sheep to canonical Soviet writer—"a saint again," in Jordan's words, before offering this rather pregnant thought: "That was because he was safely dead. You'll be safely dead yourself, he told himself." International news accounts reported the death of Russia's most prominent contemporary poet in his thirty-sixth year as a suicide by pistol over love, variously attributed to a broken heart or anguish at an inability to choose between two lovers. Eugene Lyons's widely published UP (United Press) wire-service article on the funeral described Mayakovsky's final published poem, "With a Full Voice," as obviously a "farewell poem" and asked, "Did he therefore know that he would kill himself? Or was it merely a premonition of impending death? The answer probably never will be known" (12). Other news accounts noted the irony that Mayakovsky "hated suicide on principle" ("Poet Flays" 1) and that he had once decried the suicide of a fellow poet as "a cowardly shirking of one's duties to mankind" (Deuss 3). The theory that the Soviets murdered Mayakovsky did not emerge until decades later.

This suicide allusion—in the chapter in which Jordan travels to "nowhere" during sex with Maria, challenges political orthodoxy, and convinces himself of his impending death—is striking. Hemingway knew the allusion would register for a large set of readers. "Mayakovsky's funeral procession and burial in Moscow on April 17, 1930 was the largest demonstration of public mourning since the funeral of Lenin himself: over a hundred thousand people took part, without encouragement from the State." The day before, a crowd of ten thousand showed up at the Writers' Federation memorial in Leningrad, "storming the building and tearing the doors from their hinges" to get into the hall, which was too small to accommodate them (Sundaram 79). Over the next decades, the literary set and Soviet officials endlessly revisited the meaning of Mayakovsky's work, life, and death, changing their party-line interpretations while struggling to make genuine sense of the suicide. The state established commissions to manage his legacy. Mayakovksy lived briefly in Paris in the late 1920s, and some of his poetry appeared in *The New Masses*, the major American leftist magazine of the era (the poet Langston Hughes translated one). His death made international news and shocked the literary world. Mikhail Koltsov, Hemingway's Soviet handler in Spain and the model for the novel's Karkov, weighed in on the meaning of the suicide in print and quickly republished a poem of Mayakovksy's, one of two he had recently rejected (Sundaram 82, 85). No doubt Hemingway talked about Mayakovsky's poetry and suicide with Koltsov and other communist writers in Spain, people such as Ilya Ehrenburg and Gustav Regler. Mayakovsky's four-volume *Collected Works* had just been published in 1936.

Hemingway must have been familiar with Max Eastman's 1934 book *Artists in Uniform: A Study of Literature and Bureaucratism,* which attacked Stalin's Soviet party-line aesthetics as an egregious assault on literature, citing Mayakovsky's suicide as evidence of how the oppressive party machinery destroys its artists. Eastman's language of *bigotry* and *Bohemianism* is the very language Jordan uses. Eastman's book does not doubt the suicide but expresses suspicion about the Soviet press's speedy denial of any political underpinnings. He quotes Trotsky on the absurdity of claiming "that the voluntary death of Maiakovsky [sic] was in no way related to his life, or that his life had nothing in common with his revolutionary-poetic creative work" (72). The personal was political was poetics.

Did Hemingway know that at least a couple of Mayakovsky's poems named its female addressee Maria? "The name 'Maria' was the most feminine name for him and he used it for all women as a general term" (Lila Brik in Woroszylski 126).

164:25–26 a Thermopylae, nor be Horatius at any bridge, nor be the Dutch boy: The three allusions all amount to sacrifices made to defend the homeland but with different outcomes for their causes and for their heroes.

The Battle of **Thermopylae** took place in 480 BC as a force of Greek city-states under Spartan leadership fought valiantly but futilely to defend a pass against a much larger Persian military. The last of the Greek defenders fought to the death, which inspired the famous lines from Simonides of Ceos's commemorative epitaph, "Go tell the Spartans, stranger passing by, / That here obedient to their laws we lie." Jordan, too, dies obediently in a mountain pass. Although the Greeks probably would not have prevailed, a local man betrayed them by showing the Persians a way around the pass to outflank the defenders. The Nationalists, who probably would have prevailed anyway, learned about the Republican offensive, and Pablo at least temporarily betrays the bridge mission.

In 509 BC, **Horatius** Cocles and two other officers helped defend Rome against the approaching Etruscan army at the only bridge across the Tiber River. Horatius stood his ground all but suicidally, commanded the bridge be destroyed to prevent the Etruscans from crossing, and, the bridge gone and him suffering multiple wounds from arrow and spear, and according to Polybius' *Histories,* "threw himself into the river with his armour on and deliberately sacrificed his life, because he valued the safety of his country and his own future reputation more highly than his present life, and the years of existence that remained to him" (505).

The apocryphal, anonymous "sunny-haired" **Dutch boy** became an overnight legend upon publication of the American writer Mary Mapes Dodge's *Hans Brinker; or, the Silver Skates: A Story of Life in Holland* (1865). The young boy dutifully plugs a dike with his finger and stays up all night to save the town. In Dodge's version, the story appears as a classroom lesson, "The Hero of Haarleem," with the students taking turns reading it aloud (the exchanges between the teacher and the students as they read the story feel like the telling of "A Natural History of the Dead" in *Death in the Afternoon*).

164:32 **as Doctor and Mrs. Livingstone I presume:** The Scottish David Livingstone was a prominent nineteenth-century explorer of Africa, a colonial and imperial expansionist, and Christian missionary. Like Lawrence of Arabia from the Great War, Livingstone achieved legendary status in his own lifetime. In the late 1860s the world outside of Africa lost contact with him, prompting the *New York Herald* newspaper to send Henry Morton Stanley to find him. When Stanley discovered him two years later, in 1871, he greeted him with the famous line, "Doctor Livingstone, I presume?" The wit of Stanley's line comes from the fact that Livingstone was the only white person in the region. Hemingway owned Stanley's *How I Found Livingstone,* though the line had cultural currency far beyond the memoir's literal readership. In addition to the allusion's placing of Jordan and Maria's affair within an African context, "Mrs. Livingstone" could only be a native African, Livingstone's white wife Mary having died in 1862. The line contributes to the novel's cultural association of Spain with Africa and to Jordan and Maria's relationship as interracially charged. It is perhaps too tenuous to see a racial coding in the repetition of the word "dark" in the just-concluded lovemaking (159:17, 20), although Jordan's fancy of Maria's subcutaneous "darkness" has been established (43:38).

Such an imagined lover could have been a Moor and so even more closely associated with Spain. Hemingway would have known from Stanley's memoir that Stanley found Livingstone living among natives of both African and Arabic descent. The memoir's widely reproduced illustration about the first meeting (along with its many knockoffs) depicts both, the latter eclipsing the village's African-descended inhabitants behind them. Even if Hemingway hadn't read the book, he and his generation knew the illustration, complete with a centrally prominent emblem of American global adventurism, the US flag.

Livingstone died in Africa of illness in May 1873. His organs were removed so that the body could be better preserved during transportation back to England. His heart was literally buried in Africa under a tree—to borrow Hemingway's language for Robert Jordan dying in Spain, Livingston "was completely integrated now" (471:12).

Illustration from Henry M. Stanley's *How I Found Livingstone* (1872). (Public Domain)

164:34 **Sun Valley, Idaho:** See 471:12. At this point in the drafting process, Hemingway had yet to step foot in Sun Valley, although he would work on the book there. Its landscape influenced his depictions of the novel's terrain and scenery.

164:37 **get my job back at the university:** Jordan, a professor of Spanish at the University of Montana in Missoula, worries that the university will not hire him because of his service for the communist-allied Spanish Republic. After Spain ceased to be a threat following its loss to the United States in the Spanish-American War of 1898, the study of Spanish language and culture saw a renaissance in America; Robert Jordan would have been a beneficiary of that moment, perhaps one of the 57,000 college students studying Spanish in 1922 (Rogers, *Incomparable* 26). Richard Kagan compares this new wave of Hispanism to how "nineteenth-century Americans had previously embraced and romanticized the so-called 'vanquished' or 'vanishing Indian'" (11). To this new Hispanism Jordan owes his interest and academic career as a professor of Spanish.[4]

165:1–2 **Quevedo, Lope de Vega, Galdós:** On Francisco de **Quevedo**, see 11:16. Poet, playwright, and novelist Félix **Lope de Vega** y Carpio was a contemporary and friend of Quevdo's, both writers generally considered the best of Spain's Golden Age along with Miguel de Cervantes. His thousands of titles make Lope de Vega one of the most productive authors in history. He became a Catholic priest in 1614.

Benito Pérez **Galdós** was a prolific novelist and playwright of the late nineteenth and early twentieth centuries. He shares with Quevedo and Lope de Vega a commitment to Realism and the ordinary; his global influences were Charles Darwin, Honoré de Balzac, and the French literary Naturalist Émile Zola. The line about the "**always admirable dead**" suggests a recognition of the advantages to one's reputation for being dead. It perhaps qualifies Jordan's earlier thought that the best combatants—the gay ones—were already dead (see 17:10+).

165:2–5 **Maria can tell them about how:** One of the novel's most disturbing passages. Jordan has not yet heard Maria's story of her original rape. He imagines it as an act of entertainment for younger men, for students, in a perverse incarnation of the education Jordan talks about receiving in wartime Spain. The scene superficially gives Maria a voice while scripting it into a performance for others that is literally about her being silenced, her mouth stuffed with her own skirt, an emblem of her femininity. Hemingway added these details to the draft, which originally fantasized simply about having her "tell" about being raped (MS11–003).

A more generous question: Does the novel recognize that any stories Jordan would tell or write about the war would exploit the real suffering of the people for entertainment and his own aggrandizement?

165:7–8 **ticketed as a Red:** The Communist Party of the United States (CPUSA) was responsible for recruiting and organizing the American volunteers (under the direction of the Communist International, or Comintern). Most veterans were discriminated against as communists after the war. Many who joined the American armed services during the Second World War, to continue the fight against fascism, were initially refused combat or other military assignments of consequence despite their war experience (if allowed to serve at all). They were often posted to menial labor units populated by potential subversives: "pro-fascists, Nazis, and German and Italian nationals . . . as well as assorted misfits" (Carroll, Nash, and Small 44). Veterans continued to face employment discrimination and government harassment—in some cases, fines and jail time—in the decades that followed. Former brigader and Hemingway's wartime friend Alvah Bessie became one of the Hollywood Ten, the film industry professionals who refused to cooperate with the House Un-American Activities Committee (HUAC). Their contempt citation was upheld by the US Supreme Court (see Carroll, *Odyssey* chapters 19–22).

As for Jordan's particular paranoia, American universities tended to be conservative institutions until the 1960s. For Jordan to be paranoid about blacklisting in 1937 is moderately anachronistic. The House Un-American Activities Committee wasn't created until 1938 and sat dormant during the Second World War alliance between the United States and USSR. Still, HUAC was preceded by the Fish Committee (1930) and some American businesses in the 1930s discriminated against American citizens legally affiliated with communism.

165:9–12 They've no proof . . . my passport was valid for Spain before they issued the restrictions: On 20 January 1937, the US government ordered that "not valid for travel to Spain" be stamped on passports for Americans traveling to and out of France, the gateway to Spain for most volunteers. By then, the first waves had already arrived, and because Jordan has been in the country since the beginning of the war, he possesses his valid passport. The recruited brigaders from the United States, the first group of which shipped out of New York City on 26 December 1937 aboard the *Normandie,* handed their passports over to French communist functionaries in Paris before entering Spain, to keep the passports safe, protect the identity of the volunteers, and disguise the presence of internationals in Spain.

165:15 you do not need to be back until the fall term opens: The university calendar of Jordan's job back in the United States, not the war to preserve democratic Spain, holds sway.

165:20 Just try and turn up there: This ambiguous sentence might be an honest self-appeal to survive and make it back to the university or a sarcastic rebuttal of the possibility. It either extends the sentiment of the prior line or becomes another instance of Jordan's debating himself in alternating sentences. Such grammatical indecisiveness is symptomatic of his character.

165:31+ Did big words make it more defensible? . . . You took to it a little too readily if you ask me, he told himself: Although the subject is cold-blooded murder, the distrust of rhetorical spin echoes the famous passage against war-trumpeting from *A Farewell to Arms:*

> I was always embarrassed by the words sacred, glorious, and sacrifice and the expression in vain. We had heard them, sometimes standing in the rain almost out of earshot, so that only the shouted words came through, and had read them on proclamations that were slapped up by billposters over other proclamations, now for a long time, and I had seen nothing sacred, and the things that were glorious had no glory and the sacrifices were like the stock yards at Chicago if nothing was done with the meat except to bury it. There were many words that you could not stand to hear and finally only the names of places had dignity. Certain numbers were the same way and certain dates and these with the names of the places were all you could say and have them mean anything. Abstract words such as glory, honor, courage, or hallow were obscene beside the concrete names

of villages, the numbers of roads, the names of rivers, the numbers of regiments and the dates. (184)

The novel leaves it to the reader to judge Jordan's actual maturation against his self-perception, much as *The Red Badge of Courage* does Henry Fleming's. By the end of Hemingway's novel, does Jordan still take big words like "integration" a little too readily, as he here cautions himself against "assassination"? Has the novel duped the reader into easy acceptance?

166:7 **threescore years and ten:** Psalms 90:10: "The days of our years are threescore years and ten; and if by reason of strength they be fourscore years, yet is their strength labor and sorrow; for it is soon cut off, and we fly away." So seventy to eighty years. See 169:30–31.

166:16+ **The last time I slept with a girl:** The phrase **dragging ashes** is outdated slang for meaningless sex, for nothing beyond physical gratification and release, often with a prostitute. In *A Farewell to Arms,* Rinaldi uses the expression to tempt Frederic Henry to go with him to the brothel (147). The last woman Jordan slept with may have been a prostitute. The place where it happened, **El Escorial**, served as a military support hub and contained a hospital, so the woman could also have been a nurse or another woman working for the Republic. Jordan doesn't say with whom he excitedly imagined he was with, although he has already admitted to having vivid fantasies in Spain of the film actors Jean Harlow and Greta Garbo.

"Dragging ashes" also suggests death: *ashes to ashes, dust to dust,* as the traditional Christian burial prayer says. Such a suggestion binds the sexual encounter to its location—the **Escorial**, the grandiose palace and Catholic monastery built as the burial site for future Spanish monarchs since the late 1500s, and the place where Jordan received his fateful mission and stated his resistance to the dangerous complications of a love affair behind enemy lines (4:33; 7:38+). The burial prayer has its roots in the Bible, when God casts Adam and Eve from the Garden of Eden into the world of toil and death: "for dust thou art, and unto dust shalt thou return" (Genesis 3:19). Even though Jordan contrasts casual sexual partners with Maria, the details reinforce the link between his love for Maria and his death; indeed the paragraph ends with his saying that he loves her so much he "feel[s], literally, as though I would die," in a revision of what he just told Maria, that in their lovemaking he "feel[s] as though I wanted to die" (160:3). Does he think about the Escorial now because he's been thinking about death?

For Catholic Spaniards, casual sex committed in the Escorial would have been blasphemous. Jordan's reference to "a casual piece in any country" reinforces his bourgeois cosmopolitanism and secures the impression of him as an older "young man."

166:31+ **there is only now:** Jordan's landing on the word "now" in the middle of the chapter in which he convinces himself of his upcoming death, in which he decides to love Maria "very hard" in light of his upcoming death (168:28)—arguably in which he decides to die in order to love Maria "very hard"—establishes the word's personal connotation well in advance of its star turn in the second described lovemaking passage. The repetition of "now" there, in chapter 37, can perhaps be read less as narrative description of subjective experience than as a carrying out of this thought, a direct character discourse of willful insistence, an imploring speech-act, a prayer, a hope, a plea, a pretending (see also 393:38+).

The remainder of the paragraph, Jordan's serious whimsy over the relationship between verbal sound and sense, goes nowhere. Jordan wants, for example, the English rhyme *life* and *wife* to work in French as **vie** and **mari**, because of *mari*'s resemblance to Maria—Marie being the French equivalent—but the French word means "husband." At first Jordan believes the German **todt** and **krieg** to resonate the most with their meanings, *death* and *war,* only to acknowledge their relative unfamiliarity that probably results in that impression. Against his own implicit conclusion, Jordan asserts that a rose by any other name would *not* smell as sweet: Maria, now "[t]**here was a name**" (167:2–3). Having just exposed the arbitrary relationship between word and object—signifier and signified—Jordan's defiant investment of meaning in the arbitrary signifier of her name indicates his attachment to Maria herself as a signifier or a symbol at least as much as an actual person.[5] Plus he does trade in that name, for *rabbit,* which he calls her more frequently. Does the full passage also undermine his idiosyncratic pressure on the word *now* in a way that frustrates its use in chapter 37?

For Gayle Rogers, the failure to make polyglot coherence speaks to the irony that Jordan's "many communicative failures occur despite—or because of—his imagining that his profession as a Spanish instructor and author of an ethnographical travelogue on Spain would aid him" (210). Rogers views Maria as "embod[ying] the untranslatable and ineffable that Hemingway saw in all languages—her name encodes the reference to the Virgin Mary, even as Hemingway forget the diacritical mark in the Spanish *María*—and that both fascinated and frustrated him in Spanish in particular" (213). Maria represents the exoticized ineffable otherness of Spain (and of women) that fascinated and frustrated Hemingway and Jordan.

While Jordan gets nowhere with his word game, the reader should scrutinize the underlying association of the words he chooses for his game: *now, this night, wife, life, death, war, sweetheart.* Readers interested in gender dynamics might consider the slippage to *mari*—"husband"—from Maria, Jordan's imagined wife, whose short hair approaches the Hemingway androgynous ideal that the novel expresses with Jordan's Greta Garbo fantasies.

Fenimore sees this passage not as one of semantic consternation but of "a savoring, no matter how inconclusive, of the suggestive power of particular words."

He also passes along the observation that "these lines reflect . . . the international nature of the Loyalist organization" (73). Writing in 1943, Fenimore may not have appreciated the confusion and disorganization caused by the many languages of the International Brigades.

The draft's *querida* ("dear") was probably changed to *prenda* ("sweetheart" or "darling") by Durán.

167:10 **How about that?:** Up until the galley proofs, the line reads "How about that Mister Jordan, Comrade Jordan, Captain Jordan?" and the following paragraph ends with "rather late, Mister Comrade Jordan" (167:25). A few lines later in the galley proofs, he asks himself, "Yes, what happens, my dear mister comrade captain?" Hemingway deletes "mister captain comrade" and "mister captain comrade Jordan" from the galley proofs a few paragraphs further down—after "You ask for the impossible" (168:26) and "Much more than likely" (168:35). Jordan continues to wonder about the effects of different names for the same thing while poking fun at himself.

167:36–37 **the first time you looked at her as she came out bent over carrying that iron cooking platter:** Jordan fell in love with a woman (Maria) who was shackled to traditionally gendered chores.

168:1+ **all strange inside:** On that strange feeling, see 22: 8+ and 175:35–36.

168:26+ **You ask for the impossible:** The "impossible" combines a full life of common bourgeois family domesticity (per the prior paragraph) with intense romantic love. Only a few pages earlier, when thinking about the orders he received from Golz, Jordan convinces himself to carry on by rhetorically asking himself, "How do you know they are impossible until you have tried them?" (162:25). Now, when the probably impossible thing he just might prove possible is a happy marriage of domesticity and romance, he conveniently forgets this principle. Jordan unconsciously acknowledges his forgetting it in the first sentence of the next paragraph: "This was what Golz had talked about" (168:38).

168:28+ **you had better love her very hard and make up in intensity:** Jordan makes his clearest statement yet predicating the depth of his romance upon his impending death, vowing to "make up in intensity what the relation will lack in duration and in continuity." The phrase "[t]ill death do us part" is a traditional part of Christian wedding vows.

169:30–31 **by any biblical span:** See Jordan's earlier reference to Psalms 90:10, according to which the seventy to eighty years are a lifetime full of work and sadness (66:7). An early death would prevent this long misery. Jordan's sentence rejects the

Bible as the proper instrument for morally determining a good life. The text might also play with the fact that Jordan's one life ends because of the single-span bridge he destroys. In the galley proofs, Hemingway deleted the culmination of the name game he's been playing (167:10), as the paragraph there ends with "by any biblical span, captain, instructor in Spanish, sometime engineering worker, sometime many other things, now expert in demolitions, Comrade Jordan."

170:33 **single-edged razor blade:** Maria's razor blade for suicide has relatives in the razors used by her rapists to shave her head.

171:12+ **You forget all this:** While the immediate "**beauties of a civil war**" that Jordan discusses is the possibility of killing oneself to avoid capture—the word "beauty" used sardonically—the ambiguous plural referents in the passage's pronouns allow the "beauty" to also indicate Maria (his *guapa*) and to a love like his for her. As Jordan told General Golz in chapter 1, he has no time for romance when working a mission (7:38; 8:5–6). Thus Jordan associates his death with an inevitable suicide and with the love affair with a Spanish beauty. This pronoun play occurs in the same chapter of lovemaking he experiences as "a dark passage which led to nowhere" (159:17) and links his imagined two days left to live with the language of a marriage vow, "[t]ill death do us part" (168:34).

171:27–28 **when thou art wounded I will care for thee and dress thy wound:** Eby notes that not only might Hemingway have named Maria after a nurse he met in the war (in the coastal town of Mataró just north of Barcelona, in 1938), but Maria's intention to nurse a wounded Jordan affiliates her with other war nurses in Hemingway's fiction, Brett Ashley of *The Sun Also Rises* and Catherine Barkley of *A Farewell to Arms* (*Fetishism* 139). More resonance obtains with the latter character. Both Maria and Catherine have suffered wartime trauma from their gender roles; both repeatedly insist on losing themselves in oneness with their lover; both decline formal marriage by church and state; both make themselves sexually pliant. In both cases, the lovemaking for the woman attempts to heal, mitigate, bury, or otherwise deal with the gendered wartime trauma. If Jordan renounces politics upon falling in love with Maria, then his life's trajectory begins to align with Frederic Henry's of *A Farewell to Arms.*

Comley and Scholes see in Henry's love for Catherine "a safe kind of regression . . . for his desire is always to return to the waiting Catherine, the faithful and loving mother-mistress. He is the hungry child who would devour his mother" (38–39). In this interpretation, the pregnancy spells her (and their baby's) doom: "Frederic Henry, the child-man, cannot be expected to share his mother-lover with a real baby. . . . The great calamity in this case is not so much war or death as love itself. As Hemingway observed in *Death in the Afternoon*, 'If two people love each other there can be no happy end to it'" (39). Maria's association with the Spanish earth, and Jordan's regressive desire to return to it, makes her a mother figure. It is possible too that she is or becomes pregnant, or at least that Jordan suspects her to be.

172:4+ and cut thy hair: The suggestion of cutting hair continues Maria's desire to become identical to Jordan and carries elements of violence: in the allusion to her hair being shorn by her rapists; in the line's belonging to the passage about the lovers' suicide pact; and in the threat to his self that union and sameness with another represents. Their coiffure fantasies aside, neither Maria nor Jordan likes to have their hair cut. The instruments of Maria's suicide (the razor blade) and cutting Jordan's hair (the scissors) come from Pilar, the person who just arranged their tryst.

172:11 To me it seems the same: Maria's unclear pronoun "it" appears to equate all the activities just discussed, from shooting Jordan to spare him from torture (and perhaps revealing information), tending to his illness, rolling his cigarettes, reading to him, cooking and cleaning for him, and cutting his hair, to doing nothing but watch him in the daytime and make love with him at night. The obsequiousness on her part is a selfish sort of self-abnegation, a desire to lose herself and her traumas in him.

172:11+ Oh, *Inglés*: Though Maria insists on calling Jordan her *Inglés*, this passage is also the last time she ever does it (see 159:33). She admits to following Pilar's lead (see 172:14). The rest of the group also follows Pilar's lead, but unlike Maria will continue to call him *Inglés* even unto their parting words to him (465:33).

174:18 *Cali*: Jordan probably knows Borrow's *The Zincali: An Account of the Gypsies of Spain*. *Cali* is a shortened form of Zincali, "a term by which [gypsies or Romani], especially those of Spain, sometimes designate themselves, and the meaning of which is believed to be, THE BLACK MEN OF ZEND OR IND." Borrow deduces that the word Zincali is also the etymon for Zigani (Russia), Zingarri (Turkey and Persia), and Zigeuner (Germany) (Borrow, *Zincali* 2). The mixed-language version of Romani spoken on the Iberian Peninsula is caló.

175:26 *Busnes* of thy age bore me: Young people's business bores me.

175:32–33 what tribes we came from . . . what the mysteries were in the woods: See next entry.

175:35–36 what happens to us in the nights: This sentence and the next one—which were inserted by hand to the draft (MS11–004)—fall in one of the novel's more cryptic passages. The "it" is his love for Maria, picking up the pronoun's understood referent from earlier: "When she first opened her mouth and spoke to you it was there already and you know it" (167:32+). The next paragraph especially intrigues: "It hit you then and you know it and so why lie about it? You went all strange inside every time you looked at her and every time she looked at you. So why don't you admit it? All right, I'll admit it" (167:38+). "Strange" was the first adjective he ever applied to her, the "strange thing" being her cropped head (22:6–8).

Jordan's response to Maria precurses David Bourne's response to his wife Catherine's gender and racial role-playing in *The Garden of Eden*, role-playing that includes Catherine's having her hair cut androgynously short. David debates with himself whether he likes their identity experiments. Here he admits to himself that he likes his identical haircut very much, like "it," the "it" then becoming more than just the haircut. It is very similar to how Jordan admits to himself that he loves Maria:

> "So that's how it is," he said to himself. "You've done that to your hair and had it cut the same as your girl's and how do you feel?" He asked the mirror. "How do you feel? Say it." . . .
> "All right. You like it," he said. "Now go through with the rest of it whatever it is and don't ever say anyone tempted you or that anyone bitched you." (84)

When Jordan admits his feelings, he momentarily blames Pilar for "practically push[ing]" Maria onto him (167:26+). He wonders about "whatever happened" and "what happens." In the posthumously published novel, David frets about "whatever" happens. Jordan returns to this language about accepting the things that come in the night, things one doesn't understand, in the context of alternatives to traditional heterosexual coitus (342:25+). Pilar's advice, that something does not happen to one that one does not accept, pertains (73:13–14).

Nighttime has always been the time of vulnerability for Hemingway's male characters, soldiers and veterans especially. The most famous example is the opening paragraph of the story "Now I Lay Me," in which the narrator, listening to munching silkworms, confesses, "I myself did not want to sleep because I had been living for a long time with the knowledge that if I ever shut my eyes in the dark and let myself go, my soul would go out of my body. I had been that way for a long time, ever since I had been blown up at night and felt it go out of me and go off and then come back" (*CSS* 276). In *The Garden of Eden*, Catherine Bourne leads the newlyweds on their identity adventures initially at night, when they indulge through fantasy all the taboos: miscegenation, incest, and gender-switching in which David becomes "Catherine" and Catherine "Peter," the former manually sodomized by the latter. Catherine's promise to contain those adventures to the nighttime does not last. When she announces her plans to visit the Prado as a boy in the daytime, David "give[s] up" (56).

Both novels characterize whatever happens at night with the language of **tribes** (175:32). Of the woods, the pagan, the primitive. Catherine doesn't simply visit the Prado "as a boy" but as "the young chief of a warrior tribe" (62). And Pilar has just established that earth-moving lovemaking is a Calí thing, a Gitano thing, and after all "gypsies . . . are strange enough"—there's that word again (175:30). For "it" to rear itself in the day, whether "it" be the emotion or the act of love, "*is* something." The pattern suggests that what happens to Jordan isn't simply falling in love, but is stranger, darker, and more dangerous. All these Hemingway men face a loss to their sense of control and autonomy, and to the rigid integrity of their manly (white) selfhood. They've been made vulnerable. Something threatens to penetrate or has penetrated. The silkworms munch.

176:11–12 **Whatever she saw . . . proves nothing:** In the draft, these two sentences replace two others. The first wonders if Pilar fakes her Romani lore; the second is exasperated—"to hell with gypsies" and "with mixing up with women"—when Robert has a mission to accomplish (MS11–004).

177:3 **the moon of May:** The full moon of May 1937 fell on the twenty-fifth; this scene takes place on 29 May. The end of May and most of June fall under the May moon. See 153:24.

NOTES

   1. Some government action in late March to early April aimed to close the gap between the Estremadura and Córdoba fronts; see Matthews, "Leftists Shut Gap."
   2. On Zaisser (Gomez), see Abel and Hilbert (559). The 26 June 1937 order relieving him of command: RGASPI 545/3/203,132, "Inventory 6. Lists, Personal Files of Fighters and Commanders of International Brigades," Documents of the Soviet Era (http://sovdoc.rusarchives.ru/sections/organizations//cards/95156).
   3. Although Bowers, the US ambassador to Spain, writes admiringly of Prieto (38–39).
   4. See also Richard L. Kagan (editor), *Spain in America: The Origins of Hispanism in the United States* (U Illinois P, 2002); and Faber.
   5. It's possible that Jordan the language instructor knew Ferdinand de Saussure's *Course in General Linguistics* (1916), the foundational work of semiotics that established the arbitrariness between verbal signifier and signified thing. It's less likely that Hemingway did. De Saussure trailblazed (or at least shared) modernist writers' distrust of language, of how, per Virginia Woolf, "[w]ords fluttered sideways and struck the object inches too low" (*Lighthouse* 178) (the modernist literature of ineffability preceded the postmodernist literature of exhaustion).

CHAPTER FOURTEEN

179:4 ***A mi qué?:*** What is to me? What of it?

179:14–15 **So *that's* on your mind too:** In addition to assuming that the military mission cannot happen, Pablo assumes that Jordan's and Maria's lovemaking cannot happen.

179:18–20 **cost sixty-five dollars:** On "the old eiderdowns," see 180:15. Sixty-five dollars in 1937 would be over $1,300 in 2023. Jordan's capitalist, bourgeois American soul is on full display.

179:32 **But it is bad for the work, isn't it?:** This question is ironic coming from Maria, since according to Jordan *she* is bad for his mission. Pablo's double-contentment above, connecting the snow's impact on the military operations and on the lovers' copulations, corroborates the line's irony. Rafael later tracks and kills two hares making love in the snow (274:17+).

180:15–16 **paid the Woods boys sixty-five dollars for that robe:** Again with the sixty-five dollars! The brand and price match the Woods Manufacturing Company's Three Star Arctic Eiderdown Sleeping Robe, its most popular. The Canadian company established an upstate New York factory and office in the 1920s, around the time its reputation caught hold. The Woods sleeping robe was the first modern sleeping bag. The snappable bag measured 90" x 90" unfolded and was the first bag to use internal compartments to keep the insulation in place. Using plumes instead of feathers gave it the "eiderdown" designation. Hemingway owned one, and before first traveling to wartime Spain, thought about taking it with him.[1]

180:26–27 **grain those horses or peg them out and let them dig for it:** Feed them by hand or let them forage for themselves.

181:4–5 **you two brothers in the corner whose names I've forgotten:** Andrés and Eladio, although the text doesn't name Eladio for another three chapters (218:10).

It may very well be that Jordan's confusion reflects Hemingway's while drafting, as it took him a long time to sort out the names (see 51:37). The only place where the novel lists everyone in the guerrilla band together is chapter 34, in Andrés's interior monologue (366:16–19).

181:12–13 How did it go about that cup?: Jordan forgets a quotation from Shakespeare's *Othello*: "Every inordinate cup is unbless'd, and the ingredient is a devil" (II.iii.326–27). Jordan blames the wine for the course of the conversation and his thinking. After Cassio utters it, Iago immediately praises wine, not unlike Jordan's immediately asking for another cup.

The most famous Moor in English literature, Othello is a foreigner to Venice, a war hero whose marriage to Desdemona symbolizes his union with the city-state. After being tricked into murdering her, he commits suicide in the play's final lines. According to Kathryn Swanton, "[o]f all Shakespeare's plays, *Othello* is the one that is most frequently compared to Spanish literature in the age of Cervantes." Othello could have come to Venice from Moorish Spain—the sword at the end of the play, with which he attacks the man who tricked him, is a Spanish sword that he wielded in any number of battles (V.ii.303–15). The man who tricked him, Iago, has his name from Santiago Matamoros—Saint James the Moor-Killer (Swanton)—the patron saint of Spain and its army. Othello attacks Iago, aware that doing so will lead to being killed: "Here is my journey's end, here is my butt / And very sea-mark of my utmost sail" (V.ii.318–19). He says this having just bragged about his accomplishments with the very sword now in his hand, only to then rhetorically ask, "But—O vain boast!—/ Who can control his fate? 'Tis not so now" (V.ii.315–16). He disavows personal agency, yet attacks Iago knowing the act will end his journey, and when it doesn't work, he kills himself. His conflicted sense of agency over his own fate, or perhaps a denial about his agency, corresponds to Jordan's.

Jordan's saying "that cup" three times leads Mandel to attribute the allusion to Matthew 26, where Christ speaks about a metaphorical cup three times (verses 39, 42, and 44; *Reading* 213). The day before his crucifixion, Christ prays, "O my Father, if it be possible, let this cup pass from me: nevertheless not as I will, but as thou wilt" (Mathew 26:39; also Mark 14:36 and Luke 22:42). Jesus pleads not to die on the morrow as preordained, while acknowledging God's authority on the matter. Christ's language interestingly parallels Jordan's wish to avoid the curse passed from father to son, the curse of suicide. If Jesus is God made flesh, the question of whether he wills his own death persists. Christ makes his prayer upon the ground at Gethsemane on the slope of the Mount of Olives, having walked away from his fellows. For other Biblical references to a cup as fate, see Matthew 20:22, Ezekiel 23:31–34, and Jeremiah 49:12.

181:21 **No *aviones*:** No aviation, without which a major operation couldn't take place. As in *A Farewell to Arms,* weather—indifferent nature—dictates military action, dictates whether, when, and how people die.

181:31 **from the Cantabrico:** The Cantabrian Sea off the northern coast, north of the province of Cantabria between Asturias to the west and the Basque country to the east. It is perhaps no good omen that the storm comes from the direction of the Nationalist occupation.

182:17 **arroyero:** Really *arriero,* a muleteer, or mule team driver.

182:22–23 **Asturias where they are much developed politically:** After the right won the 1933 elections, retook the Spanish parliament in 1934, and proceeded to reverse the progressive reforms of the initial Second Spanish Republic, many groups on the left—among them socialists, anarchists, and communists—allied to spark a general strike and uprising against the conservative government in October 1934. The most successful branch of the uprising took place in the northern mining region of Asturias, where the working class was best organized. To suppress it, the government called up General Francisco Franco's Army of Africa troops. The campaign to retake Asturias lasted several days, followed by a murderous punishment program against the rebelling miners and supporters. Some historians consider this event the civil war's point of no return. For many on the left, "October 1934 confirmed that parliamentary democracy was a lost cause," while for many on the right, the events "added to the conviction . . . that the 'Bolshevik' danger could only be overcome by force" (Lannon 22).

This is also the region facing conquest by the Nationalists, the military situation which the Segovia Offensive (that Jordan's mission supports) hoped to relieve.

182:28 **Finito de Palencia:** Pilar's former lover, "handicapped" as a matador by his "short stature" (184:25–26), who became a matador to earn a meager living (184:28+), and was famed for "being very valiant" (185:9), strongly resembles Hemingway's description of the novice bullfighter "Isidoro Todó, called Alcalareno II" in *Death in the Afternoon* (227). Because the fictional Finito and the real Todó suffered different deaths (years of internal damage from nonpiercing blows versus a goring, respectively), Mandel concludes that Alfonzo Gómez, though a tall matador, more closely resembles Pilar's Finito. Gómez was also known as Finito de Valladolid, a town neighboring Palencia (Mandel, *Reading* DIA 425, 176). Hemingway introduces both Todó and Gómez in the same passage of *Death in the Afternoon* as part of a 1931 corrida that he saw. Although in correspondence Hemingway associates

Finito with Rafael el Gallo, the two don't appear to have much in common except, apparently, "being impotent on his wedding night. . . . and the gypsies makeing [sic] incantations and trying to bring it up and she disgraced and him sobbing" (to Charles Scribner, ca. 15 Aug. 1940, *SL* 508).

In *The Sun Also Rises,* Hemingway treats the bullfighting ring as a rarefied space, an event staged at the center of an annual festival set apart from daily life. Its violence is aestheticized and kept at bay. In *For Whom the Bell Tolls,* Hemingway refuses to spotlight the sport in that way. This novel insists upon understanding bullfighting as part and parcel of the violence and economic class structures of Spanish society as Hemingway saw them.

182:37–38 **a red line that no one else noticed:** The no one else includes both Finito's past bullfighting audiences and Pilar's immediate conversational audience, as the novel continues its expansion of perspectives other than Jordan's (58:19+). The next pages, up to "So he wasn't a good matador?" (184:23), capture a momentary flash of memory and constitute the seven-eighths of the iceberg below the visible dramatic surface, the seven-eighths below the surface of Hemingway's spare, dialogue-heavy fiction of the 1920s. As Hemingway articulated this principle in *Death in the Afternoon:* "If a writer of prose knows enough about what he is writing about he may omit things that he knows and the reader, if the writer is writing truly enough, will have a feeling of those things as strongly as though the writer had stated them. The dignity of the movement of an ice-berg is due to only one-eighth of it being above water" (192).

On the one hand, Pilar isn't a writer of prose who, in the iceberg vein, might have omitted this passage after the red line. On the other hand, this passage is par for *For Whom the Bell Tolls*'s narrative course, as Hemingway's longest fiction by far would seem to invert the iceberg. The novel's wordiness accomplishes the same end as his other fiction's taciturnity. If the passage relies on what Pilar saw that day, it also emphasizes the unseen. No one else could see his haggard face (182:35–38); Finito himself couldn't see the spot where he aimed his sword (183:15–16). Another way of relating Hemingway's minimal and maximal prose is to regard *In Our Time,* a composite whole made of disparate stories and vignettes, and *For Whom the Bell Tolls,* a novel that integrates disconnected and sometimes competing perspectives, as two forms of narrative cubism after the visual arts style pioneered by Pablo Picasso.

Gayle Rogers interprets the novel's bizarre, impossible intercourse of English and Spanish as

> a version of cubism, a structural (rather than spoken or creolized) Spanglish that becomes a two-dimensional scaffolding for a wealth of strategies of mistranslation that the novel embodies, corrupts, and further confuses. . . . The sanctity of the single viewing plane of representation, grounded in realism's adherence to a singular version of human perception, was violated by cubism, which re-

fashioned representation around artifice, antinaturalism, and a multiperspectival collage of object and conception. (216)

In addition to its Romanticism, then, the novel's multiple perspectives structurally counter conventional Realism even as they produce their own kind of Realism. Hemingway never completed his most daring multi-perspectival work of fiction, *The Garden of Eden*.

183:20 splintered horn: This does not appear to be the bull Finito killed in Valladolid, with its "very high" and "black" horns (185:14; 188:12), or even the bull at Zaragoza that gave him the blow from which he never recovered (188:31–32). The splintered-horned bull never touched the matador.

183:22–23 his thin, clear voice: Hemingway initially typed Finito's boast about killing the bull slightly earlier, continuing the paragraph after Pilar's line, "He wasn't much of a matador?" (182:33). There, he described Finito's "thin voice, like a girl's," then the coup de grâce itself of the sword's almost sensual movement: "and then slip in, straight and easy like an angel with the steel inching in so you could watch it go in as slowly as into a tub of butter" (MS11–004).

183:31–32 as though the bull's rush plucked [the sword] into himself: Although earlier Pilar derided Finito's arrogant claim that the matador always "gored himself on the horn of the bull" (55:3–4), the bull's rush accords with Finito's claim, the bull now appearing to have gored itself on the sword of the man. The two passages combine to blur the responsibility and agency for one's own death, an appropriate blurring as Jordan watches his own voyage toward death. The bull continues the novel's study of Naturalism and Tragedy, of fate and character. The bull perhaps had little choice in the matter, but one could argue that neither do Finito or Jordan, the one driven by poverty, the other by duty (and the threat of execution). The bull's lowering its horn "magically" (183:28) suggests the Romani mysticism that informs Jordan's fate.

183:33 and she watched it move in: Hemingway added this phrase by hand to the typed draft page (MS11–005), along with an earlier insertion to emphasize her act of witness, "she could see" (184:9; MS11–004). Note the discussion of ekphrasis at 102:9–10.

184:29+ In this country where no poor man: Bullfighting was at once the domain of the wealthy to own and an arena for the poor to make a living and, for the most fortunate, to rise in station. The wealth gap in early-twentieth-century Spain was practically insurmountable, one of the civil war's root causes. Both sides found something patriotic in the bullfight, Nationalists "the church and the might of the

Right," Republicans "the triumph of the common man" (Kennedy 86)—although only Nationalist areas held bullfights during the war (Mandel, *Hemingway's* DIA 454; confirmed by searches in the *ABC* newspaper archive). In Republican areas, valuable bull-breeding pastures "were ploughed over" for farming, and the bulls slaughtered and eaten so the people could get by until the harvest (Preston, *Spanish Civil War* 104). The Republicans turned one Madrid bullring into an orchard,[2] a practical and symbolic act. In contrast to Pilar's Finito, there was Don Bernardo Escudero, the "dashing millionaire" and "amateur toreador" who opened Valladolid's war-delayed fall 1936 feria "carrying Rebel Spain's flag" as he "planted the steel point of the first banderilla" in the day's first bull. That day, "[s]oldiers in olive drab, Fascists in blue and nurses in white provided the color scheme for this strange scene of patriotism" where toreadors wore Nationalist armbands and matadors gave a Fascist salute before killing a bull (Axelsson). As Pilar's diatribe and the Club Finito story she tells make clear, however, the Republican pride in the common man was still largely class-based, the Republican middle class celebrating reluctant toreadors like Finito from the impoverished peasantry who struggled to put food on the table.

184:30 **Juan March:** The wealthiest man in Spain and one of the wealthiest in the world. March started out smuggling tobacco to mainland Spain from Morocco, and even after establishing legitimate businesses, he continued to profit from tobacco smuggling, arms trafficking, and other shady schemes. He was a chief financial patron of Franco and the Nationalist rebellion.

185:12 **a bull of Pablo Romero:** "Don Felipe de Pablo Romero founded his ranch in Seville in 1885, acquiring stock that already boasted a long and complicated pedigree. . . . distinguished by their large size, their strong heads, and their red color." At the time of the novel, the ranch was run by the founder's two grandsons (Mandel, *Hemingway's DIA* 328).

185:15–16 **in Valladolid:** Because Finito still suffers from an injury received "in his last corrida of the year at Zaragoza" (185:32–33), which takes place in October—"the last important feria of the season" (*DIA* 514)—the scene Pilar describes could have occurred at Valladolid's San Pedro Regalado feria in May. Saint Pedro Regalado was born in Valladolid in 1390 and canonized in 1746. He is the patron saint of the city as well as of bullfighting. Although Pilar mentions the purple shrouds of Easter week as a visual comparison and not as a means of dating (185:28–30), the reference is suggestive of a spring date. The Easter season extends into May with the feast celebrating Christ's Ascension. The feria dates do not correspond with the novel's time frame, but they are close enough that one is tempted to see a parallel in Finito's and Jordan's last fights (even if Finito hangs on until the next winter). Most tantalizing is the possibility—the likelihood—that Pilar's story transpired on Easter Sunday, as Valladolid held a bullfight that day (*DIA* 38): see 185:28+.

185:18 **Café Colon:** The restaurant took its name from its location, either at the Plaza Colón or on Colón Street, named after the Italian Cristoforo Colombo, known in Spanish as Cristóbal Colón and in English as Christopher Columbus. Columbus died in Valladolid in May 1507. The Columbus Monument in the middle of the plaza was inaugurated in 1905. So Hemingway employs a café named after the early European explorer of North America traveling from Spain who died in May, in his novel about a North American traveling to Spain who dies in May, for a scene over which death looms.

185:22 **Pastora, who is uglier than I am:** Pastora Imperio, the famed flamenco dancer on whom Hemingway modeled Pilar (30:24+):

> Watching Pastora Imperia, life becomes more intense, the loves and hates of other worlds pass before our eyes, and we felt ourselves heroes, bandits, hermits, or champions, shameless bullies of the tavern—whatever is highest and lowest in one. A desire to shout out horrible things takes possession of us: Gitanza! Thief! Assassin! Then we turn to curse. Finally, summing it all up, in a burst of exultation we praise God, because we believe in God while we look at Pastora Imperia, just as we do when we read Shakespeare. (Benavente qtd. in Cochran)

One can hardly read this passage and not have Pilar come to mind. Pilar's calling Pastora "uglier" than herself is a Hemingway chuckle. Photographs of Pastora in her prime show her to be, if not classically beautiful, far from unattractive, befitting Pilar's earlier statements about her own unattractiveness and her desirability by men.

185:23 **the Niña de los Peines:** Born Pastora Pavón Cruz in Seville, Andalusia, La Niña de los Peines is considered the greatest flamenco singer of the twentieth century, and one of the greatest of all time. The poet Federico García Lorca called her a "dark Hispanic genius whose powers of fantasy are equal to those of Goya or Rafael el Gallo"; during one performance, "[h]er voice was no longer playing, it was a jet of blood worthy of her pain and her sincerity, and it opened like a ten-fingered hand around the nailed but stormy feet of a Christ by Juan de Juni" (*Deep Song* 45–46).

185:28–30 **shrouded in a purple cloth . . . during the week of the passion:** Pilar's comparison of the scene to churches during the Holy Week marking Christ's last days and resurrection underscores the deep entanglement of bullfighting and Catholicism in Spain. Hemingway very well may have intentionally set this scene on Easter Sunday, the day of the resurrection (see 185:15–16). Bullfights typically "coincide with the national religious festivals and the times of the local fairs or ferias which usually commence on the [patron] Saints day of the town" (*DIA* 37). Moreover, the bullfighting season, from the spring through the fall (sometimes November), coincides with the agricultural season. Traditionally, "fiestas did mark off and separate the succession of agricultural tasks such as planting, harvesting, and storage" (Douglass 119). The community feasted on the killed bull; for some of the poor, it provided a rare meat nourishment.

Two acts of predestined sacrifice so that others can live on, in the flesh or in the spirit, through the literal body of the bull or the symbolic body of Christ. Blood must flow. The ferias conjoin the pre-Christian or pagan (non-Christian or ethnic, not necessarily polytheistic) and the Catholic in a way that is, finally, impossible to disentangle. Hemingway insists on the pagan complications of the moment by filling it with Andalusian Romani and Andalusian sherry wine (manzanilla) instead of the sacramental kind (186:18). The scene Pilar details over the next several pages reads like a blasphemous mishmash of Christian symbolism, a kind of Last Supper for Finito, resurrection for the bull whose head looks "alive" (188:14), and communion for the gathered enthusiasts. The wall-mounted bullhead resembles the crucified Christ above every altar, its stare-down of Finito a brutally honest realization of the titular Donne epigraph: the bell tolls for thee. Death spares no one. In terms of genre, Naturalism reigns here. Finito's name translates from Spanish as "finite"—in human terms, mortal. Not infinite. Against this profane interpretation, a reader inclined toward the sacred in Hemingway might regard the blasphemous mishmash as exactly the point, seeing in this Hemingway passage as in so many others a negative example, a lostness in need of Catholic salvation.

Jordan later muses on what he considers a uniquely Spanish spiritual need for killing, a pre-Christian lust that found form and legitimacy "in wars and inquisitions. They are the people of the Auto de Fé," the medieval ritual procession from the Inquisitors' examination to the accused's public humiliation, torture, and sometimes fiery death (286:37–38). Chapter 10 describes the massacre presided over by Pablo, explicitly in terms of agriculture and bullfighting and implicitly in terms of the auto-da-fé. Pilar's two great stories inform one another. Hemingway connected bullfighting and the crucifixion in *Death in the Afternoon*:

> Goya's crucifixion is a cynically romantic, wooden oleograph that could serve as a poster for the announcement of crucifixions in the manner of bullfight posters. A crucifixion of six carefully selected Christs will take place at five o'clock in the Monumental Golgotha of Madrid, government permission having been obtained. The following well-known, accredited and notable crucifers will officiate, each accompanied by his cuadrilla of nailers, hammerers, cross-raisers and spade-men, etc. (*DIA* 204)[3]

The humor does not undermine the connection. "Cynically romantic" seems an apt phrase for capturing the novel's attitude for this violent enterprise of Jordan and his *cuadrilla* of guerrillas.

The gloom and doom of this extraordinary and overlooked Easter scene might reflect the fact that on Good Friday 1938, the Nationalist army reached the Mediterranean coast, driving a wedge between the two regions comprising what was left of the Republic and thereby sealing its fate. Hemingway was covering the combat in Tortosa forty-six kilometers to the north. The government delayed releasing the news, "so pregnant with consequences," until "Easter Sunday night" (Sheean 78–79; see 41:12+).

185:33 **at Zaragoza**: The Zaragoza feria in October honors the Virgen (Nuestra Señora) del Pilar. Regardless of whether Hemingway modeled his character Pilar on the Virgen del Pilar (30:24+), Finito receives his fatal injury with his Pilar while at Saint Pilar's festival. Finito and Jordan are both fighters accompanied by their lovers, the two women themselves linked in name and icon (the Virgin of the Pilar would be Mary, or Maria) and in near-familial and near-erotic relations. Pilar describes Finito as the most terrified matador she's ever seen before a bullfight (185:4–5) and teasingly accuses Jordan of being "afraid to see the bull come out" as he makes his final preparations for the bridge battle (405:2). Finito and Jordan approach their appointment with death out of "obligation" (186:16).

185:39+ **certain details so that you will see it:** In replacing "understand" with "see" in the draft, the novel again emphasizes her ekphrastic storytelling method (see 102:9–10).

186:5 *aficionados:* Hemingway defined an aficionado as "one who understands bullfights in general and in detail and still cares for them" (*DIA* 380). Aficionados are passionate, knowledgeable followers of the sport who sometimes qualify as bullfighting insiders.

186:18 **manzanilla:** A dry sherry wine made in Cádiz, the province of Andalusia tipped by Gibraltar that reaches toward Africa at the western edge of the Mediterranean Sea (see 186:18).

186:28–29 **Pastora was prevailed upon to sing:** Pastora Pavón, the singer also known as La Niña de los Peines (185:23). *Not* Pastora Imperio, the first "Pastora" mentioned (185:22).

186:29 **El Niño Ricardo:** Born Manuel Serrapí Sánchez in 1904 in Seville, Andalusia, Ricardo was the best flamenco guitar player of his generation as well as a flamenco composer. His style changed flamenco guitar for all who followed. He and Pastora Pavón (La Niña de los Peines) often performed together. On flamenco, see next entry.

It seems improbable that the era's most talented flamenco dancer, singer, and guitar player, all from Seville, all happened to be in a restaurant-bar in Valladolid—especially if this scene occurs on Easter Sunday when there was also a bullfight in Seville. This heavily Andalusian Romani cast is supplemented by the mention of Rafael el Gallo (187:8), whose former manager, potentially another Andalusian, is in the room—not to mention by Pilar herself. Pilar the storyteller is perhaps responsible for this peopling, for its hyped effect on her audience, in a kind of mise en abyme for the novel's exaggerated style. Hemingway might also have sacrificed realism in appealing to his audience's exoticized impression of Spain.

186:32 *flamenco:* An Andalusian folk musical performance art that brings together song, guitar, poetry, and dance, with stylized arm movements involving clapping, castanet-playing, and finger-snapping. Audience participation through stomping, clapping, and shouting is part of the joy (and for some, of its vulgarity). Its development was heavily influenced by the region's Romani population. At various times since flamenco's emergence in the eighteenth century, conservative Spanish purists have campaigned against it as not representative of—and even deleterious to—proper Spanish identity because of its ethnic, common, and regional origins and because of its association with seedy urban life. The Church considered it indecent and immoral, an assault on traditional family values. Other groups, even some progressives, saw it as a backward force that worked against the nation's effort to become modern. Nationalist Spain suppressed flamenco from the start of the war until the 1950s, when the need to expand the tourist industry led to its promotion. On the politics of this scene, see 184:29+ and 187:15.

187:8 **the former manager of Rafael el Gallo:** Rafael Gómez Ortega. El Gallo, or The Rooster, was another Andalusian Romani and briefly the husband of Pastora Imperio (185:22). Mandel describes him as "a picturesque improviser, capable of great artistry and widely acknowledged as an outstanding bullfighter" as well as an "extraordinary personality" (*Reading Hemingway* 225; see also Mandel, *Hemingway's DIA* 161, 183–86). One of Hemingway's letters identifying Pilar as Pastora does so in reference to Finito: "Pilar's husband (really Rafael el Gallo)" (to Charles Scribner, ca., 15 Aug. 1940, *SL* 508). Pastora and El Gallo married in 1911. She asked for a divorce a few months later, among other reasons because he did not let her leave the house alone, much less dance in public. They separated but did not divorce until 1934, after the Republic's reforms made it possible. El Gallo had several managers during his career; it is not clear which one, if any in particular, Hemingway has in mind.

187:15 **Retana:** The Retana family wielded great power in the taurine world and beyond. The most prominent was Manuel "Manolo" Retana, who managed bullfighting in Madrid from about 1907 to 1926; according to Mandel, Pilar might reference either this Retana or his brother Matías, an agent or *apoderado* (Mandel, *Reading Hemingway* 265–66). Most people in the bullfighting industry, especially at the higher levels, sided with the Nationalists. This entire prelapsarian scene disguises the social, economic, and political tensions that erupted into the war. It would be reasonable to surmise that the members of the Club Finito (186:6) belonged to the moneyed, landed, and ruling classes who would have become Nationalists such that this scene brilliantly merges two major institutions, bullfighting and the Spanish Catholic Church, whose cults of death they wielded upon the poor—upon Finito. The flamenco occurring in the scene contributes to its complex of cultural-political dynamics.

187:22+ **Pastora intervened:** The flamenco dancer Pastora Imperio, the first-mentioned "Pastora" (185:22), who has been in the audience listening to the music of Pastora Pavón (La Niña de los Peines) and El Niño Ricardo. The bad marriage between Pastora Imperio and Rafael el Gallo festers between the lines, in El Gallo's abandoning the manager and then in the comment that "no one had ever spoken harder against" El Gallo than Pastora Imperio "had herself"—a comment made by Pilar, whom Hemingway based on Pastora Imperio herself! Pilar-Pastora sits next to Pastora, on whom she was modeled, in the presence of Pastora's matador ex-husband's manager at an event for Pilar-Pastora's matador common-law husband, Finito-Rafael—a dizzying hall of mirrors that must have made Hemingway gleeful to write. Pastora Imperio "intervened so forcibly and in such language" that Pilar had to "intervene" to "quiet" her, Pilar's intervention itself equally forceful and colorful such that another gypsy woman "intervened to quiet" her. In other words, Pilar's language toward Pastora Imperio was as loud and crude as Pastora Imperio's because Pilar was based on Pastora Imperio.

That Pilar does not bother to explain to her audience who the three flamenco stars are speaks to their fame as well as to her personal familiarity with them. That Hemingway includes two different Pastoras revisits the novel's exploration of language, about what's in a name, and whether a rose is really a rose is really a rose, or a Pastora is really a Pastora is really a Pilar.

187:28 *Gitana:* The name for a Spanish gypsy woman, the equivalent of *Roma*. Borrow writes that *gypsy* and *gitano* derive "from a general belief that they were originally Egyptians" (*Zincali* 2–3; see also 174:18).

189:7 *Qué sencillo:* How simple!

189:11+ **the naked brown body:** The visual iconography most reminiscent of this passage is that of Christ removed from the cross in descent and lamentation paintings, and also *pietà* scenes where his mother Mary cradles his naked demolished body, Mary who is also sometimes the Bride of Christ.

190:11 **the gypsy came in:** Rafael, who shares Pastora Imperio's husband's name (187:8). Hemingway can't let this chapter end without a final dash of Romani.

NOTES

1. To Lester Ziffren, 15 Feb. 1937 (PUL). On the sleeping robe details, see "The Woods Arctic Sleeping Robe—the Woodcrafter's Winter Warmer," The Woods Life: A Blog about Woodcraft & Traditional Camping," 24 Dec. 2013 (https://thewoodslife.com/?p=1768; accessed 10 Dec. 2021). See also Mandel, *Reading Hemingway,* 281.

2. "The Las Ventas Bullring Converted into an Orchard," photo by Virgil Wall, 1 Jan. 1937 (https://www.abc.es/archivo/fotos/la-plaza-de-toros-de-las-ventas-convertida-en-una-huerta-35444329.html).

3. It isn't clear what painting he is talking about. Goya's *Christ Crucified* (1780) at the Prado is an oil painting and doesn't look a bullfighting poster. As Comley and Scholes observe, the passage Hemingway discusses does not itself look at Goya's crucifixion (116).

CHAPTER FIFTEEN

191:1 **Anselmo:** Hemingway presents most of this chapter from Anselmo's perspective, transitioning back to Jordan's across the conversation after the American appears. The novel's earlier, briefer instances of narrating through other characters' perspectives, sometimes in Jordan's absence, has trained the reader, mitigating the abruptness of this chapter's opening. Like the chapter's transitioning conversation, the chapter itself transitions toward entire chapters narrated through other characters in Jordan's absence. The chapter's time frame coincides with the events of the prior chapter unless Jordan and Fernando's walk takes the same time as (or more than) Anselmo's reflections. Either way, this moment softly disrupts the classical Aristotelian unities for dramatic Tragedies: of place, time, and action.

191:13–14 **fault of the orders . . . no allowance for a change in circumstance:** Anselmo's complaint about his orders from Jordan parallels Jordan's complaint about his orders from Golz.

192:8 **Fords, Fiats, Opels, Renaults, and Citroens:** Cheaper cars, for the division level, from the United States, Italy, Germany, and France. There are no Spanish cars, although in 1920 Ford opened a plant in Cádiz, on the southern Atlantic coast in Andalusia.

192:10 **Rolls-Royces, Lancias, Mercedes, and Isottas:** Higher-end cars, for the General Staff, from the UK, Italy, and Germany. No Spanish cars.

193:2–3 **poor men as we are [who] should never be fighting against us:** Anselmo echoes a conversation among Italian soldiers in *A Farewell to Arms*:

> "But even the peasants know better than to believe in a war. Everybody hates this war."
> "There is a class that controls a country that is stupid and does not realize anything and never can. That is why we have this war." (*FTA* 51)

193:5 Gallegos: They are from Galicia, the far northwestern region of Spain with Portugal on its southern border. Like Catalonia and the Basque, Galicia has its own language and cultural identity. Farming and fishing made up its economy and way of life well into the twentieth century. With little industry, it was one of the poorest regions in Spain. The Cathedral of Santiago de Compostela, maintained as the final resting place of St. James (patron saint of Spain and the Spanish army) and one of the most holy sites in the Catholic world, is in Galicia.

193:8–9 Líster . . . from the same town as Franco: This is only one of the novel's two mentions of Francisco **Franco** Bahamonde, the Nationalist general who would become Spain's dictator from 1939 until his death (see 244:31–32). For much of his military career, Franco was an *africanista*, a member of the Spanish Foreign Legion. His leadership style was brilliant and pitiless. During the leftist October revolution of 1934 in Galicia's neighbor Asturias, the government brought in Franco and units of the Army of Africa, both Spanish *legionnaires* and Moroccan *regulares* (Moors) to crush it. Several days of retributive torture, injury, and murder followed (182:22–23). As Hugh Thomas has concluded, "After the revolution of October 1934 and the manner in which it had been quelled, it would have required a superhuman effort to avoid the culminating disaster of civil war" (137).

On Enrique **Líster** Forján, see 230:13+. The **town** is El Ferrol, a port on the northwest coast. Anselmo's association of the Republican General Líster with the Nationalist General Franco suggests the depths of the civil war, with localities divided among themselves, and connects the brutality of the two men.

193:36 like a tartar: Someone from Tartary, which covered much of medieval central Asia, which the novel treats as the vast Mongol Empire of the thirteenth and fourteenth centuries, founded by Genghis Khan, who had a most fearsome reputation (see 234:24). European literature and culture often conflated *Tartar* and *Mongol*, using both terms as racist slang tantamount to *savage* (but not *primitive*).

194:15 you have no house: Anselmo is from Ávila, in Nationalist territory. He cannot return unless the Republic wins the war.

194:23–24 almost June: On the soldiers speaking in terms of the solar (Roman) or lunar calendars, see 153:24.

195:12 Lugo: Either the geographically largest province of Galicia or the town that is its capital and one of its most populous. Today it is a small city.

195:13 *analfabetos:* Illiterates.

195:20 **inscribed. . . . Noya . . . Negreira:** Drafted or enlisted from coastal Noia or inland Negreira.

196:10 **we have formidable aviation:** Anselmo overhears—or rather, overwatches a conversation he can't hear—Nationalist soldiers using the exact language he used about his side's aviation (39:4) and expressing the same fear about their enemy's aviation. It is another way Hemingway sympathetically equates opposing soldiers caught up in a war they didn't want.

196:24 **some form of civic penance:** Penance, done to hold oneself responsible for a sin or other moral or spiritual malfeasance, is typically a religious act, and in the present context a Catholic one. For the next few pages, Anselmo continues the novel's meditation on the nature of sin. Can a secular institution be sin's arbiter? Can sin exist outside religion, outside the Church?

196:30 **a very good man:** One of the novel's occasional pronouncements from an omniscient narrator that contribute to the novel's panoply of voices and its genre play.

197:37 **In those who like it there is always a rottenness:** Jordan admits to himself that he enjoys killing (287:7). The day of the International Brigade farewell parade in Barcelona, Hemingway wrote in a letter to Max Perkins about the "carnival of treachery and rotten-ness" that was the Spanish Civil War (to Maxwell Perkins, 28 Oct. 1938, *SL* 474). Was the rottenness as inevitable, even necessary, as it was regrettable?

198:12+ **that one pays as in the days of the Church:** Anselmo smiles after issuing this standard critique of the Catholic Church as a humanity profiteer, "well organized" to make up the rules and capitalize upon them. The Church's corruption is perhaps a too-convenient way for Anselmo to exit his very serious ponderings.

198:37 **cigar store Indian:** A carved wooden statue of a Native American used by shops to advertise tobacco, an agricultural product introduced to Europeans by the indigenous people of the Americas. Jordan likens Fernando's demeanor to that of the cliché of the unsmiling, silent Indian.

199:15+ **The cave of the lost eggs:** In *Death in the Afternoon*'s glossary, Hemingway defines *huevos* (eggs) as "slang for testicles as we say balls" (410). Jordan's telling Fernando to ask Pilar implies her part in Pablo's emasculation.

200:6–7 **Agincourt:** One of England's major victories over France during the Hundred Years' War, the Battle of Agincourt took place in northern France on 25 October

1415, St. Crispin's Day. The battle is best known for the triumph of the English longbow archers over the French cavalry and infantry, which signaled a new era of long-range weaponry; and for Henry's slaughter of some three thousand French prisoners of war. In literature, Agincourt is the centerpiece of Shakespeare's *Henry V* and the setting of King Henry's famous "band of brothers" speech about his soldiers being remembered forevermore (III.3.10–12). The irony in relation to Jordan's situation may be intended: no victory, no remembrance, certainly no band of brothers in Pablo's gang. One could also see in Henry's shaming of unmanly Englanders, "now abed" rather than fighting in France (III.3.66–67), a subtle shaming of England, America, and France for not fighting in Spain, perhaps too a shaming of the United States for not yet joining the new world war against fascism.

200:29 **the Germans call an attack a storm:** The German word *sturm* means both storm and assault, attack, or charge. Hemingway calling attention to the two meanings furthers the novel's investigation of the relationship between war and Naturalism. The German operational doctrine of "lightning war," or *Blitzkrieg*, was not put into full force until the Second World War. It called for massed firepower maneuvering with great speed to overwhelm defenses, penetrate lines, and quickly reach the enemy's rear, isolating units and severing lines of communication and support. German tank support of the Nationalists was limited, and the term *Blitzkrieg* would not become widely known until Germany's astonishing military success opened the world war.

201:6 **a second Coolidge:** John Calvin Coolidge Jr., the thirtieth US president, known for his taciturnity and his deadpan wit.

CHAPTER SIXTEEN

202:8 ***No sé:*** I don't know.

203:11+ **rub thy feet . . . dry them with thy hair:** Mary, the sister of Martha and Lazarus, dries Jesus's feet with her hair after anointing them with a pound of spikenard (John 11:2; John 12:3; also Mark 14:3–9, Matt. 26:6–13). Pilar the prognosticator alludes to an event often seen as a prophetic funereal rite that occurred six days before Christ's preordained death. In Luke 7:37–38, an unnamed woman, a "sinner," bathed his feet in her tears, dried them with her hair, then "anointed them with the ointment." The woman in John connects to Maria by the shared name; the allusion in Luke fits the context of Maria's guilt and trauma over her sexual violation and the possibility of redemption through serving Jordan. "**Ex-Lord**" because of many on the Spanish left's rejection of Christianity.

203:33–34 **Blow up the fire:** Increasing the oxygen improves combustion and decreases smoke. Having just criticized Jordan for issuing commands to Maria, Pilar now attempts to assert herself over the younger woman. Maria would need to kneel, squat, or bend over, just as she would have drying Jordan's feet.

204:6+ **Roberto . . . *Inglés*:** Maria's claim invites scrutiny. Until this point, she has addressed him as "*Inglés*" in an expression of intimacy (138:7), even insisting upon it (159:33+). But by chapter 20 she calls him "Roberto" when they are alone together and continues to do so for the rest of the novel. After declaring that they are the same person, she says, "Since we are different I am glad that thou art Roberto and I Maria" (262:38); after the second ecstatic lovemaking scene, she calls him "Roberto" (381:22); in her only moment of interior monologue, in the final chapter, she calls him "Roberto" (449:25+); and in her final parting call she does so once again as she rides away with the survivors, leaving him to die (465:3).

All the guerillas except Maria and Pilar use the two names interchangeably throughout. The switch from "*Inglés*" to "Roberto" involves the Jordan-Maria-Pilar triangle. When Maria insists on *Inglés* as "my *Inglés*" (159:35), and when she insists again in the same chapter, she explains that "I call thee *Inglés* as Pilar does" (172:14), revealing the "my" as a proprietary claim against Pilar, who only ever calls him *Inglés*. Maria's switch signals an emotional movement out from under Pilar's influence to a relationship on her terms alone. Thus at some level Pilar was with the lovers for the "always and forever to nowhere" experience (chapter 13), but exorcised by the "always now, for now always" experience (chapter 37).

204:15 **Bacchus:** God of wine and drunken ecstasy, the Roman version of the Greek Dionysus.

206:1–2 **where the women eat with the men:** Pablo's Spanish *machismo* dominates the next several pages. Beyond his jealousy over Maria, Pablo taunts Jordan's manliness under the shadow of the band's accusations of his own cowardice as well as from his position of subordination to Pilar's leadership. Yet a truth lurks in his taunts: Jordan struggles with insecurities regarding his father's legacy of cowardly suicide, his anxiety about living up to his grandfather's war record, and his inferiority to Pilar's storytelling powers. For Hemingway's generation, insecurity and cowardice compromised a man's sexual as well as gender identity. As with most Hemingway male protagonists' heterosexual desire, Jordan's is not without its queer quirks.

206:4–5 **the men wear skirts as do the women . . . in Scotland:** Pablo uses kilts to question Jordan's manliness but more significantly to emphasize his foreignness. Pablo and Primitivo address him in this scene as *Inglés*. An English-speaker. To Spaniards, it is all the same—just as Spain's significant regional and ethnic differences meant next to nothing to most foreigners reading about the war in the newspapers, nor to most English-language readers of the novel. Jordan's drinking scotch might have inspired Pablo's accusation of wearing kilts. In Italy in *A Farewell to Arms*, Catherine Barkley is alternately called English and Scotch.

206:21 **Circus of Price:** Circo Price in Madrid, also known as El Price, is a permanent hall or venue for vaudeville and popular performances in the Plaza del Rey. In Pablo's era, an English family of professional entertainers, the Price family, owned the hall. They would have brought Scots who performed in kilts. Pablo's work transporting horses for the bullfights and the army, and escorting the horses into the bullring, would have taken him to Madrid (182:17+; 190:4–5).

206:37–38 **surely there are mountains:** Montana has its name from the Spanish word for mountain, *montaña*. Jordan's connection to Spain may partly stem from the country's geographic kinship with his home state.

207:8 **by living on it and declaring the intention of improving it, a man could obtain a title:** Jordan describes the Homestead Act, signed by President Lincoln in 1862 and actively used into the 1930s, which granted a person up to 160 acres. It took the American Civil War to make the act happen because Southern states had opposed it, fearing the creation of additional nonslavery states. But with secession, they had removed themselves from the US government. By 1934, some 10 percent of all US land had passed into private hands via this Act. Most homesteaders were European immigrants. The act applied to unmarried women as well, whether single, divorced, widowed, or abandoned, and after the American Civil War to Black citizens.

207:11–12 **an agrarian reform which means something:** Agustín references one of the root causes of the Spanish Civil War. Until the establishment of the Second Spanish Republic in 1931, Spain was a monarchy and much of its economy all but feudal. A small class of landowners possessed most arable land, securing its hold on wealth and power. Agrarian reform was a priority of the new Republic. Too many Spaniards were landless workers who lived at the whim of others. Almost immediately, it devised a system of land distribution managed by a central committee that proved too byzantine, with various qualifications and exceptions, and ineffective (Thomas 81–82). For the politically left of center, the reforms did not go far enough; for the right of center, they went far too far. Such reform efforts galvanized the right to retake the government in the 1934 elections and eventually support the military rebellion after the reorganized left regained the government in 1936. Agustín appreciates that the Homestead Act's simplicity made it potent and profoundly transformational.

Among other problems of the pre-Republican agrarian system, the large landowners had refused to take measures that would better the quality of life of their workers. Irrigation development, for example, would have produced greater yield, fed more people, dropped prices, and improved the lives of the working class considerably. The plot of Hemingway and Ivens's fundraising film, *The Spanish Earth,* links a village's Republic-enabled do-it-yourself irrigation project and the Republican military's battle for an important bridge. The film wisely does not mention land redistribution, as doing so would have raised the specter of communism. The Homestead Act had the advantage of offering first-time ownership, not redistribution.

208:2–3 **who do not know they are fascists but will find it out:** When conditions in a divided society arise such that the contest to control the government demands people pick a side, they must align with the power interests of that side. That alignment readily slips into identification.

210:1–2 **a false professor . . . hasn't got a beard:** Beards in Spain signified masculine authority. In a moment, Maria touches Jordan's stubbly cheek to testify to his manliness. The innuendo about the couple's lovemaking in Pablo's rejoinder, "You should know," substantiates the subtext; the matter of beard length turns the remark into a sly below-the-belt dig about a different physical shortcoming (211:7–9). Ironically, the chapter has just described Pablo as merely "stubble-faced" (205:38)—so, no different from Jordan except perhaps more visibly so because of the American's blondness. As with his joke about kilts, Pablo continues to remind everyone that Jordan isn't Spanish. Fernando's hearing an **Extremadura** accent in Jordan underscores the deeply local nature of Spanish identity politics (210:19), a nature often at odds with national projects.

211:25 **like a boar's:** Wild boars, with their size and their tusks, can be quite dangerous, ferociously so, especially when cornered—as Pablo is in this scene and much of the novel.

211:27–28 **in this war and some before:** Hemingway added this line to the draft (MS11-006). Nowhere else does the novel mention Jordan's experiences before 1936 of knowing other killers, whether in war or in peace. The circumstances remain a total mystery. The addition is in keeping with Hemingway's decision to make Jordan a more mature and worldly young man.

211:34 ***Estoy muy borracho:*** I am very drunk.

212:13 ***Sinverguenza:*** Scoundrel. Someone without shame.

212:13 **committed now:** Conveniently, Jordan commits to killing Pablo immediately after Pablo has announced his refusal to be provoked into provoking Jordan to kill him.

212:14 ***Cobarde:*** Coward. One could reasonably wonder if Jordan accuses himself of cowardice in not killing Pablo, a decision he refers to as a failure (212:22). Pablo soon enough levels that accusation at him (213:1–2).

212:21 **a *bicho raro*:** A strange one, an odd one (literally "rare").

212:25 **feeling it all moving in a circle:** At the beginning of chapter 18, Jordan will liken the cyclic experience of repeatedly wondering if he should kill Pablo to being on a merry-go-round (225:1+). That Hemingway added this phrase in hand (in red ink) to the draft suggests the edit occurred after drafting at least the beginning of chapter 18. The entire novel has a cyclic structure, beginning and ending with Jordan prone on the pine needles of the forest floor.

213:17+ ***negro:*** Black, in color, race, hue, or character. Nonwhite, or dark. Pablo notes that others call Agustín *negro*, and Agustín's denying Pablo permission suggests it could be used as a friendly nickname (213:21–22). The novel nowhere indicates that Agustín is of African descent; is from southern Spain, the part of the country geographically and culturally closest to Moorish Africa; or is Romani or Jewish. Given Agustín's incessant and endearing vulgarities, as well as his negativity and temper, the nickname could amiably connote coarse, wicked, bad, moody, gloomy, or dark. Pablo meanly calls out Agustín for his crudeness, quickness to anger, and lack of self-control, some of the stereotypical traits assigned to people of color, supposedly more prey to their own emotions and physicality. The American word *negro* comes from the Spanish word for black, from which the much more offensive slang term derived. For the Spaniards inside the text, *negro* realistically acknowledges the centuries of intermixed cultures (and bodies).

Agustín rejects **blanco,** perhaps because it does not fit his race or character, and definitely because it is the epithet for Nationalists, the Whites. Spain inherited the term from the Russian Civil War (1918–1923), where it designated the forces who fought against the communist Bolshevik "Reds." The Whites were a motley of monarchists, capitalists, and even socialist democrats uneasily allied to save Russia from the revolutionaries.

215:30 **Qué te importa:** As if you cared. What do you care.

216:1–2 **Get out and fist yourself into the snow. Take your bad milk out of here:** Pilar tells Pablo to go masturbate outside, as in "go jerk off." The Spanish word for milk, *leche,* has slang meaning of semen (i.e., cum, jism, spunk).

216:2–3 **horse exhausted *maricón*:** The adjectival "horse exhausted" picks up on Agustín's telling Pablo to go copulate with his beloved horses (215:13, 20). Western culture long associated bestiality with male homosexuality as types of sodomy—thus the modified noun, *maricón,* which Hemingway translates in *Death in the Afternoon* as "a sodomite, nance, queen, fairy, fag, etc. They have these in Spain too" (*DIA* 417). The English word *faggot* is probably a better match in terms of sheer offensiveness and ugliness. Lola de Aguado's Spanish translation of the novel writes the phrase simply as *maricón de caballos,* or "horse faggot" (256). Pilar is the only character who uses the word, a fact perhaps explained by her life among bullfighters—per Hemingway's commentary, "[i]n bullfighting circles the word is used as a term of opprobrium or ridicule or as an insult" (*DIA* 418). As in English, the Spanish word can also be applied to a heterosexual man who acts with insufficient manliness. In this case, a word like *pussy* would be equivalent; Hemingway originally typed "horse exhausted pansy" (MS11-007).

CHAPTER SEVENTEEN

218:8 *Matarlo:* Kill him.

218:23 *facciosos:* Fascists.

219:30 **bureaucracy with his mouth:** Jordan soon catches himself falling into bureaucratic euphemism in speaking about murder (220:5–8), as if word choice could render the act more agreeable, and even uses the verb "liquidate" (221:17), a word that implies political expediency or necessity. Jordan's language continues to slip in and out of political and military rhetoric regardless of his and others having already called attention to their semantic placebo effect (e.g., 132:15+; 163:38+). See other reflections on language (166:32+; 289:12+).

220:7+ **French . . . Spanish:** Jordan's ongoing concern with language, and in this case with the differences between languages, will come to a head when he distinguishes between the Spanish "La Gloria" and the French "La Gloire" (380:21). The text's efforts stumble in the need to use English to capture the "bureaucracy" apparently inherent in Spanish. Does the English "to eliminate" connote precisely what "eliminar" would in Fernando's speech (219:22)?

221:17 **liquidate:** In the draft, Hemingway replaced "kill" with "liquidate" (MS11–007).

222:6–7 **The wind has changed:** Hemingway added this line by hand to the typed draft (MS11–007). In *The Garden of Eden*, Hemingway also signifies character changes with wind changes (Eby, *Reading* 34, 174). The question of whether the wind influenced Pablo's change as a force of Naturalism or merely reflects Pablo's change as a pathetic fallacy remains ambiguous. Hemingway reinforces the ambiguity by having Pablo speak the words almost as proclamation.

222:12 **Now he is friendly:** Jordan cautioned himself about this moment upon meeting Pablo (16:31–32). "Now" marks a temporary state, a usage to keep in mind elsewhere.

223:38 *De veras:* Truly.

CHAPTER EIGHTEEN

225:1 **merry-go-round:** Jordan refers to his repetitive cycling back to the decision about killing Pablo. One wonders if the scene evokes Jordan's (or Hemingway's) ongoing psychomachy about self-murder, consciously or not. In a 26 July 1939 letter, about three months before writing this passage, he wrote to his first wife, "Important thing for me to do is not get discouraged and take easy way out like your and my noted ancestors. Because very bad example to children" (to Hadley Mowrer, *SL* 493). Jordan's back-and-forth over shooting his foil, Pablo, as well as his waffling about his responsibility for shooting his other foil, Kashkin, prefigure his back-and-forth over shooting himself.

226:24 **no more rides on it:** In the draft, Hemingway inserted and then deleted another sentence to end the paragraph: "These people have their own lives and their lives are not my business" (MS11–007). This interesting restatement of the emotional detachment he requires to do his job is just plain wrong. Their lives are literally his business in this business of the bridge.

227:4 **Grant:** Ulysses S. Grant received an appointment as brigadier general in the Union Army early in the US Civil War. In March 1864, he became a lieutenant general and commander of the entire army. After the war, he served as the eighteenth president of the United States. His *Personal Memoirs of U. S. Grant*, published in two volumes in 1855 by Mark Twain, was an enormous commercial and critical success. Historians and literary scholars consider it among the finest war memoirs from a military leader. Hemingway knew and owned the memoirs. Grant did not see its success, having died of throat cancer five days after completing it (Grant, 1160–61). He had accepted Twain's suggestion to write it to provide for his future widow; he wrote the book aware of his impending death. As he expressed during those final months, "I had been adding to my book and to my coffin. I presume every strain of the mind or body is one more nail in the coffin" (1111). In one of Grant's last letters, he wrote a phrase the spirit of which haunted Hemingway and Jordan: "The fact is I think I am a verb instead of a personal noun. A verb is anything that signifies to be; to do; or to suffer. I signify all three" (1120). Grant drank and smoked, but not to regular excess by his era's standards. His political opponents fueled the conception of him as a drunkard. As much drinking as Jordan does in the novel, he should perhaps look to himself before disparagingly comparing Pablo to the rumored Grant.

228:12+ **Florida Hotel:** Hemingway and Gellhorn lived in this Madrid hotel during the war. It was on the Plaza del Callao, off the **Gran Via** (a major avenue through downtown Madrid) only a few blocks from the Telefónica, the tallest building in the area, from which foreign journalists sent out their dispatches by radiogram. The Florida was full of journalists, other international observers, and sometimes American brigaders. The building no longer exists. Hemingway set his play *The Fifth Column* and his story "Night before Battle" in the Florida. The story's depiction of its correspondent protagonist, whose room was the social hub of the Florida, accurately reflects the role Hemingway took on at the hotel. The **Mantequerías Leonesas** (Leonese Creamery) café specialized in dairy products and, apparently, absinthe. On **Gaylord**'s, see 228:27+. The **Hotel Gran Via** at Gran Via 12 stood directly across the street from the Telefónica and was a popular restaurant and watering hole for foreign correspondents; Jordan did not care for the company of Hemingway's sort. On **Karkov**, see 231:20+.

228:27+ **Gaylord's:** The Gaylord Hotel stood at No. 4 Alfonso XI Street, on the northwest corner of Alfonso XI and Valenzuela, a block west of the Parque del Buen Retiro and several blocks east of the Telefónica. Built in the early 1930s in the Italian-inspired rationalist style, its reinforced concrete created an entirely unornamented building in sharp contrast to most of the surrounding architecture. The height of modern functionalism, with its plain flat concrete exterior forming a curved wedge to fit the street corner space, the Gaylord looked like a seven-story military bunker. Inside, it was lush, its bar "decorated with cubist panels and colored glass" (O'Keefe 57). The Soviet leadership moved into the building beginning in late September 1936. No one wore a uniform in order that Russia could maintain the pretense of military nonintervention (O'Keefe 57). Jordan's judgment of it as "too luxurious," with food "too good for a besieged city," a revolutionary city no less, is fair. Gaylord's came down in 1962. See 356:16+.

229:19 **the 1934 revolution:** The uprising in Asturias. See 182:22.

229:21 **the Lenin Institute the Comintern:** An instrument of Joseph Stalin's Soviet Union, the Communist International, or **Comintern** (1919–1943), was the organization intent on realizing a communist world order. In 1926, it established the International Lenin School, also known as the **Lenin Institute** or Lenin University, to train leaders from around the world for its global ambitions. The Institute stood opposite the British embassy, and "was one of Moscow's most modernized buildings," with such rare amenities as "steam heat" and "hot and cold showers" (Gitlow 242):

> There is no other school in any part of the world that gives such a thorough, well-rounded training in the methods of fomenting revolution, gaining power, setting up a dictatorship, operating a government under a dictatorship, and handling the forces of oppression. In addition, the Lenin University gives the student a theoretical basis and a very adequate background in international power politics. The graduates are the well-trained ambassadors of world communism, the skilled agents of world revolution.
>
> During the three years, the Lenin student is also drilled and trained in military science, OGPU espionage work and sabotage. The agenda includes a course on the organization of combat groups, how to induct people into their formations, and the training techniques which must be used. (Gitlow 246)

The **military academy** would be the M. V. Frunze Military Academy in Moscow, the name given in 1925 to an institution established in 1918.

229:31+ **Valentín Gonzalez, called El Campesino:** Jordan inaccurately accuses Gonzalez of "having never been a peasant." While he had some previous military background, he spent his childhood in relative poverty, working as a laborer to help support his family. He earned his nickname as a teenager—it was not a propagandistic invention. His father was an anarchist, and throughout his young adulthood, Gonzalez clashed with various authorities. The Second Moroccan War—the Rif War (1911–1927)—was a protracted conflict of rebellion by native Moroccans to liberate themselves from Spanish and French colonial rule. Initially Gonzalez served in the Spanish Foreign Legion, but after escaping from prison for killing a noncommissioned officer who had slapped him, he joined the forces of Muhammad Ibn **Abd-el-Krim** El-Khattabi, the leader of the Moroccan uprising. By necessity, el-Krim specialized in guerilla insurgency tactics. Although in the mid-1920s Hemingway admired the American airmen who organized out of principle to fight for the French (and thus the Spanish), his sympathies really landed on the other side, with el-Karim and his cause (Eby, "Maji Maji" 21). When those American volunteers bombed native villages in the fall of 1925, Hemingway agreed with the instant global outrage (see Eby, *Reading* 145–47). It was the bombing of Guernica a dozen years earlier and in another country. Historians regard Spain's struggles in Morocco and the end of Spain's global power as one cause of its Civil War due to the deleterious (effectively overnight) impact on the military's purpose and centuries-old identity.

Formed in 1920, the **Spanish Foreign Legion**, from which Gonzalez deserted, was the Spaniard portion of the Army of Africa—the Africanistas—that also included native Moorish troops. With its motto "Long Live Death," the Foreign Legion constituted the hard-core element of the Spanish Army that was fiercely loyal to the legacy of the Spanish Empire. The rebellion that turned into the Spanish Civil War began with the Africanistas in Morocco under the leadership of Francisco Franco, on his way to commanding the Nationalists and becoming Spain's dictator from 1940 to his death in 1975.

Recaptured by Spain in Morocco, Gonzalez benefited from the general amnesty of 1926. He later switched allegiance from the anarchist Confederación Nacional del Trabajo (National Confederation of Workers, the CNT) to the Spanish Communist Party (PCE). A member of the PCE's famed Fifth Regiment at the outset of the war, Gonzalez became the first commander of the 10th Mixed Brigade upon its formation in December 1936. He was a successful, aggressive military leader known for being harsh with his own troops. Hemingway's (or Jordan's) characterization of this ersatz peasant with a "black beard, his thick negroid lips, and his feverish, staring eyes" (230:2–3) who once sided with the Africans against the Spanish and now has a poorly disciplined tongue, has racist undertones.

230:13+ **the simple stonemason, Enrique Lister from Galicia, who now commanded a division:** Hemingway parodies his own propagandistic language from *The Spanish Earth*'s introduction of **Líster:** "Enrique Líster, a stone-mason from Galicia. In six months of fighting he rose from a simple soldier to the command of a division. He is one of the most brilliant young soldiers of the Republican Army." Born in Galicia outside Santiago de Compostela, Enrique Líster Forján in boyhood moved with his family to Cuba, where he became a stonemason. He attended the M. V. Frunze Military Academy in Moscow in the early 1930s before returning to Spain, where he joined the Spanish Communist Party and, once the war started, the Fifth Regiment, which he soon commanded. He and La Pasionaria often receive credit for rallying soldiers to the defense of Madrid at the outbreak of the war. In October 1936, he took command of the 1st Mixed Brigade, a new basic unit that could operate independently by virtue of its integrated infantry, artillery, mortar, cavalry, armored vehicles, scout, and medical, logistical, and administrative function. The brigade *mixta* system created these combined-arms units to act like miniature divisions, enabling them to function relatively independently. By the end of January, Líster commanded the new 11th Division, known as Líster's Division, which would become one of the most celebrated units of the war. The 11th took part in the battles of Jarama and Guadalajara in February and March 1937, the Republic's defensive successes just prior to the time of the novel. *The Spanish Earth* glimpses both battles.

Líster was one of the most significant Republican military commanders, albeit his career and reputation benefited from his commitment to the Spanish Communist Party. Paul Preston, a historian of the war whose sympathies are undeniably Republican and leftist, has labeled Colonel Líster a "heavy-handed Stalinist" with a rabid attitude toward suspected Fifth Columnists—Nationalist agents in the Republic—and anyone on the Republican side who threatened the order and discipline of the communist-dominated military command structure, such as anarchists and the Trotskyite POUM (*Spanish Civil War,* 277). Jordan calls him "murderous in discipline," a "true fanatic" (234:22). According to Thomas, however, Líster was also "warm-hearted . . . with a strong sense of friendship," a forgiving man to those he liked and a talented speaker "ready to lend himself to any propaganda activity" (814). He was one of Hemingway's sources, if never a great friend, and Hemingway included Líster in a short list of "true heroes" of the Republic along with El Campesino, Juan Modesto, and Gustavo Durán (to Edmund Wilson [10 Dec 1938], Outgoing).

230:15+ **Juan Modesto from Andalucía:** Hemingway considered Modesto one of the two finest Republican commanders,[1] "more intelligent than Lister or El Campesino" (see prior entries), the other being Gustavo Durán (see 335:24+). Modesto's Andalusian hometown of Puerto de Santa Maria, Port Saint Mary, sits at the mouth of the Guadalete River, where its waters feed into the Bay of Cádiz and then into the Atlantic Ocean. He worked at a sawmill before serving in the Spanish Foreign Legion in Morocco (see 229:31+). He joined the communist party in the early 1930s, and with Líster came out of the Fifth Regiment. Both commanded divisions at Jarama, but Modesto soon overpassed Líster to command the V Corps in mid-1937, then the Army of the North, the Army of the Ebro, and finally the Army of the Center. He wielded an authoritarian leadership style.[2]

The first **Berlitz** language school opened in 1878 in Providence, Rhode Island, on its way to becoming an international company.

231:8 **Marx Brothers at the Opera:** Jordan imagines taking Maria to see *A Night at the Opera* (1935), made by the slapstick comic act the Marx Brothers (Mandel, *Reading* 247–48). This was their first film after Zeppo quit the group, leaving Chico, Harpo, and Groucho. According to listings in *ABC Madrid,* the film ended a smattering of Madrid showings on 28 February 1937 and returned on 5 October 1937 for the month;[3] Gellhorn writes about it that fall (Moorehead 138). Hemingway is either misremembering or deliberately backdating the longer run.

231:17+ **"Fuente Ovejuna":** A play by **Lope de Vega** (165:1) published in 1619 and named after a Spanish town in Castile where the historical events it dramatizes occurred in 1476. In the play, a military commander representing the old order and the upper class terrorizes the village, his methods including attempted rape and forced marriage. The peasants kill and behead him. To avoid individual repercussions, they announce that Fuenteovejuna, the whole town, did it (as in Pilar's tale; see 105:35). They survive information-seeking torture by the authorities and are eventually vindicated and pardoned by the newly reunified Spain's monarchs, Isabel and Ferdinand.

The communist **Karkov** (see next entry) of course believed it "the greatest play ever written" about class struggle between the agrarian proletariat and the (fascist) oppressive aristocracy.

231:20+ **Karkov:** The real-life figure upon whom the character Karkov was based, Mikhail Koltsov, born Moisei Fridland, was Hemingway's contemporary, and like Hemingway a brilliant, charming, larger-than-life figure, a great storyteller, bon vivant, and journalist-adventurer. He had an autonomous core that variously expressed itself (or could be perceived as) admirable intellectual integrity, obstinacy, and foolhardy defiance, which exactly fits Jordan's description of him. One can easily imagine Koltsov's appeal for Hemingway; one can also easily imagine the difficulties having such a personality would have presented a committed, high-level communist in the early Soviet era.

Koltsov appeared in Madrid in early August 1936, less than a month after the start of the war as a foreign correspondent for *Pravda,* the Russian Communist Party's official newspaper. Koltsov was widely rumored to be Joseph Stalin's inside man in Spain, although scholars disagree on the exact nature of the relationship between the two.[4] Koltsov was nevertheless well-connected and hugely influential. He and Hemingway met soon after the American's arrival in late March 1937. The two men spent time together in Madrid for only about a month that spring. During that time, Koltsov strove to deepen Hemingway's knowledge of the political situation and sway him to the Soviet perspective. Koltsov's recalcitrance and occasionally blithe outspokenness suggest that the truths he imparted to Hemingway weren't necessarily the official truths. Hemingway first fictionally depicted Kolstov and his risky opining through the unnamed short bespectacled character in "Night Before Battle." Hemingway's and Koltsov's travels overlapped a second time in Spain, briefly, in the fall of 1937.

The Soviet's secret police, the NKVD, arrested Koltsov in December 1938. Stalin had him executed in February 1940. Frederick White has presented a number of reasons: Koltsov's open departures from the party line; his affair with the wife of the NKVD chief; his pre-Stalin association with Trotskyites; the popularity of his book *Spanish Diary* and its celebration of the revolutionary spirit in Spain, with the implied contrast to the Soviet Union; Stalin's appeasement of Hitler as the world war broke out; and André Marty's accusations of ongoing Trotskyite activities as well as for sleeping with a German spy (59–60). He also may have simply known too much about how Stalin operated. With respect to *For Whom the Bell Tolls,* Marty's accusation is the most pertinent reason. The French communist Marty was the top political commissar for the International Brigades (see 416:34) with whom Koltsov shared mutual disdain, dramatized by Hemingway in chapter 42, where the Russian threatens to "find out just how untouchable" Marty is (425:33–34; 426:14). The fatal denunciation may have happened the other way around. Hemingway probably did not hear about Koltsov's disappearance until after completing the novel. To Maxwell Perkins, at the galley stage, he wrote, "The whole story of Marty and Karkov would take another entire volume to tell" (26 Aug. 1940, *SL* 515).

232:7+ **Karkov's wife . . . Karkov's mistress:** Koltsov's **wife**, Elisabeta Ratmanova, was sometimes with him in Spain. Sefton Delmer, a British journalist, described her as "a neurotic-looking ex-ballerina," which fits Hemingway's description (qtd. in Preston, *We Saw Spain Die* 188). Koltsov's long-time **mistress** was Maria Osten, a German-born Russian journalist; Karkov's mistress speaks German (357:8) and strongly resembles Osten. Osten became famous in the Soviet Union for adopting a German boy with Koltsov to save him from Nazi Germany and parading him about Russia, a story she told in her 1935 book *Hubert in Wonderland: Days and Deeds of a German Pioneer*. She and Koltsov also took a young Spanish orphan boy back to Russia. The NKVD arrested Osten in 1941. She either died in prison or was executed in 1942. Ratmanova wrote for the communist youth version of *Pravda*, and Osten for the German-language *Deutsche Zentral Zeitung*. As for the "other wife" or "maybe two more," Koltsov had been married before Ratmanova and was notorious for enjoying female company.

232:34–35 **bubble reputation in the cannon's mouth:** From Jaques's "All the world's a stage" speech in Shakespeare's *As You Like It*. The soldier is the fourth role a man plays in his lifetime: "Full of strange oaths and bearded like the pard, / Jealous in honor, sudden and quick in quarrel, / Seeking the bubble reputation / Even in the cannon's mouth" (II.vii.156–60). The line suggests the ephemeral recognition of battlefield heroics sought in willing exchange for one's life. Pablo takes more interest in drinking wine than solving the tactical military challenge.

233:2 **Not the Quantrills, nor the Mosbys:** In his passing review of military leaders from the American Civil War, Jordan does not distinguish between Union or Confederate officers. His considerations are tactical and operational, not moral or political.

William Clarke **Quantrill** organized a civilian guerilla force that fought for the Confederacy, operating in Missouri and Kansas, two states at the center of the debate about extending slavery westward in the years leading to the war. A ragtag group capturing escaped slaves became, during the war, Quantrill's Raiders, whose numbers sometimes reached a few hundred men. Quantrill received a formal captaincy. As the size of his outfit indicates, he led actions of greater magnitude than the interdiction and harassment usually associated with partisan work. His methods were brutal. According to an early biographer, "Quantrill was a fatalist," and upon learning his treasured horse had been injured beyond use, he said, "Death is coming, and my end is near" (Connelley 466–67). On 10 May 1865, Union soldiers ambushed the raiders. Attempting to flee on horseback, Quantrill received two bullet wounds, the first paralyzing him from the chest down (474). As Connelley describes the scene, "[t]he guerrillas wished to carry Quantrill away, but he would not go. He knew his wound was mortal and told them so. . . . No, he would not go" (478). Unlike with Jordan, however, the enemy captured him on the spot. He died of wounds twenty-seven days later in a Louisville, Kentucky, military prison hospital (480).

John Singleton **Mosby**, like Quantrill, led a Confederate partisan unit. He operated mostly in Virginia, and he too received a commission, eventually becoming a lieutenant colonel. His politics were more complicated than Quantrill's. He argued against secession but fought for his native state of Virginia. After the war, he became a Republican and befriended President Ulysses S. Grant, the former Union Army commander. Van de Water's biography of Custer describes Mosby's methods and genius:

> Mosby's butternut troopers had no base for a heavy Blue foot to crush. The men of the 43rd Battalion, Virginia Cavalry were quartered throughout the [Shenandoah] valley in the homes of patriotic residents. They met at Mosby's order, raided, ambushed or attacked, and dissolved like a spent raincloud. Far ahead of his day, Mosby envisaged the modern purpose of cavalry. His was not a weapon of strong offense but a scouting, delaying, enemy-pestering force. The rangers had discarded the romantic saber in favor of two revolvers per man. They were as evasive as fleas and they stung like hornets. (75)

A few months before Hemingway's novel came out, F. Scott Fitzgerald published a short story about Mosby, "The End of Hate," in *Collier's* magazine (22 June 1940).

233:7 **Vicksburg:** Confederate forces at Vicksburg, Mississippi, surrendered on 4 July 1863, the day after the Confederate loss at Gettysburg, Pennsylvania. The two defeats marked the beginning of the end for the rebelling South. Major General Ulysses S. Grant's Army of the Tennessee had driven Lt. General John Pemberton's Army of Mississippi into the fortified city and laid siege for over six weeks. The victory at Vicksburg gave the Union control of the Mississippi River and cut off the Confederacy's western states. It secured Grant's path to command all Union armies. Its parallel in the Spanish Civil War was the Nationalist drive from the west to reach the Mediterranean on 15 April 1938, cutting the Republic in half.

233:12+ **Grant . . . Sherman . . . Stonewall . . . Jeb Stuart . . . Sheridan . . . McClellan:** On Ulysses S. Grant, see 227:4. The Union officer William Tecumseh **Sherman** fought at the first major battle of the American Civil War, the First Battle of Bull Run (or Battle of First Manassas) on 21 July 1861. He would go on to serve under Grant as a division commander at Shiloh, a corps commander at Vicksburg, then succeed Grant as commander of the Army of the Tennessee and again as commander of the Military Division of the Mississippi. In this role, in the fall of 1864, Sherman undertook the conquest of Atlanta and the infamous March to the Sea that ended at the coastal city of Savannah, Georgia. Believing with Grant that the quickest and most effective way to win the war was to destroy the South's will and capacity to continue, Sherman targeted supplies and infrastructure that supported civilian life in addition to the Southern war effort. The setting fire to official buildings (and some businesses and homes) in Atlanta symbolized this practice, a precursor to the total war strategy of the world wars, particularly the Second World War's massive bombing campaigns of population and industrial centers. Although sometimes regarded as personifying military cold-bloodedness, in his memoirs and other writings he expressed contempt for the cruelties the war brought about. Sherman originated the phrase *war is hell:* "There is many a boy here today who looks on war as all glory, but, boys, it is all hell" (Sherman 1115). Sherman's destruction of Atlanta figured prominently in Margaret Mitchell's popular and accoladed novel *Gone with the Wind* (1936) and its cinematic adaptation (1939). A wounded young Hemingway referred to Sherman's line in a letter home from the Milan hospital during the Great War: "I wouldn't say [war] was hell, because that's been a bit overworked since Gen. Sherman's time, but there have been about 8 times when I would have welcomed Hell" (18 Aug [1918], *Letters 1* 130).

Military historians often uphold Sherman's command as a model of maneuver warfare. After the war, Sherman oversaw the United States' western wars against Native Americans, employing a similar mindset as during the March to the Sea and authorizing the brutal tactics of Phil Sheridan and Sheridan's subordinate George Custer: "We must proceed with vindictive earnestness against the Sioux," Sherman messaged his boss, General Grant, "even to their extermination—men, women and children. Nothing less will reach the root of the case" (qtd. in Van de Water 157).

Historians rank Confederate general Thomas Jonathan **"Stonewall" Jackson** as one of the best tacticians of the war. His many successes and wartime death in May 1863—less than two months before Gettysburg—contributed to his becoming a legend, one of the Confederate trinity eventually memorialized at Stone Mountain, Georgia, along with President Jefferson Davis and General Robert E. Lee. Jackson's own troops accidentally shot him while on his horse at the Battle of Chancellorsville, the battle of Crane's *The Red Badge of Courage*. His arm was amputated, he caught pneumonia, and he died eight days after his wounding. Hemingway's next novel, *Across the River and into the Trees,* takes its title from Jackson's purported last words as referenced by the protagonist, who was once wounded by friendly fire: "let us cross over the river and rest under the shade of the trees" (*ARIT* 307). This is another war novel with a soldier protagonist—Colonel Cantwell—who knows he will die in a matter of days and who enjoys a last great soulful romance with a younger woman. Jordan dies beside a river and in the shade of pine trees from a wound received on horseback and delivered by a captured friendly tank. Mark Cirino remarks that in quoting Jackson, Cantwell "gives a practical deathbed instruction, an order to an underling, rather than a metaphysical revelation" (*Reading* 3–4). Jordan connects his own name with the crossing of the Biblical Jordan River, a common allusion to death (438:7+).

James Ewell Brown "Jeb" **Stuart** was the Confederacy's most dashing and successful cavalry officer. His reputation suffered after Gettysburg, as some blamed him for the Confederate defeat, for failing to detect the enemy, and for his absence on the first day of the battle. Historians still dispute the matter. He rose to the ranks of brigadier general, and received a bullet wound at the Battle of Yellow Tavern on 11 May 1963, dying the next day.

The Union general **Phil Sheridan** was George Armstrong Custer's superior in the Civil War from the spring of 1864 until the end of the war, first as commander of the Cavalry Corps and then the Army of the Shenandoah: "Many of the outrages committed officially by Union troops in the Shenandoah were ordered by Custer, with or without the immediate sanction but always with the subsequent approval of Sheridan himself" (Van de Water 73). The two waged a remorseless campaign of "desolation" in Virginia (84). After that war, Sheridan commanded Custer during the frontier wars of extermination against Native American tribes, where racism amplified the pair's bloodlust. Van de Water's *Glory-Hunter* paraphrases a statement attributed to Sheridan: "Dead Indians, to Sheridan, were good Indians," regardless of whether they killed any white soldiers (186). All were guilty of being Indian. Massacre was often the order of the day. Custer died while serving under Sheridan.

In the summer of 1861, General George **McClellan** organized the Army of the Potomac. On 1 November, he also became general-in-chief of all Union armies. His checkered Civil War career ended with the Battle of Antietam (Sharpsburg) on 17 September 1862. Although McClellan prevailed that day, the bloodiest in American military history, his failure to pursue the retreating Confederate forces led to his dismissal by President Lincoln. Among his contemporaries as well as historians ever since, McClellan has had a reputation for being supreme at organizing, training, and preparation but too cautious in using the military he had so expertly developed beyond the fortification of the capitol. In 1864, the war ongoing and still holding his military commission, McClellan ran unsuccessfully for the presidency against Lincoln. The perception of McClellan's lackluster battle talent and his political ambition—all talk, no action—leads to Jordan's comparison of the generals on both sides of the Spanish Civil War.

Jordan's history makes two glaring omissions. First, nowhere in the novel does he mention Robert E. Lee, the Confederate general regarded as possessing the most brilliant military mind and the most impeccable character on either side (whose first name Jordan shares). Second, he ignores the post–Civil War legacy of the US Army. This westerner is fully aware of the army's methods in prosecuting the war against the Native Americans, led by officers such as Sheridan and Custer. His family arrived in Montana, in fact, because his revered grandfather took part in those genocidally motivated campaigns (336:12+).

233:18+ Kleber, Lucasz, and Hans: Emilio **Kléber** was the alias for Manfred Stern, a Ukrainian Jew, a Red Army and Comintern veteran, and a former spy who posed as a Canadian. Kléber was the first commander of the first organized International Brigade (the XI) during the defense of Madrid in November 1936. The fighting at University City depicted in *The Spanish Earth* happened under his leadership. Jordan accurately recaps Kléber's tumble from grace that autumn. The Spanish commander in charge of defending Madrid after the government fled to **Valencia**, José **Miaja** Menant, really was "jealous" of the praise journalists heaped onto Kléber, and Kléber "*did* talk too much," criticizing superiors, subordinates, and other allies. His rivals accused him of self-aggrandizement. Unfairly and unwisely, "[b]y the end of the month Kléber had been sent off to an inconspicuous 'advisory' job on the Mediterranean coast" (Tremlett 133). He returned to command after the death of Lukács (Lucasz) in June 1937.

Máté Zalka (born Béla Frankl) was a minor Hungarian writer and a revolutionary soldier who fought in Spain under the nom de guerre Pál (or Pavol or Paul) **Lukács**. Before Spain, Zalka had fought for Hungary in World War I on the Italian front and then, after his conversion to Bolshevism, in the Russian Civil War and several later Soviet conflicts. For much of his military career, he served in the cavalry. He commanded the XII International Brigade for the November–December 1936 defense of Madrid, where Jordan could have encountered him; for the February 1937 defense of the Madrid-Valencia Road in the Jarama River Valley, the successful action depicted in the Hemingway and Ivens documentary *The Spanish Earth*; the March 1937 defeat of the Italian offensive toward Guadalajara (or Brihuega), where Hemingway met him upon first arriving in wartime Spain; and additional smaller actions in April 1937 in the Jarama Valley. It is in that last period that he appears in the Hemingway story "Under the Ridge," where one of his battalion commanders is executed for failing his mission after getting drunk (see 151:30). Zalka-Lukács became the first commander of a new division, named the 45th after his death at Huesca on 12 June 1937 from a bombing the day before. Hemingway mentions his upcoming death in "Under the Ridge." In his preface to Regler's unreliable memoir *The Great Crusade,* Hemingway writes: "The Twelfth Brigade was where my heart was. . . . I think I cried when I heard Lucasz was dead. I don't remember. I know I cried when somebody died. It must have been Lucasz because Lucasz was the first great loss. Everyone else who had been killed was replaceable" (viii–ix).

On **Hans [Kahle]**, see 233:34+.

233:30 Gall: General **Gall** was the Hungarian János Gálicz, initially commander of the XV International Brigade, then a division commander up through the Battle of Brunete in June 1937. By all accounts he was a murderous disciplinarian, an incompetent battlefield commander, and unlikeable to boot. After being pulled out of Spain, he was purged in 1938 (see 358:20–21).

233:34+ The fighting on the plateau beyond Guadalajara: Hans **Kahle** was a German veteran of the First World War, communist, and journalist. He initially commanded the Edgar André Battalion of the International Brigade's XI Brigade, but by November 1936 he took command of the XI Brigade. Hemingway arrived in wartime Spain at the end of the Battle of Guadalajara (Brihuega) in March 1937, when he and Joris Ivens toured the battlefield's aftermath with Kahle (and others). It was the Republic's first major military success, halting the Nationalist advance on Madrid from the northeast. In his war dispatches, Hemingway accurately assessed that "an encirclement of Madrid is now impossible" for the Nationalists barring a major upgrade in their force disposition (in Watson 20), but too spiritedly proclaimed that "the battle of Brihuega will takes its place in military history with the other decisive battles of the world" (in Watson 22). He and Kahle became fast friends those first couple of days. Kahle later became a division commander in the Spanish Republican Army (after the complete integration of Spanish and international units into a single command structure). Kahle is as likely a candidate as anyone for the composite model for Robert Jordan (see 3:3+).

On 11 March, the battle's third day, the Italians fighting for the Nationalists "**had broken the line near Trijueque**" against Líster's 11th division, but the International Brigades stopped them at **Torija** (234:2), and the next day Republicans regained Trijueque. By the 18th, the fascist Italians were in full retreat. Hemingway's first dispatch from Brihuega is kinder to the Italians than Kahle's remarks in the novel: "Franco . . . now finds he cannot depend on the Italians. Not because Italians are cowardly, but because Italians defending the line of the Piave and Mount Grappa against invasion are one thing and Italians sent to fight in Spain when they expected garrison duty in Ethiopia are another" (in Watson 19). Hemingway's attachment to his First World War experiences on the Italian front, defending it against Austria and Germany, shines through here (he was severely wounded at the Piave River in July 1918). Because the International Brigade's Italian unit, the Garibaldi Battalion, fought at Brihuega, the battle saw Italians pitted against Italians. Hemingway's dispatches and *The Spanish Earth* called out the Italian military units sent to fight for the Nationalists in violation of the Non-Intervention Treaty, as part of the effort to gain international support for the Republic from Western nations, but hid the presence of international volunteers by lumping them into "Government" forces.

234:24 Tartar's first invasion of the West: The Mongol Empire's initial attempt to conquer central Europe in the 1240s (see 193:36).

234:38 **Velazquez 63:** A grand mansion of four stories plus an attic floor at 63 Velázquez Street, nine blocks due north of the Parque del Buen Retiro. Part of the difference in atmosphere from between the good times at Gaylord's (228:27+) and the "puritanical communism" at Velázquez 63 stems from the difference in the buildings themselves—between a modern luxury hotel and a home. The difference was also due to the different occupants. Although the International Brigades were headquartered in and operated out of Albacete, about 160 miles south of Madrid and 100 miles west of Valencia, it housed its Madrid functions at Velázquez 63. The building had previously served as offices for the Fifth Regiment, the communist legacy militia that disbanded when the Republic organized its motley militia and other military units into the new People's Army (see next entry).

The brutal Italian Comintern agent Vittorio Vidali, under the nom de guerre Carlos Contreras, was the Fifth Regiment's commissar who continued operating in Spain after the Regiment's final dissolution in January 1937. Vidali was responsible for securing Velázquez 63 for the Fifth Regiment (O'Keefe 68). *The Spanish Earth* shows "Carlos" speaking at a troop assembly that took place in the Goya Room of the Círculo de Bellas Artes on the Gran Via.

235:3+ **the headquarters of the Fifth Regiment before it had been broken up:** Jordan has three places in mind: Gaylord's, Velázquez 63, and the Fifth Regiment's first headquarters. When he says that at "either of those places you felt that you were taking part in a crusade," he means Velázquez 63 and the old Fifth Regiment headquarters—not Gaylord's. The feeling of "being in a religious order," in a life of sacrificial vows and the most modest of living, was not the Gaylord's atmosphere. Jordan says that at Velázquez 63 and the Fifth Regiment headquarters he felt spiritually initiated such as he had not felt at his first communion, the Christian sacrament of fellowship achieved through the symbolic sharing of the body and blood of Jesus Christ.

The **Fifth Regiment** emerged from the communist party's Antifascist Militia of Workers and Peasants, or MAOC (Milicias Antifascistas Obreras y Campesinas). When the war broke out, MAOC was the only nongovernmental militia with several years of true military structure and training. Almost overnight, it transformed into the Fifth Regiment of the People's Militia for the defense of Madrid, which included holding onto the Guadarrama Mountain passes, fighting Jordan participated in months before the arrival of the International Brigades (235:32+). The Fifth Regiment continued to field combat units but turned to quickly training other military units. Its fame from its initial success made for a recruitment dream. As its ranks swelled, so did those of the Spanish Communist Party. The regiment became the structural basis for units of the Republic's new People's Army; its alumni filled many of the government army's leadership posts. That Jordan felt "the true comradeship of the revolution" defending the passes (235:33–34), and that he was familiar with the regiment's headquarters, indicates a close association with the communist-dominated outfit. Hemingway might also have understood Jordan to have fought with the Fifth Regiment in Carabanchel and Usera (see 237:14+). This passage undercuts the published novel's watering-down of his politics (see 66:14+; 163:17+).

Communist discipline was the Fifth Regiment's religion. Being in its old **headquarters before it had been broken up** also felt spiritual because it was an actual place of worship, the Salesian convent with its Church of San Francisco de Sales, built from 1926–1931 on Francos Rodriguez Street (Ibárruri 213; Juan Modesto, Enrique Líster, and Vittorio Vidali in Bolloten, 266–68). The regiment was born here, or reborn or rechristened here, from the former MAOC. Hence the feeling of "consecration":

Iglesia de San Francisco de Sales. Cropped from photo by Luis García (Zaqarbal) 2009. (WikiMedia Commons / Public Domain)

With Velázquez 63, the religious feeling came from two aspects of its occupants and mission. First, the international brigaders were volunteers, most of whom fervently believed in the Republic and no small number of whom were committed communists. Their ideological zeal exceeded that of many Spanish Republican combatants. They put their lives on the line in Spain and suffered discrimination in their home countries. Americans traveled to Spain illegally at the potential loss of their citizenship. Jordan is hardly alone in using the word "crusade." As a result, the brigaders were often assigned some of the most dangerous and ill-advised missions.

Second, the International Brigades' inspector general worked out of Velázquez 63. The IG's duties placed him squarely in the commissariat system, and the man himself, Luigi Longo (aka "Gallo"), had been the first commissar of the XII International Brigade. He and Vidali had been a part of Comintern's original, small, advanced party coordinating the establishment of the International Brigades with the Republican government. Stanley Payne places Longo as the second-ranking Comintern advisor in Spain (164). The building's new occupants also took over the propaganda work formerly carried out by the now defunct Fifth Regiment. Longo and his wife helped write the loudspeaker scripts and the leaflets dropped on the Nationalists' Italian troops (O'Keefe 68; Tremlett 259–60). Velázquez 63 bore the spirit of the Brigades' origin story and undertook a proselytizing mission.

235:15 **Bach:** Johann Sebastian Bach, German composer of the Baroque period, is considered one of the greatest composers in Western music history. Bach's prodigious output included secular and sacred music. Later in life, Hemingway named Bach as a primary influence. Hemingway's mother, Grace, was on the verge of a professional vocalist concert career when she married his father, after which she taught private music lessons in a music room attached to their home that she designed. She also wrote original music; her eldest son played a poor cello.

235:15+ **Chartres Cathedral or the Cathedral at León:** These cathedrals in France and in Spain are major stops on the Way of St. James (Camino de Santiago), the pilgrimage route to the Cathedral of Santiago de Compostela, the final resting place of the apostle Saint James, the patron saint of Spain and the Spanish army. It is the most significant Christian destination after Jerusalem and Rome. Both are gothic cathedrals dedicated to the Virgin Mary and renowned for their stained-glass windows. The Cathedral of León is known as the House of Light. The Chartres Cathedral is a pilgrimage destination in its own right. The modest rose window of the Iglesia de San Francisco de Sales (see 235:3+) reminded Jordan of the famous grandiose ones.

The reference to Chartres is more evidence of Jordan's unexplained familiarity with France. Its Our Lady of the Pillar statue, a locus of prayer, H. R. Stoneback calls an "iconographical cognate to" the Virgin of the Pillar in Zaragoza, Spain (see 30:24+). Hemingway's first visit to Chartres, in September 1925, resulted in the title of his first novel, *The Sun Also Rises*, from Ecclesiastes 1.4–7. Stoneback sees in Chartres's art "subjects that would become recurrent motifs in his work" (*Reading* 4).

235:17–18 Mantegna and Greco and Brueghel in the Prado: The **Prado** Museum, on the western edge of the Parque del Buen Retiro, was Hemingway's favorite museum in the world. The religiosity of two of these three painters' chief works should not distract from Jordan's controlling simile, from his message that a political, secular enthusiasm has usurped the spiritual. The aesthetic experience of the art matters, not its content. The overriding thematic connection among these Prado artists is death; the stylistic connection is their high stylization, their (romantic?) resistance to realism.

The Italian Andrea **Mantegna** had only one painting at the Prado, *The Transit of the Virgin*, showing St. Peter gathered with all the apostles save Thomas at Mary's deathbed (*Museo* 19). Hemingway alludes to Mantegna's far more famous painting, the *Lamentation of Christ*, in "The Revolutionist" (*In Our Time*) and *A Farewell to Arms*. Although not at the Prado, this painting of Christ's body down off the cross, the nail holes graphically prominent, informs Hemingway's Mantegna reference here.

Born Doménikos Theotokópoulos on Crete, **El Greco** relocated to Spain in 1577, settling in Toledo. In the nineteenth century, Spain began claiming him as a Spanish artist. His twenty-five paintings (plus three copies) listed in the Prado's 1933 catalog were a mix of portraiture and religious subjects, the latter predominant, and commanded their own exhibition room (*Museo* 277–86, 806). El Greco's religious works are highly stylized. As with Hemingway's prose, they can hardly be identified as any other artist's. His conservative, Counter-Reformation contemporaries rejected his religious painting for drawing attention to their own artistry rather than focusing devotion to their content. Modernist painters embraced his originality and subjectivity over uninspired verisimilitude. Even Hemingway admired El Greco's "incomparable art" for refusing to be "limited to accurate reproducing of the faces of the noblemen who were his sitters for portraits and he could go as far into his other world as he wanted" (*DIA* 204). With their intense colors and elongated, simplified, and distorted figures, his paintings are forerunners to modern expressionism, including the surrealism that many painters used when treating the Spanish Civil War. Ignacio Zuloaga's 1938 *Siege of the Alcázar* (in Toledo) bears the unmistakable influence of El Greco's *View of Toledo* (1596–1600). Because El Greco was also deeply Catholic, he was appreciated by Spanish ideological traditionalists such as Zuloaga as well as by progressive modernist artists like Picasso. In other words, by both Nationalist and Republican sympathizers (see also 380:23+).

Pieter **Bruegel** the Elder was most famous for his pioneering depictions of peasant life and his social commentary. Bruegel's village scenes and his anticlerical, Protestant spirituality and politics fit the Republican cause. The Prado's 1933 catalog includes two Bruegel paintings, *The Triumph of Death* and *The Adoration of the Magis*

Pieter Bruegel, *The Triumph of Death* (1562–1563). (WikiMedia Commons / Public Domain)

(*Museo* 420, 653). Of the two, the former, which spent time in La Granja Palace before ending up in the Prado, speaks to Hemingway's novel. The work shows Death's army destroying the land and slaughtering everyone in its path. The Christian church is ambiguously futile against or complicit in Death's advance. In the lower right corner, lovers huddle on the ground making music—making love—against their own demise's imminence. The painting accords with Jordan's love for Maria, his feelings intensified by the war and his knowledge of his upcoming death. The painting shows the clear influence of another Hemingway favorite, the Dutch painter Hieronymus Bosch.

235:21–24 something that you had never known before: In *A Farewell to Arms*, the priest predicts that Frederic Henry will know what it is to love: "When you love you wish to do things for. You wish to sacrifice. You wish to serve" (72). Henry potentially gains this emotion toward Catherine Barkley, having lost his reason for staying in the war; Jordan transfers his emotional commitment from the Republic to Maria.

235:31 The defense of a position or of a city: In the draft, Jordan contrasts defensive and offensive operations: "The defence of a position is heroic and clean. The dead are your own dead and you hold it and it is held. But the takeing of a town is like the takeing of all towns always. There is the unavoidable slaughter of civilians [sic]." He also seems to have had a specific atrocity in mind, as he added the following by hand above the typed sentences about slaughtering the innocent: "But then, later on, below Cordoba, there was the [unavoidable slaughter of civilians]" (MS11-008). Jordan has just arrived from the Córdoba front (238:37–38). This excision could be the iceberg principle in action, Hemingway expecting the reader to feel Jordan's guilt, to feel his momentary suppression of his complicity. Or it could be that Hemingway decided against involving Jordan in the slaughter—a bridge too far as it were, given the other damning evidence of his murderousness in this chapter. A third possibility is that Hemingway did not intend to place Jordan at the slaughter but realized he had suggested as much.

235:32 The fighting in the Sierras: The battle to control the passes through the Guadarrama Mountains into Madrid fought in late July and August of 1936 (the subject of Modesto Ciruelos's 1936 painting *Descubierta* or "Discovered" on this book's cover). Had the Republic's patchwork of mostly untrained militias not stopped the Nationalist advance, Madrid most likely would have fallen. The first International Brigade did not enter action until that November. Jordan was in Spain when the war broke out, fighting in league with the Spanish communist-led Fifth Regiment (see 235:3+; 236:13+).

235:35+ **enforcement of discipline . . . seen them shot:** Although reports and documentation from the war's earliest combat by ad hoc Loyalist militias are basically nonexistent, there is every reason to believe the historical accuracy of what Jordan witnessed. The novel's evidence suggests he fought alongside the Fifth Regiment (see 235:4+), whose leadership believed in battlefield executions. According to the Italian communist Vittorio Vidali, who operated in Spain as Comandante Carlos Contreras and helped create the Fifth Regiment, that authority extended to the rank and file. The regiment's new Steel Company on its way to the Guadarrama front "designed special slogans to create an iron unity. 'Never leave a comrade wounded or dead, in the hands of the enemy,' was one of these. 'If my comrade advances or retreats without orders, I have the right to shoot him.'" The regiment's oath included a pledge "to abstain from dishonorable acts and to prevent my comrades from committing them" and concluded, "If I should fail to fulfil [sic] this solemn pledge, let the contempt of my comrades fall upon me and let me be punished by the implacable hand of the law" (qtd. in Bolloten 268–69). Jordan had "**approved and understood**" such killings.

236:13+ **the Sanitarium:** Of the three passes—the northeastern Somosierra Pass, the southwestern Alto del León or Guadarrama Pass, and Navacerrada Pass (which joins the route from the Alto del León flowing toward Madrid)—Jordan must have fought in the latter two, the contiguous ones. He has been to the headquarters in the towns of Navacerrada and Guadarrama (332:21–23) and the sanitarium allusion places him there (there were none at Somosierra). The Fifth Regiment also fought at the Guadarrama and Navacerrada Passes (Ibárruri 200–01). There were several sanitariums in the Guadarramas for long-term care, particularly for pulmonary tuberculosis, because of the salubrious properties attributed to the mountain air. Most likely is the Sanatorio Hispano-Americo (Spanish American Sanitarium), on high ground in the piney woods a kilometer outside the town of Guadarrama. Republicans used it as a medical facility for the wounded and something of a logistics hub; Nationalists bombarded it in late July. This sanitarium opened in 1931 for tuberculosis patients.

Two other possibilities are the Lago Sanatorium at Tablada, the closest to the Alto del León, opened in 1921; and the Royal Sanatorium of Guadarrama, which opened in 1917 north of the town of Navacerrada and under ten kilometers south of the novel's bridge. Among the latter's patients was Hemingway's wartime friend, the poet and sometimes playwright Rafael Alberti, who stayed there for several months in the early 1920s ("El sanatorio").

237:8+ **Palace Hotel:** The Palace Hotel opened on the Plaza de las Cortes in 1912, the first luxury hotel in Madrid. The Soviet wartime delegation occupied the first floor by the end of August 1936, decamping two months later when the hotel became a military hospital. At that time the Soviet military advisory moved into Gaylord's (see 228:27+), and some Soviet officials and journalists relocated with the Republican government to Valencia; others remained in Madrid scattered to other hotels, including the Gran Via and the Florida (O'Keefe 53–54; see 228:12+).

Irún, San Sebastian, and **Vitoria** are in the Basque region of northern Spain, which, after bombardment and fierce fighting, with the same pieces of ground exchanged back and forth during hand-to-hand combat, the Nationalists captured by the first week of September 1936. The Nationalists controlled the Basque country for the rest of the war. It was a serious blow to the Republic because of the area's agricultural resources, people, and its routes to and from France. Closing that active front freed Nationalist military resources for other campaigns.

Carabanchel and **Usera** were working-class neighborhoods in southwestern Madrid described by one historian as a "cluster of villages, slums, and shanty towns" (Esdaile 132). Originally a diversion from the main attack against Madrid through the Casa de Campo woods to the north, the Nationalist assault into these neighborhoods launched on 7 November 1936, with elements of the Army of Africa, both **Moor** *regulares* and Spaniard **Tercios** (the Spanish Foreign Legion). The 8th and 9th saw vicious close-quarters combat. The fighting for the area lasted several days, ending in a stalemate, with the front line a trench through the middle of a Carabanchel street, although clearly contributing to the successful prevention of a Nationalist advance into Madrid.

The first International Brigade (the XI) marched to the front on 8 November in the areas of Casa de Campo and University City. Jordan fought in Madrid with Spanish militias, not the International Brigades. Current histories don't place the Fifth Regiment at Carabanchel or Usera, but Dolores Ibárruri's memoir reports it at both (250). Her information or memory could be faulty, and no doubt she exaggerated whatever role the regiment did play. Nevertheless, Hemingway's understanding might match her version, as his sources were her circle. This would explain the purity of Jordan's feelings in the Guadarrama and at Carabanchel and Usera (239:15–16), with Hemingway intending for Jordan to have fought with the communist-led Fifth Regiment.

237:24+ the government had abandoned the city: On 6 November, with Franco's forces at the edge of Madrid and everyone convinced of its impending fall, the government fled to Valencia, leaving General José **Miaja** Menant in charge of defending the city. Franco ended this offensive campaign on 23 November, although the Republic continued to mount attacks to dislodge the Nationalists through the end of the year as the siege of Madrid settled into local firefights.

238:6 and his hands and face so badly burned: Hemingway might be recalling his April 1937 visit to a military hospital where he met with a wounded American volunteer, Robert Raven: "The voice came from a high mound covered by a shoddy gray blanket. There were two arms crossed on the top of the mound and at one end there was something that had been a face, but now was a yellow scabby area with a wide bandage across where the eyes had been" (in Watson 31). This moment is the novel's only truly graphic depiction of what modern war does to human bodies—somewhat surprisingly so, because of the employment of photography in the 1920s and 1930s to promote pacifism through documentary images of battlefield mutilation. The most famous project was Ernst Friedrich's 1924 photobook *Krieg dem Kriege!* (*War against War!*), using photos of victims from the First World War. By contrast, the Spanish Civil War was the first war in which portable camera technology allowed photographers to capture scenes on the battlefield and in the immediate aftermath of a city's bombardment that could be distributed outside the warzone relatively quickly. Virginia Woolf's 1938 *Three Guineas* opens with her reflections on images out of Spain from the winter of 1936–1937, images of "horror and disgust" which, one would think, should only lead to the conclusion that "war is an abomination; a barbarity; war must be stopped" (Woolf 14). Yet as Hemingway knew from *The Spanish Earth*, the very same images work to mobilize violence against the other side for what it is doing to us and ours and to the innocent. Still, the absence of graphic descriptions in *For Whom the Bell Tolls*, especially in the context of the war's groundbreaking photography, raises the question of just what kind of war novel it is. The novel could not be more different from Dalton Trumbo's 1939 *Johnny Got His Gun*, told from the perspective of a soldier left paralyzed below the neck, blind, deaf, and dumb from missing his lower jaw and tongue.

238:35 **the Córdoba front:** From mid-March through mid-April 1937, Republican and Nationalist forces clashed over the Córdoba and Estremadura fronts south and southwest of central Spain. The area was rich with mining resources, plus a breakthrough on either front by either side had the potential for a deep drive into the opponent's territory. Jordan has returned from the Battle of **Pozoblanco** (239:10), a Republican defensive victory against the Nationalist Army of the South's offensive out of Andalusia. Herbert Matthews's optimistic coverage starts reporting Republican success at Pozoblanco on 27 March 1937 and continues well into April ("Pozoblanco"). If Hemingway is paying close attention to the time line, the conversation between Jordan and Karkov must have occurred before Kashkin's death in Extremadura, which happened no earlier than 11 April (23:32+; 24:2).

239:15+ **how you felt in the Sierra and at Carabanchel and at Usera:** The reader already knows that Jordan approved of the battlefield execution of "cowards" in the fight for the **Sierra** de Guadarrama Passes (see 235:35+); the reader does not yet know that Jordan murdered unarmed prisoners at **Usera** (see 304:17+). In this passage, "**corruption**" means the opposite of its presumed pejorative—it means the gaining of conscience in the loss of the purity of idealism that justified committing atrocities (see also 287:1+).

239:25+ **a certain British economist:** A few pages later, Hemingway identifies this man as "Mitchell" (242:33). The novel's draft up through the galleys identifies the character as an American journalist working for a top liberal weekly magazine. In correspondence with his publisher and editor, Hemingway changed Mitchell from "American journalist" to "British economist" and cut several lines from the novel. Fear of a potential libel lawsuit motivated the change. Because Hemingway made these last-minute changes for legal reasons rather than aesthetic ones, and because those legal reasons no longer pertain, post-copyright editions should strongly consider restoring these pages to their galley version. The 2019 Hemingway Library Edition includes much of this excised material in an appendix (506–09).

The man in question is Louis Fischer. Fischer wrote about the war chiefly for *The Nation*, to which he was an ongoing contributor on global politics and economics—so the change to "British economist" was not far off the mark. He had married a Russian and lived in Moscow for twelve years before the war. He never joined any nation's communist party, although his sympathies for the Soviet Union generated some inaccurate reporting, what Jordan calls "statistics . . . faked by wishful thinking" (239:31). The episode Jordan narrates about the tank (240:7+) parodies an episode Fischer had climbing aboard a tank during the siege of the Alcázar of Toledo. The physical description of Mitchell resembles Fischer (241:18–20), although Hemingway backed away from a more accurate description, the man's hair originally "very black," not "grey," and his "handsome face" having "big eyebrows and full lips."

Fischer took some credit for the Republican strategy at the Alcázar, as Karkov confirms (242:21+). He was very well connected with government leaders in Spain and around Europe—much more than Hemingway—traveling among them and using this access to secure even more access, as Karkov confirms (243:27–29). Preston begins a chapter on Fischer this way: "On many mornings, while shaving and then while soaking in the tub, the Republican prime minster, Juan Negrín, would discuss the international situation in German with a journalist who sat on the toilet seat" (*We Saw Spain Die* 213). The excised material adds Julio Álvarez del Vayo, who served as minister of foreign affairs and commissar-general, as one of Fischer's Republican friends.

The fear of libel stemmed from a passage in which Karkov acknowledges that Mitchell embezzled funds from Republican monies entrusted to him for deals abroad, routed through bank accounts in Paris (*HLE* 507–8). Hugh Thomas's history suggests that Fischer may have indeed profited from arms purchases (761). In the later months of the war, Fischer also moved Republican money to help pay for ocean liner passage and other needs to repatriate American volunteers. In a letter to his publisher about revising the manuscript to avoid the libel, Hemingway writes that "[t]he said Mitchell is a real crook but is still in circulation" (to Charles Scribner, ca. 15 Aug. 1940, *SL* 510). The fact that Hemingway doesn't even name Fischer to his publisher speaks to his fear, perhaps even beyond being accused of libel. Hemingway's writing conveys a career-long loathing of anyone who profits from war.

"I should have shot him at Usera that day," Jordan says, incensed by Mitchell's robbing of the Republic. Karkov quashes the implicit offer, instructing Jordan not to "shoot him" because Mitchell is useful and manageable (*HLE* 508). In the draft, Jordan initially says he "would like to have shot him" (MS11-008). Hemingway's hasty excision job has left a confusing, abrupt conversational turn from Mitchell to the Republic's gold (243:30+), for which the potentially libelous material had provided a segue. The material's removal due to legal worries means that its damning characterization of Jordan should still apply. Also excised is Hemingway's cheeky line: "Is his name really Mitchell?" (*HLE* 507). For more details, see Vernon, "Louis Fischer."

239:34-35 when they had attacked at Carabanchel: See 237:14. Within a couple of weeks after the Carabanchel fighting, Louis Fischer ("Mitchell") became the first American to volunteer for the International Brigades (see 239:26). Originally assigned to a quartermaster position as a supply officer, Fischer was forced out of the brigades by André Marty by the end of the year.

239:36 the bull ring: Possibly La Plaza de Toros de Vista Alegre in Carabanchel, opened in 1908 and severely damaged during the war. Another possibility is the venue at Tetuán de las Victorias. The Tetuán neighborhood is roughly thirteen kilometers northeast, far from the fighting but with a cityscape that would have an "apartment building on the corner of the tram-line" (240:9-10). Plus the Republic used this site to store munitions during the war, which Jordan mentions (240:25). Hemingway knew both plazas de toros well.

242:14 the combatant's hatred for the noncombatant: Note Hemingway's self-deprecation; he had never been a combatant.

242:18+ Puente de Toledo: Karkov did not cross the Toledo Bridge across the Manzanares River from Madrid into Carabanchel and Usera (237:14). He did not join the fighting.

242:21 At Toledo: Toledo is the next largest city southwest of Madrid. The **Alcázar** (Citadel) of Toledo, built as a fortress by the Moors, had centuries later become Spain's flagship military academy. Its square hulk loomed over the hilltop city. The pride of Spain's army, the bridge between tradition and the future in training the next generation of officers, the Alcázar was steadfastly conservative and sided with the Nationalists. In the opening week of the war, on 23 July, Republican forces gained control of the city and began firing into and encircling the academy. The siege of the Alcázar had begun. The final Republican assault to gain what was left of the citadel began and ended the morning of 27 September; that afternoon, Franco's Nationalist Army of Africa column began its attack on the now-fleeing Republicans. The siege ended on 28 September. Franco made his appearance the next day. Both sides invested heavily in time, resources, and bodies, in what was a battle of far more symbolic than strategic import—"the silliest part of the war," per Karkov. By diverting his column away from its direct route to Madrid, Franco might very well have given the capital the time it needed to enable its successful defense when his forces attacked in early November. On the other hand, the Alcázar became a rallying cry for the Nationalists and its global supporters. Franco's lifting the siege helped clinch his bid to become, among the several officers leading the rebellion, the Nationalists' commander in chief (*Generalísimo*) and head of state on 1 October 1936.

Throughout September, Louis Fischer, the nonfictional Mitchell, visited the Republican forces at Toledo, reviewed the situation, and discussed it with military and political leaders. At one point, he hatched the idea of getting oil inside the Alcázar and setting it aflame. The army attempted (and botched) a version of that plan (Vernon, "Louis Fischer" 68–70). Thus Karkov sarcastically claims that Mitchell "was one of the architects" of the "successful" siege—Hemingway considered it the worst siege in military history.[5]

242:27 **In America:** Several short paragraphs between Jordan's remark and the next paragraph were excised to further disguise Fischer's identity. The most direct evidence is Karkov's immediate rejoinder: "In Moscow he is supposed to be very close to Mr. Roosevelt" (*HLE* 507), the US president at the time.

243:31 **Much gold:** Early in the war, the Republic relocated its considerable gold reserves to Russia, to avoid seizure by the Nationalists and to more conveniently pay as needed for arms, equipment, and other support from the USSR. This odd passage is the remainder of a longer passage, cut from the draft, concerning the man Mitchell (see 239: 26).

244:16 **Handbook of Marxism that Emil Burns edited:** *A Handbook of Marxism*, edited by Emile Burns and originally published in Great Britain in 1935. The title page provides something of a subtitle: "Scientific Socialism as Stated and Interpreted by Marx, Engels, Lenin, Stalin." The book includes the entire *Communist Manifesto* and writings by the four major figures. Its most contemporary documents are Stalin's 1934 "Report at Seventeenth Congress of the Communist Party of the Soviet Union" (1934) and his "Address to Red Army Graduates" (1935). The book concludes with the 1928 *Programme of the Communist International,* drafted for the 1924 Fifth Congress of the

Communist International, formally adopted by the Sixth Congress in 1928, and the blueprint for the establishment of Stalin's vision for world communism.

Regarding Spain and other nations "with a medium development of capitalism," such as "Portugal, Poland, Hungary, and the Balkan countries," the *Programme* sees them as

> having numerous survivals of semi-feudal relationships in agriculture, possessing, to a certain extent, the material prerequisites for socialist construction, and in which the bourgeois-democratic reforms have not yet been completed. In some of these countries a process of more or less rapid development from bourgeois democratic revolution to socialist revolution is possible. In others, there may be types of proletarian revolution which will have a large number of bourgeois-democratic tasks to fulfil. Hence, in these countries, the dictatorship of the proletariat may not come about at once, but in the process of transition from the democratic dictatorship of the proletariat and peasantry to the socialist dictatorship of the proletariat. Where the revolution develops directly as a proletarian revolution it is presumed that the proletariat exercises leadership over a broad agrarian peasant movement. In general, the agrarian revolution plays a most important part in these countries, and in some cases a decisive role: in the process of expropriating large landed property a considerable portion of the confiscated land is placed at the disposal of the peasantry; the volume of market relations prevailing after the victory of the proletariat is considerable; the task of organising the peasantry along cooperative lines and later, of combining them in production, occupies an important place among the tasks of socialist construction. The rate of this construction is relatively slow. (791–92)

244:31–32 Calvo Sotelo . . . was a very good fascist; a true Spanish fascist [as] Franco and these other people are not: José **Calvo Sotelo** was killed by the Republican government's Assault Guard (*Guardia de Asalto*) in July 1936, such that Karkov's dig amounts to saying that the only good fascist is a dead fascist. Karkov also regards Franco as an opportunist. Sotelo had a long record of loyal service to the dictatorship of Miguel Primo de Rivera (1923–1930). After the Second Spanish Republic's electoral victory, Sotelo exiled himself to Portugal and France, returning to Spain under the Amnesty Law of 1934, whereupon he used his charisma and energy in the hopes of uniting the anti-Republican Spanish conservative factions under a single banner. Franco, on the other hand, remained in the army of the Second Republic. Karkov's qualifier "Spanish" suggests the fact that Sotelo did not live to fall under the influence of international fascism sponsored by Germany and Italy. Karkov's qualifier thus ridicules the Nationalists' pro patria brand. Hemingway's irony is sharp, given the Russian Karkov's presence in Spain as a leading figure of international communism's corruption of the Republic. Although Franco and his coconspirators were already planning their rebellion, Sotelo's murder inspirited the coup that commenced several days later whose failure led to the war.

245:4+ **Bukharinite:** Initially allied with Leon Trotsky, Nikolai Ivanovich **Bukharin** moved to Stalin's camp, but disagreements led to his being cast out of the Soviet government's inner circle. He was arrested in February 1937, a couple of months before this conversation, and eventually executed. Grigory Yevseyevich **Zinoviev** was another Stalinist who came to have significant differences with the Soviet leader, although unlike Bukharin, Zinoviev responded to his ouster by allying with Trotsky. Zinoviev was arrested, tried, and executed in 1936 alongside Lev **Kamenev** at the start of the Great Purge. Alexei Ivanovich **Rykov** was yet another Stalinist against whom Stalin turned and had arrested and executed with Bukharin.

245:37 **Mundo Obrero:** The newspaper of the Spanish Communist Party. See 397:5.

246:12 **it is very rotten:** See 197:37.

246:14 **Durán:** On Gustavo Durán, see 335:24+.

247:1+ **romantic revolutionists:** Karkov is talking about the Trotskyite POUM militia, the anarchist militias with their red and black scarves, and their suppressed uprising against Republican control and Stalinist communist discipline—the **POUM putsch** of early May in Barcelona. For challenging the Republican government and its Comintern support, the POUM was accused of being secretly working with the fascists. See 120:6-8. The failed uprising had the unintended consequence of making the Comintern a more powerful force in the Republic. It was the summer after Barcelona, for example, that the Republic created its internal security force for rooting out the supposedly untrustworthy. This was the SIM, the Servicio de Inteligencia Militar (Military Intelligence Service)—Jordan's papers anachronistically bear the SIM seal (10:12).

247:24-25 **Trotskyite murderers:** A Trotskyite followed the communist ideas of Leon Trotsky. Along with Vladimir Lenin and Joseph Stalin, Trotsky was a key figure in the founding of the Soviet Union (USSR), having successfully led the Red Army during the Russian Civil War (1918-1920). Stalin succeeded Lenin as the premier of the Soviet Union after Lenin's death in 1924. Trotsky was sent into exile in 1929, landing in Mexico in January 1937, where Stalinist agents murdered him in August 1940. As popularly understood, the complex ideological rift between Stalin and Trotsky involved the means of achieving the communist vision: Stalin believed in establishing communist governments one country at a time through democratic processes;

Trotsky sought an international workers' revolution. For Trotskyites, Stalin had merely replaced the monarchy with a dictatorship, one exploitative ruling class with another. For Stalinists, the violence of Trotskyite revolution and its abandonment of democratic processes made for **fascist machinations**. The democratic victory of the Spanish left in 1931, which created the Second Spanish Republic, fit the Soviet's incremental global plan and motivated intervention in Spain's civil war. Stalin's hold on power in a one-party system, however, was hardly democratic, and it turned to disposing of its political opponents in the Great Purge of 1936–1938. Trotsky had supported the Red Terror against political opponents during the Russian Civil War. The tactics of disappearances and executions infiltrated Republican Spain during its civil war, as Karkov admits in the next entry.

247:26 **Nin was their only man:** Andrés Nin was the POUM leader killed after the failed uprising (247:1+). "We say he *is* in Paris," Karkov says in present tense, but he "*was* a very pleasant fellow" in past tense (247:29, emphasis added). This is an example of Koltsov-Karkov boldly speaking against the party line (see 231:20).

247:37–38 **St. Jean de Luz . . . people from Burgos:** Burgos was the capital of Nationalist-occupied Spain; Saint-Jean-de-Luz is a coastal French Basque town just over the border.

248:5 **their fine people behind our lines:** The term *fifth column*, for an enemy's forces working incognito inside one's own controlled areas, originated in the Spanish Civil War and was in circulation during the time frame of this conversation. In October 1936, having taken Irún and San Sebastián in the north (237:11) and lifted the siege at Alcázar to the south (242:21), the Nationalists marched on Madrid from both directions with a total of four columns. The first English reference in print to the term dates to 10 October: "The Socialist newspaper *Informaciones* in Madrid said Fascists had claimed assistance from a 'fifth column inside the capital'" ("Loyal Forces"). Although commonly credited to General Emilio Mola, the northern commander, the earliest US newspaper attributions cite General Franco, the newly installed commander in chief ("Nightmare")—which does not mean that Franco hadn't picked up on Mola's language, or that the newspapers weren't confusing or compressing information.

From that first mention, the press reported on the immediate Republican response: "Dispatches concerning the 'inside' column were cut drastically by the Spanish censor although indications were given that mass arrests of Fascist suspects followed the newspaper's story" ("Loyal Forces"). Hemingway titled his only full-length play *The Fifth Column*; the term's absence from this long novel is somewhat surprising. Hemingway credited his play with resurrecting the term (as if), and he believed Mola to be the source.[6]

248:20–21 He knew the Basque country, Navarre, Aragon, Galicia, the two Castiles and Estremadura well: Mostly northern and central Spain. In other words, the more historically Christian and "European" parts of Spain, not the Spain with the longer Moorish dominance. That Moorish southern Spain is less familiar to Jordan could contribute to his and the novel's exoticization of it. Jordan operated in Extremadura (west-southwest of Madrid) earlier in the war, perhaps in the time during which he developed his familiarity here. Although Jordan separates Navarre from the Basque country, a mountainous region defined ethnolinguistically (that crosses into France), historically Navarre—especially northern Navarre, down to and including Hemingway's beloved Pamplona—is Basque. During the Second Spanish Republic, Navarre separated itself politically from the Basque, choosing not to belong to the new autonomous region. The Navarrese strongly supported the Nationalists, and Navarre was a critical launching point for the 1936 uprising. Jordan later says he likes the Navarrese people better than any other Spaniards (304:2–3), though he does not account for the division between Navarre's Basque north the more Castilian south. Perhaps that division and ambiguity bespeak some of the novel's and Jordan's own.

248:22 such good books written by Borrow and Ford: George Borrow traveled Spain for five years (1835–1840) to distribute Bibles and spread Protestantism on behalf of the British and Foreign Bible Society. His two travelogues from that time are *The Zincali* (1841), about the Spanish Romani (gypsies), and *The Bible in Spain* (1843). Even more so than Borrow's work, Richard Ford's *Hand-book for Travellers in Spain, and Readers at Home* (1845) connects Spain to the Orient, to Africa, to the past, and to nature. After a prefatory description of Spaniards as "incurious semi-orientals [who] look with jealousy on the foreigner" (vii), Ford likens Spain to the Orient and the East over three hundred times.

Hemingway owned nearly thirty twentieth-century English-language books about Spain and bullfighting, an impressive collection that was a fraction of what was available. Not to mention the modern Spanish-language books that Jordan could have read more ably than Hemingway (Mandel, "Literary Backgrounds"). Hemingway's choice to color Jordan's view of Spain through two Orientalizing nineteenth-century Anglophone writers appears deliberate.

248:25 why I bother with you: Karkov bothers with Jordan for the sake of the book about the war the American will someday write, the same reason Hemingway once wrote that Koltsov bothered with him (to Bernard Berenson, 14 Oct. 1952, *SL* 789).

NOTES

1. To Edward Garnett [c. May 1938] (HRC).
2. "Despotic" in Thomas, 814; "domineering" in Preston, *The Spanish Civil War,* 288.
3. *ABC Madrid* (28 Feb 1937), 15; *ABC Madrid* (5 Oct 1937), 10.
4. Paul Preston finds the idea of Koltsov as Stalin's spokesperson "absurd" (*We Saw Spain Die,* 182), while Frederick White sees him and "the journalist and writer Il'ia Ehrenburg [as the] two important intermediaries between Stalin's regime and the outside world in the 1930s" (46), with Koltsov as Stalin's "close associate" and "unofficial mouthpiece" (47).
5. To Lambert Davis, 7 May 1940 (Boston University Library).
6. To Maurice Speiser, 19 June 1940 (USC).

CHAPTER NINETEEN

249:11–12 **hundreds of thousands:** The Soviets provided 2,000–3,000 military personnel over the course of the war (Payne 160). As Payne notes, this contribution "was far exceeded by the approximately 16,000 Germans and 70,000 Italians who at one time or another served in Spain" (153). International participation on the fascist side more than doubled the approximately 40,000 members of the Soviet-backed International Brigades.

251:16 **smelt of death:** Later in the chapter, Pilar offers an extended graphic description of this smell (254:22+). He needed, he told his editor, to "make the idea of the odour earthily and concretely and vulgarly believable—instead of seeming to be gypsy-cross-my-hand-with-silver nonsense" (to Maxwell Perkins, 26 Aug. 1940, *SL* 513). To his publisher, he wrote that some people do carry about them a portentous aura—it is Realism, not Romanticism—and that he didn't put in half of how awful Madrid can be, including a story about a man paying for a leprous prostitute missing most of her face, and the crude clash with a gypsy afterward (to Charles Scribner, ca. 15 Aug. 1940, *SL* 508–09). The scent of death section attempts to bridge the divide between Naturalism and Tragedy, with the malodorousness a matter both of nature and of character (see introduction). The odor of death is reminiscent of the "vapour" of death from John Donne's *Devotions*'s "Meditation XII" (see front matter: title and epigraph).

251:19 **Blanquet:** Enrique Belenguer Soler, "Blanquet," was a banderillero, one of four toreros (bullfighters) who work on foot to stick a pair of banderillas—the harpoon-like short spears—"in the humped muscle at the top of the bull's neck as he charges the man"; the purpose "is not only to force the bull by hooking to tire his neck muscles and carry his head lower but also, by placing them at one side or another, to correct a tendency to hook to that side" (*DIA* 96–97) The banderillos are used after the horse-mounted picadors with their lances and before the matador with cape and sword. *Peón* is another term for banderillero; **peón de brega** refers to anyone in a matador's cohort (*cuadrilla*). According to Mandel, "[i]n spite of his intelligence and skill," Blanquet "was unable to rescue the great matadors José Gómez

Ortega (Joselito), Manuel Granero, or Miguel Baez (Litri), all of whom were killed in fights at which Blanquet was serving as banderillero" (Mandel, *Reading* 206).

251:21 **Manolo Granero:** The professional name of Manuel Granero Valls, a talented violinist turned bullfighter from Valencia who showed great promise but died in the ring on 7 May 1922: "He was twenty years old when he was killed by a Veragua bull that lifted him once, then tossed him against the wood of the foot of the barrera and never left him until the horn had broken up the skull as you might break a flowerpot" *(DIA* 45). Pilar likely ate pastries named after him on a Valencia beach (85:7–9).

251:28+ **Juan Luis de la Rosa:** He, **Marcial** Lalanda, and **Chicuelo** (Manuel Jiménez Moreno) were the other matadors present the day Manolo Granero died in the ring (see prior entry). Hemingway had the impression that these three "all fought as though they were condemned to it rather than as if they had chosen it" *(DIA* 74) None were as talented as Granero. Mandel notes that Juan Luis de la Rosa "may have descended from gypsies" (*Reading* 268), which would explain his ability to smell death as Pilar does (252:19).

251:38 **José at Talavera:** José Gómez Ortega, known as Joselito or Gallito, "probably the greatest bullfighter who ever lived" *(DIA* 39, 69), died on 16 May 1920 in the ring at Talavera de la Reina. "Joselito nearly always placed banderillas in the bulls he killed" *(DIA* 78). Despite Hemingway's admiring descriptions of Joselito's talents in *Death in the Afternoon,* the writer did not see his first *corrida de toros* until after Joselito's (and Granero's) deaths.

252:1+ **the bull *Pocapena*:** See Hemingway's description of Granero's death from *Death in the Afternoon* (at 251:21). **Tendido** two is the second section of a bullring's seating, open to the sun between the red-painted fence or barrier (***barrera***) and the covered gallery *(DIA* 454, 387). The ***estribo*** is "the ridge of wood about eighteen inches above the ground which runs around the inside of the barrera which aids the bullfighters in vaulting the wooden fence" *(DIA* 406–07).

252:4+ **The horn entirely destroyed:** Hemingway added this graphic sentence by hand to the typed draft along with other sentences on this page that ekphrastically insist upon Pilar's eyewitness and that then assert the truth of the unseen: "It was thus, being at an angle, that I could see all that happened" (252:10–11); "I was present when this happened" (252:15); and from "But I could tell thee" to the end of that paragraph (252:24+; MS11–009).

252:12+ Joselito: The matador José Gómez Ortega (see 251:38). Café **Fornos** stood on the corner of Alcalá and Calle de la Virgen de los Peligros, near Puerta del Sol in central Madrid. In *Death in the Afternoon,* during a conversation with the Old Lady while they watch the mingling bullfighters, Hemingway characterizes the café as "frequented only by people connected with the bullfights and by whores" (*DIA* 64–65). A 1932 *ABC Madrid* article paints a different scene: "The heights of Fornos! The coffee! With its lively and noisy gatherings of writers, artists and students, the military and the hunters. It was the astonishment of provincials, a paradise—with snakes—of geniuses in agraz and a meeting point for young people." This article locates the bullfighting crowd at the nearby Café Inglés ("Urbanismo"). Fornos closed in the early 1930s. On **banderilleros** and **picadors,** see 251: 7; **all of the *gente*** would be all the matador's people, all the *peón de brega* who make up his *cuadrilla* (see 251:19).

253:29 Ignacio Sanchez Mejias: A protégé and brother-in-law of Joselito (251:38), Sánchez Mejías was killed by a bull in August 1934. He distinguished himself from other matadors "by deliberately courting danger in the ring. He would put himself in difficult positions, such as fighting with his back against the barrera or sitting on its railing, and then flaunt the intellectual and technical prowess that enabled him to survive such situations" (Mandel, *Hemingway's DIA* 386). This is one reason Jordan challenges the smell-of-death business (253:32+). Sánchez Mejías also loved literature, writing several plays and other works (Mandel, *Hemingway's* DIA, 387).

254:2–3 Villa Rosa . . . Ricardo and Felipe Gonzalez: Ricardo could be el Niño Ricardo, the flamenco guitarist included in Pilar's story about the *Club Finito* (186:29). The café or saloon and the person Felipe Gonzalez are as yet unidentified.

254:8 a well-known thing among us: Beyond its evocation of ideas about Romani, the chapter's discussion of fate evokes ideas about Spaniards (about the conflation of Romani and Spaniard in the non-Spanish European and Anglo imaginations). At the beginning of the war, in trying to explain the anarchist church burnings throughout Catalonia, the English writer Ralph Bates recalled a conversation "in the Enchanted Mountains" with "two [illiterate] cowherds . . . [with] unadulterated imaginations" whom he labels "authentic Spaniards." Bates concluded about their "*natural* curiosity" (emphasis added): "You've got to get a legendary feeling into your imagination to grasp the quality of these events. . . . There is a sense of Fate, or, better put, of the Inevitable about Spain at all times, and it is that which makes this war so grim, it is something which reason cannot modify, nor sentiment ameliorate" (683).

254:30–31 to Mexico and to Venezuela: Pilar presumably accompanied Finito or a different bullfighter.

254:36+ **Puente de Toledo:** The Toledo Bridge across the **Manzanares** River. El **Matadero** y Mercado Municipal de Ganados (Municipal Slaughterhouse and Cattle Market) was a relatively new structure for the Madrid cityscape, having opened in the mid-1920s.

256:8+ **Calle de Salud:** Health Street, off the Gran Via, four blocks east of the Plaza del Callao and the Hotel Florida where Hemingway stayed during the war. He walked past the street on his way to the Telefónica to file dispatches or on his way to some of his favorite places to eat and drink, such as Chicote's (the setting for two of his Spanish Civil War stories, "The Butterfly and the Tank" and "The Denunciation") and the Hotel Gran Via, on the southeast corner of Calle de la Tres Cruces (Three Crosses Street). Health Street has its name because its residents survived a fifteenth-century bubonic plague outbreak. **Casas de putas** are brothels.

256:10 **love's labor lost:** Pilar references the aforementioned brothels on Calle de Salud; Hemingway references Shakespeare's *Love's Labor's Lost,* an early comedy from the 1590s often mischaracterized as his only play set in Spain because of its setting at the court of Navarre. If as most scholars believe the play's king is Shakespeare's contemporary, Henry III of Navarre, the play takes place in Lower Navarre, the sliver of the kingdom north of the Pyrenees that survived annexation by Spain's Ferdinand of Aragon in 1512, thus effectively a part of France, and formally so once Henry III of Navarre became Henry IV of France in 1589. Prior to 1512, Navarre was Navarre, not Spain. Indeed the play includes a character described as "a refinèd traveler of Spain" (I.i.167). What scholars have read in Shakespeare's fictional court is commentary on French and English royalty, not Spanish royalty.

The Navarrese are Robert Jordan's favorite Spaniards (304:2–3). *Love's Labor's Lost*'s ambiguous geography straddling the Pyrenees Mountains fits the novel's Sierra de Guadarrama setting, between northern and southern Spain, between historical Realism and heightened Romance. Shakespeare's traveler comes from "tawny Spain" (I.i.177), using Jordan's favorite adjective for his beloved Spain and his beloved embodiment of Spain, Maria. William C. Carroll's commentary reminds readers of the romantic comedy's "rather somber, even apocalyptic frame," a death obsessed frame for a love-obsessed story:

> *Love's Labor's Lost* begins with the young King of Navarre anticipating the "disgrace of death," when he and his courtiers will succumb to "cormorant devouring time" and become "heirs of all eternity" (1.1.3–7); the play ends with the stunningly dramatic entrance of Marcade, whose brief "tale" (5.2.796) announces the death of the old King of France, and with the futile efforts of the young courtiers to "make a world-without-end bargain" (5.2.866) with the ladies they have courted. (253)

The play's story and silly fun has almost nothing in common with the novel. The death frame serving as a raison d'être for romance, however, can be seen in the Jordan-Maria romance. *Love's Labor's Lost* opens with the men of the Navarre court forswearing women, oaths they all in short order break, apparently against their better judgment, when they meet lovely ladies visiting from the court of France. Jordan too initially rejects romance, a resolve he also breaks—against his better judgment—when he meets Maria. The play's language's lighthearted likening of seduction to hunting takes a dark twist in the novel (e.g., 378:7–10). The women chased by the men spend much of Shakespeare's play mocking the men's overly romanticized attitude, Hemingway's allusion perhaps suggesting his awareness of how such an attitude troubles Jordan's and Maria's relationship. *Love's Labor's Lost* is a Romance that pokes fun at Romance.

256:12 **Jardín Botánico:** The Royal Botanical Garden of Madrid is adjacent to El Buen Retiro Park and the Prado Museum in Madrid. Hemingway replaced Parque del Buen Retiro with Real Jardín Botánico in the galley proofs, perhaps at Durán's suggestion.

CHAPTER TWENTY

259:11+ **"Then sleep well on it," she had said:** Pilar knows that Jordan prepares the bed for Maria, thus her offer to sleep with the explosive material and her hushed offer of sheep hide for the bed (259:32–35). The chapter's structure communicates as much, this moment being a flashback after the opening sentence's announcement that he waits for Maria (258:1)—in other words, Hemingway assures that the reader knows that Pilar knows. Jordan does not object to her guarding the explosives; he allows himself to be distracted from his mission for romance, against his own judgment (7:38+). Jordan's public "good night" signals to Maria to join him (259:25). Note the potential colonialist dimension of Jordan's attitude in preparing their bed "as in [his] country" (259:10), an odd thing for someone who desires to integrate with the Spanish earth via Maria's body. Making the bed involves similar actions as making defensive preparations, especially machine gun placement, in cutting down a small tree and using its boughs to nestle among the rocks (258:19+).

260:25+ **the odor of nostalgia:** The pine boughs and the camping remind Jordan of his Montana home. Politically and culturally speaking, nostalgia is a conservative emotion, appropriate for a man engaged in a clichéd love, who reads nineteenth-century travelogues about Spain, and whose bourgeois soul is askance from his cause. Inherent in nostalgia is a hope of restoration, a common motivation for nationalist movements. His musing on the smell of "the sweet grass the Indians used in their baskets" as possibly a more preferred odor carries a note of racism in its fondness for a people Jordan's culture violently diminished, largely in the very western states for which he pines. It is interesting to speculate on whether the word pine as in "to pine" led Jordan or Hemingway to the passage's nostalgia, on the potential for an unconscious word association to determine a mood. This night with Maria sets the stage for El Sordo's last stand and the novel's evocation of George Armstrong Custer.

260:31 **as you come in toward Cuba:** The second reference to Jordan's firsthand knowledge of the Gulf Stream between Florida and Cuba (87:5). Hemingway first fished off the Cuba coast in 1932. In 1934, he began taking his new boat the *Pilar* to Cuba. He took up residence in Havana in February 1939, where he plunged into writing *For Whom the Bell Tolls*. In August he returned stateside, but in December he left Key West and his second wife (Pauline Pfeiffer) on his way to Cuba and his next wife (Martha Gellhorn). He finished the novel in Cuba in July 1940. He probably drafted this passage shortly after his return to Cuba that December on the *Pilar*.

260:37–38 **you must be hungry, he thought [as he] watched the entrance of the cave:** Hemingway has lent the sentence a Spanish syntax, connecting nouns by prepositions instead of apostrophes, as Jordan waits for his Spanish paramour. He is hungry for sex with Maria. His nostalgia for certain meals feeds the sexual longing, which in turn reinforces the attribution of nostalgia to Jordan's feelings for her. However genuine, nostalgia always risks giving way to the saccharine, to the clichéd, and to its violent defense. He welcomes her into the bed by calling her "little rabbit" (261:37), at once the crude sexual term as well as the link between sex and consumption—of Maria, of Spain—through the rabbit stew. Cannibalistic metaphors involving colonized or otherwise subjugated bodies, particularly racially othered bodies, bear a homoerotic aspect whereby who consumes whom is beside the point of the double-edged fear-fantasy (see 22:37).

261:28 **my wedding shirt:** The shirt Maria wore when she and Jordan consummated their love.

262:22 **as one animal of the forest:** For Mark Spilka, the fused identities of Jordan and Maria, in the overall context of "their grounding in the pagan religion of love" and "the wild spirit of Nature . . . removes them from the Christian purview and suggests, rather, their romantic origin in Emily Brontë's novel" *Wuthering Heights* (139). Spilka does not quote this line, which joins other lines comparing the lovers to animals (e.g., 93:13–14). While Hemingway has Brontë's novel in mind, a compatible if more expansive way to read the couples' animalistic love is through the novel's larger meditation on the nature of love—through the rhetorical juxtaposition of animal physicality and transcendent spirituality—as well as on questions of literary genre (Naturalism, Romance, Realism, Tragedy, etc.). See next entry.

262:26+ **I am thee and thou art me and all of one is the other:** See the above entry. Spilka quotes Catherine in *Wuthering Heights*: "I *am* Heathcliff. . . . Whatever our souls are made of, his and mine are the same" (in Spilka, 138). For Spilka, Brontë's Catherine's tomboy quality and her lovers' near-sibling relationship deepen the connection between the two writers. Such language of lovers becoming the other, of changing to match the other's desire, is not unique in this Hemingway novel. It characterizes the romantic coupling of his two Catherines, Barkley of *A Farewell* to Arms and Bourne of *The Garden of Eden*.[1] In the interest of Realism, these two women share with Maria traumatic histories that all three seek to remedy by relieving the burden of themselves. Readers who find Maria the most cloying of Hemingway's male characters' love interests should keep in mind that she is the most traumatized and the most recently traumatized. Her apparent two-dimensionality is commensurate with her suffering and shock.

"You're my religion, you're all I've got," Catherine Barkley tells Frederic Henry (*FTA* 116). Maria, a good Republican, has also rejected Christianity. For Ernest Becker in *The Denial of Death*, the post-Darwin death of God at the end of the nineteenth century led to the relocation of meaningful transcendent love into the heterosexual love relationship, a way of denying that a person is "a mere fornicating animal" (163) in making the beast with two backs. One can apply this idea to Hemingway's novels regardless of whether one interprets their characters' religious lostness as negative examples—and so evidence of a Christian universe—or as indicative of a world that has accurately dispelled the God fantasy. For Lewis and Roos, *A Farewell to Arms* reveals that Barkley "does not believe in any other world but this, and in this world, love, the realm of emotion, reigns supreme. It is her spirituality," a "middle way" between reason and faith (142). One could say the same thing about Maria, although this later novel emphasizes romantic love's animal physicality. Lewis and Roos's middle way too tidily, too assuredly, solves Hemingway's complex engagement with the nature and spirit of human love in all its messy, ugly, beautiful ambiguity.

During the era historians have identified as having invented homosexuality and heterosexuality, the merging of heteronormative eros and the transcendent became a cultural weapon against same-sex desire and gay identity. For some readers, Jordan's and Maria's sameness, as a kind of mirroring or twinning, reflects this novel's slippage into the homoerotic and the queer (see Moddelmog on queer slippage in *A Farewell to Arms*).

The other predominant relationship that Hemingway figures in terms of *oneness* is the one between bullfighter and bull (e.g., *In Our Time*; *The Sun Also Rises*). As Comley and Scholes argue, "the connection between bulls and manliness, already present in the textuality of Spain itself, was appropriated by Hemingway in a manner that allowed him to explore aspects of manliness, including male desire expressed toward other males, to an extent that no other cultural context available could have provided" (109). The connection to Jordan and Maria, beyond the grounding in Spain itself and under the shadow of Pilar and Finito, is the predator-prey relationship and danger built into much of Jordan's language about her. The bullfighter is at risk too, of course, and heterosexual romantic love in Hemingway is a dangerous game. One could argue that entering the arena of love destroys (to use Catherine Bourne's word) the male lovers of the two Catherines and Maria, each text in its own fashion. The predator-prey dynamic is one of identical rivals, interchangeability of roles, and merged selves—of oneness, as Hemingway romanticized between the matador and the bull in "Chapter XII" of *In Our Time* and in *The Sun Also Rises*. Oneness is the attraction and the danger.

263:23 **Como tu:** Like you. As you are. As you did. As with you.

263:26 **But I loved it more. One does not need to die:** They have made love for the third time ("Then afterwards . . ."). Maria references her feeling of having "died" their second time together (160:4–6). Interestingly, she asserts her preference for this third time, even though it did not warrant description and was not the powerful experience of the earlier one.

263:31 **With a man there is a difference:** Jordan continues the afternoon's conversation when he said he did not die during sex as Maria had (160:5). For Jordan, men experience the finality of death more literally than women do. He can't even accept a metaphor of orgasm as death. For Maria, the metaphor is more than metaphor. The interchangeability or equivalence, for her, suggests a fluidity or porousness of being, a cyclic process of being, related to Western culture's long association of women with nature. She is the Spanish earth; she is also Pilar.

264:6 **an alliance against death:** The sentence's language, particularly this phrase, evokes the image of the lovers in Bruegel's painting *The Triumph of Death*, with which Jordan was familiar (see 235:17–18). In the moment, Jordan feels that their love has acquired a significance greater than death, and in that significance achieves a kind of immortality. See 262:26+.

264:18 **lay there in the night thinking:** Hemingway's longest novel, much of which consists of Jordan's unceasing interior monologue (that at times reads like a dialogue with "you"), spares readers these nighttime thoughts.

Those thoughts are available in a rare piece of surviving discarded writing, an "insert" of five handwritten pages that would have taken the place of the chapter's published final paragraph.[2] In these pages, Jordan tells himself he loves Maria and that his life has changed. He thinks about taking her to Madrid, where she doesn't know anybody, where she'll need papers and new clothes. He knows they should marry, and afterward he'll bring her home to Missoula grateful that she won't need the razor blade once they cross the border out of Spain. He imagines getting identical haircuts in Madrid long before he says it aloud in the published novel in very similar language; the fact that in the later chapter he tells Maria "I thought we could go together to the coiffeur's," past tense (345:33–35), reveals the discarded pages as faithful to the text. The later scene reads as if he had these discarded pages on his desk as he wrote, in his vision of her hair down "to [her] shoulders" (346:5), hair "like sun burned corn silk." Her suggestion of styling it as "Garbo in the cinema" (346:7) picks up on and specifies his curiosity (in the insert) about the length of time needed for her hair to reach "glamour girl length" and intuits his visceral response to Garbo. The discarded bit closes with Jordan's telling himself to get some sleep. The pistol from the published paragraph does not appear in the discarded insert.

NOTE

1. On *Wuthering Heights* and *FTA*, see Tyler, "Passion and Grief in *A Farewell to Arms*" (summarized in Lewis and Roos 140–41).
2. JFK #356: MEHC-001-002-002 (Museum Ernest Hemingway Collection).

THE THIRD CALENDAR DAY

[30 MAY 1937]

CHAPTER TWENTY-ONE

265:25 the scarlet of the formalized device he wore on the left breast: The bright red Sacred Heart emblem (269:29) stands out on the badge's white background against the soldier's dark uniform top.[1] The Sacred Heart is a Catholic symbol of devotion to Christ for His compassionate sacrifice. In its most basic form, a red cross rises from the red heart. Variations include encircling the heart with a thorn crown, having flames emerge from the heart, piercing it with a sword, dripping blood from it, and topping it with a sovereign's crown. Theologically, suffering in this life in imitation of Christ brings one closer to Christ and to the resurrection (e.g., Philippians 3:10–11). It is the route to salvation and grace. Jordan touches on this theological idea in a later reference to San Juan de la Cruz (St. John of the Cross) (see 380:21+).

This soldier was a Carlist militiaman, also known as a *requeté* (301:7; 302:15). Carlism formed after the death of King Ferdinand VII in 1833, the sonless Ferdinand having nullified the Salic law to make his daughter Isabel his heir instead of his younger brother Carlos. Upset by the liberalism of Ferdinand's legacy, traditionalists took up Carlos's claim to the throne as their own, leading to the Carlist wars of 1833–1840, 1846–1849, and 1872–1876. The Catholic Church was fundamental to Carlism, whose adherents bore the Sacred Heart long before the Spanish Civil War. During the 1930s' war, the opposing monarchist factions set aside their fundamental difference as much of the Nationalist military adopted the Sacred Heart image—on badges, banners, and military vehicles. The crown invokes Christ as King of Kings and the monarchist elements of the Nationalist cause. In military use, the Sacred Heart casts death in battle as martyrdom, with the resurrection implied by the symbolism suggesting the political restoration of traditional Spain.

268:8–9 *Qué caballo más bonito . . . más hermoso*: Pablo says "What a good-looking horse" twice, although elevating his appreciation from pretty or lovely to gorgeous or beautiful.

268:11+ the light automatic rifle: The description of the 9mm submachine gun with a ventilated barrel is not particularly helpful for identification, as there were several such weapon types around. Because it takes different ammunition from his own submachine gun, Jordan implies it is not of German make (269:1–4). Most such weapons in the war, however, derived from German design or license. Pablo claims this cavalry saddle gun for himself (see 404:2+). His acquisition might further embolden him to steal the dynamite and desert the mission.

269:4 old Kashkin's gun: Jordan has inherited the weapon of his predecessor, Kashkin, whom he first says shot himself, but then admits to having shot. It might be the very weapon used to kill its previous owner. Hemingway builds an interesting parallel to Jordan's having inherited the pistol his father used to commit suicide. Jordan carries Kashkin's gun in the final battle, wielding it in his last moment. Hemingway inserted the material from "Robert Jordan carried" to the end of the paragraph by hand to the draft (MS11-010). This is not the captured Nationalist cavalry 9 mm automatic rifle, the saddle weapon with the different ammunition, which Pablo takes (268:11+).

269:29 Sacred Heart: See 265:25.

270:3–4 I want to go to hold the legs of the gun and while it speaks love thee all in the same moment: Take your pick: Maria's desperation for union, and for inflicting violence, reflects her ongoing trauma. This moment connects to their aggressive lovemaking against her past violations. Or: Maria resists Jordan's rigid emotional compartmentalization, insisting on the oneness of their union. The moment expresses her danger to him. Or: the line challenges yet reinforces traditional gender spheres—as she is there on the gun but still in a supporting role. Or: it acknowledges the connection between heteronormative romantic love and war from time out of mind. Or:—

270:25 She lifted her fist: Maria's fist had been "clenched tight" in Jordan's "pocket" (270:18). Now she raises it to make the clenched-fist Republican salute, adopted from the traditional gesture of workers' solidarity from the late nineteenth century.

NOTE

1. "Part Four" appears at the top of the manuscript draft page (MS11-009) and the Armstrong typescript.

CHAPTER TWENTY-TWO

274:7+ **two big hares:** Hares are not rabbits, but might as well be in this scene, whose heavy-handed symbolism should not bother readers at ease with the novel's place in the Romance tradition: two hares tracked in the snow, a pair beyond the gypsy's dreams (275:14) that he kills during their mating, more or less at the same time Jordan and his rabbit Maria, make love, all while the Nationalists track El Sordo's guerrillas in the snow. Jordan is Maria's rabbit partner since they became a single, indistinguishable creature, "one animal of the forest" (262:22). The hares' fornication brought their fate upon them, perhaps suggesting that Jordan's lovemaking brings his death upon him.

Hemingway must have realized that switching from rabbits to hares for this scene would make for a clumsy, ineffectual misdirection. Granted that the hare "has provided writers and artists an unusually flexible symbolic device" (Carnell 45), it is fair to ask how this brace might resonate. With two cautions. First, because of what Simon Carnell calls the hare's "historical multivalence, the archive of associations which it has generated" (45), it would be far too easy to cherry-pick among them to fit an interpretive agenda. Second, because one cannot know what associations Hemingway, consciously or not, wanted to generate. Hare symbolism, writes Carnell in *Hare*, "tend[s] to cluster around a number of areas more or less troped upon its natural history: sex, death, speed and vitality; super-sensitivity, elusiveness, and cunning; untamable 'wildness,' with only their sinister portentousness bucking the trend" (45–46). Did Hemingway remember that a hare spooked Don Quixote? Had he read that Napoleon "fell from his horse while reconnoitering the banks of the Niemen when his mount was startled by a running hare," which some took to mean "that the invasion should not take place" (50)?

In addition to hare as portent, the cluster that best fits the novel involves sex and death. The animal's "fleetness and vitality" sometimes serve "as reminders of the fleetingness of existence" (47). Sexually, hares are linked to hermaphroditism, homoeroticism, and lasciviousness; in Greek myth, "we find the origin of the idea that if hunting was like war, it was also like sexual pursuit" (61). Christian symbolism figured the hare both ways, as the miracle of reproduction (even of virgin birth) but also as "lustfulness and 'unnatural' proclivity" (71). From the latter stemmed connections to the devil and witchcraft. In terms of Jordan and Maria, Bosch's *The Garden of Earthly Delights* comes to mind: damnation as consequence of vigorous sexuality, or, per Eby, the more complex convergence of innocence, sex, and death (see 4:33). Elsewhere Eby connects the homophonic terms *hare* and *hair* in a psychoanalytic reading of hair fetishism throughout Hemingway's works (*Fetishism* 113–14).

274:15 **hijo de la gran puta:** Son of the great whore.

274:23 **Rediós!:** Oh God! Good God! An expression of unwelcome surprise or setback. Although the Spanish term isn't exactly obscene, a late-twentieth- or twenty-first-century English speaker might burst out with Crap! Shit! or Fuck! Changed in the galley proofs from *Me cabra*, probably Durán's suggestion.

275:4 **Qué tio!:** What a guy! What a fellow!

275:27 **Anda!:** Go!

276:3 **No one was exempted:** Although many Spaniards on both sides volunteered, many did so reluctantly, and forced conscription was often the order of the day. Spanish soldiers did not always believe in the cause for which they fought. It could be a matter of simple geography (what side of the lines your village found itself), of avoiding imprisonment, or of protecting threatened family members.

276:33 **Me voy:** I'm going.

277:1 **Pues, to load it:** Well, to load it.

277:22 **Menuda matanza!:** What a slaughter or massacre.

279:5 **the crow fly up:** Because the Nationalist cavalry patrol approaches. Jordan has been paying attention to the crow for a while now, waiting for just such a sign (275:30+; 277:37+). Ending the chapter here operates both as a cliff-hanger—"Get thee down," the next chapter opens (which could have begun with the flight of the crow)—and also as an omen hanging beyond this moment. Crows aren't ravens, but in their popular symbolism they similarly forebode ill, as in *Macbeth* when the "Light thickens, and the crow / Makes wing to th' rooky wood" (III.ii.56–57). In Shakespeare's play, the death-fated Macbeth has just divulged his "affliction" every night by "terrible dreams" that make him think it "[b]etter [to] be with the dead" in peaceful slumber (III.ii.21–23); here, Agustín has just called Segovia the place where Jordan's "bad dream waits . . . to become a reality" (279:1–2). The deaths of both works' protagonists involve an ambiguous interplay between prophecy and choice.

As a monogamous species with a distinct mating ritual, crows symbolize conjugal love. In this chapter with the two killed hares, in advance of Jordan and Maria's final parting, the original crow pair has separated. Hemingway loses track of the third crow (275:31), who joined the pair but is now unaccounted for, unless it be a subtle reference to the resurrected Christ from Luke 24:13–31, who appeared unrecognized to two followers on the road to Emmaus before vanishing. Crane's *The Red Badge of Courage* and Eliot's *The Waste Land* allude to this Biblical encounter.

The cavalry unit is on its way to carry out El Sordo's last stand (chapter 27). Jordan will later muse on George Armstrong Custer, the army colonel who infamously died leading his unit to slaughter at the Battle of the Little Bighorn by a combined force of Lakota and Cheyenne in June 1876. Custer's last stand occurred on the Crow Nation Indian Reservation in Montana, not far from Jordan's childhood home, and Custer relied on Crow scouts, perhaps figured in this scene as Jordan's crow "sentinels" (275:32).

CHAPTER TWENTY-THREE

280:18 **the four horsemen:** An allusion to the Four Horsemen of the Apocalypse, the harbingers of the end of days and the Second Coming of Christ. The Book of Revelations (6:1–8) only names the fourth rider, Death. The others are usually called the Conqueror, War, and Famine.

284:23 *Cómo qúe no?:* What? How so? What do you mean? What are you talking about?

284:26 **to continue to exist:** Pablo's strategy matches that of the Republic and of the picaro.

285:21 **but Señor and Señora:** A return to traditional honorifics against the egalitarian spirit of revolution.

285:28 **the most grand *carajo*:** The most grand fucking or hell. In other words: We're screwed.

286:4 **reformed by work:** Anselmo previously made this argument (41:33).

286:23–24 **like a mare in the corral waiting for the stallion:** Agustín describes the bloodlust in sexual terms and in reversed gendered terms—he anticipates being the mare receiving the bloodlust in ecstasy. Jordan tacitly concurs that life affords "no stronger" feeling (286:31–33). Does this line at all interact with others that assert agency when something happens to one (55:3–4; 73:13–14)?

286:38 **Auto de Fé:** In a book Hemingway knew, Havelock Ellis defines this "act of faith" as "the great festival of joy in a glorious service to God, at which the Inquisition publicly enacted the final scene in the condemnation of the heretic, before he was 'relaxed,' that is, abandoned to the secular arm, to be burned at the *quemadero* outside the city, the execution of heretics being a matter entirely of secular law" (53). Ellis's description appears in his chapter "The Spanish People" from *The Soul of*

Spain as evidence of "the love of formalism and ritual and ceremony" that is "characteristic" of the Spaniard's "savage attitude toward life" (52). Jordan's thoughts are in keeping with Ellis's (see also 104:26–27; 185:28–30).

Fittingly, Jordan thinks about the auto-da-fé after the appearance of the Carlist cavalry, a Nationalist militia whose monarchist roots has deep ties to the Catholic Church (see 265:25), and more specifically the arrival in this chapter of the Biblically resonant four horsemen (280:18).

286:38+ **Killing . . . you have never been corrupted by it? . . . Sierra . . . Usera . . . Estremadura . . . every train:** Readers do not yet know that Jordan at Usera murdered unarmed prisoners (304:17+). Here, *corruption* means the suspension of conscience in falling under the suasion of killing for a greater cause, or perhaps just for the ecstatic pleasure of it (or some mixture of cause and pleasure)—in other words, the word bears the traditional pejorative meaning, the exact reverse of the first time he discussed it in connection with Usera (239:15+). That Jordan applies the same word to opposed ideas (in the same context) reveals the extent of his confusion in his moral reckoning with the war and himself. Hemingway uses Jordan to ruminate over his own moral code, specifically the casual code of *Death in the Afternoon*: "So far, about morals, I know only that what is moral is what you feel good after and what is immoral is what you feel bad after" (13) (Jake Barnes makes a very similar statement in *The Sun Also Rises*).

287:6+ **Berbers and the old Iberians:** The **Berbers** are the indigenous people of Mediterranean North Africa west of Egypt, sometimes called the Barbary Coast. The term Moor was imposed upon the region's population after its Arabization (which began in the sixth and seventh centuries), when over centuries it intermixed Berbers, Arabs, Africans to the south, and Europeans. All Berbers are Moors, but not all Moors are Berbers. The Berbers mostly became Muslim. The initial Moorish conquest of Spain involved more Berbers than Arabs, and the dynamic between the two groups fluctuated widely between friendly integration and open warfare. They often vied for control over Moorish Spain. In his *Hand-book for Travelers in Spain and Readers at Home,* Ford says that the Berbers

> at different times allied themselves with the Spaniards, French and Christians against the Cordovese Moors. . . . Brave and martial, these barbarians, barbarous in name and deeds, were at once the strength and weakness of the Moors; first they aided in the conquering of the Goths, and then turning against their allies, in upsetting the most elegant and accomplished dynasty Spain has ever witnessed. (297)

The twentieth-century Moroccan rebellion leader Abd el-Krim was Berber (229:34). Europeans often elided the difference between "Berber" and "Moor." Ford regards

Spanish Berbers (Muslim or pagan) as noble and ferocious. In describing Spain as "between the hat and the turban," he calls it "*Berberia Christiana*" (ix), a phrase he also uses just for Andalusia (224), reinforcing the non-Spanish penchant for locating the Spanish character in Moorish Spain.

The "**old Iberians**" refers to the original inhabitants of the Iberian Peninsula, the land mass south of the Pyrenees (France), the land occupied by Spain and Portugal. Technically, this would exclude the Basque, whose traditional territory extends into modern France and whose roots are more Celtic than Iberian. Ford's *Hand-book* uses the term "old Iberian" many times, with several variations: "original" Iberians, "aboriginal" Iberians, "old autochthonic" Iberians, "primitive" Iberians. Geographically isolated Spanish communities, such as those deep in the mountains, he thinks of as still essentially Iberian of spirit. Ford at times tilts romantic in his language, affixing to Iberian adjectives such as "true," "pure," and "genuine."

Jordan thinks "Berbers" to avoid the wartime baggage of "Moors," but primarily to evoke the premodern pagan past of "Berbers and old Iberians," of whom his imagination makes "**dubious literature**" by portraying them as bloodthirsty savages. His tendency to romanticize everything south of the Pyrenees and older than the industrial age should not be forgotten. Jordan owes his understanding to Ford's book, something his reference to "dubious literature" might recognize.

287:7+ **admit that you have liked to kill:** The novel's conversation about hunting and killing, in dialogue and monologue, continues until the novel's end. The present passage reinforces the difference between Anselmo the hunter and Jordan the irregular volunteer soldier. At this point, he has fallen in love with Maria, slept with her, and begun imagining life with her after the war. Jordan's insistence that he has liked killing people also admits a dissatisfaction with postwar normalcy and domesticity. Jordan's insistence also operates in conjunction with his romantic belief that he will die at the bridge, a belief that at once intensifies the relationship with Maria and, in its self-fulfillment, succeeds in permanently avoiding the discontent of postwar ordinariness.

287:14 **Something very rare in Catholic countries:** Because historically, Catholic countries such as Spain have taken their religion and their nationalism deadly seriously, more than willing to kill in the name of Christ, the Prince of Peace.

CHAPTER TWENTY-FOUR

288:28 **onion out of his side jacket pocket:** In Spain, whenever he could, Hemingway carried an onion or two in his jacket pockets to enjoy raw.

289:10 **The odor. Nothing more. Otherwise it is like the rose:** The focus on smell and roses invites consideration of Shakespeare's *Romeo and Juliet,* the most famous romance in English literature. The entire action of play and novel occurs in less than four full days. Juliet bemoans the fact that Romeo's surname categorizes him as a family enemy (in a feud one might see as analogous to a civil war): "What's in a name? That which we call a rose / By any other word would smell as sweet" (II. ii.46–47). These lovers' "star-crossed" romance ends in death for both, their fate at once foredoomed and by their own hands. Jordan and Maria's romance is equally star-crossed, instantaneous, and overwrought. Hemingway's lovers make a suicide pact (170:24+), and Jordan's death has a self-murder aspect related to his love for Maria. The Shakespeare allusion leads the text to a Gertrude Stein allusion (next entry) in strange imitation of Shakespeare's rose wordplay.

289:12+ **A rose is a rose is an onion:** An allusion to Gertrude Stein's line, "Rose is a rose is a rose," originally from her 1913 poem "Sacred Emily." The appearance of the word "stein" a few lines later confirms the allusion (289:16). Hemingway had been distancing himself from Stein since the mid-1920s and really dismissed her after her portrait of him in *The Autobiography of Alice B. Toklas.* To his great frustration, he still found himself reading assertions of and answering questions about her influence on his writing. Jordan's onion serves as a public rebuke of that influence. His private rebuke came in the form of his inscription to the copy of *Death in the Afternoon* he mailed her in 1933. Beneath "To Gertrude Stein" appears a circle made of the words "a bitch is a bitch is a bitch is a bitch" (*Letters* 5 548–49).[1] Ironically, it was Stein who had sent him to Spain to experience the bullfights in the first place, as *Death* acknowledges on its first page. The maximalism of *For Whom the Bell Tolls* only superficially differs from the Stein-influenced minimalism of Hemingway's early work. This new novel also pressures words in the spirit of Stein, to foreground the dynamic between sound and sense; the present passage doesn't quite divorce itself from the verbal associative writing Stein practiced and preached.

Two comments by Stein best reflect her line's purpose: "When I said. A rose is a rose is a rose is a rose. And then later made that into a ring I made poetry and what I did I do I caressed completely and addressed a noun" (*Lectures* 231). As with much of her poetry, "Sacred Emily" revels in language, turning over words as one might turn over dough or a picked-up pebble. The poem caresses all kinds of words, from proper names to a verb like *curls,* which she separates from its object—"curls the butter" becomes "curls" and then "curls" again, each its own line—in order to relish the word as object, as sound, as potential, the word now neither verb nor noun but both, perhaps noun as word-object whose repetition effects a kind of curling in on itself. Stein's omission of an article before the first "Rose" plays with the possibility of the word as a name (ambiguously capitalized as either a proper noun or the beginning of the sentence), and so lovingly teases the relationship between a person's name and the thing for which they are named. The novel most closely follows Stein's method in the two lovemaking scenes, with their rhythmic repetitions whereby the urgently caressed, turned-over words stand in for Maria's body.

Stein's other comment admits the difference between functional and poetic language: "Now listen! I'm no fool. I know that in daily life we don't go around saying 'is a . . . is a . . . is a . . . ' Yes, I'm no fool; but I think that in that line the rose is red for the first time in English poetry for a hundred years" (*Four* vi). For Stein, the rose had become such a mainstay literary device that readers no longer envisioned an actual rose in the mind's eye, its redness, its petals, its texture. To say that every repetition of the word *rose* changes it by refining attention is to say that every repetition returns us to the thingness of the thing that exists only in individual roses, in unique, discrete iterations. To say *a rose is a rose is a rose* is also, then, to say that *one rose is not another rose is not another rose.*

Jordan's riff, in replacing the last "a rose" with "an onion," accomplishes the same goal. His sentence reads as nonsensical only because the reader reflexively sees, touches, and smells roses and onions. The novel's preoccupation with the question *What's in a name?* has real political and human ramifications. A Nationalist is a Nationalist is a Nationalist, a Republican is a Republican is a Republican, and yet not: as the text clearly depicts, there are as many varieties of Nationalists and Republicans as there are Nationalists and Republicans. Characters muse on the names of things throughout the novel (e.g., 132:15+; 166:32+).

The text never answers the diegesis question: Has Jordan read Gertrude Stein, or does the allusion belong solely to Hemingway? The circularity of Stein's line about roses finds its way structurally into *For Whom the Bell Tolls,* which begins, returns to several times, and ends on the pine-needled forest floor.

289:16–17 **a stone is a *stein*:** See 289: 12+. Hemingway's translating the German word *stein* to the English *stone* and then introducing the closely related words *rock* and *boulder*, potentially recollects his impression of Pilar as a granite monument and Pablo's of her as a rock (30:27; 64:3). Josephs contends that nothing about this allusion links Stein with Pilar (*Undiscovered* 74). Josephs's rebuttal to this observation notes that Jordan's associative play ends with pebble, and there is nothing pebble-like about Pilar. This rebuttal depends upon the logic that the list's last item works as conclusion rather than mere association. Josephs is right that Pilar is absent from the scene, from the conversation, and nothing about the conversation has any interpretative bearing on her. One twist in the wordplay is the English word *stein,* for a mug.

The word might even point to Hemingway, whose youthful nickname *Hemingstein* he and his friends sometimes shortened to *Stein*. Before traveling to Spain, Hemingway wrote to Max Perkins that he had already paid the way for two volunteers to go, and if he arranged for a few more and went himself, he'd be "corporal of the Hemingstein legion" (15 Dec. 1936 *SL* 455). During the civil war years, he occasionally signed letters "Stein."

290:9 **Carmelites:** The Order of the Brothers of the Blessed Virgin Mary of Mount Carmel, dating to the twelfth century, demands a life of constant prayer and devotion; no owned things, including money; much solitude; work; and chastity. The order's dictate of silence between the last evening prayer and sunrise, and its emphasis on as little talking as possible the rest of one's existence, is interesting in light of this novel's windy verbosity: "talkativeness is . . . to be carefully avoided, for as it is written—and experience teaches no less—In talkativeness sin will not be lacking; and, the one who is careless in speech will meet with evils; and again, The one who uses many words injures his own soul" (Carmelite Rule 21).

290:15 **to *joder*:** To fuck. In Spanish the "to" is redundant, as *joder* is the full infinitive. In the draft, Hemingway wrote and crossed out "make love to," replacing it with "*joder*" (MS11–012).

291:9–10 **how such a girl would be:** If by "such a girl" Agustín means no longer a virgin, regardless of the violence she suffered, the result in conservative Spain would be a severe diminishment of marriage prospects and possibly an unwanted life as a mistress or prostitute. If he means nubile in terms of sexuality, the result might not be much different. If he means nubile in terms of marriageability, the result would be a life confined to domesticity effectively as property to a husband she might not be fond of. Her beauty potentially increases the desire for ownership of her. Even though she and Jordan genuinely love one another, the novel predicts that her life with him would still be life as domestic helpmate.

291:14 **no need for that under the revolution:** For many on the left, marriage oppressed women, treating them as property. Its abolishment as a state and church function was fundamental to women's liberation. Free love meant giving "the right of both men and women freely to choose a sexual relationship without benefit of clergy or state and freely to end it when it was no longer mutually satisfying" (Ackelsberg 51). Another ideological argument maintained that lower-class women were forced into prostitution not just because of economic need but because the bourgeois cult of virginity and propriety depended upon it (Nash 158). If marriage and prostitution exploited women, eliminating state- and church-controlled marriage and divorce addressed both social ills. The Republic reformed the laws to make marriage a civil matter and to ease the divorce process, but did not adopt Agustín's more radical free love position whereby marriage as an institution requiring state or church sanction would no longer exist, as people authorized their own unions and, as necessary, disunions. Nationalist rhetoric equated ideals of women's equality and liberation with promiscuity, using it to justify rape as giving the women what that rhetoric said they wanted and also as punishing them all at once—as they did to Maria.

291:16 **I will marry her:** This is the second of three scenes in which Jordan says he wants to marry Maria (164:33). Here he insists upon it after Agustín's revolutionary notion about romantic union. In the third scene, Maria reminds him that institutionalized marriage is irrelevant; he again says he wants to marry her anyway (344:17). Later in that scene, he declares them married privately but "truly," seemingly acceding to the revolutionary idea (354:19–22), yet by the end of the scene he reverts to his wish that they traditionally wed (355:28–29). Jordan's habits of thought inevitably reveal a more traditional than revolutionary character.

291:30 **No:** Jordan lies. See 166:16+.

293:2–3 ***Es muy hombre!:*** He is much man, very much a man, very much of a man. Better, less literal translations: What a man!; He's quite a man; He's a hell of a man; He's a stud. Changed in the galley proofs from *Mucho! Mucho!* on Durán's advice. Hemingway explained that it means "terrific," and that many of the words and expressions Durán corrected, Hemingway had from "Basques who really do not know Spanish any more than I do."[2] Hemingway wrote much of the novel in Cuba, where he spent time with the Basque community, including Spaniards displaced by the war. The novel's Spanish is thus influenced by his Cuban and Basque environment.

NOTES

1. Hemingway included the bitch circle in a letter to Archibald MacLeish (ca. 17–20 Nov. 1933, *Letters 5* 546).
2. To Gustavo Durán [ca. 20–27 Aug. 1940] (Residencia).

CHAPTER TWENTY-FIVE

295:25 **behind two boulders:** Hemingway replaced the word "rocks" with "boulders" in the draft to be consistent with all earlier references in the paragraph (MS11–014). Apparently, a stone is not a stein is not a rock is not a boulder is not a pebble (289:16–17).

298:1 **He's *jodido?*:** He's fucked? He's screwed? In the draft, this word replaces "obscenitied" (MS11–014). The same replacement occurs further down the page (298:24).

298:3 **Pobre:** Literally *poor,* in this case something like, Poor man, or What a pity.

298:37 **high Indian cheekbones:** Jordan also likens Pilar to an Indian because of her bedding's odor (360:28). Besides Pilar, he likens El Sordo and Fernando to Native Americans (141:12; 198:37). See the conversation about Romani and Indian beliefs regarding bears (40:15). All of these comparisons are complicated by the fact that the grandfather Jordan idolizes took part in the United States' war to eradicate the continent's indigenous people.

299:5+ **He should learn:** This paragraph follows and replaces one written and crossed out in the draft: "'He should write novels,' Pilar said. 'Such a novel as I have just heard from the gypsy. You should learn to read and write and write novels'" (MS11–014).

299:18 ***Total, qué?*:** Idiomatic: So? What of it?

300:26 ***puchero*:** Stew.

300:36 ***Ya lo sé*:** I know. I get it. I understand.

301:5 **a physic:** A medicine.

CHAPTER TWENTY-SIX

302:1–2 **It was three o'clock in the afternoon before the planes came. The snow had all been gone by noon:** At the end of the chapter, it turns "three o'clock" and Jordan hears and sees the planes (306:8–9). Whether the novel intends the chapter's contents to represent all three hours isn't clear—that "the rocks were hot now in the sun" indicates that some time has passed since noon. The first sentence indicates either that the narrator has knowledge of the story's future, and thus narrates past events, or that the chapter's content is a kind of flashback that occurs at three o'clock. Either way, the rupture of the novel's straightforward chronological storytelling jars. The result isn't understood until several pages into the next chapter, when the Carlist captain checks his watch: "ten minutes to three o'clock" (315:9–10). In addition to fragmenting perspective throughout, the novel now fragments time with concurrent scenes presented linearly. In this chapter, Jordan reads the letters off the body of the man he killed and he reflects on others he has killed in the war; in the next chapter, Hemingway inverts those reflections by entering the headspace of those who know they are about to be killed. These simultaneous, parallel scenes connect Jordan to the fascist officer (Captain Mora) as the two men who check their watches. Both men die needlessly.

302:12 **Tafalla:** A town in the plains south of Pamplona, part of the Navarre province that does not identify as Basque. See 248:20–21.

302:13 **Nth cavalry:** Hemingway initially intended to specify a regiment, as he left a large blank before "cavalry" up through the galley proofs and in the margin asked the publisher to ask Gustavo Durán to fill in the blank (MS17–006). He also told his editor to expect an actual designation by cable ("Memorandum" enclosure in letter to Maxwell Perkins, 26 Aug. 1940, *SL* 516). Within a couple of weeks he changed his mind, cabling Perkins to use "Nth" because of "THE BUSINESS ABOUT THE HEADS."[1]

302:15 **Carlist:** See 265:25.

302:18 **Feria in Pamplona:** A several-day fair coinciding with the July celebration of San Fermín, Pamplona's patron saint, and the occasion of the town's annual bullfights. Before the Spanish Civil War, Hemingway attended the fiesta de San Fermín for five consecutive years beginning in 1923 and then again in 1929 and 1931. His 1926 novel *The Sun Also Rises* immortalized and popularized the festival, especially its dramatic running of the bulls.

303:2+ **Saint Anthony:** Saint Anthony of Padua, the patron saint of lost and stolen things and of travelers, is one of the most well-known saints. In Spain, France, Italy, and Portugal, he is the patron saint of sailors and fisherman. On the **Blessed Virgin of Pilar**, see 30:24+. On the **Sacred Heart**, see 265:25.

304:2–3 **the people of Navarra:** See 248:20–21. Here is Ibárruri (La Pasionaria) on Navarre:

> The political history of Navarre has always been different from that of other provinces in Spain. Navarre was a fortress of reaction where neither the restoration of the Republic nor the progress of Spain counted a farthing. It had been traditionally resistant to democratic forms of government. . . .
> Navarre had hardly changed from what it had been in 1876. The only difference was that in 1936 it was armed, not with the old muskets and pistols buried at the end of the Carlist Wars, but with modern Mausers and machine guns.
> In Navarre there lived the descendants of the old Carlists, organized in armed bands called *Requetés*, characterized by iron discipline, religious fanaticism and untouchable hierarchies. A combination military, Carlist and fascist organization, the *Requetés*, held constant drills, target practice, military parades and maneuvers, to which the authorities shut their eyes. (Ibárruri 180–81)

That was before the war. Long before. Ibárruri voices the communist party-line opinion, which most Republicans shared, such that Jordan's sympathy for Requetés, both this dead one and the soon-to-be-dead Lt. Paco Berrendo (322:34–35; 326:2+), is remarkable.

304:17+ **I had to shoot them when we took them prisoners at Usera:** Let's be perfectly clear: our hero has just admitted to murdering two unarmed prisoners in explicit violation of the 1929 Geneva Convention Relative to the Treatment of Prisoners of War, not to mention of basic human morality and decency. Readers disposed to romanticize Jordan would do well to reflect upon this episode. It dares readers to overlook the real in their taste for the romantic. The episode transplants a scene in *A Farewell to Arms* in which that novel's protagonist initiates a categorically unjustifiable battlefield execution—a murder—of two soldiers from his own army but not under his command. What Margot Norris has contended about the earlier novel applies to this one as well, in that both "challenge the desires and resistances that readers bring to war novels" and in both "a love story seduces readers into misreading and misprising a war story" (59, 61). In other words, the readers' desire for romance, plus genre conventions about the moral fiber of the romantic hero, lead to overlooking violences that must not be brooked.

The novels enact opposite if equal silences. *A Farewell to Arms* provides minimalist, blow-by-blow reportage of the scene by its retrospective first-person protagonist but no reflection whatsoever, no admission of guilt—the text deflects any acknowledgment to a joke by his partners in the murder about what they would say in a Catholic confessional. The hero of *For Whom the Bell Tolls* gives a declaration of his act with zero description and an ambiguous acceptance of responsibility. The text never mentions the incident again, making it far easier to overlook these four lines in this substantially longer novel. Jordan has already taught the reader how to read such moments in his appraisal of Pilar's tale, which he esteems for avoiding mere statements and for the vivid details that made him see the atrocities "we did" to others (134:38+). The four lines dance clumsily around guilt and regret: Jordan says he "had to shoot them" but does not offer why. He tells himself that he "did not mind it" but also that he "did not like it" and so has chosen not to repeat it—yet he didn't seem to have a choice at Usera? Was it his choice or not? How does one not mind something that he doesn't like? The noncommittal regret resembles Pablo's, who wishes he could bring back to life all those he killed, yet also says, "We should have killed all or none" (209:20). Nor does Jordan express regret over having killed nonfascists, such as the unwilling apolitical or even Republican-sympathizing conscripts who served in the Nationalist military. Hemingway added the last line of the paragraph to the draft to emphasize that Jordan has stopped killing the unarmed (MS11–015).

The action in Usera, a district in the southwest quadrant of Madrid east of Carabanchel, took place in November 1936 (237:14; 239:15+). In early November, Koltsov orchestrated the slaughter of around 2000 Nationalist prisoners by their guards just northeast of Madrid (Thomas, 463, 463n2; Wyden, 205–06). Hemingway might have known about a possible actual event from a year later, the so-called Crime of the Tunnel of Death. Purportedly, Republicans tricked Nationalists living in Madrid to flee Madrid through a tunnel, where they killed at least sixty-seven by gunshot or rope strangulation. Jordan's calling El Sordo's plight in this chapter "a passageway with no exit" is suggestive (305:38–39). There is some controversy about whether the postwar Franco government fabricated the tunnel murders. Thomas removed references to it after the first edition of *The Spanish Civil War* (1961). A memorial site still exists. That Hemingway references an atrocity at Usera, when his information came entirely from the Republican side (including Soviet agents and SIM), suggests that something like it happened. LaPrade points out that Hemingway's novel appeared three years before "the publication of the official rumor" by Franco's government in *The General Cause* in 1943 (156). Hemingway's personal sources included Pepe Quintanilla, the assistant to the chief of counterespionage, and Gustavo Durán, briefly the head of SIM in Madrid at the time the Crime of the Tunnel reportedly transpired.[2]

305:8+ Liberty, Equality, Fraternity . . . Life, Liberty, and the Pursuit of Happiness: The first three terms constitute France's national motto, which emerged during the French Revolution and was formally adopted in the late nineteenth century. The second three terms are the "inalienable rights" of all mankind according to the US Declaration of Independence. Jordan believes in capitalist democracies such as those of these nation-states, not communist systems of government derived from Marxism. He's a mainstream bourgeois American. By **dialectics**, Jordan refers to dialectical materialism, a fundamental aspect of Marxist philosophy that considers oppositional relationships in the material (economic) and the social worlds as primary in historical development, not the evolution of ideas divorced from their material conditions.

NOTES

1. To Max Perkins, 9 Sep. 1940 (PUL).
2. On Quintanilla's role and its exaggeration by Hemingway and subsequently others (who took Hemingway literally), see Preston, "Hemingway's Forgotten Spanish Civil War Play." On Durán's SIM role in October 1937, see LaPrade (157); Ruiz (300).

CHAPTER TWENTY-SEVEN

307:1 **El Sordo was making his fight:** This is the first chapter entirely devoted to characters other than Jordan, who is absent. Previous chapters integrated the other character's point of view within Jordan's story, such as Pilar's tale (chapter 10) and Anselmo's reflections (chapter 15). As the novel progresses, as it nears Jordan's death, it outlives him by constructing perspectives belonging to characters who survive.

In terms of El Sordo's last stand's connection to George Armstrong Custer's (introduction; 8:4), the more parallel event would be Major Reno's separate battle that day in June 1876: "One hundred-odd men were surrounded by thrice their number and more Indians continually were arriving from the village. It was now about three-thirty p.m. Where was the promised support? Where was Custer?" (Van de Water 343). Unlike El Sordo, Reno escaped death, although he also was chased to take defensive positions on high ground, and his help, as with Robert Jordan's guerillas, also never came. Hemingway's novel follows Van de Water's narrative by having participants check their watches and providing the reader the time. The Reno battle and the El Sordo battle commenced at the same time of day, around three in the afternoon. (Custer's last stand began very shortly thereafter, and while Jordan's takes place twelve hours after El Sordo's, it is approximately the same clock time.)

309:9 *Mierda:* Shit. Hemingway does not translate offensive words such as shit and fuck as he does much of the novel's other Spanish, a decision emphasized here by the text's translation of *vencer* in the immediately prior line. He did not want to give anyone a reason (excuse) not to distribute or read the book. Read diegetically, these omissions suggest Jordan did not need to translate them for himself.

309:11–12 **Pasionaria says it is better to die on your feet:** Ibárruri's memoir dates her motivational rhetoric to an evening radio broadcast she gave on 18 July 1936, at the beginning of the war. It was the same broadcast in which she first exhorted ¡No pasarán!—They shall not pass! (195; see 54:3–4).

309:15–16 **a son thy age in Russia:** Rubén Ruiz Ibárruri and his sister Amaya moved to the Soviet Union in the spring of 1935. Their mother had been arrested once already, the new rightist government constantly hounded her, and according to her memoir the communist party would not let her return home to the Basque countryside because they needed her in Madrid:

> My two country-raised children were used to the fresh air, the sea and the mountains of the Basque country. I couldn't bear to see them cooped up in a stuffy, dark Madrid house, or lost in the crowded city selling *Mundo Obrero* [the communist newspaper], without knowing anyone but a small group of Pioneers [communist youth organization], without being able to attend school, and constantly worrying about their mother. The party leaders thought the matter over and proposed to send my children to the Soviet Union, where they could lead a normal life together with the children of Soviet workers, though they would not have the presence and comfort of their mother.
>
> It was another sacrifice I had to make. (Ibárruri 151)

Rubén eventually slipped back into Spain to fight in the Republican Army, but after the novel's timeframe (July 1938, per Mandel, *Reading* 231–32). He attended aviation school while in Moscow (311:24).

311:31 **Me cago en tal:** I shit on such. Replaced *Me cabra* in the galley proofs, on Durán's strong suggestion. Hemingway explained to Durán why he had used it and other invented versions of *I shit*:

> Me Cabra or me Cabo or Me Caba are words invented by healthy cursers to cover the real word. I would rather, always, use the real word.... You see I would wish to treat one language as seriously as another and if I cannot say shit in English it is cheating to say it in Spanish.[1]

312:37+ **But living was a field of grain:** El Sordo paints a pastoral fantasy of Spanish life. The "field of grain" is suggestive of Jordan's repeated descriptions of Maria, as is perhaps the following line that "[l]iving was a horse between your legs" (313:2+).

313:38+ **9mm. Star:** A 1931 Star Model B pistol, of Spanish manufacture, the standard military sidearm in Spain. This second edition of the Model B resembles the famous Colt 1911A1—the Colt .45. The original Star adopted John Moses Browning's design for the original Colt 1911, the US handgun from the Great War.

315:9–10 **ten minutes to three:** Precisely twelve hours later, Jordan will check his watch (382:6–7). Both men die in the fighting that follows. They share death-foreshadowing names (see 318:20+), have blond hair and blue eyes (319:15+), and use French to demean (fellow) Spaniards (317:25).

315:26 **mortars:** Mortars are short-ranged portable indirect fire artillery weapons that do not require a direct line-of-sight because they lob their explosive munitions upward in an arcing trajectory rather than shooting them straight at target as a cannon or rifle does. They are ideal for targeting dead space—depressions, trenches, ravines, craters, the other side of a ridge or hill. One can use them from a position of safety from direct fire weapons, as they travel over one's defensive cover and concealment (entrenchment, wall, sandbags, bushes, boulders) and the enemy's. In this case, the dead horses.

317:1–2 **pushed the pistol against the small of the man's back:** Leadership by gunpoint was not uncommon by both sides of the war, or historically by any military force for that matter (by gunpoint or swordpoint). In *A Farewell to Arms,* Hemingway's protagonist, Frederic Henry, infamously shoots a disobeying sergeant on the spot during a retreat in World War I.

317:25 **canaille:** Scum would be a good translation or synonym for this loanword. The captain's use of the derogatory French term for riffraff or rabble, as in a group of vulgar commoners (rascals or scoundrels), is perhaps explained by this unit's hailing from Navarre. The medieval Kingdom of Navarre included what is now upper Spain and lower France on the other side of the Pyrenees. His use of French to assert himself over Spaniards also associates him with Jordan (see 16: 37–38; 404:22–23).

317:36 **Captain Mora:** Hemingway might have borrowed the surname of Constancia de la Mora (Constance or Connie Mora), a Spanish aristocrat with familial Nationalist ties, but a communist and staunch Republican. Her prominence stemmed from her background, her marriage to the general in command of the air force (Ignacio Hidalgo de Cisneros y López de Montenegro), and her role as the director of the Foreign Press Bureau. Her language skills initially led to her work in the bureau providing information and support to foreign correspondents—along with censoring their outgoing dispatches—from its Valencia office. When the government moved to Barcelona in the fall of 1937, she became its director. She only had nice things to say about Hemingway in her memoir *In Place of Splendor,* although she either remembered differently from Hemingway or invented conversations with him about bullfighting, for he claimed they never had them. The memoir came out in November 1939, three months before Hemingway drafted this chapter. To Gustavo Durán he called de la Mora "a god-damned Prima-Donna" in a letter written around the time he finished the chapter.[2] The death in the novel of the prima donna Captain Mora could have been retribution or simple meanness. He was probably jealous and irritated by the praise reviewers lavished on *In Place of Splendor*. Charles Poore in the *New York Times* called it "one of the most vivid and dramatic" books about Spain, its author "a legendary figure." How could Hemingway not have bridled at Poore's praise of her war writing? "Many have described what it is like to be under bombardment from the air," Poore wrote, "but I don't suppose any one has ever described it more precisely than Constancia de la Mora's account of the three days when squadrons of fascist planes bombed Barcelona with clocklike precision every three hours, day and night." Hemingway's journalism described city life under artillery bombardment in "Hemingway Describes Shelling of Madrid" (12 Apr. 1937) and "Hemingway Finds Madrid Callous to Bombardment" (23 Apr. 1937).[3]

On the name Mora, see also 318:20+.

318:20+ **bad luck:** As with Jordan's several mistakes in his relationship with the guerillas and in his anxiousness preceding his death, bad luck and "ill fortune" do indeed follow the captain's "blasphemies." He dies in the next few minutes, and Lt. Berrendo, crouching with the sniper who has this thought, will die on the imagined page after the novel's last. The novel's Gitano superstition and Catholic superstition have the same folk roots. Jordan's palms register his forthcoming death ambiguously by fate's, or by his own, hand.

What's in a name? Captain Mora and Jordan both have death embedded in their names: Mora from the Latin word for death, *mors,* the source of the Spanish *muerte,* French *mort,* and English *morgue* or *mortuary;* Jordan from the River Jordan, the crossing of which gains one freedom from toil, in the Promised Land. As does a third character who willingly places himself in harm's way, Finito, which means *finite*—so not infinite, that is, mortal. Hemingway continues to play with ideas of plot causality, character, and literary genre. This "bad luck" thought comes from an anonymous sniper as Hemingway adds yet another voice to the novel's array.

On Berrendo's name, see 471:33.

319:6 *caza mayor:* Big game. The war-as-hunting discourse continues.

319:8 **This one coming now makes the same voyage I do:** El Sordo's last stand sets up Jordan's. Both men, doomed to die, wait with a dead horse to kill an approaching enemy officer. Both men reflect on their last moments. El Sordo fakes suicide; Jordan pretends to himself that his death isn't self-murder. Paco Berrendo is a witness here and is the dead man walking in the later scene.

319:15+ **the face of an *Inglés*:** With Mora's blonde hair and blue eyes, the novel further connects Captain Mora and Jordan the *Inglés* (see 315:9–10).

319:23 **tripoded automatic weapon:** See 320:33.

320:15 **At this moment:** Perhaps the novel's most realistic moment, certainly one of its most Naturalist moments, in the reminder of the utter arbitrariness of who lives and who dies in war. The line refreshingly contrasts with the novel's ponderous Tragic elements.

320:26 ***Cabrones! Hijos de puta!:*** Bastards! Sons of whores! Sons of bitches! In the galley proofs, replaces "Me cabra. Me cabra. Me cabra." Hemingway used one iteration of this phrase a little earlier, but again in the galley proofs changed it to *Cojones!* (318:2). See 311:31.

320:33 **three legs of that tripod:** In the draft margin, Hemingway wrote "bipod" and, just beneath it, "two leg." This is the gang's Lewis gun (145:3); El Sordo adds the bipod's support arm in counting the legs (see 27:11). This fact clarifies how Ignacio can grasp the tripod legs with only two hands (321:1)—he's holding the two legs proper. Hemingway corrects himself in the draft: "gathered the ~~three~~ legs of the tripod" (MS12-002).

321:7+ **Hail Mary, full of grace:** In Catholicism, the Hail Mary prayer is part of daily devotions and the central part of the Rosary, a set of prayers regarded as a defense against evil and a common remedy after confession. Joaquín doubly rejects Pasionaria, in the turn to Mary and in the very language of the prayer: "Blessed art thou among women and Blessed in the fruit of thy womb, Jesus"—in contrast to Pasionaria's son (309:15–16). Joaquín then moves into the prayer of **contrition**, of which there are several variations: "O my God, I am heartily sorry for having offended Thee, and I detest all my sins because of Thy just punishments, but most of all because they offend Thee, my God, Who art all-good and deserving of all my love. I firmly resolve, with the help of Thy grace, to sin no more and to avoid the near occasions of sin." Contrition is part of the Sacrament of Penance, a necessary step for salvation: "But except you do penance," He says, "you shall all likewise perish" (Luke 13:5); "Be penitent, therefore, and be converted, that your sins may be blotted out" (Acts 3:9). Joaquín's chief sin would be his rejection of the Catholic God, his idolatrous secular replacement of the Virgin Mary with Pasionaria.

321:20+ **at the hour of our death:** In the intensity of the moment, Joaquín either forgets the words of the Hail Mary he just uttered or he recourses to a different prayer: "O Mary, Mother of grace and Mother of mercy, do thou protect us from our enemy, and receive us at the hour of our death." In "Chapter VII" of *In Our Time,* an unnamed narrator also under bombardment (presumably Nick Adams) prays to be delivered from death. This being that 1925 book's only gesture toward God or religion, from a character who seems to be embarrassed by it and after the battle heads for comfort to a brothel (*CSS* 109), into sin, works against seeing that moment as devotion or acknowledgment of God's existence—against seeing it as anything other than a reflexive response to fear. Upon Hemingway's wounding during a bombardment during the First World War, in expectation of death he received divine unction from a priest. Nick's fear and Hemingway's genuine battlefield experience inform Joaquín's prayers.

321:24+ **the earth rolled under his knees:** The earth figuratively moves during Jordan's and Maria's lovemaking at least once—"out and away from under them" (159:26)—and probably twice, and it literally moves thrice: here; in the train mission that rescued Maria (29:25); and at Jordan's death. According to Pilar, the earth "never moves more than three times in a lifetime" (174:30).

322:36 **Our Fathers:** In addition to "**five Hail Marys**" (321:7+), Berrendo recites five Our Fathers, also known as the Lord's Prayer: "Our Father, Who art in Heaven, hallowed be Thy name; Thy Kingdom come, Thy will be done on earth as it is in Heaven. Give us this day our daily bread; and forgive us our trespasses as we forgive those who trespass against us; and lead us not into temptation, but deliver us from evil. Amen."

NOTES

1. To Gustavo Durán [ca. 20–27 Aug. 1940] (Residencia).
2. To Gustavo Durán, 5 Mar. 1940 (Resedencia).
3. In Watson, where he titles them "Battle in the Casa de Campo" and "Bombardment of Madrid."

CHAPTER TWENTY-EIGHT

323:15 **pistol shot did not carry that far**: An omniscient narrator intrudes here.

323:21+ **stewed hare:** Pilar and Maria have cooked and now serve the hares that Rafael trapped (274:7+). Shortly before his death, the doomed El Sordo compares the hilltop position to a "flayed rabbit" (310:34). This moment between Jordan and Maria is obscene in context. He watches her "climbing lithely" with "her cropped head bright in the sun" (323:28–30), the adjective "lithely" and the focus on her titillating hair betraying his appreciative (sexual) gaze, before "ladling out" the stew while dishing out news of El Sordo's fate (324:1–2). Compare Jordan to Primitivo, who has lost his appetite (324:6). For readers sympathetic to DeGuzmán's argument about Jordan's colonialist consumption of Spain (22:37), this scene bites sharply. Later Jordan supposes that Pablo "always intended to muck off but he knew we were *cooked* when Sordo was attacked" (385:19–20; emphasis added).

324:34+ **religious instruction:** Pilar is giving Maria a crash course in sex education, "of things one can do for a husband" (349:24–25). Jordan's "patt[ing] her on the head" reinscribes the sexual stimulation he receives from the visible sign of her sexual violation. Maria's original rapists twisted religious language to justify their cruelty, to teach her, school her: "This is how we make Red nuns. This will show thee how to unite with thy proletarian brothers. Bride of the Red Christ!" (352:9–11). Probably unintended by Hemingway, Jordan's gesture within Christian discourse recalls the countless paintings of the Annunciation, when the angel Gabriel announces to Mary her pregnancy, the act of annunciation literally also the act of conception. In these scenes, the ray of light carrying Christ into Mary's body strikes either her lap or, just as often, her head—because it is the Word of God entering her. Either way, the asexuality of the Christian tradition is a far cry from Jordan and Maria's relationship. The chapter contrasts their joking about sex and religion with the novel's most heartfelt expression of Catholic faith, Lt. Berrendo's devotions (326:22+).

326:2+ **felt no arrogance:** The declaration of "no arrogance" reinforces Berrendo's humility and decency, pointedly rebuking Jordan's presumption and making clear that "lashed arrogantly" (325:38) was Jordan's opinion, not the fact of the matter. If anything, the presumption of another person's frame of mind reveals *Jordan's* arrogance. Coincidentally, the draft and the published version begin a new page with this new paragraph—one reads Jordan's perspective, then starts a fresh page to discover Berrendo's true one. The structural predecessor is Pablo's horse's annoyance with Pablo's cooing (64:14+). Berrendo's deeply felt adjective, "barbarous," recasts Jordan's easy rhetoric of "barbarians" (134:14+). Besides distinguishing between Jordan's and Berrendo's perspectives, the passage also converges them. Berrendo's "hollowness" matches Jordan's "hollow feeling" (323:17). The last few lines eavesdrop on Berrendo's tactical reflections as he talks back and forth with himself in a moment of free indirect discourse that sounds exactly like so many of Jordan's. It is a brilliant paragraph.

326:22+ **Hail, holy queen:** This passage is perhaps the most Catholic-affirming of any in Hemingway's oeuvre. Berrendo offers up the *Salve, Regina* (Hail, Holy Queen) as an expression of grief for the dead as well as of his Catholic spirituality, humility, and duty. Among other employments, the prayer concludes the Rosary and structurally expresses finality and the end of a cycle. The recognition of finality relates to the John Donne epigraph from which the novel's title comes: the bell "tolls for *thee*." The prayer invokes the reciter's eventual death—"after this our exile ended, show unto us the blessed fruit of thy womb." In the mundane case of this story, it foreshadows the lieutenant's death the next morning. As he prays here, Berrendo rides into a patch of ground where the sunlight verily turns the pine trees into "the columns of a cathedral" (326:26–27), setting up his last moment on earth as he rides into "the sunlit place where the first trees of the pine forest joined the green slope of the meadow" (471:33–34). Anselmo could not have heard Berrendo but resumes the prayer exactly where Berrendo left off (327:12).

326:26–28 **pine needles . . . the columns of a cathedral:** See 326: 22+. The line might additionally allude to Stephen Crane's *The Red Badge of Courage*. The ambiguity of Christian spirituality in Crane's thoroughly Naturalist novel does not fit the sincerity of Berrendo's journey, although it certainly plays into *For Whom the Bell Tolls*'s overall religious inquiry (see introduction). Berrendo's **flankers** would be the two men riding slightly ahead of the column, one on each side (flank), perhaps suggestive of the two men crucified with Christ: "Where they crucified him, and two other with him, on either side one, and Jesus in the midst" (John 19:18).

327:12 **Most kind, most sweet, most clement Virgin:** Anselmo's prayer begins with a version of the apostrophe to the Mother of God that concludes the *Salve, Regina*. Although he has recited the entire prayer (327:9–10), as Berrendo has (326:25), the fact that Anselmo concludes the prayer begun by Berrendo testifies to their shared

Catholic-infused Spanish culture, if not a more spiritual fraternity. The shared prayer also portends their shared fate, as both men depart earthly life in the last chapter.

The *Salve, Regina* has appeared in many variations due to evolution over the centuries; translations and regional differences, particularly with nonliterate societies and as their languages have developed; and adaptations to liturgical functions, including hymns. The following version appears in Thomas Smyth's *Mary Not a Perpetual Virgin, Nor the Mother of God*, originally published in 1846:

> Hail! Hail! then, all Holy Queen, Mother of Mercy, our life, our sweetness, and our hope, to thee do we cry, poor banished sons of Eve; to thee do we send up our sighs, mourning and weeping in this valley of tears; turn then most gracious advocate, thine eyes of mercy towards us, and, after this our exile ended, show unto us the blessed fruit of thy womb, Jesus. Oh! most clement—most pious—most sweet Virgin Mary; pray for us, O Holy Mother of God, that we may be made worthy of the promises of Christ.—Amen. (5)

The reference to the supplicants as Eve's banished son Cain connects the war to the original civil war between the brothers Cain and Abel, incarnated here by Berrendo and Anselmo. The lamentation speaks to the newly dead from El Sordo's last stand. Although "banished" and "exile" signify mortal life outside the Garden of Eden and God's kingdom, they speak to the wartime displacement of Spaniards forced to leave villages and town and kin (such as Anselmo himself; 39:20–21). The request to "be made worthy" has an immediate application in Anselmo's prayer that follows.

327:15+ But let me be close to him, O Lord: Whereas the *Salve, Regina* appeases Berrendo in his quiet reflection on death and the eternal, Anselmo can't stop "thinking of the next day" and his own behavior facing death in battle on the morrow (327:13). Anselmo replaces the prayer's final supplication to be made worthy of Christ's promises with one to be worthy of Jordan's instructions. If Jordan ever uttered a prayer, it would sound like this one in its anxieties over manly comportment in the face of death. There's a self-centeredness to Anselmo's prayer not present in Berrendo's.

The text appears to pass judgment through a description of physical movement. Both characters have been moving through the dark. But whereas during the *Salve, Regina* Berrendo rides into the cathedral-like light accompanied by his soldiers (326:26–28), after Anselmo finishes his personal prayer, he walks "in the dark alone" (327:25). Only after resuming his prayers for others, for "the people of Sordo" (perhaps with the *Salve, Regina*) does Anselmo find company at "the upper post where Fernando challenged him" (327:29). Even this rejoined company, however, is qualified by two reiterations of still being "in the dark" (327:34; 328:6).

Perhaps Anselmo, caught between rejecting the abuses and power of the Spanish Catholic Church while harboring a genuine Christian faith, resorts to a personal prayer that either of necessity compromises or that approaches a Protestant theology requiring no priest and refusing what Smyth calls the "*inexcusable* idolatry" of Mary in acknowledging God as "the only object of prayer" (Smyth 6, 15)—"O Lord," Anselmo repeatedly directs his prayer. Still, Anselmo's momentary return to the comforts of his Spanish-Catholic upbringing is not in and of itself proof of the text's belief in a Christian God, or of a deep-seated belief within Anselmo contrary to his professed wish for the comfort of faith in the certainty of a godless universe (41:20). The text does not directly pass judgment, as the two characters' contrasting spiritual reckonings both belong to Hemingway, in whom Catholicism's light and *nada*'s darkness coexisted.

Hemingway cut several lines from the draft that followed "as a man tomorrow in the day of the battle" (327:21–22), in which Anselmo pleads defensively that in fighting for the Republic he has never opposed God, as the cause itself doesn't oppose God or the Holy Mother (MS12–003).

328:13 **alone with his dignity:** The line immediately references the sarcastic use of dignity for inflicting upon the Nationalist soldiers the same indignities to which they subjected El Sordo's guerrillas. It is also either the narrator's or Anselmo's furtherance of the group's regard of Fernando as their overly serious member. Finally, one might consider it a subtextual conclusion to the chapter's religious meditation. Readers disinclined to seeing a deep Catholicism in Hemingway's works might interpret it as upholding the possibility of the lone man's dignity despite the *nada* of individual existence, in accord with Anselmo's earlier assertion that "a man must be responsible to himself" (41:20); readers convinced of the pervading Catholicism would perhaps understand it as offering that such dignity risks the sin of pride, of the spiritual arrogance of believing one does not need God.

CHAPTER TWENTY-NINE

331:23 **Estado Mayor:** The headquarters.[1]

331:34+ **Brigades, Divisions, Army Corps:** Despite Anselmo's confusion, Hemingway lists the units in increasing size and hierarchy: a corps consists of more than one division, a division of more than one brigade. The situation for the Republic was especially confusing because at the start of the war the militias that defended it used their terms for themselves: **columns**, **regiments**, and **brigades**. The arrival of the International Brigades confused matters more. At the time of the novel, the Republic's military was still transforming into its single, government-controlled People's Army with standard unit designations. Some units were redesignated, some remnant designations persisted, and old units were intermixed with new ones. Anselmo's understanding that a "place was a place" underscores how armed forces restructure or remap the landscape; it isn't the Nationalist machine versus the Republican salt of the earth, but modern international militaries versus Spain (see 1:13). The line echoes the famous one from *A Farewell to Arms* inveighing against the "obscene" abstractions "glory, honor, courage" when "only the names of places had dignity" (185).

332:15 **the seal of the S.I.M.:** The Servicio de Información Militar. See 10:12–13.

332:38 ***picardia:*** Cleverness, slyness, craftiness. Pablo's use of the word further associates it and the related term *picaro* with him. See 11:16, 95:1, and 95:11.

333:13–14 **only a holding attack:** The Segovia Offensive was a holding attack and diversion to relieve pressure in the north, where the Nationalists were pressing toward Bilbao to conquer the Basque country. Since 1512, Guernica was the seat of the central assembly for all Basque communities; its bombing by the Nationalist-allied Condor Legion on 26 April was a symbolic act as much as a one of terror. Guernica had zero military value.

NOTE

1. At the top of this page in the draft, above the title, it reads, "End chapter 28 or short between-chapter" (MS12–004).

CHAPTER THIRTY

334:20 **Soria . . . Siguenza:** Two towns northeast of Madrid. An attack from this direction would travel between the Guadarrama and the Cuenca mountain ranges toward **Guadalajara**, the same route the Italians fighting for the Nationalists tried unsuccessfully in March (233:35+).

334:25 **Cádiz:** A small port town up the Atlantic coast from Gibraltar that the Nationalists seized the third day of the rebellion (19 July 1936) with the arrival of Army of Africa soldiers. Thereafter it became an entry point for Nationalist forces. Hemingway filed his second war dispatch on 15 March 1937 from Toulouse, France, before entering Spain, reporting "12,000 Italian troops [had] landed at Málaga and Cádiz" on a single day, the total number now at 88,000, information he had "from a most reliable source" (in Watson 14).

334:31+ **the Arganda offensive:** Part of the Battle of Jarama. After failing to enter Madrid through the Guadarrama from the northwest in July and August 1936, and then from the west in November and December 1936 (through Carabanchel, Usera, and Casa de Campo), the Nationalists in February 1937 tried to encircle Madrid to the south, with the hope of seizing the **Valencia Road** and severing Madrid from the Republic's new capital. The contested bridge in *The Spanish Earth* is the Arganda Bridge, a steel bridge some readers believe to be the physical model for the bridge of *For Whom the Bell Tolls*.

335:11 **The orders on this are very clear. Too very clear:** The stark emphasis on the clarity of his orders suggests the possibility of Jordan's execution were he to fail, a possibility he earlier expressed as a certainty (151:30; also 6:16+).

335:24+ **Durán:** Gustavo Durán-Martínez was a thirty-year-old pianist, composer, and linguist "dubbing foreign films into Spanish when the war broke out," whereupon he became an army officer for the Republic (Ruiz 300). Durán helped lead the initial defense of Madrid in the fall of 1936, initially in the communist's Fifth Regiment, then as a commander of a mixed brigade as well as an International Brigade staff officer under the Hungarian Emilio Kléber. He commanded the 69th Division during the Segovia Offensive that Robert Jordan's mission supported. Historians share Jordan's estimation of Durán's considerable military leadership talents. His very brief leadership of Madrid's Military Investigation Service (SIM) in the fall of 1937 ended due to a purported excessive appointment of communists into its ranks (see also 304:17–18). Preston calls him a "playboy intellectual" and a close friend of the poet Federico García Lorca (*Spanish Civil War* 112). Hemingway described him at length with great admiration and love in a letter to the American poet and International Brigade veteran Edwin Rolfe. Given Durán's background as a pianist, man about town, and Chicote's regular, one could be forgiven for assuming he'd be a fascist, a fellow like the fascist pilot in Hemingway's story "The Denunciation" who sneaked back to the Madrid bar during the war, a man with whom the American narrator once shot pigeons, gambled, and drank. But Durán was a Republican officer from the get-go. He was wounded during the Segovia Offensive, "where his brigade and the 14th I. B. had such a horrible balls up and Walter shot so many damned people." He led a division at the Battle of Teruel from December 1937 to February 1938. In April, he was cut off in the mountains near Vinaròs when the Nationalists reached the Mediterranean to split the Republic in half. Somehow, Durán managed to save his division and rejoin the defensive fight: "Almost Christ. It was a piece of soldiering such as you couldn't believe." At war's end, he commanded a corps,

> [and] when Passionaria decided it was better to fly in an airoplane than die on your knees and the plane seats were whacked up and the privelegiados got them (I understand why it was necessary to save the cadres to fight again. You don't need to explain that to me) Am just telling you how things go.) Duran was still holding solid as a fucking rock at Segorbe. Nobody had told him it was over. Well he made it finally behind the boilers from Valencia to England. I staked him and now he is o.k.I wish the hell you could know him.[1]

Jordan has no illusions about surviving the mission to see Durán again. After the war, Durán moved the United States, where he and Hemingway resumed their friendship while Hemingway was writing *For Whom the Bell Tolls*. Hemingway might very well have known of Durán's plans to relocate from London to New York City in May 1940 when he drafted this chapter around mid-March (see appendix A), writing, "It would be good to see Duran again" (335:33–34).

On 13 August 1940, Hemingway wired his publisher from Cuba to send the galley proofs to Durán in New Hampshire to correct the novel's Spanish.[2] The friends had just spent three days together in New York City, where he asked Durán in person to check the galleys over.[3] Hemingway then transferred Durán's corrections onto his own copy of the galley proofs (the set at the JFK).[4] Durán fixed spelling errors (such as Hemingway's *machina* to *máquina* and *Augustín* to *Agustín*), fixed grammar problems, and in some cases supplied better phrases.

335:32 the War of the Rebellion: The Union's official name in US war records for the American Civil War. Grandfather and grandson thus share a certain political kinship: both fight for the legitimate Republic against a rebellious body whose economic system was based upon a conservative, quasi-feudal landed gentry and its labor exploitation.

336:5–6 just finishing your first year in this war: The war is just over ten months old (17 July 1936 to today, 30 May 1937). More accurately, he is just finishing his year in Spain, on leave for the academic year from his university.

336:12+ Fort Kearny after the war: The US Army established Fort Kearny, Nebraska, along the Oregon Trail in 1848. After the Civil War, the US war against the Native Americans moved farther west, to Wyoming and Montana, taking Jordan's grandfather with it. He served in the 7th Cavalry Regiment (see 337:10–11), perhaps under George Armstrong Custer—Jordan's language isn't clear on this point: "They said if he had been with Custer that day," the day of Custer's death at the Little Bighorn, "he never would have let him be sucked in that way" (337:38+). Custer had divided the 7th into three columns. One possibility is that Jordan's grandfather was with one of the other two, under Major Marcus Reno or Captain Frederick Benteen (or with the company assigned to the supply trains), and so not "with Custer that day." Another possibility is that the grandfather's and Custer's postings to the 7th didn't coincide.

The rest of the paragraph, about "the cabinet in your father's office" displaying Native American weaponry and clothing from Jordan's grandfather, raises a question the novel never answers: How did the grandfather come into possession of them? In purchase or trade, or as war (genocide) trophies? That he doesn't care to talk about the people he killed is suggestive of an answer to this question (337:4).

Jordan dresses as a Spanish local, his "peasant's trousers" and alpargatas (3:5), the cultural equivalent of the displayed "leggings" and "moccasins" that function as fetish objects. Jordan sensuously recalls "how the bundle of shafts felt when you closed your hand around them." In the draft, Hemingway rewrote the initial language—"how the shafts clicked when you picked an arrow out of the quiver" (MS12-004)—then added "bundle of" to the galley proofs.

336:25+ Grandfather's Smith and Wesson: Jordan's grandfather used this pistol in the American Civil War and again during the wars in the American West against the Sioux, Cheyenne, Kiowa, and Arapaho. This was the Smith and Wesson Model No. 2 Army Revolver, first manufactured in 1861 (the first year of the Civil War), whose revolving cylinder housed six rounds. The pistols were not army-issue, but many soldiers who could afford to bought them as personal sidearms. Custer owned a pair, and while historians don't know which of his weapons he carried at the Little Bighorn, paintings of his last stand often depict him with one or two No. 2s. This was Hemingway's grandfather's pistol from the Civil War, the pistol with which Hemingway's father, like Jordan's, committed suicide, and which both Hemingway and Jordan inherited (337:5+). Clarence Hemingway shot himself in the (right) temple (Reynolds, *Homecoming* 209; coroner's description at 257n57). The fatal bullet wound to Custer's (left) temple led to decades of speculation as to whether he killed himself to spare himself. The text juxtaposes Jordan's detailed memories of the frontier war artifacts in the prior paragraph with his attention in this paragraph to the pistol with "the softest, sweetest trigger pull you had ever felt." The language leans ominously into attraction and temptation. This memory segues into the memory of Jordan's ridding himself of the pistol in an attempt to rid himself of the suicide temptation (see 337:31).

337:10–11 **when he first came out with the Cavalry:** Up through the galley proofs, Hemingway named the "Seventh Cavalry." He probably crossed out the word for conversational realism—the coroner would not have said it. It read clunkily. In that part of Montana, it would have been redundant and unnecessary. The preserved capital "C" in Cavalry indicates the proper noun of a specific unit. Nearby Custer National Forest was so-named in 1908.

337:16 **Red Lodge, with Chub:** Leland Stanford "**Chub**" Weaver was a native of Red Lodge, Montana, Robert Jordan's hometown, whom Hemingway met at the L-Bar-T ranch outside **Cooke City** in 1930. They became fast friends. A hunter and fisherman, Weaver knew the land. He had traveled the world a little too, adding to his appeal for Hemingway. In the late summer of 1936, Weaver traveled from Red Lodge to work for Hemingway and Pauline during their extended hunting stay (August-October). He also spent time with Hemingway when the writer returned alone in 1939 (August-September). He was with Hemingway during the early phase of the Spanish Civil War and in the months before Hemingway started writing the novel.

"For its first four decades," writes historian Bonnie Christensen, "**Red Lodge** was a town whose public identity centered around industrialization, workers, and immigrants—all coated in the dust and grime of coal." At the turn of the twentieth century, most of its working men mined coal (40–41). It wasn't until the 1920s that Red Lodge and much of the region began cultivating an identity based upon "formerly despised symbols and characters of the Wild West and particularly around the multi-layered imagery of the greatest of all American heroes, the cowboy" (92). Christensen characterizes this mythos as "a twentieth century interpretation of the nineteenth century past" (89). To the degree that Jordan sought to embody some version of this mythos in Spain, he would have been chasing an inauthentic, revisionist vision, a nostalgia for a nineteenth century that never existed. Jordan was as much his own invention as Hemingway's. He was following the cultural lead of his home, inventing a self that twentieth-century Montana couldn't accommodate—but that Spain could. With its mining industry roots, Red Lodge might be where Jordan first acquainted himself with explosives.

337:31 **I know why you did that with the old gun:** Hemingway disposed of his grandfather's pistol, which his father used to commit suicide, as described in this passage by dropping it into Froze to Death Lake in the Beartooth Mountains, between Red Lodge and Cooke City, Montana, on a horseback trip with Chub Weaver (Warren 12, 24, 103–4).[5] Jordan's act can be read as a simple rejection of his father's choice (Warren 104). Yet Chub intimates that Jordan must rid himself of the symbol and means of suicide because he hadn't banished the temptation. No temptation, no need to ditch the pistol. According to Carlos Baker, one evening on a hunting trip in the fall of 1932, sated with elk meat and local whiskey, Hemingway told Chub that "he would never hesitate to kill himself if conditions were bad enough" (*Life Story* 232). Jordan recalls Chub once more, in the morning darkness on the day he dies (381:8).

337:32 **we don't have to talk about it:** The word suicide never appears in the novel. In declining to talk about his source of shame, Jordan mimics his grandfather, whom he just remembered declining to talk about his source of shame in the people he killed (337:4).

337:34 **He still had the saber:** A curved sword used by cavalrymen. Jordan holds onto the romantic emblem of pre-twentieth-century warfare, the weapon of aristocrats and the cavalry. His thinking about the saber leads him to think about George Armstrong Custer, the cavalry officer in command of the most legendary and romanticized suicidal military mission in US history. In other words, he has not stopped thinking about arranging his own death (see 337:38+). Contrast with Frederic Henry in *A Farewell to Arms,* who passes on a chance to purchase an officer's sword on his way back to the front in the First World War but does buy a pistol.

338:3 **in the draw along the Little Big Horn:** The Battle of the Little Bighorn, or Custer's Last Stand, took place on 25 June 1876 in the Montana Territory. See the introduction. The parallel with El Sordo's death might distract readers from seeing the correspondence with the protagonist's (unless Hemingway meant El Sordo's fight to parallel Major Reno's before Custer's death; see 307:1). See 339:18–19. The Little Bighorn is a river. A **draw** is a terrain feature, the sloping low ground between two spurs that descend from higher ground like tributary ridges. *Draw* and *spur* are commonly used terms in the military.

F. Otto Becker, *Custer's Last Fight* lithograph (1896) from an 1888 painting by Cassilly Adams commissioned by Anheuser-Busch Brewing Association. (WikiMedia Commons / Public Domain)

338:7 **and I'm sure there isn't, he thought:** Hemingway added this language by hand to the draft (MS12–004).

338:21 **Lâche:** *Lâche* is French for coward or cowardly. Jordan plays another what's-in-a-name game, trying out the Spanish *cobarde* before landing on the English "coward" (338:37).

338:22–23 **You have to be awfully occupied with yourself:** Hah! Already Hemingway's longest novel with still over a hundred pages to go, much of which represents Robert Jordan thinking about being Robert Jordan; the irony and dark humor couldn't be clearer. Jordan meets his own criterion for suicide. Hemingway added this clause to the draft by hand (MS12–004).

339:3 **not let her bully him:** Hemingway blamed his mother for his father's suicide, a murder by henpecking.

339:18–19 **Anheuser-Busch lithograph that hung on the poolroom wall in Red Lodge:** In his youth, Jordan idealized and romanticized the image of Custer in his final battle. *Custer's Last Fight* was an 1896 lithograph by F. Otto Becker, commissioned by the Anheuser-Busch Brewing Association for an advertisement, made from an 1888 painting by Cassilly Adams, and widely reproduced.

To aspire to the heroic message of the lithograph is to aspire to death in battle. Jordan's declining a proper military haircut leaves it resembling Custer's famous locks (8:4). Dean Rehberger contends that at novel's end, "Jordan, like Custer in the lithograph, is left waiting on a hill—frozen in a timeless moment before the inevitability of his death." For Rehberger, the novel critiques Jordan's battlefield romanticism; it becomes "an exorcism that cuts away a remaining visage of the Custer myth by making us skeptical of the heroics and mythic qualities of last stands." He sees Hemingway as conflicted about the role of the American "adventure ethos" and frontier mythology in the modern world, simultaneously valuing it and invalidating it (180–81). The Adams image has been endlessly reproduced, giving it a clichéd quality of childhood aspirations.

Eby also sees Jordan responding to Custer as a "complex and ambivalent" model, quoting Richard Slotkin's characterization of Custer as a "liminal hero,"

> the meeting point of the positive and negative forces in American culture—masculinity and femininity, adulthood and childhood, civilization and savagery, sanity and madness, order and disorder. As one who balances on a turning point between these orders and qualities, he is able to draw knowledge and power from both; but that very position makes him the embodiment of trouble and conflict, unstable and dangerous as a moral reference point. (*Fetishism* 219)

Jordan's potential affinities for an exploitative, even fascist outlook have been proposed by scholars such as DeGuzmán and Strychacz. Eby is interested in Hemingway's personal gender identity, focusing on accounts of Custer's androgynous appearance and his flamboyancy. The long hair is a critical element of the androgynous appearance, and of Jordan's memory of the lithograph, those "yellow curls blowing." Ironically, by 1876 Custer wore his hair short, and he had it cut—after his wife's prompting—before the campaign that ended his life.

339:20 **great ability to get himself in and out of trouble:** The implication is battlefield trouble. Custer also got himself in trouble with his own military, usually for ignoring orders he didn't like and for recklessness, yet his superiors invariably restored him to duty and awarded him with commands. This habit started when he was a cadet at West Point and followed him during the Civil War and to the frontier. He was court-martialed in September 1867 for deserting his own command, injuring horses, failing to pursue the enemy and recover his soldiers' bodies, ordering the murder of deserters, and not allowing the wounded to receive medical attention (Van de Water 175). Within a year, Custer had his command reinstated.

339:23–24 **Phil Sheridan:** On Sheridan and **Jeb Stuart**, see 233:12+. On **John Mosby**, see 233:2.

339:26 **Killy-the-Horse Kilpatrick:** Hugh Judson Kilpatrick was a Union cavalry officer during the American Civil War. The novel's nickname is an adaptation of "Kilcavalry" (or "Kill-Cavalry"), an epithet he earned for leading his troops into hell-bent, seemingly suicidal charges. Although Kilpatrick survives his war, Hemingway's allusion appears to be more substantive than casual. The altered nickname suggests the death of Jordan's own horse during the risky bridge-blowing mission. During the Chancellorsville Campaign of 1863, which also occurred in May (the battle depicted in *The Red Badge of Courage*), Kilpatrick conducted operations behind Confederate lines, disrupting railroads and burning bridges, in a failed effort to distract Confederate General Robert E. Lee. The Republic's Segovia Offensive also ended in failure, in its own territorial aim and its goal to distract the Nationalists' northern campaign.

339:32+ **Lenin Institute ... military academy:** See 229:21.

340:1 **Napoleon and Wellington:** Two figures whose names are synonymous with military genius. **Napoleon** Bonaparte was a military hero of the French Revolution (1789) and the subsequent Revolutionary Wars against other European nations (1792–1802). He ruled France as First Consul (1799–1804) and then Emperor (1804–1814; 1815). He is often considered one of history's greatest military leaders.

Arthur Wellesley, First Duke of **Wellington**, was an extremely successful British commander who dealt Napoleon two decisive defeats during the Peninsular Wars, first at the Battle of Vitoria (1813) and then at the Battle of Waterloo (1815). The latter ended Napoleon's reign. Wellington went on to a successful career as a statesman.

Hemingway's imagination was under the influence of the Peninsular Wars. In February 1939, one of the three stories Hemingway planned to write in Cuba would have treated the successful 1808 capture of the Somosierra pass through the Guadarrama Mountain by the 1st Polish Light Cavalry Lancers, part of Napoleon's Imperial Guard, a victory against the Spaniard's effort to restore the legitimate Spanish sovereignty (to Maxwell Perkins, 7 Feb. 1939, *SL* 479). In a letter to Gustavo Durán, written about a month after he finished drafting the novel, Hemingway compared his "chickenshit" protagonist with Wellington's subordinate Major Colquhoun Grant, the far more competent soldier who scouted in Spain behind enemy lines. The letter believes it quotes Wellington on Grant:

> He was proficient in their provincial dialects, intimately acquainted with their songs, their music, and their domestic habits. He was an enthusiastic admirer of the Spanish character, well read in their literature, and he even danced their national dances most admirably. He was such a favourite with priests and peasantry, his name was so widespread, and the devotion felt to him so strong, that far in the rear of the French posts he slept secure. His knowledge of the enemy's army was exact. He knew not only the regiments, but the character of every superior officer, almost of every *chef de bataillon*.[6]

The letter quotes Sir Charles Oman's 1930 *Studies in the Napoleonic Wars,* which doesn't quote Wellington but Grant's brother-in-law, Sir James McGrigor. Oman's quotation digests and slightly misquotes two pages from McGrigor's memoir (283–84). Hemingway might have remembered from his copy of Douglas Bell's new book *Wellington's Officers* (1938) that Grant spent a cold February night in the mountains "with his head in the lap of Juana de Leon, a Spanish girl whose lover he was." He was working with guerillas in central Spain. In the morning, Grant kissed her goodbye before he and her brother, with the enemy sentries firing after them, scampered on their horses across a ford to "a friendly wood" (36–37).

According to Yuval Noah Harari, during this era (1740–1865) the idea of combat delivering a revelatory experience emerged. Whether called truth, reality, wisdom, epiphany, or even ecstasy, this cultural narrative came about as "the Enlightenment, the culture of sensibility, and Romanticism led soldiers to begin seeing war as an agent of revelation" (22). Harari emphasizes that battlefield revelation, always based in embodied experience, "has no essential connection to religion. Revelation denotes a particular *method* for gaining knowledge rather than a type of knowledge" (10; also 260). Harari's breakdown of war literature's four new elements reads like a blueprint for *For Whom the Bell Tolls:* "the richness of sensory descriptions"; "changing concepts of fear and courage"; "detailed descriptions of pathetic scenes . . . to illustrate that they and their fellow soldiers were men-of-feeling"; and "sensations and experiences resulting from the natural setting" which "shaped not only the mood of individual people, but the character of entire nations and the outcome of great enterprises" (199–207).

340:16 **Quatorzième Brigade:** Jules Dumont's XIV Brigade and Gustavo **Durán's** Mixed Brigade fell under Golz's (Walter's) division command (the 35th) during the Segovia Offensive. Jordan uses French for "fourteenth" because Dumont was French and the unit was primarily composed of French and Belgians. Jordan's noun *clochards,* for tramps or bums, comes from French even though English and Spanish have imported it. One can almost hear a sneer in Jordan's "Quatorzième." The mixed review he gives the brigade, a gaggle of ne'er-do-wells and "heroes," accurately conveys the unit's mixed reputation. Walter was irate at the brigade's performance during the Segovia Offensive, while Dumont was angry that Walter sent his brigade unprepared into a disastrous situation (Tremlett 43, 309–16).

340:36 **the festival would not be cancelled:** Spanish bullfights typically occur in conjunction with festivals (*festivals*), fairs (*ferias*), and *fiestas* (holidays). An American soldier's colloquial equivalent would be "the show," which Jordan uses twice (137:4; 467:27). Only Jordan uses "festival" for the battle, although it is not the novel's only comparison to a bullfight (e.g., 405:2).

NOTES

1. To Edwin Rolfe [April 1940] (University of Illinois Library).
2. Western Union Cablegram of 13 Aug. 1940 to Max Perkins (PUL).
3. Three days in NYC: to Hans Kahle (c. late Aug 1940, Kvam 18). Hemingway's letter of 13 Aug. 1940 telling Durán to expect the galleys followed-up from an in-person conversation.
4. To Gustavo Durán, 13 Aug. 1940 (Residencia). Hemingway tells Durán that the galleys are incomplete because of "a little part at the end" he is "still working over trying to make it good"; the galley proofs at the JFK toward the end of the published chapter 41, at the line "lashing the grenades firmly" (409:37).
5. It's not known on which of Hemingway's five trips this event happened: 1930, 1932, 1936, 1938, or 1939. On the long 1936 trip, he seems to have been especially preoccupied with suicide (Warren, 89; Reynolds, *The 1930s*, 238–39).
6. To Gustavo Durán [c. 20–27 Aug. 1940] (Residencia). As quoted from the probable Hemingway source, Oman's 1930 *Studies in the Napoleonic Wars* (164), not the letter to Durán. The US edition was published by Hemingway's publisher, Charles Scribner's Sons. Hemingway often requested that his publisher send him some of its new titles, particularly in military history.

CHAPTER THIRTY-ONE

342:20+ **any oversupply of that for tomorrow:** The "that" references semen. Offering a few lines comically riffing on Maria's willingness to give Jordan noncoital sexual release, most likely through manual stimulation, this paragraph gives reason to pause. Jordan draws on the age-old equating of a man's sexual energy with his heroic energy, a myth made visible in Botticelli's painting *Venus and Mars* (ca. 1485): behind a postsex, dead-to-the-world Mars, two satyrs carry off his lance and helmet. Jordan regards as folly the intermingling of lovemaking and warmaking. The "pine needles" that do not need his semen "now" evoke the pine needles upon which he and Maria sleep together and his conflation of Maria with the Spanish earth—the word "now" suffuses their final lovemaking (378:1+; 379:6+). These pine needles further evoke those on which he lay in the novel's opening sentence and those on which he will lie, dying, in its final sentence (Maria the Venus to Jordan's Mars).

In Genesis, Judah instructed his son **Onan** to bear a child by Onan's widowed sister-in-law. But "when he went in unto his brother's wife, . . . he spilled it on the ground"—he withdrew before ejaculation. This decision "displeased" God, who "slew him" (Genesis 38:8–10). It is theologically debatable whether God capitally punished Onan for disobedience and violating his levirate obligation or for wasting his sacred seed in a nonprocreative sexual act. The term *onanism* has come to mean masturbation (and all forms of noncoital male ejaculation) as well as coitus interruptus. Hemingway knows full well how Onan fared, and Jordan probably does as well, as expressed by his knowing smile "in the dark." Hemingway really directs the question about Onan's fate to his readers, to ensure they don't miss the allusion and to tease them with the foreshadowing. Like Onan, Jordan finds a way not to become a father: to pull out, as it were. Perhaps a certain onanism, a certain fruitlessness or narcissism, has always afflicted Jordan's Spanish pursuit. That Onan's partner is his sister-in-law renders their relationship akin to incest and to the sibling resemblance between Jordan and Maria (67:12).

The Onan lines were added by hand to the typed draft (MS12–005).

342:25+ **and let himself slip into it:** In the draft, this handwritten phrase replaces the typed "and started to speak," with the rest of the published paragraph also inserted by hand before Jordan says—as originally typed—"My beloved" (MS12–005). The draft clarifies that the "it" to which he surrenders is the fantasy of life in Madrid with Maria. The irony and oddity is the simile of the "voluptuousness" of "sexual acceptance of something that could come in the night when there was no understanding, only the delight of acceptance," when Jordan is trying to take his mind off the fact that he can't have sex. Hemingway inserted this paragraph at the same time he inserted the lines above about Onan (342:20+). With death upon him, Jordan uses very similar language about acceptance, unreality, and slippage (452:3+; 470:38).

The text does not clarify the nighttime "something" Jordan or Hemingway imagines with sexual pleasure but without understanding. Some readers might find this paragraph prescient of the yet-to-be-written and posthumously published *The Garden of Eden,* in which at night the male protagonist surrenders to his wife's genderplay, becoming Catherine to her Peter, and being anally penetrated by her fingers. David Bourne struggles to understand those nights but does not deny his enjoyment. Much of that later unfinished novel occurs in Madrid; Jordan's "unreality" is his Madrid fantasy. The sequence could support such a reading: having learned he cannot have traditional coitus with Maria and then having declined other ways he might be stimulated to release, by her or by himself, Jordan's imagination (at some level that even it doesn't understand) fetches this alternative mode of penetrative intimacy. The things one doesn't understand that happen "in the night" here repeat in language and intimation the earlier passage about tribes, mysteries, woods, and "what happens to us in the nights" (see 175:35–36).

342:32 the hotel of the Russians: On Gaylord's, see 228:27+.

342:36 the Seguridad: The Republic's internal intelligence and security, its paranoid zealotry for policing the Fifth Column threat (248:5), led to torture and permanent disappearances. Hemingway explored the moral dilemma of the Seguridad, of ends justifying the means and the collateral damage to the innocent, in *The Fifth Column.*

343:5 on the Plaza del Callao: Jordan is talking about the Hotel Florida (see 228:12).

344:17–18 since we no longer have the Church: On no longer having the Church, see 41:12+. On marriage being obsolete, see 291:14 and 291:16 (see also 355:28–29).

344:31 that I could love one deeply: In crossed-out drafted lines, Maria replies by telling Jordan how "handsome," "brave," and "gay" he is. He demurs. She reports that Pilar told her he's the bravest and gayest man she's ever met, which Jordan dismisses as "nonsense" (MS12–005). The excised dialogue recalls Jordan's thinking that the "best ones" were all "gay," most of them now dead (17:10+), as well as his dismissal of Pilar's forecasting his death as nonsense.

345:22 **just lying to his girl:** In the next chapter, the communists in Madrid offer feel-good lies to make propaganda and boost morale. The text invites comparison.

345:34–35 **go together to the coiffeur's . . . as they cut mine:** Jordan thought about getting her hair shaped by a Madrid coiffeur at the end of chapter 20, in a drafted insert he replaced with the published paragraph (see 264:18).

In other Hemingway works in which a lover proposes that the beloved get an identical haircut, the woman makes the proposal. In this novel, as Eby has observed, "the identical haircuts are proposed by the man in the relationship, not by some more safely dissociated half-crazy woman" (*Fetishism* 26). Thus Jordan takes on the role of the more blatantly fragile character—not incidentally the one who ends up dead, as Catherine Barkley did in *A Farewell to Arms* and Catherine Bourne probably would have in *The Garden of Eden*—reinforcing the pattern in which the desire to erase differences masks a deeper desire to erase the self (see 262:26+). Jordan's remedy for Maria's shorn hair resembles the remedy for her rape, a reversal through a structurally similar act: tender, intimate, consensual hairstyling and tender, intimate, consensual lovemaking. Within the novel's symbolic embodiment of Maria as Spain, the control of and violence to the country characterizes the activities of both warring sides (the Nationalists still emerging as crueler and more extreme). Jordan's control of her hairstyle does not escape the violence in his vision of her retelling her rape story to his students (165:2–5). Jordan just compared her hair's new growth to "the fur of an animal" when he touches it (345:28), an affectionate sentiment with predation lurking inside—the throat-swelling fondling of her hair he soon likens to fondling the fur of a marten pulled from the jaws of his hunter's trap (378:7–8).

Although Jordan takes pleasure in this new growth, in Maria's hair "now" (345:27), the original violence to her head and body remains the founding condition of his eroticization of her hair. This conversation disturbingly anticipates in this same chapter, by a matter of mere pages, Maria's description of her brutal head-shaving and rape (351:25+). Even though both Jordan and the reader know the basic facts, they have not yet heard the story. The sensuality of this moment in the conversation becomes the rape story's antecedent in a way that arguably implicates Jordan's desire and the reader's desire, or at least shapes the reading experience: from sensual touching, to talking about merged identities through hairstyling that becomes a titillating fantasy involving the film star Greta Garbo (346:7–8), to a fantasy of looking at themselves together in a mirror (346:27–29), that simultaneously anticipates the story to come while echoing the past happening in the barber's chair which she watched in a mirror (351:26–28), all of it a prelude to the gang rape elided from the text (353:12–13), visualized solely by the reader's own imagination.

One of the Lynd Ward lithographs in the 1942 Limited Editions Club illustrated edition of *For Whom the Bell Tolls* manifests the novel's troubling confusion about the relationship between sexual violence and that violence's anticipation. The illustration falls as the frontispiece to chapter 12, the brief chapter when Pilar leaves Jordan and Maria alone to make love in chapter 13. In other words, it anticipates the first detailed lovemaking as well as the eventual rape story even as the rape forms the erotic image's very background: Ward's image depicts Maria glowingly bare-chested, full lips imperceptibly parted, eyes closed, while over her shoulder her violent recent past plays out—civil guards executing her parents (presumably) while several Falangists rape her.[1] The image literally bisects her body, offering the eroticized top half to the gazing readers and her bottom half—her kicking legs—to the Falangists.

Why does her head tilt sensually *toward* the violence? The saving grace of Ward's image could be Maria's closed eyes, as they will be closed when she and Jordan sleep together in the following chapter (159:9–10), her interiority not yielding itself in either scene to any man. Is she lost to herself inside herself, traumatically transported? Does the image participate in what she later calls *la gloria* (379:37) potentially linked to the suffering of Christ on the cross (see 380:21+)? Ward's illustration verily quotes artistic representations of St. Teresa of Ávila in ecstasy and the theological positing of suffering as the condition of ultimate divine union.

Ward's image warps time. Perhaps this Maria is Jordan's Maria, not the rapists', their presence in the background her memory? Is she both at once? She wanted to die while being raped (73:14–15); she achieves death while making love with Jordan (160:4). The deep problem with the image is how the eroticized female body dominates the frame and informs the rape, where she becomes the backdrop for the rape, not the other way around.

346:5 **to thy shoulders:** The preferred hair length and skin hue resemble a tanned Martha Gellhorn. In a letter of 7 July 1943, Hemingway wrote to Gellhorn: "I will love you short and curly haired, brown and thin. . . . I wish I could see you so beautiful and curly and brown and lovely in front of the magnificent pink house" (Outgoing). As described, the hairstyle looks a lot like Ingrid Bergman's in her role as Maria in the 1943 film adaptation, which premiered a week after Hemingway's letter (on 14 July 1943 in New York City). Hemingway's fascination with short hair and dark skin becomes increasingly associated with gender play and race play, Africa and Spain, literarily culminating in *The Garden of Eden*. In a 15 July 1954 letter, he asked his fourth wife, Mary, to get "a good boy safari haircut the way you had . . . to please me in Madrid" (Outgoing). As Jordan's and Maria's conversation about her hair wraps up, Jordan proposes that they retire from the war to an apartment on the street that runs alongside the Buen Retiro Park (346:36–37)—very possibly Alfonso XII Street, two blocks from the Prado Museum, whose artworks inspire Catherine Bourne's gender experiments in *The Garden of Eden*.

346:7+ **As Garbo in the cinema:** The actor Greta Garbo, on whom Jordan projects a special attachment (see 137:16+). The word "thickly" communicates his reflexive arousal to the mention of his fantasy object by his flesh-and-blood lover. The text acknowledges that Jordan's attraction to Maria relies on fantasy—Maria's "in the cinema" language repeats his earlier fantasy's involving Garbo, when he can't help but mention Garbo's hair. The next line takes the reader there: "Now the making believe was coming back in a great rush." The Pygmalion-like transformation of Maria also arouses Jordan. This woman who embodies Spain becomes palatably Westernized, domestically translated, like Garbo the Swede becoming American and her character Queen Christina of Sweden becoming Spanish. The transformation of the Spanish Maria into the Nordic Garbo admits the foreign aspect of Jordan's attraction to her even as racially it safely turns her white. Garbo's gender and sexual flexibility enhance Jordan's arousal, a flexibility that the novel quietly imparts to Maria. Jordan has already fantasized about Maria starring in a show of her own as she retells her story to an audience of his undergraduates.

346:26+ **and look into the mirror:** Although the novel has not yet presented Maria's account of her violent head-shaving, this piece of dialogue about looking into the mirror ahead of sexual contact reflects and distorts that scene (351:26). This envisioned image in the armoire mirror reenacts the hope that making love with Jordan annuls her repeated rapes. Alas, it also prefigures the graphic account and once again places Jordan proximate to those who did violence against her. The novel's other major mirror imagery involves Jordan looking at his reflection in the lake's still water as he disposes of the pistol his father used to kill himself (337:23).

346:32 **all those things that he knew could never happen:** The stuff of domestic life with Maria. Jordan knows "those things" can't ever happen because he believes he will die in the morning's battle. In the novel's genre logic, domesticity has no home in high Romance. This formal reason Jordan must die dovetails with Lydia Davis's insight into why Flaubert's Emma Bovary kills herself: *Madame Bovary*'s "whole project is opposed to the romantic. The heroine, infatuated with romanticism, comes to grief because of it—because of her craving for impossible dreams, her refusal to accept the ordinariness of her own life and its limited possibilities for happiness" (327). Hemingway's war novel bears the added complication of expressing the international volunteers' romanticized political cause and of its publication a year before the United States finally entered the fight against fascism.

346:37+ **Parque of the Buen Retiro:** Park of the Pleasant Retreat (or Good Leisure or Good Retirement). The original 353-acre park was created in the early sixteenth century by and for the royal family. It expanded over the centuries with additional gardens, water features, tree-lined walkways, riding paths, and sculpture. It transferred to public ownership in 1868. At the time of its creation, the park sat on the eastern edge of the city, but by Hemingway's day it had become the green heart of

Madrid. Finished in 1922, the artificial recreational lake (347:7) was a monument to Alfonso XII, the father of the king who fled the country upon the birth of the Second Spanish Republic in April 1931.

347:33 **Petra:** The name of the actual chambermaid at the Hotel Florida. Petra shows up by name in *The Fifth Column*. Jordan elsewhere refers to Luis, the hotel's actual porter (228:14).

348:11+ **as I love all that we have fought for:** As much as he loves Madrid and his comrades—the passage follows on the heels of two comparisons by Jordan of Maria's hair to the wheat fields of Spain (345:29; 346:13). This chapter is the most blatant in dramatizing Maria's abstract, symbolic value to Jordan, who wants to make her his bride in a church (344:16+; 355:28–29). For Maria's rapists, she is also a symbolic object, a "Bride of the Red Christ" (352:11). The chapter interrogates Jordan's attitude toward Maria, the shared textual space revealing a shared psychological space with her Church-insistent Falangist rapists.

349:4 **as though I were a bullfighter:** Comley and Scholes's *Hemingway's Genders* devotes a long chapter to the indivisibility for Hemingway of bullfighting and gender performance. "The topics of homosexuality and decadence are so prevalent in *Death in the Afternoon* that Hemingway finds it easy to stray far from the bullring as long as he sticks to these other interests" (123). The matador "is so macho and so narcissistic that he turns himself into the object of the gaze, so much a man that he effeminizes himself" (139), a gender conflation Maria exposes in watching her figure the way a matador watches his. Comley and Scholes remind their readers that Gertrude Stein introduced Hemingway both to homosexuality and to the bullfight (127). And, one should add, to Spain. Pilar, herself a person of conflated genders associated with bullfighting, facilitates the Jordan-Maria romance. Maria's slight simile also suggests the inevitably fatal danger she represents to Jordan. The bullfight, Hemingway writes, is a "tragedy," the story of "the certain death" of the bull (*DIA* 16).

350:19+ **Never did I submit to any one:** The word "never," plus the repeated word "always," testifies emphatically to multiple violations by multiple men, which would have happened during her months-long imprisonment in Valladolid (22:24+; 23:21+). Peter Wyden believes Hemingway took Maria's name and this part of her story from a woman he met in Mataro, Catalonia, in 1938, the "prettier" of two nurse's aides whom Fred Keller introduced to Hemingway: "shy, serene, about 24. She was a Communist, like her father, who had been executed in Andalusía when the war broke out. María had been imprisoned and, over the months, raped 24 times" (468).

350:25–26 **mayor of the village:** Though Maria's village is never named, we can safely locate it near Valladolid in Old Castile. After her initial rape, she is imprisoned in Valladolid before being shipped south by train (23:22–24). Valladolid is northwest of where Pablo's band hides out, and Falangist soldiers actively perpetrated atrocities in Valladolid even though the area was firmly and early in Nationalist hands (Beevor 93).

350:33 *Viva la República y vivan mis padres:* Long live the Republic and long live my father.

350:38 *matadero:* Slaughterhouse.

351:14 **Falangists:** The original fascists of Nationalist Spain. Falangism upheld a unified Spanish identity centered upon the supreme authority of the State, in league with the Spanish Catholic Church and advocating for a restoration of Spain's glorious imperial past. Violence was a legitimate means to their goals. On 19 April 1937, Franco issued the Unification Decree which merged the monarchist Carlists and the dictatorian Falangists into a single political party, the only legal political party, Falange Española Tradicionalista y de las Juntas de Ofensiva Nacional Sindicalista (FET y de las JONS; Traditionalist Spanish Phalanx of the Councils of the National Syndicalist Offensive). Needless to say, it was the party of Francisco Franco.

351:14 **herded us away and up the hill:** Hemingway has already mentioned the forced march up the hill and he repeats it in the next sentence. Often with Hemingway, emphasis by repetition secures symbolism. Maria's path could be read as a condensed perversion of the Stations of the Cross. She sees her mother, who is shot (351:10–12). Her group of condemned souls is marched up a hill first described as "steep" (350:38), the town's "main square" (*plaza mayor*) serving as Calvary (Golgotha). In the barbershop at the top of the hill, Maria is held down by two soldiers while another soldier shaves her head (and two others watch), effectively turning it into a bloodied crown of thorns as they transform her into a "Bride of the Red Christ" (352:11). The Latin abbreviation of Jesus of Nazareth, King of the Jews, which paintings typically depict above Jesus's head on the cross, INRI, is replaced with the initials for the radical left-wing Unión de Hermanos Proletarios (Union of Proletarian Brothers), UHP, written on Maria's forehead with iodine by one of the soldiers "as though he were an artist" (352:35–36). They finally take her down from the barber's chair, now almost beyond recognition. Instead of being laid in the mother's lap, in this perversion of the Pietà "they laid [her] onto the couch," her murdered father's office couch, where "the bad things were done" (353:12–13). The animal husbandry language of being "herded" complicates any spiritual suggestiveness.

351:28 **were leaning over me:** Hemingway added by hand everything after this to the end of the published paragraph, replacing Maria's seeing in the mirror the body of the shot barber by the door (MS12–005).

351:35+ **my hair in two braids and as I watched:** The description of the violent head-shaving acts as a surrogate for the rape, which Maria does not describe (353:12–13).

352:9–11 **This is how we make Red nuns:** The raping of women known, presumed, or conveniently labeled Republican or Republican sympathizers was fallaciously justified by the Nationalists as punishment for the Republic's progressive politics regarding women's equality. The illogic of raping Maria to make her a celibate nun partakes of the same illogic whereby Jordan's sleeping with her restores her virginity. While the Falangists' intent is vile and Jordan's loving, the shared illogic recalls how Jordan and the Republic must acquire fascist modern militancy to fight fascist modern militancy for possession of the Spanish earth that Maria embodies. On "**Bride of the Red Christ**," see 348:11+.

352:34 **U.H.P.:** Unión de Hermanos Proletarios (Union of Proletarian Brothers)— see 351:14. Hemingway did not invent this detail. The shaving of women was a com-

Alfonso Daniel Rodríguez Castelao, "¡*Cobardes! ¡Asesinos!*" / "*Cowards! Assassins!*" (1937). (Public Domain / Author's collection)

mon practice. The inscribing of the acronym on the forehead was either commonly known or rumored enough to be depicted elsewhere, such as in the 1937 print *¡Cobardes! ¡Asesinos!* ("Cowards! Assassins!") by Alfonso Daniel Rodríguez Castelao.

Hemingway might have seen the print in *Galicia Mártir: Estampas por Castelao*, published in February 1937 in Valencia by the Republic's Ministry of Propaganda, the month before Hemingway's arrival in Valencia for his first trip to wartime Spain. If so, it could have contributed to his earliest conception of Maria's story. If not, he would have seen it in 1939 while working on the novel, when it appeared in *Somebody Had to Do Something: A Memorial to James Phillips Lardner*, a fundraising book he cosponsored and which included his essay "On the American Dead in Spain" (see 471:12). In this case, assuming he had written the novel's early references about Maria's shaving before seeing the image, he would have seen it by the time he wrote this scene. Castelao's drawing very well could have provided the UHP detail and the image of the barber's body "in the doorway" (352:28–30).

354:1 **I will marry thee:** Jordan's statement later on this page that he and Maria are already "truly" married is lip service, as he will shortly whisper to himself that he still wants to marry her (355:28–29). See 348:11+.

354:32–33 **we did dreadful things to them too:** Jordan's distinction between the ignorant Republican atrocities and the calculated Nationalist ones agrees with most historians' assessments, especially for the first months of the war (see 99:18–19). See the above entry on the Seguridad, however (342:36). The Red Terror was as real as the White Terror.

354:37–38 **Cortez, Pizarro, Menéndez de Avila:** Hernando **Cortez** (or Cortés) was a sixteenth-century Spanish explorer to the New World: "Commissioned to explore and conquer Mexico, he at various times disregarded the orders of the Spanish king as well as those of the colonial rulers, in order to advance his own interests"; he also broke his word with the Aztecs (Mandel, *Reading* 212). Another sixteenth-century New World explorer, Francisco **Pizarro** (or Pisarro), betrayed the Incas for his own personal gain, only to be killed himself by other Spaniards (Mandel, *Reading* 259). Durán might have suggested including Pizarro, as the name is inserted in the galley proofs. Pedro **Menéndez de Avilés** was another merciless sixteenth-century Spaniard for whom personal gain trumped all motives, including loyalty to the Spanish crown. Installed as the governor of Florida in 1565, he began a slaughter-for-slaughter war against French forces, which led to the decimation of his own Spanish colonizers (Mandel, *Reading* 250; see also 355:12). Hemingway greatly admired Cortez and Pizzaro but had serious reservations about de Avilés.[2]

355:6–7 **Otra Virgen más:** Another virgin more.

355:12 **the reformation . . . Inquisition:** The Protestant Reformation (1517–1648) was one of the most profound periods in European history, when the emergence of Christian Protestantism challenged the power and theology of what for centuries had been the dominant Christian religion in western Europe, Roman Catholicism. When Menéndez de Avilés massacred French soldiers in Florida (354:37), he "display[ed] their bodies under an announcement which explained that they had been killed 'not as Frenchmen but as Lutherans'" (Mandel, *Reading* 250) referring to Martin Luther, whose *Ninety-Five Theses* of 31 October 1517 against the Church is considered the start of the Reformation. The story that he nailed the Theses to church doors in Wittenberg, Germany, might inform Anselmo's nailing a bear paw to his village's church door (39:34+). Historians use the end of the Thirty Years' War to mark the end of the Reformation. That was the war Queen Christina of Sweden inherited from her father; she relinquished the throne of her Protestant country upon conversion to Catholicism (on Christina, see 137:16+).

The Spanish **Inquisition** (Tribunal of the Holy Office of the Inquisition, 1478–1874) preceded the Reformation, having been established by Queen Isabel and King Ferdinand, the Catholic Monarchs of the Reconquista, the Reconquest of Spain from the Moors. The Inquisition's chief means of converting or dispensing with whomever it deemed a heretic was the auto-da-fé (104:25–26). Franco's Falange party adopted Isabel's and Ferdinand's iconography for their own as a signal of their twentieth-century version of the Reconquest and their commitment to the Catholic Church as fundamental to Spanish identity and social order (39:28+).

355:28–29 **I'd like to marry you, rabbit:** After just assuring Maria that they already are married (354:19+), and in the context of just hearing her rapists' language of making her a Bride of the Red Christ, Jordan's last word on the subject expresses his desire for reversion to a bourgeois belief in institutional marriage (see 291:16). At best, Jordan's marriage-wish carries a salvation fantasy related to his love's restoring her virginity, a fantasy some readers will regard as genuine and loving, others as sexist paternalism. At worst, the framing intermixes the marriage-wish with the sexual violence against her that he has just envisioned, two parts of a single fantasy. The first time he told himself he wants to marry her (164:33), he instantly imagined her retelling this story of her first gang rape as evening entertainment for his undergraduate students to accompany their fraternal cigar-smoking (165:2–5). Jordan's use of the "rabbit" pet name here warrants consideration.

NOTES

1. The firing squad and the rapists are distinguished by their headgear—the former appear to wear the famous *El Tricornio* hats of the *guardia civil,* the latter the tasseled garrison caps of the Falange. The illustration appears between pages 164 and 165.
2. To Gustavo Durán [ca. 20–27 Aug. 1940] (Resedencia).

CHAPTER THIRTY-TWO

356:16 The apartment where he lived in Gaylord's: Martha Gellhorn remembered the actual room the same way: "Koltzov's sitting-room was well and expensively furnished like any sitting-room in a first-class hotel in peacetime. It was lit by table lamps and warm." Guests lounged on sofas. The food "tidbits" included "dabs of caviar on real bread" ("Memory").

357:12 Dolores . . . Carmen: Dolores is the Republic's communist firebrand and organizer **Dolores Ibárruri**, La Pasionaria (see 30:24+), as evidenced by her "radiant exultation," "great face," and the power of her speech (357:31+), not to mention her presence at Gaylord's. Ibárruri sometimes visited troops at the front lines and field commanders in their headquarters. The doomed soldiers of El Sordo's last stand were debating her integrity and value, and here at Hotel Gaylord she delivers the misinformation that "the fascists have been fighting among themselves" (357:23–24), when in fact the battle sounds were those of El Sordo's gang's destruction.

Carmen is a very common Spanish name, and Hemingway provides no identifying information. Yet the fact that everyone else in this chapter is a historical figure and the association with Dolores suggests a real person, making it the only chapter in the book without fictional characters. A very good candidate is Ruth Kahn, a German who called herself "Carmen" in Spain and whom Karkov's German mistress would know. The information about the offensive came from another German, Richard Staimer (see next entry). Kahn directed the Communist Youth International (KIM), the parent organization of the Spanish Unified Socialist Youth (Juventudes Socialistas Unificadas, or JSU), created in 1936. During the war, Kahn fell in love with and married a Spanish communist Pedro Martínez Cartón, who at the time of the novel had recently, as commander of the 16th Mixed Brigade, succeeded in ending the months-long siege of the sanctuary of Nuestra Señora de la Cabeza. He then assumed command of the 64th Division. His military role perhaps explains why Karkov's mistress assumes Carmen can get her to the front. According to Fernando Hernández Sánchez, a preeminent historian of the Spanish Communist Party during the war and the source of this suggested identification, "The other JSU leaders hated [Kahn] and gave her the insulting name of Carmen La Gorda (The Fat Girl Carmen)."[1]

A Carmen Martínez—probably Kahn, Pedro Martínez's wife—published a 1937 New Year's letter in the Soviet paper Izvestia along with messages from Ibárruri and other prominent Spanish communists ("La Prensa"). There was also Carmen Loyola, with Ibárruri a member of the National Committee of Women Against War and Fascism (Ibárruri 134).

357:17 **Richard:** A German recently given command of a brigade (358:30–31), this would be Richard Staimer, who assumed command of the XI International Brigade after Hans Kahle's promotion to division commander of the 45th. Staimer appears in almost no English-language histories of the war, although Giles Tremlett's *The International Brigades: Fascism, Freedom, and the Spanish Civil War* portrays him as a Stalinist ideologue "who tended to disappear in the heat of battle" (188; see also 352, 364). It fits that the novel finds this rigid communist at Gaylord's and not in the field.

357:19 **a man of middle height:** The physical description, his writing for the Soviet paper *Izvestia* (357:37), and his propagandizing match the Russian novelist and journalist Ilya Ehrenburg, whom Hemingway knew in Madrid.

358:20–21 **divisional commander and . . . a Hungarian:** Probably General Gall, the Hungarian Jânos Gálicz (233:30+), who received division command over the International Brigades during the Battle of Jarama in February 1937. Stalinist Russia executed him in 1938 or 1939. Hemingway learned about it as late as April 1940, as he mentions it in the same letter where he reports finishing draft chapter 32 (published as 33).[2] Mikhail Koltsov—the Karkov he speaks with—was disappeared in December 1938 on his way to execution in February 1940. Hemingway suspected Koltsov might have been or might soon be killed. Thus the line, "Perhaps you and me should be shot too. It is possible" (358:32–33).[3] Mandel cites as evidence Gall's age, at about forty-seven close to the character's "about forty-eight," and his unpopularity in life and the novel (233:30+; 359:1; 421:9–10) (*Reading* 231–32, 221).

Hemingway muddies the waters, however. The "short" and "jovial-looking" man with a mustache fits Hemingway's friend General Paul Lukács (233:18+), whom Mandel calls "short" and "cheerful" (*Reading* 244). The character's "gay mouth" conforms to Jordan's thesis that "there were not many of the gay ones left" (17:13–14)—Lukács was killed about two weeks after this fictional moment. Gall, on the other hand, was pitiless and mean of mien. Perhaps, as in this scene, Gall turned on his version of charm for people with power. This character's joking about shooting people accords with Gall's leadership: "For him, anyone who committed a mistake deserved the firing squad" (Tremlett 214), Lukács did not receive a division until after the Segovia Offensive, just before his death, at the age of 41 (not that the novel strictly obeys the historic timeline).

358:31 **Richard . . . that Sunday *függler*:** Richard Staimer (see 357:17). *Függler* appears to be a form of fugelman—German *flügelmann*, literally "file leader"—used for a political rabble-rouser or an exemplar soldier. That Richard only leads occasionally, the way nominal Christians show up for church on Sundays to save face, matches Staimer's derelictions, while the term's political aspect matches his haughty and punishing party loyalty.

NOTES

1. Personal email, 21 June 2022.
2. Hemingway to Edwin Rolfe [Apr. 1940] (UIL).
3. Gellhorn remembers at some unremembered point learning Koltsov had been executed ("Memory," 3). In a letter of 14 October 1952, Hemingway wrote that "Kolzov himself, of course, ended up in Siberia if he is still alive" (to Bernard Berenson, *SL* 789).

THE FOURTH AND FINAL CALENDAR DAY

[31 MAY 1937]

CHAPTER THIRTY-THREE

360 **Chapter Thirty-Three:** Pablo betrays Jordan in this chapter. Jesus's betrayal by Judas Iscariot, which led to Christ's death, resurrection, and return to God everlasting, happened in his thirty-third year. The betrayal by Pablo leads to Jordan's final "forever now" lovemaking with Maria "that they were not to have" had (379:10+); in the following chapter, Pablo reappears, and Pilar likens him to Judas (391:5).

360:23 **electric torch:** A flashlight. It is not clear why Hemingway uses the British term; the Spanish word would more closely translate as *lantern*. Spaniards speaking in English would have used the British term. Perhaps the language is intended to be Jordan's, in which case he is thinking in English as a Spaniard would.

360:27–28 **stale and sweat-dried and sickly-sweet the way an Indian's bed does:** Another of the novel's pejorative comparisons of Spaniards to Native Americans. Readers never learn how Jordan knows what an Indian's bed smells like.

361:31–32 **The big bay and the gray were gone:** This is the first time Pablo steals horses within the novel's timeframe. Earlier, Jordan accused Pablo and some of the Republican leaders of having "the politics of horse thieves" (163:33). He has perhaps taken a second horse because of his love for horses—especially the big bay (63:34+)—but equally likely: because doing so might discourage Jordan and the remaining Spaniards from attempting the high-risk mission.

CHAPTER THIRTY-FOUR

364:34 **in those village *capeas*:** Local amateur bullfights, with local traditional formats, and on which the massacre of Pilar's tale was structured (103:25). Hemingway's return to it now, as part of Andrés's peacetime pastoral fantasy, raises the question of bullfighting's relationship to the war, to what Jordan has typified as a Spanish proclivity to violence and killing (286:34+).

365:29 **Villaconejos:** A village southeast of Madrid, in the area of the Jarama River. In the draft, Hemingway replaced Zafra, a town in Extremadura, with Villaconejos (MS12–009).

366:21–22 **the accident of a message:** Another Naturalist and realistic reminder of the role of chance in human lives. Andrés survives the battle he doesn't fight, the battle in which his brother Eladio dies.

367:19 **soldiers now with the fascists:** With Andrés, Hemingway presents a fully, humanly complex character. Andrés has just reflected on the simultaneous shame and pride toward the same thing (365:36–37; 366:5), contradictory emotions that a person can experience as a singular, multifaceted response. He is eager to get back to the fight; he is grateful for having been sent away. In the present passage, Andrés admits to the attraction of fascism as well as his belief in the Republican cause. Paradoxically, the brothers end up as Republicans out of respect for paternal authority—a trait one would associate with fascism. Living in Nationalist territory at the beginning of the war, they otherwise would have been recruited (or conscripted) to fight for the Nationalists (see 375:32). Andrés corroborates Jordan's death epiphany as one of the novel's enduring messages: "There's no *one* thing that's true. It's all true" (467:20).

CHAPTER THIRTY-FIVE

369:15 **bloody woman:** Replaces "unutterable bitch" in the draft (MS12-010).

369:28–29 **Largo, Prieto, Asensio, Miaja, Rojo:** The socialist Francisco **Largo** Caballero was the prime minister of the Second Spanish Republic and its minister of war until just before the events of the novel (4 Sept. 1936—17 May 1937). On Indalecio **Prieto** Tuero, see 163:30+. José **Asensio** Torrado was an army general before the war, one of the very few *Africanistas* loyal to the government. He led troops in the defense of the Guadarrama passes (the Somosierra), became Caballero's ministry of war subsecretary in October 1936, then the commander of the Army of the Center in November 1936. Asensio organized the Republic's motley military into the single-command Republican Army, notably not under communist control. The military's mixed results on the battlefield gave the communists the excuse they needed to smear him; he lost command in February 1937. On José **Miaja** Menant, see 233:18+; it was under Caballero (and Asensio) that the government fled Madrid for Valencia, leaving Miaja in charge of the defense of Madrid. On Vicente **Rojo** Lluch, 6:32.

None of these Republican leaders whom Jordan tells to "muck" off was a communist. The line "Much the whole treachery-ridden country" has a printer's error—it should be "Muck..."

370:3 **Pablo Iglesias:** Pablo Iglesias Posse was a founder of the Spanish Socialist Workers Party (Partido Socialista Obrero Español; PSOE) in 1879 and would go on to serve as its secretary-general and its president. A decade later, he spearheaded the creation of the General Workers Union (Unión General de Trabajadores; UGT), for which he also served as president. The latter was officially apolitical, but clearly leftist—PSOE and UGT were affiliated organizations, and Iglesias was a Marxist socialist decades before the Spanish Communist Party gained a real foothold in Spain (which wasn't until the civil war). He was also an editor and a prolific journalist of and spokesperson for the labor movement. Jordan understands that the comparison to wartime leaders is rhetorical and unfair, since Iglesias died in 1925: "How do we know how he would have stood up in this war?" This question and the next sentence, about Largo, Hemingway inserted in the draft (MS12-010). See 163:30+.

370:6 Durruti: Buenaventura Durruti Domínguez was a militant anarchist long before the civil war. When the war started, his leadership in the anarchist CNT-FAI helped defeat the Nationalist seizure of Barcelona, an early Republican victory of inestimable significance. His anarchist militia of a few thousand, known as Durruti's Column, marched to Madrid to participate in the city's defense, where he was killed on 19 November 1936. The **Puente de los Franceses** is the bridge across the Manzanares River between University City and Casa de Campo. The actual circumstances of his death are unknown. Jordan's accusation that his subordinates shot him out of their cowardice was an early rumor, perhaps spread by the communists to undermine the anarchists further in light of Durruti's fame. Hemingway's comment that he didn't shoot Durruti, in a 1940 letter defending the novel's depiction of anarchists (to José Alemany, 8 Nov. 1940, Outgoing), suggests he believed the rumor. Durruti's funeral in Barcelona drew a crowd upward of half a million Catalans.

370:12 Cortez and Menedez de Avila: See 354:37.

370:13 what Miaja did to Kleber: See 233:18+.

370:20 If that were true: Hemingway inserted this sentence and the next three (up to "fine ones") by hand in the draft (MS12–010).

370:26–27 sharp, cold-seeing as a man is after he has had sexual intercourse with a woman that he does not love: After the first depicted lovemaking between Jordan and Maria (chapter 13), Jordan says his mind has become "clear and hard and sharp as when a camera lens is brought into focus" (161:26). So he doesn't love her? On the other hand, the next several pages evidence his unfocused musings. So he does love her? After the second depicted lovemaking scene (chapter 37), Jordan calls his mind—not Maria—his "best companion" (380:20), and very quickly returns to thinking about the mission as he walks into the cave, leaving her to roll up his expensive sleeping bag. So he doesn't love her?

CHAPTER THIRTY-SIX

372:8 *milicianos:* Militiamen, or just militia.

373:1 **bomb:** A hand grenade.

373:14 *Me cago en la leche:* I shit in the milk. An idiomatic Spanish expression for which an English speaker might say something like: Damn it! Shit! What the hell?! What the fuck?!

373:22 **zigzag belt of wire:** Barbed concertina wire used to surround a defensive position or protect an entrance, with switchback lanes—envision a switchback security or ticket queue—to allow those inside the wire to send soldiers out but to significantly slow down and turn sideways enemy soldiers trying to enter so they can be easily stopped, in this case by a machine gun or a hand grenade.

373:35 **Peter nor of Paul:** Two of the twelve original disciples, the Apostles, of Jesus Christ. Saint **Peter** is considered the chief Apostle, and the first Bishop of Rome—the first pope, to whom Christ said: "And I say also unto thee, That thou art Peter, and upon this rock I will build my church; and the gates of hell shall not prevail against it. And I will give unto thee the keys of the kingdom of heaven: and whatsoever thou shalt bind on earth shall be bound in heaven: and whatsoever thou shalt loose on earth shall be loosed in heaven" (Matthew 16:18–19). Thus, although Peter denied Christ three times, he is the "rock" of the Church and the gatekeeper to Heaven, so an ironically appropriate saint to be invoked by these atheist anarchist entrance guards. Saint **Paul** started out as a persecutor of Christians, but after his conversion (see 392:26+) became the fledgling religion's most prominent messenger and proselytizer, one of the principal authors of the books of the New Testament.

374:29+ **black-and-red scarves:** The identifying clothing of anarchists, as the text immediately confirms with their shouted allegiance to *la Libertad*—liberty—and the **FAI**, **CNT**, and *anarco-sindicalismo* (anarcho-syndicalism). See 120:6–8.

375:24 **Aranjuez:** A town south of Madrid near Villaconejos, originally built up as exclusively a royal retreat and palace for the nobility.

375:32 **Villacastín:** The first major town on the northern side of the Guadarrama Pass (Alto del León) through the mountains, in Nationalist territory since early in the war. This explains why Andrés and Eladio found themselves behind enemy lines among Pablo's guerillas (see 367:19).

375:39 *tomate:* Commotion. Its literal meaning, *tomato,* is suggestive of blood, in this case the blood of El Sordo's men. (La Tomatina Festival is an annual tomato fight in the streets that started in August 1945 in Buñol, Valencia, Spain.)

376:7 **Libertarian discipline:** Hemingway is being funny, the officer dead serious. Beyond the oxymoron of an anarchist military, the phrase suggests the absurdity of anarchists in the Republican government, perhaps the futility of Republican cohesion, and the challenge of any liberty-spewing populist movement that requires ideological conformity.

376:18 **thirty-fifth:** This is the correct division, historically speaking. Through the galley proofs, Hemingway used two different names, the thirty-third here and the forty-first later (416:12). Both could have been honest misrememberings that Durán corrected, having been a brigade commander in the division for the battle. It is also possible that Hemingway initially disguised the historical division but later changed his mind.

377:12 *carabine:* A carbine rifle. See 9:16–17.

CHAPTER THIRTY-SEVEN

378:1+ **Now:** Although Jordan observes his watch's movement throughout the paragraph, the text never registers the time. Pilar woke him at two in the morning (360:1), and at the end of this chapter he notes the time: ten until three (382:6–7). The attention Jordan pays to "time passing" as he kisses Maria awake so that they can have sex together recalls the quotation from Andrew Marvell's "To His Coy Mistress" (see 72:26). Marvell's poem ends by acknowledging that the lovers can't make the sun "[s]tand still" in its rotation, just as Jordan understands he can't still the cycling of the watch hand. The lovemaking ends with an aubade, a poetic acknowledgment of "the morning of the day to come" (379:26–27), the end of the lovers' frolic, and mortality (e.g., Donne's "The Sun Rising"). Jonathan Vincent argues that the novel charts Jordan's progress toward "political disillusion" and a commitment to personal sensation and experience: "Chronological or dialectical registers of 'span' and 'duration'—and thus purpose or cause—disappear as he revels in the war's effects on his emotions, his consciousness, its shrinking of a historicized 'value of time' into an intensified, ever more ecstatic and concentrated 'now'" (136). In other words, the insistent *now* of the upcoming lovemaking scene becomes less an instant of transcendence than a devotion to the immediate, but either way to remove oneself temporally is to remove oneself politically.

378:7+ **as when a marten's fur rises under the caress of your hand:** Variants of this small mammal from the weasel family live throughout Europe, but Jordan is remembering home and the American marten native to the northwestern United States, to Montana (Hemingway worked on the novel in Sun Valley, Idaho, which is also marten country). Jordan's frequent likening of Maria to mammals bears on this passage. The marten is hunted primarily for its pelt. That Jordan finds the throat-swelling feeling of Maria's hair against his cheek similar to a hunter's stroking the fur of a small mammal he has trapped and intends to kill injects violence into his erotic regard for her even as the language suggests a freeing of the marten and Maria from their pain. This moment becomes troublingly difficult to divorce from the head-shaving that preluded her rapes, especially because the couple couples as soon as she wakes, the few words they speak referencing the rapes through the residual pain (378:31–32; 379:1+).

In his initial manuscript draft, Hemingway compared Jordan's touching Maria's head to caressing a cat "on a cold night in winter," but then revised it to the more violent imagery involving the marten (MS12–012). Hemingway decided against a marten pelt in favor of a beaver pelt for Jordan's first impression of Maria's hair (22:8+).

378:31 **firm and hard and pressing:** Hemingway inserted this language to the draft, crossing out "and there was a fierceness, and desperateness and haste"; he then inserted—and then crossed out—"desperately and in haste" after "and she said" (MS12–012).

379:1+ **Nay, there is no pain:** Jordan is suspicious of Maria's denial of the pain during intercourse. Readers might well share his suspicions. See 379:36–37 below.

379:6+ **Then they were together:** Josephs points to precedent language from *Green Hills of Africa*, Hemingway's nonfiction book about safari hunting (and writing) from 1935:

> All I wanted to do now was get back to Africa. We had not left, yet, but when I would wake in the night I would lie, listening, homesick for it already.
>
> Now, looking out the tunnel of trees over the ravine at the sky with white clouds moving across in the wind, I loved the country so that I was happy as you are after you have been with a woman you really love, when, empty, you feel it welling up again and there it is and you can never have it all and yet what there is, now, you can have, and you want more and more, to have, and be, and live in, to possess now again for always, for that long, sudden-ended always; making time stand still, sometimes so very still that afterwards you wait to hear it move, and it is slow in starting. But you are not alone, because if you have ever really loved her happy and untragic, she loves you always; no matter whom she loves nor where she goes she loves you more. So if you have loved some woman and some country you are very fortunate and, if you die afterwards it makes no difference. (*GHOA* 52; Josephs, *Undiscovered* 102)

For many readers, the "**now**" of Jordan and Maria's lovemaking is an eternal now, which is to say a mystical or sacred union, an entrance into mythic time, into the absolute. Josephs reads the spiritual achievement as inclusively catholic;[1] other scholars have read it as more exclusively Catholic. Matthew Nickel, for example, hears the language "[e]choing the [Gloria Patri lesser] doxology" with "all past and present in this union, the Alpha and Omega" (166). One might frame this passage in terms of Mircea Eliade's ideas of the "eternal return" as an escape from the "terror of history." Or through Henri Bergson, whose ideas about time influenced such modernist crafters of stream-of-consciousness as James Joyce, Virginia Wolf, and William Faulkner. For Bergson, *durée,* or pure duration, is interior time uncorrupted by the passing of time as dictated by clocks. If one submits entirely to clock time, a particular moment cannot endure because the next moment usurps it. One experiences the real time of *durée* qualitatively, not quantitatively, and qualitative time endures outside the framework of clock time.

There are other precedents. In an article on fishing, Hemingway discovered that "it is not the duration of a sensation but its intensity that counts. If it is of enough intensity it lasts forever no matter what the actual time was." He learned this lesson in Spain, probably in the 1920s, from a Spaniard who stopped to watch him. Pulling the trout in gradually, by tiring it, does not provide the same heightened emotion as yanking it out of the water and pitching it through the air, *al vuelo,* onto the bank. The intensity of landing a big fish *al vuelo,* the Spaniard says, "is an emotion that kills you." Hemingway agrees with him (JFK #570a; MS54–014).

As Hemingway writes in *Death in the Afternoon,* the *faena,* the finale that delivers the bull unto death, "takes a man out of himself and makes him feel immortal while it is proceeding, that gives him an ecstasy, that is, while momentary, as profound as any religious ecstasy" (206). The *faena* is the ground zero moment of a religious fiesta lasting for several days whose purpose, for Josephs, is "to stop profane time, clock time, historical time. . . . A fiesta is time out of time, sacred time, original time, primal time"; it is the "still center of sacred time" (Josephs, "*Toreo*" 93, 98). The instant of the sword's fatal plunge Hemingway calls "the original moment of truth, or of reality" (*DIA* 174), a moment of pure "spiritual enjoyment" to which the killer brings "a sense of glory" and which blesses him with "the feeling of rebellion against death" (*DIA* 233). Maria expresses her gratitude for having "been another time in *la gloria,*" seemingly a metaphysical destination (379:37).

Bringing bullfighting into the lovemaking combats the critical habit of divorcing these scenes from the violence of the rest of the novel, from the violence potentially inherent in the romantic relationship. Reconciling the affectionate and the predatory aspects of the relationship is as challenging as reconciling *Death in the Afternoon*'s claims about ecstatic truth with its statement that "any over-metaphysical tendency in speech" is "horseshit" (95).[2]

Because there are more prosaic, more profane, ways to read this scene.

In the first line, who says, "**Then they were together**," the third-person omniscient narrator or Jordan? Evidence points to Jordan. His interiority's freewheeling synonymizing of first-, second-, and third-person pronouns throughout the novel readily allows this "they" to signify *we.* He has been the one watching his now "unseen" watch; he is aware of his elbows and admits that everything unsaid here "was only in his head" (the words "for the other" through "had said nothing" were inserted in the draft; MS12–012). Inasmuch as the rhythmic repetition repeats his perspective's voice in chapter 13's lovemaking scene, the constant return to the word "now" simply extends his awareness of his watch's ticking minute hand, which he had already involved in the sex by watching it as he licked Maria's cheek and earlobe, "the hand of the watch now mounting in sharp angle toward the top" (378:19+). The idea that the lovers have only the now that must last forever comes straight from his earlier postcoital postulations (see 166:31+). While one could understand his subjectivity in this passage as faithfully expressing a spiritual truth of the novel, one could instead understand it as an earthbound expression of Jordan's active effort to live that compensatory proposition. His "for now always one now" becomes an imploring, an attempted speech act, rather than an omnisciently narrated fact, the repeated "now" not far afield from the repeated "*please*" begging God to let its speaker survive a bombardment in "Chapter VII" of *In Our Time*. The cynical reader might rephrase Queen Gertrude's line from *Hamlet:* This caballero doth insist too much. Jordan's similarity to the Hemingway from *Green Hills of Africa* becomes ironic, perhaps even an act of self-interrogation or self-deprecation on the writer's part.

In the draft, after "this was what had been and now and whatever was to come" (379:9–10), the passage continued in a different direction, which Hemingway crossed out: "They did not know that ^Robert Jordan knew that^ if there is any reward this is the reward, that only those have it who merit it, that it is only to be given and only by giving can it be received. He felt proud and humble and happy with the ecstasy of fulfillment. There are no words for such things" (MS12–012). Perhaps he deleted these words after writing himself to the conclusion that words fail feelings. The deletion reinforces the fact of Jordan's narration, a narration not always reliable or particularly self-aware. Does the reader agree with Jordan that he deserves bliss?

The text frames the sexual congress on both sides with concern for Maria's pain. At no point during the act, however, does Jordan's interiority ever worry about her or otherwise wonder about her physical or emotional experience. The rhythmic insistence is all his.

379:36–37 **Nay . . . another time in *la gloria:*** It is possible that Maria "miraculously" loses the genital pain of her months of wartime rape (Josephs, *Undiscovered* 134), but improbable. Even religious interpretations of Hemingway's texts ought to obey his code of realism. The novel practically dares readers to obliviate her pain in their desire for a star-crossed romance rather than to conclude realistically that she denies her pain to Jordan for his sake (as she does all things). Maria's "nay" does not directly answer the question of whether she experienced physical pain but why she "held him tight and turned her head away." That, not the pain, is the referent to the pronoun "it." The glory—*la gloria*—might signal an ephemeral heaven on earth, a spiritual ascension experienced with corporeal ecstasy, but even within the metaphorical frame of Christ's ascension, it involves crucifixion. Pain. The passion of Christ is a path of suffering, as St. Paul testified. It involves Saint John of the

Cross's imprisonment and torture (reminiscent of Maria's). Profoundly indebted to Saint Teresa of Ávila, Saint John's theology testifies to the requirement of pain for the attainment of divine union (see 380:21+). It involves the pain that Elaine Scarry observes as the gist of Christian religious ecstasy: "As in dying and death, so in serious pain the claims of the body utterly nullify the world. . . . It is the intense pain that destroys a person's self and world, a destruction experienced spatially as either the contraction of the universe down to the immediate vicinity of the body or as the body swelling to fill the entire universe" (33, 35)—or both at once. For Maria to die each time is for Maria to be killed each time; the dissolution of the self, even in another, destroys the self. Perhaps Maria experiences spiritual, even Christian, ecstasy. Or perhaps she, too, clings to a compensatory proposition in her ongoing quest for release from her trauma, for a reborn self. Perhaps she simply defaults to what she knows—a Catholic vocabulary for her trials.

Hemingway inserted her sentence about *la gloria* to the draft (MS12–012).

380:21+ **La Gloria:** In the draft, Jordan reflects that he's never known "it" before, but only "together" have they experienced it, and now for the second time—all of which Hemingway excised (MS12–012). One should not assume that *la gloria* means the same thing for Maria as it does for Jordan. Their interiors were not in sync during or after the first extended lovemaking passage (see 159:8+; 160:2–3; 160:6–7)—his presumption in this crossed-out material that they were is itself revealing. For her, whose best companion is him, it is a physical experience, maybe of pain; for him, whose "best companion" is "his mind" (ouch), it is an idea (380:20).

The paragraph begins with Jordan's revisiting his practice of mulling over a word's translations based on its cultural heritage (e.g., 166:31+). He distinguishes the Spanish term from the English "**glory**"—individual heroic fame—and from the French "**La Gloire**"—pride in the French nation, especially its long history of global imperialism and European cultural dominance. Whatever *la gloria* means to the Spanish Maria, it means something about being Spanish to the American Jordan.

The ***cante jondo***, or deep song, is considered the pure folk expression of Andalusia. Flamenco song derives from it, but the "profound difference," according to the poet Federico García Lorca, is that of flamenco's "local color," a "modern song" whose "emotional interest fades before that of deep song," whose "spiritual color" is "the mysterious color of primordial ages" (*Deep Song* 25; on flamenco, see 186:32). Lorca wrote his *cante jondo*–inspired *Poem of Deep Song* (*Poema del cante jondo*) in 1921 but did not publish a version of it until 1931. He defined deep song in a 1922 lecture written for a gathering he and his friend the Andalusian composer Manuel De Falla organized at the Alhambra Castle in Granada.[3].

Deep song's Iberian roots precede the Romani (27). The tradition is pagan, primitive, and pantheistic: "Deep song is akin to the trilling of birds, the song of the rooster, and the natural music of forest and fountain. It is a very rare specimen of primitive song, the oldest in all Europe, and its notes carry the naked, spine-tingling emotion of the first Oriental races" (25). Their subjects are temporal love, death, the solo journey of life, and pain. (And an "obsession with hair," which Lorca relates to the ghazals of the Persian poet Hafiz. Lorca offers this deep song exemplar:

> If I should happen to die, I order you,
> tie up my hands
> With the tresses of your black hair.

"There is nothing more profoundly poetic than those three lines," Lorca writes, "with their sad, aristocratic eroticism" (38).[4])

Carlos Bauer defines the **saeta** as "as a musical prayer that is sung during Holy Week in Sevilla" to the figures of Christ or the Virgin "carried through the streets on hand-held floats" during the stops along the procession (ii). *Poem of the Deep Song* includes *saeta*-inspired poems as a subgenre of the deep song. Drawing on the image of the gowns and tall conical caps worn by the processing penitents, Lorca's "Procession" makes clear the *saeta*'s indebtedness to Andalusia's pre-Christian soul: "Down the narrow street / comes strange unicorns. / From what field, / from what mythical forest?" (47). As Bauer notes, "Saeta means arrow or barb" (ii), and Lorca takes full advantage of that language to express the pain inherent in the *cante jondo* tradition.

On **El Greco**, see 235:17–18. El Greco falls squarely in Spain's Golden Age of artistic and literary flourishing from the sixteenth to the mid-seventeenth centuries, the era following the Reconquest and coeval with the Catholic Revival—the Counter-Reformation—throughout Europe. The Generation of '98, the Spanish intellectuals and artists regarded as bringing Spanish culture into the modern world, who shaped the views of modernists like John Dos Passos and Ernest Hemingway, saw El Greco's religious painting as of a piece with the mystical poetry of Santa Teresa de Jesús—Saint Teresa of Ávila—and **San Juan de la Cruz** (Saint John of the Cross). Saint Teresa and Saint John belonged to the Carmelite Order, a mendicant order committed to a life of poverty, prayer, and contemplation (see 379:36–37). Saint Teresa mentored Saint John, and in 1562 the pair founded the Order of the Discalced (shoeless) Carmelites in Spain to return to the original vision of the Carmelites, whose asceticism had been mitigated over the centuries. The Discalced Carmelites maintain a stronger commitment to abstinence, poverty, fasting, cloistered solitude, continual prayer, and divine contemplation. Privation and suffering lead to God's graces. Much of Saint John's theology and poetry focused on the union with God through trials of physical suffering or by metaphors of love, marriage, and intimacy.

For some readers, Jordan's defining La Gloria by the examples of the *saeta*, El Greco, and Saint John, solidifies a Catholic interpretation (379:6+; 379:36–37). Josephs focuses on the nonsectarian mysticism of these three in seeing a universal spirituality in such rapture (*Undiscovered* 103, 136–37). The Catholic interpretation is problematic, because Maria and Jordan don't exactly follow the path of privation set by Saint Teresa and Saint John, and because it ignores the earthy, pagan *cante jondo*. For Lorca, the *cante jondo* represented a protest to oppressive Spanish Catholicism, to the threat to its pantheist, folk heart.

When Jordan references what is "in San Juan de la Cruz," he surely means Saint John's poetry, with all four examples—and the other unnamed examples—being artistic expressions of the Spanish essence. The Catholic allusions are of *Spanish* Catholicism, the religion of the auto-da-fé, which Jordan sees as an updated expression of the primitively violent, abiding Spanish character (286:34+) just as the *saeta* is a vessel for the *cante jondo*. As Jordan has said, "Spain has never been a Christian country" (355:5). For him, the Spanish essence of *la gloria* he discovers in Maria.

All four of Jordan's named examples allude to the transformation of pain into the consolation of art. Three of them—the *cante jondo,* the *saeta,* and San Juan de la Cruz—have Andalusian connections, Saint John having done a great deal of missionary work in the latter part of his life there. It befits Jordan's romantic foreign sensibility to equate Spain's essence with Andalusia, the land of Romani and Moors. The fourth is neither Andalusian nor technically even Spanish, yet the *Inglès* who desires to become Spanish includes El Greco, literally The Greek, the Greece-born painter adopted by Spain as one of its own greats. Male homosexuality inhabits two of the allusions. *Death in the Afternoon* shows Hemingway preoccupied with the androgynous and apparently queer figures of El Greco's painting (117–20). "Viva El Greco El Rey de los Maricónes," he writes (205): Hail El Greco, King of the Fairies. Lorca's homosexuality was widely known.

In the next chapter, Jordan retracts his musing about *la gloria* as "nonsense" (386:26), just as earlier he caught himself unduly romanticizing the spirit of the primitive peoples of Spain before there was a Spain but that nevertheless lives on in modern Spaniards (287:6–7). The earlier comment reinforces the conclusion that *la gloria* for Jordan means pre-Christian Spain.

381:8–9 **Charles ... Chub ... Guy ... Mike:** Charles Thompson, Chub Weaver, Guy Hickok, and Mike Strater were Hemingway's friends. This allusion string is an autobiographical slippage more direct than Jordan's familiarity with France. With the exception of Chub Weaver (see 337:16), one should not make too much of Hemingway's using the first names of his friends for the first names of Jordan's friends, in this case a name being nothing more than a name, an authorial shout-out to friends. All were buddies first and only; none were professional rivals. Three of the four referenced men aptly compare to Anselmo, because they were hunting and fishing companions of Hemingway's, and presumably—though not necessarily—of Jordan's, who claims not to like hunting much (39:14). They crossed paths with each other at some point while in Hemingway's company. Hickok is the odd man out, although he published an interview with Hemingway about the 1933–1934

African safari. The chapter begins with the comparison of Maria's hair to the fur of a trapped (hunted) marten as prelude to lovemaking during which Maria experienced physical pain, then recalls these hunting friends in the same breath that Jordan calls Maria his "true love and wife" (381:11). Jordan's idea that Maria is also his sister and daughter suggests, perhaps, the manifold ways animals signify to people: predator, prey, pet, helpmate, relation.

Charles Thompson, a Key West native, introduced Hemingway to sea fishing, which became a lifelong passion; the easygoing Thompson also became a lifelong friend. He hunted and fished with Hemingway and Pauline in Montana in 1932 and accompanied them on the African safari, where he outshot Hemingway. Hemingway openly portrayed his bruised ego in *Green Hills of Africa* (1935), with "Old Karl" as Thompson's avatar. In addition to hunting and fishing with Hemingway in Montana and Wyoming, Leland Stanford **"Chub" Weaver** spent the first part of 1931 living and fishing in Key West, a constant companion. Chub's witness to Jordan's throwing into a lake the pistol with which the father killed himself makes his appearance in Jordan's mind now, before first light on the day Jordan moves toward certain death, noteworthy. Hemingway befriended **Guy Hickok** in Paris in 1921, when Hemingway wrote for the *Toronto Star* and Hickok worked as the bureau chief for the *Brooklyn Daily Eagle*. In 1922, the two covered the Lausanne Peace Conference. Hemingway's 1927 story "Che ti dice la patria?" treats an episode he and Hickok experienced on a trip to Italy that March. On that trip, Hemingway visited with Don Giuseppe Bianchi, the priest who had performed extreme unction on him after his severe wounding in 1918 (see Trogdon, "'Legend'").

Hemingway and **Henry Hyacinth "Mike" Strater** met as young men in Paris. They had a great deal in common: both served in ambulance units during the Great War; both were aspiring artists who emulated Cézanne; both were sportsmen, boxing and playing tennis together in the twenties, and sea-fishing together in the thirties. Strater painted the first portraits of Hemingway. Hemingway initially invited Strater and Archibald MacLeish along for the 1933–1934 safari. When they declined, he asked Thompson. Strater was aboard Hemingway's boat the *Pilar* in April 1935 when Hemingway accidentally shot himself in both legs with a pistol while shooting a shark. The following month, as Strater was bringing in an enormous marlin, Hemingway shot up the incoming sharks with a Tommy-gun, resulting in a large shark convergence tearing apart Strater's catch. Hemingway's action and his neglect of mentioning it in an article for *Esquire*—"The President Vanquishes," July 1935—soured their friendship for Strater (Baker, *Life Story* 272–73).

As Hemingway's voice, the line speaks to the living reality fictional characters such as Anselmo had for the artist, in contrast to the mystery posed by living people the artist knew quite well—especially in the *now* of the act of literary creation, Hemingway at his typewriter, outside the march of time, bringing his inventions to life while relegating real people to the abstraction of pastness.

381:21 **coming fast now:** The text propels the reader forward to the book's conclusion and hurries Robert Jordan to his death. The chapter began with a lovemaking scene rife with the word "now"; and as the story moves to its climax, the sexual innuendo is hard to ignore.

382:6 **ten minutes to three:** Precisely twelve hours earlier, Captain Mora checked his watch just before being killed in action (315:9–10; see also 318:20+). This isn't a coincidence—Hemingway changed it from "twenty minutes" in the draft (MS12-012). Also, unlike with the prior lovemaking scene (161:24+), Jordan now appears to have achieved the postsex clarity of mind, this chapter being significantly shorter than that one (chapter 13).

NOTES

    1. Josephs, *Undiscovered,* 100–109, 134–38. Josephs's language of "mandala" (107), "tantric" sexuality (107), the gypsies's "Indian past" (109), and "Eastern enlightenment" (109) risks an Orientalizing perhaps in keeping with Jordan's own. See Broer for an extended analysis of *DIA* and *FWBT* in terms of *GHA* (*Spanish Tragedy,* chapters 5 and 6, 68–97).

    2. See *DIA*'s critique of Waldo Frank's excessively mystical writing about Spain and the bullfight (53–54) and Mandel's interpretation of that criticism (*Reading DIA* 149–50).

    3. De Falla's 1915 work *Nights in the Gardens of Spain* was a Hemingway household standard. See Justice, "Music" 202. Justice's essay discusses Hemingway listening to De Falla in the 1950s. More than likely, he became familiar with the piece in the 1920s, when "it was performed all over Paris and Spain, and the solo piano part for it was published in 1923" (Justice, personal email, 7 July 2022). His wife at the time, Hadley, was a pianist; his mother was a classical singer; and this was the period he started traveling to and falling in love with Spain.

    4. Hemingway's 1935 edition of Lorca's *Romancero Gitano* included the "Poema del cante jondo" (Reynolds, *Hemingway's Reading* 128).

CHAPTER THIRTY-EIGHT

383:33+ **oval Mill bomb type:** A hand grenade, properly spelled "mills" in the draft (MS12–013). The 1915 No. 5 Mark 1 Mills Bomb was manufactured by the British in the First World War. Egg-shaped, sized and fitted to the palm, with rigged squares for easy gripping, the fragmentation grenade functioned as Jordan describes. The pin-and-ring acted as a safety to hold in place the springed lever—the published word "**level**" is another printing error from the draft's proper spelling (Hemingway inserted "lever" to replace "handle"). The thrower's grip held the lever in place after the other hand pulled out the pin. Once the grenade left the hand, the lever sprang away, activating the blast cap and fuse inside. The grenade exploded about five seconds later. The Mills grenade was typically a defensive weapon, as its blasted fragments were effective in injuring multiple attacking soldiers in the open. The Mark 2 "Pineapple" hand grenade was the US version from the Second World War, featured in most films with infantry combat.

384:7 *Valen más que pesan:* They are worth more than their weight. Changed from *Famoso* (famous) in the galley proofs, perhaps by Durán.

384:13 **the post at Otero**: The raid during which Anselmo first killed a man (193:18+).

384:25 **soup-tin-shaped bomb:** Hemingway doesn't provide a name or nomenclature, but Eladio's description of this grenade as "all flash and no fragments" identifies it as either a concussion grenade or more likely a thermite grenade rather than a fragmentation grenade (see 383:33+). Concussion grenades were designed for offensive trench warfare in the First World War, as they produced shock waves that could travel through trenches (and other enclosed spaces) in ways that fragments could not. Thermite grenades generate an intense heat blast useful for igniting flames or melting metal weaponry. The Thermite Mark 1 looked like a soup can. Since guerrillas did not attack fortified trench positions, they would not have found concussion grenades very useful, and thermite grenades only moderately so.

386:5 **John Mosby:** See 233:2.

386:26 ***gloria:*** See 380:21+.

386:30+ **to bite on the nail:** To bite on any hard object, or something like a belt, to endure pain without vocalizing. Twice the paragraph suggests suicide: there "always" being "ways out," and the "damned snake with a broken back biting at itself," the latter suggestive of Jordan's broken leg at the end of the novel (with the double meaning of "damned"). Snakes do sometimes bite their own tail when under duress or pain. It's possible Hemingway intended to imply the ouroboros, an ages-old symbol of the endless death and rebirth cycle, for some of eternal life. As a symbol of regeneration through fertility—through propagation—it acquires the self-sufficiency of the hermaphrodite. This would be appropriate for Jordan, who after sleeping with Maria calls his own mind his "best companion" (380:20). Although referencing a fish, the Spanish proverb *la pescadilla que se muerde la cola,* "the hake [or whiting] that bites its tail," expresses faulty circularity of logic, the futility of a line of thought that always returns to its beginning.[1] Jordan, perhaps, on the subject of suicide.

387:31 **political commissar:** Units in the International Brigade and the People's Army of the Republic had a commissar to motivate the soldiers and ensure proper political thinking. At their best, they were morale officers who genuinely looked out for the soldiers. At their worst, they were informants and disciplinarians of the harshest sort, pernicious Comintern agents. They held military rank and could countermand a commander's orders. At the higher levels of command, the commissar wielded a great deal of power. Stalin's purges were under way, after all.

387:35 ***Ni tu, ni Dios:*** Neither you, nor God.

388:12 ***Bueno, y qué?:*** Well, so what?

389:12–13 **five from the bands of Elias and Alejandro:** It is about three in the morning. Jordan entered the cave at ten to three (382:6–7); Pablo left about one in the morning (360:1; 360:15). Readers will need to suspend their disbelief that in two hours Pablo left the cave, gathered up his horses, dumped the explosives materials, changed his mind, plodded about the forested mountains (one horse in tow) at night to two different guerrilla camps, woke the guerrillas, made his recruitment pitch, waited for them to prepare themselves and their horses, and made the way back to the cave. With a waning crescent moon, at least it wasn't totally dark.

391:4 ***Hombre! Qué mal lo pasé!:*** Man, what a hard time! Changed from *Hombre! Muy malo* (Man, very bad) in the galley proofs.

391:5 **Judas Iscariot:** The disciple whose betrayal of Christ to the Romans led to the crucifixion. Because Christ's death brought about his resurrection and the salvation of the world, Judas Iscariot's betrayal was a rather significant contribution to the spiritual history of the world. Despite Pablo's return, his initial betrayal has already contributed to Jordan's death, a death Jordan and many readers perceive as spiritually redeeming (if not necessarily in Christian terms). Judas and Pablo share ambiguous, controversial reputations. Their treason made the final victory come to pass, and their foils, Christ and Jordan, allowed it.

Christ and Jordan martyr themselves knowing death is coming. From the moment they met, Jordan suspected Pablo might betray the mission; by two Biblical accounts, Jesus knew Judas would betray him (John 6:64; Matt. 26:25). Christ's willing death is why John Donne argues that self-murder cannot ipso facto be sinful, but one would be hard-pressed to argue that Jordan's self-murder qualifies as Christ-like by Donne's definition (see front matter: title and epigraph). Judas hanged himself (Matt. 27:3–5); Pilar is basically telling Pablo to go hang himself, but in a chapter where she and Jordan revisited the question of her prognostication in his hand of his fated death, in a sense by his hand (387:20).

391:12 ***Son buenos:*** They are good.

NOTE

1. Real Academia Española, *El diccionario de la lengua española* (https://dle.rae.es/pescadilla).

CHAPTER THIRTY-NINE

392:22 **five horses, *sabes?*:** Five horses, you know? Pablo is telling Jordan that they will have enough horses for their people after all. See 392:26+.

392:26+ **conversion on the road to Tarsus:** Saint Paul the Apostle's conversion to Christianity occurred on the road from Jerusalem to Damascus, not to his hometown of Tarsus. The swap was surely no accident. Paul's conversion is a popular Biblical story, so Hemingway, his typist, his editor and publisher, and everyone else who worked on the book would have to have missed the error. Either Jordan is not particularly well-versed in the Bible, or Jordan quips that when Pablo deserted he was running from the war, figuratively if not literally running home, to his personal Tarsus. Paul is his Latin name, Saul his Hebrew name.

Paul witnessed and condoned the stoning to death of a Christian convert, then "made havock of the church, entering into every house, and haling men and women committed them to prison" (Acts 8:3). After, "breathing out threatenings and slaughter against the disciples of the Lord, [he] went unto the high priest, and desired of him letters to Damascus to the synagogues, that if he found any of this way, whether they were men or women, he might bring them bound unto Jerusalem," presumably for execution (Acts 9:1–2). The conversion to Christ and away from violence occurred when Christ appeared on the road and blinded him for three days.

Pablo initially led the massacre of a priest and other Christians, then retreated to his cave and, most recently, from the war, in the form of the bridge mission. His return is to violence against the Christian-aligned Nationalists. He is preconversion Paul and worse: Pablo intends to murder the fellow Loyalist guerrillas he has recruited, people he knows on a first-name basis, to steal their horses for his people's escape. Jordan, realizing Pablo's plan, sarcastically calls it his latest **"revelation"** (393:6): Pablo underwent no "complete conversion" in returning; one needn't worry about a **"canonizing"** (392:28–29). Jordan's wry allusion does not evidence an inclining toward Christ by Pablo or the novel (contra Stoneback, "Priest" 104–05).

393:38+ **And you, he said to himself:** While this is not the first nor last time Jordan talks with himself (e.g., 161:24+), the voices or selves have increased beyond the bifurcated consciousness of self-debate. From "our work" (393:37), which means his work, Jordan thinks, "We were all in bad shape. You and me and both of us. . . . One at a time, now" (394:2–4). Who all is *we all?* Awareness of a dialogue between two selves implies a third, the aware and spectating self (and so on). One might well ask about his need to insist to himself on his unity of being with language that admits a "**schizophrenic**" fragmentation (394:4) as he approaches death and as the novel increasingly structurally fragments among perspectives. A romantic claim would see his fragmentation as a condition of Maria's absence—that she completes him. After all, he precedes this confusion by declaring about them, "But that is over and done with now" (393:36). Or does this "now" work to undermine the eternal "now" of their recent lovemaking (379:6+; see also 166:31+)? Hemingway inserted into the draft the sentences beginning with "But you were pretty bad" to "One at a time, now," including the schizophrenia language (MS12–014).

395:4 ***Que me maten:*** Let them kill me. An English speaker would say, Kill me now, or I'll be damned.

CHAPTER FORTY

397:5 **Mundo Obrero:** *The Working World*, the official wartime publication of the PCE, the mainstream Communist Party in Spain, was the proper newspaper for a Republican soldier to be seen reading. As this scene unfolds, characters employ the names of news outlets to establish or challenge another's ideological bona fides and loyalty. Twenty-first-century American readers should be familiar with how consuming certain news sources could be "tantamount to proclaiming one's political affiliation" (Mandel, *Reading* 199).

398:6 **El Debate:** Hemingway added by hand to the typed draft the line describing this paper for his reader as "the leading Catholic-Conservative organ published in Madrid before the movement" (MS12–0015). *El Debate* was not as far-right as the novel suggests. It started in the first decade of the twentieth century. According to Mandel, "[d]uring the Spanish Civil War it managed to offend both sides of the conflict. The Republicans suspended its publication several times because the Church supported the Nationalists. The Nationalists also suppressed it in Nationalist-held territories because the paper, although Catholic in orientation, presented moderate views" (Mandel, *Reading* 214) After 1936, it moved publication outside Republican-controlled Madrid; after the war, it did not survive long under Franco's totalitarian regime.

398:12 **A.B.C.:** Per Mandel: "Madrid's oldest daily newspaper was founded in 1903 as a weekly and became a daily in 1905." Before the war, "ABC consistently supported the monarchy and the Church." In Madrid, the Republic allowed it to continue wartime publication, "albeit under Republican censorship." The Seville edition was a rare Nationalist-aligned paper published in the Republic without government "interference" (Mandel, *Reading* 199).

398:19 **By any name:** The semantic question pesters Jordan throughout the novel, because in such politically charged circumstances as civil war, connotations can prove a matter of life and death. The euphemisms *eliminate, purge,* and *liquidate* don't rise to the outlandish level of Orwellian doublespeak, but George Orwell's experiences fighting for the Republic in the Spanish Civil War catalyzed his disenchantment with the communism of Stalin and the Comintern. That totalitarian communist rhetoric, along with the totalitarian fascist rhetoric of the Nationalists and their Nazi Germany and Italian brethren, inspired the doublespeak of his political satire *Animal Farm* (1945) and the dystopian novel *Nineteen Eighty-Four* (1949).

398:38+ in Morocco, and became a Republican: Miranda is one of the exceptional *Africanista*s (regular army officers from the Spanish Foreign Legion) who remained loyal to the Republican government. His personal reason is only indirectly political—because the traditional Nationalists didn't allow divorce.

399:10 *milicianas*: At the beginning of the war, a woman who took up arms against the rebellion was called a *miliciana*—a female militia member—whether in uniform or in mufti. They had the conjoined political motives of fighting against fascism and for gender equality: "Most of these young women appear to have come from politicized anarchist or communist youth backgrounds and were already integrated into political circles. . . . It is impossible to ascertain the number of militia women who carried out military or auxiliary roles at the war fronts. However, all the existing testimonies suggest that there were relatively few (Nash 107–08).[1] Relative to their actual warfront numbers, they initially played an outsized role in Republican propaganda imagery. However:

> Very quickly, attitudes changed. . . . A clear gender division of roles emerged. . . . For once, there was a consensus among severely divided political parties, unions, and even women's organizations on the need to oblige milicianas to withdraw from the war fronts, and, by September [1936], a policy was being implemented to coerce them to leave the fronts [such that] by the beginning of 1937 their number had been drastically reduced. (Nash 110)

The novel realizes conflicting attitudes toward women, gender roles, and the movement to uphold traditional femininity and domesticity, in its depictions of Pilar and Maria, the older woman permitted to join the planning and bear a rifle to fight at the bridge, the younger woman assigned to stay with the horses, truly a *camarada de la retaguardia* (comrade [female] of the rear guard). Both survive the battle, but the future rides away with the more gender-conventional Maria. In terms of the novel's consideration of the aesthetic relationship between form and function (e.g., 87:2), the uglier, more mannish woman (by conventional standards) perpetrates violence and violent storytelling, while the novel protects the prettier young woman from such acts except as victim. On Pilar and Maria as *milicianas*, see Guill, "Pilar and Maria."

400:11 **Cercedilla:** A town in the Guadarrama Mountains just northwest of Navacerrada. The two towns straddle the southern end of the Navacerrada Pass.

400:23 **Peguerinos:** A town in the Guadarrama Mountains west of the Guadarrama Pass (Alto del León). Miranda fought in defense of the Guadarrama Pass to prevent the Nationalists from taking Madrid at the beginning of the war (399:4–5), when he met Golz. Jordan fought there too (235:32+).

401:1 **Andrés:** The chapter begins and ends with Andrés's perspective, seamlessly touring other perspectives along the way.

NOTE

1. Nash claims that "[w]omen's entry into the militia seems to have been entirely spontaneous, as there was no official recruitment policy for women" (107), yet there's evidence to suggest otherwise in the "Les milicies, us necessiten!" poster—"The Militias Need You!"—featuring a rifle-wielding *miliciana* pointing at the viewer. The background has two anarchist flags and one Catalan flag; the woman's scowl, finger, and blue overalls seems a direct borrowing from the famous American "Uncle Sam Needs You" Great War poster (she also looks like Greta Garbo). See Greeson, *Gendering the Republic,* figures 1.1 and 1.2, p. 23; and "Spanish Women Called to Arms" photo, ca. 1936, Barcelona, Spain (Hulton-Deutsch Collection/CORBIS/Corbis via Getty Images; www.gettyimages.com/detail/news-photo/propaganda-posters-in-barcelona-spain-encouraging-women-to-news-photo/613513882).

CHAPTER FORTY-ONE

403:22 *De la primera:* Of the first.

403:34–35 **Or does he think I did not understand him the first time:** In case the reader missed it the first time, Hemingway emphasizes that Jordan is fully aware of Pablo's plan to sacrifice their guerilla allies to get their horses (see 392:22; 392:26+).

404:7 *Suerte:* Good luck.

404:22–23 *au fond:* At bottom, or Deep down, in French. One effect of Jordan's using French is to assert a difference from, even a superiority to, Pablo after the two just shared a connection through the handshake. It certainly emphasizes Jordan's bourgeois cosmopolitanism. Jordan switched to French to distance himself from Pablo when they met (16:37+). See the next entry.

404:31 *maricones:* See 216:23. Curiously, Pilar's accusation of homosexuality follows from Jordan's interior use of a French phrase (404:2223). What does Pilar intuit? Homosexuality was condescendingly associated with the (nonwhite) supposedly uncivilized, but also with the excessively civilized, a *vice aristocratique*.

The familiarity and similarities between Jordan and Pablo, their rivalry, and their shared desire for (possession of) Maria make *For Whom the Bell Tolls* a good fit for the understanding of literary history advanced by Eve Kosofsky Sedgwick's groundbreaking *Between Men: English Literature and Male Homosocial Desire*. Sedgwick's study focuses mostly on nineteenth-century English literature, the very Romantic and Victorian eras that shaped Hemingway. The texts her study chooses to include "are specifically *not* meant to begin to delineate a separate male-homosocial literary canon" because "the European canon as it exists is already such a canon, and most so when it is most heterosexual" (17).

405:1–2 *Me cago en tu padre:* I shit on your father (another changed *Me cabra* in the galley proofs). Pilar's casual insult stings Jordan deeply, as it is followed immediately by Pilar's charge of cowardice and then by Jordan's only actual memory of his father in the novel. Pilar has turned her joking accusation of homosexuality (404:31) into a joking accusation of fear—"thou art afraid to see the bull come out"—drawing on the genderist stereotype of male homosexuality as unmanly, simpering, and cowardly. Don Faustino is the other man accused of being afraid to face the bull, in Pilar's tale of the massacre (113:1–2). He was the preening aspirant bullfighter who attached himself to Romani, dressed in Andalusian clothes, and trained to fight bulls the Andalusian way. He "had no courage and was considered a joke" (112:27).

405:13 **as though it were a train:** Jordan's description of his déjà vu with a train simile, followed by a remembered hometown moment of saying goodbye at a train station to the suicided father who embarrasses him, connects with the death of Kashkin—wounded after a successful train mission, then shot by Jordan (149:17), who first reported his companion had killed himself (21:1). This chapter ends with Jordan heading into his own successful mission that results in his death after a postmission fatal wounding, putting his lips to the muzzle of Kashkin's former weapon and feeling the inserted magazine "click home" (411:5).

405:34+ **May the Lord watch:** Genesis 31:49. Besides his fantasy of marrying Maria properly in a church, Jordan nowhere expresses religious sentiment. In addition to his surety that there is no afterlife (338:7) and his embarrassment at his father's religiosity, he excludes himself from those who have the comfort of religion at the hour of death (468:32–33). His recalled embarrassment is entangled with the greater shame of his father's suicide. For the next several paragraphs, Jordan conflates the parting from his father at the train station with his parting from Maria and his appointment with death—"the meeting he was going to" (406:24–25). Taken out of Biblical context, the verse asks that God watch over father and son while separated, reflecting Jordan and Maria's separation during the pending battle as well as his and his father's separation. Perhaps Jordan anticipates their reunion in death.

The Genesis story is far more complicated. Jacob labored for Laban for twenty years, in his eyes never fairly compensated, but also became Laban's son-in-law by marrying two of his daughters, Rachel and Leah. Commanded by God, Jacob flees, taking his wives and their children (Laban's grandchildren); Rachel has also secreted away with them her father's idols. Laban gives seven days' chase. The two men finally declare peace, on two conditions: neither Laban nor Jacob crosses the border between their lands, and Jacob never mistreats Laban's daughters or takes any other woman as a wife. In their covenant, the watching God serves not as caretaker but as surveillance, ensuring Jacob keeps his end of the truce terms. The implication for Jordan, then, is of an inescapable, internalized, threatening paternal gaze and a tense détente.

These paragraphs exacerbate the ambiguity of Jordan's role in his upcoming death. Is he leaving his paternal inheritance behind? Or reconciling himself to it?

He can "hardly bear" his pity for his father (406:3), and what burdens one can or cannot bear is the very question of Hamlet's "to be or not to be" soliloquy. Jordan refers to his upcoming death as a meeting but also reflects on "do[ing] it" (406:28+). There is a sense that he wishes to die to avoid becoming his pathetic father even as, in effecting his death, he becomes his father.

The presence of Maria, the simile of parting with a girl as a schoolboy, and the language of "the meeting he was going to" suggests *Appointment in Samarra*, either the 1934 sexually frank novel by John O'Hara about a man's road to suicide or the W. Somerset Maugham version of a Mesopotamian fable from which O'Hara's novel has its title and which it includes as epigraph:

Death speaks:
There was a merchant in Bagdad who sent his servant to market to buy provisions and in a little while the servant came back, white and trembling, and said, Master, just now when I was in the marketplace I was jostled by a woman in the crowd and when I turned I saw it was Death that jostled me. She looked at me and made a threatening gesture; now, lend me your horse, and I will ride away from this city and avoid my fate. I will go to Samarra and there Death will not find me. The merchant lent him his horse, and the servant mounted it, and he dug his spurs in its flanks and as fast as the horse could gallop he went. Then the merchant went down to the marketplace and he saw me standing in the crowd and he came to me and said, Why did you make a threating gesture to my servant when you saw him this morning? That was not a threatening gesture, I said, it was only a start of surprise. I was astonished to see him in Bagdad, for I had an appointment with him tonight in Samarra. (Maugham in O'Hara 3)

The Arab-world setting, the ambiguity of the servant's hand in his death, the woman as embodying the death from which and toward which he rides, galloping to his fate on a borrowed horse, resemble Jordan's story.

407:3+ crouched on his haunches: Fernando is defecating just off the path, "but he spoke with great dignity." The typed draft clarifies his business, as before Hemingway's handwritten changes, Fernando returns from completing "a natural function" (MS12–016). This explains why Jordan and Agustín jokingly wish Fernando good luck in everything he does.

410:3 *de acuerdo?*: Agreed? Right?

410:30+ Robert Jordan lay on the pine-needle floor of the forest: The paragraph's opening line repeats with slight difference the novel's opening line (1:1) and will be repeated with slight difference by the novel's last line (471:35–36). The suicidal imagery is undeniable: Jordan puts the weapon's muzzle to his mouth and feels the magazine "click home." The cyclic imagery echoes the merry-go-round of indecision that begins chapter 18 (225:1+) as well as the snake eating its own tail (386:32–33). Jordan's and Hemingway's fathers may have put pistol to temple, but Hemingway will put a shotgun in his mouth in Ketchum (Sun Valley), Idaho, one of the places he worked on the novel and where he hunted with Gary Cooper, the actor who played Jordan in the film adaptation.

The weapon Jordan touches to his lips belonged to Kashkin (269:4). Writing to his publisher, Hemingway confuses the matter of who finally shot Kashkin: "You remember there is a whole dark business about that from the very start. The man Kashkeen who has killed himself, the same necessity which faces Jordan" (to Charles Scribner, ca. 15 Aug. 1940, *SL* 508). Intended or not, the confusion only underscores the irrelevance of who pulled the trigger. By whoever's hand, the event amounts to a kind of suicide. Jordan only uses the word "home" in relation to himself two other times, both times in terms of self-inflicted death. First, at his childhood home where the coroner bequeaths him the pistol his father had recently used to kill himself (337:6); and second, in reference to the bridge whose destruction will be his own: "A home away from home" (438:11–12).

The sensuous nature of the scene on the pine-needle floor, in the predawn dark, also associates it with Jordan's times with Maria.

For Whom the Bell Tolls could have ended here. In a sense it does. The novel already knows that Jordan dies; that by carrying out the fatal mission, Jordan has chosen the time and place of his death; and that the bridge mission's outcome is inconsequential to the battle and the war. By this reading, his dispute with himself about suicide in the last chapter is superfluous. The next two chapters confirm what the novel has already determined and satisfy the reader's curiosity about the bridge mission while providing a conclusion at once disquietingly Naturalist (chapter 42) and heroically Romantic (chapter 43). They are sleight of hand; they form the epilogue that made redundant the epilogue Hemingway decided against (see 58:12–13).

CHAPTER FORTY-TWO

412:1 **During the time that Pablo had ridden back:** The chapter opens with an omniscient narrator unabashedly setting the stage, aware of simultaneous actions in different places, as had two recent earlier chapters (32 and 40). This may be the most Naturalist chapter in the book in establishing deterministic forces, accidental as well as mechanistic, external, and indifferent to the characters and beyond their ken.

413:1 **a smash-up:** It remains unclear how much the truck accident slows down Gomez and Andrés, preventing them from getting the message to Golz to stop the attack (and save Jordan's life). Such fate-inducing accidents frequently occur in Naturalist novels to demonstrate not just the universe's indifference but its absolute randomness, whether with the inexplicable locking of a safe that commits an indecisive man to become a thief and ruin his life in Theodore Dreiser's *Sister Carrie* (1900), or the caprices of ocean waves and currents that determine which members of a shipwrecked crew live or die in Stephen Crane's "The Open Boat" (1897).

416:12 **Thirty-Fifth Division:** This was General Walter's (Golz's) division, although in the draft Hemingway disguises it, calling it the Forty-First (MS12–017). Oddly, the first time Andrés names the division in the draft, it is the Thirty-Third (see 376:18).

416:34+ **A large man, old and heavy, in an oversized khaki beret, such as** *chasseurs à pied* **wear:** *Chasseurs à pied,* literally "hunters on foot," is the French term for light infantry who specialize in small-unit, high-mobility operations such as reconnaissance, foraging, and disruption behind enemy lines. The text identifies this character as the Frenchman André Marty (417:36). Marty joined the French Communist Party in 1923, rapidly rising to its leadership circle, and in 1931 joined the Comintern, where he again rose to prominence. The French communists provided much of the organizational and logistical leadership to the International Brigades, France being the geographic gateway to Spain. As the highest-ranking commissar in Spain during Stalin's Great Purge, Marty became a paranoid zealot who ordered the executions of scores of soldiers, usually on hasty charges of cowardice and fascist collaboration. He earned the epithet the Butcher of Albacete, after the town where the internationals were headquartered. After the war, Marty "admitted that he had ordered the shooting of about 500 Brigaders, nearly one-tenth of the total killed in the war, but some question this figure" (Beevor 161).

In the exchange of letters with his publisher and editor about the potential libelous portrait of Louis Fischer as the character Mitchell (see 239:25+), Hemingway asked Scribner whether the depiction of Marty was also legally imprudent:

> He has fled from France to Russia under sentence of death. . . . He could never come to the U.S. under any circumstances. He cannot go back to France unless the Communists come to power. Can he sue? Ask your lawyer. He has been publicly accused of murder in several books and numerous articles in France before he fled the country and did not sue. He was under investigation by the chamber of deputies when he fled the country when the Communist party was outlawed.
>
> Nick Guillen accused him of murder in Marianne (a large French Weekly) in article after article; each time nameing [sic] who Marty had shot. He accused him of the same thing in a book entitled Le Mercenaire [sic] published in 1938. I have a copy. Marty took no action against him. He really had the people shot and is in no position to sue. Also he is a fugitive from justice. (to Charles Scribner, ca. 15 Aug. 1940, SL 509–10)

417:11+ **the mutiny of the French Navy in the Black Sea:** Shortly after the end of the First World War, France dispatched a naval fleet to Odessa to support the Russian government (the Whites) against the communist revolution (the Reds). Under the leadership of **Comrade Marty** and a few others (416:34+), the crews of several French ships mutinied because of poor conditions aboard ship as well as their sympathies for the Russian communists. The French government conceded to the major demands, but afterward sentenced Marty to twenty years in a labor prison. He received a pardon and release in 1923.

418:32 **mania for shooting people:** True fact. See 416:34+.

418:34 *Como lo oyes:* As you hear it. It's true what you hear. It's true what they say.

419:2+ **at Escorial we shot I don't know how many:** Jordan received his orders for the bridge mission at El Escorial from General Golz, this corporal's division commander. The possibility of execution is a major factor motivating Jordan to continue the bridge mission (see 151:30). On El Escorial as a symbol of death in and of itself, see 4:33.

419:7+ *Tiene mania de fusilar gente:* He has a mania for shooting people. **Salvarsan** was a drug compound available in 1910 for treating syphilis. The corporal either bitterly jokes that Marty has killed more people than the extremely large number of syphilis cases the drug cured, the joke playing with the language of purification or cleansing; or he references the fact that the injections could be fatal. Salvarsan, also known as Ehrlich's 606, was the world's first chemotherapeutic compound, very much a symbol of modernity and progress (a mantle the communists wore).

420:10+ **The corporal and the soldier:** In the typed draft, this sentence replaces one about two soldiers having been "disarmed and searched" while standing next to Andrés and Gomez (MS12–017).

421:4+ **that winter with Lucacz in Siberia:** During the 1918 Russian Civil War, General Walter, the nom de guerre in Spain of Karol Świerczewski—the novel's Golz—did indeed fight in Siberia with Pál **Lukács** (see 233:18+), the nom de guerre in Spain of Máté Zalka, on the Bolshevik (Red) side. Their principal enemy was Alexander Vasilyevich **Kolchak**, who became the supreme leader of White Russia's government (1918–1920) based out of Omsk, Siberia. Polish by birth, Golz-Walter-Świerczewski fought in **Poland** for the Soviets in the 1919 Polish-Soviet War. The 1918 fighting in the **Caucasus** occurred during the Russian Civil War. The Soviet Union did not militarily enter **China**'s civil war (which began in 1927), yet another conflict between White Nationalists (Kuomintang) and Red Communists, but it did provide the communists logistical, material, and other support. Nicknamed the Red Napoleon, Mikhail Nikolayevich **Tukhachevsky** fought in the First World War and for the communists in the Russian Civil War before commanding Soviet forces in the Polish-Soviet War and going on to achieve major staff officer duties. On 22 May 1937, shortly after the novel's action, Stalin had Tukhachevsky arrested for treason as a Trotskyite. He was tried and executed in June. Kliment Yefremovich **Voroshilov**, another veteran communist commander from the Russian Civil War and the Polish-Soviet War who rose to military prominence, survived the purges. On **Gall**, see 233:30.

The Belgium-born Joseph **Putz** fought for the French in the First World War. In Spain, he began in 1936 as the Henri Barbusse Battalion's commander under Walter's (Golz's) XIV International Brigade. In February 1937, he replaced Walter as brigade commander, Walter having received a division command, only to lose command upon being wounded at the Battle of Jarama. Vladimir **Ćopić**, a Yugoslavian communist, commanded the XV International Brigade at Jarama (February 1937) and Belchite (August 1937). The American and Canadian battalions belonged to the XV; the North Americans found Ćopić too reckless with their lives.

Walter-Golz's chief of staff was not a Frenchman named **Duval** but a German communist, Ludwig Renn, who had originally been Hemingway's friend Hans

Kahle's XI International Brigade chief of staff (233:34+). Renn's novel of the First World War, *Krieg* (*War*), brought him much acclaim when it came out in 1928, the year before Hemingway's *A Farewell to Arms*. Hemingway has deliberately kept Renn out of the novel. **Varloff** (421:30) appears to be entirely fictional.

421:37 **Me cago en su puta madre:** I shit on his fucking mother; I shit on his whore of a mother **Está loco**: He is crazy.

422:8 **Hijo de la gran puta:** Son of the great whore.

422:9+ **The stupidity of this man:** In the draft, this sentence replaces by hand a typed one revealing Andrés's optimism about his fate—about not getting executed—"because his heart was good and his papers were in order," although he worries that his fate was tied to Gomez's, plus "the son of a bitch" Marty "was a foreigner" (MS12-017).

423:28+ **It is doubtful:** This is a rare third-person omniscient pronouncement. As Hemingway wrote to his editor, "I don't like to write like God. It is only because you never do it, though, that the critics think you can't do it" (to Maxwell Perkins, 26 Aug. 1940, *SL* 515). The paragraph's original draft focused on Marty's unwelcome interferences in military matters (*HLE* 515). The published declaration on the juggernaut of military operations once set in motion, against which the individual is powerless and inconsequential, in whose machinery he is churned through, is the stuff of Naturalism, of Stephen Crane's *The Red Badge of Courage*.

424:29 **dégonfler:** Deflate. Puncture.

425:6 **anyway?":** The closed quotation mark is a publication error; it should not be there.

425:33 **Tovarich Marty:** Russian for Comrade Marty.

425:38+ **(this was a lie):** This parenthetical remark, along with the following one—**(this was the truth although it was the corporal who had spoken)** (426:1–2)—are either additional narratorial intrusions or Karkov's asides to himself.

426:7 **Azerbaijan:** An area of the Caucasus that, at the time of the novel, was a Soviet republic.

426:14 **just how untouchable you are:** Like Koltsov, the actual man behind the fictional name, Karkov could be arrogantly incautious (see 231:20+).

426:19–20 ***Et maintenant fiche moi la paix:*** And now leave me in peace (alone), which sets up Karkov's sarcastic next line, "I leave you to your military labors."

427:32 **Their 45-mm. guns:** Almost certainly Soviet-made T-26 tanks. See 459:4.

428:6–7 **position Segovia:** As with "**position Avila**," these are the military names for observation posts, not the actual cities in Nationalist territory, most likely invented by Hemingway.

428:37–38 ***Nous sommes foutus. Oui. Comme toujours. Oui. C'est dommage. Oui:*** We are screwed. Yes. As always. Yes. That's too bad. Yes.

429:3+ **our planes:** These Republican aircraft have come from the Soviet Union.

429:37 ***Rien à faire. Rien. Faut pas penser. Faut accepter:*** Nothing to do. Nothing. Don't think. Accept it. Recall Pilar's claim that nothing ever happens to one that one does not accept (73:13–14).

430:3 ***Bon. Nous ferons notre petit possible:*** Good. We will do what little is possible.

CHAPTER FORTY-THREE

431:1 **Robert Jordan lay behind the trunk of a pine tree on the slope:** The final chapter opens the way the novel opened (1:1) and will end (471:31+).

432:3+ **as long as we can hold them here:** The rest of the paragraph is one of the novel's saddest, angriest moments, but not for its characters. As Hemingway writes it, then his readers read it, the Republic has lost its fight against fascism, and the fascist Axis powers of Germany, Italy, and Japan have launched the Second World War. If only France and the United States (and Great Britain) would have materially helped the Republic in 1937, perhaps the democracies of the world would not now, in 1940, be fighting for their lives. "The Time Now, the Place Spain," Hemingway titled an April 1938 article. The plea was too optimistic. One of his saddest, angriest nonfiction pieces is the preface to Luis Quintanilla's *All the Brave*, written by candlelight in Spain the night of 18 April 1938. Days earlier, the Nationalists had reached the Mediterranean Sea, severing the Republic between Valencia and Barcelona. The war was all but over: "Compared to the necessity of holding the line of the Ebro everything, including drawings of war by a great artist and one of your best friends, seems like chicken crut, and that is what makes this an unpleasant and churlish piece of writing" (in Trogdon, *Reference* 210). Before the United States entered the world war in 1941, some embittered American supporters of the Republic argued against their country's aiding the Western Allies, seeing such support as hypocritical and cowardly profiteering. In March 1939, Hemingway no longer felt obliged to fight for France, after its abandonment of the Spanish Republic (to Maxwell Perkins, 25 Mar. 1939, *SL* 482).[1]

433:17 **Zeiss 8-power glasses:** Binoculars from a German company established in 1846.

433:23+ **Jordan watched the squirrel:** The squirrel potentially alludes to the squirrel Henry Fleming watches in *The Red Badge of Courage*. In Crane's novel, Fleming uses the squirrel's flight reaction from a thrown pine cone to justify as natural—and therefore wise and right—his own flight from combat. Jordan, his squirrel scurrying away, does not follow suit. In this paragraph, as Jordan "trie[s] not to think at all," the squirrel becomes a model of nonthinking, nonworrying existence. The desire to be an unthinking forest creature belongs to the fantasy of union with Maria (e.g., 72:5–6; 262:22). Jordan's desire to have "the squirrel with him in his pocket," something "he could touch," recalls her fist clenched in his pocket and pressed to his thigh (270:18). His determination that "his elbows against the pine needles ... was not the same" appears to mean not the same as having a squirrel or something else warm to fondle in his pocket, but also or instead not the same as being with Maria. His body memory recalls making love to Maria on the pine-needled forest floor; his elbows are the only parts of his body the lovemaking scenes show awareness of (159:19; 379:24–25). The fantasy of unthinking existence and the two body memories deliver the feeling of loneliness that prompts him to think about Maria (434:1).

The draft contains a crossed-out passage following "not the same" (433:37), one of the strangest bits from the composition. In it, Jordan rails against "Mother Earth." She is not the place where life begins but the unfriendly place where people end up, lacking the comfort and consolation of something one can touch: "What shit, old Mother Earth and Santa Claus." He prefers the friendship of water and fire—of the real—even though one could drown him and the other burn him. His imagined pocketed squirrel could bite him, after all (*HLE* 518).

434:19 the sudden, clustered, thudding of the bombs: The prior chapter ends with the officers who are coordinating the offensive listening to their bombers head toward their targets. The timing across the two chapters does not skip a beat. The commas reinforce the feeling and rhythm of the thudding.

435:24 *Buena, caza:* Good hunting.

435:31–32 *Sin novedad:* No news. There's nothing to report or worry about. Anselmo killed the sentry: "I had to finish him" (***Tuve que rematarlo***).

436:33 like a bloody Tarzan: The title character of Edgar Rice Burroughs's *Tarzan of the Apes: A Romance of the Jungle*, which debuted in the October 1912 issue of *All-Story Magazine*. Burroughs lived in Hemingway's hometown of Oak Park, Illinois, at the time he created Tarzan; in a letter from 1919, Hemingway suggests having had at least one encounter with Burroughs (to William D. Horne [3 Feb. 1919], *Letters 1* 167–68). Hemingway had grown up on lectures and tales of white men's African adventures; he was fascinated by white men like Teddy Roosevelt and David Livingstone as well as (his image of) Africans (Reynolds, *Young Hemingway* 230–32). The son of British nobles abandoned by mutineers on the African coast and dead within a year, Tarzan was born in Africa and raised by an ape-creature tribe. By dint of his aristocratic breeding, he triumphs over Africa's native inhabitants, both animal and human. He becomes aware of his humanity and, eventually, of his noble birthright.

By 1940, Burroughs had published twenty-one Tarzan books and the US film industry had cranked out sixteen films (counting serials as single films). Burroughs was the first writer to incorporate himself and license related products and merchandise, not to mention the radio shows, comics, and the Boy Scout–inspired Tribe of Tarzan and Tarzan Clan of America (Vernon, *On Tarzan* 34). In the twentieth century, Tarzan was the most recognized fictional figure in the world.

The 1930s were the golden era for Tarzan films, both in the United States and abroad. When the film adaptation of *A Farewell to Arms* premiered in 1932 in Piggott, Arkansas (Hemingway's wife's hometown), it shared the marquee with *Tarzan, the Ape Man*, the first film starring the Austrian Olympic swimming sensation Johnny Weissmuller. Tarzan pictures played in Madrid throughout the war, sometimes more than one at a time: *Tarzan of the Apes* (1932), *Tarzan and his Mate* (1934), *The New Adventures of Tarzan* (1935), and *Tarzan Escapes* (1936). A "Tarzan" keyword search for *ABC Madrid* between 1 August 1936 and 30 November 1938 yields eighty-six hits.

Tarzan embodies the hybrid soul Jordan aspires to gain, the Great White Hope who saves the day, often saving Africans from other white invaders, yet also a fully integrated native. Jane Porter, the love interest, initially mistakes him for an African, as he dresses in native garb and sports black hair and a deep tan. The Tarzan imaginary flirts with the same race, gender, and sexual curiosities that piqued Hemingway, in the wings in *For Whom the Bell Tolls* and fully onstage in *The Garden of Eden*: miscegenation, homoeroticism, and incest.[2] The debate over the difference between killing animals and people—the difference between animals and people—in this novel riddles *Tarzan of the Apes* too. Both novels also dramatize the troubling and potentially self-destructive nature of human consciousness, of worrisomeness. Both novels are troubled by their participation in discourses of racist colonialism and colonial consumption.

437:7 **A bloody dream bridge:** The repetition of "dream" could point to Hamlet's suicide soliloquy: "To die, to sleep; To sleep, perchance to dream." See 452:6+.

437:36 **He gave them hell:** After this sentence, the draft included and deleted this assessment of Pablo: "He's good. He's bloody good and bloody awful" (MS13–002). The language suggests William Tecumseh Sherman's characterization of war as "hell" and "cruelty," and the suspension of morality sometimes required to wage it effectively (233:12+).

438:7+ **Roll Jordan, Roll:** Robert Jordan's name and his river-related mission link him to the Jordan River, the Israelites' crossing of it into the Promised Land, and its widespread symbolism of entering Heaven (see 4:6). "Roll, Jordan, Roll" was a nineteenth-century Black spiritual anthem of freedom attained by escaping into Heaven or across the Ohio or Mississippi Rivers into free states. The savior fantasy that the Republic's fate follows from Jordan's success or failure—"As Jordan goes, so go the bloody Israelites"—is rather self-centered. The recollection of the football spectators cheering him on, presumably in high school, calls back to his not having felt so young since leaving home for school (presumably college) (405:28+). An excised sentence in the draft corroborates that Jordan has death on his mind, as he regrets that his "strange" brain can't be preserved—unless maybe, he jokes to himself, "in alcohol" (MS13–002).

438:14 *Para qué?*: For what? What for?

438:15 **As Maine goes so goes the nation:** A political maxim from the American Civil War into the 1930s that saw Maine's September elections as predicting the November presidential election. Franklin D. Roosevelt's crushing defeat in November 1936 over Alf Landon, who won only Maine and Vermont, voided the maxim. "As Maine Goes" was the title, or was included in the title, of newspaper articles across the country. In the spring of 1937, the slogan's death knell was a current event. Jordan's employment of it could suggest his defeat and failure, or his success since Roosevelt was a Democrat sympathetic to the leftist Republican loyalists.

The word "Maine" would have had another resonance for Hemingway, the military history buff who had recently moved into a home outside Havana. The USS *Maine* sank in Havana Harbor in February 1898. Sensationalist newspapers blamed Spain. The spirit behind rallying cries like "Remember the *Maine!* To hell with Spain!" helped motivate the United States to launch the Spanish-American War. This was the war in which Col. Theodore Roosevelt led his "Rough Riders"—the 1st US Volunteer Cavalry—to victory at San Juan Hill (a cavalry allusion Jordan surprisingly never makes). This was the war Stephen Crane covered as a journalist and where he caught the yellow fever that probably contributed to his death two years later. This was the war that inspired the new Hispanism that created Robert Jordan, professor of Spanish (see 164:37). Spain's defeat sounded the death knell of its recent imperial past and the subsequent existential crisis of the Spanish army that led to the Spanish Civil War. As the *Maine* goes, so goes this novel. The *Maine* story also seeded a deep distrust of jingoist wartime journalism.

438:30 **brown three days ago:** After this sentence in the draft, Hemingway inserted and then cut an allusion to military history: "Take it easy Jordan meet Sir Francis Drake Sir Comrade Robert Jordan of the Spanish Armada" (MS13–002). The allusion is to the 1588 English naval victory over the Spanish Armada, which crushed King Philip II's plan to take the English throne. Vice Admiral Drake commanded the English. Philip II built El Escorial (4:33).

439:26 **At the bridge he pulled the:** In the draft, with the page break after these six words also comes a chapter renumbering, from 42 at the top of this page to 43 at the top of the new page (MS13–002). See appendix A.

441:5+ **Leave me here:** Fernando's fatal wounding, his decision to be left behind with his weapon, and his bearing the pain, prelude Jordan's fate.

443:1+ **now thou has what thou asked for last night coming home across the hills:** Anselmo references his prayer to "comport" himself "as a man" during the battle (327:21–22). He then asks to die "**quickly**" but takes it back, the prior prayer having been the last one he said he would make. Perhaps it is because he takes back the prayer, honoring his promise, that the prayer is granted in the upcoming pages.

444:19 ***Vaya mandanga!*:** What slowness! What sluggishness!

444:28 ***Es muy concienzudo!*:** He is very conscientious, exacting, or precise. Hemingway's draft language was *Es scientifico,* which matches the English in-text translation (MS13–002).

444:32 **Jordan's imaginary actions:** Crossed-out language in the draft clarifies that Pilar accuses Jordan of masturbating under the bridge: "*haciendo puñetas,*" which the draft then translates as his "committing the sin of a man" (MS13–002). Jordan earlier thought about masturbation and wondered what happened to the Biblical Onan, who sinned by letting his seed fall on the ground (42:20+). Combined with her prophesying ability, Pilar's accusation is as bleak as it is funny. Earlier in the chapter, Jordan wondered about a "superstition" concerning spitting into the gorge and thinks about how "prov[ing] it doesn't work" (432:33+).

The muting of references to ejaculating and defecating onto the Spanish earth (407:3+), the very earth Jordan enters into union with at novel's end, plus the removal of Jordan's rejection of a romantic return to Mother Earth as an idea as ridiculous as Santa Claus (433:24+), suggests a superficially romantic conclusion that dares the reader to deny the ugly, messy reality of it all.

446:37 **I don't forget anything:** The draft continues with an excised reflection that Jordan's "heart always felt dead" when things like combat ended, but never this dead (MS13–002).

447:4–5 **Fernando and Eladio were men, too:** In the draft, this line replaces Pilar's accusation of Jordan having no more feeling for dead comrades than he might for a killed pet (MS13–002). See prior entry.

448:13 *Sigue tirando:* Keep firing. Keep shooting.

448:37 the planes: Nationalist planes from Segovia coming to counter the Republican offensive (450:21–27).

448:38+ Maria had been with the horses: Maria's staying with the horses calls back to Pablo's and Jordan's thinking of her in terms of horses (see 16:34). Yet for the first time, the novel grants Maria an interior life. Soon hereafter, she defies his command (458:35); soon thereafter, he dies.

451:37 with Golz up at the pass: Hemingway drafted and then deleted a paragraph after this one and before the next published one. In it, Jordan admits that he had expected to die. He realizes that the offensive would not breach the Nationalist front line and that it had never been anything other than a diversion. He fails to make himself feel better by imagining that the Nationalist planes had been rerouted from the Nationalist campaign to conquer the Basque, providing some relief there (MS13-004).

452:3+ He had accepted being killed so completely that all of this now seemed unreal: "So completely" could modify either Jordan's complete acceptance of his death or the completeness of his death; technically it ought to modify the latter, to which it is grammatically more closely attached. Dying "completely" suggests completion as fulfillment—in this case, the text reveals that he has premeditated his response when he actually lies dying, "completely integrated now" (471:12).

The feeling of unreality **"through the absolute reality"** describes the material world "becoming like a dream" as Jordan imagines departing it for death's absoluteness (see 437:7), recalling the metaphor of life as a dream from Shakespeare's *The Tempest*: "We are such stuff / As dreams are made on, and our little life / Is rounded with a sleep" (IV.i.173–75). The language also suggests the moment of the bull's death in the ring, which Hemingway regards as "the original moment of truth, or of reality" (*DIA* 174; see 379:6+). A religious interpretation would equate the dreaminess to the ephemerality of earthly life and the "absolute reality" to the eternal truth of God.

The line also expresses the general trope of the surreality of war occasioned among other things by the proximity to death—the intensification or heightening of one's sensory and psychological experience during combat, which participants often describe as somehow more real and authentic than ordinary experience. As described by Yuval Noah Harari:

> When veterans try to give a detailed description of combat, they often describe it as an epiphany. The flow of time changes, slows down, or stops altogether. Unfamiliar sensations appear, and familiar sensations mutate. Awareness becomes completely absorbed in the present moment, and combatants feel more alive than

ever before. As the most basic laws of physics seem to bend and change, combatants are exposed to hitherto unknown layers of reality. (2)

The experience, sometimes described as a kind of ecstasy, grants truths unavailable except through the combat experience. For Harari, such experiences partake of the Romantic sublime encounter with the awesomeness of nature, "Yet war fitted the definition of the sublime far better than mountains" (155).

453:16 **whippet tank:** The term "whippet" designated smaller, lighter, faster, more maneuverable tanks, first developed by Great Britain during the Great War. "Tank" here should be understood to indicate tracks (instead of wheels) rather than armament type, as most of these lightly armored vehicles, sometimes called tankettes, carried mounted machine guns, not large-bore cannons. This Italian Fiat (458:24) is a CV 3/33 or CV 3/35, the most common Italian tanks in the war, their nomenclature designating their first production year. The CV 3 (or L3) series had a crew of two. Its fixed (nonrotating) turret, its height of less than two meters, and its hull's acute front slope match Jordan's description (453:12–13). Jordan aims his Lewis gun at "the slit above the machine gun" (454:17); some photographs clearly show a vision slit for the machine gunner above where the weapon projects from the turret. While the 1935 model was far more common in Spain, Jordan's mentioning a single

CV 33 tankettes at the Battle of Guadalajara (or Brihuega), 1937. (Public Domain)

CHAPTER FORTY-THREE · 309

machine gun points to the 1933 model, whose single 6.5mm machine gun the later model replaced with two 8mm guns.

456:37 where he never had slapped her: On her ass, as one would a horse to get it moving. Throughout this passage, with several comrades having just died, including his new best friend Anselmo, and the survivors not yet escaped to safety, Jordan apprizes Maria's breasts. Seriously, my guy?

To be more precise, Jordan thinks about the physical sensation of their bodies pressed together and notes that Maria's breasts could not "know" about the battle (a verb the Bible uses for sex). His attention to the comfort of her body divorced from the war could be read sympathetically as a reflexive emotional response to what he has just experienced and is still processing.

458:35 "Nay," she told him: Maria refuses Jordan's demand that she move up in line to cross the road sooner to reduce the danger the tankette poses. Her refusal puts her fate closer to his. This is the second time in the novel she asserts herself against him; the first time brought about the little death of his orgasm, almost typologically structuring this disobedience (157:26). The sequence of Jordan's fatal wounding after Maria's willful resistance suggests a symbolic consequence. In dying, he avoids a future with a spouse capable of acts of defiance, albeit trivial ones. In dying, he avoids the loss of independent selfhood uncompromised by oneness with another. One could argue that this is the book's climax, the moment the subsequent becomes consequent. Jordan, like Hemingway, blames his bullying mother for his father's suicide (339:2–3). Perhaps this is the moment Maria becomes a woman, the moment she claims her adult personhood—not the sex in which they fantasize the restoration by him, and then the yielding to him, of her virginity. The text connects these scenes when the Nationalist tanks make the "earth rise" (459:6, 25–26; see also the association of Greta Garbo, death, and a Republican tank [137:16+]). Jordan chooses integration with the earth rather than domestic union with Maria. The novel has raised the specter of a baby (79:29; 89:1+). After receiving his fatal wound and commanding her to ride away, he says, "Now thou art obeying" (464:7). In death, he secures his male prerogative.

Such a reading comports with other Hemingway texts, from for example the very early story "The End of Something," in which a youth breaks up with his girlfriend because she doesn't need his instructions anymore; to the novels *The Sun Also Rises* and *A Farewell to Arms*, which creatively and poignantly orchestrate avoidance of family life; to his famous stories from the 1930s that kill off unhappily married, "bitched" middle-aged male protagonists, "The Snows of Kilimanjaro" and "The Short Happy Life of Francis Macomber." In two letters written two years apart, Hemingway revealed that the heart of *The Fifth Column* wasn't the war in Spain, but the male protagonist's dilemma between a life of domesticity and a life alone but for his work.[3]

Soviet BT-5 used by the Spanish Republican Army. (Wikimedia Commons / Public Domain)

459:4+ **sweeeish-crack-boom!:** A second tank is now firing at the fleeing band. From sound and impact, Jordan identifies the munition as a "**47 mm**" shell (459:32) before seeing the "big" tank (460:20). No such tank existed, but the error belongs to the publisher or the printer, not Hemingway, as his typed draft and the Armstrong typescript accurately call the round a 45mm (MS15–011).[4] The two contenders with 45mm guns are Soviet tanks that the Nationalists would have captured from Republican forces, a T-26 or a BT-5, both crewed by three. Although practically the same height, the BT-5 fits the "heavy, squat" description (460:36) better because of the shorter length from hull-top to turret-top—in effect, a shorter neck.

The BT-5 would be a slight anachronism, since these tanks did not arrive in Spain until 10 August 1937, about nine weeks later. Nevertheless, their newness explains Jordan's failure to recognize the tank, as would never have happened with a T-26, which the Soviets had been shipping to Spain since October 1936 (Zaloga 27). Its image appeared everywhere. His familiarity with the T-26 also explains how he knows the 45mm round by sound and impact.

How unheard of: a Hemingway hero not to know or not to show he knows a detail like the kind of a tank. The deliberate choice to make him unaware yet not entirely unaware—whether from a BT-5 or a T-26, the 45mm shell still indicates a captured Republican vehicle—dramatizes a certain suppression of knowledge while still providing its trace (through the rounds' trajectory), as the novel does with Jordan's death drive. Determined to avoid capture, determined to die but not by his own hand, Jordan is killed by a captured Republican tank.

463:6 I go always with thee: Jordan repeats this sentiment several times during this final conversation, in terms of either going with Maria or being with her after his death. For Cleanth Brooks, this language secures Jordan's atheism: "The human spirit still craves its immortality. In his trying to tell her that she must now live for both of them, that the only wisp of immortality that he can have will be what remains of him in her mind, there is the touching though finally desperate effort to secularize the conception of immortality and bring it down to some naturalist possibility" (18). Brooks's position aligns Jordan's spirituality with his understanding of Hemingway, whom he sees as "too thoroughly committed to naturalism and too honest a man to try to delude himself into thinking that one can ever get outside the dimension of time; yet he is aware of what other men have meant in saying that an experience of completeness, wholeness, and power and delight may convey an aspect of eternity" (18). Hemingway and Jordan don't necessarily share the same attitude about the divine and the eternal. Jordan's rhetoric could also be mundane. His belief in immortality with Maria might be a very limited belief, or simply lip service in the interest of getting her to safety while leaving him behind (see 466:22).

465:11 *Quieres?*: Do you want?

465:12 *No hace falta*: No need. It is not necessary.

465:14 *Me cago en la leche que me han dado!*: I shit in the milk I've been given!

465:31 *Qué puta es la guerre*: *Puta* can translate to "bitch" or "whore." The latter is the better translation than Hemingway's provided "bitchery," because of how *whore* speaks to the temptation, to war's seduction, as well as to the financial motive for wars, which Hemingway detested.

465:33 "*Salud, Inglés*," Agustín said, clenching his right fist: The final words any character says to Jordan repeat the nickname denoting foreignness even as it expresses solidarity. A raised fist was the wave and salute throughout Republican Spain.

466:7+ Now, finally and at last, there was no problem: The problem of the bridge enlarges to become "any problem" or all problems—in the words of Hamlet, "the slings and arrows of outrageous fortune," a "sea of troubles," the "heart-ache and the thousand natural shocks / That flesh is heir to," the "whips and scorns of time" (III. ii.3–13). More specifically, the problem of suicide that plagued both Hamlet and Jordan. In the final stage of preparing the book for publication, Hemingway wrote his editor that Jordan started the novel, there on the forest floor, with the problem he had always suffered from, the problem that plagued him his whole life and this whole novel, the problem that only death could put behind him there again on the forest floor (to Maxwell Perkins, 26 Aug. 1940, *SL* 514). The repetition of "now" three times in four lines faintly echoes the second lovemaking scene (379:6+) and perhaps resonates with Hamlet's soliloquy's labeling death "a consummation / Devoutly to be wish'd" (III.ii.8–9). The word "devoutly" offers a tantalizing recontextualization of *la gloria*, the word the lovers apply (separately) to their sexual union (379:37; 380:21+).

Another problem now behind Jordan is how to dispatch Maria. The draft originally ends the paragraph with his admitting he wasn't sure what he told her was true but that he had to come up with something to say "awfully fast" (MS13-005). The published novel confirms a rhetoric of expediency, not romance, when he tells himself to "try to believe" it anyway (466:22).

466:21–22 **no good to think about Maria:** After this paragraph, Jordan references her by name once (467:31) and by pronoun one other time (469:8).

467:7 **for a year now:** The rebellion began on 17 July 1936, and today is 31 May 1937. Jordan came to Spain in the summer of 1936 on a one-year leave from his university (165:13–15).

467:8–9 **The world is a fine place . . . I hate very much to leave it:** A lovely line completely at odds with John Donne's understanding of the proper attitude for a holy death. See front matter: title and epigraph.

467:13–15 **I wish there was some way to pass on what I've learned, though. Christ, I was learning fast there at the end:** The text could pass on what Jordan has learned—where has that omniscient narrator gotten off to?—except that it doesn't, because Jordan can't, dead or still alive: for all the time the audience spends inside Jordan's headspace, what he has learned is to a great extent a matter of embodied experience, of incommunicable flesh-witnessing—

> What is it about war that reveals truth? Most late modern veterans point to the extreme bodily conditions of war: hunger, cold, exhaustion, injury, the presence of death—and occasionally the thrill of killing and the exhilarating rush of combat. Eschewing the rationalist authority of logical thinking, and the scientific authority of objective eye-witnessing, veterans lay claim to the visceral authority of "flesh-witnessing." They are neither thinkers nor mere eye-witnesses. Rather, they are men (and occasionally women) who have learned their wisdom with the flesh. . . .
>
> [A] flesh-witness can never really transmit her knowledge to other people—she cannot really describe what she witnessed, and the audience cannot really understand. (Harari 7)

The reader learns what Jordan has learned only by nature of having experienced Jordan's last days with him, by its being embodied in the reader, word made flesh—if Hemingway is as good a storyteller as Stendhal and Pilar, anyway (134:33+).

467:20 There's no *one* thing that's true. It's all true: This is an astonishing epiphany. The Spanish Civil War erupted due to irreconcilable truth-claims. The two sides, Nationalist and Republic, suffered their own internal truth-conflicts. Jordan's epiphany is not a Catholic truth but a catholic truth that admits the Catholic. The novel, over its long course and despite its primary allegiance to the truth of Jordan's subjectivity, has presented other people's truths and has given reasons to question Jordan's. As Hamlet said, "there is nothing either good or bad but thinking makes it so" (II.ii.268–70). All people's truths, all subjectivities, are true; or no one individual thing or truth is true by itself, because truth resides only in the aggregate. Truth involves ideas, embodied experiences, and objects (things). Perhaps only the dying can afford this epiphany.

Its context begins with a vision of the landscape, of Madrid "**Just over the hills there**" (467: 15+). In alternating between the "beautiful" and the "true," the passage evokes John Keats's famous closing lines from "Ode on a Grecian Urn," a classic ekphrastic poem that muses on mortality, history, romantic love, and art:

> "Beauty is truth, truth beauty,"—that is all
> Ye know on earth, and all ye need to know.

For Jordan in this passage, the beautiful and the true include Madrid, the pastoral Guadarrama landscape, old women drinking blood, the warplanes on both sides, and everything else in creation. It's all true. It's all beautiful. True because beautiful, beautiful because true, true and beautiful simply because they exist. But also because they have been transformed into art, *into this novel in our hands,* as with the stories depicted on Keats's poem's urn. The urn's two scenes, its two faces, correspond to the novel's intertwined stories of romance and sacrificial violence: the lovers for whom time stands still, forever now as object of art; and the heifer led to slaughter to preserve the community, the dark passage to nowhere. What the novel offers, then, is what the *cante jondo* and the *saetas,* and the paintings of El Greco and the poetry of Saint John of the Cross, provide amid death and suffering: the consolation of art (380:21+). The first time Jordan paid attention to his own process of describing enemy aircraft, ending with "mechanized doom," it made him want to write (87:8–9). It is a forlorn consolation, because the urn, itself a vessel of the dead, teaches the poem's narrator that the slowing of time, the forestalling of death, can only transpire in art.

In the passage's final line, Jordan gruffs, "**the hell they are**"—a reversal in the spirit of his earlier reversal of the *gloria* "nonsense" (386:26)—in order to yank himself back to urgent reality. Art and meditation must wait. He has enemies to kill, comrades to save. The epiphany belongs to the dead, which he isn't, not just yet. And because it is all true: the planes are beautiful in form, if ugly in function; inspiriting to Nationalists, repugnant to Republicans. The romance of abstract, aesthetic sentiment; the realism of people slaughtering people. *For Whom the Bell Tolls* is a meditation, not a treatise or parable, whose only certainty is uncertainty.

In the draft, the paragraph ends with the beauty of the planes "no matter what they drop" (MS13–005). Hemingway changed the line and added the final rejoinder.

470:38 **slipping away from himself as you feel snow:** Perhaps an allusion to Meditation II of Donne's *Devotions upon Emergent Occasions:* "The heavens are not the less constant, because they move continually, because they move continually one and the same way. The earth is not the more constant, because it lies still continually, because continually it changes and melts in all the parts thereof. Man, who is the noblest part of the earth, melts so away as if he were a statue, not of earth, but of snow" (8). When the four horsemen appeared, his shirt wet from the "melting snow," Jordan had "a hollow feeling in his chest" (282:32–33).

Compare this "slipping away" language with Jordan's slipping "into" the "unreality" of his Madrid-with-Maria fantasy, a slipping he writes in terms of "sexual acceptance" (342:25+); compare that "unreality" and "acceptance" with the "unreal" of "all of this now" he feels once he has "accepted being killed" (452:3+).

471:3 **Jordan's luck held:** Jordan receives his wish to remain conscious for a few moments longer. It appears his pain has greatly abated as he bleeds out and slips toward death. With the end minutes if not seconds away, the suicide question has become moot. The "Robert Jordan" that begins the next two paragraphs marks the narrative's final departure from a contorted first-person approximate point of view. Sensory observation replaces cogitation. After his feeling of complete integration (471:12), an observing witness, even a motion camera, could mostly report this final passage.

471:12 **completely integrated now:** The mountains of Sun Valley, Idaho, where Hemingway worked on the novel in the fall of 1939, bear a striking similarity to the Guadarrama Mountains. A community of Basque immigrants lived in the area. Hemingway drew on his present environs in his descriptions of the Spanish terrain, tapping into the sights and smells and mood around him. A month after Hemingway's arrival, one of the people who invited him, Gene Van Guilder, died in a hunting accident. Van Guilder had instantly won over Hemingway, who in a letter to his brother described Van Guilder as "a swell guy (best friend out here)."[5] His widow asked Hemingway to give the eulogy. Although he was still several months from drafting Jordan's death, the language of the graveside eulogy anticipates this moment in the novel. Van Guilder's hunting gear and saddle went with him into the ground (Baker, *Life Story* 343). After detailing Van Guilder's love for the country in all four seasons, Hemingway concluded:

Now those are all finished. But the hills remain. Gene has gotten through with that thing we all have to do. His dying in his youth was a great injustice. There are no words to describe how unjust is the death of a young man. But he has finished something that we all must do.

And now he has come home to the hills. He has come back now to rest well in the country that he loved through all the seasons. He will be here in the winter and in the spring and in the summer, and in the fall. In all the seasons there will ever be. He has come back to the hills that he loved and now he will be a part of them forever.[6]

The last line serves as Van Guilder's epitaph.

Hemingway's language for Jordan's death also draws on his elegy "On the American Dead in Spain" published in the 14 February 1939 number of the *New Masses,* on the two-year anniversary of the Abraham Lincoln Brigade's first combat, at the Battle of Jarama. Robert Merriman, on whom some readers believe Hemingway based Jordan, was wounded at Jarama. The fighting was so fierce that the British dubbed their defensive turf "Suicide Hill." The winter conditions of the Jarama battle neatly coincide with the novel's May snow in the Guadarrama, such that the elegy's references to cold and snow more or less fit the scene of Jordan's death. When Hemingway wrote the elegy, the war was all but lost for the Republic. Franco's dictatorship and the Second World War loomed. The elegy looked backward and forward in its conclusion:

> The Spanish people will rise again as they have always risen before against tyranny.
>
> The dead do not need to rise. They are a part of the earth now and the earth can never be conquered. For the earth endureth forever. It will outlive all systems of tyranny.
>
> Those who have entered it honorably, and no men ever entered earth more honorably than those who died in Spain, already have achieved immortality. (3)[7]

For all its beauty, the novel's rendering of one man's now-consummated life borrows its central conceit from an abundance of wartime rhetoric. It is an unoriginal staple of speeches, propaganda, and poetry: Those who died for the Republic merged with the land itself. They became Spain; they would be the seed of its democratic reflowering (Vernon, *Second War* 58). The Spanish communist leader and spokesperson Dolores Ibárruri (La Pasionaria) used it in her 28 October 1938 farewell address to the International Brigades, thousands of whom "are staying here with the Spanish earth for their shroud" (Ibárruri 313–14).[8] If Hemingway hadn't seen the text of her speech before, he read it in *Somebody Had to Do Something,* the slender memorial booklet for Jim Lardner that Hemingway cosponsored, published in 1939. "On the American Dead in Spain" is the book's lead piece, whose first lines begin beneath a drawing with the caption, "It is not corpses they bury, but seed" (3).⁹ On the Lardner book, see 352:34.

While Jordan's line can be understood as matter-of-fact resignation, the words "completely integrated" suggest to many readers a more profound embrace. Josephs encapsulates the various reconciliations and incorporations:

> *Integrated:* knowing la gloria; having felt the earth move; being selfless and giving completely of himself; accepting that he can have had his whole life in seventy hours; believing now in the intuitive along with the rational, the female side of him and the male, the dark along with the light; feeling himself a part of humanity, bridged to John Donne's *Mankinde;* lying on the Spanish earth in touch with nature; sacrificing; saving. (*Undiscovered* 153)

Other scholars are skeptical, such as Lawrence Broer (see introduction) and Jeffrey Walsh, who read Jordan as disillusioned with the cause and retreating to individual fulfillment. Broer evokes the matador, Walsh the American frontiersman (96).

For Jonathan Vincent, Jordan's death is a nostalgic enterprise that compensates for—or liberates him from—industrial militarization's subjugation of individuals to the modern nation-state's war machine, what Crane's *The Red Badge of Courage* calls the "blue demonstration." Vincent's analysis takes in Jordan's perspective all novel long:

> While Jordan subordinates himself to communist discipline, attempting to shed his self-concern and submerge himself in the larger cause, his commitment to the resistance gradually erodes, more prominently manifesting as an experiment in self-enlargement. . . . Ever more the aesthetic tourist, he comes to relish the war's immediacy and aesthetic "intensity," recodifying its experience as an event expressly for him. (136)

Much analysis of Jordan's final reverie overlooks the depth to which Jordan has infused Maria with his vision of Spain (and vice versa). Jordan achieves "aesthetic 'intensity'" with her because he has foredoomed his life, for Spain and for this ephemerally everlasting love. And vice versa: the religious ecstasy Jordan feels embracing Maria can be viewed as political rather than spiritual. As Vincent demonstrates, the modern era in which Hemingway and Jordan grew up was steeped in the language of militant, religious nationality, which framed warmaking

> as sense participation in an enduring national soul: life through death. . . . Such an understanding highlights the religious dimensions of modern nationalism as a kinship of love, not simply contract, or law, or territoriality. Thus did some mobilization literature tap into what [Paul] Kahn calls, variously, the "erotic" or "sacred"

character of the political. In times of existential crisis, he contends, "forgotten ultimates"—residual, miraculous "faculties of soul" retained from repressed origins in divine and monarchical sovereignty—spring to life anew under the returned signs of love and sacrifice. (63)

Spain's imagined embrace, not Maria's, completes him "now," in contrast to the ticking time bomb of "now" in the couple's last lovemaking.

There are less theoretical ways to be suspicious. The novel has educated its readers to scrutinize Jordan's subjective use of the word "now," to probe whether it simply marks a temporal instant or reaches for the everlasting, whether that everlasting now is ever anything more than his earnest, desperate reaching. See 452:3+ on Jordan's prior use of the adverb "completely" in relation to death. The novel has also established a pattern of realistic reversals by Jordan of his romantic conceits. He spurned his ideas about Berbers and premodern Iberians (287:6+), of *la gloria* (386:26), and of the beautiful truth of all things (467:21–22). Who's to say that he won't reverse himself again before he dies, that he won't overturn this fantasy of complete integration as one more dollop of wishful poppycock? To his Soviet translator Ivan Kashkin, Hemingway wrote about his difficulty composing "On the American Dead in Spain" because there's "not much to say about the dead except that they are dead" (23 Mar. 1939). If Jordan has resorted in his final hour to the Republican cliché about living forever in the Spanish earth, does he know he's using a bit of rhetoric "like enemies of the people" that "came into his mind without his much criticizing them in any way" (164:4–5)?

471:22–23 The officer was Lieutenant Berrendo: Readers might find Berrendo's appearance at novel's end ludicrously convenient, a bit like Jane Porter's being cast ashore by a mutinous crew on the Africa coast at the exact same spot where baby Tarzan's parents were cast ashore by a mutinous crew eighteen years earlier in Burroughs's *Tarzan of the Apes*. Tarzan is all Romance, of course. At this moment, perhaps *For Whom the Bell Tolls* lets its Romance trump its Realism. For some readers, Berrendo's presence fits a religious understanding of the novel, whereby coincidence evidences the hand of God.

471:33 He was waiting: The bullfighting term is *recibir*, which Hemingway defines in *Death in the Afternoon*: "to kill the bull from in front awaiting his charge with the sword without moving the feet once the charge has started; . . . Most difficult, dangerous and emotional way to kill bulls; rarely seen in modern times. I have seen it executed completely three times in almost three hundred bullfights" (442).

471:33+ the sunlit place: Rod Romesburg finds that the text troubles harmonious integration with the natural world, as Jordan, duty-bound to people, "gives the physical beauty of the natural world as a sighting for one last killing. His last act condemns humanity to a fundamental separation between us and nature. His integration is not himself into the order of nature, but an assimilation of that order into the chaos of humanity" (148–49). In this vein, one might read tension in the novel's last line, when Jordan "feel[s] his heart beating against the pine needle floor" (471:35–36), *against* meaning *touching* and *adjoining* but also possibly *in opposition to*.

Lt. Berrendo's approach is redolent of his earlier moving through the pines into a place of sunlight, the narrator likening the beams through the branches to "the columns of a cathedral" (see introduction; 326:27–28). Berrendo's plaintive Ave Maria intercessory prayer in that passage juxtaposes now with Jordan's recent farewell to his earthly Maria. Jordan's spiritual crossing is less obviously indicated. His feeling of complete integration is subjective; the novel provides no omniscient validation. Or, not *either/or,* but *both,* Berrendo's heaven-bound Christian sacrifice is as true as Jordan's earthbound, more pagan one.

The Spanish word *berrendo* means pronghorn, an ungulate related to antelopes and goats and native to the American northern plains, including the states of Montana and Wyoming. The final encounter of Jordan's life, then, is a kind of homegoing for him as well as a parting continuance of the book's mediation on hunting (animals) and killing (people).

471:35–36 He could feel his heart beating against the pine needle floor of the forest: The novel ends almost exactly as it (and this final chapter) began, with Robert Jordan lying on the "pine-needled floor of the forest" (1:1), looking down from a gentle mountainside slope toward the site of a violent future he triggers and that secures his inevitable death. Readers love to observe that the novel has thus come full circle, to use the ready phrase. The spiritual view of the novel detects in this cyclic language the spirit of the funeral service of the Anglican Church's *Book of Common Prayer*—"we are mortal, formed of the earth, and unto earth shall we return. . . . All we go down to the dust; yet even at the grave we make our song: Alleluia, alleluia, alleluia." Josephs presents a less spiritual but no less triumphant and transformative view in calling attention to the word *heart:* "Jordan's heart, absent from the beginning description, becomes our final image; and it is the hero's heart, the beating of which still gives him life. It is the lover's heart, which he has found in this round of seventy hours." Josephs continues:

> By giving up his idea for an epilogue to tie up the loose ends, Hemingway was able to leave Robert Jordan there on the Spanish earth, at the still point of the turning world, in that eternal present, his heart still beating, suspended artfully on the edge of death just as the lovers were suspended in ecstasy, undefeated by time. Only in the true undiscovered country of the imagination . . . can such a vicarious release from human bondage and mortality take place. (*Undiscovered* 154)

Is it disingenuous to turn the reader's eyes away just shy of the flesh-rending spray of bullets? Or does the novel acknowledge the inevitability of human brutality while insisting on moments of personal and even transcendent triumph? Can Romance and Realism coexist? Can it all be true, in art if nowhere else?

NOTES

1. Louis Fischer felt the same way (letter to "Kingsley," 20 July 1939 [Princeton University, Seeley G. Mudd Manuscript Library, Louis Fischer Collection, MC#024]).

2. See Vernon, *On Tarzan*, chapter 4, "Native Son" (miscegenation); chapter 6, "Monkey Business" (homoeroticism); chapter 5, "All in the Family" (incest).

3. To Maurice Speiser, 11 July 1938 (USC); to Mr. Langner, 19 Mar. 1940 (Yale Collection of American Literature, Beinecke Rare Book and Manuscript Library, Yale University).

4. The extant galley proofs do not have these pages. The first edition includes the error, as does the Hemingway Library Edition. Future editions, postcopyright, should correct it.

5. To Leicester Hemingway, 2 Nov. 1939 (David Meeker Collection, The Community Library, Ketchum, Id.).

6. *Idaho Statesman* (2 Nov. 1939), 4; reprinted in Trogdon, *Reference* 216–17.

7. The *New Masses* issue included an advertisement for a Memorial Meeting "in Honor of All Americans Who Died Fighting for Democracy in Spain," listing Hemingway as a speaker, on Wednesday 22 February (George Washington's birthday) at the Manhattan Center. The event was a fundraiser for the Rehabilitation Fund for veterans of the war. The other speakers were Vincent Sheean, Lt. Col. John Gates, and Langdon Post, the event chairperson (25).

8. Ibárruri incorrectly dates it 15 November. Tremlett prints the entire speech (513–15).

9. All the drawings "*are taken from a portfolio titled* Galicia Martir *by a Spaniard, Castelao*" (x). Five hundred copies of the book were printed, to raise money for the James Lardner Memorial Fund, organized to repatriate Americans stuck in France or in Nationalist prison camps and "to rehabilitate the wounded" (inside back cover). The fund's officers were Will Rogers Jr. (chair), Ring Lardner Jr. (vice-chair), and Howard Goddard (executive secretary). In addition to Hemingway, the other sponsors were: Jay Allen, Ralph Bates, Heywood Broun, James Cagney, Langston Hughes, John Howard Lawson, Andre Malraux, Carey McWilliams, Tom O'Connor, Dorothy Parker, Ludwig Renn, Frank Scully, Vincent Sheean, and Donald Ogden Stewart (iv).

APPENDIX A

Composition

The novel's inception has two contenders: October 1938 and March 1939.

Two letters from late October 1938 report from Paris that he has written two chapters of a novel (to Arnold Gingrich, 22 Oct. 1938, *SL* 472; to Maxwell Perkins, 28 Oct. 1938, *SL* 474). In the preceding months, Hemingway's correspondence shows him eager to begin writing a novel. Then nothing until 7 February 1939, when he let his editor Maxwell Perkins know that he'll return to the novel as soon as he finishes a trio of stories (for the money to carry the family once he dedicates himself to the book; *SL* 479). A week later, he sailed his boat *Pilar* from his home in Key West to Havana, Cuba, where he settled into the Hotel Ambos Mundos before eventually moving outside the city into an old house and his future home, the Finca Vigía, with Martha Gellhorn.

In late March, Hemingway wrote two letters announcing a new novel, already swelled to 15,000 words (to Ivan Kashkin, 23 Mar. 1939, *SL* 480; to Maxwell Perkins, 25 Mar. 1939, *SL* 482). The letter to Perkins says that the novel emerged from a short story he'd been reluctant to write (*SL* 482); as he wrote to another friend on April 4, he hadn't intended to write a novel (to Thomas Shevlin, 4 Apr. 1939, *SL* 484). The top of the very first draft page records its beginning as the first day of March, a date affirmed by future letters referencing the novel's anniversary. When he gifted the draft to Gus Pfeiffer, his wife Pauline's uncle, Hemingway documented its origins in March 1939 in Cuba (JFK Item 83 Description: MS10-008). The first clear section of the draft—what will be the published novel's first two chapters—is about 13,000 words. This section's typescript ends on page 46, where it continues by hand for several lines onto page 47. Hemingway's notes in his marginalia that he stopped typing on 19 March—a few days after returning to Key West—and resumed by hand on 9 April—a few days after returning to Cuba (though there's good reason to believe he wrote those final lines, onto page 47, before he got back to Cuba). The two chapters he wrote in the fall of 1938 appear to have been permanently sidelined. This material perhaps survived in the two "rabbit" fragments set in a wartime Madrid hotel (JFK Items 522a & 824; see frontmatter: Martha Gellhorn); the first one is actually divided into two chapters, perhaps the chapters Hemingway wrote about to Gingrich and Perkins.

The following table presents a timeline of the novel's composition, based mostly on the extant draft's chapters and pagination, and references to chapters and pages in Hemingway's letters. Occasionally, the draft includes a date scribbled at the top of a page or in a margin. Hemingway added a word count to many (but crucially not all) draft pages, and calculated totals for select dates on a few of the folders containing drafted material. The letters also document progress based on the total word count. This is the least accurate dating tool, because Hemingway constantly circled back to make revisions, doing line edits, inserting new pages, doubtless discarding pages, and we don't know whether, when, or how he recalculated the ongoing total. The daily word count calculations on surviving folders include inserted revisions to some earlier point in the draft, perhaps replacement material, and so do not necessarily reflect forward progress. The daily count for 17 July 1939 adds up the count for seven pages that turn out to be draft pages 295–301, when his forward progress has moved past page 340 (679 words, MS12-005 folder). The letters also approximate the word count by thousands, no finer. Comparing the published novel's chapter-by-chapter and page-by-page word counts with the correspondence's ongoing total sometimes approximately matches his progress but often significantly diverges. On 7 May 1940, he wrote Lambert Davis that he was finishing chapter 37—published Thirty-Eight—and had reached 170,000 words. The published novel's word count through Thirty-Eight, however, is about 144,000 words. The number he reported to Davis is closest to the novel's total word count of about 175,000.

The early chapter divisions did not fall into place until about one-third of the way through the novel—although at the time, Hemingway imagined a much shorter book than it wound up becoming. On 10 May, for example, in the middle of writing the published chapter Eight, he considered the novel half-completed.[1] Except for chapter VIII (published as Ten), the Armstrong typescript leaves a blank after the word *CHAPTER* from published Three to published Fifteen. By the end of 1939, the chapters seemed to have settled to Hemingway's satisfaction, as the letters begin to report progress in terms of chapters. Armstrong filled in the blank for VIII because Hemingway wanted to show it off. Rightly so—this is Pilar's tale from the beginning of the war (chapter Ten).

Hemingway sorted out the early chapter divisions in the late summer or early fall of 1939. Until this moment, draft chapters Three to Fourteen trailed the published book by two. The Armstrong typescript for draft Fourteen is blank, but after two pages of draft chapter Fourteen, Hemingway rebooted the chapter by inserting pages from the Armstrong typescript with "Fifteen" inserted by hand, in red ink, in the blank. Beginning with draft chapter Three, he promoted all chapters by hand, in red ink, by one. This may have been when Hemingway split those first forty-seven pages into two chapters (although that split, plus draft Two's promotion to Three, were made in pencil, not red ink). At this point, then, the revised draft chapters, as well as the Armstrong typescript and the galley proofs, trail the published book chapters by one.

The published chapters become finalized when Hemingway split chapter Three from the galley proofs into chapters Three and Four and bumped up all that followed. Hemingway informed his editor about the split in his letter of 26 August 1940, upon the airmailed return of corrected galley proofs, but he might have made the decision before he finished writing the book, sometime in June. On 21 May, Hemingway informed Perkins a "Chapter 40" was done, and two days later wrote him again to say that he expected two more chapters; on 31 May, he wrote Perkins that he was at work on draft Chapter 42, "It's either the last or next to last" (Trogdon 209). On 7 June, over six weeks before he finishes the published Forty-Three, the novel's last chapter, Hemingway wrote to Mike Strater of "43 chapters done and one more to do," the final bridge fight in a forty-fourth chapter.

Draft Forty is the first chapter where the Armstrong typescript matches the draft's chapter number. That it becomes Forty-One perhaps indicates that the splitting of chapter Three into Three and Four happened after he drafted Forty, so after 21 May.

In the middle of draft chapter Forty-One, the paragraph that begins "It is doubtful if the outcome of Andrés's mission would have been any different" (with a preceding phrase)—from published Forty-Two (423:28+)—begins a new chapter on a typed page headed "Chapter 43." But this new chapter heading is crossed out, and the page numbers on this and the next typed page are replaced by hand with 41—so page 43-2 (typed) becomes page 41-18 (written)—and all the following handwritten chapter draft page numbers indicate draft Chapter 41 (MS12–017; MS12–018). Hemingway's letter to Strater must have been referring to this aborted Chapter 43, these two surviving typed pages that wound up a continuance of draft Chapter Forty-One (published Forty-Two) and perhaps several pages discarded and now lost. The letter a week earlier to Perkins might have referred to a discarded and now lost draft Chapter 42 that preceded the aborted Chapter 43.

There's another wrinkle. In the middle of draft Chapter Forty-Two, Hemingway changed the pagination to indicate Chapter Forty-Three, as the page after 42-30 becomes 43-31 (published page 439) and all subsequent pagination for the chapter follows suit. Because Hemingway did not change "Forty-Two" to "Forty-Three" on the draft chapter's first page, Armstrong replicated the title she saw when she began typing Chapter Forty-Two, even as her typescript text matches the manuscript text after the pagination switch. In other words, it appears that Hemingway split Three into chapters Three and Four to create Forty-Three before Armstrong finished her typescript.

Was there a drafted chapter 42, lost forever now to the trash can? Did Hemingway initially envision an arrangement for the final chapters, of basically the same material spread over forty-four instead of forty-three chapters and a different alteration sequence? Whatever the case, the split of Three into Three and Four must have happened during June's dizzying rewriting and restructuring. It perhaps resulted from the decision not to serialize the novel in *Cosmopolitan* magazine, a decision that probably happened in mid-May[2] (a magazine would have required the longer chapter).

Hemingway cabled Perkins "BRIDGE ALL BLOWN AM ENDING LAST CHAPTER" on 1 July 1940. Two weeks later, Hemingway wrote that he was working on the last four pages (to Michael Lerner, 13 July 1940, Outgoing). Although he would continue to fiddle with the ending into August, he finished the draft on his forty-first birthday: Sunday, 21 July 1940.[3]

The following table assumes that draft page numbers match page references in Hemingway's correspondence. From 21 July to 2 November 1939, Hemingway only reported word counts. These counts appear to reasonably date the draft's progress. The table's inclusion of reported word counts, in relation to the published novel's word count, should be understood to be inexact if nevertheless generally helpful for the timeline. A similar imprecision should be understood when matching up his location in the draft as he changed physical locations. Boldfaced type indicates handwritten text; the text within braces was originally in red.

Pub. Chpt.	Date	Draft Page	Draft	Armstrong typescript "CHAPTER"	Galley Proofs	Source
Cuba then Key West						
1	1 Mar. 39	1	[blank]	I	ONE	
2	19 Mar. 39	46	**Chapter Two** insert/split finished first section to "after thy equipment" (34:29)	II	TWO	MS10–009
3			**Chapter ~~Two~~ Three**	—	THREE	
Cuba						
4	9 Apr. 39	46	resumed drafting		insert/split: FOUR	MS10–009
5		94	**Chapter ~~Three~~ {Four}**	—	~~FOUR~~ FIVE	
6		110	**Chapter ~~Four~~ {Five}**	—	~~FIVE~~ SIX	
	2 May 39	111	"That's the way to talk," the woman said . . . (65:25+)			to M. Speiser
7		118	**Chapter ~~Five~~ {Six}**	—	~~SIX~~ SEVEN	

Pub. Chpt.	Date	Draft Page	Draft	Armstrong typescript "CHAPTER"	Galley Proofs	Source
8		132	**Chapter Six {Seven}**		SEVEN EIGHT	
	5 May 39		on p. 135: then drew them together . . . (74:25+)			to M. Speiser
	10 May 39		on p. 149: thee (77:20)			to M. Speiser and to M. Perkins
	10 May 39		150 pages done			to G. Durán
	12 May 39	149	thee." ¶ Anselmo came out of the cave (77:20+)			
	17 May 39		179 pages done			to J. Ivens
9		180	**Chapter Seven {Eight}**		EIGHT NINE	
	22 May 39		199 pages done: to "Pilar slapped him on the shoulder" (93:18)			to M. Speiser
			on p. 199: begins "'Thou never never had one,' Pilar told"			to C. Scribner
10		208	**Chapter Eight {Nine}**	VIII	NINE TEN	
	26 May 39		on p. 212: "'Then let us talk of what . . .'" (98:32)			to G. H. Hemingway

Pub. Chpt.	Date	Draft Page	Draft	Armstrong typescript "CHAPTER"	Galley Proofs	Source
	30 May 39		on p. 213: "'Much;' the woman said. 'Much . . .'" (99:2)			to M. Perkins
	13 Jun. 39		on p. 243: "'A peasant who had left the lines . . .'" (120:12)			to C. Thompson
	13 Jun. 39		p. 243 done, to "against the door to try to see" (120:33)			to S. Murphy
11		257	Chapter ~~Nine~~ {Ten}		~~TEN~~ ELEVEN	
	30 Jun. 39		about 280 pages done, to about "Nor I', . . ." (144:7)			to G. & P. Hemingway
12		296	Chapter ~~Ten~~ {Eleven}		~~ELEVEN~~ TWELVE	
13		307	Chapter ~~Eleven~~ {Twelve}		~~TWELVE~~ THIRTEEN	
	14 Jul. 39		on p. 340: "All right, Robert Jordan said . . ." (175:29)			to G. & P. Hemingway
	17 Jul. 39		manuscript insert final pages of pub. Chpt.11, from "We'll see,' Pilar said" (150:36) to end, per word count on manuscript (MS11–002) corresponding to date count on folder at MS12–005			

Pub. Chpt.	Date	Draft Page	Draft	Armstrong typescript "CHAPTER"	Galley Proofs	Source
14			Chapter ~~Twelve~~ {Thirteen}	——	~~THIRTEEN~~ **FOURTEEN**	
	28 Jul. [39]	343	first page of chapter draft			MS11-004
	28 Jul. [39]		approaching 70,000; "; the very hardest part to write"			to P. & M. Pfeiffer
15		364	Chapter Thirteen	——	~~FOURTEEN~~ **FIFTEEN**	
	16 Aug. 39		73,000 (pub. ch. 14 ≈ 70,000; pub. ch. 15 ≈ 75,000)			to M. Speiser
	23 Aug. 39		74,000			to P. & G. Hemingway
	27 Aug. 39		74,000			to M. Perkins
			Chapter Fourteen	FIFTEEN		
		380	[two pages]	[Second Armstrong typescript]		
			CHAPTER {FIFTEEN}			
16			[Armstrong typescript]		~~FIFTEEN~~ **SIXTEEN**	

Pub. Chpt.	Date	Draft Page	Draft	Armstrong typescript "CHAPTER"	Galley Proofs	Source
	16 Sep. 39		80,000 words (published Chpt 16 ≈ 80,000)			to M. Speiser from Cooke City, MT
Sun Valley, Idaho						
	7 Oct. 39		80,000 words			to E. Rolfe
17		404	Chapter Sixteen	SIXTEEN	~~SIXTEEN~~ **SEVENTEEN**	
18		416	Chapter Seventeen	SEVENTEEN	~~SEVENTEEN~~ **EIGHTEEN**	
19		447	{Chapter Eighteen}	EIGHTEEN	~~EIGHTEEN~~ **NINETEEN**	
	27 Oct. 39		over 90,000 words (published ch. 18 ≈ 92,500 words)			to M. Perkins
	2 Nov. 39		into 90,000			to L. Hemingway

Pub. Chpt.	Date	Draft Page	Draft	Armstrong typescript "CHAPTER"	Galley Proofs	Source
20		460	Chapter Nineteen	NINETEEN	~~NINETEEN~~ **TWENTY**	
	[5 Nov. 39]		on p. 474: "and it was true. But she was sleeping . . ." (264:13)			to M. Perkins
21		475	Part Four **Chapter Twenty**	PART FOUR: TWENTY	TWENTY **ONE**	
22		493	**Chapter Twenty-One**	TWENTY-ONE	TWENTY-~~ONE~~ **TWO**	
	18 Nov. 39		Over 100,000 (pub. ch. 21 ≈ 100,000)			to A. Gingrich
	24 Nov. 39		Over 100,000			to H. Mowrer
	4 Dec. 39	508	"Robert Jordan said." (277:4)			
23		515	{**Chapter Twenty-Two**}	TWENTY-TWO	TWENTY-~~TWO~~ **THREE**	
	7 Dec. 39	517	"Robert Jordan heard his heart beating" (280:24)			
	8 Dec. 39	522	"Primitivo was raising and lowering his" (282:17)			

Pub. Chpt.	Date	Draft Page	Draft	Armstrong typescript "CHAPTER"	Galley Proofs	Source
Cuba						
24		538	**Chapter Twenty-Three**	TWENTY-THREE	TWENTY-~~THREE~~ FOUR	
	21 Jan. 40		finished ch. 23			to E. Rolfe
25	25 Jan. 40	551	**Chapter Twenty-Four**	TWENTY-FOUR	TWENTY-~~FOUR~~ FIVE	
	26 Jan. 40	556	… stopped. If we go there we are lost too. (296:23)			
	27 Jan. 40	565	"He should learn to control them,' Pablo said." (299:5)			
26	9 Feb. 40	573	**Chapter Twenty-Five**	TWENTY-FIVE	TWENTY-~~FIVE~~ SIX	
27		593	**Chapter Twenty-Six**	TWENTY-SIX	TWENTY-~~SIX~~ SEVEN	
	18 Feb. 40		writing Sordo's last stand			to M. Perkins
28		653	**Chapter Twenty-Seven**	TWENTY-SEVEN	TWENTY-~~SEVEN~~ EIGHT	

Pub. Chpt.	Date	Draft Page	Draft	Armstrong typescript "CHAPTER"	Galley Proofs	Source
29		676	**Chapter Twenty-Eight**	TWENTY-EIGHT	TWENTY-EIGHT NINE	
	10 Mar. 40		28 chs. done			to W. Seward
30		689	**Chapter Twenty-Nine**	TWENTY-NINE	TWENTY-NINE **THIRTY**	
31		699	**Chapter Thirty**	THIRTY	THIRTY ONE	
32		1 [700]	**Chapter Thirty-One**	THIRTY-ONE	THIRTY-ONE **TWO**	
33		1 [707]	{Chapter Thirty}-Two	THIRTY-TWO with insert	THIRTY-TWO **THREE**	
	6 Apr. 40		ch. 32 done; "well into" ch. 33			to M. Perkins
34		1 [712]	**Chapter Thirty-Three**	THIRTY-THREE	THIRTY-THREE **FOUR**	
35		1 [736]	**Chapter Thirty-Four**	THIRTY-FOUR	THIRTY-FOUR **FIVE**	

Pub. Chpt.	Date	Draft Page	Draft	Armstrong typescript "CHAPTER"	Galley Proofs	Source
36		1 [747]	Chapter Thirty-Five	THIRTY-FIVE	THIRTY-FIVE **SIX**	
37		1 [757]	Chapter Thirty Six	THIRTY-SIX	THIRTY-SIX **SEVEN**	
38		1 [773]	**Chapter Thirty-Seven**	THIRTY-SEVEN	THIRTY-SEVEN **EIGHT**	
	1 May 40		on ch. 37			to A. Jenkinson
	7 May 40		finishing ch. 37			to L. Davis
39		1 [801]	**Chapter Thirty-Eight**	THIRTY-EIGHT	THIRTY-EIGHT **NINE**	
40		1 [814]	Chapter Thirty-Eight Nine	THIRTY-NINE	THIRTY-NINE **FORTY**	
41		1 [815]	Chapter Forty	FORTY	FORTY ONE	

Pub. Chpt.	Date	Draft Page	Draft	Armstrong typescript "CHAPTER"	Galley Proofs	Source
	21 May 40		finished ch. 40			to M. Perkins
42		1 [840]	Chapter Forty-One	FORTY-ONE	FORTY-ONE TWO	
43		1 [863]	Chapter Forty-Two	FORTY-TWO [916 pp.]	FORTY-TWO THREE	
			pagination switches to ch. 43 at "wire back out through the hitch" (439:26+)			
	31 May 40		writing [discarded] ch. 42 (see above)			to M. Perkins
	7 Jun 40		discarded ch. 43 done (see above)			to M. Strater
	1 Jul 40		bridge blown			to M. Perkins
	13 Jul 40		on final four pages			to M. Lerner
	21 Jul 40	[1002]	finished			to C. Spiegel 23 Aug. 40; also JFK Item 83 description (MS10-008)

NOTES

1. To Gustavo Durán, 10 May 1939 (Residencia); to Maurice Speiser, 10 May 1939 (USC).

2. Trogdon interprets Hemingway's letter to Perkins of 13 May 1940 as Hemingway having learned that *Cosmopolitan* declined serialization. Nothing in Hemingway's letter, however, directly says the magazine made a decision, only that Harry Burton "tried to jew me down to a 30,000 serial price and no decision until he has it all" (*Lousy Racket* 208). Which couldn't happen for another several weeks. Hemingway's letter then asks about the Book of the Month Club possibility. In a later letter, Hemingway says he decided against serialization in order to better angle for the book club sale (to Charles Scribner, 12 Sept. 1940 [PUL]).

3. On fiddling: letter to Gustavo Durán, 13 Aug. 1940. On birthday: letter to Clara Spiegel, 23 Aug. 1940, *SL* 510]; and inscription to Gus Pfeiffer (JFK #83 headnote; also JFK 0630).

APPENDIX B

In Memoriam Frank G. Tinker Jr.

By 28 July 1939, well into writing the novel, Hemingway had another suicide in mind. Frank Tinker was a volunteer American pursuit (fighter) pilot for the Republic. Hemingway met him soon after the writer arrived in Spain in the spring of 1937. According to Tinker's war memoir, after getting out of Spain he had trouble establishing his US citizenship with the American consulate in Paris. He, like most American volunteers, had relinquished his passport before entering Spain, because joining the International Brigades violated American law:

> Finally, [the vice-consul] said that if I could get some American citizen who knew me to identify me, his department would condescend to give me the passport.... But luck was again on my side. I went over to Harry's Bar that night and the first person I saw after entering was my old Madrid friend, Ernest Hemingway. When he heard what I needed, he immediately offered to make the required identification. After a few further delays and obstacles I was at last formally identified on August 25 and a passport was made out in my name. (311)

If Hemingway hadn't known it before, he would have learned from Tinker's 1938 memoir that Tinker had flown as part of a fighter escort to bombers during the Segovia Offensive (232–39).[1] Hemingway included an excerpt from the memoir in *Men at War*, titling it "The Italian Debacle at Guadalajara" (939–46).

A bellhop found Frank Glasgow Tinker dead in a Little Rock, Arkansas, hotel room in June 1939. Newspapers reported his death as a suicide from a .22 caliber pistol ("Aviator"). Hemingway probably got the news from his Piggott, Arkansas, in-laws, the recipients of his 28 July 1939 letter: "Was sorry I did not see Frank Tinker before he took such a drastic step. Have argued myself out of that so often that I think I could have kicked the idea out of his head. He was a good fellow; very brave and a truly fine flyer" (to Paul and Mary Pfeiffer, 28 July 1939, *SL* 495). The word count in the letter locates Hemingway around the start of chapter 16. In a letter a year earlier, about the memoir, Hemingway described Tinker as fearless in the air.[2] Family and friends did not believe Tinker killed himself—for one thing, because he always carried a .45 Colt pistol in his suitcase ("Frank"). He was twenty-nine.

Frank Tinker, standing far left; Whitey Dahl, squatting center, white hair. (Reproduced from F. G. Tinker Jr., *Some Still Live*)

Tinker titled his memoir *Some Still Live*. His DeWitt, Arkansas, tombstone reads "¿Quien Sabe?" (*Who knows?*).

Between the memoir's publication and Tinker's death, Hemingway wrote "Night before Battle." Tinker's memoir misremembers the chronology, placing Hemingway in Spain before the famous writer actually arrived. Still, moments in Hemingway's story and Tinker's memoir closely resemble one another. Both feature a pilot carrying champagne in an elevator who recently had to bail out of his shot-up plane. The story calls him Baldy, a "rummy fake Santa Claus" (*CSS* 452); the real person, Whitey Dahl, sported Santa-white hair.

The Frank character in Hemingway's story never shows up:

"'Where's Frank?'" Baldy asks, and asks again: "'Listen, where's Frank?'" (*CSS* 452).

NOTES

1. Reviews appeared in late May 1938. See, for example, F. James, "The Fighting in Spain," *Democrat & Chronicle Sunday Magazine* (Rochester, NY; 29 May 1938), 11; and Paul Swensson, "The Daredevil Airmen Who Fight in Spain," *Minneapolis Tribune* (29 May 1938), 9.

2. To Edward Garnett [1938].

APPENDIX C

"For Whom the Gong Sounds"

Cornelia Otis Skinner

(With apologies, somewhat, to Mr. Hemingway)

Robert Jordan snapped the lock of his revolver, made certain the machine-gun at his hip was handy, gripped his màquina and continued to crawl up the Guadarrama hills on his belly. Robert Jordan grinned. You're almost there, he told himself. He'd been telling himself things like that all day. Robert Jordan was hunching over a rocky ledge now, hanging on by the bristles of his chest. The warm Spanish earth scraped his belly. Robert Jordan could feel a pine-cone in his navel. It was a resinous pine-cone, the kind they grow in Catalan. These people, Robert Jordan thought, turn out to be people. There's no getting away from that. Sure there isn't. Hell, no.

A gypsy was sitting on a rock strumming a guitar. With one bare foot he practiced range-finding with a sub-machine gun. The other foot lay idly on his màquina. The gypsy's face was the color of old Virginia ham.

"Salud," Robert Jordan said.

Fernando eyed him through the barrel of a Lewis gun. Robert Jordan made certain his Mauser was uncocked. The gypsy's voice was like golden Amontillado gurgling out of a wineskin.

"Thou wast of the street car, camarada?"

"Comé no? Why not?" Robert Jordan thought of the last street car he had blown up. They had found arms and legs all over the roofs. One femur had gone as far as Valladolid.

"Quien sabe," said Jacinto. "Who knows."

"Each according to each," said Ignacio. "Street cars I have a boredom of. We have heard what we have heard. Si. Yes." He flung some hand grenades into a nose-bag, trampling them firmly with his rope-soled feet.

"Hombre," said Anselmo, squinting down the barrel of a 45mm. gun. "One goes to the cave."

"Bueno," said Robert Jordan. "Good."

Robert Jordan and the gypsy continued to scrabble up the hill past a deserted saw-mill. Juanito burrowed his way, Andalusian fashion, into a pile of saw-dust, and emerged after a little while, grinning sweatily. Robert Jordan opened his pack, making sure that all was as it had been. He unlocked the grommet, untied the drawstrings, uncoiled the insulating wire and tossed the caber. His groping fingers came in reassuring contact with a bunch of bayonets. His automatic pistols were safe, so were the hand grenades, the old French '75 and his father's sawed-off shotgun. His father had been a preacher, a man of God back in Ohio. He drew forth a bottle of TNT and a quart of Haig and Haig. It might come in handy when the time came for blowing up the boardwalk. He studied the bottle of Haig and Haig and thought, no. They'll take me for a fascist. A bloody fascist, that's what they'll take me for. He put the bottle of Haig and Haig back into the bandolier of ammunition, screwing it down with a grenade pin, a belaying pin and a Skull and Bones pin. Then he got out a magnum of Courvoisier. This is more their stuff, he said to himself. Then to make sure, he pulled out a carton of Abdullas and a box of Corona Coronas. That was all he had in his knapsack except, of course, his sleeping bag, a case of Old Grandad, three pairs of rope-soled shoes and an asbestos suit for when he blew up the boardwalk.

An old man sat at the mouth of the cave guarding the entrance with a Mauser, a Howitzer, a Winchester and a Fly-swatter.

"Salud, camarada," said the old man.

"Equally," said Robert Jordan, then added, "Hola!" for good measure.

"Thou. Thou wast of the street-car?"

"Wast."

He is old, Robert Jordan said to himself. And the gypsy is old, too, and some day I will be old. But I'm not old yet, not yet, I'm not old.

"He knows of which whereof he speaks of, old one," the gypsy was saying.

"Que va, young one."

"It makes well to joke, old one."

"Pass, middle-aged one."

The mouth of the cave was camouflaged by a curtain of saddle-blankets, matadores' capes and the soles of old espadrilles. Inside it smelt of man-sweat, acrid and brown . . . horse-sweat sweet and magenta. There was the leathery smell of leather and the coppery smell of copper and borne in on the clear night air came the distant smell of skunk.

The wife of Pablo was stirring frijoles in a Catalonian wineskin. She wore rope-soled shoes and a belt of hand grenades. Over her magnificent buttocks swung a 16th century canon take from the Escorial.

"I obscenity in the obscenity of thy unprintable obscenity," said Pilar.

"This is the Ingles of the street car. He of the boardwalk to come soon."

"I obscenity in the unprintable of the milk of all street cars." The woman was stirring the steaming mess with the horns of a Mura bull. She stared at Robert Jordan and then smiled. "Obscenity, obscenity, obscenity," she said, not unkindly.

APPENDIX C · 339

"Que va," said Robert Jordan. "Bueno. Good."

"Menos mal," said El Sordo. "Not so good."

"Go unprint thyself," said Pilar. The gypsy went outside and unprinted himself.

The girl with the shaved head filled a tin pail full of petite marmite and handed it to him and she gave him a great swig from the wine-skin and he chewed the succulent bits of horsemeat and they said nothing.

And now Esteban stood beside him on the rim of the gorge. This is it, Robert Jordan said to himself. I believe this is it. I did not think it was this to be it but it seems to be it, alright. Robert Jordan spat down the gorge. Pablo watched the fast disappearing globule of man-saliva then slowly, softly spat down the gorge. Pilar said obscenity thy saliva then she too spat down the gorge. This time it was Pablo's gorge.

The girl was walking beside him.

"Hola, Ingles," she said. "Hello, English."

"Equally, guapa," said Robert Jordan.

"Que va," said the girl.

"Rabbit."

Robert Jordan pulled the pistol lanyard up, cocked his màquina and tightened the ropes of his rope-soled shoes.

"Vamos," he said. "Let's go."

"Si," said Maria. "Yes."

They walked on in silence until they came to a rocky ledge. There were rough rocks and thistles and a wild growth of Spanish dagger. Robert Jordan spread his buffalo robe out for himself and allowed Maria to lie near him on a bed of nettles. The earth moved.

"Rabbit," said Robert Jordan. "Hast aught?"

"Nay, naught."

"Maria," he said. "Mary. Little shaved head."

"Let me go with thee and be thy rabbit."

The earth moved again. This time it was a regular earthquake. Californians would have called it a temlor.

Robert Jordan had reached the boardwalk. He lay in the gorse and rubble. He had his infernal machine beside him, some hand grenades, a blunderbuss, an arquebus and a greyhound bus. His màquina was held securely in his teeth. Across the ravine Anselmo was sniping off sentries as they passed.

Listen, Robert Jordan said to himself, only the fascist bombs make so much noise he couldn't hear. You had to do what you did. If you don't do what you do now you'll never do what you do now. Not now you won't. Goltz was right. A real surprise surprised people. Sure it does. He lashed the wire through the rings of the cotter pins of the release levers of the wires of the main spring of the coil, insulating it with a piece cut off the bottom of his rope-soled shoes.

What about the others . . . Eladio and Ignacio . . . Anselmo and St. Elmo? And Rabbit? I wonder how Rabbit is. Stop that now. This is no time to think about Rabbit . . . Or rabbits. Better think about something else. Think about llamas. It's better to breathe, he thought. It's always much better to breathe. Sure it is. The time was gradually, inevitably drawing near. Someone in the valley was singing an old Catalonian song. A plane crashed quietly overhead. Robert Jordan lay still and listened for the gong to sound.

(Skinner, *Soap behind the Ears* 88–96)

WORKS CITED

Abel, Werner, and Enrico Hilbert. *Sie werden nicht durchkommen: Deutsche an der Seite der Spanischen Republik un der sozialen Revolution.* Verlag Edition AV, 2015.
Adams, J. Donald. "The New Novel by Hemingway." *New York Times Book Review,* 20 Oct. 1940, p. 1.
Ackelsberg, Martha A. *Free Women of Spain: Anarchism and the Struggle for the Emancipation of Women.* AK Press, 2005.
Allen, Jay. "Slaughter of 4,000 at Badajoz, 'City of Horrors,' Is Told by Tribune Man." *Chicago Tribune,* 30 Aug. 1936, p. 2.
Álvarez, José E. *The Spanish Foreign Legion in the Spanish Civil War, 1936.* U Missouri P, 2016.
Archibald, David. *The War That Won't Die: The Spanish Civil War in Cinema.* Manchester UP, 2012.
Auden, W. H. *W. H. Auden,* poems selected by John Fuller, 80th anniversary edition. Faber and Faber, 2009.
"The Avatar." Episode 2, *Hemingway.* Directed by Ken Burns and Lynn Novick, written by Geoffrey C. Ward, Florentine Films, 2021.
"Aviator Kills Self at Hotel." *The Blytheville Courier* [Arkansas], 14 June 1939, p. 1.
Axelsson, George. "Rebel Spain Sees a Bullfight Again." *New York Times,* 20 Oct. 1936, p. L15.
Baker, Carlos. *Ernest Hemingway: A Life Story.* Charles Scribner's Sons, 1969.
———. "Hemingway's Empirical Imagination." *Individual and Community: Variations on a Theme in American Fiction,* edited by Kenneth H. Baldwin and David K. Kirby, Duke UP, 1975, pp. 94–111.
———. *Hemingway: The Writer as Artist.* Princeton UP, 1972.
Bataille, Georges. *Erotism: Death and Sensuality.* Translated by Mary Dalwood, City Lights, 1986.
Bates, Ralph. "Companero Sagasta Burns a Church." *The Left Review,* vol. 2, no. 13, Oct. 1936, pp. 681–87.
Bauer, Carlos. "Introduction." *Poem of the Deep Song,* by Frederico García Lorca, translated by Carlos Bauer, City Lights, 1987. pp. i–iii.
Becker, Ernest. *The Denial of Death.* Free Press Paperbacks, 1997.
Beebee, Thomas O. *The Ideology of Genre: A Comparative Study of Generic Instability.* Pennsylvania State UP, 1994.
Beevor, Anthony. *The Battle for Spain: The Spanish Civil War 1936–1939.* Penguin, 2006.
Bell, Douglas. *Wellington's Officers.* Collins, 1938.
Bolloten, Burnett. *The Spanish Civil War: Revolution and Counterrevolution.* U of North Carolina P, 2001.

"'Books That Shaped America' Exhibition to Open June 25." *News from the Library of Congress*, 21 June 2012 (revised 2 July 2012), https://www.loc.gov/item/prn-12-123/.

Borrow, George. *The Bible in Spain*. With the notes and glossary of Ulick Ralpf Burke, John Murray, 1907.

———. *Zincali; or, An Account of the Gypsies of Spain*. John Murray, 1908.

Bowers, Claude G. *My Mission to Spain: Watching the Rehearsal for World War II*. Simon & Schuster, 1954.

Brenner, Gerry. *Concealments in Hemingway's Works*. Ohio State UP, 1983.

Broadwell-Gulde, Anna. "Pilar's Turn Inward: Storytelling in Hemingway's *For Whom the Bell Tolls*." In *Teaching Hemingway and War*, ed. Alex Vernon. Kent State UP, 2016, pp. 224–37.

Broer, Lawrence R. *Hemingway's Spanish Tragedy*. U Alabama P, 1973.

Brogan, Jacqueline Vaught. "Parody or Parity: A Brief Note on Gertrude Stein and *For Whom the Bell Tolls*." *The Hemingway Review* vol. 15, no. 2, spring 1996, 89–95.

Brontë, Emily. *Wuthering Heights*. Modern Library, 1994.

Brooks, Chris. "An Analysis of American and Canadian Volunteers Compiled by the International Brigades in Spain." *The Volunteer*, 26 Sept. 2017, https://albavolunteer.org/2017/09/an-analysis-of-american-and-canadian-volunteers-compiled-by-the-international-brigades-in-spain/.

Brooks, Cleanth. *The Hidden God: Studies in Hemingway, Faulkner, Yeats, Eliot, and Warren*. Yale UP, 1963.

Burnam, Tom. "Primitivism and Masculinity in the Work of Ernest Hemingway." *Modern Fiction Studies*, vol. 1, no. 3, Aug. 1955, pp. 20–24.

Carnell, Simon. *Hare*. Reaktion, 2010.

Carroll, Peter N. *The Odyssey of the Abraham Lincoln Brigade: Americans in the Spanish Civil War*. Stanford UP, 1994.

Carroll, Peter N., Michael Nash, and Melvin Small, editors. *The Good Fight Continues: World War II Letters from the Abraham Lincoln Brigade*. New York UP, 2006.

Carroll, William C. "*Love's Labor's Lost*: A Modern Perspective." *Love's Labor's Lost* by William Shakespeare, edited by Barbara A. Mowat and Paul Werstine, Folger Library Edition, Washington Square Press, 1996, pp. 253–68.

Chamberlin, Brewster. *The Hemingway Log: A Chronology of His Life and Times*. UP of Kansas, 2015.

Christensen, Bonnie. *Red Lodge and the Mythic West: Coal Miners to Cowboys*. UP of Kansas, 2002.

Cirino, Mark. *Ernest Hemingway: Thought in Action*. U of Wisconsin P, 2012.

———. "One True Sentence #26 with Illan Stavans." *The Hemingway Society*, produced by Michael Von Cannon, 2023, https://www.hemingwaysociety.org/podcast.

———. *Reading Hemingway's* Across the River and into the Trees: *Glossary and Commentary*. Kent State UP, 2016.

Cirino, Mark and Robert K. Elder. "Was Ernest Hemingway the Original American Sniper?" *Huffington Post*, 6 Sept. 2016 (https://www.huffpost.com/entry/was-ernest-hemingway-the-original-american-sniper_b_57cecfc8e4b06c750ddbbf1f).

Cochran, Charles B. Letter. *The Times* (of London), 30 June 1948.

Comley, Nancy R., and Robert Scholes. *Hemingway's Genders: Rereading the Hemingway Text*. Yale UP, 1996.

Connelley, William Elsey. *Quantrill and the Border Wars*. Torch Press, 1910.

Cortada, James W., editor. *Modern Warfare in Spain: American Military Observations on the Spanish Civil War, 1936–1939*. Potomac Books, 2012.
Cowles, Virginia. *Looking for Trouble*. Harper & Brothers, 1941.
Crane, Stephen. *The Red Badge of Courage*. Edited by Donald Pizer, Norton Critical Edition, 3rd ed., Norton, 1994.
Dale, Helen. "Two Queens Were Born in Sweden." *Photoplay*, vol. 44, no. 5, Oct. 1933, pp. 28–29, 113.
Davis, Lydia. *Essays One*. Farrar, Straus and Giroux, 2019.
Dearborn, Mary V. *Ernest Hemingway: A Biography*. Alfred A. Knopf, 2017.
DeGuzmán, María. "Hemingway in the Dirt of a Blood and Soil Myth." Eby and Cirino, pp. 9–27.
———. *Spain's Long Shadow: The Black Legend, Off-Whiteness, and Anglo-American Empire*. U Minnesota P, 2005.
Deuss, Edward L. "Poets Suicide Bares Strange Love Triangle." *San Francisco Examiner*, 15 Apr. 1930, p. 3.
Dickenson, Victoria. *Rabbit*. Reaktion, 2014.
Donaldson, Susan V. *Connecting Voices: The American Novel 1865–1914*. Twayne, 1998.
Donne, John. *Biathanatos*. With Introduction and Commentary by Michael Rudick and M. Pabst Battin, Garland, 1982.
———. *Devotions Upon Emergent Occasions and Death's Duel, with The Life of Dr. John Donne by Izaak Walton*. Preface by Andrew Motion, Vintage, 1999.
Dos Passos, John. *Travel Books and Other Writings 1916–1941*. Library of America, 2003.
Douglass, Carrie B. *Bulls, Bullfighting, and Spanish Identities*. U Arizona P, 1997.
Eagleton, Terry. *Sweet Violence: The Idea of the Tragic*. Blackwell, 2003.
Eastman, Max. *Artists in Uniform: A Study of Literature and Bureaucratism*. Alfred A. Knopf, 1934.
Eby, Carl P. "Gardens of *Eden* and *Earthly Delights*: Hemingway, Bosch, and the Divided Self." *Hemingway Review*, vol. 37, no. 2, spring 2018, pp. 65–79.
———. *Hemingway's Fetishism: Psychoanalysis and the Mirror of Manhood*. SUNY Press, 1999.
———. "'In the Year of the Maji Maji': Settler Colonialism, the Nandi Resistance, and Race in *The Garden of Eden*." *Hemingway Review*, vol. 39, no. 1, fall 2019, pp. 9–39.
———. *Reading Hemingway's* The Garden of Eden: *Glossary and Commentary*. Kent State UP, 2023.
Eby, Carl P., and Mark Cirino. *Hemingway's Spain: Imagining the Spanish World*. Kent State UP, 2016.
Eby, Cecil D. "The Real Robert Jordan." *American Literature*, vol. 38, Nov. 1966, pp. 382–83.
Ehrenreich, Barbara. *Blood Rites: Origins and History of the Passions of War*. Virago, 1998.
Ellis, Havelock. *The Soul of Spain*. Houghton Mifflin, 1924.
Esdaile, Charles J. *The Spanish Civil War: A Military History*. Routledge, 2019.
Faber, Sebastiaan. *Anglo-American Hispanists and the Spanish Civil War*. Palgrave MacMillan, 2008.
Fenimore, Edward. "English and Spanish in *For Whom the Bell Tolls*." *ELH*, Mar. 1943, vol. 10, no. 1, pp. 73–86.
Fitch, Noel Riley. *Walks in Hemingway's Paris: A Guide to Paris for the Literary Traveler*. St. Martin's Griffin, 1989.
Ford, Richard. *Gatherings from Spain*. John Murray, 1851.

———. *Hand-book for Travellers in Spain, and Readers at Home*. Part I. John Murray, 1845.

"Frank Glasgow Tinker (1909–1939)." *Encyclopedia of Arkansas*, https://encyclopediaofarkansas.net/entries/frank-glasgow-tinker-4581/.

Frank, Waldo. *Virgin Spain: Scenes from the Spiritual Drama of a Great People*. Horace Liveright, 1926.

Fraser, Ronald. *Blood of Spain: The Experience of Civil War, 1936–1939*. Penguin, 1981.

Frederic, Harold. Review of *The Red Badge of Courage*, by Stephen Crane. *New York Times*, 26 Jan. 1896, p. 22.

Frye, Northrop. *Anatomy of Criticism*. 1957. New foreword by Harold Bloom, Princeton UP, 2000.

———. *The Secular Scripture: A Study of the Structure of Romance* Harvard UP, 1976.

Fuller, Sam. *A Third Face: My Tale of Writing, Fighting, and Filmmaking*. With Christa Lang Fuller and Jerome Henry Rudes, Alfred A. Knopf, 2002.

Gallagher, Matt. "Ernie and Me." *The Paris Review*, 2 Feb. 2016, https://www.theparisreview.org/blog/2016/02/02/ernie-and-me/.

Gautier, Théophile. *A Romantic in Spain*. Interlink, 2001.

Gellhorn, Martha. "Memory." *London Review of Books*, vol. 18, no. 24, 12 Dec. 1996, https://www.lrb.co.uk/the-paper/v18/n24/martha-gellhorn/memory.

Gitlow, Benjamin. *The Whole of Their Lives: Communism in America, a Personal History and Intimate Portrayal of Its Leaders*. Foreword by Max Eastman, Charles Scribner's Sons, 1948.

González Rosado, Carlos, and Juan García del Río Fernández. *Grupo de Fuerzas Regulares de Ceuta nr. 3. 1915–1985, 70 años al servicio de España*. Ceuta, 2012.

Graham, Helen. *The Spanish Civil War: A Very Short Introduction*. Oxford UP, 2005.

Grant, Ulysses S. *Ulysses S. Grant: Memoirs and Selected Letters*. Library of America, 1990.

Greeson, Helen M. *Gendering the Republic and the Nation: Political Poster Art of the Spanish Civil War, 1936–1939*. 2012. Master's thesis, Georgia State University, https://doi.org/10.57709/2767981.

Guill, Stacey. "'Los Aviónes!': The Interpretation of a New Warscape in *The Spanish Earth*, Picasso's Guernica and *For Whom the Bell Tolls*." *Hemingway Review*, vol. 34, no. 1, fall 2014, pp. 13–29.

———. "Pilar and Maria: Hemingway's Feminist Homage to the 'New Woman' of Spain." *Hemingway Review*, vol. 30, no. 2, spring 2011, pp. 7–20.

———. "The Red and White Terrors: Civil War and Political Savagery in Ernest Hemingway's *For Whom the Bell Tolls*." *Hemingway Review*, vol. 40, no. 1, fall 2021, pp. 29–52.

Guttmann, Allen. *The Wound in the Heart: America and the Spanish Civil War*. Free Press of Glencoe, 1962.

Haapakamaki, Michele. "Writers in Arms and the Just War: The Spanish Civil War, Literary Activism, and Leftist Masculinity." *Left History*, vol. 10, no. 2, fall 2005, pp. 33–52.

"Half-Naked Moors Leave Trail of Carnage in Irun. Knives, Guns: The City Is Now in Flames." *Daily News* (Australia), 5 Sept. 1936, p. 2.

Hardorff, Richard G. *The Custer Battle Casualties: Battles, Exhumations, and Reinternments*. Upton and Sons, 1989.

———. *The Custer Battle Casualties, II: The Dead, The Missing, and a Few Survivors*. Upton and Sons, 1999.

Harari, Yuval Noah. *The Ultimate Experience: Battlefield Revelations and the Making of Modern War Culture, 1450–2000*. Palgrave Macmillan, 2008.

Haver, Ronald. "Finally, the Truth about *Casablanca*." *American Film*, June 1976, pp. 11–16.

"Hemingway: *Life* Documents His New Novel with War Shots." *Life*, 6 Jan. 1941, pp. 52–57.
Hemingway, Ernest. *Across the River and into the Trees*. Charles Scribner's Sons, 1950.
———. "The Cardinal Picks a Winner." *Ken*, vol. 1, no. 3, 5 May 1939, pp. 38–39.
———. *Death in the Afternoon*. Simon and Schuster, 1996. 1932.
———. *A Farewell to Arms*. Scribner, 1995.
———. *For Whom the Bell Tolls*. Scribner, 2003.
———. *The Garden of Eden*. Scribner, 1986.
———. *Green Hills of Africa*. Hemingway Library Edition. Scribner, 2015.
———. *The Letters of Ernest Hemingway Volume 1, 1907–1922*. Edited by Spandra Spanier and Robert W. Trogdon, Cambridge UP, 2011.
———. *The Letters of Ernest Hemingway Volume 3, 1926–1929*. Edited by Rena Sanderson, Sandra Spanier, and Robert W. Trogdon, Cambridge UP, 2015.
———. *The Letters of Ernest Hemingway Volume 5, 1932–1934*. Edited by Sandra Spanier and Miriam B. Mandel, Cambridge UP, 2020.
———, editor. *Men at War: The Best War Stories of All Time*. Introduction by Ernest Hemingway, Crown, 1942.
———. *A Moveable Feast: The Restored Edition*. Edited by Seán Hemingway, Scribner, 2009.
———. *The Nick Adams Stories*. Edited by Philip Young, Charles Scribner's Sons, 1972.
———. "On the American Dead in Spain." *New Masses*, vol. 30, no. 8, 14 Feb. 1939, p. 3.
———. "On the Blue Water: A Gulf Stream Letter." *Esquire*, April 1936, pp. 31, 184.
———. *Selected Letters*. Edited by Carlos Baker, Charles Scribner's Sons, 1981.
Herbst, Josephine. *The Starched Blue Sky of Spain and Other Memoirs*. Northeastern UP, 1991.
Hochschild, Adam. *Spain in Our Hearts: Americans in the Spanish Civil War, 1936–1939*. Houghton Mifflin, 2016.
Hohenberg, John. *The Pulitzer Prizes: A History of the Awards in Books, Drama, Music, and Journalism, Based on the Private Files over Six Decades*. Columbia UP, 1974.
hooks, bell. "Eating the Other: Desire and Resistance." In *Black Looks: Race and Representation*. Routledge, 2015. pp. 21–39.
Hotchner, A. E. *Papa Hemingway: A Personal Memoir*. Carroll & Graff, 1999.
Holman, C. Hugh and William Harmon. *A Handbook to Literature*. 6th ed, MacMillan, 1992.
Hugo, Victor. *Les Orientales, Les Feuilles d'automne*. Librairie Générale Française, 2000.
Hutchinson, George. *Facing the Abyss: American Literature and Culture in the 1940s*. Columbia UP, 2018.
Hutchisson, James M. *Ernest Hemingway: A New Life*. Pennsylvania State UP, 2016.
Hutton, Paul Andrew. "Introduction." Van de Water, pp. 11–14.
Hynes, Samuel. *The Unsubstantial Air: American Flyers in the First World War*. Farrar, Straus and Giroux, 2014.
Ibárruri, Dolores. *They Shall Not Pass: The Autobiography of La Pasionaria*. International Publishers, 1966.
Josephs, Allen. *For Whom the Bell Tolls: Ernest Hemingway's Undiscovered Country*. Twayne, 1994.
———. "*Toreo*: The Moral Axis of *The Sun Also Rises*." *Hemingway Review*, vol. 6, no. 1, fall 1986, pp. 88–99.
Juntunen, Kim A. "U.S. Army Attachés and the Spanish Civil War, 1936–1939: The Gathering of Technical and Tactical Intelligence." 1990. Master's thesis, Temple University. http://www.dtic.mil/dtic/tr/fulltext/u2/a222347.pdf.

Justice, Hilary K. "Music." *Ernest Hemingway in Context,* edited by Debra Moddelmog and Suzanne del Gizzo, Cambridge UP, 2013, pp. 193–205.

Kagan, Richard L. *The Spanish Craze: America's Fascination with the Hispanic World, 1779–1939.* U Nebraska P, 2019.

Kale, Verna. *Ernest Hemingway.* Reaktion, 2016.

Kalyvas, Stathis N. *The Logic of Violence in Civil War.* Cambridge UP, 2006.

Kennedy, A. J. *On Bullfighting.* Anchor Books, 1999.

Knapp, Bettina L. *Gertrude Stein.* Continuum, 1990.

Kvam, Wayne. "Ernest Hemingway and Hans Kahle." *Hemingway Review,* vol. 2, no. 2, spring 1983, pp. 18–22.

Lannon, Frances. *The Spanish Civil War, 1936–1939.* Osprey, 2002.

LaPrade, Douglas Edward. *Hemingway and Franco.* Universitat de València, 2007.

Leff, Lenonard J. *Hemingway and His Conspirators: Hollywood, Scribners, and the Making of American Celebrity Culture.* Rowman & Littlefield, 1997.

Lewis, Robert W., and Michael Kim Roos. *Reading Hemingway's* A Farewell to Arms: *Glossary and Commentary.* Kent State UP, 2019.

Link, Alex. "Rabbit at the Riverside: Names and Impossible Crossings in Hemingway's *For Whom the Bell Tolls.*" *Hemingway Review,* vol. 29, no. 1, fall 2009, pp. 134–39.

Lorca, Federico García. *Deep Song and Other Prose.* Edited and translated by Christopher Maurer, New Directions, 1980.

———. *Poem of the Deep Song.* Translated by Carlos Bauer, City Lights, 1987.

"Loyal Forces Begin Counter-attack Near Saint Martin." *St. Louis Post-Dispatch,* 10 Oct. 1936, p. 1.

Lusk, Norbert. "The Screen in Review." *Picture Play,* vol. 40, no. 2, Apr. 1934, pp. 40–41.

Lynn, Kenneth S. *Hemingway.* Simon & Schuster, 1987.

Lyons, Eugene. "Capitol News." *Daily Times and Daily Journal-Press* (St. Cloud, MN), 12 May 1930, p. 12.

Malcolm, Janet. *Two Lives: Getrude and Alice.* Yale UP, 2007.

Mandel, Miriam B., editor. *A Companion to Hemingway's Death in the Afternoon.* Camden House, 2004.

———. *Hemingway's Death in the Afternoon: The Complete Annotations.* Scarecrow Press, 2002.

———. *Reading Hemingway: The Facts in the Fiction.* Scarecrow Press, 1995.

———. "Subject and Author: The Literary Backgrounds of *Death in the Afternoon.*" In Mandel, *Companion,* pp. 79–119.

Matthews, Herbert L. "Leftists Shut Gap on Cordoba Front." *New York Times,* 9 Apr. 1937, p. L1.

———. "Pozoblanco Siege Is Broken in Spain; Loyalists Say They Pushed Back Five Miles a Force Including 10,000 Italians." *New York Times,* 27 Mar. 1937, p. 7.

Mazzeno, Laurence W. *The Critics and Hemingway, 1924–2014: Shaping an American Literary Icon.* Camden House, 2015.

McGrigor, James. *The Autobiography and Services of Sir James McGrigor, Bart: Late Director-General of the Army Medical Department; with an Appendix of Notes and Original Correspondence.* Longman, Green, Longman, and Roberts, 1861.

McLoughlin, Kate. "War and Words." *The Cambridge Companion to War Writing.* Ed. Kate McLoughlin. Cambridge UP, 2009.

Michaels, Walter Benn. *Our America: Nativism, Modernism, and Pluralism.* Duke UP, 1995.

Moddelmog, Debra A. "'We Live in a Country Where Nothing Makes Any Difference': The Queer Sensibility of *A Farewell to Arms*." *Hemingway Review*, vol. 28, no. 2, spring 2009, pp. 7–24.

Moorehead, Caroline. *Martha Gellhorn: A Life*. Vintage, 2004.

Mora, Constancia de la. *In Place of Splendor: The Autobiography of a Spanish Woman*. Harcourt, Brace and Company, 1939.

Motion, Andrew. "Preface." Donne, *Devotions*, pp. xi–xxi.

Muller, Gilbert H. *Hemingway and the Spanish Civil War: The Distant Sound of Battle*. Palgrave Macmillan, 2020.

Murad, David. "The Conflict of 'Being Gypsy' in *For Whom the Bell Tolls*." *Hemingway Review*, vol. 28, no. 2, spring 2009, pp. 87–104.

Museo del Prado Catálogo. Blass, S.A., 1933.

Nash, Mary. *Defying Male Civilization: Women in the Spanish Civil War*. Arden Press, 1995.

Nelson, Cary, editor. *Remembering Spain: Hemingway's Civil War Eulogy and the Veterans of the Abraham Lincoln Brigade*. U of Illinois P, 1994.

Nickel, Matthew. *Hemingway's Dark Night: Catholic Influences and Intertextualities in the Work of Ernest Hemingway*. New Street Communications, 2013.

"Nightmare in Madrid." *Boston Globe*, 16 Oct. 1936, p. 11.

Norris, Frank. "Three Essays on Naturalism." *Documents of American Realism and Naturalism*, edited by Donald Pizer, Southern Illinois UP, 1998, pp. 167–74.

Norris, Margot. *Writing War in the Twentieth Century*. UP of Virginia, 2000.

O'Brien, Tim. *Dad's Maybe Book*. Houghton Mifflin, 2019.

O'Hara, John. *Appointment in Samarra*. Introduction by Charles McGrath, Penguin, 2013.

O'Keefe, Ken. *International Brigade Sites in Central Madrid: The Spanish Civil War*. Asociación de Amigos de las Brigadas Internationales, 2013.

Oman, Sir Charles. *Studies in the Napoleonic Wars*. Charles Scribner's Sons, 1930.

Ong, Walter J. *Orality & Literacy: The Technologizing of the Word*. Routledge, 1982.

Ortega y Gasset, José. *Meditations on Quixote*. Introduction and notes by Julián Marías, translated by Evelyn Rugg and Diego Marín, W. W. Norton, 1961.

Orwell, George. *Homage to Catalonia*. Introduction by Lionel Trilling, Harcourt Brace, 1980.

Payne, Stanley G. *The Spanish Civil War, The Soviet Union, and Communism*. Yale UP, 2004.

Perez, Steven Jay. "Once and For All: The Spanish Civil War and the Nationalist Concentration Camps." *Undergraduate Humanities Forum 2013-2014: Violence*, no. 5, 2014, https://repository.upenn.edu/uhf_2014/5.

"Poet Flays Suicide, Then Decides to Take Own Life." *San Bernardino Daily Sun*, 15 Apr. 1930, p. 1.

Poliquin, Rachel. *Beaver*. Reaktion, 2015.

Polybius, *Histories of Polybius*. vol 1. Translated by Evelyn S. Shuckburgh, Macmillan, 1889.

Poore, Charles. "Books of the Times." *New York Times*, 18 Nov. 1939, p. 15.

"La Prensa de Moscú publica páginas de Largo Caballero, José Díaz, Dolres Ibarruri, Erembourg y Carmen Martinez." *ABC Madrid*, 3 Jan. 1937, p. 6.

Preston, Paul. "Hemingway's Forgotten Spanish Civil War Play to Be Produced for Only Second Time Ever." *The Guardian*, 18 Mar. 2016, https://www.theguardian.com/stage/2016/mar/18/ernest-hemingway-the-fifth-column-spanish-civil-war-play-revived-first-time-70-years.

———. *The Spanish Civil War: Reaction, Revolution, and Revenge*. Revised and expanded edition, W. W. Norton, 2006.

———. *The Spanish Holocaust: Inquisition and Extermination in Twentieth-Century Spain.* W. W. Norton, 2012.

———. *We Saw Spain Die: Foreign Correspondents in the Spanish Civil War.* Constable, 2008.

Prudlo, Donald. "American Catholics in the Spanish Civil War." *Faith and Reason,* vol. 31, no. 2, summer 2006, pp. 243–73.

Quintanilla, Luis. *Franco's Black Spain.* Drawings with a commentary by Richard Watts Jr., Reynal & Hitchcock, 1946.

Quintanilla, Paul. *Waiting at the Shore: Art, Revolution, and Exile in the Life of the Spanish Artist Luis Quintanilla.* Lulu Press, 2003.

Rankin, Ruth. "They're All Queening It." *Photoplay,* vol. 45, no. 1, Dec. 1933, pp. 34–36, 89–90.

Regler, Gustav. *The Great Crusade.* With a preface by Ernest Hemingway, translated by Whittaker Chambers and Barrows Mussey, Longmans, Green and Co., 1940.

———. *The Owl of Minerva: The Autobiography of Gustav Regler.* Translated from the German by Norman Denny. Farrar, Strauss and Cudhay, 1959.

Rehberger, Dean. "'I Don't Know Buffalo Bill' or Hemingway and the Rhetoric of the Western." Sanderson, 159–84.

"Reports 800 Slain by Leftists." *New York Times,* 26 Sep. 1936, p. 10.

Reynolds, Michael. *Hemingway: The Final Years.* W. W. Norton, 1999.

———. *Hemingway: The Homecoming.* W. W. Norton, 1999.

———. *Hemingway's Reading 1910–1940.* Princeton UP, 1981.

———. *Hemingway: The 1930s.* W. W. Norton, 1997.

———. "Ringing the Changes: Hemingway's Bell Tolls Fifty." *Virginia Quarterly Review,* vol. 67, no. 1, winter 1991. *VQR Online,* 12 Dec. 2003.

———. *The Young Hemingway.* W. W. Norton, 1998.

Richardson, R. Dan. *Comintern Army: The International Brigades and the Spanish Civil War.* UP of Kentucky, 1982.

"Robert Jordan, Hemingway's Bipartisan Hero." *National Public Radio,* 14 Oct. 2008, https://www.npr.org/templates/transcript/transcript.php?storyId=95604448.

Roberts, C. V. "Hemingway Lets Down Followers." *Dayton Daily News,* 10 Nov. 1940, p. 33.

Rogers, Gayle. *Incomparable Empires: Modernism and the Translation of Spanish and American Literature.* Columbia UP, 2016.

Rogers, W. G. *When This You See Remember Me: Getrude Stein in Person.* Rinehart, 1948.

Romesburg, Rod. "Shifting Orders: Chaos and Order in *For Whom the Bell Tolls.*" *Hemingway and the Natural World,* edited by Robert E. Fleming, U of Iowa P, 1999, pp. 139–52.

Roth, Joseph. *Joseph Roth: A Life in Letters.* Translated and edited by Michael Hoffman, W. W. Norton, 2012.

———. *Report from a Parisian Paradise: Essays from France, 1925–1939.* Translated by Michael Hoffman, W. W. Norton, 1999.

Ruiz, Julius. *The 'Red Terror' and the Spanish Civil War: Revolutionary Violence in Madrid.* Cambridge UP, 2014.

Sales, Juan. *Uncertain Glory.* Translated by Peter Bush, NYRB Classics, 2017.

"El sanatorio 'fantasma' que inspiró a Cela y Machado." *ABC,* 16 June 2016, https://www.abc.es/espana/madrid/abci-sanatorio-fantasma-inspiro-cela-y-machado-201606162208_noticia.html.

Sanderson, Rena, editor. *Blowing the Bridge: Essays on Hemingway and* For Whom the Bell Tolls. Greenwood Press, 1992.

Scarry, Elaine. *The Body in Pain: The Making and Unmaking of the World.* Oxford UP, 1985.

Sedgwick, Eve Kosofsky. *Between Men: English Literature and Male Homosocial Desire.* With a new preface by the author, Columbia UP, 1985.

Seidman, Michael. *Republic of Egos: A Social History of the Spanish Civil War.* U of Wisconsin P, 2002.

Sheean, Vincent. *Not Peace But a Sword.* Doubleday / Doran, 1939.

Sherman, William Tecumseh. *Memoirs of W. T. Sherman.* Library of America, 1990.

Skinner, Cornelia Otis. *Soap Behind the Ears.* Drawings by Alajalov, Dodd, Mead & Company, 1941.

Slotkin, Richard. *Fatal Environment: The Myth of the Frontier in the Age of Industrialization, 1800–1890.* Atheneum, 1985.

Smyth, Thomas. *Mary not a perpetual virgin, nor the mother of God.* B. Jenkins, 1846.

Somebody Had to Do Something: A Memorial to James Phillips Lardner. James Lardner Memorial Fund, 1939.

Sontag, Susan. *Against Interpretation and Other Essays.* Picador, 1996.

———. *Regarding the Pain of Others.* Farrar, Straus and Giroux, 2003.

Spilka, Mark. *Hemingway's Quarrel with Androgyny.* U of Nebraska P, 1990.

Stein, Gertrude. *Four in America.* Books for Libraries Press, 1969.

———. *Lectures in America.* Beacon Press, 1957.

Stone, John A. "Hemingway Sets the Style." *American Weekly,* 8 Sept. 1946, pp. 6–7.

Stoneback, H. R. "'The Priest Did Not Answer': Hemingway, the Church, the Party, and *For Whom the Bell Tolls.*" Sanderson, pp. 99–112.

———. *Reading Hemingway's* The Sun Also Rises: *Glossary and Commentary.* Kent State UP, 2007.

Strychacz, Thomas. *Hemingway's Theaters of Masculinity.* Louisiana State UP, 2003.

Stuckey, W. J. *The Pulitzer Prize Novels: A Critical Backward Look.* U of Oklahoma P, 1966.

Sundaram, Chantal. *Manufacturing Culture: The Soviet State and the Mayakovsky Legend, 1930–1993.* 2009, University of Toronto, PhD dissertation.

Swanton, Kathryn. "Cervantes, the Moors of Spain, and the Moor of Venice." *Shakespeare & Beyond* [Folger Shakespeare Library blog], 15 Mar. 2016, https://www.folger.edu/blogs/shakespeare-and-beyond/cervantes-the-moors-of-spain-and-the-moor-of-venice/.

Thackeray, William Makepeace. *Vanity Fair.* Norton Critical Edition, edited by Peter Shillingsburg, W. W. Norton, 1994.

The Life of St. Teresa of Jesus, Of the Order of our Lady of Carmel, Written by Herself. Translated from the Spanish by David Lewis, Burns, Oates, & Co., 1870.

Thomas, Hugh. *The Spanish Civil War.* Revised Edition. Modern Library, 2001.

Tinker, F. G., Jr. *Some Still Live.* Funk & Wagnalls, 1938.

Tompkins, Kyla Wazana. *Racial Indigestion; Eating Bodies in the 19th Century.* New York UP, 2012.

Tremlett, Giles. *The International Brigades: Fascism, Freedom, and the Spanish Civil War.* Bloomsbury, 2021.

Trogdon, Robert W., editor. *Ernest Hemingway: A Literary Reference.* Carl & Graff, 1999.

———. *The Lousy Racket: Hemingway, Scribners, and the Business of Literature.* Kent State UP, 2007.

———. "'I Am Constructing a Legend': Ernest Hemingway in Guy Hickok's *Brooklyn Daily Eagle Articles.*" *Resources for American Literary Study,* no. 37, 2014, pp. 181–207.

———. "Money and Marriage: Hemingway's Self-Censorship in *For Whom the Bell Tolls.*" *Hemingway Review*, vol. 22, no. 2, spring 2003, pp. 6–18.

Tyler, Lisa. "Passion and Grief in *A Farewell to Arms:* Ernest Hemingway's Retelling of Wuthering Heights." *Hemingway Review*, vol. 14, no. 2, spring 1995, pp. 79–97.

"Urbanismo Madrileño en 1931." *ABC Madrid*, 1 Jan. 1932, p. 32.

Valaik, J. David. "Catholics, Neutrality, and the Spanish Embargo, 1937–1939." *Journal of American History*, vol. 54, no. 1, June 1967, pp. 73–85.

Valis, Noël. "Hemingway's War." *Teaching Representations of the Spanish Civil War*, edited by Noël Valis, Modern Language Association, 2007. pp. 258–66.

Van de Water, Frederic F. *Glory-Hunter: A Life of General Custer*. U of Nebraska P, 1988.

Vernon, Alex. "Afterthoughts on 'The Rites of War and *The Sun Also Rises*' Inspired by *For Whom the Bell Tolls*." *Hemingway Review*, 28 Oct. 2015. https://www.hemingwaysociety.org/afterthoughts-%E2%80%9C-rites-war-and-sun-also-rises%E2%80%9D-inspired-whom-bell-tolls.

———. *Hemingway's Second War: Bearing Witness to the Spanish Civil War.* U of Iowa P, 2008.

———. "Louis Fischer as 'Mitchell' in *For Whom the Bell Tolls.*" *Hemingway Review*, vol. 36, no. 2, spring 2017, pp. 65–78.

———. *On Tarzan*. U Georgia P, 2008.

———. "The Rites of War and *The Sun Also Rises*." *Hemingway Review*, vol. 35, no. 1, fall 2015, pp. 13–34.

———. "*The Spanish Earth* and the Non-nonfiction War Film." *Hemingway Review*, vol. 34, no. 1, fall 2014, pp. 30–46.

Vincent, Jonathan. *The Health of the State: Modern U.S. War Narrative and the American Political Imagination, 1890–1964*. Oxford UP, 2017.

Warren, Chris. *Ernest Hemingway in the Yellowstone High Country*. Riverbend, 2019.

Watson, William Braasch. "Hemingway's Spanish Civil War Dispatches." *Hemingway Review*, vol. 7, no. 2, spring 1988, pp. 4–121.

Watts, Henry Edward, "Quevedo and His Works with an Essay on the Picaresque Novel." *Pablo de Segovia, The Spanish Sharper*, Unwin Press, 1892. Project Gutenberg online. https://www.gutenberg.org/files/46125/46125-h/46125-h.htm.

Webb, Ruth. *Ekphrasis: Imagination and Persuasion in Ancient Rhetorical Theory and Practice*. Ashgate, 2009.

White, Frederick H. "Ideological Profit: Hemingway, Kol'tsov, and the Spanish Civil War." *Hemingway Review*, vol. 41, no. 1, fall 2021, pp. 43–67.

———. "The Most Outstanding Work of an Idealistic Tendency: Hemingway, Pasternak, and the 1958 Nobel Prize for Literature." *Hemingway Review* vol. 40, no. 1, fall 2020, pp. 10–28.

Williams, Wirt. *The Tragic Art of Ernest Hemingway*. Louisiana State UP, 1981.

Woodard, Vincent. *The Delectable Negro: Human Consumption and Homoeroticism within U.S. Slave Culture*. Edited by Justin A. Joyce and Dwight A. McBride., foreword by E. Patrick Johnson, NYU Press, 2014.

Woolf, Virginia. *To The Lighthouse*. Harcourt Brace Jovanovich, 1955.

———. *Three Guineas*. Harvest/Harcourt, 2006.

Worden, Daniel. *Masculine Style: The American West in Literary Modernism*. Palgrave, 2011.

Woroszylski, Wiktor. *The Life of Mayakovsky*. Translated by Boleslaw Taborski, Orion Press, 1970.

Wyden, Peter. *The Passionate War*. Simon and Schuster, 1983.

Yeats, W. B. *The Collected Poems of W. B. Yeats.* Macmillan, 1982.
Zaloga, Steven J. *Spanish Civil War Tanks: The Proving Ground for Blitzkrieg.* Osprey, 2010.

INDEX

Page numbers in *italics* refer to illustrations.

ABC, 48, 128n2, 128n3, 158, 164n2, 179, 203n3, 206, 291, 305
Abd el-Krim, 177, 223
Abraham Lincoln Brigade (Lincoln Battalion), xi–xii, xx, 16, 70, 72, 108, 127, 145, 176, 316
Abrams, David, 116
Absalom, Absalom! (Faulkner), xvi, 62
absinthe, 61
Ackelsberg, Martha, 228
Across the River and into the Trees (Hemingway), 11, 67, 133, 183
Adams, Cassilly, 251
Adams, Donald J., xi
Adams, Nick (character), 99, 238
Adoration of the Magis (Bruegel), 190, 192
agency and acceptance, xxvii, 63, 78, 80, 92, 151, 154, 157, 222, 255–56, 302, 308, 315
Agincourt (battle), 167–68
Agustín (character), 27, 42, 46, 77, 94, 171, 172–73, 222, 296, 312
aircraft and air forces, 51–52, 83–85, 90–92, 155, 167, 246, 302, 308
Albacete, 16, 70, 138, 187, 299
Alberti, Rafael, 193
Alcázar of Segovia, 22, 53
Alcázar of Toledo, 21, 53, 190, 196–98, 201
Alfonso XII, 260
All the Brave (L. Quintanilla), 303
Allen, Jay, 41, 320n9
All Saints' Church, 54
All-Story Magazine, 304
Alto del León, 87, 124, 193, 276, 293. *See also* Guadarrama Pass
Álvarez, José E., 108–9
Álvarez del Vayo, Julio, 196
American Civil War, xxiv, 28, 54, 60, 63, 72, 108, 171, 175–76, 181–85, 247–48, 252
American Communist Party. *See* Communist Party of the United States (CPUSA)
American Revolutionary War, 63
Amnesty laws (Spain), 178, 199
anarchists and anarchism, xviii, xxiii, 37, 66, 87, 97, 104, 109–11, 117, 155, 177, 178, 200, 206, 274–76, 292, 293n1
Andalusia, 30, 67, 86, 97, 111, 137, 161, 165, 179, 195, 260, 281–83, 295, 334; Moorish association, 38, 40, 55, 224, 283; Romani association, 46, 159, 160, 162, 283
Andrés (character), 42, 61, 64, 94, 153, 272, 276, 293, 298, 300–301
Anheuser-Busch Brewing Association, *250,* 251
Animal Farm (Orwell), 292
animals and animal symbolism (mammals, birds, fish), xxix, 85; bears, 35, 54, 58, 229; beavers, 38; crows, 220–21; eagle, 52–53; geese, 84; hares, 219–20, 240; hawk, 136; horses; Jordan and Maria as, 94, 210; martens, 38, 84, 136, 257, 277–78, 284; pronghorns, 319; sharks, xxix, 84, 90, 284; squirrel, xxx, 136, 303–4. *See also* rabbits and rabbit symbolism
Anna Karenina (film), 120
Anselm (Saint), 55
Anselmo (character), 15, 18, 25–26, 31, 33, 40, 53, 55, 83, 85, 106, 165–67, 222, 224, 241–42, 244, 284, 286, 304, 310; judgment of Pablo, 42; recollection of bear, 54, 264; religion, 53–57, 242–43
Antietam (battle), 184
anti-fascists, xi, xviii, xx, 70–71
Appointment in Samarra (O'Hara), 296
Aragon front, 66–67, 109–10, 200
Aranjuez, 276
Arapaho, 247
Archibald, David, 119
Arevalo, 30
Arganda Offensive and bridge, 12, 245. *See also* Jarama (battle)
Army of Africa, 31, 108, 155, 166, 177, 194, 198, 245, 273. *See* Spanish Foreign Legion
Arnold, Ruth, 48
Arroyo del Puerto del Paular, 12
Artists in Uniform (Eastman), 141
Asensio, Torrado, José, 273
Asturias, xxxiii, 155; Asturian campaign (Nationalists), 86, 109; October Revolution, 155, 166, 176
As You Desire Me (film), 120
As You Like It (Shakespeare), 181

353

Auden, W. H., xxi–xxii, xxxiii
Autobiography of Alice B. Toklas, The (Stein), 225
auto-da-fé, 8n1, 92, 101, 103–4, 160, 222–23, 264, 283
automobiles, 165
Ávila, 26, 30, 52–53, 104, 124–25, 166
Axelsson, George, 158
Aztecs, 263

Bach, Johann Sebastian, 189
Badajoz, 41, 63, 102
Baez, Miguel, 205
Baker, Carlos, xxv, xxvi, 65, 107, 249, 284, 315
Bakunin, Mikhail, 109
Balzac, Honoré de, 144
Barcelona, 18, 56, 66–67, 166, 236–37, 274, 293n1, 303; fighting in May 1937, 110, 117, 200
Barco de Avila, 15, 125
Basque, xviii, xxxiii, 86, 92, 103, 155, 166, 194, 201, 202, 224, 235, 244, 308, 315; community in Cuba, 15, 67, 228; community in Idaho, 315
Bataille, George, 134
Bates, Ralph, 206, 320n9
"Battler, The" (Hemingway), 75
Bauer, Carlos, 282
Baym, Nina, xvi
Beartooth Mountains, 249
Becker, Ernest, 211
Becker, F. Otto, *250*, 251
Beebee, Thomas O., xv–xvi
Beevor, Anthony, 19, 83, 87, 127, 261, 299
Béjar, 125
Belchite (battle), 300
Bell, Douglas, 253
Benteen, Frederick, 247
Berbers, 223–24, 318
Bergman, Ingrid, 119, 258
Bergson, Henri, 279
Berlitz language school, 179
Bernini, Gian Lorenzo, 26
Berrendo, Lt. Paco (character), xii, xxx, 7, 237, 239–42, 318–19
Bessie, Alvah, 144
Bianchi, Giuseppe, 284
Biathanatos (Donne), 6–7
Bible in Spain, The (Borrow), xxxii, 77, 202
Biblical references, 6, 18, 146, 148, 149, 154, 169, 190, 221, 222, 295, 310; Onan, 255, 307; St. Paul, 275, 289. *See also* Jesus; Judas Iscariot
Bilbao, 244
Blitzkrieg, 168
Bogart, Humphrey, xi, xxxviin1
Bolloten, Burnett, 188, 193
Bolshevik and Bolshevik Revolution, 19, 137, 140, 173, 300
Bonaparte, Napoleon, 22, 219, 252–53
Book of Common Prayer, 319
Book of the Month Club, 37, 70, 335n2
Borrow, George, xxxii, 43–44, 55, 77, 150, 163, 202
Bosch, Hieronymus, 20–21, 77, 192, 220

Botticelli, 255
Bourdon, Sébastien, *121*, 122, 129n4
Bowers, Claude, 108–9, 139, 152n3
Brandt, Harold, 118
Brenner, Gary, xxvi
Bride of the Red Christ, 240, 260–62, 264
bridges: Hemingway's invention, xxxi–xxxii, 51; Puenta de la Toledo, 197, 207; Puente de la Cantina, 12–13; Puente de los Franceses, 274. *See also* Arganda Offensive and bridge
Brihuega (battle). *See* Guadalajara
Britain (battle), 92
Broadwell-Gulde, 115
Broer, Lawrence, 5, 285n1, 317
Brogan, Jacqueline, 135
Brontë, Emily, xiii, 210
Brooklyn Daily Eagle, 284
Brooks, Chris, 70
Brooks, Cleanth, xxx, 312
Broun, Heywood, 320n9
Bruegel, Pieter the Elder, 190, *191*, 192, 212
Brunete, 138
Buitrago, 26
Buitrago del Lozoya, 26
Bukharin, Nikolai Ivanovich, 200
bullfighting, xxvii, 41, 43, 63, 97, 100–102, 105, 107, 155–58, 160, 163, 204–6, 211–12, 254, 260, 272, 295; capeas, 61, 100–101, 104, 272; Catholicism and, 159–60; coleta, 24, 113–14; faena, 279; ferias, 88, 158, 160; peon de brega, 204; recibir, 318; Valencians and, 88
Burnam, Tom, 42
Burns, Emile, 198
Burns, Ken, 134
Burroughs, Edgar Rice. *See* Tarzan (Burroughs)
Butte Chamont, 60
"Butterfly and the Tank, The" (Hemingway), xviii, 32–33, 112n2, 118, 120, 207

Cabaret Le Jockey, 32
Cádiz, 8, 161, 165, 245; Bay of, 179
Café Colon, 159
Café Fornos, 206
Cagney, James, 320n9
Calvo Sotelo, José, 199–200
Camille (film), 120
Camino de Santiago/Way of St. James, 189
Cantabria and Cantabrian Sea, 155
cante jondo/deep song, 281–82
Carabanchel, 188, 194, 195, 197, 245
Cardsharps and Fortune Teller (Régnier), 44
Carlists and Carlism, xxx, 217, 223, 230, 231, 261
Carmelite Order, 227, 282
Carmen (character), 265–66
Carnell, Simon, 219
Carroll, Peter N., 70, 144
Carroll, William C., 207
Cartón, Pedro Martínez, 265
Casablanca (film), xi, xxxviin1

Casa de Campo, 194, 239n3, 245, 274
Castelao, Alfonso Daniel Rodríguez, 262, 263, 320n9
Castro, Fidel, xx
Catalonia and Catalonians, xii, xviii, 55, 66–67, 110, 118, 166, 206, 260, 335, 337. *See also* Barcelona
Cathedral-Basilica of Our Lady of the Pillar, 47, 68
Catholicism, 52–55, 106–7, 146, 167, 190, 222–24, 237–39, 240–43, 278, 282–83, 291, 314, 319; American Catholicism and the war, 71–72; and bullfighting, 88, 159–61, 163; Counter-Reformation and the Inquisition, 264; and Hemingway, 56; in Hemingway studies, 6–7; and Nationalism, 30, 31, 39, 217, 261, 264; as not Christian, 224; Queen Christina and the Thirty Years' War, 119; and the Republic, 46–47, 53–56
Catholic Worker, 72
Cercedilla, 293
Cervantes, Miguel de, 27, 116, 143, 154
Chamberlin, Brewster, 91
Chancellorsville (battle), xxviii–xxix, 11, 183, 252
Chanson de Roland, 23
"Charge of the Light Brigade, The" (Tennyson), xii
Charles I, 20
Charles Scribner's Sons, 254n6
Charterhouse of Parma (Stendhal), 114
Chartres Cathedral, 189–90
"Che ti dice la patria?" (Hemingway), 284
Cheyenne, 221, 247
Chicote's Bar, 32–33, 99, 207, 246
Chicuelo, 205
China's civil war, 300
Christ Crucified (Goya), 164n3
Christensen, Bonnie, 248
Christian inquiry, xxx. *See also* Catholicism
Christina (Queen), 120–22, 259, 264
Christina of Sweden on Horseback (Bourdon), 121, 122, 129n4
Chrost, Antoni "Antek," 16
Circo Price, 170
Cirino, Mark, 15, 45, 52, 108, 183–84
Ciruelos, Modesto, 192
Civil Guard/*guardia civil*, 30, 47, 57, 100, 106, 258, 264n1
"Clean, Well-Lighted Place, A" (Hemingway), 49
Club Finito, 158, 163, 206
"¡Cobardes! ¡Asesinos!"/"Cowards! Assassins!" (Castelao), 262, 263
Cochran, Charles B., 159
Cody, Buffalo Bill, 60–61
Collier's magazine, 3–4, 182
Colmenar Viejo, 85
colonialism. *See* race
Columbia University, xix
Columbus, Christopher/Colombo, Cristoforo/Colón, Cristóbal, 159
Comley, Nancy R., 42, 47, 131–32, 149, 164n3, 211, 260
commissars, 21, 127, 287
Communist International (Comintern), 21, 25, 137, 144, 176, 185, 187, 189, 198–99, 200, 287, 292, 298

Communist Party of the United States (CPUSA), 70–71, 144
Communist Youth International (KIM), 265
Confederacíon Nacional del Trabajo (National Confederation of Workers, the CNT), 109, 178, 273, 275
Connelley, William E., 181–82
Conquest (film), 118
Conquest of Bread (Kropotkin), 109
Čopić, Vladimir, 300
Contreras, Carlos ("Vittorio Vidali"), 187–89, 193
Cooke City, 248–49
Coolidge, John Calvin, Jr., 168
Cooper, James Fenimore, xxiv
Cooper, Gary, xiii, 17, 123, 297
Córdoba and Córdoba front, 111, 127, 137, 152n1, 192, 195
Cortada, James W., 16, 84
Cortes (Spanish Parliament), 71, 110
Cortez, Hernando, 263, 274
Coughlin, Charles, 72
Counter-Reformation, 282
Cowles, Virginia, 122
Crane, Stephen, 306
"Crime and Punishment" (Hemingway), 67
Crow Nation, 221
Cuenca mountain range, 245
Cur Deus Homo (Anselm), 55
Custer, George Armstrong, xxiv–xxv, 23–24, 54, 60–61, 182, 183, 184, 209, 221, 234, 247–52
Custer National Forest, 248
Custer's Last Fight (Becker), 250, 251

Dahl, Whitey, 337
Daily News (Perth, Australia), 108
Dale, Helen, 122
Darwin, Charles, and Darwinism, xxvii, 144, 211
Davis, Lydia, 259
Dead Soldier, The (anonymous), 28–29
de Aguado, Lola (translation), 45, 93, 173
Dearborn, Mary V., 79
Death in the Afternoon (Hemingway), xvii, xxxiii, 18, 47, 88, 97, 100–101, 105–6, 114–15, 142, 149–50, 155–56, 158–61, 167, 173, 190, 204–6, 223, 260, 279, 283, 308, 318
deep song/*cante jondo*, 281–83
De Falla, Manuel, 281, 285n3
DeGuzmán, María, xxxiii–xxxiv, 39, 47, 50n4, 54, 77, 240, 252
de la Mora, Constancia, 3, 236–37
de la Rosa, Juan Luis, 205
Delasalle, Gaston, 127
de Leon, Juana, 253
Delmer, Sefton, 16, 181
Denial of Death, The (Becker), 211
"Denunciation, The" (Hemingway), xviii, 32–33, 62, 112n2, 207, 246
de Saussure, Ferdinand, 142n5
Descubierta (Ciruelos), 192

Deuss, Edward L., 140
Deutsch Zentral Zeitung, 181
Devil Is a Woman, The (film), xxxv, 123
Devotions Upon Emergent Occasions (Donne), 5–7, 204, 315
Dickenson, Victoria, 77
Dietrich, Marlene, xxxv, 17, 122–23
Dodge, Mary Mapes, 142
Donaldson, Susan, xxxv
Don Faustino (character), 105, 107, 295
Don Juan Tenorio: Drama religioso-fantástico en dos partes (Zorrilla), 94
Donne, John, 5–8, 8n1, 63, 106–7, 134, 160, 204, 241, 277, 288, 313, 315, 317
Don Quixote (Cervantes), xvi, 27, 219
Don Ricardo (character), 105, 107
Dos Passos, John, xxi, xxxv, 21, 23, 59, 61–62, 109–10, 117, 123, 282
Douglass, Carrie B., 160
Drake, Francis, 306
Dreiser, Theodore, 298
Dumont, Jules, 254
Durán Martinez, Gustavo, 236; help with the novel, 15, 42, 67, 83, 87, 94, 107, 130, 148, 208, 220, 228, 230, 235, 246, 253, 254n3, 254n4, 254n5, 263, 276, 286; in the war, 127, 179, 233, 245–47, 254
Durruti Domínguez, Buenaventura, 274
Duval (character), 300

Eagleton, Terry, xxvi
Eastman, Max, 141
Eby, Carl, 21, 24–25, 38–39, 42, 47, 58–61, 77–79, 131–32, 149, 174, 177, 220, 251–52, 257
Eby, Cecil, 15
Ecstasy of Saint Teresa (Bernini), 26
Ehrenburg, Ilya, 141, 203n4, 266
Ehrenreich, Barbara, 102–3
ekphrasis, 100–101, 104, 114–15, 157, 161, 205, 314
Eladio (character), 42, 61, 64, 153, 272, 276, 307
El Campesino, 177, 179
El Debate, 107, 291
Elder, Robert, 52
El Escorial, 19–21, 25–26, 64, 85, 127, 146, 299, 306, 339
El Ferrol, 166
el Gallo, Rafael, 50n3, 156, 159, 162–63
El Gitano, 97
El Greco (Domenikos Theotokopoulos), 190, 282–83, 314
Eliade, Mircea, 278–79
Eliot, T. S., 4, 221
El Jaleo (Sargent), 50n4
El-Krim, Abd, 223
Ellis, Havelock, xxi, xxxiii, xxxv–xxxvi, 19, 28–29, 58, 222–23
El Matadero y Mercado Municipal de Ganados (Municipal Slaughterhouse and Cattle Market), 207
El Niño Ricardo, 161–63, 206

El Sordo (character), 24, 59, 75, 87, 94, 111, 124–26, 136, 209, 219, 240, 243, 249, 276; last stand, xxviii, 221, 234, 237, 242, 265
"End of Hate, The" (Fitzgerald), 182
"End of Something, The" (Hemingway), 310
energeia, 101
epic literature. *See* genre
Esdaile, Charles J., 194
Escudero, Don Bernardo, 158
Esquire magazine, 32, 59n2, 284
Extremadura/Estremadura, 30, 41, 137, 152n1, 172, 195, 202, 223, 272

Faber, Sebastiaan, 152n4
Falange Espanola Tradicionalista y de las Juntas de Ofensiva Nacional Sindicalista (FET y de las JONS; Traditionalist Spanish Phalanx of the Councils of the National Syndicalist Offensive), 39, 54, 261, 264, 264n1
Falangists, 39, 41, 105, 108, 258, 260–61, 264n1. *See also* Falange Espanola Tradicionalista y de las Juntas de Ofensiva Nacional Sindicalista (FET y de las JONS; Traditionalist Spanish Phalanx of the Councils of the National Syndicalist Offensive)
Fallola, Roberto Domingo, 18
Farewell to Arms, A (Hemingway), xiv, 15, 22, 43, 56, 155, 165, 190; Catherine Barkley, 33, 74, 133, 149, 170, 192, 210–11, 257; film adaptation of, 17, 123, 305; Frederic Henry, xxii, xxviii, 17, 33, 73, 79, 123, 138–39, 146, 149, 192, 211, 249; Rinaldi, 146
"Fathers and Sons" (Hemingway), 58, 67
Faulkner, William, xvi, 62, 79, 279
Federacion Anarquista Iberica (FAI; Anarchist Federation of Iberia), 109, 274–75
Fenimore, Edward, 14, 45, 92–93, 147–48
Ferdinand of Aragorn, 22, 53, 179, 207, 264
Ferdinand VII, 217
Fernando (character), 42, 64, 68, 87, 167, 172, 242–43, 296, 307
fifth column, 179, 201, 256
Fifth Column, The (Hemingway), xviii, 17, 61, 128, 176, 201, 256, 260, 310
Fifth Regiment, 70, 138, 178, 187–89, 192–94, 245
"Fight on the Hilltop, The" (Hemingway), xxviii
Finca Vigía, 18, 321
Finito (character), xxvii, 63, 91–92, 155–58, 160–61, 163, 211
1st Polish Light Cavalry Lancers, 253
1st US Volunteer Cavalry, 306
Fischer, Louis, 196–98, 299, 320n1
Fish Committee, 144
Fitch, Noel Riley, 32
Fitzgerald, F. Scott, xvi, 182
flamenco, 35–36, 46, 50n4, 159, 161–63, 206, 281
Flaubert, Gustave, 259
Flesh and the Devil (film), 123
Ford, Henry, 71
Ford, Richard, xxxiii, 38–39, 77, 202, 223–24

Foreign Press Bureau, 3, 236
foreshadowing, omens, and prognostication, xxvii, 15, 17, 19–21, 27, 37, 43–45, 49, 62, 79, 80, 83, 86, 111, 119–20, 125, 136, 152–53, 155, 169, 174, 204, 235, 237, 219–20, 241, 252, 255–56
Fortune Teller, The (Caravaggio), 44
Fort Kearny, 247
For Whom the Bell Tolls: circularity, 11, 172, 296, 319; composition, 321–35; dates and chronological setting, xxv, 11, 92, 130–31; epilogue, 64–65, 297, 319; international bans, xx; maximalist prose, xvii, 156, 225; naming the guerillas, 42–43, 64, 153–54; narrator, xxix, 18, 64, 167, 240, 279–80, 298, 301, 315; obscenities, 36–37, 77; reception and reviews, xi–xii, xix–xx, xxxi; title and epigraph, 4–9 (*see also* "undiscovered country" [from Shakespeare's *Hamlet*]); use of Spanish, xvii, xx, 13–15, 26–27, 40, 57, 86, 156–57; widening perspectives, 64–65, 68–69, 156, 165, 234, 240–41, 265, 293, 308
For Whom the Bell Tolls (film), xiii, 17, 119, 258, 297
"For Whom the Gong Sounds" (Skinner), 134, 334–37, 338–41
Franco Bahamonde, Francisco, xviii, xx, 5, 20, 30, 35–36, 39, 54, 57, 62, 67, 109, 113, 155, 158, 178, 186, 194, 198–201, 232–33, 261, 264, 291, 316
Franco's Black Spain (L. Quintanilla), 59
Frank, Waldo, 104, 285n2
Frank Fairlegh (Smedley), 38
Fraser, Ronald, 109
Frederic, Harold, xxx–xxxi
French Communist Party, 145, 180, 298
French Foreign Legion, 24
French Line, 32
French Revolution, 233, 252
Fridland, Moisei (Koltsov/Karkov), 180
Friedrich, Ernst, 195
frontier, American, and frontier wars, xxiv, xxxv, 60, 184, 247–48
Froze to Death Lake, 249
Frye, Northrop, xiii–xiv, xxvi–xxvii, 73
"Fuente Ovejuna" (Lope de Vega), 179–80
Fuentidueña de Tajo, 35, 56
Fuerte cosa es (Goya), 115
Fuller, Sam, 128

Galdós, Benito Pérez, 144
Galicia, xxxiii, 166, 178, 202
Galicia Mártir: Estampas por Castelao, 263, 320n9
Galicz, Janos. *See* Gall, General
Gall, General, 185–86, 266, 300
Gallagher, Matt, xi
Garbo, Greta, 42, 118–23, 146–47, 213, 257–59, 293n1, 310
Garcia, Don Saturnino, 56
Garden of Earthly Delights, The (Bosch), 20–21, 77, 220
Garden of Eden, The (Hemingway), xvii, xxxiii, 22, 39–40, 51, 74, 132, 157, 174, 258, 305; Catherine Bourne, 25, 58, 132–33, 151, 211, 256–58; Colonel Boyle, 24–25; David Bourne, 38–39, 42, 114, 132, 137, 151, 256; Marita, 38–39, 42; transgressions in, 74, 151
Gatherings from Spain (Ford), 77
Gautier, Théophile, 19–20
Gaylord Hotel, 176, 187, 194, 256, 265–66
Gellhorn, Martha, 3–4, 16, 37, 48–49, 56, 93, 96, 112n1, 176, 179, 210, 258, 265, 267n3
gender: androgynous or fluid, xxxvin4, 3, 42, 47–48, 74–75, 96, 120–22, 131–32, 170, 173, 211, 258–60, 294, 295, 308; conventional/traditional, 96, 148, 227; emasculation and challenge, xxxiv–xxxv, 23–24, 45, 48, 79–80, 93, 113, 119–20, 132, 148, 167, 308, 310
General Workers Union (Union General de Trabajadores; UGT), 273
Geneva Convention Relative to the Treatment of Prisoners of War, 231
genre, xii–xvii, xxiv–xxxii, xxxiv–xxxvi, 23, 26–27, 32, 63, 73, 135, 160, 167, 210, 232, 237, 259; Romance, 17, 128, 134, 207–8, 219, 297, 318, 320; Realism, 134, 142, 157, 204, 210, 272, 280; Naturalism, 90, 136, 144, 157, 160, 168, 174, 204, 238, 241, 272, 298, 301, 312; Tragedy, 11, 63, 157, 165, 204, 238, 260; imagined Spanishness, xx–xxii, 206, 208
Gilbert, Jack, 119–20, 123
Gitano. *See* Romani people (Gitano, Zincali, gypsy)
Gitlow, Benjamin, 177
Glory-Hunter (Van de Water), xxiv–xxv, 24, 184
Goddard, Howard, 320n9
Golz, General (character), 19, 21, 23, 64–65, 127, 137, 148–49, 165, 254, 293, 298–300, 308
Gomez (character), 298, 300–301
Gómez, Alfonzo, 155
Gomez, General (Zaiser), 137–38, 152n2
Gone with the Wind (Mitchell), 183
Gonzalez, Filipe, 206
Gonzalez, Ricardo, 206
Gonzalez, Valentín, 177–78
González Rosado, Carlos, 109
Gorge of the Guadalevin, 98
Goya y Lucientes, Francisco José de, 114–15, 129n4, 159–60, 164n3
Graham, Helen, 86
Grand Cross of the German Eagle, 71
Grand Hotel (film), 120
Granero, Manuel, 88, 205
Grant, Colquhoun, 253
Grant, Ulysses S., 175–76, 182
Grapes of Wrath, The (Steinbeck), xix
Great Crusade, The (Regler), xiii, xxviii, 185
Great Gatsby, The (Fitzgerald), xvi
Great Purge, 25, 200–201, 298
Gredos Mountains (Sierra de Gredos), 15, 30, 35, 125–26
Green Hills of Africa (Hemingway), xvii, xxviii, 278, 280, 284

Greeson, Helen M., 293n1
grenades, 254n4, 275, 286, 338–40
Guadalajara, 245; battle (or Brihuega), xxv, *309*
Guadarrama (town), 25
Guadarrama Mountains. *See* Sierra de Guadarrama (Guadarrama Mountains)
Guadarrama Pass, 87, 124–25, 193, 195, 273, 276, 293. *See also* Alto del León
guardia civil. *See* Civil Guard/*guardia civil*
guerilla warfare, xxii, 13, 16, 22–23, 41, 125, 177, 181, 253
Guernica (town), 92, 177, 244
Guernica (Picasso), 92
Guill, Stacey, 92, 99, 292
Guillen, Nick, 299
Guttman, Allen, 33n1
gypsy. *See* Romani people (Gitano, Zincali, gypsy)

Haapamaki, Michele, xxii
Hafiz, 282
Hail, Mary, 238–39
hair signification, 23–24, 48–49, 58, 60, 75, 78–80, 84, 113–14, 118, 122, 133, 137, 139–40, 147, 150–51, 169, 212–13, 220, 240, 251–52, 277–78, 282, 284
Hamlet (Shakespeare), xxxii, 4–5, 39, 280, 296, 305, 312–14
"Hamlet and His Problems" (Eliot), 4
Handbook of Marxism, A (Burns), 198–99
Hand-book for Travelers in Spain and Readers at Home, A (Ford), xxxiii, 39, 202, 223–24
Hans Brinker; or, the Silver Skates (Dodge), 142
Harari, Yuval Noah, xxvi, 22–23, 253–54, 308–9, 313
Hardorff, Richard G., 34n9
Harlow, Jean, 118–19, 122, 146
Harmon, William, xiii, xvi
Hartwig, Eva Brigitta, 119
Haver, Ronald, 119
Hawthorne, Nathaniel, xvi
Hays Code, 36
Hemingway, Clarence (father), 48; suicide, 4, 73, 79, 248–49, 251, 284, 297
Hemingway, Ernest: African Otherness complex, 42; Catholicism and, 6, 56, 243, 312; divorce from Martha Gellhorn, 3; divorce from Pauline Pfeiffer, xii, 3, 37, 56; ego, 78; fishing, 209–10, 279, 284; in France, 24, 60, 245, 284; grandfather, 249; hair as a reoccurring theme, 23–25, 37–38, 257–58; homes, 37, 210; in the hospital, 194–95; hunting, 52, 283–84; journalism, xviii, 43, 117–18, 228, 237; marriage to Martha Gellhorn, 3, 4, 37, 48–49, 56, 176, 210; marriage to Pauline Pfeiffer, 48, 56, 210, 284; moral code, xii; paper doll caricature of, 78, 129n5; politics, xix, 117–18; sketches, 85; in Spain, xviii, 16, 23, 52, 62, 66, 93, 117–18, 176, 190, 207, 225, 263, 285n3; suicide, 4, 249, 297
Hemingway, Grace Hall (mother), 48, 73, 189, 251, 285n3

Hemingway, Hadley (first wife), 4, 175, 285n3
Hemingway, Leicester (brother), 99, 112n2, 320n5
Hemingway, Marcelline (sister), 75, 107
Henry III, 207
Henry IV, parts 1 and 2 (Shakespeare), 45
Henry IV, 207
Henry V (Shakespeare), 168
Herbst, Josephine, 45–46
Hickok, Guy, 283–84
Historia de la vida del Buscón, llamado Don Pablos, ejemplo de vagamundos y espejo de tacaños (Quevedo y Villegas), 26–27
Hitler, Adolf, 5, 65, 109, 180
Hochschild, Adam, 71
Hohenberg, John, xix
Hollywood Reporter, 118
Hollywood Ten, 144
Holman, C. Hugh, xiii, xvi
Holocaust, 36
Homage to Catalonia (Orwell), xvii, 110
Homestead Act, 170–71
homophobia and the homosocial, 79, 170–73, 283, 294–95
hooks, bell, 40
Horatius, 141–42
horses, 27–28, 31, 33, 44, 52, 111, 125, 127–28, 136, 139, 170, 173, 252–53, 271, 287, 289, 292, 308; colt, 31, 42, 68, 72, 76, 83
Hotchner, A. E., 97
Hotel Florida, 176, 194, 207, 256, 260
Hotel Foyot, 60
Hotel Gran Via, 176, 194, 207
House Un-American Activities Commission (HUAC), 144
How I Found Livingstone (Stanley), 142, *143*
Hubert in Wonderland (Osten), 181
Hughes, Langston, 140–41, 320n9
Hugo, Victor, xxxiii
Hundred Years' War, 167
hunting: Hemingway as hunter, 52, 248–49, 278, 283–84; and love/sex, 38, 84, 208, 219, 257, 277, 284; versus killing (in war), xxix, 30, 51–52, 57, 84–85, 102–3, 136, 224, 237, 304, 319
Hutchinson, George, xxxvi
Hutchisson, James M., xxxvin4, 14
Hutton, Paul Andrew, xxiv
Hynes, Samuel, 51

Ibárruri, Dolores (La Pasionaria), 18, 178, 188, 193–94, 231, 234–35, 238, 246, 265–66, 316; as model for Pilar, 45–46, *48*, 49, 62, 68, 94, 114, 139
Iberians, 223–24, 318
Iglesias Posse, Pablo, 139, 273
Ile de la Cité, 60
Imperio, Pastora, 46, *48*, 159, 162–64
Incas, 263
incest, 40, 58, 73–75, 151, 255, 305, 320n2
Indian Wars (frontier wars), xxv, 60, 184, 247

In Our Time (Hemingway), xvii, 156, 211; "Chapter VII," 238, 280; "Chapter IX," 114; "Chapter XII," 212, 238–39, 280; "The Revolutionist," 190; "Soldier's Home," 22
In Place of Splendor (de la Mora), 3, 236–37
Inquisition, Spanish, 6, 36, 103–4, 160, 222, 264
Instituto Valencia of Don Juan, 27
International Brigades, xi–xii, xiv, xviii, xxii, xxxvi[n]1, 21–22, 110, 111, 180, 192, 197, 204, 246, 287; XI, 16, 118, 194, 266, 301; XIII, 137, 138; XV, 16; farewell parade, 167; Franco-Belgian battalion, 118; headquarters, 16, 138; La Pasionaria's farewell address to, 18, 316; leadership, 70; Mixed Brigade, 254; Quatorzième Brigade (XIV), 19, 127, 254, 300
Irún, 108, 194, 201
Isabel I/Isabel la Católica/Isabella (Queen), 21–22, 53–54, 179, 217, 264
Ivens, Joris, xviii, 62, 96, 171, 185, 186
Izvestia, 266

James, Henry, xxviii
James, Saint, 26, 47, 126, 154, 166, 189
James Lardner Memorial Fund, 320n9
Jarama (battle), xx, 83, 245, 266, 300, 316
Jardín Botánico, 208
Jay, Martin, 12
Jesus, and crucifixion/resurrection/Easter, 11, 18, 92, 154, 158–62, 164, 187, 221, 241, 261, 271, 275, 288
Joaquín (character), 113–14, 123, 238–39
Jockey Club of Paris, 32
John the Evangelist, 53
Johnny Got His Gun (Trumbo), 195
Jordan, Robert, 3–4, 96; appeal of character, xi, xx; aspiration to be Spanish, xx, 17, 281–83, 317–18; based on, 15–17; beard, 79–80, 171–72; bourgeois and fascist strains, 12, 72, 79, 136–37, 153, 230, 260, 264; backstory (Montana), xxiv, 15, 17, 28, 32, 52, 143, 145, 170, 185, 209, 221;
Jordan, Robert (*cont.*)
247–49, 277, 319; epiphany, xiv, xxxvi, 314–15; father, inheritance, and suicide, 4–5, 15, 20, 65–66, 71–73, 78–79, 126, 133, 135, 154, 170, 218, 248–49, 259, 284, 295–97; grandfather, xxiv, 54, 72–73, 79, 170, 185, 229, 247–49; interior dialogue/monologues, 58, 107, 116, 127, 212, 289–90, 294; killing Kashkin, 126, 128, 175; killing Pablo, xvi, 61–62, 67–68, 112, 172, 175; likeness to Kashkin, xxv, 49, 58, 59, 125–26, 175, 218, 295, 297; likeness to Pablo, xxx, 31, 33, 68, 294; love for Maria, 4, 31, 44, 49, 58, 77–78, 146, 150–51, 192, 212–13, 224, 227–28, 256, 259–60, 264, 284, 295, 304, 311–12, 317; marriage/domesticity, xxxiv, 73–75, 144, 148–49, 154, 168, 228, 255, 259, 264, 310; mission focus and motive, 64, 75, 80, 127–28, 149, 153, 155, 168, 245–46, 259, 281, 299, 310; murderousness, 61–62, 67–68, 193, 195, 197, 223, 231–32, 289;
name, 17–18, 75, 113, 116, 169–70, 237; politics, xix, 31, 42, 70–72, 110, 117–18, 138–39, 149, 187–89, 252; previous combat, 123, 137–38, 192–93, 195–97, 231–33; religion, 6, 7, 282–83, 295, 312, 314; Spain, identification with/love for/consumption of, xx, 13, 17, 27, 38, 40, 75, 77, 96, 125, 128, 134–35, 170, 172, 240, 247, 281–83, 317–18; suicide references, xxi, xxiv, xxix, 4–7, 57, 65, 126, 133, 218, 140–41, 149–50, 154, 175, 225, 237, 248, 251, 287, 296–97, 305, 308, 312–13, 315–16; travels, 32, 60–61, 91, 209; violence toward Maria, 78, 84, 144, 257; worrying and anxious, xxiv, 4–5, 7, 33, 49, 58, 62, 79, 91, 125–26, 251, 303, 305, 318; as a writer, 91, 117, 202
Jordan River, 18, 184, 305
Josephs, Allen, xix, xxxi–xxxii, 5, 13, 46, 77, 115, 134, 278–80, 282, 285n1, 317, 319
Joyce, James, 80, 279
Judas Iscariot, 271, 288
Jungle Book (Kipling), xxxiv
Juntunen, Kim A., 88
Justice, Hilary K., 285n3

Kagan, Richard L., 143, 152n4
Kahle, Hans, 16, 118, 185–86, 254n3, 266, 300–301
Kahn, Paul, 317
Kahn, Ruth, 265
Kale, Verna, xxvii
Kalyvas, Stathis N., 105, 123
Kamenev, Lev, 200
Karkov (character), 65, 68, 141, 180–81, 195–202, 266, 301–2
Kashkin (character), xxv, 30, 40–41, 49, 58–59, 62, 113, 125–26, 128, 137, 175, 195, 218, 295, 318
Kashkin, Ivan, 15, 30, 37, 59, 318, 321
Keats, John, 69, 100, 314
Keller, Fred, 260
Ken magazine, 61–62
Kennedy, A. J., 158
Khan, Genghis, 166
Kiki, 32
Kilpatrick, Hugh Judson, 252
Kiowa, 247
Kipling, Rudyard, xv–xvi, xxxiv–xxxv
Kléber, Emilio, 185, 246, 274
Knapp, Bettina L., 47
Kolchak, Alexander Vasilyevich, 300
Koltsov, Mikhail, 118, 141, 180–81, 202, 203n4, 265–66, 267n3, 301
Krieg (Renn), 301
Krieg dem Krieg! (Friedrich), 195
Kropotkin, Pyotr, 109
Kvam, Wayne, 254n3
Kyd, Thomas, 4

Lady Chatterley's Lover (Lawrence), 77
la gloria, 92, 174, 258, 279–83, 313, 317–18
la Gloriosa, xvii

La Granja, xxxi, 19, 25, 127; palace, 192. *See also* Segovia (La Granja) Offensive
Lakota, 221
Lalanda, Marcial, 205
Lamentation of Christ (Mantegna), 190
Landon, Alf, 306
language, semantics, rhetoric, and lies, 51–52, 88, 113, 145–48, 168, 174, 225–27, 257, 265, 281, 291–92, 312, 318
La Niña de los Peines, 159, 161–63
Lannon, Frances, 155
La Plaza de Toros de Vista Alegre, 197
LaPrade, Douglas Edward, xx, 232, 233n2
Lardner, James, 16, 33n2, 263, 316–17, 320n9
Lardner, Ring, 16
Lardner, Ring, Jr., 320n9
Largo Caballero, 273
Lausanne Peace Conference, 284
La Vanguardia, 139
Lawrence, D. H., 77
Lawrence, T. E. ("of Arabia"), xxii, 22, 41, 142
Lawson, John Howard, 320n9
L-Bar-T ranch, 248
Lee, Robert E., 28, 183–84, 252
Leff, Leonard J., 122–23
Left Review, xxii
Le Mercenaire (Guillen), 299
Le Morte d'Arthur (Malory), 23
Lenin, Vladimir, 140, 198, 200
Lenin Institute (University), 176–77, 252
Lerroux García, Alejandro, 139
Le Stade Buffalo, 60
Lewis, Robert, 211, 213n1
Lewis, Sinclair, xiv–xv, xxviii–xxxiv
Lewis machine gun, 43, *44,* 124, 238, 309
Library of Congress (US), xi
Life magazine, 16–17
Light That Failed, The (Kipling), xxxiv–xxxv
liminality, xxxi–xxxii
Limited Editions Club, 257–58
Lincoln, Abraham, 72, 170–71, 184
Lincoln Battalion. *See* Abraham Lincoln Brigade (Lincoln Battalion)
Link, Alex, 77
Líster Forján, Enrique, 166, 178–79, 186, 188
Little Bighorn (battle), 23, 221, 247–49
Livingstone, David, 142, 304
Livingstone, Mary, 142
Llosa, Mario Vargas, 134
Lope de Vega y Carpio, Félix, 143–44, 179–80
Lorca, Federico García, 159, 246, 281–83, 285n4
Los desastros de la Guerra (Goya), 115
Louis-Philippe, Emperor, 60
Love (film), 123
Love's Labor's Lost (Shakespeare), 207–8
Loyola, Carmen, 266
Lukács, Paul, 185, 266, 300
Lusk, Norbert, 122

Luther, Martin, 54, 264
Luxembourg Gardens, 60
Lynn, Kenneth, 75
Lyon, Eugene, 140

Macbeth (Shakespeare), 220
MacLeish, Archibald, 59n1, 228n1, 284
Madame Bovary (Flaubert), 259
Madrid, xxxi, 15, 19, 23, 25, 27, 85, 87–88, 120, 122, 138, 163, 170, 176, 178, 192–94, 197–98, 201, 206, 245–46, 257, 276, 291, 293; romantic vision of, xxxvi
Malcolm, Janet, 47
Malory, Thomas, 23
Malraux, Andre, 320n9
Mamsurov, Hadji, 16
Mandel, Miriam B., 33n5, 154–55, 158, 162–63, 164n1, 179, 202, 204–6, 235, 263–64, 266, 285n2, 291
Mantequerías Leonesas, 176
Manzanares el Real, 85
Manzanares River, 197, 207, 274
maquis, 13
March, Juan, 158
Maria, xii, xxxv, 33, 87, 96, 170, 292, 295–96, 313; androgyny, 39, 42, 49, 123; blushing, 42; comparison to a colt/horse, 31, 42, 68–69, 76, 83, 308; father, 71, 73, 106; hair, 24, 37–41, 80, 84, 118, 137, 149, 150, 212–13, 240, 257, 259–60, 262–63, 277–78, 284; hometown, 104, 261; inspiration for character, 3, 149, 260; lovemaking with Jordan, xiv, 5, 7–8, 20, 24, 37, 39, 42, 45, 58, 76, 78–80, 84, 94, 111–12, 132–33, 134, 136, 138–40, 149, 153, 171–72, 210, 212, 239, 255, 258, 271, 274, 277–81, 285, 290, 318; mother, 104; "rabbit" nickname, 3, 39, 75, 76, 78–79, 146, 219, 264; rape and trauma, 24, 39, 41, 75, 78, 99, 104, 107–8, 111, 135–36, 144, 149–50, 169, 211, 218, 240, 257–61, 264, 277–78, 280–81; rescue, 40, 45, 130; Spain, association with, 37–38, 40, 60, 77, 93, 134–35, 142, 150, 207, 209–10, 212, 257, 260, 317–18; suicide pact, 149–50
Martínez, Carmen, 266
Marty, André, 65, 127, 180–81, 197, 298–301
Marvell, Andrew, 79, 277
Marx Brothers, 179
Mary Not a Perpetual Virgin, Nor the Mother of God (Smyth), 242
Mata Hari (film), 120
Mategna, Andrea, 190
Matthews, Herbert, 16, 152n1, 195
Maugham, W. Somerset, 296
Mayakovsky, Vladimir Vladimirovich, 140–41
Mazzeno, Laurence W., xix
McCain, John, xi, xx
McClellan, General George, 182–84
McGrigor, James, 253
McLoughlin, Kate, 111
McTeague (Norris), xxxv

McWilliams, Carey, 320n9
Mead, Margaret, 58
"Meditation XII" (Donne), 6
"Meditation XVII" (Donne), and novel's epigraph, 5–6, 106, 160, 204, 241
Melville, Herman, xvi. See also *Moby-Dick* (Melville)
Menéndez de Avilés, Pedro, 263–64
Men at War (Hemingway), xxiv, xxviii, 33, 36, 91, 99, 114, 128, 332
Men without Women (Hemingway), 114
Mera, Cipriano, 118
Merriman, Robert, 15–16, 18, 316
Miaja Menant, José, 185, 194, 273–74
Michaels, Walter Benn, 74, 75
milicianas, 292, 293n1
Ministry of Propaganda, 263
Miró, Joan, 49
Miró, Maria, 49
Miró, Pilar, 49
Mitchell (character), 196–98, 299
Mitchell, Margaret, 183
Moby-Dick (Melville), xvi, 15
Moddelmog, Debra, 211
Modesto, Juan, 179, 188, 192
Mola, General, 108, 201
Mongol Empire, 166, 186
Monk's Cave (Cueva del Monje), 35, 83
Moorehead, Caroline, 179
Moors, 31; in the civil war (Army of Africa/*regulares*), 59, 63, 108–9, 166, 177–78, 194; in *Othello*, 154; racist associations with Romani (and others), Africa, and Andalusia, 35, 38, 47, 54–55, 58–59, 66, 142, 173, 202, 223–24, 283; rape of Maria, 39, 41, 107–8; Spanish history and legacy, 21–22, 23, 53, 104, 197, 223–24, 264
Mora, Captain (character), 230, 236–37, 285
Moreno, Manuel Jiménez, 205
Morocco, 24, 31, 98, 109, 158, 177–79, 292
Morocco (film), 123
Mosby, John Singleton, 181–82, 252, 286
Motion, Andrew, 7
Motion Picture Production Code, 36
Motril, 137
Moveable Feast, A (Hemingway), xvii, 47, 104
Muller, Gilbert H., 61
Mundo Obrero, 200, 235, 291
Murad, David, 35, 37
Murray Butler, Nicholas, xix
Mussolini, Benito, 5, 71, 95n1
M. V. Frunze Military Academy, 177–78

nada/nothing and nowhere, 49, 56, 94, 132, 134, 140, 149, 170, 243, 314
NANA (North American Newspaper Alliance) dispatches, xviii; "Hemingway Describes Shelling of Madrid" (Hemingway), 237; "Hemingway Finds Madrid Callous to Bombardment"

(Hemingway), 237; "Hemingway Lets down Followers" (Roberts), xii
Nash, Michael, 144
Nash, Mary, 23, 228, 292, 293n1
Nation, The, 196
National Committee of Women Against War and Fascism, 266
Nationalists (rebels/insurgents), xviii, xx, 12, 47, 59, 71, 88, 96–97, 111, 113, 120, 124, 130–31, 155, 161, 163, 166–67, 178, 182, 195, 198, 219–20, 243–46, 252, 257, 263, 272, 289, 292, 303, 308, 310, 314; bullfighting and, 102, 157–58; Catholic Church and, 31, 39, 223, 291–92; espionage, 26; Fifth Columnists, 179, 256; General Staff, 25–26; offensive toward Madrid, 19, 49, 192, 194, 201, 293; racism of, 35–36, 108, 172–73; territory, 13, 26–27, 30, 41, 98, 194, 201, 245, 261, 274, 276, 302; weapons used, 43, 83, 218; women and, 104, 262
National Legion of Decency, 36
Native Americans (Indians), xxv, 32, 54–55, 58, 60–61, 124, 143, 167, 184, 209, 221, 229, 247–48, 271
naturalist literature/Naturalism. See genre
Navacerrada and the Navacerrada Pass, 12, 25, 193, 293
Navarre, 23, 202, 207–8, 230–31, 236
Nazis and Nazism, 56, 70–71, 122–23, 144, 181, 292
Negrín López, Juan, 139, 196
Nelson, Cary, xii
Nevada Mountains, 137
New Deal, 71–72
New Masses, The, 18, 140, 316, 320n7
New York Herald, 142
New York Times, xix, xxxi, 16, 97, 158, 236–37
New York Times Book Review (Adams), xi
Nickel, Matthew, 6, 278
Night at the Opera, A (film), 179
"Night before Battle, The" (Hemingway), xviii–xiv, 176, 180, 333
Nights in the Gardens of Spain (De Falla), 285n3
Nin, Andrés, 110, 201
Nineteen Eighty-Four (Orwell), 292
Ninety-Five Theses (Luther), 54, 264
NKVD, 180–81
Non-Intervention Pact (Treaty), xviii, 43, 108, 186
Norris, Frank, xxxv
Norris, Margot, 232
No se puede mirar (Goya), 115
Novick, Lynn, 134
"Now I Lay Me" (Hemingway), 151
Nuestra Señora de la Cabeza, 265
Nuestra Señora del Pilar/Virgen del Pilar, 47, 161

Obama, Barack, xx
O'Brien, Tim, xii–xiv, 107
Observer, The, xlii
O'Connor, Tom, 320n9
October Revolution (Asturias), 155, 166, 176
"Ode on a Grecian Urn" (Keats), 69, 100, 314

O'Hara, John, 296
O'Keefe, Ken, 176, 187, 189, 194
Old Man and the Sea, The (Hemingway), 11, 126
Oman, Charles, 253–54
"On the American Dead in Spain" (Hemingway), xx, 18, 263, 316, 318
Onan and onanism, 255, 307
"On the Blue Water" (Hemingway), 52
oneness/sameness, xiii, 73, 133, 135, 149–50, 210–12, 218, 257–58, 281, 310, 312
Ong, Walter, 116
"Open Boat, The" (Crane), 298
Ordonez, Cayetano, 102
Oregon Trail, 247
Ortega, José Gómez "Joselito," 204–6
Ortega y Gasset, José, xxvi–xxviii
Orwell, George, xvii, 66, 110, 291–92
Osten, Maria, 181
Othello (Shakespeare), 154
Our Lady of the Pillar, 47, 68, 189
Owen, Wilfred, xiii, xiv
Oxford Book of English Prose, The, 5

Pablo (character), xvi, xxiii, 13, 15, 17, 24, 26–27, 33, 51, 61–62, 67–69, 79, 84, 97, 103–4, 106, 125–26, 153, 160, 167, 170–75, 218, 222, 298; betrayal, instances and plans for, 28, 271, 288–89, 294; death, 93; guerilla band, 28, 30–31, 37, 40, 60, 91, 126, 154, 261, 276, 287, 294; horses, 28, 31, 44, 64, 83, 111, 125, 139, 173, 271, 289, 308; relationship with Pilar, 4, 43–44, 48, 63, 94, 173, 271; reputation, 26, 42–43, 305
Pablo Romero, Don Felipe de, 158
Painted Veil, The (film), 119–20
Palace Hotel, 193–94
Paramount Pictures, 17, 119
Parc Montsouris, 60
Parker, Dorothy, xxxi, 320n9
Parque del Buen Retiro (Madrid), 176, 187, 190, 208, 258–60
Parque del Oeste, 139
Paul, Saint, 275, 289
Payne, Stanley G., 39, 189, 204
Pegerinos, 293
Pemberton, John, 182
Peninsular Wars, 22, 253
People's (Popular) Army of the Republic, 287; Army of the Center, 179, 273; Army of the Ebro, 179; Army of the North, 179; 1st Mixed Brigade, 178; V Corps, 179; 11th Division, 178; 16th Mixed Brigade, 265; Thirty-Fifth Division, 276, 298; Forty-First Division, 276, 298; 69th Division, 246
Perez, Steven Jay, 30
Perkins, Max, xxviii, 4–5, 18–19, 24, 33n4, 50n1, 55, 64–65, 112n2, 125, 167, 181, 204, 227, 230, 233n1, 253, 254n2, 301, 303, 313, 321–24, 335n2
Personal Memoirs of E. S. Grant (Grant), 175
Peter, Saint, 275

Pfeiffer (Hemingway), Pauline, xii, 3, 37, 48, 56, 210, 248, 284, 321
Pfeiffer, Gus (uncle-in-law), 321, 335n3
Pfeiffer, Mary and Paul (parents-in-law), 56, 66, 93, 118, 336
Philip II, 20, 306
Philip IV, 28
picaro, *picardia*, picaresque, 26–27, 94, 222, 244
Picasso, Pablo, 92, 156, 190
Picture Play, 122
Pilar (boat), 48, 91, 209–10, 284, 321
Pilar (character), 3–4, 15, 42, 64, 65, 70–71, 75, 77, 80, 87, 104, 112–14, 122, 125–26, 133, 138, 150–52, 209, 211, 239–40, 258, 277, 292, 302, 307; bullfighting story, 88, 103, 156, 158–59, 205–6, 272, 295; comparison to stone, 46–47, 68, 227; as the emasculating woman, xxxv, 48, 167; inspiration for character, 45–46, 48–49, 62, 94, 114, 135, 159, 161–63, 227; on Jordan killing Pablo, 67–68, 91, 112; leadership role, 47, 73–74, 94, 150, 169–70; palm reading, xxvii, 43, 45, 49, 111, 125, 256; relationship with Pablo, 4, 26, 63, 91, 94, 103–4, 173, 271; Romani blood, xxiii, 35, 43–44, 47, 54, 62, 97, 126, 152, 162; on the scent of death, xxv, 204–5; sexuality, 44–45, 47–49, 58, 73–74, 76, 96, 131, 212, 294–95; story about the start of the war, 43, 98–100, 106–8, 111; storytelling skill, 101, 114–17, 128, 161, 170, 314
Pizarro, Francisco, 263
Plasencia, Spain, 125
Plaza Colón, 159
Plaza de las Cortes, 193
Poem of Deep Song (Lorca), 281, 285n4
Polikarpox I-16, 52
Poliquin, Rachel, 38
Polish-Soviet War, 24, 300
Polybius, 141
Poore, Charles, 236–37
Popular Front, Spanish, xviii
POUM (Partido Obrero de Unificacion Marxista; the Workers' Party of Marxist Unification), 66, 110, 179, 200–201
Pozoblanco, 123, 137–38, 195
Prado Museum (Museo Nacional del Prado), 25, 104, 115, 121–22, 129n4, 151, 164n3, 190–92, 208, 258
Pravda, 180–81
"President Vanquishes, The" (Hemingway), 284
Preston, Paul, 31, 87, 89n2, 89n3, 97, 111, 158, 178–79, 181, 196, 203n2, 203n4, 246
Prieto Tuero, Indalecio, 62, 139, 152n3, 273
Primitivo (character), 42, 61, 64, 170, 240
Primo de Rivera, Miguel, 86, 199
Prince Baltasar Carlos on Horseback (Velázquez), 28
Protestant Reformation, 54, 264; Counter-Reformation, 190, 282
Proudhon, Pierre-Joseph, 109
Prudlo, Donald, 72
Pseudo-Martyr (Donne), 6
Pulitzer Prize, xix

Putz, Joseph, 300
Pyrenees Mountains, xxxiii, 73–74, 207, 224, 236

Quantrill, William Clarke, and Quantrill's Raiders, 181–82
Queen Christina (film), 119–21
Queipo de Llano y Sierra, Gonzalo, 86–87, 89n2, 97, 99, 111
Quevedo y Villegas, Francisco Gomez de, 26–27, 116, 143–44
Quintanilla, Luis, 59, 102, 139, 233, 233n2, 303
Quintanilla, Paul, 102
Quintanilla, Pepe, 233

rabbits and rabbit symbolism, 3, 37, 39, 75–78, 131, 136, 147, 210, 219, 240, 264, 321
race: miscegenation, colonialism, consumption, and the exoticized other, xxxii–xxxiv, 38–40, 58–59, 73–75, 93, 108–9, 119, 131–32, 142, 150–52, 209–10, 240, 258–59, 271, 305. *See also* Moors; Native Americans (Indians); Romani people (Gitano, Zincali, gypsy)
Rafael (character), 37, 42–43, 45, 73, 79, 112, 124, 153, 156, 164, 240; Romani blood, xxiii, 35, 55, 65, 86
Rankin, Ruth, 122
rape, 39, 41, 59, 86–87, 107–8, 133, 135, 144, 228, 258–62
Ratmanova, Elisabeta, 181
Raven, Robert, 195
Realism/realistic fiction. *See* genre
Real de Nieva, Spain, 30
"Real Robert Jourdan, The" (Eby), 15
Reconquista/Reconquest, xxxiii, 22, 31, 53, 104, 264, 282
Red Badge of Courage, The (Crane), xxiii, xxvi, xxviii–xxxi, 11, 18, 57, 87, 146, 183, 221, 241, 252, 301, 303, 317
Red Lodge, 248–49, 251
Regaldo, San Pedro, 158
Regler, Gustav, xiii, xxviii, 16, 141, 185
regulares, 31, 86–87, 109, 166, 194. *See also* Army of Africa
Rehberger, Dean, 251
Reiber, Torkild, 71
religious inquiry, xxx, 240–43
Renn, Ludwig, 300–301, 320n9
Reno, Major Marcus, 247, 249
Republicans, xviii, xxxi, 11–12, 21, 30–31, 40, 71, 106, 108, 110–11, 117–18, 127, 166, 192, 194–96, 198, 222, 244, 246–47, 252, 262–63, 273, 274, 276, 291, 302, 314; American versus Spanish, 71–72; anticlericalism, 55–56, 72; Assault Guard, 199; bullfighting and, 102, 158; *guerrillos*, 13, 28, 37, 62, 124–25; literacy campaigns, 57; morale-building disinformation campaign, 52; postwar labor units, 57; religion and, 169, 256; salute/salutations, 25, 70, 218, 312; social hierarchy, 70, 96; territory, *xli*, 12, 85–86; weapons used, 43, *311*; women and, 292–93

Retana, Manuel "Manola," 163
Revolt in the Desert (Lawrence), 41
Reynolds, Michael, xiv, xviii, xix, 15, 24, 248, 254, 285n4, 304
Richardson, R. Dan, 137
Rif Wars (Moroccan uprising), 17, 24, 177
Roberts, C. V., xii, 134
Robles, José, 61–62
Rogers, Gayle, 27, 117, 143, 147, 156–57
Rogers, W. G., 47
Rogers, Will, Jr., 320n9
Rojas Monje, Pastora, 46
Rojo Llusch, Vincente, 21, 273
Rolfe, Edwin, 127, 129n7, 246, 254n1, 267n2
"Roll, Jordan, Roll," 305–6
romance literature/Romanticism. *See* genre
Romancer Gitano (Lorca), 285n4
Romani people (Gitano, Zincali, gypsy), xii, xiii, xxiii, 35–37, 45, 46, 65, 86, 97, 150–52, 163–64, 202, 206, 281, 295, 338–41; from Andalusia, 55, 160, 162, 173, 283; association with Moors, Native Americans, and others, 47, 54, 55, 66, 229, 285n1; mysticism, intuition, and foresight, 43–44, 62, 126, 156–57, 169, 204–5, 319
Romantic in Spain, A (Gautier), 19
Romeo and Juliet (Shakespeare), 113, 225
Romero, Pedro, 102
Romesburg, Rod, 318–19
Ronda, Spain, 87, 97, *98*, 102, 106, 107, 111
Roos, Michael Kim, 211, 213n1
Roosevelt, Franklin D., 71–72, 198, 306
Roosevelt, Theodore, 304, 306
Rosinante to the Road Again (Dos Passos), xxi, 109–10
Roth, Joseph, 65n1
Rough Riders, 306
Ruiz, Julius, 245
Ruiz Ibárruri, Amaya, 234–35
Ruiz Ibárruri, Rubén, 234–35
Rukeyser, Muriel, 113
Russia. *See* Soviet Union (USSR)/Russia
Russian Civil War, 19, 173, 185, 200–201, 300
Russian Communist Party, 180, 299
Rykov, Alexei Ivanovich, 200

Sacred Heart emblem, 217–18, 231
saeta, 282–83, 314
Saint-Jean-de-Luz, France, 201
Saint Pilar's festival, 161
Sales, Joan, xii
Salic law, 217
Saltando la Barrera (Domingo Fallola), 18
Salvarsan, 300
Salve, Regina, 241–42
Sánchez Mejías, Ignacio, 206
San Fermin, Fiesta de, 103, 105
Sanitariums, 193
San Juan de la Cruz (Saint John of the Cross), 217, 280–83, 314

San Sebastian, 194, 201
Santa María del Real, 30
Santiago (name), 124, 126, 154
Santiago de Compostela, 178; Cathedral of, 166, 189
Sargent, Singer, 50n4
"Satire 3" (Donne), 8n1
Savage Coast, The (Rukeyser), 113
Scarlet Letter, The (Hawthorne), xvi
Scarry, Elaine, 350
Scholes, Robert, 42, 47, 131–32, 149, 164n3, 211, 260
Scribner, Charles, xxvi, 4, 46, 50n3, 156, 162, 197, 204, 297, 299, 335n2
Scribner's magazine, 36, 49
Scully, Frank, 320n9
"Second Coming, The" (Yeats), 65
Second Italo-Ethiopian War, 95n1
Second Moroccan War, 177
Second Spanish Republic, xvii, xxi, xxxvi, 55, 71, 86, 110, 123, 155, 171, 199, 201–2, 260, 273. *See also* Republicans
Sedgwick, Eve Kosofsky, 68, 294
Segovia, xxxi, 19, 21–22, 25, 27, 30, 53, 57, 85, 87, 124, 220, 302, 308. *See also* Segovia (La Granja) Offensive
Segovia (La Granja) Offensive, xxv, xxviii, 11, 12, 19, 21–22, 86–87, 92, 109, 127, 130, 155, 244, 246, 252, 254, 266, 336
Segundo, 42, 43
Seguridad, 256, 263
Seidman, Michael, 13, 66, 109
Serrapí Sánchez, Manuel, 161
Seven Pillars of Wisdom, The (Lawrence), xxii, xxv, 41
7th Cavalry Regiment, 54, 247–48
sex and sexuality: Jordan and Maria's times together, 80, 133–34, 212, 278–80; Jordan with other women, 80, 194; masturbation, 173, 307; non-coital, 255–56; queer desire, 58, 122, 131–32, 211. *See also* gender; homophobia and the homosocial; incest; race
Shakespeare, William, xvii, 26–27, 120, 159. *See also As You Like It* (Shakespeare); *Hamlet* (Shakespeare); *Henry IV*, parts 1 and 2 (Shakespeare); *Henry V* (Shakespeare); *Love's Labor's Lost* (Shakespeare); *Macbeth* (Shakespeare); *Othello* (Shakespeare); *Romeo and Juliet* (Shakespeare); "undiscovered country" (from Shakespeare's *Hamlet*)
Sheean, Vincent, 56, 161, 320n9
Sheridan, General Phil, xxv, 54, 182–84, 252
Sherman, General William Tecumseh, 182–83, 305
"Short Happy Life of Francis Macomber, The" (Hemingway), 310
Siege of the Alcázar (Zuloaga), 190
Sierra de Gredos (Gredos Mountains), 15, 30, 35, 125–26
Sierra de Guadarrama (Guadarrama Mountains), xiii, xxxi, xxxii, xxxiii, xxxv, 13, 15, 19, 25–26, 28, 31, 35, 49, 65, 67, 85, 87, 124, 127, 187, 192–93, 194–95, 207, 245, 253, 293, 314–16, 338
Sierra de Paramera, 125
Siguenza, 245
SIM (Servicio de Información), 25–26, 200, 233, 233n2, 244, 246
Simonides of Ceos, 141
Sioux, 247
Sister Carrie (Dreiser), 298
Skinner, Cornelia Otis, 134, 338
sleeping robe (bag), 153
Slotkin, Richard, 61, 251
Small, Melvin, 144
Smedley, F. E., 38
Smyth, Thomas, 242–43
"Snows of Kilimanjaro, The" (Hemingway), 310
Society for the Improvement of Horse Breeding in France, 32
"Soldier's Home" (Hemingway), 22
Soler, Enrique Belenguer, 204–5
Somebody Had to Do Something, 263, 316–17, 320n9
Somme, the (battle), 133
Somosierra Pass, 193, 253, 273
Sontag, Susan, xi, xii, xxvii, 100, 105, 122
Soria, 26, 245
Soul of Spain, The (Ellis), xxi, xxxv–xxxvi, 19, 28–29, 58, 222–23
Sound and the Fury, The (Faulker), 62
Soviet Union (USSR)/Russia, xx, 30, 43, 52, 173, 176, 180, 181, 196, 198, 200, 234, 235, 266, 299, 300, 302
"Spain" (Auden), xxi–xxii, xxxiii
Spanish Alpine Club, 25
Spanish-American War of 1898, 59n2, 143, 306
Spanish Armada, 306
Spanish Army (pre–civil war), 43, 178, 189, 306; patron saint of, 47, 166
Spanish Civil War, xvii–xviii, xix–xx, xxxv, xxxvin1, 4, 17, 28, 32–33, 46, 52, 55–57, 63, 123–24, 155, 157–58, 166, 171, 178, 182, 190, 199–201, 220, 291, 314; American response to, 71–72; British narratives of, xxii; executions, assassinations, and murders, xvi, 21, 56, 127–28, 232–33, 252, 298–99; massacres and atrocities, 56, 59, 87, 97–99, 118, 155, 166, 179, 186, 192, 263; photography, 195; propaganda in, 31, 35, 43, 86–87, 96, 109, 118, 179, 189, 263, 292, 316
Spanish Communist Party/Communist Party of Spain (PCE), 49, 62, 110, 138, 178, 200, 265, 291–92. *See also* Fifth Regiment
Spanish Diary (Koltsov), 180
Spanish Earth, The, xviii, 3, 12, 43, 46, 56–57, 96, 104–5, 117, 171, 178, 195, 245
Spanish Foreign Legion, and legionnaires, 31, 86, 108–9, 166, 177–79, 194, 292. *See also* Army of Africa
Spanish Foreign Legion in the Spanish Civil War, 1936, The (Álvarez), 108–9

Spanish Renaissance, 26
Spanish Republic (1873–1874), xvii, 198
Spanish Socialist Workers Party (Partido Socialista Obrero Espanol; PSOE), 273
Spanish Tragedy, The (Kyd), 4
Spanish Unified Socialist Youth (Juventudes Socialistas Unificadas; JSU), 265
Sparre, Ebba, 121
Spilka, Mark, xiii, xxxiv, 210
Staimer, Richard, 266–67
Stalin, Joseph, xviii, 25, 141, 176, 110, 180, 198–201, 203n4, 266, 287, 292, 298, 300
Stanley, Henry Morton, 142, *143*
Stavans, Ilan, 14–15, 44
St. Crispin's Day, 168
Steel Company (Fifth Regiment), 193
Stein, Gertrude, 47–48, 68, 122, 131, 135, 225–27, 260
Steinbeck, John, xix
Stendhal, 114, 116, 314
Stewart, Donald Ogden, 320n9
Stone, John A., 48
Stone, Robert, xi
Stoneback, H. R., 47, 55, 60–61, 106, 189–90, 289
storytelling and art, xv–xvi, xxxvi, 69, 98, 99–100, 104, 114–16, 128, 314, 320. *See also* ekphrasis; genre
"Strange Country, The" (Hemingway), 61
Strater, Henry Hyacinth "Mike," 283–84, 323
Strychacz, Thomas, 12, 86, 252
Stuart, James Ewell Brown "Jeb," 182, 184, 252
Stuckey, W. J., xix
Studies in the Napoleonic Wars (Oman), 253, 254n6
Sun Also Rises, The (Hemingway), 36, 51, 56, 74, 101–3, 105, 190, 212, 310; Brett Ashley, 122, 149; bullfighting in, 156; film adaptation, 122; Jake Barnes, 103, 223
Sundaram, Chantal, 140, 141
Supreme Court (US), 144
Swanton, Kathryn, 154
Sweeny, Charles, 16, 24
Świerczewski, Karol Wacław (General Walter), 19, 127, 300

Tablada, 193
Talavera de la Reina, 205
Talbot, Francis X., 72
tanks and armored vehicles, 33n1, 85, 120, 168, 196; BT-5, 311; CV-3/whippet/tankette, 309–10; T-26, 302, 311
Tartary, 166
Tarzan (Burroughs), xiv, 40, 304–5, 318
Telefónica, 176, 207
Tennyson, Alfred, xii
Teresa of Ávila, Saint, 26, 258, 281–83
Teruel, 35; battle, 66, 246
Tetuán de las Victorias, 197
Texaco, 71
Thackeray, William, 38

Thalberg, Irving, 122
Thermopylae (battle), 141
Thompson, Charles, 283–84
Three Guineas (Woolf), 195
3rd of May 1808 in Madrid, The (Goya), 115
Thomas, Hugh, 55, 89n3, 97–99, 102, 111, 127, 139, 166, 171, 179, 196, 203n2, 232
"Time Now, the Place Spain, The" (Hemingway), 303
time and watches, 79, 80, 84, 86, 147, 230, 235, 258, 277–80, 285, 314, 316
Tinker, Frank G., 336–37
Todo, Isidoro, 155
To Have and Have Not (Hemingway), 36
"To His Coy Mistress" (Marvell), 79, 277
Toklas, Alice, 47
Toledo, 21, 67, 190, 196–98
Tompkins, Kyla Wazana, 40
Toronto Star, 284
Torrents of Spring, The (Hemingway), 74
tragic literature/Tragedy. *See* genre
Transit of the Virgin, The (Mantegna), 190
trauma, 39, 78, 113, 136, 149–50, 169, 210–11, 218, 258, 281
Tremlett, Giles, 13, 127, 185, 189, 254, 266, 320n8
Triumph of Death, The (Bruegel), 190, *191*, 212
Trogdon, Robert, xix, xxxi, 33n2, 36–37, 70, 284, 303, 320n6, 323, 335n2
Trotsky, Leon, 141, 200–201
Trotskyites, xviii, 66, 110, 179–80, 200–201, 300
Trouble I've Seen, The (Gellhorn), 3
Trumbo, Dalton, 195
Tukhachevsky, Mikhail Nikolayevich, 300
Turner, Victor, xxxii
Twain, Mark, xxviii, 175
Tyler, Lisa, 213n1

Ulysses (Joyce), 80
Uncertain Glory (Sales), xii
"Undefeated, The" (Hemingway), 114
"Under the Ridge" (Hemingway), xix, 62–63, 128, 185
"undiscovered country" (from Shakespeare's *Hamlet*), xxxii, 4–5, 39, 319
Unification Decree, 261
Unión de Hermanos Proletarios (Union of Proletarian Brothers), 261–63
University City (Madrid), 185, 194, 274
UP (United Press), 140
Usera (Madrid), 188, 194–95, 197, 223, 231–32, 245
USS Maine, 306

Valaik, J. David, 72
"Valediction: Forbidding Mourning, A" (Donne), 7–8, 134
Valencia, 33n5, 47, 88, 185, 187, 194, 205, 236, 245–46, 263, 273, 276, 303
Valentino, Rudolph, 123

Valis, Noël, 14
Valladolid, 30, 39, 41, 87, 104, 108–9, 155, 157–58, 162, 260–61
Valle de los Caídos/Valley of the Fallen, 20, 57
Valsaín, 12
Van de Water, Frederic F., xxiv–xxv, 24, 182–84, 234, 252
van Gennep, Arnold, xxxii
Van Guilder, Gene, 315–16
Vanity Fair, 38, 78, 122, 129n5
Varloff, 301
Velázquez, 63, 70, 187, 189
Velázquez, Diego, 27–29
Velázquez, Eugenio Lucas, 104
Venus and Mars (Botticelli), 255
Verdun (battle), 63
Vernon, Alex, 15, 16, 40, 49, 56, 58, 74, 102–3, 118, 197–98, 305, 316, 320n2
Versuch über den Roman (von Blanckenburg), xxvi
"Veteran, The" (Crane), xxix
Vida del Buscón (Quevedo y Villegas), 26–27
Vidali, Vittorio (Carlos Contreras), 187–89, 193
Vietnam War, xi, xii, 107
View of Toledo (El Greco), 190
Villacastín, 124, 276
Villaconejos, 272, 276
Vinaròs, 246
Vincent, Jonathan, xxiii, xxiv, 277, 317–18
Virgen del Pilar, 47, 161
Virginian, The (Wister), xiv–xv, xxv; film adaptation of, 17
Virgin Mary, 47, 92, 147, 189, 227, 238, 241–42
Virgin Spain (Frank), 104
Vitoria, 194; battle of, 253
von Blanckenburg, Friedrich, xxvi
von Rothman, Kaja, 122
Voroshilov, Kliment Yefremovich, 300

Walsh, Jeffrey, 317
Walter, General (Karol Świerczewski), 19, 127, 300
Ward, Lynd, 257–58
Warren, Chris, 249, 254n5
Warren, Robert Penn, xvi
Waste Land, The (Eliot), 221
Waterloo (battle), 253
Watts, Henry Edward, 27
Weaver, Leland Stanford "Chub," 248–49, 283–84

Webb, Ruth, 100–101, 114
Weissmuller, Johnny, 305
Wellington, Arthur Wellesley, First Duke of, 63, 252–53
Wellington's Officers (Bell), 253
Wendorf, Paul, 71
What Mad Pursuit (Gellhorn), 3
White, Frederick, xx, 30, 180, 203n4
White Horse (Velázquez), 28–29, 29
White House, 3
Williams, Wirt, xxvi
Wister, Owen, xiv, xvi, xxiv, 17
"With a Full Voice" (Mayakovsky), 140
Wolff, Milton, xii
Woman of Affairs, A (film), 123
Woodard, Vincent, 40
Woods Manufacturing Company, 153
Woolf, Virginia, 152n5, 195, 279
World Enough and Time (Warren), xvi
World War I/Great War/First World War, xvii, xxii, xxxiv, 22, 24, 41, 43, 51, 92–93, 137, 142, 183, 185–86, 195, 235–36, 239, 249, 284, 286, 293n1, 299, 300–301, 303, 309
World War II/Second World War, xix, xxxvin4, 4–5, 36, 52, 65, 71, 92, 118, 128, 144, 168, 303, 316
Woroszylski, Wiktor, 141
Writers' Federation memorial, 140
Wuthering Heights (Brontë), xiii, xxviii, xxxi, 210, 213n1
Wyden, Peter, 232, 260

Yeats, W. B., 65
Young Communist League, 70

Zafra, 272
Zaisser, Wilhelm "Gomez," 137, 138, 152n2
Zalka, Máté (Lukács"), 185, 266, 300
Zaloga, Steven J., 311
Zaragoza, 47, 111, 157–58, 161, 189
Zincali. *See* Romani people (Gitano, Zincali, gypsy)
Zincali (Borrow), 150, 202
Zinoviev, Grigory Yevseyevich, 200
Zola, Émile, xv, xxviii, xxxiv, 144
Zorina, Vera, 119
Zorrilla, José, 94
Zuloaga, Ignacio, 190